Other books by Martin Middlebrook
in Allen Lane

The First Day on the Somme

The Nuremberg Raid

Convoy
The Battle for Convoys SC.122 and HX.229

Martin Middlebrook
and Patrick Mahoney

Battleship

The Loss of the Prince of Wales
and the Repulse

Allen Lane

ALLEN LANE
Penguin Books Ltd.
17 Grosvenor Gardens, London SW1W 0BD

First published in 1977

Copyright © Martin Middlebrook
and Patrick Mahoney, 1977

ISBN 0 7139 1042 9

Set in Monotype Bell by
Western Printing Services Ltd, Bristol
Printed photolitho in Great Britain by
Ebenezer Baylis & Son Ltd., The Trinity Press,
Worcester, and London

Contents

List of Maps and Text Figures

List of Plates

Introduction

At 11.00 on Wednesday, 10 December 1941, the crews of a formation of Japanese Navy Mitsubishi Type 96 aircraft sighted two large warships escorted by three destroyers steaming on an easterly course some fifty miles off the coast of Malaya. One merchant ship could also be seen near by, but there was no sign of any aircraft protecting the warships. The two larger ships were both British; they were the battleship H.M.S. *Prince of Wales* and the battle cruiser H.M.S. *Repulse*. Two of the escorting destroyers were also Royal Navy ships, but the third was Australian. It was only the third day of the war that Japan had started in the Far East. The weather was fine and clear. Lieutenant Yoshimi Shirai, the pilot of the leading Mitsubishi, ordered his formation to attack.

That night there were great parties at two Japanese-held airfields near Saigon to celebrate a momentous victory against the hated British.

This is not the first book to be written about the loss of the *Prince of Wales* and the *Repulse*, but history is a subject that takes many years to unfold, both in the increasing availability of documents and in the continuing repercussions of events and the gradual realization of their implications. In particular, the publication in 1969 by the Japanese of their Official History and the release in 1972 of the British Second World War documents at the Public Record Office have thrown new light on this decisive action and justify a fresh study.

This book will aim to pass fairly quickly over those aspects of the subject which are common knowledge or are not controversial; it will concentrate more on those areas which earlier writers may not have been able to cover in depth. An attempt will also be made to tell the reader not just what happened on that sunny morning off Malaya, but what it was like for the men involved. One hundred and ninety-three officers and men who were serving in the warships attacked have been traced, together with others who were stationed at Singapore or other relevant places at the time of the disaster. We are fully aware of the pitfalls of relying on the human memory for descriptions of an episode full of confusion and emotional stress – an episode furthermore that occurred more than thirty years ago. But the basic framework of the book has been formed from reliable contemporary records; the participants in the battle provide descriptions of smaller incidents never included in the official records and, perhaps more importantly, tell of their emotions at that dramatic time. The contributions of these men put flesh on the bare bones of the story and bring it more to life.

Our choice of title may need some explanation. We realize that the *Repulse* was a battle *cruiser* and that battleships and battle cruisers were designed for different roles in the event of a fleet action, but on 10 December 1941 neither the *Repulse* nor the *Prince of Wales* was operating in the strict role for which it had been built. Our title – *Battleship* – has been chosen for other reasons. Since 1918 the leaders of most of the world's navies had been under pressure, sometimes in the bitterest of circumstances, to accept the argument that heavily gunned and armoured capital ships – what may be called battleships, whether true battleships or dreadnoughts or battle cruisers – had outrun their useful lifespan and that new weapons and their means of delivery – the torpedo, the bomb, the submarine, the aircraft – had rendered the battleship obsolescent. In Britain this argument had been put even before 1914. But in no country had the theory been fully accepted and vast quantities of money from national budgets had continued to be spent on battleships.

The clearest warning of all had been given by a famous American, Brigadier-General Billy Mitchell, Assistant

Chief of the U.S. Army Air Corps between 1919 and 1925. After the First World War the U.S. Navy had wanted to re-equip with a fleet of new battleships. Mitchell argued, as forcefully as he could, that aircraft could sink by bomb or by torpedo any ship afloat. He proved it, though not to the U.S. Navy's satisfaction, in trials during which his aircraft sank two empty ex-German warships – a battleship and a cruiser – in 1921, and then three old American battleships during the next two years. The experiments were naturally followed with great interest by other naval powers, but Mitchell and the other anti-battleship critics did not prevail. Billy Mitchell continued to agitate until exiled to a remote command for pressing his ideas too strongly, and then was court-martialled and suspended from duty for publishing his views in the press without permission. At least thirty-four battleships were launched and completed after this time at a cost of around £250–300 million or $1,000 million, and many more of the older battleships were refitted and modernized at further massive cost. Most of the countries engaged in this battleship bonanza started their wars in 1939 or 1941 desperately short of aircraft carriers and anti-submarine vessels.

The action started by Lieutenant Shirai on 10 December 1941 proved conclusively that the battleship could no longer live with the bomb, the torpedo and the aircraft. The validity of this theory, so hated and resisted by traditionalist naval officers of so many countries, had taken a remarkably long time to find its proof.

The tenth of December 1941 was the end of the battleship era.

PATRICK MAHONEY
MARTIN MIDDLEBROOK

1

'A Sword at Our Hearts'

In the years following the First World War, the victorious but exhausted Allied nations took stock of the much-changed world over which they held virtual rule. There were at least three urgent tasks to be undertaken: clear up the mess in Europe, exact suitable penalties from the defeated Germans and Austrians, and plan for the future. There was a genuine and sincere desire by the victors to make sure that the four-year holocaust just ended would never need to be repeated. To unscramble the tangled web of new allegiances, the thirsts for vengeance, the debts to be honoured and secret promises to be kept, to rebuild anew the delicate balances of power and spheres of influence – these were the daunting tasks facing the statesmen. Events twenty years on were to show that the decisions reached, so often achieved by compromise between politicians whose national desires overcame their grasp of the world's needs, were the wrong decisions. The conferences and treaties of the five years or so following 1918 are as good a starting point as any to the story of the *Prince of Wales* and the *Repulse*.

The Pacific was hardly touched by the First World War, but the role of Japan in that war should be studied. Britain had had a friendship and mutual aid alliance with Japan since 1902, and when she found herself fighting Germany in August 1914, the Japanese had honoured the treaty and joined Britain in attacking the German-held colony of Tsingtao on the coast of China. Tsingtao fell quickly, but this proved to be the limit of the Japanese Army's support; the mutual-aid clauses of the alliance only covered India and the Far East. No Japanese troops were ever sent to France or any other front where British troops were fighting. The Japanese Navy did, however, send warships in 1917 to help the hard-pressed Royal Navy on convoy escort work in the Mediterranean.

The Japanese had meanwhile taken advantage of the great powers' preoccupation with the European war by gaining important footholds in mainland Asia. The conquered German colony of Tsingtao was retained and China was forced to give up other land in the area. Further moves into China were blocked by British and American political pressure, but the Japanese were allowed to move into southern Manchuria to extend their existing control of Korea. Finally, when the ex-German island colonies in the Pacific were being divided among the victors after 1918, the Japanese had to be given the Marianas, the Carolines and most of the Marshall Islands in return for the naval help given to Britain in 1917 – a typical example of the settling of debts that took place after the war.

So, for the modest outlay of possibly a battalion of infantry at Tsingtao in 1914 and a few escort vessels in 1917, Japan had gained important footholds in mainland Asia and the Pacific Islands. Japan was one of the few countries to do well out of the First World War. She also showed that her aims were expansionist. The Japanese Empire was clearly on the move.

This Japanese attitude posed a dilemma for two of her wartime Allies, Britain and the United States. Communications to important members of the British Empire – Australia, New Zealand, New Guinea, Borneo and Malaya – could be threatened by an expanding Japan, and the United States' interests in the Philippines were similarly at risk. Both countries were also heavily dependent upon South-East Asia for two essential commodities: Malaya and the Dutch East Indies produced three quarters of the worlds' raw rubber and two thirds of its tin. The political and commercial consequences of Japanese moves into this area were immense. The American and British dilemma was how to check the Japanese without directly antagonizing their former ally.

The threat to Britain and the United States was closely bound up with sea power; political and military progress by the Japanese away from mainland Asia could be achieved with naval cover. At the end of 1921, the United States, using her new-found influence as a major world power, invited the other four naval powers – Britain, France, Japan and Italy – to a joint conference. This meeting, the Washington Naval Conference, took only a few weeks to reach agreement. The outcome was that the existing strengths should not be altered, nor existing spheres of influence be extended by the construction of new bases outside the old spheres.

No doubt to the relief of Britain and the United States, the Japanese signed, without demur, this agreement which limited their naval strength to 60 per cent of that of both the Royal Navy and the United States Navy while forbidding them to build bases in their newly acquired island possessions in the Pacific. Although the British were not permitted to build a new base at Hong Kong nor the Americans one in the Philippines, they could do so in Malaya or Hawaii. This question of bases was all-important. The Pacific was so vast that a naval power could only expand within certain distances from proper bases.

The Washington Naval Agreement had limited the Japanese dream of expansion – at least for the moment.

The post-war period posed particular problems for the British Admiralty. The old enemy, Germany, had lost her navy and was no longer a threat in European waters; the old ally, Japan, now posed a potential threat in the Far East and the Pacific. Britain had enough warships but no base in the Far East with a dry dock capable of taking the largest capital ships; and even if these docks had existed, it would be an expensive burden to maintain permanently an Eastern Fleet which contained battleships. The Admiralty solution was to press the government to build a new base in the Far East but to retain all the battleships in the Home and Mediterranean Fleets. The British naval presence would be made up, as in the past, of cruisers and smaller vessels; capital ships would make no more than the occasional flag-showing visits. It was hoped that if ever war in the East threatened, capital ships could be rushed out in time to meet that threat. The proposed new base would service and repair these ships both on arrival and during subsequent operations. This combination of a permanent modern base in the Far East and rapid reinforcement by capital ships from England was to be the cornerstone of British and Empire defence policy in the area for exactly twenty years.

The British Cabinet accepted the Admiralty plans and also the choice of a site for the base. Hong Kong was soon dismissed as too isolated and vulnerable, and Trincomalee, in Ceylon, as too remote from the area to be defended. Singapore and Sydney were both given more serious consideration, but the final choice fell on Singapore as having the better strategic position. At the Imperial Conference of 1921 Mr Arthur Balfour, representing the British government, said:

We have come to the conclusion that one of the pressing needs for Imperial defence is that Singapore should be made into a place where the British Fleet can concentrate for the defence of the Empire, of our trade interests in the East, our interests in India, our interests in Australia, our interests in New Zealand, our interests in the small possessions there and for that purpose it is absolutely necessary to undertake works at Singapore. *

It is interesting to note that this decision had been taken in June 1921, five months before the Washington Naval Conference was convened. Britain was thus able to agree at the conference that no new naval bases would be built by her 'east of the 110 degrees meridian'. Singapore was just west of this line.

There were two possible sites at Singapore for the great new base: at the existing small naval base at Keppel Harbour, among the commercial wharves just south of

* Public Record Office WO 106/2530.

Singapore city, or at a new site in the remoter northern
part of the island on the Johore Strait. The Admiralty
asked for the Johore Strait site since it was remote enough
from the open sea to be free from the danger of naval
bombardment, and also because it would be clearer of
commercial shipping. The Admiralty's recommendation
was approved, and it was also decided to construct an air
and seaplane base at near-by Seletar.

The next thing to be settled was how the base should be
protected from enemy attack, and here an unhappy story
begins, the main ingredients of which are well known. It
was at this time that the Royal Air Force was striving to
establish itself as the third major service and to get the
principle accepted that air power would be a major factor
in any future war. The 1920s and 1930s were difficult
economic times, and the allocation between the three
services of the limited defence budgets was bitterly contested. The R.A.F. did have some friends in British
governments of the time, but not enough. Of the £1,938
million in the defence budgets for the fifteen years from
1920 to 1934, the Navy received the lion's share of 47 per
cent, the Army 40 per cent, and the R.A.F. only 13 per
cent.

When the defence of Singapore was being considered in
the 1920s, belief was almost unanimous that any threat
would come from naval bombardment, possibly followed
up by a landing directly on the island of seaborne troops;
the jungle-covered mainland of Malaya to the north was
believed to be impenetrable. The R.A.F. contended that
the best defence against naval attack was the presence at
Singapore of a strong force of torpedo bombers protected
by fighters, but the Navy and the Army believed that heavy-
calibre guns in fixed positions would provide a better
defence. The 'big-gun' lobby won and Singapore's main
line of defence was entrusted to artillery in fixed emplacements and capable of covering all sea approaches to Singapore, but most being unable to train back on to the mainland of Malaya.

The actual work of building the base and its defences was slow to start. The newly elected Labour government of 1924 decided to abandon the scheme completely, but Labour were out of office again within the year and their Conservative successors reinstated the plan. So it went on for several years, with successive governments slowing down or speeding up construction according to financial pressures, political outlook or changing world events. The main work was not completed until 1938, but the result was the fine, modern Singapore Naval Base. The 1,006-foot King George VI Graving Dock and the 858-foot No. 9 Floating Dock were both capable of dry-docking the largest Royal Navy ships then afloat or planned, while a smaller floating dock would care for destroyers and other small vessels. There were great towering cranes, workshops and stores to cater for a whole fleet, huge oil tanks and the F.S.A. (Fleet Shore Accommodation) with facilities for housing up to 3,000 men when their ships were undergoing major repair. The total area of the base covered one and a half square miles and there were twenty-two square miles of anchorages. The final cost came to more than £60 million.

This fine outpost of the Empire was formally opened on 15 February 1938 by Sir Shenton Thomas, Governor of the Straits Settlements, in the presence of many distinguished visitors. It is recorded that Mr Okamoto, the Japanese Consul-General in Singapore, attended the opening ceremony but left before the reception. Eighteen naval vessels made a fine sight with the cruiser H.M.S. *Norfolk* flying the flag of the Eastern Fleet and the United States and the Indian Navies were each represented by three ships. But no battleships were present. The new Singapore Naval Base stood ready to receive these should the British Empire in the Far East ever be threatened.

The Japanese were not happy. The Singapore Naval Base, which the British saw as a vital link in the *defence* of the Empire, appeared to the Japanese to be more a base for aggression against them – or, at least, that was the public line they took in the 1930s.

Relations between Britain and Japan had undergone great changes after 1918. The alliance and solidarity that had existed between the two nations for almost twenty years had begun to crumble even before the end of the First World War. Britain's belief in Japanese good faith had been shaken by the Japanese moves in China and Manchuria while the attention of most of the world was still concentrated on the fighting in Europe. Japan's expansionist policy had provoked not only the 1921 Washington Naval Conference – which, as already described, limited her naval strength – but also two political treaties: the Four-Power Treaty, defining and regulating the positions in the Pacific of Britain, the United States, France and Japan; and the Nine-Power Treaty, which was intended to protect China from Japanese aggression. At the same time, Britain informed Japan that she would not be renewing the long-standing Anglo-Japanese Alliance, giving as the main reason the view that the new League of Nations rendered such alliances obsolete. All these changes were undertaken while Japan was under a government where civilians dominated and whose outlook was commercial rather than military. This government accepted all these great changes without demur.

The treaties of the 1920s were to keep the peace for eight years, but a succession of seemingly isolated events meanwhile gradually eroded the post-war stability of Japan's civilian government. Japan was accorded the status of a major power by the League of Nations and a permanent seat on the League's Council, but the League failed to pass Japan's requested declaration of racial equality, mainly on opposition from Australia's prime minister, Billy Hughes. A great earthquake in 1923 caused the deaths of approximately 100,000 people in Yokohama and Tokyo. Hot on the heels of this disaster came a widely circulated rumour that Communists and Korean Nationalists were combining to overthrow the government; this caused a bloody witch-hunt and badly rocked the government. Then, Crown Prince Hirohito was photographed in western clothes playing golf with the Prince of Wales while on a visit to England – a seemingly innocent event, but one which upset the traditionalists in Japan. In 1924, the United States government passed a Bill banning further immigration from oriental countries, which caused the Japanese Ambassador in Washington to threaten 'grave consequences' to this second racial insult to his country. These were just some from an intricate series of events that rocked the stability of Japan in the 1920s. The final blow came when Japan suffered more severely than most countries from the world slump of 1927 and its government fell in 1928; a new party, the Seiyukai, came to power with General Tanaka Giichi as prime minister.

General Tanaka's party had strong support from the young army officers, the traditional malcontents in any country emerging slowly to full democratic status. What did they see around their country? They found the West classifying them as 'inferior orientals', their naval strength being limited to a level well below that of other world powers, their expansion on the mainland of Asia and their desire to build an empire deliberately blocked by countries that had already built their own empires, their centuries-old standards and traditions threatened, their trade in ruins, their civilian government failed. And how had Britain, their old ally, behaved? Britain had torn up the alliance which had been so useful in gaining Japanese help in the First World War. Britain had connived with the United States to keep Japan in an inferior naval position and was now building this great new base at Singapore, the only reason for which could be distrust of Japan. A proud nation had been deeply hurt. The Singapore Naval Base, it was said, was 'a sword at our hearts'.

The situation deteriorated fast in the 1930s. Japan renewed her expansion in Manchuria in 1931 and in China the following year. A full-scale military attack on China was undertaken in 1937. The Western Powers were appalled by the savagery with which the Japanese treated the captured Chinese cities, but were unable to stop the fighting. When the League of Nations protested, the Japanese withdrew from the League. Japan then refused to renew the conditions of the Washington Naval Conference when these came up for renewal in 1934 and commenced a great modernization and expansion of her navy, though details of how this was implemented were largely kept secret. At home in Japan, personal freedom and democracy went and the country moved towards a military dictatorship that the Emperor seemed powerless to check. The behaviour of the Japanese during these years matched closely that of the Germans under Hitler and the Nazis. These two countries, although so dissimilar in character, were taking almost parallel paths to outright aggression, to the military alliance of the Axis – and to their own eventual self-destruction in 1945.

The Japanese made no secret of their intentions. A remarkable book written by an officer of the Imperial Japanese Navy, *Japan Must Fight Britain*, was translated into English in 1936 and sold at least 11,000 copies in Britain. The English publisher's introduction stated:

The Pan-Asia movement to establish Tokyo as the pivot of an empire 1,000,000,000 people strong . . . The author discusses the inevitable war between the two powers, detailing the relative strengths and weaknesses of their Army, Navy, Air Force, a comparison from which Britain emerges as definitely the weaker. He claims that the Singapore Base is an insult to Japan, that the Dominions are apathetic and of little material aid in the event of war, that the British Navy is decadent . . . He urges Britain to realize the terrible disadvantages under which she would labour in such a struggle, and to avoid it by making such concessions as will satisfy Japan, concessions that will assure Japan's domination of the Pacific. If she will not give way, then war is inevitable, and the result will be that the British Empire will be broken up for ever.*

* Tota Ishimaru, *Japan Must Fight Britain*, Paternoster Library, London, 1936.

The whole point of the book, of course, was to persuade the British government, through public opinion, to stand aside in China and the Pacific while Japan created her empire.

The governments of Britain and the Empire were well aware of the Japanese threat, but the mid and late 1930s were difficult years with threats to peace from many other quarters – Italy invaded Abyssinia (now Ethiopia), there was the Civil War in Spain, Germany had reoccupied the Rhineland. Britain was ill-prepared to meet the danger of a new war. She was only slowly recovering from the terrible years of the Depression; a constitutional crisis culminated in the abdication of Edward VIII; and public sentiment had far from forgotten 1914–18 – 'the war to end all wars'. But, as that decade moved on, Britain did reluctantly start to rearm and the Far East qualified for part of the expenditure.

The Singapore Naval Base continued to be regarded as the vital position in the Far East and further attention was given to its defence. More heavy coastal guns were installed; two more military airfields were built in the north of Singapore Island at Tengah and Sembawang; and a further five airfields were built up-country in Malaya. The purpose of these last airfields was to extend air cover out over the sea. When they were planned in 1935 and 1936, any Japanese attack was still expected to be purely seaborne and directed only on Singapore Island. It was not until 1937 that Major-General W. G. S. Dobbie, General Officer Commanding in Malaya, came to the conclusion that the jungle on the mainland was not after all impassable to well-trained troops and that the Naval Base could one day be threatened by a Japanese landing on the east coast of Malaya and by a subsequent attack on Singapore from the north. A paltry £60,000 was thereupon allocated to General Dobbie for the construction of ground defences on a stretch of coastline a hundred miles long.

Britain's naval policy for the Far East remained almost

unaltered throughout these years. The defence of the homeland would come first; the Mediterranean, with its vital oil and other trade communications, took second priority; and a threat by Japan came only third. By the late 1930s it was hoped that Japan would keep quiet at least until the completion of the five new battleships and six aircraft carriers of the emergency building programme. The main strength of the Royal Navy's capital ships continued to be retained in the Home Fleet and the Mediterranean Fleet; nothing larger than a cruiser was allocated to the Far East. The policy remained unchanged: in the event of trouble a squadron of capital ships would be sent immediately to Singapore. To make sure that this reinforcement could still be carried out if the Mediterranean or the Suez Canal became closed, extra fuelling facilities were constructed at Freetown, Sierra Leone, and at Simonstown in South Africa.

Over and over again during these years the Admiralty was pressured to change this policy and to station capital ships permanently at Singapore. Australia and New Zealand were constant petitioners; the Australians once considered building their own battleships, but nothing came of it. British Ambassadors in Far Eastern capitals wrote many reports asking for battleships to be sent on prolonged cruises, or, even better, to be stationed permanently at Singapore – anything to impress the Japanese. The Foreign Office passed the correspondence on to the Admiralty. The Navy's answer remained the same. It could not spare battleships for the Far East; Europe and the Mediterranean came first; Germany and Italy were the more likely to attack first. Perhaps, when the new battleships and aircraft carriers were completed, the situation would be more favourable.

Germany put an end to some of the uncertainty in September 1939 by invading Poland and starting the long-anticipated war in Europe. Britain's Far East Empire was now in extreme danger, with every possibility of an opportunist Japanese attack while her main forces were tied up by the Germans. Singapore would have to rely on Britain being able to release heavy naval forces in time and get them out to the Naval Base; if the Japanese arrived before the capital ships, then Singapore's coastal guns, and the slender Army and R.A.F. strength would have to hold off the Japanese until the Royal Navy arrived.

2

'Sinister Twilight'

There were to be just two and a quarter years of war in Europe before the conflict spread to the Far East. What therefore were the principal actions in which capital ships* became involved in European waters during the period between the German invasion of Poland in September 1939 and the early days of December 1941?

Britain started the war with a seemingly impressive strength of capital ships: twelve battleships, three battle cruisers and six aircraft carriers. These twenty-one ships, with five French battleships and one French carrier, faced five German battleships and battle cruisers. These were odds well in favour of the Allies, though the summer of 1940 would add six Italian battleships to the Axis strength while the French fleet would be as good as lost to the Allies. But it was not just a question of relative numbers; of the fifteen British battleships and battle cruisers, only three – *Nelson*, *Rodney* and *Hood* – were post-1918 ships, and *Hood* was only just so. The carriers, too, were an assorted lot, mostly converted to this role after being laid down and partly built as battleships. All the German and most of the Italian ships were of modern construction, and these countries also had the great advantage of being Continental powers with the ability to feed and supply themselves from the mainland of Europe for many years without need for overseas trade. They could keep their ships in harbour until ready to strike while the Royal Navy had to guard a huge arc from the Red Sea round to Scandinavia against enemy attacks on the overseas trade shipping that kept Britain alive. Britain's main hope for the future lay in five modern battleships and four aircraft

---

* Capital ships are taken here to include aircraft carriers as well as battleships and battle cruisers.

carriers which started to come into service after the outbreak of war. The Germans were building only two battleships – the powerful *Bismarck* and *Tirpitz* – and one
carrier, the *Graf Zeppelin*, though this ship would never be
completed.

How had capital ships fared in their encounters before
the Japanese joined in this deadly game of war?

After the sinking of the *Prince of Wales* and the *Repulse* in
action in December 1941, one of the leading questions was
whether the admiral in charge of the operation had been
justified in risking the two ships in an area where friendly
air cover could not be guaranteed and over which enemy
aircraft were likely to be operating. Although it became
painfully obvious after the event that some of the admiral's
decisions were misjudged, an examination by him of the
main actions in which capital ships had been involved up
to that time would not have led him to that conclusion
before the event. Twelve capital ships were in fact sunk
between the opening of the war in September 1939 and the
end of November 1941.

17 September 1939. The British aircraft carrier *Courageous*
was torpedoed off Ireland by the German submarine, U.29.
The *Courageous* would probably have outrun the submerged
U-boat, whose presence was not suspected, had the
carrier not turned to 'fly on' her aircraft and given the
U-boat captain a lucky shot.

14 October 1939. The British battleship *Royal Oak* was
torpedoed at anchorage in Scapa Flow by U.47. The
defences of Scapa Flow against submarine entry were not
yet complete and the attack was made with great skill.

17 December 1939. The German battleship *Admiral Graf
Spee* was caught by three cruisers – H.M.S. *Exeter* and
H.M.S. *Ajax* and H.M.N.Z.S. *Achilles* – off the River Plate
while commerce raiding and seriously damaged. The *Graf
Spee* put into Montevideo for repairs but was then scuttled
on the order of Hitler.

8 June 1940. The British aircraft carrier *Glorious*, with only two escorting destroyers, was caught off Norway by the German battle cruisers *Scharnhorst* and *Gneisenau*. For reasons not known, the *Glorious* was not flying reconnaissance air patrols at the time. All three British ships were soon sunk by shellfire, but not before one of the destroyers, *Acasta*, had damaged *Scharnhorst* in a torpedo attack.

3 July 1940. The French battleship *Bretagne* blew up in Oran harbour when French warships were bombarded by the Royal Navy to prevent them being used by the Germans.

12 November 1940. Three Italian battleships – *Littorio, Conte Di Cavour* and *Caio Duilo* – were torpedoed in a night attack by Fleet Air Arm Swordfish aircraft while moored in Taranto Harbour. All three sank in shallow water.

24 May 1941. The British battle cruiser *Hood* blew up and sank after a surface gun action with the German battleship *Bismarck* and the cruiser *Prinz Eugen* in the North Atlantic. H.M.S. *Prince of Wales* also took part in this battle and scored two hits on the *Bismarck* before herself being hit and forced to break off the action.

27 May 1941. After being damaged by *Prince of Wales*, then hit by torpedoes of three Fleet Air Arm aircraft and two more fired by destroyers, the *Bismarck* was crippled by the battleships *King George V* and *Rodney* and finally finished off by the cruiser *Dorsetshire*'s torpedoes.

13 November 1941. The British aircraft carrier *Ark Royal* sank in the Mediterranean after one torpedo, fired by U.81, struck her engine room.

25 November 1941. The British battleship *Barham* was torpedoed in the Mediterranean by U.331 and her magazines blew up at once.

Twelve capital ships were thus lost between the beginning of the war and the end of November 1941 – four to submarine attack, four to surface gun action, three (the Italian battleships) sunk in harbour by Fleet Air Arm torpedo-carrying aircraft and one (the *Bismarck*) succumbing to a combination of shells and torpedo hits.

It therefore seemed at the time that the main danger to capital ships remained the gunfire of other capital ships. It might have been reasonable to assume that the four ships lost to submarine attack had all been unlucky – *Royal Oak* at anchor at Scapa Flow, *Courageous* turning into the U-boat's sights to fly on her aircraft, *Ark Royal* and *Barham* sunk by single torpedo hits which caused disproportionate damage. At least four other battleships – *Nelson*, *Barham* (in an earlier attack), *Scharnhorst* and *Gneisenau* – had shrugged off torpedo hits by submarines. It was still believed, and correctly so, that a battleship could elude most submarine attacks if she kept up her speed, and that her armoured belt or watertight compartments could usually survive any but the most unfortunate hit if torpedoes did strike home.

Attack by aircraft had not yet loomed large as a danger to capital ships. None had as yet succumbed to bombing attacks, though plenty of smaller ships, including five British cruisers and twenty-eight destroyers, had done so, while the British battleships, *Barham* and *Warspite*, had withstood direct hits by bombs while at sea, and the German ships, *Scharnhorst* and *Gneisenau*, had done the same while in port. The British aircraft carrier *Illustrious* had sailed on in the Mediterranean after being hit by six heavy bombs and near-missed by three more. Torpedo bombers had been active since the outbreak of war, but, apart from the Taranto Harbour action, had achieved no outright sinkings of capital ships.

Any survey carried out in early December 1941 might thus have come to the following three conclusions:

First, capital ships were at risk when faced with a superior force of enemy capital ships.

Secondly, capital ships were vulnerable to submarine

attack only if they slackened speed or suffered unlucky hits in vulnerable spots.

Thirdly, and despite the forecasts of Billy Mitchell and his like, no capital ship, Allied or Axis, had yet been sunk at sea by any form of aircraft attack.

These are important and not unreasonable conclusions for that time. But, more than this, there had been several occasions when the vigorous use of capital ships by both sides had brought positive success. The sending of *Warspite* with a party of destroyers into the enclosed waters of Narvik Fjord in April 1940 had led to the destruction of eight German destroyers and a U-boat, the only outright British success of the Norwegian campaign. Three battle-ships – *Warspite* again, *Barham* and *Valiant* – had, with the aircraft carrier *Formidable*, humiliated the Italian Fleet at the Battle of Cape Matapan and sunk three cruisers without loss. The Germans, too, had had their triumphs. Their fast, modern battleships and battle cruisers had claimed the *Glorious* and the *Hood*, and the bold use of their capital ships as commerce raiders had resulted in the sinking or capture of fifty-one merchant ships, though they had paid for this with the loss of the *Graf Spee* and the *Bismarck*.

The new war in Europe did not seem to have altered the basic nature of naval warfare. The battleship still appeared to have a future.

This second European war in twenty-five years was again a golden opportunity for the Japanese, hungry as always, to expand their empire. Britain was by now almost totally involved in Europe; the United States were watchful but still neutral. When Holland and France fell to the Germans in the summer of 1940, the Far East possessions of these two countries lay almost defenceless. The Japanese could be excused for thinking that before long Britain would also be defeated and another Far Eastern empire could become theirs for the taking. So the Japanese were able to continue their conquests of China and to start actively planning to take over rich European possessions. An even more military-dominated government came to power in July 1940 with General Tojo as Army Minister. A Tripartite Pact was signed with Germany and Italy later that year, and a Neutrality Pact with Russia early in 1941.

The Japanese were not yet ready for outright war with a Western country, but they made steady progress in other ways. The Dutch were persuaded to step up raw-material exports from the Dutch East Indies to Japan, though not by as much as the Japanese would have liked. The British were pressed to close the Burma Road along which most of American war aid entered China, and also to withdraw the British garrisons from Tientsin and Shanghai. The British did close the Burma Road for three months, but only during the monsoon season when the road would have suffered from heavy lorries. And the small garrisons at Tientsin and Shanghai were withdrawn, but for the excellent military reason that, in the event of war, they would have been eliminated in a few hours anyway; the troops could be better employed elsewhere and were moved to Singapore.

Within weeks of the fall of France in 1940, the Japanese demanded that Japanese troops in China be allowed to move into the northern part of French Indo-China. The French Governor-General had to agree, and in April 1941 the Vichy government in France, under German as well as Japanese pressure, had to allow the Japanese the use of air and naval bases in southern Indo-China. Without firing a shot, the Japanese had secured bases only 450 miles from Malaya and 700 miles from Singapore itself. The British possessions were now well within range of Japanese bombers.

Even before the war, doubts about the speed at which capital ships could reinforce Singapore from England had led to a warning that the island might, in the event of attack, have to hold out for ninety days rather than the earlier estimate of seventy days. At the outbreak of war in 1939, Royal Navy strength in the Far East consisted only of the old aircraft carrier *Eagle*, four cruisers, nine destroyers and some submarines; and most of these were soon withdrawn to Europe. After the crisis of the Battle of Britain had passed in 1940, the Far East situation was again reviewed. The commanders of the three services there were asked for their assessment of the minimum military and air force strength needed to hold Singapore until the Navy could arrive. This 'Singapore Defence Conference' was held in October 1940, with Vice-Admiral Sir Geoffrey Layton, Commander-in-Chief China Station, in the chair. (Layton would later be involved, though in a minor way, with the *Prince of Wales* and *Repulse* affair.) Lieutenant-General L. V. Bond and Air Vice-Marshal J. T. Babbington represented the Army and R.A.F. Commander A. C. Thomas, the American Naval Attaché at Bangkok, was sent by his government to Singapore, ostensibly to consult a doctor, though he attended the conference in civilian clothes.

The truth was that the British were in a pathetic position just over one year before full-scale war would begin in the area. The Japanese were known to have occupied two French military airfields near Saigon, to have over 400 land-based aircraft and 280 carrier-based aircraft available for operations, and to be expanding this strength fast. The combined strength of the British and U.S. Navies in South-East Asia was weaker now than the British strength alone had been before the war. The conference decided that, with the Japanese now in Indo-China, the potential danger to Singapore was no longer from a sea attack but from a land advance through Siam and down the Malayan peninsula. The conference also decided that it would now be most prudent for the main defence of Singapore to rely on a strong force of aircraft, and so asked for 582 modern aircraft to be provided. Given these, together with additional Australian and Indian army units earmarked for Malaya, it should be possible to hold off a Japanese offensive until the Navy arrived. The actual air strength in Singapore and Malaya was at that time only eighty-eight aircraft, of which only forty-eight were modern machines.

The vast majority of those 582 aircraft was never provided. They existed, in England, but the recent experiences of the Battle of Britain and the London 'Blitz', coupled with the desire of the R.A.F. leaders, with Churchill's full support, to create a huge bomber force with the hope of bombing Germany into defeat, kept them at home. When the Japanese eventually did strike just over a year after the Defence Conference, Malaya and Singapore would only have 158 operational aircraft, the best of them being a slow American fighter, the Brewster Buffalo, and the Bristol Blenheim bomber – hardly modern aircraft in 1941. At that moment, the R.A.F. would have at least a hundred squadrons of modern fighters in England, very much under-employed since the main Luftwaffe strength would have been moved to Russia and the Mediterranean. Only three months after Singapore fell, R.A.F. Bomber Command would mount the first of its Thousand Bomber Raids on Germany. But such errors are easy to see in hindsight.

Immediately after the Singapore Conference, a new command system for the Far East was instituted. For the first time a joint commander for the British forces in the area was appointed. Air Chief Marshal Sir Robert Brooke-Popham, who had retired from the R.A.F. in 1937 to become Governor of Kenya, but who was now back on the active list, was in November 1940 appointed as Commander-in-Chief, Far East. His imposing title gave him command of all British army and air units in Burma, Malaya, Singapore and Hong Kong. It was a measure of the reliance now being placed on the R.A.F. to defend Singapore until the Navy's battleships could arrive that the choice for this important post should fall on an air force and not an army officer. But the Royal Navy's ships in the Far East were expressly excluded from his joint command!

The second of the future participants in the tragedy of the *Prince of Wales* and the *Repulse* had thus arrived on the scene. Pity poor Brooke-Popham, whose parent service allowed him to go out to carry this burden in the Far East but which kept its aircraft at home.

The five-month period from July to November 1941 was destined to be the last period of peace in the Far East and the Pacific. During these months three of the Western powers with interests in the area finally said 'No' to further Japanese expansion, even at the risk of provoking a war which two of them certainly could not afford. For Winston Churchill, the Japanese threats made these months a period of 'sinister twilight' in the Far East. The crunch came over a country and over a commodity that, by coincidence, were both to threaten world stability in entirely different circumstances a quarter of a century later. This country was Indo-China, part of which is now Vietnam, and the commodity was oil.

In July 1941 the Japanese Ambassador to the Vichy government in France was instructed to inform the French that Japan demanded further military and economic concessions in Indo-China. Such an extension of the Japanese sphere of influence would bring Japanese army units much closer to the Americans in the Philippines and the British in Malaya. The Americans had succeeded in deciphering the radio instructions from Japan to her Ambassador at Vichy and informed Britain that the United States was not prepared to let Japanese troops move south in Indo-China and would stop all trade with Japan if it happened. Before taking this drastic step, the United States proposed to Japan that Indo-China should be regarded as neutral, but this proposal was ignored. Vichy soon submitted to the Japanese demands and the Japanese troops did march into southern Indo-China. The Americans immediately stopped all trade with Japan and froze Japanese assets in the United States. The British and Free Dutch followed suit, wanting to keep in step with the Americans at all costs, but desperately alarmed at the prospect of war if the Japanese refused to withdraw from Indo-China.

The Japanese were appalled at this firm American action,

which was entirely unexpected. Their main problem was oil. Japan produced a mere 10 per cent of her own oil needs; 80 per cent of her oil imports came from the United States and 10 per cent from the Dutch East Indies. Although she had stockpiled oil steadily over the past ten years, these reserves could only last for three years, even with the strictest economies. For this modern industrial country, striving hard to build up its forces for a later confrontation with the West at the same time as continuing the war in China, the American and Dutch oil embargo was intolerable. The Japanese decided that they could take one of three courses: (a) back down and withdraw their army units from southern Indo-China; (b) attempt to negotiate with the Americans; or (c) take the ultimate step and prepare for an all-out war in which they could invade the oil-rich countries of South-East Asia and set up their much desired 'Greater East Asia Co-Prosperity Sphere' – the Japanese dream of a federation of Asiatic countries under Japanese leadership.

The proud Japanese had suffered enough insults at the hands of the West over the years; they were not prepared to lose face further and refused to withdraw from Indo-China. Instead, a negotiating team was sent to Washington in the hope that the Americans might relax the trade embargo. At the same time, however, preparations were made for war if the Americans would not cooperate. It is interesting to note that it was the Army in Japan which was keenest for war while the Navy wanted to continue negotiations. There was no separate air force and the civilian politicians and the Emperor were now without influence. As it turned out, neither side was prepared to offer any real compromise.

On 5 November a decision was taken in Tokyo: if no agreement could be reached with the Americans by the 25th, Japan would launch surprise attacks on the Americans, the British and the Dutch at many points, the operations to start as soon as possible after 1 December. Time was now of the essence for the Japanese; with each day that passed her oil reserves were being run down, her potential enemies were reinforcing their garrisons, the monsoons expected at the end of November would make more difficult the operations being planned.

British and American naval plans of twenty years' standing were about to be put to the test. It would be very much a naval war and the battleships would soon be in action.

3

'A Decisive Deterrent'

No large British warship had visited the Far East since long before the war, but with the Battle of Britain safely weathered in 1940, the *Bismarck* sunk in May 1941, and the new King George V Class battleships coming into service, the Admiralty decided upon a long-term plan to assemble a force of heavy warships in the Indian Ocean; then to send it to Singapore as Britain's third fleet – the 'Eastern Fleet'. Public Record Office documents reveal that this fleet was to consist of no less than seven battleships or battle cruisers, one aircraft carrier, ten cruisers and twenty-four destroyers. Together with the American Pacific Fleet based at Pearl Harbor, this force would be a formidable deterrent to Japanese aggression.

But there were several weaknesses in the Admiralty plan. The battleships selected were *Nelson* and *Rodney* with the four old and slow R Class ships, *Ramillies*, *Resolution*, *Revenge* and *Royal Sovereign*, and the equally old but faster battle cruiser *Renown*. No King George V Class ship was included; quantity rather than quality would be the keynote. Then, it was found necessary to refit or repair many of the ships chosen, and also to fit them with the latest radar. And finally, the destroyers could not yet be released from the Home and Mediterranean Fleets or from convoy work. The earliest date given by the Admiralty for the assembly of the Eastern Fleet was March 1942. This document is undated, but undoubtedly refers to the Admiralty policy for the summer of 1941 after the *Bismarck* had been sunk.*

Alas, events would move too fast for this paper fleet ever to become a reality. The next move came on 11

* The document is Public Record Office A D M 199/1149.

August 1941, while the Prime Minister was attending the Atlantic Conference with President Roosevelt in Newfoundland, having been taken across the Atlantic by the battleship *Prince of Wales*. Roosevelt had informed Churchill that the American attitude to Japan, which had already led to the trade embargo, was about to be stiffened further and that war in the Far East might result. Churchill immediately signalled this information to his planners in London.

Even while Churchill was still in Newfoundland, work began. On 12 August the Joint Planning Staff started to prepare a plan for the immediate reinforcement of the Far East with a force 'including capital ships'. The twenty-year-old-plan to send battleships out to the Singapore Naval Base was about to be put into effect. The proposal was passed to the Naval Staff, and they met the following day, presumably under the First Sea Lord, Sir Dudley Pound. The naval leaders produced a plan which became the basis of their policy for the next two months – until, in fact, they were argued out of it by the politicians. This was that only the old battle cruiser *Repulse*, now more easily available than *Renown* of the previous plan, and the four old R Class battleships be sent to the Indian Ocean. This plan reflects the great reluctance of the Admiralty to let any of their modern battleships leave European waters. Their fear was that the fast German battleship *Tirpitz*, or the battle cruisers *Scharnhorst* and *Gneisenau*, might sail to attack the Atlantic trade convoys; it was a good example of the way a handful of German capital ships was able to tie down the Royal Navy for years without actually leaving harbour.

These deliberations in August 1941 were taking place at a time when the Americans were quietly taking over some responsibility for the protection of North Atlantic convoys. Sir Dudley Pound and the Naval Staff decided to lay down their terms for the release of a modern British battleship for the Eastern Fleet. At the First Sea Lord's meeting at the Admiralty on 20 August, it was concluded that should the U.S.A. provide a sufficiently strong striking force of modern battleships capable of engaging *Tirpitz* and be prepared to allow one of these ships to replace one of our own King George V Class if damaged, then it would be possible to send one of the King George V Class to the Far East or Indian Ocean in addition to *Nelson, Rodney*, four R Class and *Renown*. *

In other words, if the Americans were prepared to send not just escort vessels to protect convoys but several modern battleships to Scapa Flow to serve with the British Fleet at a time when the United States was not at war with Germany, then the Admiralty would send one modern British battleship to the Far East to defend Singapore in the event of a Japanese attack. It was a condition that the Admiralty knew could hardly be met, and amounted to a virtual refusal to release a modern battleship.

Churchill was back in London by the end of the month, and soon made his views known to the First Sea Lord in one of his celebrated 'Action This Day' personal minutes.

It should become possible in the near future to place a deterrent squadron in the Indian Ocean. Such a force should consist of the smallest number of the best ships. The most economical disposition would be to send *Duke of York* as soon as she is clear of constructional defects, via Trinidad and Simonstown to the East. She could be joined by *Repulse* or *Renown* and one aircraft carrier of high speed. This powerful force might show itself in the triangle Aden-Singapore-Simonstown. It would exert a paralysing effect upon Japanese Naval action. The *Duke of York* could work up on her long voyage to the East, leaving the C.-in-C. Home Fleet with two K.G.V.s which are thoroughly efficient. It would be in my opinion a more thrifty and fruitful use of our resources than to send *Prince of Wales* from regions where she might, though it is unlikely, meet *Tirpitz*.†

Several implications of this important minute should be looked at more closely. Churchill clearly wanted a small fleet of quality – a fast, hard-hitting combination of battleship, battle cruiser and aircraft carrier. In later documents on the same subject it becomes clear that Churchill did not

* Public Record Office ADM 199/1149.
† Public Record Office PREM 163/3.

fear a direct Japanese attack on Singapore or Malaya, seeing the greatest potential danger as coming from Japanese ships attacking British trade shipping in the Pacific and Indian Oceans. Churchill therefore wanted a fast *offensive* or 'hunting-down' force on the lines of that which had so recently destroyed the *Bismarck*. The Admiralty wanted a larger *defensive* force of ships to protect Malaya and Singapore. Churchill's choice of *Duke of York* is an interesting one. This was the third of the five King George V Class battleships, only recently completed, and Churchill was obviously saying to the Admiralty, 'Give me one aircraft carrier and this latest, unready, King George V Class battleship and I will leave you with *Nelson*, *Rodney* and the two more experienced modern battleships, *King George V* and *Prince of Wales*, to look after any German ships coming out into the Atlantic.'

Churchill was badly in error over two major parts of his reasoning. First, the Japanese were already planning an attack on Malaya and, through it, on Singapore; and secondly, had the Japanese limited themselves to raiding actions against British shipping, just three British ships would have been of very little use against the Japanese Navy with its strong force of battleships and aircraft carriers. His reference to the exertion by his three ships of a 'paralysing effect upon Japanese Naval action' was soon to look a little ludicrous, but Churchill was not the only one in these months to so seriously underestimate Japanese intentions and capabilities.

Churchill's note was followed three days later by a long reply from Sir Dudley Pound in which the Admiralty put forward many, quite valid, reasons why all three King George V battleships should remain at home and repeated their intention of building up the larger force of older ships in the East. Churchill did not accept this without a counter-blast on the following day. It contained no new views, but several powerful arguments in support of his original position. It is worth recording in full the contents of this minute, for not only does it set out fully Churchill's policy which eventually resulted in the dispatch of the *Prince of Wales* and the *Repulse* to the Far East, but is also a good example of the vigorous way Churchill set about his service leaders, without mincing words:

1. It is surely a faulty disposition to create in the Indian Ocean a fleet considerable in numbers, costly in maintenance and manpower, but consisting entirely of slow, obsolescent or unmodernized ships which can neither fight a fleet action with the main Japanese force nor act as a deterrent upon his modern fast heavy ships, if used singly or in pairs as raiders. Such dispositions might be forced upon us by circumstances but they are inherently unsound in themselves.

2. The use of the four R's for convoy work is good as against enemy 8-inch cruisers. But if the general arrangements are such that the enemy is not afraid to detach an individual fast modern battleship for raiding purposes, all these old ships and the convoys they guard are easy prey. The R's in their present state would be floating coffins. In order to justify the use of the R's for convoy work in the Indian and Pacific Oceans, it would be necessary to have one or two fast heavy units which would prevent the enemy from detaching individual heavy raiders without fear of punishment. No doubt the Australian Government would be pleased to count the numbers of old battleships in their neighbourhood, but we must not play down to uninstructed thought. On the contrary, we should inculcate the true principles of naval strategy, one of which is certainly to use a small number of the best ships to cope with a superior force.

3. The potency of the dispositions I ventured to suggest in my minute M 819.1 is illustrated by the Admiralty's own extraordinary concern about the *Tirpitz*. *Tirpitz* is doing to us exactly what a K.G.V. in the Indian Ocean would do to the Japanese Navy. It exercises a vague, general fear and menaces all points at once. It appears, and disappears, causing immediate reactions and perturbations on the other side.

4. The fact that the Admiralty consider that three K.G.V.s must be used to contain *Tirpitz* is a serious reflection upon the design of our latest ships, which though being undergunned and weakened by hangars in the middle of their citadels, are evidently judged unfit to fight their opposite number in a single ship action. But, after making allowances for this, I cannot feel convinced that the proposal to retain the three K.G.V.s in the Atlantic is sound, having regard (a) to the American dispositions which may now be counted upon and (b) to the proved power of aircraft carriers to slow down a ship like

Tirpitz if she were loose. It also seems unlikely that *Tirpitz* will be withdrawn from the Baltic while the Russian Fleet remains in being; and further, the fate of the *Bismarck* and all her supply ships must surely be present in the German mind. How foolish they would be to send her out, when by staying she contains the three strongest and newest battleships we have, and rules the Baltic as well! I feel therefore that an excessive provision is being made in the Atlantic, and one which is certainly incomparably more lavish than anything we have been able to indulge in so far in this war.

5. The best use that could be made of the R's would be, even at this late date, to have them re-armoured against aircraft attack and used as a slow-moving squadron which could regain for us the power to move through the Mediterranean and defend Malta indefinitely.

6. I must add that I cannot feel that Japan will face the combination against her of the United States, Great Britain and Russia, while already preoccupied in China. It is very likely she will negotiate with the United States for at least three months without making any further aggressive move or joining the Axis actively. Nothing would increase her hesitation more than the appearance of the force mentioned in my minute M 819-1, and above all a K.G.V. This might indeed be a decisive deterrent.

7. I should like to talk these matters over with you.

W.S.C. 29.8.41*

These views were sent to the First Sea Lord, but, strangely, the talk that Churchill wished to have on the subject does not seem to have materialized. It was nearly seven weeks before the issue was raised again. During these weeks it was the Admiralty plan for the collection of the force of old battleships in early 1942 that was quietly being proceeded with.

By the middle of October, no one could ignore further the developing events in the Far East. The Americans had kept their British friends informed of all diplomatic moves, and British Intelligence had gleaned a few items from the Japanese side, even though the Japanese were making their preparations under conditions of unprecedented secrecy. As early as 3 June, a British naval intelligence officer at

* Public Record Office PREM 163/3.

Cape Town had reported a considerable increase in Japanese cipher cable traffic between Tokyo and Japanese consuls as far afield as Singapore, Mombasa and Beirut. Another intelligence officer, at Mombasa, reported that Japanese businessmen in Kenya were selling off their businesses and belongings at prices well below their true value and leaving for home. Reports from elsewhere in August and September told of Japanese merchant ships having all their sailing schedules cancelled, painting out all house flags and national markings and being gathered in large numbers at Japanese ports. Japanese naval reservists were being called up and were reporting for duty at naval bases. All Japanese shipping had disappeared from the Indian Ocean. These sundry reports are all recorded in naval documents; no doubt there were many other intelligence hints that the Japanese were actively preparing for war.

On 16 October, a new government with General Tojo as Prime Minister took power. All over the world, diplomats warned their governments that this event had brought war appreciably nearer. The British War Cabinet met the following day to hear the views of Anthony Eden, the Foreign Minister. Eden asked that the possibility of sending capital ships to the Far East be once more examined. No firm decision was taken at this meeting, and there was not much more than the restating of old views. Churchill, supported by Eden, and also by Clement Attlee, the Labour leader in Churchill's Coalition government, all wanted one modern battleship of the King George V Class as a deterrent, Churchill quoting to the sailors how,

we had before us the example of the battleship *Tirpitz* which now compelled us to keep on guard a force three times her weight in addition to the United States forces patrolling the Atlantic. The presence of one modern capital ship in Far Eastern waters could be calculated to have a similar effect on the Japanese Naval authorities, and, thereby, on Japanese foreign policy.*

* Public Record Office CAB 69/2.

Mr A. V. Alexander, First Lord of the Admiralty (equivalent to Navy Minister), pointed out that the two situations cited by Churchill were not comparable; it was not Britain's intention to go raiding Japanese trade convoys as the *Tirpitz* was threatening to do in the Atlantic. This piece of logic was ignored. The First Sea Lord, Admiral Sir Dudley Pound, was not present, and the Admiralty's views were put by Vice-Admiral Sir Tom Phillips, the Vice-Chief of the Naval Staff. Phillips merely repeated the long-held Admiralty view that the older battleships should be sent East. Churchill heard Phillips out, then said he was not going to impose a decision on the Admiralty in the absence of Sir Dudley Pound, but, 'in view of the strong feeling of the committee', he 'invited' the Admiralty to consider the proposal to get one King George V battleship and one aircraft carrier out to Singapore as quickly as possible to join the old battle cruiser *Repulse*, already on her way to the Indian Ocean. Churchill hoped 'that the Admiralty would not oppose this suggestion', which would be finally debated at the committee's next meeting three days hence. There is no record of the Army or R.A.F. leaders, General Sir John Dill and Air Chief Marshal Sir Charles Portal, expressing an opinion on this naval matter.

And so, at 12.30 p.m., on Monday, 20 October 1941, what was to be a fateful meeting of the War Cabinet's Defence Committee took place at 10 Downing Street. Admiral Sir Dudley Pound was present. Sir Tom Phillips, who had represented Pound at the previous meeting, was also there, knowing already that he would command whatever fleet was established as a result of this protracted debate.

Churchill started on a belligerent line. He had clearly heard quite enough of the *Tirpitz* and the Admiralty's desire to keep three King George Vs at home in case the *Tirpitz* came out into the Atlantic. 'The War Cabinet', Churchill said, 'are quite prepared to face the loss of shipping which might take place if the *Tirpitz* comes out

into the Atlantic.' Sir Dudley Pound restated the Admiralty
position at length. While his statement contained little
that was new, he took care to 'note that the War Cabinet
are prepared to face this responsibility' – for shipping
losses caused by *Tirpitz* should a King George V battleship be sent East. (The King George V battleship now
under consideration was *Prince of Wales*; it had been
accepted that *Duke of York* was too new and unready.)
Anthony Eden backed Churchill. 'From the political point
of view there is no doubt as to the value of our sending a
really modern ship. The weakness of our political position
at present is that the Japanese are not faced with the
certainty that the United States and ourselves will act, if,
for example, they go into Thailand (Siam) or attack
Russia.'*

The absence of any reference by Eden to a danger to
Malaya shows how he, like Churchill, had little idea of
Japanese intentions, or of how mightily audacious would
be the opening Japanese moves.

It is difficult to interpret the full force of emotion
through the recorded, written record of the discussion. The
Prime Minister said that he did not believe that the
Japanese would go to war with the United States and ourselves. He would like to see the *Prince of Wales* sent and
the situation reviewed when the *Nelson* had been repaired.
It seems innocent enough, and the War Cabinet secretaries
have probably condensed Churchill's full statement for the
minutes, but it must have been said with enough emphasis
for Sir Dudley Pound to know that he was beaten and the
Admiralty overruled.

The First Sea Lord's surrender was couched in the form
of a compromise. He would send *Prince of Wales* to Cape
Town so that the full publicity value of its arrival there,
ostensibly *en route* to the Far East, could be gained, but he
would not authorize any further movement by *Prince of
Wales* to the East until that time so that the current

* Public Record Office C A B 69/8.

situation could then be assessed. Nothing had been said at the meeting about an aircraft carrier to accompany *Prince of Wales*. Like the dispatch of the battle cruiser *Repulse*, this had been taken for granted, and the committee had confined itself to debating the one outstanding item of disagreement between the two sides: that of the type of battleship to be sent. In fact it was planned that H.M.S. *Indomitable*, a new aircraft carrier then working up in the West Indies, would be included in the force.

So the decision was taken. The Navy were to dispatch as quickly as possible H.M.S. *Prince of Wales* and H.M.S. *Indomitable* to Cape Town, and a decision would then be taken about the advisability of sending these two ships into the Indian Ocean to join H.M.S. *Repulse* and proceed to Singapore. Only three people Churchill, Eden and Sir Dudley Pound, had taken part in the discussions; once again, the Army and the R.A.F. had remained silent. The Committee proceeded to its next item of business, which was to consider 'Operation Crusader', General Auchinleck's proposed offensive in the North African desert.

There was one strange and, so far, unexplained sequel to the decision. Although Pound's proviso was that the *Prince of Wales* should not proceed past Cape Town without further consideration, Admiralty orders to various headquarters on the day following the meeting announced that *Prince of Wales* would be sailing for Singapore, with no mention of Cape Town. This has always been one of the small mysteries of the *Prince of Wales* and *Repulse* story. Churchill, sending out his round of telegrams to the Empire governments, was quoting the Cape Town plan. Perhaps the Admiralty's references to Singapore as the destination were deliberately spread around in the hope that the Japanese would pick up the information and be suitably impressed that the British meant business.

It should be emphasized that the Public Record Office documents show quite clearly that Churchill, well backed up by Eden and the Foreign Office, had insisted on sending this force of only three ships, from three widely separated points, to Singapore in the belief that it would persuade the Japanese to make no further moves in South-East Asia. Churchill and Eden clearly did not consider Malaya and Singapore to be threatened by direct attack. The Admiralty had concurred with the general intention of this move, but had consistently opposed, until overruled, the inclusion of the King George V Class ship in this force on the grounds that its dispatch would encourage the *Tirpitz* to come out. In fact the Admiralty were probably more realistic in their assessments of the danger to Malaya, though they did not make much of this argument.

Time was running out. Within a week of the War Cabinet decision, Naval Intelligence was reporting that the Imperial Japanese Navy had fully mobilized on a war footing and was concentrated at Sasebo Naval Base in southern Japan.

4

Force G

Even under the pressure of imminent war in the Far East, it would take several weeks to assemble the three large ships of Force G and their attendant escorts. The *Prince of Wales* was at Scapa Flow, having only recently returned from operations in the Mediterranean. The new aircraft carrier *Indomitable* was three days out into the Atlantic from Greenock on her way to the quiet waters of the Caribbean. Once there, she would complete the working up of her ship's company and Fleet Air Arm squadrons before proceeding round the Cape of Good Hope to join the remainder of Force G. Only the battle cruiser *Repulse* was even part-way to Singapore, having arrived in the Indian Ocean earlier in the month. There were in the Far East only the ships of the China Station, with Headquarters ashore at Singapore, and nothing heavier than three old light cruisers. The Eastern Fleet could come into being only when the various ships of Force G reached Singapore.

H.M.S. *Repulse* was just a quarter of a century old, having been launched at John Brown's Clydebank yard on 8 January 1916 and being completed ready for service in August of that year. It was originally intended that she would become one of the seven R Class battleships, the first of which were already under construction in 1914, but it was decided to alter drastically the design of two of this class from battleships to battle cruisers. Hence *Repulse* and her only sister ship, *Renown*, finished up more lightly protected and less heavily gunned but a clear 8 knots faster than the R Class battleships. *Repulse*'s main armament consisted of six 15-in. guns in two double turrets forward and one aft, and the secondary armament consisted of twelve 4-in. guns. Her weight was 32,000 tons – 36,800 fully loaded – and the top speed was 32 knots. As usual with capital ships built at that time, underwater bulges up to fourteen feet wide were built outside the main hull to absorb the force of a torpedo hit.

With her graceful lines and slim beam, this fast battle cruiser was pleasing in appearance. She and the *Renown* were certainly the most elegant big ships in the Royal Navy at the time and, with the *Hood*, built two years later, remained so for many years. In the summer of 1916 *Repulse* reported for service with the Grand Fleet at Scapa Flow just after the Battle of Jutland. As three battle cruisers had been blown up under German shellfire in the battle, the new arrival was immediately sent back for more armour plating, even though battle cruisers were intended to have a fast, roving commission in war and should not have been expected to withstand the slogging match of a fleet action on Jutland lines. Before the First World War ended, *Repulse* did manage to take part in one brief, inconclusive action with German ships in the engagement off the Horn Reefs in the Heligoland Bight in November 1917. She covered the retirement of a squadron of British light cruisers and her 15-in. guns scored a hit on the German cruiser *Königsberg*. That single hit was destined to be the only one scored by *Repulse*'s great guns in her whole career.

From 1918 to 1939, *Repulse* lived the typical peacetime life of a Royal Navy capital ship with a mixture of home service and foreign cruising. She took Edward, Prince of Wales, to South America and South Africa in 1925, and another voyage included a call at Singapore, many years later to be the starting-point of *Repulse*'s last voyage. There were two extensive refits costing over £2 million in all; these kept *Repulse* in good shape for the next war, but she was never re-engined like the *Renown*, although her ageing machinery was still capable of producing a useful 29 knots when required. During her last refit, *Repulse* had been fitted with special accommodation to take the newly crowned King George VI and Queen Elizabeth on the 1939

Royal Visit to Canada, but a last-minute decision not to allow the battle cruiser to leave European waters in that year of crisis meant that she could do no more than escort the King and Queen on the first part of their voyage aboard the liner *Empress of Australia*.

So the coming of war in September 1939 found the *Repulse* ready, in sound condition and still fast, with a powerful armament and accommodation fit for a king. If she had one drawback other than the thin armoured protection of all battle cruisers, it was the quantity and quality of her anti-aircraft armament. This was composed of just eight hand-operated high-angle 4-in. guns and two sets of eight-barrelled 2-pounder 'pom-poms'.

Repulse was at sea within four days of the outbreak of war, serving on the Northern Patrol between Scotland and Iceland, guarding against German naval units trying to get out into the Atlantic and among the British merchant shipping there, and also against blockade-running merchant ships trying to reach Germany. When German raiders did get into the Atlantic, *Repulse* sailed as heavy escort with trade convoys and formed part of the escort for the convoy of five liners which brought the 20,000 soldiers of the 1st Canadian Division safely to England in December 1939. Then, in 1940, she took part in the naval operations off Norway, but without making contact with any German ships. More Northern Patrol and convoy work followed, and in 1941 *Repulse* narrowly missed being in action with the *Bismarck* when sent out with the rest of the Home Fleet in the hunt for the German battleship. A combination of tired engines and shortage of fuel eventually forced her to break off and put into Newfoundland while other ships had the satisfaction of finishing off *Bismarck* and revenging the *Hood*.

Just as *Repulse* was a representative of the pre-war Royal Navy, so were most of her crew. The ship had recommissioned early in 1939 after a long refit, and the crew had been bitterly disappointed to miss the glamour of the Royal Visit to Canada that summer. This 1939 crew, a large proportion of whom were still aboard *Repulse* when she sailed East in 1941, had been provided by the Devonport Manning Depot at Plymouth. It is said that when the Navy had first come to Devonport many years earlier, the sailors were much impressed by the local peoples' appetite for Devonshire cream and 'Tiddley Oggies' (Cornish pasties), and had ever since called the Devonport people 'Guzzlers'. The naval base thus became 'Guz', and *Repulse* what is known in the Royal Navy as a 'Guz ship'.*

Repulse had been built for a crew of 1,181 men with extra accommodation for an admiral's staff of twenty-four if required. Like all wartime ships, she had been forced to take more men aboard for extra weapons and equipment. She would eventually sail into action with sixty-nine officers and 1,240 petty officers and ratings. The increase of 104 over her intended capacity was much less than in many wartime ships, so *Repulse*'s men probably had as spacious and comfortable accommodation as any ship in service at that time. Since she had better ventilation than *Prince of Wales*, she would not be so troubled by a voyage to the tropics.

Captain E. J. Spooner had commanded *Repulse* for the first years of war, but was then posted to Singapore as Rear-Admiral, Malaya, where he would soon be welcoming his old ship to the Naval Base. Spooner was succeeded by Captain W. G. (Bill) Tennant, a tall grey-haired officer of fifty-three, seemingly stern and reserved in character but found on closer acquaintance to be a warm-hearted man and a fine leader. By reputation he was one of the Navy's finest navigators. Captain Tennant had done well at Dunkirk, where he had served ashore as Senior Naval Officer throughout the evacuation and been one of the last to leave. The *Repulse* men were quite proud of their new captain's exploits at Dunkirk and called him affectionately 'Dunkirk Joe'.

* Of the other two manning depots, Portsmouth is known as 'Pompey' and Chatham as 'Chats'.

Repulse's Heads of Departments when she sailed East in 1941 were as follows:

The Commander: Commander D. G. V. Williams

Gunnery: Lieutenant-Commander C. H. Cobbe

Torpedo and Electrical: Lieutenant-Commander K. R. Buckley

Navigation: Lieutenant-Commander H. B. C. Gill, D.S.C.

Engineering: Engineer-Commander H. Lang

Medical: Surgeon-Commander D. A. Newberry, M.R.C.S., L.R.C.P.

Supplies: Paymaster-Commander L. V. Webb

Royal Marines: Captain R. G. S. Lang

Chaplain: Reverend Canon C. J. S. Bezzant

Repulse's more junior officers were quite typical of large naval ships at this time, being mainly a mixture of regular officers and R.N.V.R.s, with three Royal Marine and three Fleet Air Arm officers, the latter for the ship's two Walrus amphibian reconnaissance aircraft. An unusual element among the midshipmen were five Australians who had been sent to join the Australian cruiser *Australia*. On arrival in England in February 1941, they found that their intended ship had departed to the Indian Ocean, and they were posted instead to *Repulse*, then on the Clyde.

It is a little difficult to remember exactly one's impressions on that particular afternoon of joining one's first ship. Naturally to a Midshipman she looked enormous, impressively powerful, and capable of high speed. It was not possible to comprehend how we would ever find our way about or fit into the organization, and one had the inevitable feeling of apprehension about the future, from the personal aspect rather than from operational activities. On arrival we were welcomed by the 'Snotty's Nurse' – then Lieutenant Joc Hayes – and Sub-Lieutenant Dicky Pool, Sub of the Gunroom. (Midshipman G. R. Griffiths) *

---

* Ranks used in this and the following quotations are those held in December 1941. The 'Snotty's Nurse' was the officer in charge of midshipmen.

Probably 60 to 70 per cent of *Repulse*'s lower deck were pre-war regulars, the remainder being recalled reservists or 'Hostilities Only' men. There were about 130 Royal Marines, and the usual complement of 120 or so of the sixteen- and seventeen-year-old boy seamen carried by all capital ships and cruisers. It is clear, from contact with many of the men who served in her, that *Repulse* was a well-disciplined and happy ship under a popular captain. Not one criticism of any aspect of the ship's equipment or organization was to be heard. Rather there was immense pride in the old ship, especially in her gunnery – 'we could straddle any battle practice target at 26,000 yards' – and also in the fact that their ship was one of the élite battle cruisers and not just a 'common' battleship. There was pride also in the fact that *Repulse* had protected many a convoy in her 30,000 miles of steaming since 1939 and had not lost a single ship from those convoys or had otherwise let down any ship in which she had been in company. But there was regret that her main armament had yet to be fired in this war, and it was the great desire of *Repulse*'s ship's company that they would soon meet an enemy warship against which to try out those six 15-in. guns.

While his ship was undergoing a short refit at Rosyth in August 1941, Captain Tennant was summond to London and told that *Repulse* was now destined for the Indian Ocean as one of the first members of the new Eastern Fleet. On 28 August, *Repulse* received her orders to sail as senior ship of the escort of Convoy WS. 11,* carrying troops and military equipment for Suez via the Cape. On the last day of the month, *Repulse* slipped quietly out of the Clyde to join her convoy and commence her voyage to the East.

The five ships of the much-vaunted King George V Class of battleships formed part of Britain's emergency rearmament

---

* Each regular convoy run was identified by initials, usually denoting the starting or finishing points of that run. The WS. Convoys were an exception; the initials stood for 'Winston's Specials'.

programme of the late 1930s and were the first battleships
to be built since *Nelson* and *Rodney* had been launched in
1925. The Royal Navy was no longer building battle
cruisers; battleships could now achieve almost 30 knots,
so these new vessels had the best of both worlds – armour
and speed. The biggest drawback to the new battleships
was the limitation on their tonnage and on the size of their
main gun armament imposed by the latest naval treaty.
The London Naval Treaty of 1936 had restricted ships to
a weight of 35,000 tons and their guns to 15-in. calibre,
and Britain had complied. Germany on the other hand, who
had also signed, was designing the battleships *Bismarck*
and *Tirpitz* which would eventually turn out at 45,000 tons
and 56,000 tons respectively and be armed with 15-in.
guns; and the Japanese, who had refused to sign at all,
were soon to build their two Yamato Class monsters of
64,000 tons with 18-in. guns! It was such adversaries that
the King George Vs might one day be called upon to fight.

But the King George Vs did have some advantages,
especially in their main armament. Each ship had ten guns.
The original design had even envisaged twelve, but the
tonnage limitation had posed the choice of armour plating
or guns, and two guns had been dropped to give more
armour. The 14-in. guns were also of an advanced design,
had a range of 36,000 yards (over twenty miles) and a
higher rate of sustained fire – two shells per gun per
minute – than had ever been achieved before. The weight
of shell that could be delivered in a stand-up fight would
thus still be formidable. There were few doubts about the
King George Vs' secondary and anti-aircraft armament.
They had four twin 5·25-in. turrets mounted on each side
of the main deck, each gun being capable of firing eighteen
rounds a minute at either a ship or aircraft target. These
5·25-in. guns had a highly sophisticated control system
and were reckoned to be the last word in anti-aircraft
armament. The close-range anti-aircraft armament varied
slightly from ship to ship, but *Prince of Wales* carried six
sets of eight-barrelled 2-pounder pom-poms, a 40-mm.

Bofors gun and a number of Oerlikon light cannons and Lewis machine guns.

The anti-torpedo bulge of the older battleships and battle cruisers had now been replaced in the King George.V Class by a sophisticated system of bulkheads and watertight compartments intended to limit any flooding following a torpedo hit to very small areas. Out of a total weight of 35,000 tons, no less than 12,500 tons was armour plating, but most of this was above the waterline. Unofficial propaganda claimed that the King George Vs were unsinkable.

THE KING GEORGE V CLASS BATTLESHIPS

King George V: launched 21 January 1939

Prince of Wales: launched 3 May 1939

Duke of York (originally named *Anson*): launched 24 February 1940

Anson (originally named *Jellicoe*): launched 28 February 1940

Howe (originally *Beatty*): launched 9 April 1940

It is interesting to note that three of the class had their names changed before being launched; it was perhaps thought that Jellicoe and Beatty were names involved in too recent and controversial an action – Jutland – to be used so soon. The Prince of Wales and the Duke of York were the two sailor sons of the old King George V, who had died in 1936 while the class named after him was being planned. There may have been some embarrassment at the choice of name for H.M.S. *Prince of Wales* when the prince became King Edward VIII in 1936, then abdicated in the same year over his proposed marriage to the American divorcee Mrs Simpson, but the choice of name was allowed to stand.

Prince of Wales was laid down on New Year's Day 1937 by Cammell Lairds at their Birkenhead shipyard, and the hull took just over two years to build. She was launched on

4 May 1939 by the Princess Royal in glorious spring weather and before a crowd of 50,000. At the luncheon following the launching, the Princess Royal, who had launched the *Rodney* from the same yard fourteen years earlier, said she now had 'two splendid God-children', and Mr R. S. Johnson, Managing Director of Cammell Lairds, said: 'If I were in Hitler's shoes and heard about the wonderful work and speed with which we are turning out new ships, I believe I would turn on my "Axis" and think twice before coming to grips with this country.'*

But the building and subsequent fitting-out period was not a happy one and the new and complicated design of hull and equipment caused difficulties. After the war started, a heavy German bomb burst between *Prince of Wales* and the quay of the fitting-out basin during the 1940 Liverpool Blitz and caused leaks in the hull; dockyard officials and naval officers were much concerned at the amount of water that entered the ship, causing a list which one observer stated to be 14 degrees, though this was probably an over-estimate. It was the first of many incidents that were to bring *Prince of Wales* a reputation for bad luck.

It was decided to get *Prince of Wales* away from Liverpool and the danger of further German bombs as soon as possible. She was commissioned on Sunday, 19 January 1941, but her departure for Rosyth the following day was delayed when her four tugs pulled her on to an unsuspected sandbank before she could even get under her own power. *Prince of Wales* then sailed with two of her four screws lashed down to the upper deck; there had been no time to fit them at Liverpool. There were more unhappy incidents at Rosyth – a pom-pom crew fired two rounds in error while reloading and a nearby dockyard worker was injured, though not seriously; small fires broke out three times in the shell room of B Turret, but were soon extinguished; two men had bad falls and were injured.

The Admiralty had obviously selected with care the

* *Liverpool Daily Post*, 5 May 1939.

officer to command one of its precious modern battleships. Captain John C. Leach was a tall, broad-shouldered West Countryman, sometimes called 'Trunky' on account of a large nose. He was a superb athlete – Racquets, Squash and Tennis Champion of the Navy in the late 1920s – a good cricketer, keen fisherman and gardener. As with Captain Tennant of *Repulse*, there have been no adverse comments on Captain Leach's qualities of leadership. His naval specialist occupation was that of gunnery and, like many gunner officers, he was slightly deaf. Leach had served in battleships in the First World War, had commanded the cruiser *Cumberland*, flagship of the China Fleet, before the Second World War, and then served, appropriately for a future battleship captain, as Director of Naval Ordnance at the Admiralty.

Captain Leach's Heads of Departments in December 1941 were as follows:

The Commander: Commander H. F. Lawson

Navigation: Commander M. Price*

Gunnery: Lieutenant-Commander C. W. McMullen

Torpedo and Electrical: Lieutenant-Commander R. F. Harland

Engineering: Commander (E) L. J. Goudy, D.S.O.

Medical: Surgeon-Commander F. B. Quinn, M.B., B.Ch.

Supplies: Paymaster-Commander A. J. Wheeler

Royal Marines: Captain C. D. L. Aylwin

Chaplain: Reverend W. G. Parker

Paymaster-Commander Wheeler found that his son, John, was appointed to *Prince of Wales* as a midshipman, but did not think that father and son should serve together and persuaded the Admiralty to move his son. The two Wheelers were one of the few father and son combinations

---

* Commander Price was also Navigation Officer on Admiral Phillips's staff.

to have served in the same Royal Navy ship in the Second World War.

Prince of Wales would sail into action with 110 officers, including an admiral's staff, and 1,502 men. The crew were provided by the Devonport Manning Depot, so, like *Repulse*, *Prince of Wales* was a 'Guz' ship, but a far higher proportion of *Prince of Wales*'s crew were 'Hostilities Only' men. The best-known rating in the crew was undoubtedly the Manchester-born boxer Johnny King, the reigning British and Empire Bantamweight Champion. Among the 180 or so boy seamen were two sets of twins.

There was no hanging about for *Prince of Wales*. Within two months of sailing from Rosyth for Scapa Flow, she was pitchforked into action even though she had not completed her working-up period: there were still numerous defects in her equipment and dockyard workmen were still aboard. Several books have been written about the dramatic engagement between *Hood*, *Prince of Wales* and the German battleship *Bismarck* and heavy cruiser *Prinz Eugen*. When the Germans were sighted, Vice-Admiral L. E. Holland, in command aboard *Hood*, turned towards the enemy. The range at this time was about on the 36,000-yard limit for *Prince of Wales*'s 14-in. guns, but not yet inside the range of *Hood*'s eight 15-in. guns. Admiral Holland ordered a new course that would converge on that of the Germans, but this would only allow the forward guns of his two ships to bear. For fifteen minutes, *Hood* and *Prince of Wales* closed the range without opening fire, not even when *Hood* did come within range.

It has been suggested that Admiral Holland, who died a few minutes later, was unwilling to try a long-range action in case the unarmoured deck of *Hood* were to be exposed to the plunging fire of German shells when an engagement at shorter range would result in shells arriving with a flatter trajectory. Admiral Sir John Tovey, Commander-in-Chief of the Home Fleet, who was at sea in his flagship *King George V*, was aware of what was happening and nearly sent a signal ordering *Prince of Wales* to take the lead so that her more heavily armoured deck could take the brunt of the German fire. But he was reluctant to interfere, the signal was never sent and Admiral Holland kept *Prince of Wales* tucked in close astern of *Hood*.

During the lengthy run-in, Admiral Holland ordered both ships to aim at the left-hand enemy ship. This was the *Prinz Eugen*, mistaken by Holland for the *Bismarck*. The *Prince of Wales*'s gunnery officers, however, had been training their guns on the more important target of the *Bismarck* and ignored the order. Holland only realized his mistake at the last moment and hurriedly amended the aim to *Bismarck* when all four ships opened fire at the comparatively close range of 26,000 yards.

It was a sorry story. The German ships obtained the correct range almost at once, while *Prince of Wales*'s first five salvoes all fell beyond the *Bismarck*. One of her 14-in. guns developed a fault after the first round and never fired again, and, because of the angle of Admiral Holland's approach, the four guns of the rear turret could not open fire at all. No one is certain where *Hood*'s opening salvoes landed, but they were not on the enemy. The Germans were firing full broadsides. *Hood* was hit almost at once, then again, and this fine ship blew up and disappeared only seven minutes after the first shell of the action had been fired. Three men out of the 1,419 aboard were later picked up by a destroyer. *Prince of Wales* continued to fight on and scored two hits on *Bismarck*, but was herself hit seven times by German shells, one of these making a bloody shambles of her bridge. The four-gun turret aft was now bearing on the enemy, but soon broke down and could not fire.

With the loss of Admiral Holland, *Prince of Wales* had come under the command of Rear-Admiral W. F. Wake-Walker in the cruiser *Norfolk*. He decided that *Prince of Wales* should discontinue this one-sided fight and join the cruisers shadowing the enemy until the main strength of the Home Fleet came up. Although *Prince of Wales*'s log showed that she did open fire again later that day while

shadowing, the action was as good as over for this ship.*
She buried her dead at sea and was detached to Iceland to
land her wounded. Among the thirteen dead were two
midshipmen and one boy seaman, none aged more than
eighteen years; and one of the wounded officers was
Esmond Knight, a well-known actor who was blinded
though he later recovered the sight of one eye.

The men on the *Prince of Wales* felt they had done well
in this their first action. Despite the technical failures
caused by teething troubles in unproved equipment and
their own inexperience, they had identified *Bismarck*
before *Hood*, their guns had hit the *Bismarck* twice and
their ship had withstood the effects of German gunfire. One
of their hits on the *Bismarck* had affected the German ship
by causing a serious oil leak, which later made the German
admiral give up the idea of raiding in the Atlantic and was
a major link in the chain of events that led to the *Bismarck's*
own destruction three days later. Unfortunately, none of
this was known at the time and *Prince of Wales* was not
credited with the hits. Her crew were very bitter at the
way they had been prevented from using the greater range
of their guns and believed that the *Hood* had been unwilling to allow another ship the privilege of opening fire
first.

When we put into Iceland to patch up the shell holes in our hull and
take in fuel, we were naturally feeling unhappy about the inconclusive nature of our *Bismarck* encounter, but worse was yet to come.
Knowing that we had been obliged to act under the orders of two
admirals throughout the crucial part of the engagement, we could
hardly blame ourselves for failing to sink the *Bismarck* on our own
initiative. We went into action as ordered, opened fire when
ordered, and withdrew only when the *Hood* had been blown out of
the water and we (by then heavily damaged) would have been
inviting a similar fate had we not sensibly lengthened the range.

Unfortunately this simple interpretation of the facts was not available to the rest of the fleet, who could only darkly deduce what had

---

* *Prince of Wales*'s log for the *Bismarck* action is Public Record
Office ADM 53/114888.

occurred from such cryptic signals as were intercepted from the battle area. Thus, when the cruiser *Kenya* secured alongside us that day, we found ourselves on the receiving end of some extremely hurtful and unfounded accusations of being unduly cautious in the presence of the enemy. Some of *Kenya*'s marines were misguided enough to couch these comments in blunter terms and in the ensuing skirmishes our marines amply proved that their zeal for combat was still unimpaired. Even so, it was a bitter experience. It was bad enough having to watch such a promising encounter with the enemy's prize battleship turn into a total disaster without having to stagger back with our dead and wounded and be blamed for decisions we had never made. (Leading Telegraphist B. G. Campion)

But *Hood* had been an extremely popular ship in the Navy, and although the charge was completely without foundation, *Prince of Wales* was felt to have let *Hood* down and immediately took on the reputation of being a 'Jonah'.

After *Prince of Wales*'s battle damage had been repaired, she was chosen to take Mr Churchill across the Atlantic for the famous meeting with President Roosevelt in Newfoundland at which the Atlantic Charter was drawn up. Churchill's choice of a battleship recently scarred by battle made quite an impression on the Americans; President Roosevelt came in a cruiser. After bringing Churchill home, *Prince of Wales* was soon in action again, this time in the Mediterranean on 'Operation Halberd' in which a convoy of merchant ships carrying vital reinforcements and supplies from Gibraltar to the besieged island of Malta was escorted by no less than three battleships – *Prince of Wales*, *Nelson* and *Rodney* – the aircraft carrier *Ark Royal*, five cruisers and eighteen destroyers. It was a major naval operation designed to fight the convoy through at all costs. There were numerous air attacks in which *Prince of Wales*'s anti-aircraft armament had plenty of opportunity to take part. The guns and gun crews performed well and at least two Italian torpedo bombers were shot down by *Prince of Wales*, but unfortunately one of the *Ark Royal*'s fighters followed up too closely and was also shot down. The Italian

Fleet was reported to be at sea, and *Prince of Wales* and *Rodney* were detached to give battle; *Nelson* had to be left behind, having been hit by an aerial torpedo. *Prince of Wales* worked up to 31½ knots in this chase, but the Italian ships, as so often, turned back and were never seen. The merchant convoy eventually reached Malta, with the exception of only one ship hit by a torpedo bomber in a moonlight attack. *Prince of Wales* returned to Gibraltar and thence home.

'Operation Halberd' may not have made a big impact on naval history, but it was of considerable significance to *Prince of Wales* in the light of her own last operation, now a mere ten weeks away. Here was a convoy, albeit well protected, that had withstood and fought off repeated bombing and torpedo attacks by aircraft, and the Italians were certainly neither inept nor cowardly in their attacks. It was realized that *Ark Royal*'s aircraft had been an important factor in the defence, but there was still no hint that well-fought battleships had much to fear from aircraft. The torpedo hit on *Nelson*, which had done little more than slow her down slightly, tended to confirm this.

There was another aspect of this operation that attracted attention. Soon after returning to Scapa Flow from 'Operation Halberd', the Commander-in-Chief, Home Fleet, was warned by the Admiralty that *Prince of Wales* was to be sent out to the East. Admiral Tovey protested to the Admiralty that:

the recent operations in the Mediterranean made it clear that, when under way, ventilation in King George V Class is most inadequate in a hot climate and health and efficiency of ship's company will be seriously affected, which will be aggravated by lack of awning and side screens in harbour. Evaporator power is inadequate for long periods at sea and there is every reason to expect failure of V.S.G. [Variable Speed Gear] Pumps for 14-inch turrets which is liable to have a serious effect on the efficiency of the main armament.*

It is unlikely that any newly commissioned battleship had

---

* Public Record Office ADM 199/2232.

ever been worked so hard in the first months of her service as the *Prince of Wales*, but the ship had survived without serious harm, at least not to her structure, but there is some evidence that the morale of her crew was not all it might have been. The lack of time allowed to work up the ship peacefully, the trauma of seeing the *Hood* blown to pieces, the recurring mechanical defects for which time for proper rectification was never allowed, few opportunities for leave – all these had impaired the settling down of the crew. Much has been made of this by other authors; it has been strongly contested by some *Prince of Wales* men, but supported by others. Perhaps this view by one of her crew may be a fair summing up of what the lower deck felt.

When we joined the ship originally at Scapa, starry-eyed and ideal-istic, straight from initial training, we soon formed the impression that it wasn't a well-run-in ship. It had never been given a chance. I was also conscious that there was not that confidence between the officers and senior ratings – nostalgic for peacetime Navy manning perhaps – on the one hand and the predominantly 'hostilities only' crew on the other, many of whom came from that stratum of society which had good cause to resent the 'gaffers' and upper class gen-erally. I often wondered just what one of my friends from the Liverpool slums was 'fighting to defend'.

The Navy had never had to face this sort of problem on so large a scale. Given a lot of time and training and the elimination of mech-anical faults, all would have been O.K., but the ship was hustled from one commitment to another, with petty, demoralizing setbacks. Discipline and *esprit de corps* were no better but no *worse* than could be expected. In the *final* analysis everyone knew the job expected of him and did it. (Ordinary Seaman D. F. Watson)

We will leave *Prince of Wales* at Scapa Flow in October 1941 so as to look at the remainder of the proposed Force G.

The third of the major ships allocated to Force G was the aircraft carrier *Indomitable*, commanded by Captain H. E. Morse, D.S.O. This was one of the modern 23,000-ton Illustrious Class carriers, and she had only been launched at Vickers Armstrong's Wallsend-on-Tyne yards the previous year. *Indomitable* was still not fully worked up and had just been sent to the West Indies to complete her working-up period at Bermuda and Kingston, Jamaica. There were four Fleet Air Arm squadrons on board: 800 Squadron with twelve Fulmars, 827 and 831 Squadrons each with twelve Albacores and 880 Squadron with nine Hurricanes. With these aircraft and her speed of 31 knots, *Indomitable* would have been an ideal partner for *Prince of Wales* and *Repulse*.

But on 3 November, only one week after *Indomitable* reached Bermuda, the Admiralty received the following signal from the aircraft carrier:

REGRET TO REPORT SHIP GROUNDED AT 16.21R/3 WITH STEM IN POSITION 174 DEGREES 600 FEET FROM RACKUM CAY BEACON. WAY WAS NEARLY OFF BUT SHIP IS FAST FROM STEM FOR ABOUT 100 FEET. AM LIGHTENING SHIP. NO TUG AVAILABLE HERE. WEATHER AND SEA CALM. NO WIND.

Indomitable had run aground on the reef just before entering Kingston harbour. It must have been a badly charted area as the tiny corvette *Clarkia*, escorting *Indomitable*, also went aground at the same spot. *Indomitable* managed to get off the reef by her own efforts the next morning and went into Kingston for an inspection by divers. The hull plating was found to be badly torn, and, once her aircraft had flown off to a local airfield, *Indomitable* was ordered to the United States for dry-docking and repair. She reached Norfolk, Virginia, within the week and became Job No. S.139 in the U.S. Navy Dockyard there.

The Americans were to do a fast job on *Indomitable*, and she would be away again twelve days later. After picking up her aircraft at Kingston, she would set off for the Cape of Good Hope and Singapore, but it would be too late. By the time she reached the Indian Ocean the Japanese would have attacked and *Prince of Wales* and *Repulse* be beyond the help of *Indomitable*'s aircraft. *

The composition of the destroyer escort allocated to Force G would eventually change from that originally ordered by the Admiralty. The first members were the E Class ships *Express* and *Electra*, 4·7-in. guns, 1,375 tons, 35 knots, modern ships built in the mid-1930s. *Electra* (Commander C. W. May) and *Express* (Lieutenant-Commander F. J. Cartwright) were detached from the Home Fleet at the same time as *Prince of Wales*, and would sail out from England with the battleship. Both destroyers had already had an eventful war. On the very first day, *Electra* had helped to rescue survivors when the liner *Athenia* was sunk by a German submarine; and it had been *Electra* that picked up *Hood*'s three survivors in the *Bismarck* action. *Express* had served at Dunkirk, and later in 1940 had her bows blown off by a mine when a flotilla of British destroyers ran into a German minefield off the Dutch coast; two other destroyers, *Esk* and *Ivanhoe*, were lost in that incident, but *Express* returned to have new bows fitted at Hull.

The Mediterranean Fleet was ordered to give up two of its destroyers to join Force G later in the Indian Ocean. Those chosen were *Encounter* (Lieutenant-Commander E. V. St J. Morgan), another E Class ship, and *Jupiter* (Lieutenant-Commander N. V. J. T. Thew) of the slightly

---

* *Indomitable* was diverted to the Sudan and took on a further fifty Hurricanes as belated reinforcements for the R.A.F. in the Far East. These were later flown off from a safe position south of Java and flew to Singapore by way of Batavia, but they arrived too late in Singapore to have any great effect on the outcome of the fighting there. *Indomitable* gave honourable service during the remainder of the war, mostly in the Far East and the Mediterranean. She was seriously damaged by bombs dropped by German aircraft off Sicily in 1943, and in 1945 a Japanese Kamikaze suicide aircraft bounced off her deck without exploding. The Illustrious Class – *Illustrious, Indomitable, Implacable, Indefatigable, Victorious* and *Formidable* – were lucky; they all survived the war.

larger J Class. The choice of these two was ostensibly that they were recent arrivals in the Mediterranean Fleet and were more easily spared than older members, and also that most of the Mediterranean Fleet's destroyers were F Class ships, so an 'E' and a 'J' could be more easily spared. It was later said, however, that the Mediterranean Fleet had given up its poorest destroyers. Both ships were later plagued with mechanical troubles, and neither was to be available to sail out with *Prince of Wales* and *Repulse* from Singapore.

Since there was already a naval command system in existence at Singapore – that of the China Station with Vice-Admiral Sir Geoffrey Layton as Commander-in-Chief – it might have been expected that, because of his knowledge of local conditions, this officer would take command of the Eastern Fleet that would come into being when Force G reached the Far East. As we have seen, however, the Admiralty had someone else in mind, someone who had had far more contact with the realities of modern war: Rear-Admiral Sir Tom Spencer Vaughan Phillips, K.C.B., then Vice-Chief of the Naval Staff. In this position he had attended the two important War Cabinet meetings that had made the decision to send *Prince of Wales* and *Indomitable* to join *Repulse* in the Far East. It may be assumed that Phillips had supported his chief, Sir Dudley Pound, in opposing so bitterly the inclusion of *Prince of Wales* in this force.

Sir Tom Phillips was fifty-three years old and had been a naval officer for thirty-seven of those years. His early speciality had been navigation, so often in the Royal Navy a stepping stone to high rank. He had served in the First World War as a lieutenant in the cruiser *Bacchante* at the Gallipoli landings in 1915, but had missed the great naval action at Jutland in 1916. He was a captain and in command of his own ship before the war finished. After the war, a spell at the Staff College was followed by a variety of staff positions, mostly of some importance. He was

Assistant Director of Plans at the Admiralty, Chief of
Staff to Commander-in-Chief, East Indies, and finally
Director of Plans at the Admiralty from 1935 to 1939.
Then came his first big command position: Commodore
Commanding Home Fleet Destroyer Flotillas.

Just before the outbreak of war, Phillips had come to the
important post of Deputy Chief of the Naval Staff, a post
redesignated Vice-Chief of the Naval Staff in 1940. In this
position, for the whole of the German war to date, he had
acted as immediate deputy to the First Sea Lord with
special responsibility for operational matters, and would
certainly have been well up on all the latest operational
principles and thinking. Phillips had also been very close
to Churchill, First Lord in 1939 and Prime Minister from
1940, but their relationship had cooled after disputes over
the effectiveness of the R.A.F.'s heavy bombing of
German cities – Phillips did not place a high value on this
as a means of waging war – and over the decision to go to
the aid of Greece, which Phillips opposed. Phillips had
always shown an interest in the Far East and was realistic
about the danger from Japan. He had supported the
Admiralty plan to create an Eastern Fleet, although one to
be composed of older battleships only, and had long been
earmarked as Commander-in-Chief of such a Fleet when it
could be assembled. Churchill was probably not too sorry
to see him leave the Admiralty.

Much has been written about this officer. His intellect
and determination had always been recognized as first
class. He liked to take firm, centralized control of any
situation, did not delegate much, and was a stickler for
detail. He was a man of small stature, and his nickname in
the Navy was 'Tom Thumb' Phillips. In general, it
might be said that he was well experienced in naval
strategy, highly respected but not unduly popular and
certainly not an easy man to get on with.

There were at least two reservations to be made about
the appointment of Sir Tom Phillips to command the
Eastern Fleet. First, he had seen no action since 1917 and

had not been to sea since 1939. Secondly, he had no great opinion of the effectiveness of the modern aeroplane or the danger it posed to warships. We have already seen how no capital ship had yet been sunk, or even seriously damaged, by aircraft while at sea and Phillips's views on the many smaller ships that had succumbed to aircraft attack was that they had been unlucky to be caught alone or had not been properly handled. But Phillips was clearly not the only Royal Navy officer to underestimate the danger of aircraft, and later events in the Pacific would soon show that the Royal Navy was not the only navy to contain such officers. Yet it is probable that Phillips's views were considerably more out of touch and mistaken than those of most of his contemporaries.

The following illuminating quotation is by General Lord Ismay – in 1941 Major-General Sir Hastings Ismay, Chief of Staff in the office of the Ministry of Defence and a participant in many of the discussions leading up to the dispatch of Force G. Before studying it, the reader must take into consideration the fact that these views are those of an army officer and an R.A.F. officer about a naval officer and may be touched with anti-naval prejudice. The Arthur Harris mentioned in the passage became Commander-in-Chief of Bomber Command in 1942, and when he worked with Ismay and Phillips before the war had certainly objected to the huge expenditure on the Navy between the wars and the failure to recognize the R.A.F. as an equal service. Here is what Hastings Ismay wrote after the war:

After a good deal of discussion with the Admiralty, it was decided that an Eastern Fleet would be formed and consist of the *Prince of Wales*, the *Repulse* and the aircraft carrier *Indomitable*. This Fleet was to be under the command of Admiral Sir Tom Phillips. We had worked together for many years in peace and war and I had always greatly admired his courage, industry, integrity and professional competence. His whole heart and soul were in the Navy, and he believed that there was nothing that it could not do. In particular, he refused to admit that properly armed and well-fought ships had anything to fear from air power. Nor was he alone in that opinion. Even Winston Churchill, whose forecasts were not often at fault, was one of the many who did not 'believe that well-built modern ships properly defended by armour and A.A. guns were likely to fall a prey to hostile aircraft'.

The battles royal which raged between Tom Phillips and Arthur Harris when they were Director of Plans in their respective departments were never-ending and always inconclusive. On one occasion, when the situation which would arise in the event of Italy entering the war on the side of Germany was under discussion, Tom Phillips insisted that our Fleet would have free use of the Mediterranean however strong the Italian Air Force might be. Bert Harris exploded, 'One day, Tom, you will be standing on a box on your bridge (Tom was diminutive in stature) and your ship will be smashed to pieces by bombers and torpedo aircraft; as she sinks, your last words will be, 'that was a . . . great mine!'

Tom Phillips came to say goodbye to me before he sailed. He was blissfully happy at the prospect of flying his flag after so many years in Whitehall. As he left the room I suddenly felt sad. I am not psychic, nor am I given to having presentiments. But for some unaccountable reason I had a feeling that I would not see him again.*

It should not be thought that Harris and Phillips were enemies; they were the greatest of friends, sharing the same 'diggings' in London. Harris was also a friend of Captain Leach of the *Prince of Wales*; they had met while Harris was at the Staff College at Camberley.

Admiral Phillips would be taking his own staff out to Singapore. His Chief of Staff was Rear-Admiral A. F. E. Palliser, a former gunnery specialist. There would be the usual team of experts and their assistants, including a strong team of communications and cypher officers and ratings. The assembly of this staff was codenamed 'Party Piano', and they were to sail in *Prince of Wales* with Admiral Phillips. A batch of eight R.N.V.R. sub-lieutenants of the Paymaster Branch, newly commissioned from H.M.S. *King Alfred* at Hove, were chosen as cypher officers,

---

* Lord Ismay, *The Memoirs of General The Lord Hastings Lionel Ismay*, Heinemann, London, 1960, p. 240.

and the communications ratings came from the Wireless School at Chatham.

Prince of Wales had been at Scapa Flow when the War Cabinet decided at its lunchtime meeting on Monday, 20 October, that the battleship should become part of Force G. No time was lost, and before the afternoon was out Captain Leach was summoned to *King George V* to receive preliminary orders from Admiral Tovey. That evening the first ammunition lighter was alongside *Prince of Wales*. For the next two and a half days, the crews of *Prince of Wales* and those of the destroyers *Electra* and *Express* worked to fill their ships with ammunition, water and stores for the long voyage east. At dawn on Thursday the three ships sailed out of Scapa Flow, making for Greenock, where Admiral Phillips and 'Party Piano' would come aboard. Greenock was reached on Friday morning and *Prince of Wales* moored out in the river where a succession of ships topped her up with oil, water and stores. A group of R.A.F. men, probably taking passage for Freetown or South Africa, also came aboard, and a last-minute consignment of Oerlikon light anti-aircraft cannons with ammunition arrived. Admiral Phillips and his staff duly arrived and the Admiral's flag was hoisted in the new flagship.

Two men, one of the newly commissioned cypher officers and the other an older reservist rating recalled for war service, remember what it was like arriving in *Prince of Wales* before she sailed:

There were eight Cypher officers aboard *Prince of Wales*. I think two lived in the Gun Room and the rest of us in the Ward Room. She was not a particularly happy ship. We seemed to be shunned by the other officers in the Ward Room. We had to sling our hammocks even though there were many empty cabooses. We kept our kit in our suitcases until we 'purloined' chests of drawers. (Sub-Lieutenant H. J. Lock)

Our draft fell in outside Greenock Station and marched straight down to the Dockyard where a trawler was already being loaded with our bags and hammocks. We made a last effort to send a message back home but failed and found ourselves packed on board the trawler, on the water once again. As we cleared the entrance to the break-water, quite a number of ships came into view – naval and merchant – and included one big battleship, H.M.S. *Prince of Wales*, and it was towards this that the trawler steered – much to our disgust for most of us, at least our little gang, were reservists or pensioners and had no wish to join up with the 'Real Navy'.

We found everyone on board knew no more than we did and, until they saw the tropical helmets attached to our kit, had been expecting a trip to Northern Russia. The crew had not had much leave during the previous eighteen weeks although many rumours had been cir-culating concerning a long leave whilst the ship docked, so that our coming aboard smashed their hopes. (Telegraphist C. V. House)

5

The Voyage East

At 13.08 hours on Saturday, 25 October 1941, *Prince of Wales* hauled up anchor and steamed down the Clyde towards the open sea; it was only six days, almost to the minute, since the War Cabinet had decided to send this ship to the Far East. It was 'a good Scottish day, one could see for miles'. The battleship had three destroyers as escort – *Electra* and *Express*, her permanent escort, and *Hesperus* (Lieutenant-Commander A. A. Tait), loaned by Western Approaches to provide additional protection for the first part of the voyage. There were mixed emotions among those aboard the ships and those ashore who knew their destinations. The lower deck of the battleship were not particularly happy at the prospect of going 'foreign' without the usual leave; the destroyer crews did not even know that they were setting out on such a long voyage. One young officer in *Prince of Wales* remembers:

I was not alone amongst the young, fired with enthusiasm to do our bit, who thought we were being sent away from the fighting war – and our families – to take part in a 'Fleet-in-being' containment of the Japanese along with the Americans. We were a bit cheesed off. I reacted by embarking some personal luxuries, extras like shotgun, cricket gear, some decent personal oddments – studs, links etc. Others did too. More fool us?

I dare say that those higher up saw the future differently. Admiral Noble said to my father, then a Rear-Admiral on his staff in the Western Approaches Command, as we sailed from Greenock, 'I'm very sorry for those chaps.' He didn't know that his Rear-Admiral's son was on board *Prince of Wales*. As one who had recently been in command in the Far East, I expect he read the tea leaves successfully and rightly. (Lieutenant D. B. H. Wildish)

Admiral Sir Percy Noble had been Commander-in-Chief China Station until September 1940. His Western

Approaches Command was responsible for the sailing arrangements of *Prince of Wales* from Greenock.

The four warships, now known as Force G, made out to the west, passing north of Ireland and getting well out into the Atlantic before turning south to avoid long-range German aircraft operating from France. Because the through passage of the Mediterranean was too dangerous at this time, Freetown in Sierra Leone would be the *Prince of Wales*'s first port of call. The battleship settled down to a steady 18 to 20 knots, any greater speed would have caused the destroyers to use too much fuel. Various patterns of zig-zag were steamed to confuse the aim of any German U-boat that might be lucky enough to find itself ahead and try a long-range torpedo shot; no U-boat could travel fast enough, submerged or surfaced, to catch up from astern. The crews soon dropped into the shipboard routine of a long voyage – four hours duty on, eight hours off, many practice Action Stations, two hours' gun drill every day, much vigilance by lookouts and radar, all incoming signals decoded but radio silence observed and no outgoing signals. The occasional long-range Coastal Command aircraft – Sunderlands, Catalinas or Liberators – turned up to give added protection. Most of the men believed they were off on a prolonged 'flag-waving exercise', and on *Prince of Wales* Admiral Phillips was looked upon as 'a supernumerary and a very much respected nuisance'.

Prince of Wales's log gives details of one or two incidents on the first leg of the voyage. On the first day out from Greenock *Express* caused a stir when she opened fire and signalled 'submarine in sight' but her 'submarine' turned out to be a large floating spar. Two days later a fourth destroyer H.M.S. *Legion* (Commander R. F. Jessel), joined the escorts; *Legion* had been detached from a Gibraltar–U.K. convoy to cover *Prince of Wales* while *Express* and *Electra* went off to refuel from a tanker at Ponta Del Garda in the Azores. Later that night, while *Express* and *Electra* were away, what appeared to be the track of a torpedo was seen passing astern of *Prince of Wales*, but the War Diary of the German U-boat Headquarters does not record any attack by one of their boats; perhaps it was an Italian submarine or perhaps a mistake by the *Prince of Wales* lookout. If it was a torpedo, it is fascinating to speculate what the future course of events in the Far East or *Prince of Wales*'s own fortunes might have been if the submarine commander had calculated his target's speed more accurately and put a torpedo into *Prince of Wales*. This would probably have done no more than damage the battleship but it would have meant a period of repair and would certainly have delayed the ship's arrival in the Far East by weeks if not by months.

Express and *Electra* returned the following day, and the *Hesperus* and *Legion* parted company for Gibraltar; their involvement with Force G was now over.*

Mr Churchill was kept informed at the progress of Force G and complained to the Admiralty at the comparatively slow speed *Prince of Wales* was making, urging that she push on faster. Churchill also wasted no time in informing the heads of various governments that he was sending Britain's most modern battleship to deter the Japanese, and a spate of his famous 'personal telegrams' was soon on its way. Looked at in the light of subsequent events, Churchill's hopes at the time seem a little optimistic. As Stalin was informed:

With the object of keeping Japan quiet, we are sending our latest battleship *Prince of Wales*, which can catch and kill any Japanese ship, into the Indian Ocean and are building up a powerful battle squadron there. I am urging President Roosevelt to increase his pressure on

---

* *Hesperus* went back to her normal convoy work and sank a U-boat, U.93, off Portugal in January 1942; she survived the war, though her captain, Lieutenant-Commander Tait, later a successful Escort Group Commander in the Battle of the Atlantic, was lost when his next ship, *Harvester*, was torpedoed in March 1943. *Legion* returned to Force H at Gibraltar, but was sunk by German aircraft off Malta in March 1942 with the loss of eleven men.

the Japanese and keep them frightened so that the Vladivostok route will not be blocked.

And President Roosevelt was told:

As your naval people have already been informed we are sending that big ship you inspected into the Indian Ocean as part of a squadron we are forming there. This ought to serve as a deterrent on Japan. There is nothing like having something that can catch and kill anything. I am very glad we can spare her at this juncture. It is more than we thought we could do some time ago. The firmer your attitude and ours, the less chance of their taking the plunge.

I am grieved at the loss of life you have suffered with *Reuben James* [an American destroyer lost in the Atlantic]. I salute the land of unending challenge.*

Churchill addressed himself to a wider audience on 10 November when he spoke at the Lord Mayor's inaugural luncheon at the Mansion House, the traditional evening banquet of pre-war years having been dropped as a war-time economy. In a rousing speech, Churchill referred to the 'splendid new battleship and aircraft carriers of the largest size' coming into service, and went on to announce that 'a powerful naval force of heavy ships' was being provided for service in the Indian and Pacific Oceans. 'Should the United States become involved in war with Japan, the British declaration will follow within the hour.' This was fully reported, as Churchill intended it should be, and was all part of the plan to persuade the Japanese not to go to war.

On 5 November, eleven days out from Greenock, *Prince of Wales* with her two destroyers put into Freetown. This was one of the intermediate refuelling points established by the Admiralty well before the war in the event of the Mediterranean being blocked to the safe passage of a fleet being sent to Singapore. Although Force G was hardly a fleet, this was a good example of the steady unfolding of the twenty-year-old plan to reinforce the Far East. Some

* Both these documents are from Public Record Office C A B 65/24.

shore leave was given in Freetown that night, and a few men failed to return to *Prince of Wales* when the battleship sailed next day.

Sunderland flying boats of 95 Squadron, based in Sierra Leone, flew further anti-submarine patrols until the range became too great. Sergeant Fowler was a signaller in the last Sunderland to escort Force G.

I recall our last moments with the battleship. She looked a magnificent sight and, despite wartime livery, her lines, armament and decks stood out giving an impression of speed, strength and impregnability. As was our practice on leaving a big ship, we 'beat up' her bows at low level – probably about 100 feet – making two or three runs and then informally waved to the crew. We had been under a tightly enforced communications silence throughout these patrols; however, prior to our final departure we flashed by Aldis lamp to the battleship, 'Good Luck KG5', meaning King George the Fifth. The response was an immediate, 'Thank You – but we are the POW.' We were highly amused at being caught out, although the two ships were very similar in every way. We then gave the POW a final 'beat up' and turned for our base.

Soon after leaving Freetown, the traditional 'Crossing the Line' ceremony was performed for the many men on board who had never before crossed the Equator, but conditions on board were by now becoming extremely uncomfortable in the hot climate because of the ship's poor ventilation.

Conditions inside the ship were getting rather trying by then. Our mess deck had no portholes and was just above one of the boiler rooms so that the constant temperature was about 95 to 100 degrees. The only time my skin was dry was when I got onto the upper deck. The hammock soon became impossible – unable to sleep with pillow and bedding damp with perspiration. Conditions were much the same in the wireless office and reading signals was a sticky job. My hands suffered with prickly heat in the shape of small blisters spread all over them but, as most of the ship's company were suffering from the same complaint, it was just a case of carrying on. (Telegraphist C. V. House)

Surgeon-Commander F. B. Quinn, the Fleet Medical

Officer, had earlier warned Admiral Phillips of the dangers of heat exhaustion and asked that ratings in positions between decks should not be kept closed up at Action Stations for long periods unless it was absolutely essential. Many men took to sleeping on deck, but, while on duty, they were subject to great hardship, particularly the engine and boiler-room men, and several stokers collapsed despite the introduction of two-hour spells of duty in the hotter compartments.

Just before reaching Cape Town, the second port of call, rough weather was encountered. A man on *Express* records that the seas were the heaviest he ever met in six years of naval service, and one member of the destroyer's crew was washed overboard and lost. The two destroyers certainly had to slow down because of the weather, and *Prince of Wales* pressed on alone. The battleship's crew were told that a number of shore-based aircraft would carry out dummy air attacks as their ship approached Cape Town to exercise the gun crews, but the 'attackers' could not locate *Prince of Wales* in poor visibility and the exercise was abandoned. *Prince of Wales* came into Table Bay soon after breakfast time on 16 November, having taken ten days to steam from Freetown. *Electra* and *Express* put into the near-by Simonstown Naval Base that afternoon.

It had been intended that Force G would remain at Cape Town for a week. Churchill wanted Admiral Phillips to meet Field-Marshal Smuts, the Empire states-man whose opinion and support Churchill valued so highly. He also wanted Smuts to visit *Prince of Wales*. There was, besides, the promise to the Admiralty to recon-sider the future movements of *Prince of Wales* at this point. Finally, the crew would have benefited from a period of rest. Alas, it was not to be. Phillips did meet Smuts, but only briefly at Pretoria where Phillips flew by air with his secretary and valet. After the meeting, Smuts sent a telegram to Churchill which showed that, of the two, the South African had a clearer insight into the Far East situation.

ADMIRAL TOM PHILLIPS HAS BEEN HERE FOR MOST
USEFUL TALKS AND WILL REACH CAPE TOWN
BEFORE NOON TODAY. HE HAS MUCH IMPRESSED
ME AND APPEARS ADMIRABLE CHOICE FOR MOST
IMPORTANT POSITION . . . IN PARTICULAR, I AM
CONCERNED OVER PRESENT DISPOSITION OF TWO
FLEETS, ONE BASED ON SINGAPORE AND OTHER
ON HAWAII, EACH SEPARATELY INFERIOR TO
JAPANESE NAVY WHICH THUS WILL HAVE AN
OPPORTUNITY TO DEFEAT THEM IN TURN. THIS
MATTER IS SO VITAL THAT I WOULD PRESS FOR
REARRANGEMENT OF DISPOSITIONS AS SOON AS
WAR APPEARS IMMINENT. IF JAPANESE ARE
REALLY NIPPY THERE IS HERE OPENING FOR
FIRST CLASS DISASTER. *

No records have been released giving details of the
promised reconsideration whether *Prince of Wales* should
now proceed to Singapore. At home the naval situation
was quiet, while the situation in the Far East continued to
deteriorate. If there had been close cooperation between
Germany and Japan at this time – which there was not –
the Germans could have caused real difficulties by making
threatening moves with *Tirpitz* which might have induced
the Admiralty and Churchill to bring *Prince of Wales* back
to Europe. However, nothing of the sort took place and,
after only a two-day stay instead of the proposed week,
Admiral Phillips was ordered by the Admiralty to leave
Cape Town.

It had still been a very happy two days for the men of
Prince of Wales and the two destroyers. The *Prince of
Wales* had arrived on a Sunday and an estimated 600 cars
had been waiting at Cape Town harbour to carry away the
crew to private homes, farms and sightseeing trips; most
men had at least one night ashore and the survivors of the
Prince of Wales cannot speak too highly of the hospitality

* Public Record Office PREM 3 163/3.

shown to them. For the many men who were not to survive, this South African hospitality was their last taste of
civilian conviviality.

Some events planned for the Cape Town visit had to be
rushed or cancelled. Workmen fitted the four Oerlikon
light anti-aircraft guns put aboard at Greenock, two near
the bridge and two on the quarterdeck. It had been
arranged that selected officers and ratings would be interviewed by the local press, but this was cancelled, as was a
visit to the ship by press photographers. The local papers
were allowed to report the visit the day after *Prince of
Wales* left and to identify the battleship by name, though
the local censor only allowed vague references to the ship's
future movements.

The censor had earlier been ordered to treat Force G's
visit as 'Most Secret' and to arrange that all cables in
cypher to Japan, France and Spain be held up for seven
days. The local police were also alert, and picked up the
radio operator of a Greek merchant ship who had broken
regulations and taken a photograph of *Prince of Wales*.
The Greek was charged at the Cape Town court and sentenced to three weeks in prison or a fine of £10.

Prince of Wales took on thirty-nine fresh ratings, most
of whom were naval prisoners who had 'jumped' previous
ships visiting South Africa. Captain Leach welcomed these
men to *Prince of Wales*, promised them a fresh start and
let it be known that their previous bad records would not
henceforth be mentioned. The battleship sailed on the
afternoon of 18 November, short once again of a few crew
members who had deserted. Ironically, the aircraft carrier
Hermes had that morning come into Simonstown Naval
Base for a refit after recent service in the Indian Ocean.
Although *Hermes* was the smallest of the Royal Navy's
carriers, with room for only fifteen aircraft, it is strange
that no consideration at all seems to have been given to
attaching her to Force G as a replacement for the recently
damaged *Indomitable*. *Hermes* was not performing any
vital duty in the Indian Ocean and she could eventually

have refitted at Singapore as well as at Simonstown. She would certainly have added to the deterrent effect of Force G. But no changes were made, and *Prince of Wales* sailed out of Cape Town even as what was virtually a spare aircraft carrier sailed into Simonstown a few miles away.

It took another ten-day voyage for Force G to reach Colombo. It was, again, a cruise under the hot weather conditions that were such a trial to the crew. *Prince of Wales's* Engineering Officer, Commander L. J. Goudy, and her Meteorological Officer, Instructor-Lieutenant T. W. Smith, took readings of the temperatures in some of the worst-ventilated positions. These are some examples of the temperatures found:

Engine Rooms – 105 to 122 degrees
Boiler Rooms – 125 to 136 degrees
X and Y Action Machinery Rooms – above 150 degrees when machines run for more than four hours.
Stores and Workshops – considerably above 100 degrees
Torpedo Working Spaces – 100 to 110 degrees
Mess decks – 95 degrees
Officers' Cabins – 75 to 80 degrees*

The voyage to Colombo was broken by short calls at Mauritius and at Addu Atoll (now known as Gan) so that Force G could refuel. Ashore at Addu Atoll was a small detachment of Royal Marines. Sergeant Eric Winter tells how pleased they were to see *Prince of Wales*.

We had been here for something like two months building defences and installing emplacements for 6-inch guns, living on hard-tack biscuits with tins of herrings, sardines, tomatoes and powdered egg. Our water ration was two pints a day for drinking and washing. The *Prince of Wales* did us proud; they cooked us a Christmas dinner, sent ashore fresh bread, fruit, meat, vegetables and other fresh food. Not only that, they sent beer and a tot of Navy Rum; this proved too much for some of those who drank and dined too well; most of them

* The temperature readings report is from Public Record Office ADM 199/1149.

went down with dysentery and diarrhoea. I was one of the few left standing the following day.

Repulse was waiting at Ceylon; the battle cruiser had been out in the Indian Ocean, killing time by escorting convoys off the East African coast and holding gunnery practices. There was a certain amount of shuffling around of the two ships between Colombo and Trincomalee, and orders had been given to the press that *Repulse* was not to be mentioned by name; she was to be reported only as 'a large warship'. This order, originating from the Admiralty, caused much resentment among *Repulse*'s crew. They viewed the arrival of *Prince of Wales* and the prospect of serving in her company with considerably less than enthusiasm. The battleship's 'Jonah' reputation among the lower decks of the Royal Navy had preceded her and the crew of the old battle cruiser, who thought their ship's gunnery the best in the Royal Navy, did not care to be serving under the orders of an admiral in such a recently commissioned and apparently unlucky battleship. One man from *Repulse* recollects that 'there was an instant and bitter rivalry between the two ships'.

The reason for the decision not to mention the *Repulse* by name was a wish to conceal from the Japanese both the strength and the quality of the force about to sail for Singapore. The Admiralty had earlier suggested that not only *Repulse* but also *Revenge*, which was also available in the Indian Ocean, should accompany *Prince of Wales* to Singapore, but Admiral Phillips had given his opinion that *Revenge* should not go.

The two fast battleships in Singapore would cause Japan concern but would be regarded by her as a raiding force rather than as an attempt to form a line of battle against her.

The addition of one 'R' Class battleship might give the impression that we were trying to form a line of battle but could only spare three ships, thus encouraging her.*

It is curious to see this old-fashioned phrase, 'a line of

* Public Record Office ADM 119/1149.

battle', used as late as November 1941. And so the old and slow *Revenge* remained behind in the Indian Ocean to survive the war while the old but fast *Repulse* went on to Singapore. The destroyers *Encounter* and *Jupiter* were expected to arrive shortly from the Mediterranean, but Admiral Phillips was ordered by the Admiralty not to wait for them but to fly on immediately to Singapore to discuss the latest Japanese situation with the commanders there and, if possible, with Admiral T. C. Hart, Commander-in-Chief of the American Asiatic Fleet in Manila. The day after the arrival of *Prince of Wales* in Ceylon, Admiral Phillips flew on to Singapore in a Catalina flying boat.

Prince of Wales herself was to stay little longer. The Admiralty was now urging that *Prince of Wales* and *Repulse* get to Singapore as soon as *Encounter* and *Jupiter* arrived. Several fresh ratings were put aboard both ships to fill various gaps. One *Prince of Wales* telegraphist had been given permission to visit his sister in up-country Ceylon and missed his ship when the sailing time was brought forward; he hoped then to be given a comfortable shore job in Ceylon, but was packed off on another ship and later rejoined *Prince of Wales* just before she sailed from Singapore into action. He survived. One of *Jupiter*'s stokers, Tom Cairns from Liverpool, missed his ship by a few minutes and just had time to be put aboard *Prince of Wales*. He never went back to *Jupiter* and did not survive. After *Prince of Wales* sailed, Captain Leach congratulated his ship's company on the fact that, for the first time since leaving Greenock, there had been no desertions from shore leave.

. On 29 November, *Prince of Wales* sailed with *Electra*, *Express*, *Encounter* and *Jupiter* from Colombo, and *Repulse* left Trincomalee. What would soon become known as Force Z assembled at sea and set a south-easterly course for Singapore. With Admiral Phillips absent, Captain Tennant was now senior officer, so *Repulse* preceded *Prince of Wales* on this occasion, much to the satisfaction of *Repulse*'s crew.

There were no incidents of note during this last stage of the voyage. Singapore was reached three days later on the afternoon of 2 December, and the impressive line of ships steamed up Johore Strait and entered the Naval Base. It was without doubt a historic moment. The years of naval planning and the vast expenditure of money spent on the Base had at last borne fruit.

Singapore had been warned that, should Japan attack, it would probably have to hold out for ninety days before the Navy could get there. Now, with the judicious decision of the War Cabinet and the subsequent hard driving by Churchill and the Admiralty, this new fleet had arrived before the first shot had been fired.

6

Singapore

Prince of Wales, being the flagship, was given the best berth alongside the West Wall of the Naval Base, opposite the main office buildings. *Repulse* was left moored out in the stream like the poor relation. Sir Tom Phillips had watched the berthing of *Prince of Wales* and was first of the large welcoming party up her gangplank. It had been announced publicly the previous day that Phillips had been promoted to full admiral and was to be Commander-in-Chief of the new Eastern Fleet.

The arrival of the ships, long heralded in the world's press, caused much interest at Singapore. The Naval Base, officially H.M.S. *Sultan*, was also manned from Devonport, and many men there soon renewed old friendships in *Prince of Wales* and *Repulse*. It had been decided that the exact composition of the new fleet should remain a secret, and local newspapers were directed to refer to the arrival of *Prince of Wales* 'with other heavy ships and auxiliary vessels'. The identity of *Repulse*, the only other 'heavy ship' nearer than Ceylon, was once more concealed – much to the disgust of her crew when they bought local papers.

Only a few press reporters were initially allowed into the Naval Base, and the remainder had to be content with a long-distance view from vantage points outside the base and the handouts of the Naval Press Officer. These restrictions were bitterly criticized in some local newspapers and the authorities relented two days later when *Prince of Wales* threw a big party in the wardroom for the general body of the press. Officers were asked to be particularly friendly to the reporters on account of the earlier 'social error' in not allowing better press facilities. It was all part of the dream world in which the men from wartime Britain found themselves.

The local newspapers gave enthusiastic coverage to the Fleet's arrival.

It is big news not only for Singapore and Malaya but for the whole of the democratic countries bordering on the Pacific; it is bad news for Japan which may begin to see the shattering of her hopes for an unopposed naval advance to the south.*

The *Malaya Tribune*'s military correspondent, Major Fielding Eliot, wrote on the same day:

A Far Eastern detachment [of the Royal Navy] of the size suggested would not be able to seek out the Japanese Navy in Japanese waters and force it to battle, but neither would the Japanese Navy dare venture into the South China Sea . . . In fact, the arrival of some British battleships at Singapore would render the Japanese naval problem in the Pacific quite hopeless . . . Naval aviation is, of all its departments, that in which the Japanese fleet is weakest as compared with the American, and Japanese aircraft production is so small as to be utterly unable to replace the losses of war . . . The Japanese are caught in a trap of their own making and neither by land nor sea nor in the air do they have even a glimmer of a chance of victory if they now appeal to arms against the preponderant forces which encircle them.

Yet Japan had built 5,088 military and naval aircraft in 1941 alone! Such unrealistic optimism was not confined to naval and air prospects. The *Singapore Free Press* had sent a reporter to visit Australian troops preparing positions in northern Malaya against a possible Japanese landing and informed the people of Singapore that

an enemy force invading this area has a poor chance of escaping complete ruin . . . A back-door entrance to Singapore will be closed to the enemy with the same determination which has characterized the fighting of Australians in other spheres of the present war.

The reporters were keen to talk to the recently arrived sailors. One *Prince of Wales* man was found to be 'itching for someone to start something so that we can show him what we have on board'. Much interest was shown in

* *Singapore Free Press*, 3 December 1941.

Johnny King, the Bantamweight Champion in *Prince of Wales*, who was recognized 'in spite of his huge growth of beard' and was found 'eager to fight in Singapore provided permission is given by my Commander'; but Johnny admitted that he was now over the weight for his old class and would have to fight as a lightweight.

By day the crews of *Prince of Wales* and *Repulse* were kept hard at work taking on stores and overhauling boilers and engines after the long voyage from England, though at night there was plenty of shore leave. *Repulse* was standing by to sail to Australia, but the crew of *Prince of Wales* could get to Singapore city fifteen miles away – a 30-cent bus ride or $2 by taxi (there were nine Malayan dollars to the £ at the time). Although a State of Emergency had been declared in Malaya and Singapore the day before the fleet arrived, social life in the city was proceeding as normal. Those men who had never been in the Far East before found it fascinating to walk through the noisy, smelly, but lively Chinese quarter. Many comment that, while the Chinese and other local races were friendly enough, the Europeans were not, in stark contrast to the hospitality the sailors had so recently been shown by the white South Africans. One young sailor wrote to his mother: 'The English-speaking people are very wealthy and won't have anything to do with the Servicemen who are out here to defend them, but we get on very well with the natives.'

There were opportunities a-plenty in Singapore for the sailors to enjoy themselves.

THE HAPPY CABARET
Charming, Happy Girls Ready to Greet and Dance with You
Miss Venus Chong – An Overnight Sensation
Nowhere else such Cheerfulness and Friendliness
Carnival Night in Honour of the Military
Non-stop Dance 8–12pm Nightly

NEW WORLD CABARET
Singapore's Premier Dance Palace De Luxe

And, possibly for officers only:

THE CATHAY RESTAURANT
The Finest Ballroom in the East – Air Conditioned Orchestral Concert by the Band of the Gordon Highlanders (by kind permission of Lt.-Col. W. J. Graham, M.C., and officers). Followed by Dancing to Harry Hackmire's Band with Lisette the popular vocalist.

RAFFLES HOTEL
Dinner and Dance Tonight
Saturday – Tiffin-Time Orchestral Concert

SEAVIEW HOTEL
Tonight – Romantic Night
Dinner Served in the Moonlight
Dancing in the Ballroom

And were any of the sailors invited to the Singapore Rotary Club Meeting at the Adelphi Hotel to hear Dr J. W. Scharff speak on 'Vegetables For All'?

At various cinemas were showing films such as *Blood and Sand* with Tyrone Power and Linda Darnell, *International Squadron* with Ronald Reagan, *Belle Star* with Gene Tierney and Randolph Scott, *A Woman's Face* with Joan Crawford and Mervyn Douglas.

The *Prince of Wales* men certainly enjoyed themselves in those few days of peace at Singapore. There were the usual troubles, including a fight at the Union Jack Club involving sailors, Australian soldiers and the Gordon Highlanders, and thirty men finished up in the Alexandra Military Hospital. Captain Leach had to talk to the ship's company of *Prince of Wales* about the publicity their ship was receiving and warned them not to get 'swollen-headed', particularly when in company with the men from the *Repulse*, which had seen more war service than *Prince of Wales*, or from the old cruisers *Danae*, *Durban* and *Dragon*, which had been doing dull local patrol duties for many months. Captain Leach also warned against rumours that *Prince of Wales* might soon return home. The captain who commanded *Prince of Wales*'s Royal Marines remembers this time.

Viewed from home, Singapore would appear to be remote from war
and I believe officers and ship's company alike were looking forward
to settling down to a peacetime routine. I had been given to understand that the purpose of *Prince of Wales*'s presence in the Far
East was largely political. It was also rumoured that public morale
in Australia was at a rather low ebb and the presence of substantial naval reinforcements at Singapore was intended to bolster
it up.

So the ships' companies present had visions of goodwill cruises to
Sydney and other Australian ports, Manila in the Philippines, and
various ports in the Netherlands East Indies. Certainly the vast
quantity of champagne, red and white wines and 10,000 bottles of
beer that were embarked and stored in the wardroom wine store
during the first few days at Singapore gave credence to this idea. The
Commander set about having a quarterdeck awning made in the
dockyard. The seeming remoteness of air raids would permit a
quarterdeck awning to be spread to shelter from the tropical sun
those who walked it. (Captain C. D. L. Aylwin)

The diners, dancers and cabaret singers, sailors and
soldiers, the Rotary Club members and all at Singapore
were about to find a veritable whirlwind blowing through
their well-ordered lives.

When negotiations between the United States and Japan
approached their climax in November 1941, the Japanese
had already taken the decision that, should no agreement
be reached by the 25th, they would go to war as soon as
possible after 1 December. In the event, Japan extended
the deadline to the 29th, but the extra few days made no
difference; there was no agreement of any kind. A so-
called Imperial Conference was held in Tokyo on 1
December, and no one disagreed when General Tojo
insisted there was no option but for Japan to go to war.
Because she was unwilling to give up her ambitions in
China and other parts of Asia, because she could not live
with the resulting economic embargo – especially that on
oil – and because she was tired of being treated as an
inferior power by the white nations, Japan was prepared
to take on the United States, the British Empire and the

.Dutch. The Japanese decided that their attacks were to commence on 8 December.*

The scale and boldness of the proposed Japanese attacks can only be described as breathtaking. No less than five separate operations, or groups of operations, were planned to commence on that first day.

1. Pearl Harbor: The United States Pacific Fleet was stationed at this naval base in Hawaii. A Japanese force of six aircraft carriers protected by battleships, cruisers, destroyers and submarines was to launch 360 aircraft to carry out what was hoped to be a surprise attack on the American warships in Pearl Harbor. It was known that the Pacific Fleet usually returned to port at the weekend, and the timing of this attack, at dawn on Sunday, 7 December, governed the whole timetable of the Japanese attacks elsewhere.

2. The Philippines: Air attacks from airfields in Formosa were planned to cripple the aircraft strength on the American airfields in Luzon. These air strikes were to be followed almost immediately by the full-scale invasion of the Philippines.

3. Guam, Wake Island and the Gilbert Islands: These American island-outposts, situated between Pearl Harbor and the Philippines, were to be first attacked by air and then occupied by troops. Airfields were then to be built to cut off the Philippines from seaborne reinforcements from Pearl Harbor or the United States.

4. Hong Kong: This isolated British outpost on the coast of that part of China already occupied by Japan was to be attacked by Japanese troops.

5. Siam, Malaya and Singapore: A Japanese naval force was

---

* Because of the International Date Line, the first attacks would occur on 7 December by United States and British times, but on the 8th in Japan and South-East Asia. The times used here will be the local times for the location involved unless otherwise stated.

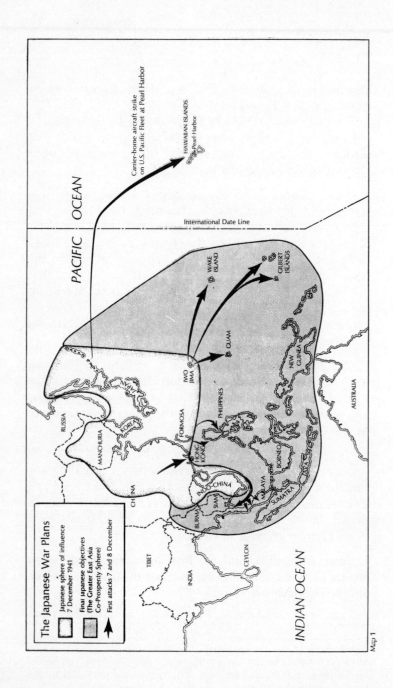

The Japanese War Plans

Japanese sphere of influence 7 December 1941

Final Japanese objectives (The Greater East Asia Co-Prosperity Sphere)

First attacks 7 and 8 December

PACIFIC OCEAN

Carrier-borne aircraft strike on U.S. Pacific Fleet at Pearl Harbor

HAWAIIAN ISLANDS

Pearl Harbor

International Date Line

WAKE ISLAND

GILBERT ISLANDS

GUAM

IWO JIMA

NEW GUINEA

PHILIPPINES

AUSTRALIA

FORMOSA

HONG KONG

BORNEO

JAPAN

KOREA

MANCHURIA

RUSSIA

CHINA

INDO-CHINA

SIAM

BURMA

MALAYA

Singapore

SUMATRA

JAVA

TIBET

INDIA

CEYLON

INDIAN OCEAN

Map 1

to land troops at several points in Siam and northern Malaya as a preliminary to the advance down the Malayan peninsula with the eventual aim of eliminating the British naval and air bases on Singapore Island.

For these attacks, excepting only that on Hong Kong, the Japanese were completely dependent on the use of naval forces, and much of their air strength would be made up of carrier-borne or land-based naval aircraft.

This, then, was to be the first phase of the Japanese bid in South-East Asia. Their only serious fear was that American or British warships might escape the initial attacks and break up the various invasion fleets. But, provided the first objectives were successfully achieved, the Japanese planned to go into a second phase and invade New Guinea, Borneo, the Dutch East Indies and Burma. It was calculated that all of these, except Burma, could be taken within 150 days of the opening attack. In less than six months, the Japanese intended to dispossess the United States, Britain and Holland of their entire colonial territories in South-East Asia. There could have been few outside Japan who, if they had known of the Japanese intentions, would have credited that such a grand plan was possible, especially since the Japanese were already fighting a major war in China. But the Japanese, by daring and skill coupled with a savagery that their national code encouraged but which the rest of the world found loathsome, were to prove capable of achieving most of these aims.

Looking back on the whole affair, however, it seems incomprehensible that the Japanese should have expected to hold on permanently to what they called their 'Greater East Asia Co-Prosperity Sphere'. It was reasonable for them to assume that German-occupied Holland could do little to regain the Dutch possessions, but Britain was far from being beaten by the Germans and the vast resources of British India were right on the border of what would become the Japanese outpost of Burma. And did the

Japanese really expect the Americans to retreat into their shell on the mainland of North America without any attempt to make a comeback in South-East Asia? Did the Japanese, who themselves placed so much store on national prestige and 'face', really believe that the Americans had so little of these qualities? Japanese judgement in these matters was clouded by a hatred of the West so deep that they seemed incapable of realizing the consequences of their actions.

It was not going to be any ordinary war.

The Japanese intended to put ashore strong forces of troops at the narrowest part of the Malaya–Siam peninsula with three aims in view: to cut communications between Burma and Malaya, to develop the attack on Singapore to the south and, later, the attack on Burma to the north. Siam was militarily a weak country, so the landings there were not expected to be resisted strongly, but Malaya and Singapore would be a different matter.

The Japanese army units to be involved do not much concern us here. Most had seen active service in China, where they had carried out several previous amphibious landings and had since been trained in jungle warfare. They would perform their task well and were destined to appear at the gates of Singapore a few weeks later.

The naval units involved had been on the move since 21 November. The arrival at Singapore of *Prince of Wales* and *Repulse* had become known to the Japanese, as Churchill intended it should, and had been confirmed by a Japanese reconnaissance aircraft which had flown over Singapore on 3 December. Although there is no evidence that the last-minute appearance of these two ships at Singapore led the Japanese to reconsider their decision to go to war, it did cause them much concern as all their aircraft-carrier force had been committed to the Pearl Harbor operation 5,000 sea miles away to the east and the best of the Japanese battleships were also committed elsewhere.

The Malaya–Siam operation was the responsibility of
Vice-Admiral Nobutake Kondo's Southern Force. Kondo
himself would keep a distant watch both on the Malaya–
Siam landings and on the Philippines operation. He had
two battleships in Southern Force: the old ships *Kongo*
and *Haruna*, both launched before 1914. The *Kongo* had
actually been designed and built by the British during the
long period when the two countries had been friendly, and
the remainder of the Kongo Class, of which *Haruna* was
one, had then been built in Japanese yards to the same
design. Both ships had been modernized between the wars,
were armed with eight 14-in. guns and were capable of
making 30 knots, though they were not reckoned by the
Japanese to be a match for *Prince of Wales* and *Repulse*.
The closer protection of the Japanese landing forces was
provided by Vice-Admiral Ozawa's 'Malaya Unit', and
he had nothing heavier than Takao Class 8-in. gun
cruisers.

To help to counter the threat posed by *Prince of Wales*
and *Repulse*, the Japanese made three amendments to their
plans. Two minelayers, the *Tatsumiya Maru* and the
Nagasa, were sent south to lay a minefield between the
island of Tioman and the Anamba Islands – in other
words, across the direct route that *Prince of Wales* and
Repulse might take if they came out from Singapore to
attack the Japanese invasion fleets. The two minelayers
accomplished their task and laid 1,000 mines during the
night of 6/7 December, forty-eight hours before the outbreak of war.

The next move was to dispatch every submarine available in the area to form patrol lines north of the minefield.
The ten submarines concerned sailed from Hiroshima and
Sasebo late in November, and by 2 December were formed
up in three patrol lines while two more submarines were
on station near the approaches to Singapore. A further
four submarines are believed to have arrived as reinforcements on 8 December.

The third step taken by the Japanese to protect the

invasion convoys from *Prince of Wales* and *Repulse* was to reinforce the air units assigned to the area. Since there was no separate Japanese Air Force, an earlier plan had called for army planes to cover the landings. Yet the Japanese Navy had no confidence in the Army to provide the necessary scale of air cover, and Admiral Yamamoto, Commander-in-Chief of the Japanese Navy, had ordered the 22nd Koku Sentai – the 22nd Air Flotilla – to move from its airfields in Formosa to Indo-China. Rear-Admiral Sadaichi Matsunaga, the 22nd Flotilla's commander, had moved his headquarters to Saigon and his aircraft had followed. The Genzan Kokutai – the Genzan Air Corps – flew into Saigon airfield with thirty-six twin-engined Mitsubishi Navy Type 96 G3M2 bombers, and the Mihoro Air Corps, with another thirty-six aircraft of the same type, flew into Tu Duam airfield north of Saigon. Thirty-six fighters and six reconnaissance aircraft at Soc Trang to the south of Saigon completed the concentration of Admiral Matsunaga's flotilla. But, when the arrival of the two large British ships at Singapore became known, Admiral Yamamoto decided to strengthen this force by taking part of the Kanoya Air Corps away from the 21st Air Flotilla in Formosa. In this way, twenty-seven Mitsubishi Navy Type 1 G4M1s flew into Saigon just in time for the new war.

This redeployment of the Kanoya aircraft was at the expense of the forces supporting the Philippines attack. The aircraft of Kanoya Air Corps became the most modern and effective of the aircraft supporting the Malaya operations, and Admiral Matsunaga now had a total of ninety-nine bombers, thirty-six fighters and six reconnaissance planes with which to protect the landings.

There are several points concerning these Japanese naval air units that ought to be clarified at this point. The Japanese word *kokutai* is normally translated as 'Air Corps', but this is unfortunate as the English 'corps' is usually a much larger unit than the Japanese *kokutai*. The English word 'wing' – a unit containing two to four squadrons – would have been better, but, to avoid confusing readers who have become used to seeing these Japanese naval air units described as 'air corps', we will continue to use that translation. It should be borne in mind, however, that these 'air corps' contained only three or four squadrons, normally of nine aircraft each.

The Japanese did not have different ranks for their Army and Navy. In our translations we use the nearest equivalent to Royal Navy ranks. This will solve most problems, though American readers will know the 'Sub-Lieutenant' and 'Midshipman' better as 'Lieutenant (Junior Grade)' and 'Ensign'. The Japanese warrant officer and petty officer system is a complicated one with many subsidiary grades, and the general term 'petty officer' will be used here for all these.

The British and the Americans code-named all the Japanese aircraft types with English Christian names. The Mitsubishi Type 96 G3M2 became known as the 'Nell' and the Mitsubishi Navy Type 1 G4M1 became the 'Betty'.

There are considerable differences between various sources, including the British Official History,* over the exact number of bombers in the three Japanese air corps, and many works give higher figures. Details quoted above are from the Japanese Official History† and are partly confirmed by the number of aircraft recorded as taking part in subsequent operations. It is possible that the larger strengths quoted elsewhere were the full establishment of the units and that some of these aircraft had been left behind at home bases.

The title of each air corps is derived from the name of its home base. Genzan and Kanoya are in Japan and Mihoro is in Korea.

.   .   .

* S. Woodburn Kirby, *The War Against Japan*, vol. I, H.M.S.O., London, 1957; subsequently referred to throughout the text as the British Official History.

† Japanese Defence Agency, Research Section, *The Book of Military History: The Malayan Area*, Tokyo, 1969; subsequently referred to throughout the text as the Japanese Official History.

The Japanese plans were based on the hope that the landings and subsequent army operations in northern Malaya would rapidly draw into battle the R.A.F.'s aircraft and that the Mitsubishi Bettys and Nells – whose crews had been thoroughly trained in torpedo as well as in bombing work – could, with the two Japanese battleships, take care of *Prince of Wales* and *Repulse* if the British ships ever got past the minefield and the submarine patrols. The main fear of the Japanese was that their invasion convoys might be spotted *en route* to the landing areas, and that the British ships would come out to intercept the convoys before the Japanese actually started hostilities.

Soon after dawn on 4 December, the main convoy of nineteen troop transports with an escort of cruisers and destroyers left Hainan for the four-day voyage to the area of operations. Nine more transports sailed from Saigon and other Indo-Chinese ports on the 5th and the 7th. These twenty-eight merchant ships, together with no less than thirty-five warships giving close and distant cover, sailed on to the south and then west around Cape Cambodia. The troop transport convoys were then to sail north-west towards Bangkok as a feint before coming to the splitting point in the middle of the Gulf of Siam. It was the earnest hope of every man aboard those ships, and of every other Japanese connected with this operation, that Allied reconnaissance aircraft or ships would not sight the invasion convoys. Should this happen, and should the Allies decide to jump the gun and attack first, the whole Japanese invasion plan would be in jeopardy.

The Allies had been aware of many of the Japanese moves, but it is clear that there was still a great reluctance to accept that war was inevitable. A few realistic decisions were taken in those last few days of peace, but many more moves were made on the assumption either that everything would turn out all right in the end or that more time was available than was actually the case. This attitude was the product of two factors: the first-class security being practised by the Japanese and the continuing underestimate by the Western nations of their true ability and potential. To the average European the Japanese were seen as buck-toothed, short-sighted, physically poor specimens with inferior equipment and a clumsy attitude to mechanical devices. The thought of such a people seriously challenging the sophisticated nations of Great Britain and the United States was not a serious consideration in the minds of many of the men making decisions at that time. It was not just a matter of faulty intelligence, but also of an attitude of mind rooted deep in generations of colonial rule and military supremacy. (Dare one mention the more recent underestimate by the French and then by the Americans of the people of Vietnam?)

The following paragraphs detail the various moves made by the Allies during the first week of December 1941, particularly those that would affect the fortunes of the British ships which arrived at Singapore on the 2nd.

Monday, 1 December

A State of Emergency was declared in Malaya. The Admiralty sent a signal to Admiral Phillips, who had just arrived at Singapore by air from Colombo, suggesting that either *Prince of Wales* or *Repulse*, or both ships if possible, should leave Singapore soon after their arrival and cruise in waters east of Singapore. The purpose of this was ostensibly 'to disconcert the Japanese', but there was probably also a fear that the two ships might be caught in harbour at Singapore by a surprise Japanese air attack which would cripple the new Eastern Fleet igno-miniously before it ever sailed on operations.

Tuesday, 2 December

American patrol aircraft from the Philippines sighted twelve Japanese submarines off Indo-China; all were pro-ceeding south and it was thought likely that the submarines were bound for the Singapore area to keep watch on the movements of the capital ships just arrived. Other Allied intelligence reports stated that twenty-one transport vessels were seen in Camranh Bay, a large anchorage north of Saigon, and that there were now no Japanese merchant ships in the whole of the Pacific, Atlantic or Indian Oceans and that Japanese air strength in southern Indo-China had reached 180 aircraft, including ninety heavy bombers.

Wednesday, 3 December

The Admiralty again signalled Phillips, suggesting that *Prince of Wales* and *Repulse* should be got away from Singapore. This second urging was probably because of the possibility that the Japanese submarines sighted off Indo-China might reach Singapore and attack the capital ships as they came out in the event of war. The Admiralty also urged Admiral Phillips to ask Admiral Hart, commanding the U.S. Asiatic Fleet at Manila, if the eight American destroyers then in the Dutch East Indies and Borneo areas could be moved to Singapore to strengthen the British naval forces there. This last suggestion is interesting and shows how British policy was always to attempt to involve the Americans in any outbreak of war and to show the Japanese that an attack on one was an attack on both. The British were certainly prepared to join with the Americans in the event of war; they probably still had doubts about reciprocal American willingness.

Admiral Phillips informed the Admiralty that he was soon to visit Admiral Hart and would discuss the destroyer suggestion there, and also that he intended to sail *Repulse* on a short visit to Darwin in Australia. This would at least get one of his two ships away from Singapore. Phillips also asked the Admiralty if the old battleships *Revenge* and *Royal Sovereign* as well as *Ramillies* and *Resolution*, previously earmarked for his Fleet, could now be sent to Singapore; he also asked if *Warspite*, which was due to return to England from repair in the United States, could call in at Singapore and remain one week to give a further impression of strength. He informed the Admiralty that he was anxious to commence 'Fleet training of battleships'. *

Thursday, 4 December

Admiral Phillips with two members of his staff left Singapore by air for Manila to meet Admiral Hart and General MacArthur and to plan for future cooperation. This meeting was intended to be the first of several with the Americans and the Dutch to draw up a long-term plan for mutual naval aid in South-East Asia.

Friday, 5 December

Repulse sailed from Singapore for Darwin, accompanied by the destroyers *Vampire* and *Tenedos* (Lieutenant R. Dyer). The crews of all three ships were delighted at the prospect: the *Repulse* and the *Tenedos* for the opportunity to visit Australia and the *Vampire* because she was an Australian ship. It was hoped by the crews that this trip to Darwin was only the start of a longer visit to Australia and there was some talk of being in Sydney for Christmas. The true purpose of the voyage was twofold: *Repulse* could be got away from Singapore, as the Admiralty had twice requested, and Admiral Phillips was hoping to persuade the Australians to send H.M.A.S. *Hobart*, one of their cruisers, to join the Eastern Fleet. Phillips had earlier been counting on receiving H.M.A.S. *Sydney*, another Australian cruiser, but this ship had just been lost with her entire crew in an action with a German raider, the *Kormoran*, off the coast of Western Australia. But the dispatch of *Repulse* to a destination well outside the potential war area shows how little the proximity of war was appreciated at Singapore.

Admiral Phillips met Admiral Hart at Manila on this day and the two discussed the possibility that the British Eastern Fleet might do well to join the Americans at Manila, which would make a suitable base for combined

* Public Record Office ADM 199/2234.

offensive operations in the event of war against Japan. This view, a little over forty-eight hours before the Japanese struck in the Pacific and South-East Asia, again illustrates the naïvety of Allied thinking. The two admirals agreed that this joining of their fleets would have to remain a long-term plan dependent upon more British aircraft being sent to replace the Navy and protect Singapore.

Saturday, 6 December

Admiral Hart and Admiral Phillips continued their talks in Manila. Admiral Hart agreed to send the four ships of his Destroyer Division 57 (Commander E. M. Crouch) from Balikpapan in Dutch Borneo to join Phillips's ships at Singapore if Phillips would call into Singapore the three British destroyers stationed at Hong Kong. It was agreed. The four Americans – U.S.S.s *Whipple* (Lieutenant Commander E. S. Karpe), *John D. Edwards* (Lieutenant Commander H. E. Eccles), *Edsall* (Lieutenant J. J. Nix) and *Alden* (Lieutenant Commander L. E. Coley) – were told to prepare to sail from Balikpapan, ostensibly for Batavia for their crews to have shore leave, but in reality for Singapore. Admiral Phillips must have agreed in principle to moving the Hong Kong destroyers, though they were nominally part of China Station and so still under Vice-Admiral Layton's command, because two of them, *Scout* (Lieutenant-Commander H. Lambton) and *Thanet* (Lieutenant-Commander B. S. Davies), proceeded to Singapore on the outbreak of war. This was hard luck on Hong Kong, but its position was regarded as indefensible and its garrison as good as written off should war break out. The third Hong Kong destroyer, *Thracian* (Commander A. L. Pears), was under repair and remained at Hong Kong.*

This was the last item discussed at Manila before an

---

* *Thanet* and *Thracian* were both sunk within the next few weeks, although *Thracian* was later salvaged by the Japanese and used by them as a patrol boat. *Scout* survived the war. The four American destroyers will be met later in this narrative.

American officer brought a dramatic message into the meeting. A convoy of Japanese merchant ships, previously located by air reconnaissance at Camranh Bay, had now been spotted at sea by an Australian-crewed Hudson aircraft flying from Malaya. The Hudson's captain, Flight Lieutenant J. C. Ramshaw, had reported seeing, first, three Japanese ships steaming south, and then what Ramshaw estimated to be a convoy of no less than twenty-five merchant ships escorted by one battleship, five cruisers and seven destroyers (Ramshaw's 'battleship' was actually a heavy cruiser). This convoy was well south of Saigon and steaming a westerly course. The ships Flight Lieutenant Ramshaw had seen could only be making for Siam, which was still neutral, or Malaya. If this was not war, then it was as near as one could get to war without it actually breaking out.*

There was a flurry of action. The four American destroyers at Balikpapan were ordered to sail at once and were on their way to Singapore within twenty-four hours. Admiral Phillips sent a signal to his Chief-of-Staff, Rear-Admiral Palliser, ordering that *Repulse* should be recalled, but Palliser had already done this. Within an hour or so, Phillips was himself on the way back to Singapore by air, departing so hurriedly that one member of his aircraft's crew who was out in Manila city was left behind. More sightings of Japanese ships at sea came in, and three convoys had now been spotted, believed to contain twenty-nine merchant ships and to be guarded by a similar number of warships.

These sightings by Allied aircraft of the invasion convoys were the last thing the Japanese wanted at this stage, but their luck still held. Now was undoubtedly the time for the British to throw their warships and aircraft at the Japanese convoys, but Admiral Phillips had been in Manila, *Repulse* had been steaming south towards Australia

* Flight Lieutenant Ramshaw was to be killed in action on the first day of the Japanese War.

and the convoys were still beyond the range of most of the obsolete British aircraft in Malaya. In addition, there was the deep-rooted desire by the British to believe that this was not yet war and they were certainly unwilling to take the first step and attack the convoys. But, if Admiral Phillips and all his ships had been at Singapore, and if he had sailed at once for the Gulf of Siam, the appearance of these ships might well have persuaded the Japanese to turn back their vulnerable convoys, which would at least have upset their whole timetable.

The R.A.F. were ordered to fly more air patrols from Malaya, but low cloud and bad weather prevented any more sightings that day.

Sunday, 7 December

Admiral Phillips arrived back at Singapore in the early hours and found waiting to consult him the First Naval Members of both the Australian and the New Zealand Naval Boards. This was about the last thing the harassed British admiral wanted, but he did meet his visitors, if briefly, in company with Dutch and American naval liaison officers.

There was much relief at Singapore when *Repulse* and her two escorting destroyers arrived back after a high-speed run. The British cruiser *Exeter* (Captain O. L. Gordon), with a convoy in the Bay of Bengal, was ordered by the Admiralty to make for Singapore at her best speed.

More air reconnaissance sorties were flown, but the weather had become even worse with the low clouds and tropical downpours of the north-east monsoon. Several fleeting glimpses were obtained of Japanese ships, however, although the reports were so scattered that no clear picture of the Japanese movements could be deduced. As a last resort, two Catalinas of 205 Squadron were sent even farther to the north to examine the bays on the western coast of Indo-China in case the Japanese convoys had put in there. One Catalina returned without having sighted anything useful, but the second was never seen again. A Japanese fighter had shot it down. Its crew were all killed, the first casualties of this new war.

The town of Kota Bharu is situated near the mouth of the Kelantan river at the most north-easterly point of Malaya. The beach, six miles away, was defended by the Indian troops of the 3/17th Dogra Regiment. Just after midnight of 7/8 December the Indians spotted three large merchant ships anchoring two miles off their beach, and a few minutes later were being shelled. The sea was rough, and some of the Japanese troops drowned, but this did not prevent their main force from reaching the beach in landing craft. The invaders were the veteran soldiers of the Japanese 56th Infantry Regiment. The Dogras were mostly young recruits, not fully trained, who had never before been in action. The fighting was fierce and the Japanese eventually gained a firm foothold ashore.

The timing of this Japanese landing, at 00.45 hours local time, was probably dictated by the need to land in the dark and at high tide. It was actually the very first open attack of the new war, preceding the attack on Pearl Harbor by seventy minutes. This was a considerable risk for the Japanese; had news of the Kota Bharu landing been flashed around the world, the American defences at Pearl Harbor might have been alerted. Yet the Japanese guessed correctly that the information could not be passed on so quickly. (In London, Winston Churchill was furious on hearing of the landings; his advisers had repeatedly told him that once the north-east monsoon on this coast started such landings would be impossible until spring.)

What the Japanese were really after at Kota Bharu was the airfield. It lay half-way between the town and the invasion beach and was the home of the R.A.F.'s 36 Squadron, with twelve ancient Vildebeeste torpedo bombers, and of No. 1 Australian Squadron, with thirteen Hudson bomber–reconnaissance aircraft. It is a measure of the Japanese awareness of air power and the vulnerability of their ships at sea that this airfield was their first objective. The Australian Hudsons took off almost at once, and in the bright moonlight they, and the army artillery firing from the shore, managed to hit all three Japanese merchant ships and some of the landing craft. But, when daylight came, the Japanese troops started advancing inland and Japanese aircraft from Indo-China bombed and machine-gunned the airfield. The Indian troops fought well, but there was panic among the ground personnel at the airfield. Disheartened by the constant strafing by the Japanese aircraft and by stray bullets whizzing out of the near-by jungle across the airfield, the R.A.F. men set fire to buildings and equipment, although no order to do so had been given, and departed in lorries. Soon afterwards the eighteen aircraft that had survived the Japanese air attacks were ordered to leave and the army gave up trying to defend the airfield. The airfield in Malaya which was best placed for aircraft to operate against the Japanese invasion convoys had fallen in less than twenty-four hours.

The action at Kota Bharu was typical of the Japanese successes that day. At Pearl Harbor the Japanese aircraft carrier fleet approached undetected, the warnings of a U.S. Army radar station which picked up the Japanese aircraft 130 miles out having been ignored. The Japanese swept in and caused tremendous havoc. Their torpedoes and bombs sank or crippled all eight battleships of the American Pacific Fleet together with several other smaller vessels. One hundred and eighty-eight American aircraft were destroyed, parked wing-tip to wing-tip and mostly caught on the ground. The Japanese lost twenty-nine aircraft. It was a brilliant stroke, marred only by the fact that the three American aircraft carriers were not in harbour and escaped to fight another day. It was much the same story on a smaller scale in the Philippines, in Siam and at Hong Kong. Despite the great risk to the Japanese of committing so many of their forces to slow seaborne convoys, some of which had been sighted several days earlier, the Allies had failed to act quickly enough and the first Japanese moves were everywhere successful.

Singapore was the target of one of the earliest Japanese strikes. Some of the aircraft from the Japanese naval air units at the airfields around Saigon had spent the past few days flying long reconnaissance patrols over the sea to give warning if the British capital ships left Singapore. Others had stood by, loaded with bombs or torpedoes in case that did happen. There had been intense dismay among the Japanese airmen when it was reported that their troop convoys had been spotted on 6 December, and amazement that no air attack developed either on the ships at sea or on their own airfields and that there was no sign of the British ships coming out of Singapore. When this strained period of waiting had passed safely, the Japanese aircrews were able to revert to their main role for the first day of the open war: the bombing of Singapore.

Fifty-four Mitsubishi bombers of the Mihoro and Genzan Air Corps were loaded with bombs for the first strike, the targets being the airfields at Tengah and Seletar. Once again, the attempt to neutralize British air strength was seen as having paramount importance. The attack was to be carried out in the bright moonlight of early morning of the 8th, partly because Singapore was beyond the range of any Japanese fighter aircraft and partly because the Japanese wanted to get this first raid in before the British were fully alerted by other Japanese operations.

But the Singapore operation did not go as planned. Heavy cloud and turbulent conditions forced all of the Genzan and some of the Mihoro aircraft to turn back, and only seventeen of the Mihoro crews struggled through to find themselves in the clear sky over Singapore soon after 04.00. Because the defence system at Singapore had never practised joint operations between night fighters, search-lights and anti-aircraft guns, the defence of the island was left to searchlights and guns only, and the night-fighter crews, who had been alerted by radar while the Japanese were still 140 miles away, were forbidden to take off. The Japanese were picked up by searchlights and thousands of people on the ground watched the neat formation fly steadily over the island. Many bombs were dropped around the airfields, but the only serious damage was the destruction of three Blenheims at Tengah. Some bombs were dropped into the middle of Singapore city, where the blackout did not function until after the raid was over, and 200 people, most of them Chinese, were killed or wounded. The Japanese aircraft flew away; not one had been hit by the anti-aircraft fire.

The crews of *Prince of Wales* and *Repulse* were among the spectators of the raid.

I had been ashore with some of my mates on the Liberty boat to the big wet canteen at the Naval Base. We had been drinking Lion or Tiger beer – I forget which – and had had plenty. When I got back to the ship I went to sleep on the upper deck. I was woken up by gunfire and the sirens ashore and heard the bugle calling us to Action Stations. For a moment I wondered where I was and what was going on. 'Blimey. What am I doing here?' (Able Seaman S. E. Brown, H.M.S. *Repulse*)

I was returning to the ship following a pleasant, sociable day in Singapore. It was a night of quiet, warm and peaceful calm, when all hell let loose and all the guns and sirens sounded off. We watched *Prince of Wales* in action as we ran back – a little surprised to see the multiple pom-poms firing away at the minuscule high-level targets. I remember our absolute astonishment at the time. (Lieutenant D. B. H. Wildish, H.M.S. *Prince of Wales*)

I can remember quite clearly various areas of the Dockyard blacking out whilst others remained fully lit. As one area was blacked out, so another would be switched on, and this continued for a considerable time, during which people were forever running hither and thither, presumably looking for some sort of shelter. (Able Seaman R. H. James, H.M.S. *Prince of Wales*)

We had turned in, very merry from a Canteen Leave and not very worried, and were awakened by the almost forgotten sound of wailing air-raid sirens in the Dockyard followed by distant gunfire. This

could only mean Japs? My waking thoughts were merely, 'Damn it!
The silly blighters have gone and started it!' How our little world
was bound to change. I watched very high-flying planes lit by
searchlights – far too high to be hit by the wasteful volume of Ack-
Ack. Strangely, they dropped no bombs near the Dockyard.
(Ordinary Seaman D. F. Wilson, H.M.S. *Prince of Wales*)

In fact the Japanese aircraft had been within range of
Prince of Wales's high-angle 5·25-in. guns, and after the
raid the battleship was moved away from the quayside so
that these guns could operate more freely in any future air
raid.

The crews of *Prince of Wales* and *Repulse* had already
seen much of the war, and this new development was soon
accepted by them if not by the civilian population of
Singapore. The recent arrival of the two capital ships and
the presence on the island of so many aircraft and troops,
coupled with the poor opinion that the Europeans at least
held of the Japanese, had led the civilians to believe that
their peaceful existence in this tropical haven would continue undisturbed. Now, Japanese aircraft had appeared
from nowhere, bombed the city, caused many deaths, and
flown off undamaged. The shattering event was to be
followed by a whole string of disastrous news items during
the hours ahead.

At 06.30 a special Order of the Day was published by
all military units and civil authorities in the British
possessions of the Far East.

Japan's action today gives the signal for the Empire Naval, Army and
Air Forces, and those of their Allies, to go into action with a common
aim and common ideals.

We are ready. We have had plenty of warning and our preparations are made and tested. We do not forget at this moment the
years of patience and forbearance in which we have borne, with dignity and discipline, the petty insults and insolences inflicted on us by
the Japanese in the Far East. We know that those things were only
done because Japan thought she could take advantage of our supposed
weakness. Now, when Japan herself has decided to put the matter to
a sterner test, she will find out that she has made a grievous mistake.

We are confident. Our defences are strong and our weapons efficient. Whatever our race, and whether we are now in our native land or have come thousands of miles, we have one aim and one only. It is to defend these shores, to destroy such of our enemies as may set foot on our soil, and then, finally, to cripple the power of the enemy to endanger our ideals, our possessions and our peace.

What of the enemy? We see before us a Japan drained for years by the exhausting claims of her wanton onslaught on China. We see a Japan whose trade and industry have been so dislocated by these years of reckless adventure that, in a mood of desperation, her Government had flung her into war under the delusion that, by stabbing a friendly nation in the back, she can gain her end. Let her look at Italy and what has happened since that nation tried a similar base action.

Let us all remember that we here in the Far East form part of the great campaign for the preservation in the world of truth and justice and freedom; confidence, resolution, enterprise and devotion to the cause must and will inspire every one of us in the fighting services, while from the civilian population, Malay, Chinese, Indian, or Burmese, we expect that patience, endurance and serenity which is the great virtue of the East and which will go far to assist the fighting men to gain final and complete victory.

> R. BROOKE-POPHAM, Air Chief Marshal,
> Commander-in-Chief, Far East
>
> G. LAYTON, Vice-Admiral,
> Commander-in-Chief, China *

This document had actually been prepared several months earlier so that it could be translated into the various languages spoken in the Far East, but, in the light of what had happened and what was about to happen, it reveals a failure by the British leaders in the area to appreciate the strength of their new enemy.

When the Admiralty in London had heard of the sightings of the Japanese convoys at sea two days earlier, a signal had been sent to Admiral Phillips asking what action he proposed to take. It was a good question. The sending of

* Quoted in the British Official History, p. 525.

the two capital ships to Singapore had always been intended as a political deterrent and no detailed planning had taken place about what was to be done if that deterrent failed.

The overall Commander-in-Chief of the Far East forces, Air Chief Marshal Sir Robert Brooke-Popham, was due for routine replacement when events put him in the unenviable position of having to cope with the Japanese attacks. Despite his title, as we have seen, Brooke-Popham exercised command only over the Army and the R.A.F. units in the Far East; the Admiralty had insisted that their ships remain purely under naval command. And even in this independent naval command there was an element of ambiguity. Admiral Phillips had been appointed Commander-in-Chief Eastern Fleet on his arrival at Singapore, but there still remained Vice-Admiral Sir Geoffrey Layton, who was Commander-in-Chief China Station. The Admiralty had ordered that Phillips would take over command and administration of China Station at 00.30 on 10 December, two days hence. Admiral Layton was to strike his flag that evening, and had planned to sail at once for England on a liner. He is reputed to have been very disappointed at not being given command of the new Eastern Fleet, and the imminent departure at this critical time of an officer so experienced in local conditions was a great waste. As soon as the Japanese opened their attacks, however, Admiral Phillips, by prior order of the Admiralty, brought forward the take-over from Layton. Poor Admiral Layton does not appear to have been much consulted by Admiral Phillips in the momentous decisions about to be taken, though in the event it is unlikely that the outcome would have been much different if he had been. However, Layton was not yet out of the story.

On the relationship between Brooke-Popham and Phillips, there is clear documentary evidence of their respective positions since both had received detailed directives from London on 2 December. Brooke-Popham's position as Commander-in-Chief Far East was reaffirmed and he was told that he was to be 'jointly responsible with Commander-in-Chief Eastern Fleet to H.M. Government for the conduct of our strategy in the Far East'. Phillips was similarly directed to become 'jointly responsible with the Commander-in-Chief Far East to H.M. Government for the conduct of our strategy in the Far East'.* In other words, because the Admiralty was unwilling to place its ships under a unified command and under an R.A.F. officer, even though one of higher rank, the war in the Far East was to be fought under divided command. Admiral Phillips, who had spent not much more than a few days in the Far East and only a few hours at Singapore, need only *consult* Brooke-Popham and was then completely free to decide on the action to take in the naval side of the war.

It is known that Phillips and Brooke-Popham met for a short while at the Naval Base in the late evening on 7 December, just two hours before the Japanese landed in northern Malaya, and discussed the latest situation. Soon after this meeting Phillips sent the following signal to the Admiralty:

IF THE RELATIVE STRENGTH OF THE ENEMY FORCE PERMITS, ENDEAVOUR WILL BE MADE TO ATTACK THE EXPEDITION BY NIGHT OR BY DAY. IF WE ARE INFERIOR IN STRENGTH A RAID WILL BE ATTEMPTED AND THE AIR FORCE WILL ATTACK WITH BOMBS AND TORPEDOES IN CONJUNCTION WITH OUR NAVAL FORCES.†

It is probable that this signal was not sent until after the Japanese actually landed and that it merely represents Phillips's preliminary intentions. There is one aspect of the signal which is of interest. During his years as Vice-Chief of the Naval Staff, Phillips had seen many examples

* British Official History, pp. 485 and 487.
† Public Record Office ADM 199/1149.

of the Admiralty taking detailed control of operations at sea; indeed, he had probably exercised such control in the name of the First Sea Lord on numerous occasions. Although London was now half a world away, it was quite possible that the Admiralty might try the same methods here; they were certainly asking to be informed of every move. It is only conjecture that the vague wording of this signal reflects the desire of Phillips to retain as much freedom of action as possible, but this aspect will be met again.

By midday of the 8th, with the war now nearly twelve hours old, more news of the widespread Japanese moves had come in to Singapore. Information from more distant areas was still lacking in detail but it had become quite clear that the Japanese had landed in northern Malaya and at several points in Siam and that units of the Army and the R.A.F. were involved in heavy fighting. It was time for Phillips to decide what the Royal Navy should do. At 12.30 Admiral Phillips opened a meeting aboard *Prince of Wales*. Besides the admiral and his immediate staff, there were Captain Leach of *Prince of Wales*, Captain Tennant of the *Repulse*, and the captains of several destroyers. No representative of Air Chief Marshal Brooke-Popham's Far East Headquarters was invited, and nobody from the local R.A.F. command. It was purely a naval occasion. No minutes were kept of this council of war, but there is little doubt of how it went.

Admiral Phillips had already counted up the strength of warships available to him. The Admiralty were now making desperate efforts to get more ships to Singapore, but these would take days or even weeks to arrive. Fortunately Phillips's two capital ships, *Prince of Wales* and *Repulse*, were free of any serious defect and ready to sail within an hour or so of receiving orders. There were also four cruisers in the Naval Base at Singapore. Three of these were *Durban* (Captain P. G. L. Cazalet), *Danae* (Captain R. J. Shaw) and *Dragon* (Commander D. H. Harper) of the China Station force which Phillips had taken over that morning, but they were old ships built for patrol and scouting work and not for hard fighting, though each carried six 6-in. guns and had the speed to keep up with *Prince of Wales* and *Repulse*. Only one of them, however, the *Durban*, was actually ready to sail. The fourth was a more modern cruiser, the *Mauritius* (Captain W. D. Stephens), with twelve 6-in. guns. She was undergoing refit, and although orders were issued to hurry this along as fast as possible, she could not be available for some time. The *Exeter*, a powerful eight 8-in. gun cruiser, was on the way from the Indian Ocean at top speed and was expected to arrive within thirty-six hours, as was the Dutch 5·9-in. gun cruiser *Java*, coming up from the Dutch Indies.

The destroyer situation was not much better. Two of the four that had escorted *Prince of Wales* and *Repulse* into Singapore were out of action with defects. These were the two ships provided by the Mediterranean Fleet, and while *Encounter* would be ready in three days' time, *Jupiter*, described by Phillips in a signal as 'a notorious crock', would take three weeks to complete repairs. However, *Express* and *Electra*, the two destroyers provided by the Home Fleet, were both fit for action. There were two other destroyers on hand at Singapore: H.M.A.S. *Vampire* (Commander W. T. A. Moran) and H.M.S. *Tenedos* (Lieutenant R. Dyer). Moran and Dyer were both in Phillips's cabin, surprised, perhaps, to find their old First World War destroyers being considered for a major fleet action with these glamorous capital ships fresh out from England. Another local destroyer, H.M.S. *Stronghold* (Lieutenant-Commander G. R. Pretor-Pinney), had recently completed repairs and was also available. Moreover, if Admiral Phillips could wait two more days, he would have the four American destroyers from Balikpapan and the two British destroyers that had been sailed from Hong Kong that morning as they could do little to decide the outcome there.

So, when Admiral Phillips surveyed the warships available that morning, he found that he had one battleship, one

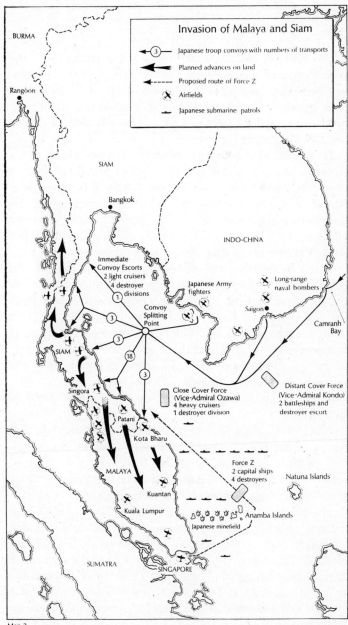

Invasion of Malaya and Siam

←③	Japanese troop convoys with numbers of transports
←	Planned advances on land
←----	Proposed route of Force Z
✕	Airfields
‒‒‒	Japanese submarine patrols

BURMA

Rangoon

SIAM

Bangkok

INDO-CHINA

Immediate
Convoy Escorts
2 light cruisers
4 destroyer
① divisions

Japanese Army
fighters

Long-range
naval bombers

③

Saigon

Convoy
Splitting
Point

③

Camranh
Bay

③

18

SIAM

Singora

③

Close Cover Force
(Vice-Admiral Ozawa)
4 heavy cruisers
1 destroyer division

Distant Cover Force
(Vice-Admiral Kondo)
2 battleships and
destroyer escort

Patani

Kota Bharu

Force Z
2 capital ships
4 destroyers

Natuna Islands

MALAYA

Kuantan

Kuala Lumpur

Anamba Islands

Japanese minefield

SUMATRA

SINGAPORE

Map 2

battle cruiser, one light cruiser and five destroyers immediately on hand, with several more cruisers and destroyers becoming available in the following days. But there was no chance of capital-ship reinforcement within the next week, and no aircraft carrier could become available for an even longer period.

It is obvious from the available documents that the British were in possession of remarkably sound intelligence on many of the Japanese moves, partly through a U.S. Naval radio unit at Honolulu, which was monitoring and deciphering Japanese naval signals, and partly through effective R.A.F. air reconnaissance during the past few days. Phillips knew that the Japanese troop convoys were escorted by cruisers and destroyers, and that there was a covering force of heavier warships containing at least one Kongo Class battleship. (There were actually two battleships of this class, *Kongo* and *Haruna*.) Phillips also knew with some degree of accuracy the number of Japanese bombers and fighters stationed around Saigon, and was aware of the recently laid Japanese minefield and the Japanese submarine patrols. There were therefore few gaps in his knowledge of what his ships might have to face.

Admiral Phillips had two decisions to make: on the timing of any move he made and on the composition of the force with which he made it. He had already decided on both of these points, and had summoned the meeting more to inform those present of his decision than to consult them. It was an undramatic scene. The officers sat quietly around the long mahogany table in the Admiral's dining cabin. The atmosphere was hot and humid; Phillips looked strained and weary. He quietly announced that he intended to sail that evening in his flagship *Prince of Wales* in company with *Repulse* and just four destroyers – the faithful *Express* and *Electra* that had escorted Force G all the way from Greenock, and with *Tenedos* and *Vampire* of the local ships to complete the destroyer screen. The cruiser *Durban* was to be left behind. It would be a small but fast striking force. His intention was to sail north into the Gulf of Siam and, on the morning of 10 December, attack the Japanese shipping carrying out landings on the coasts of Malaya and Siam.

Phillips then asked for opinions on his plan, though it is unlikely that he expected serious argument from professional naval officers, and unlikely also that this determined personality needed the reassurance of juniors. The question was a formality and was treated by those present as such. Captain Tennant of *Repulse* was the first to support the decision. Hardly anyone else spoke.

There were, in any case, only two real alternatives to Phillips's proposed course of action: first, that the Eastern Fleet should remain at Singapore to see how the situation developed and gather further strength, but at the same time risking an air attack like the one which had finished off the American battleships in Pearl Harbor that same morning; or, secondly, that it should sail for safer waters and await events. With the Army and the R.A.F. fighting for their lives in northern Malaya, however, these were not really valid alternatives.

During the research for this book it was possible to contact the last two men still alive who had been among those present at the meeting.

The atmosphere was calm and quietly thoughtful – fatalistic perhaps. To the best of my recollection I remember Admiral Phillips saying, 'Gentlemen, this is an extremely hazardous expedition and I would liken it to taking the Home Fleet into the Skagerrak without air cover. Nevertheless, I feel that we have got to do something.'

There was a very long silence after this and I suspect that others were feeling the same as I at the time. My own thoughts were 'Yes, indeed you have got to do something but this is quite against your own reasoning and the position in which you find yourself must be laid at Churchill's feet.' I suppose we were all thinking of ourselves and forgetting other priorities, the North Atlantic, Mediterranean, Home Defence and so on. (Lieutenant R. Dyer, H.M.S *Tenedos*)

After all the discussion was over, Admiral Phillips summed up in words something like this. 'We can stay in Singapore. We can sail away to the East – Australia. Or we can go out and fight. Gentle-men, we sail at five o'clock.' (Lieutenant-Commander F. J. Cart-wright, H.M.S. *Express*)*

The meeting had lasted half an hour at the most, and those present returned to their ships or duties ashore to prepare for sailing. Even before the meeting, Admiral Phillips had sent a signal to the Admiralty stating that he intended to sail that evening and to attack Japanese shipping off Kota Bharu on the morning of the 10th. Now he turned his attention to the question of air cover. There are several references to discussions that day between Admiral Phillips or his staff and the R.A.F. over air support for the coming operation, but there are no documents recording what was actually said because most of the Singapore headquarters war diaries and signal files were later lost. It is probable that Air Vice-Marshal C. W. H. Pulford, Air Officer Commanding Malaya, had earlier indicated that the R.A.F. would do its best and asked for the Navy's specific requirements. After the meet-ing on *Prince of Wales*, one of Phillips's staff officers put the naval requirements into writing and this was delivered to Air Vice-Marshal Pulford:

1. Reconnaissance 100 miles northward of the force at daylight on the 9th December,

2. Reconnaissance off Singora at first light on 10th December,

3. Fighter protection off Singora during daylight of the 10th December.†

It is of interest that Admiral Phillips had already in-formed the Admiralty that he intended to attack Japanese shipping at Kota Bharu; now he was telling the local R.A.F. command that his target was the Japanese shipping off Singora, 120 nautical miles farther into the Gulf of Siam. Up-to-date intelligence had probably indicated that

---

* Unfortunately Lieutenant-Commander (later Captain) Cart-wright died before this book was ready for publication.

† Public Record Office A D M 199/1149.

the Singora landings were more serious than those at Kota Bharu, though Phillips was now planning a more ambitious operation than the one he had signalled to the Admiralty that morning. But in this new theatre of war the fortunes of the R.A.F. were already running low. The obsolete aircraft of their squadrons were being battered to pieces on the ground or shot to pieces whenever they took to the air. The forward airfields were being evacuated under Japanese attack, and the R.A.F. was fast diminishing as a major element in the defence forces of the Far East. There is no need to labour the point that the Air Ministry had consistently failed to send any modern aircraft to Malaya and that their men out there were now paying the penalty.

It is not easy to be certain about the precise developments following the arrival of this message at R.A.F. Headquarters. The airmen were well aware of the risks the sailors were taking if they ventured into the Gulf of Siam without air cover, and they were becoming more aware by the hour of how difficult it would be for the needed aircraft to be found. It would look very bad for them simply to say that air cover could not be provided; it would look even worse later if they allowed the ships to sail and then could not provide the requested air cover, particularly in two days' time when the ships would be closest to the known Japanese air bases in Indo-China.

It is probable that Air Vice-Marshal Pulford talked with Air Chief Marshal Brooke-Popham about his dilemma, and it is still believed in Singapore that there was an argument that afternoon between Brooke-Popham and Phillips, presumably with Brooke-Popham warning Phillips that the operation was in danger and that the R.A.F. would not be able to fulfil all the Navy's demands. But, with the divided command at Singapore, Brooke-Popham, although Commander-in-Chief Far East, could not order Phillips to give up the operation. There is also evidence, albeit hearsay, that one of Brooke-Popham's staff, Group Captain L. Darvall, was dispatched on a special visit to *Prince of Wales* that afternoon 'to make it quite clear to him that he could not have or expect shore-based air cover. Admiral Sir Tom Phillips, therefore, having been left in no doubt, took a calculated risk and sailed.' These words were spoken by Darvall to a colleague later in the war, but Darvall (later an Air Marshal) is now dead and they cannot be verified.

His difficulties with the R.A.F. made no difference to Admiral Phillips's resolve to sail, though he would still be free to cut short the operation between the time of sailing and the arrival in the area of maximum danger in thirty-six hours' time. Yet some sympathy is due to the tired admiral on that afternoon. Given time, much that was not yet clear would have become so. More ships would be arriving. Indeed, if Phillips had waited only forty-eight hours, the expedition could have sailed with two cruisers and four extra destroyers. It would then also have been a true Allied force, with American and Dutch as well as British ships; whether Phillips would have thought that an asset cannot be guessed, but the anti-aircraft defences of such an increased force would have been far stronger. But time was the one element Tom Phillips did not have. With every hour that passed the Japanese were securing their landings in the north. Also, as one naval officer rightly comments, the effect on morale in Singapore if the ships had remained in harbour would have been 'devastating'. True, there was danger from the air, but how great was that danger? It is said that Phillips did not believe that any Japanese torpedo bomber had the range to fly the 400 miles from Saigon to the area off Siam he was heading for. If this was Phillips's belief, then he did not realize that the Japanese aircraft that had bombed Singapore the night before had flown nearly twice the distance and that these same aircraft could operate as torpedo bombers when required.

But perhaps Admiral Phillips let his thoughts wander over the various capital ships that had been sunk since 1939 and dwelt on how not one had succumbed to air attack while at sea. Mines, submarines and old Japanese battleships he would face as a matter of course. He could steer clear of the area where the mines were believed to be. He could steam fast enough to outrun any submarine. His ships could stand up to any of the Japanese warships known to be in the area. And, if he could get into the right position, the big guns of *Prince of Wales* and *Repulse* could inflict a veritable slaughter on the Japanese merchant ships off the invasion beaches. If he could achieve this, then it would be a great victory for the Royal Navy and for British interests in the Far East.

In retrospect, it might have been better to have proceeded more cautiously, but there are few who will say that, on the evidence available, Phillips actually went wrong. Retrospectively again, it might have been better if Air Chief Marshal Brooke-Popham had been in overall command and, with his airman's sense of reality, could have imposed a decision on Phillips and made him wait. But the Admiralty had demanded its freedom of action in operational matters, and it was this freedom which Phillips was now exercising.

There remained only a few hours before the ships sailed. For signal purposes it was decided to call the squadron 'Force Z', an unhappy choice which had a ring of finality. Admiral Phillips's Chief-of-Staff, Rear-Admiral A. F. E. Palliser, was ordered to remain ashore to provide Phillips with a link between the ships at sea and the various headquarters at Singapore during the operation. Palliser was to keep his chief as fully informed as possible, by signal, of any developments after Force Z sailed, but Phillips would want to maintain radio silence for as long as possible and the two must have discussed the various moves that Phillips might make in the event of changing circumstances. The degree to which Palliser could read Phillips's mind after the ships had sailed would be of great importance.

The two capital ships were completely ready and could have sailed at once, but Admiral Phillips wanted an evening departure to conceal the sailing from possible Japanese agents on the island. An officer in *Prince of Wales* remembers the afternoon as being filled with 'much preliminary scampering of staff officers'.

There was more work still to do on the destroyers, particularly on the *Express*:

Prior to 8 December, the ship's company had been busy de-ammunitioning ship to enter drydock for urgent repairs. When the order was given to reverse the whole operation and prepare for sea – shells half in and half out of portholes – you can imagine the verbal chat that followed. 'Do these idiots know what they are doing?' The intense heat didn't help. Shipshape and Bristol fashion, we were soon ready to leave harbour to head for all sorts of mysterious adventures as rumour had it – communication hadn't been invented then. One version was we were heading home. Bloody good job! (Able Seaman J. M. Farrington)

An Admiralty press officer, Lieutenant Horace Abrahams, reported aboard *Repulse*, complete with camera. Two civilian journalists, O'Dowd Gallagher of the *Daily Express* and an American, Cecil Brown of the Columbia Broadcasting System, followed, having been offered an 'unknown assignment' lasting up to five days. Many of the pressmen at Singapore had turned down this offer; only Gallagher had had a hunch that it might be something big and had persuaded his friend Brown to keep him company.

Captain Leach of the *Prince of Wales* managed to get ashore that afternoon and met his son whose own ship was refitting at the Naval Base.

I saw little of my father that day, but we did manage to meet at the Base swimming pool in the late afternoon. I am a poor swimmer and merely splashed about to get cool but I remember my father saying, 'I am going to do a couple of lengths now; you never know when it mightn't come in handy', a remark which in retrospect was both prophetic and consistent. Afterwards we had a final Gin Sling (the popular local drink at the time subsequently to be replaced by Gin and Tonic) and he introduced me to Captain Bill Tennant of the *Repulse*, a charming, kindly man. The two were good friends and clearly saw very much eye to eye. We then parted, my father to the

Prince of Wales and I to the shore accommodation that is now called
H.M.S. *Terror*. I never saw him again. (Midshipman H. C. Leach,
H.M.S. *Mauritius*)

It is difficult to generalize about the morale and feelings
of the men aboard the six ships preparing to sail. Most had
been involved in dozens of wartime sailings, and no one
had yet told the lower deck one word of what was happening, although many must have had some idea that they
were off to look for the Japanese.

Only two quotations are needed to round off this
chapter. Surgeon-Commander F. B. Quinn, the Fleet
Medical Officer who was sailing aboard *Prince of Wales*,
later prepared a report commenting on the physical state
of the ship's company following the long, high-speed
voyage from England in a badly ventilated ship and then
the strenuous working while at Singapore.

Though the morale of the ship's company was good, I am of the
opinion that the men were fatigued and listless and their fighting
efficiency was below par.*

And Ordinary Seaman Cecil Jones, a New Zealander
stationed ashore at the Naval Base, recollected:

I was on one of the many working parties from the Fleet Shore
Establishment and other ships who helped to provision *Repulse* and
Prince of Wales before they sailed. I remember them sailing, as it
was with deep regret that I did not get a draft on to one of them.
Only two N.Z. seamen did so; one survived.

The ships left the Dockyard with our honest thoughts that they
were unsinkable.

* Public Record Office ADM 199/1149.

7

The Sweep

'Close all scuttles and deadlights. Special seamen to your stations.' Over the Tannoy loudspeakers of four warships came these instructions alerting the crews that they would soon be putting to sea. A third call, 'Hands fall in for leaving harbour', then set in motion the procedure that most of the sailors had gone through so often before.

The Australian destroyer *Vampire* was first away at 17.10, followed closely by another destroyer, *Tenedos*. Then came *Repulse* and *Prince of Wales*. *Electra* and *Express* had been out exercising their minesweeping gear since mid afternoon, and would rendezvous outside the boom off Changi Point. As the two capital ships left the Naval Base, an official photographer took photographs of each but not of the escorting destroyers. All the ships flew the Royal Navy's White Ensign, but from the main mast of *Prince of Wales* also flew a red cross of St George on a white background – the flag of a commander-in-chief taking his fleet to sea. It was a fine but hot evening, already starting to grow gloomy, and the sun was near to setting behind the palms and low hills of Singapore Island. When the ships turned east to steam away down Johore Strait towards the sea, there were many spectators on shore to wave them on their way. With this new war not yet twenty-four hours old, it was a sight to stir any breast, and there can have been few among the onlookers who did not believe that they were watching these warships deliberately going out to find and fight the Japanese. Six warships: one new battleship that had already been involved in a dramatic battle, one battle cruiser that had not fired her big guns in action since 1917, two destroyers that had been in constant action since the war began and two more which had passed just as many peaceful months in the East and whose crews must have been still in a daze over being plunged so suddenly into action.

Once clear of the land, Force Z formed into its cruising pattern for the first night. *Prince of Wales* had overtaken and passed *Repulse* and the battle cruiser was now in position four cables (800 yards) astern of the flagship. On reaching the open sea, *Express* moved ahead to take up a position well in front of *Prince of Wales* and streamed her high-speed minesweeping gear, but this broke down almost at once and *Electra* had to take her place. The six warships steamed on into the night at 17½ knots.

Many men have recorded their feelings on this first evening at sea with the prospect of action within days or, possibly, hours. There was every point of view between the extremes of blind optimism and a belief in imminent doom.

I experienced that tense awareness of one's heart beating; that rather pleasurable, bittersweet enjoyment – I wonder is it pleasure? It's difficult to say, for I am quite sure no man gets any kick out of being shelled or bombed. I certainly don't, but I do know that these occasions give you an intense comradeship with your shipmates and a rather selfless exaltation which appears to be pleasurable.

We went to routine Dusk Action Stations and then many of us stood on deck talking long after darkness had fallen. What was ahead of us? How did the Japs fight? Were they truly fanatical? Did they make suicidal attacks? (I recalled the last time I personally had seen a Jap – he was playing snooker at Edinburgh.) I talked to an old friend of mine, who had joined the ship at Singapore, and we watched the escorting destroyers winking a few signals at us, then went through the screen into the bright, chattering Wardroom for a drink. (Surgeon Lieutenant-Commander E. D. Caldwell, H.M.S. *Prince of Wales*)

We had been led to believe that the Japs would be quite unorthodox and not nearly equal to the German Air Force. We should be able to pick them off like pigeons. The only misgivings I had were the small rumours which had come up from the 'Plotting Tables' that things were not as coordinated as they would like them to be during some of the practice shoots. But putting all doubts on one side we quietly eased away to meet the tropical darkness and silence. (Ordinary Seaman W. E. England, H.M.S. *Prince of Wales*)

We had left Singapore in glorious weather but I had this premonition that the *Prince of Wales* would never again return to Singapore or any other port. I had this feeling that this was the end as far as the ship was concerned. (Boy Seaman W. S. Searle, H.M.S. *Prince of Wales*)

This uneasy feeling of trouble ahead was even stronger on the *Repulse*.

It was a funny thing, I don't know if anyone else has memories of this but a 'buzz' seemed to go round the ship that this was one trip we wouldn't be coming back from, this stemming from the fact that we were in company with the *Prince of Wales* who was generally considered by many as a 'Jonah'. (Ordinary Seaman H. J. Hall)

We all knew that with the *Prince of Wales* with us we were never coming back again in one piece. (Chief Petty Officer E. L. Smith)

Many other men on *Repulse*, however, would say that this gloomy talk was not prevalent and that the greater number of men on the battle cruiser were only too anxious to see their ship in action at last and had no doubts about the outcome.

The feelings of the British sailors about their enemy was that there was really nothing to fear.

Well, here we come you Jap bastards. Get ready!

The popular conception was that the Japanese were pushovers.

Afraid? Not really; perhaps excited is the word. After all, this is the battle cruiser *Repulse* and they are only Japs.

Their ships were supposed to be old and top-heavy, liable to roll over if they fired a full broadside; their aircraft were even slower than our old Swordfish, so what had we to worry about?

We talked quite a lot of sharks and jokingly said they are going to have a beanfeast – on Japs.

We didn't really know what we were up against and just passed them off as slant-eyed so-and-so's.

Eight hours after sailing, the first of several signals sent by Rear-Admiral Palliser in Singapore was received in *Prince of Wales*. It was not a signal to increase Admiral Phillips's confidence.

TO C IN C E.FLEET   FROM CHIEF OF STAFF
                                                E.FLEET

IMMEDIATE
MY 2253/8TH PART 1 BEGINS. R.A.F. RECONNAISSANCE TO A DEPTH OF 100 MILES TO THE NORTH WESTWARD OF YOU WILL BE PROVIDED BY 1 CATALINA FROM 08.00 ONWARDS 9TH.

(II) IT IS HOPED THAT A DAWN RECONNAISSANCE OF COAST NEAR SINGORA CAN BE CARRIED OUT ON WEDNESDAY 10TH.

(III) FIGHTER PROTECTION ON WEDNESDAY 10TH WILL NOT, REPEAT NOT, BE POSSIBLE. MY 2253/ 8TH PART 1 END. PART 2 FOLLOWS.

MY 2253/8 PART 2

(IV) JAPANESE HAVE LARGE BOMBER FORCES BASED SOUTHERN INDO-CHINA AND POSSIBLY ALSO IN THAILAND. C IN C FAR EAST HAS REQUESTED GENERAL MACARTHUR TO CARRY OUT ATTACK WITH HIS LONG RANGE BOMBERS ON INDO-CHINA AERODROMES AS SOON AS POSSIBLE.

(V) KOTA BHARU AERODROME HAS BEEN EVACUATED AND WE SEEM TO BE LOSING GRIP IN OTHER NORTHERN AERODROMES DUE TO ENEMY AIR ACTION.

(VI) MILITARY POSITION NEAR KOTA BHARU DOES NOT SEEM GOOD BUT DETAILS ARE NOT AVAILABLE. *

* Public Record Office ADM 199/1149. Further operational signals will be from the same Public Record Office reference unless otherwise stated.

Palliser was telling his chief in as clear a manner as possible that the R.A.F. could supply limited reconnaissance support but there was no chance at all of fighter cover on the 10th, the day on which Force Z would be most at risk from the Japanese air units known to be in Siam. The R.A.F. had been blamed many times from Dunkirk onwards for leaving the Army or the Navy in the lurch without air cover; on this occasion they were leaving the Navy in no doubt that if their ships ventured too far north then it must be entirely at the Navy's risk.

There was one factor to this affair that Admiral Phillips did not then know. On 8 December, the previous day, Japanese aircraft had made a successful air attack on Clark Field, Manila, and destroyed half the American B-17 Flying Fortresses there; these were the American aircraft that Air Chief Marshal Brooke-Popham had asked General MacArthur to use in bombing attacks on the Japanese airfields near Saigon. The American air attack referred to in Palliser's signal was thus never to take place.

The signal placed a further heavy burden of decision on Admiral Phillips's shoulders. It is believed, however, that he did not anguish for long and his mind was soon made up. The earlier fine weather had now broken and there was low and heavy cloud with frequent rain squalls. Phillips would continue to sail north throughout the next day, the 9th, and then, if the bad weather continued to shield his ships from Japanese reconnaissance aircraft, he could still turn west and make the intended dash at high speed to one of the Japanese invasion areas at dawn on the 10th. After attacking whatever Japanese shipping could be found, Force Z could then retire at speed to the south and fight off whatever air or surface vessel attack the Japanese could mount while it was withdrawing. But, if the Japanese spotted his ships during the daylight hours of the 9th, Phillips could always give up the operation and return to Singapore. In retrospect it seems as prudent a course as was possible in the circumstances.

One account says that Admiral Phillips did not do much

more than shrug his shoulders over the 'no fighter cover' signal and declared that it was 'best to get on with it'. But this is probably a simplification and the decision taken was certainly the product of some careful thought. Admiral Phillips decided there was no need to reply to this signal and thus break wireless silence; he assumed that Palliser would realize that no signal meant the operation was proceeding.

There is one important point to be emphasized. The R.A.F. had not abandoned the Navy altogether in the matter of fighter support. Although their fighter squadrons were being drawn into the land battle in northern Malaya, No. 453 (Australian) Squadron, with their Brewster Buffalo fighters at Sembawang airfield on Singapore Island, was earmarked to support Force Z. There was no question of this handful of aircraft providing permanent air cover over the British ships, but they would remain at readiness throughout the hours of daylight for as long as the naval operation continued. Whether the Australian pilots would be able to intervene in the event of a Japanese air attack on the British ships depended on how much advance warning they would receive and how far north the attack on the ships took place.

It was a quiet night free of any incident. Dawn came at around 06.00 and there was much satisfaction when it was found that the low cloud, rain showers and generally misty conditions that so favoured the concealment of the British ships from air reconnaissance showed no signs of breaking up. Force Z had now been at sea for almost twelve hours and had covered 220 nautical miles of the proposed route to the area of action. There still remained 520 miles to steam in the whole of the coming day and night. Admiral Phillips believed that he had avoided being spotted by the Japanese and everything now depended upon his ability to remain concealed for the coming fourteen hours or so of daylight. When dawn broke, Phillips ordered that a zig-zag course be adopted with a speed of 17½ knots. This speed would achieve the arrival in the area of the Japanese landings in twenty-four hours' time, while the combination of speed and zig-zag would prevent a Japanese submarine getting off anything but a lucky snap torpedo shot. The course was still the north-easterly one needed to pass east of the Anamba Islands and avoid the Japanese minefield. *Electra* was still ahead of the big ships, sweeping for mines, but there were none on this route.

There was a moment of alarm soon after daylight had broken when *Vampire* signalled the flagship that she had sighted an aircraft. Immediately came this reply from *Prince of Wales*:

TO VAMPIRE   FROM C IN C

ARE YOU CERTAIN OF AIRCRAFT SIGHTING. REPORT ALL DETAILS.

This incident was obviously of paramount importance and Phillips's inquiry must have been followed by some close questioning of the lookout who had spotted the plane and much consultation of aircraft recognition books aboard the Australian ship because it took Commander Moran thirty-eight minutes to draft his reply.

TO C IN C   FROM VAMPIRE

YOUR 06.21. AIRCRAFT WAS SEEN BY ONE RELIABLE LOOKOUT FOR ONE MINUTE, BEARING 135 DEGREES, ANGLE OF SIGHT 8, AND THEN DISAPPEARED INTO CLOUDS. TYPE NOT RECOGNIZED.

Admiral Phillips had now to assess whether his force had been spotted by a Japanese aircraft and, if so, decide whether to continue or abandon the operation. Again, there are no documents to support Phillips's decision, but it is obvious that he decided that the aircraft may not have been Japanese and that, even if it had been, the sighting was so brief that the aircraft may not have seen the ships. It is possible that *Prince of Wales*'s radio room was also

1. Winston Churchill and Admiral Sir Tom Phillips – two of the central figures in the *Prince of Wales* and *Repulse* story. This photograph was taken in February 1940, when Churchill was First Lord of the Admiralty and Phillips was Vice-Chief of the Naval Staff.

2. H.M.S. *Repulse*. This photograph, taken at Portsmouth in May 1939, shows the elegant lines of the First World War battle cruiser. She had just been specially fitted out to take King George VI and Queen Elizabeth on the Royal Tour of Canada. The masts of Nelson's *Victory* can be seen beyond *Repulse*'s two forward 15-in. turrets.

3 and 4. The launching of H.M.S. *Prince of Wales* at Birkenhead, May 1939. The lower photograph shows the recesses in her hull side that will be covered with the 15-in. side-armour meant to protect her engine and boiler rooms and her magazine from shell fire. The force of any

torpedoes striking below this armour plating was intended to be absorbed by a double system of watertight compartments.

The 20 feet of black-painted hull still above the waterline represents the extent to which the battleship will settle when fitted out with armour plating, gun turrets and the remainder of her superstructure and stores.

5. *Repulse* in wartime camouflage. On this occasion she is forming part of the escort of WS.11, a valuable troopship and trade convoy, sailing round the Cape of Good Hope to Suez. It was after this convoy that *Repulse* joined *Prince of Wales* to form the nucleus of the new Eastern Fleet.

6. This photograph, taken from *Repulse* on the same convoy, shows one of *Repulse*'s 4-in. anti-aircraft guns. Eight of these old, hand-operated guns in exposed, unprotected positions, like the one shown here, comprised the ship's main anti-aircraft defence.

7. 'X' Engine Room of *Prince of Wales*. Rear, the Senior Engineer, Lieutenant-Commander (E) Lockley, monitoring the repeater gauges from all four engine and boiler rooms. Right foreground, Engine Room Artificer Chesworth at the throttle, controlling the speed of 'X' propellor shaft; watching him, Lieutenant (E) Pybus, who left *Prince of Wales* before the ship sailed to the Far East. Left, an unidentified petty officer writing up the Engine Room Register.

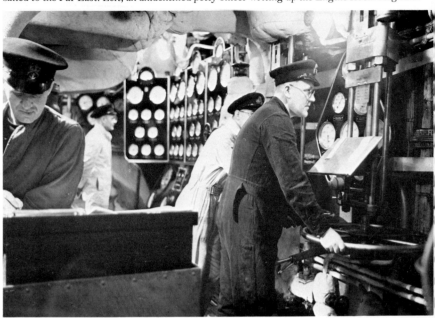

8. *Prince of Wales* docks at Cape Town on her way to Singapore. This photograph shows the camouflage pattern and the thick armour side-plating. The wartime censor has blotted out the radar aerials.

9. Admiral Sir Tom Phillips and his Chief of Staff, Rear-Admiral A.F.E. Palliser, wait on the quayside at the Singapore Naval Base for the arrival of *Repulse* and *Prince of Wales*.

10. *Prince of Wales* reaches Singapore, her hull paint showing signs of the long voyage from Britain. The censor has not obliterated the radar aerials, but the picture was probably not published. The Fiji Class cruiser at the quay is H.M.S. *Mauritius*, under repair for engine defects, and alongside *Mauritius* is the yacht used by the Commander-in-Chief, Far East. The land in the background is Johore on the mainland of Malaya.

11 and 12. *Prince of Wales* (upper) and *Repulse* (lower). These sombre photographs show the two capital ships of Force Z in the Johore Strait just after sailing from the Naval Base to seek out the Japanese invasion forces. The top flag on the mainmast of *Prince of Wales* is the Red Cross of St George, the flag of a full admiral.

13, 14, 15 and 16. The destroyer escorts of Force Z.
H.M.S. *Tenedos* (H04), H.M.S. *Express* (H61), H.M.S. *Electra* (H27),
H.M.A.S. *Vampire* (D68). All these are pre-war photographs.

17. Gun drill (1). This photograph, taken from the port wing of *Prince of Wales*'s bridge, gives a good view of two of the ship's six sets of multiple 2-pounder 'pom-poms', sometimes called 'Chicago pianos'. Also in view is P2 5.25-in. gun turret with its guns in the 'high-angle' anti-aircraft position. These guns could also operate in the 'low-angle' role against surface targets.

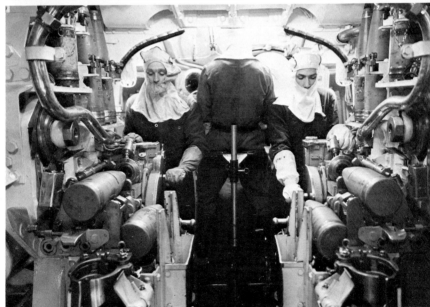

18. Gun drill (2). The interior of a 5.25-in. turret's gunhouse, believed to be in *Prince of Wales*. This photograph was taken from the rear of the turret. The two men facing the camera are the ratings who set the fuses on the shells coming up from below. The third man is the 'Turret Trainer'. Not visible are the Turret Captain – a Petty Officer or a Royal Marine Sergeant – and the remaining five members of the gunhouse crew.

19. Japanese submarine I.65 (later I.165), the first Japanese naval or air unit to sight Force Z at sea. This photograph was taken at sea off Hiroshima in 1932, soon after I.65 was built.

20. Japanese naval air crews run to their Mitsubishi G3M2 ('Nell') bombers. It is not known where or when this photograph was taken, but it was with this type of aircraft that the Genzan and Mihoro Air Corps were equipped.

23

24

21. A 'Nell' in flight.

22. A formation of Mitsubishi G4M1 ('Betty') bombers in the type of loose formation in which the Kanoya Air Corps would have flown while searching for Force Z.

23. The opening of the Japanese attack on Force Z. A salvo of bombs has just exploded around *Repulse,* and one hit – the dark smoke – has been scored. The white smoke is funnel smoke. The wake of *Prince of Wales* (top of picture) shows the rapid course changes ordered by Admiral Phillips during this first attack.

24. The heavily listing *Prince of Wales* seen from the bridge of the destroyer *Express* in a photograph taken by Sub-Lieutenant P.F.C. Satow. The 5.25-in. turret visible is S3. The plate seen below the glass screen of *Express*'s bridge contains the half-eaten sandwiches of Lieutenant-Commander Cartwright's lunch.

25. *Prince of Wales* survivors trying to get across to *Express* just before the increasing heel of the battleship forced the destroyer away.

26. 'That magnificent but awful picture.' This dramatic photograph of the German battleship *Blucher* sinking at the Battle of the Dogger Bank in January 1915 is often mentioned by survivors of *Repulse* and *Prince of Wales* as being similar to the scene when their own ships heeled over before sinking. *Blucher* was less than half the tonnage of *Repulse* or *Prince of Wales*. Only one-fifth of the German sailors survived the cold waters of the North Sea in mid-winter.

27. The Brewster Buffalo fighter aircraft of the Australian 453 Squadron drawn up for review.

28. 453 Squadron in the air over Malaya accompanied by one Bristol Blenheim. The censor has obliterated the squadron identification letters.

29 and 30. Lucky survivors of the sinkings. These are probably *Repulse* men on board the destroyer *Electra*.

1. Captain W. Tennant and Canon J.S. Bezzant, captain and chaplain of *Repulse*, sitting on depth charges in the stern of the Australian destroyer *Vampire* after their rescue.

The future of peoples is not decided by organised demonstrations of emotion, but by the hard facts of life. Future allegiances in the Pacific were settled in 1941 when the British battleships REPULSE and PRINCE OF WALES were sunk off Malay peninsula.—
U.S. CANDID FRIEND

HURRY 'TONIA, OR YOU'LL LOSE 'EM

32. The political effects of the sinkings still being quoted in one of David Low's famous political cartoons thirteen years later. 'Tonia' is the British Foreign Secretary, Anthony Eden, and the 'nanny' who is making off with Australia and New Zealand is the United States Secretary of State, John Foster Dulles. The occasion is a conference at Geneva in April 1954 at which the future of Indo-China and other Far East problems were to be discussed.

33. The White Ensign secured to the port inner propellor shaft of the wreck of *Repulse* ninety feet below the surface of the South China Sea.

34. The Memorial to the Missing on The Hoe at Plymouth. The names of the men lost in *Repulse* and *Prince of Wales* are recorded on this memorial, both ships having been manned from the near-by Devonport Naval Barracks.

consulted and asked whether it had picked up a signal near by. Phillips weighed the evidence, decided that Force Z had not been spotted and took no action. He was right to do so. The identity of the aircraft is not known; if it was a Japanese, it did not see the warships.

At 07.13, Force Z at last 'turned the corner' to the east of the Anambas and settled on to a new course of 330 degrees. The next two hours were incident free and allowed everyone to have breakfast. The dawn Action Stations had been relaxed to 'Second Degree of Readiness' with all guns still loaded and at least partially manned but some men off duty, sleeping, reading, writing letters, playing cards, 'someone playing the old guitar'. It was important that the crews be given as much rest as possible at this stage, particularly in the poorly ventilated *Prince of Wales*; a later emergency or the action expected on the morrow night required that First Degree of Readiness of full Action Stations be maintained for hours on end.

There were a few medical incidents. In *Repulse*, an R.N.V.R. officer missed his footing on a ladder while changing watches at the Air Defence Position, fell to the deck below and had to be taken to the Sick Bay with a broken arm and several bruised ribs. In *Prince of Wales* a young gunnery rating had recently been operated on for appendicitis. The ship's doctors advised that he should not serve at his action station in one of the 5·25-in. turrets because the scar would still be weak and the sailor was ordered to remain below decks in the event of action. Both the officer and the young gunner were later caught below when the action did come. It is also known that Admiral Phillips was in some pain on this day. When Boy Seaman Millard reported for duty that morning as Admiral's Messenger, he was told by the coxswain to 'be very quiet and not make any noise because the Admiral was suffering from a severe bout of toothache'. Phillips sought no treatment for this, but may have asked for a few aspirin or codeine tablets.

The six British ships steamed on through the damp,

claggy weather. Lookouts strained hard but more reliance was placed on the various radar sets aboard *Prince of Wales* and *Repulse*. The British radar sets could detect surface vessels at ranges up to twenty-five miles, depending on the size of the ship involved, and could pick up a high-flying aircraft eighty miles out or lower aircraft at closer ranges, though these were still early days for radar and the sets did not always function satisfactorily. Japanese ships and aircraft had no operational radar at all at this time. The Asdic sets of the four British destroyers could in theory pick up submarines, but Asdic was a very imperfect device and could only cover a small arc in front of each destroyer; a submerged submarine more than 2,500 yards away was fairly safe from detection. On balance, however, the conditions of that morning of 9 December could not have suited the British purpose more admirably.

At 09.06 the quiet was broken, but only by a long signal flashed out by *Repulse*'s signal lamp to the flagship.

TO C IN C   FROM REPULSE

A VERY CONVENIENT SKY TO PREVENT US BEING SPOTTED. AT WHAT SPEED WILL YOU OPERATE AT DAWN TOMORROW. PRESUMABLY WE SHALL BE CLEAR OF ALL MINEFIELDS. WOULD IT HELP IF TENEDOS SPENT TOMORROW WELL TO THE SOUTH EASTWARD AT ECONOMICAL SPEED, SHE MIGHT THEN BE AVAILABLE TO SWEEP US HOME. PROPOSE TO HAVE ONE AIRCRAFT FUELLED AND AT SHORT NOTICE TO FLY FOR SPOTTING IF ANYTHING WORTH OUR METAL APPEARS. AIRCRAFT, IF FLOWN OFF, TO LAND AT PENANG OR ELSEWHERE. SHOULD BE VERY GRATEFUL FOR ANY INFORMATION YOU MAY HAVE DURING THE DAY ABOUT JAPANESE OPERATIONS ON THE SIAM—MALAYA COAST.

It is always useful to try and read between the lines of signals, and this one is full of interest. The message

Captain Tennant had sent to Admiral Phillips was almost a public one in that it could be seen and read by anyone on *Prince of Wales* who understood Morse Code. Tennant's message had opened with a chatty comment on the weather in true English style, but had then gone on to make several major suggestions and ask pointed questions about the future of the operation, questions to which Captain Tennant might normally have expected to receive answers as a matter of course later in the day. It is only conjecture that Captain Tennant was feeling a little left out of things on *Repulse* and might have imagined that Captain Leach on *Prince of Wales* was being frequently consulted by Admiral Phillips on the future course of the operation and Tennant wished to put his experience and thoughts also at the disposal of the overall commander. What is evident from the signal is that Captain Tennant was showing no apprehension about the danger of air attack on nearing the Japanese airfields. Tennant had seen many Royal Navy ships sunk by German aircraft at Dunkirk, but, if he was having qualms about the danger of the current operation, he would certainly not reveal these in a signal that so many people could read.

Captain Tennant had to wait nearly two hours for this brief reply to his signal.

TO REPULSE   FROM C IN C

YOUR 09.06. POLICY SIGNAL IS BEING MADE SHORTLY.

What followed next was not a policy signal but several exchanges about the possibility of *Repulse* refuelling *Tenedos* and *Vampire*. *Repulse* reported that speed would have to be reduced to 8 knots to refuel *Tenedos* because of the nature of this old destroyer's equipment, but that *Vampire* could be refuelled at 11 knots. In each case it would take about one and a half hours to refuel. Admiral Phillips decided to take no action; he was unwilling to reduce speed and lose time in this way and the problem of his destroyers' fuel endurance would have to be solved in another manner.

Soon after midday a Catalina flying boat appeared over *Prince of Wales* and, having been identified as friendly, came in low and flashed a message by Aldis lamp. This message is reputed to have read:

JAPANESE MAKING LANDING NORTH OF SINGORA.

But no copy of this signal has been found in the Public Record Office. It is unlikely that the Catalina had itself been to Singora, way up north in the Gulf of Siam. It was probably the aircraft detailed (requested by Admiral Phillips before leaving Singapore) to provide reconnaissance a hundred miles ahead of Force Z during this day. It is not known why this method of relaying information from Singapore to Admiral Phillips was used. The Catalina disappeared into the mist to continue its reconnaissance.

Force Z had recently altered course to 345 degrees and was now keeping farther to the east than the intended route, presumably to keep well away from the more obvious direct route of approach to the Gulf of Siam which the Japanese might be searching. The half-way mark from Singapore to the area where Japanese shipping might be found was passed at 13.00. Admiral Phillips had still to make up his mind on the exact course of action to take that night and on the next morning, and a decision would have to be taken shortly about *Tenedos*, whose fuel position would not allow her to keep up the present speed much longer. Force Z was now only 360 miles from the airfields around Saigon and within very easy range of the Japanese aircraft there. Every hour's steaming took them nearer to this danger and to the many Japanese warships guarding the invasion routes but, thanks mainly to the weather conditions, the British ships had still not been spotted.

The Japanese had drawn up three incomplete patrol lines of submarines to cover the routes from Siam to the

invasion areas. The most easterly submarine in the second
of these patrol lines was I.65. This submarine was actually
the command boat of the 30th Submarine Flotilla and was
carrying the flotilla commander, Captain Masao Teraoka,
as well as the boat's own captain, Lieutenant-Commander
Hakue Harada. At 15.15 by Tokyo Central Time (one
and a half hours ahead of the time by which the British
were working), I.65's officer of the watch caught a glimpse
through his periscope of the dim shapes of two ships to
the east and almost at the extreme limit of visibility. The
Japanese assumed that the two ships were destroyers and
immediately called the two senior officers. Both looked
carefully through the periscope, but had difficulty making
a surer identification as the two ships kept disappearing
into the mist and squalls and rain kept dashing over the
periscope's outer lens. Eventually, after much staring and
consulting of identification books, Captain Teraoka
decided that the ships he was looking at were not destroyers
but a British battle cruiser and a more modern type of
battleship. To save time, Teraoka ordered the following
signal to be transmitted:

TWO REPULSE TYPE ENEMY BATTLESHIPS SPOTTED.
THEIR POSITION KO.CHI.SA11. COURSE 340. SPEED
14 KNOTS.*

This was a good piece of work by I.65, and a fairly
accurate assessment; the British ships were then steaming
345 degrees at 18 knots. The Japanese submarine waited
for them to pass, came to the surface and settled down to
shadow the British ships for as long as it could.

This was the cruellest of luck for the British. If their
course had carried them just a few miles more to the east,
Prince of Wales and *Repulse* would not have been spotted.

---

* All Japanese signals quoted here are from the Japanese Official
History. The position given is part of the Japanese naval grid
reference system.

As it was, Force Z was so far from I.65 that the four destroyers were invisible to the submarine.

There is no doubt that, from the very beginning, the Japanese commanders in the Malaya–Siam operation had been extremely apprehensive about the two big British ships known to have arrived at Singapore. The elaborate Japanese war plans had not allowed the release of aircraft carriers or modern battleships from the Pearl Harbor operation, and the Japanese would have to take care of the British ships with the two old battleships keeping a distant watch on the landing areas, with the collection of cruisers and destroyers giving close escort or support to the troops and supply ships and with their aircraft and submarine forces. Although the Japanese warships were numerous, no individual ship or group of ships had anything like the combination of speed and gun power of *Prince of Wales* and *Repulse*. The landings on the Malayan and Siamese coasts may have been progressing well, but every Japanese commander had the fear in the back of his mind that the British capital ships might intervene.

During most of 9 December the Japanese had had no idea that the British were at sea. A reconnaissance plane had flown over Singapore on the previous afternoon and spotted the two ships still in harbour. There had been surprise among the Japanese that the British ships had not put to sea to catch their invasion forces in the first critical hours of the landings. Then, on the morning of the 9th, another Japanese aircraft flew high over Singapore and its pilot thought that he could see the British capital ships still in harbour. He radioed this report to Saigon. Until this moment the Japanese had been particularly concerned over their landing at Kota Bharu. The landings farther north had all gone according to plan, but the vigorous action of the Australian-crewed Hudsons and the army artillery battery in attacking the Japanese ships off the Kota Bharu beaches had thrown the timetable there into some confusion. Now Vice-Admiral Ozawa received two vital messages. One told him that during the past night the main landings at Kota Bharu had been successfully completed, and the second told him that the British capital ships still appeared to be at Singapore. The Japanese Official History tells of the Japanese satisfaction at this stage.

Since a British aircraft had spotted our invasion fleet [before the landings] Vice-Admiral Ozawa judged that it was highly likely that the British naval force would make a preventive attack on our forces and thus he paid the greatest attention to this possibility. However, the British had failed to attack and our units had now succeeded in landing at various points. At this moment only a small amount of resupplying was continuing. Even if the British attacked from now onwards, there would be no damage done to the military units already landed and any damage would only be to empty ships and to a small quantity of supplies. In other words, the British naval force had lost their best chance and the critical time for our naval units had already passed without serious difficulty.*

The Japanese were now free to plan the next stage of their operations, and once again their audacity and speed were breathtaking. The troops ashore were left almost to their own devices to fight their way into Malaya with a bare minimum of resupplying and reinforcement. The Japanese had no need for the huge logistical build-up considered essential in Western armies. At around midday on the 9th, Vice-Admiral Ozawa issued his next orders. Most of his warships were ordered back with the empty transports to Camranh Bay in Indo-China to take on fresh troops for the invasion of Borneo. Only a few light warships were left behind to protect the invasion beaches. The air units at Saigon and the submarines were left with the main responsibility for dealing with the British warships at Singapore. At 13.30, while *Prince of Wales* and *Repulse* were steaming steadily north, and just before I.65 sighted the British ships, Admiral Ozawa's orders had gone out and many Japanese warships would soon be on their way

* Japanese Official History, p. 247.

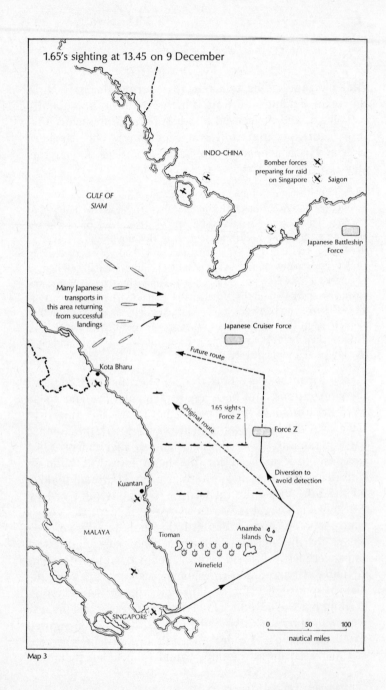

1.65's sighting at 13.45 on 9 December

INDO-CHINA

Bomber forces
preparing for raid
on Singapore   Saigon

GULF OF
SIAM

Japanese Battleship
Force

Many Japanese
transports in
this area returning
from successful
landings

Japanese Cruiser Force

Future route

Kota Bharu

Original route

1.65 sights
Force Z   Force Z

Diversion to
avoid detection

Kuantan

Anamba
Islands

MALAYA   Tioman

Minefield

SINGAPORE

0   50   100

nautical miles

Map 3

east, steaming directly into the area towards which
Force Z was heading.

The false news that the British ships were still in harbour at Singapore had been received by the Japanese
airmen at Saigon.

Everybody relaxed; our troopships were free of the threat of the big
British guns. Although we had nothing to fear from the warships as
long as they remained in Singapore, at any moment the British might
move the ships out to sea where they would be in a position to
attack.

Rear-Admiral Matsunaga called a staff conference in his headquarters to determine the feasibility of our bombers making a mass
torpedo attack against the warships while they remained within the
base.

All pilots and aircrew members were in high spirits. We had found
the battleships, and the opportunity to gain even more glorious fame
than the men who had successfully attacked Pearl Harbor beckoned
to us. Everybody was busy investigating the water depths at the
Singapore Naval Base, the best directions from which to attack, and
the most advantageous flight formations to utilize. (Lieutenant
Sadao Takai, Genzan Air Corps)*

Of the 138 Mitsubishis at the airfields near Saigon, nine
were away attacking the British airfield at Kuantan and
three more were flying reconnaissance sorties. Ground
crews were working hard on the remaining aircraft, preparing them for what the Japanese airmen hoped would be
a second Pearl Harbor in the morning.

But while the ground crews sweated on the airfields, the
Japanese were suffering a major setback elsewhere. I.65
was just managing to keep in visual touch with the two
ships she had spotted, but at 15.50 a squall obscured the
view and contact was lost. Although the British ships
were seen once more an hour later, the contact was lost for
good at 18.00 when a seaplane approached the Japanese
submarine as though to attack. Lieutenant-Commander

---

* This and further quotations by Lieutenant Takai are from *Zero,
The Story of the Japanese Naval Air Force*, Cassell, London, 1957.

Harada dived, and when he came back to the surface half an hour later he could see nothing of the British ships. The aircraft which forced him to dive had, ironically, been a Japanese scouting seaplane from the cruiser *Kinu* which was acting as a flagship to some of the Japanese submarines.

Unfortunately for the Japanese, there had been a two-hour delay before I.65's sighting signals had been received – a delay that became the subject of some comment in the Japanese Official History. It seems that only *Kinu* and *Yura*, another cruiser acting as a submarine flagship, together with a unit described as the '81st Communications Unit', were tuned to I.65's wavelength. Either through poor radio reception conditions or by confusion in the signals arrangements, nobody at all picked up I.65's signals for an hour and a half, and it was two hours before *Kinu* managed to pass on to Vice-Admiral Ozawa the vital news that a British battleship and a battle cruiser were at sea and steaming north.

When it did arrive, I.65's signal startled Ozawa. Thinking that the British were still at Singapore, he had released most of his warships from their escort duties with the transports and they were now steaming in non-battle formation back to Camranh Bay. The air units at Saigon were mostly loading bombs for the air raid next morning on Singapore. Now, here were two powerful British ships almost into an area full of Japanese shipping with only a few hours of daylight left. No doubt the Japanese admiral roundly cursed the two-hour delay in receiving I.65's signal, and cursed still further when the submarine reported that it had lost contact with the British ships.

The first thought of the Japanese was that I.65 had been mistaken and that the British really were still at Singapore. It was an easy matter to clarify this. A reconnaissance aircraft just about to land at one of the outlying airfields at Saigon was ordered instead to land at Saigon itself, and the photographs it had taken over Singapore were rushed to the developing room. They showed a large floating dock, possibly mistaken by the aircrew for a battleship, some cruisers and a large merchant ship – no battleships! I.65's report must be true. *

The Japanese reacted quickly to this alarming situation. Vice-Admiral Ozawa, in his flagship the cruiser *Chokai*, was himself only about 120 miles from the reported position of the British ships and decided on the simple expedient of ordering every available Japanese warship to search for the British during the four remaining hours of daylight and on during the coming night, despite the fact that a hastily prepared night action can be the most confusing of naval engagements. Once more Ozawa's orders went out by radio. Scouting planes from *Chokai* herself and from *Mogami*, *Mikuma*, *Kumano* and *Suzuya* – the four cruisers of the 7th Cruiser Squadron – were ordered to be catapulted off and to rediscover, if possible, the British ships. Unknown to Ozawa, a sixth cruiser, the *Kinu*, the submarine flagship already referred to, also sent off its seaplane. The nearest warships were then pulled into some sort of order and it was found that there were seven cruisers and at least five destroyers to join in the hunt for the British.

Vice-Admiral Kondo's battle squadron, with the old battleships *Kongo* and *Haruna*, were farther north, but these could not arrive until the early hours of the following day. A further six cruisers and several more destroyers would also be able to join in the morning. The nearest submarines were also ordered to the sighting area. The transports off the invasion beaches were ordered to stop unloading immediately and to scatter to the north. A further Japanese ploy was to order the frequent use of the

* I.65 will not be met again in this book. She was renumbered I.165 in May 1942 and remained in service as an operational boat until December 1944, sinking several Allied ships. She then served for a few months as a training boat, but in April 1945 was equipped to carry two Kaiten midget submarines; the Kaitens were the naval equivalent of the Kamikaze suicide aircraft. It was while on a Kaiten mission that I.165 was sunk with all her crew off Saipan by U.S. Navy aircraft on 27 June 1945.

radios in those of their warships which were well out to
sea in a deliberate attempt to lure the British to battle and
away from the invasion beaches. But there is no British
record that any of these radio signals were picked up.

Hurried new plans were also made at the Saigon airfields, and Rear-Admiral Matsunaga decided on his own
initiative to prepare his aircraft to join in this grand hunt
that evening. The last reported position of the British
ships had been only 300 miles from Matsunaga's airfields.
Once more there was a delay because the aircraft had
mostly been loaded with bombs and these now had to be
taken out and replaced with torpedoes. Once more the
ground crews sweated and heaved to get the attacking
aircraft ready.

The first aircraft to get away were four reconnaissance
planes which were ordered to take off at once and search
for the British ships. Three formations of fifty-three attack
aircraft managed to take off in the late afternoon and early
evening. There had been no time to remove the bombs
from nine of these aircraft, but all the others were armed
with torpedoes. Local army units near Saigon had heard of
what was happening and a large group of Japanese army
officers came out to Saigon airfield and cheered the airmen
on their way.

The position, then, in the early evening of 9 December,
was that *Prince of Wales*, *Repulse* and the four destroyers
were still on their northerly course, unaware as yet that
they had been sighted by I.65. Attempting to find them
were several more submarines, six Japanese scouting seaplanes from the cruisers, and the four search aircraft from
Saigon. Intending to attack the British ships if they could
be found again, were seven Japanese cruisers, at least five
destroyers, several submarines, forty-four torpedo-carrying
aircraft and nine bomb-carrying aircraft.

At 18.09 the sun would set. At 22.38 the moon would
rise. At dawn Admiral Phillips hoped he would have the
Japanese shipping off the invasion beaches under his guns.

.   .   .

It had been an afternoon of planning and preparation for the British. Following his earlier decision to persist with the operation, providing the Japanese did not detect the presence of his force, Admiral Phillips had finalized his plans for the coming night and for the critical first hours of daylight on the following day. Five signals had blinked out from *Prince of Wales*, some addressed to the captains of ships, some intended for every man in the crews of the ships.

TO FORCE Z   FROM C IN C E.F.

1. BESIDES A MINOR LANDING AT KHOTA BHARU WHICH WAS NOT FOLLOWED UP, LANDINGS HAVE BEEN MADE BETWEEN PATANI AND SINGORA AND A MAJOR LANDING 90 MILES NORTH OF SINGORA.

2. LITTLE IS KNOWN OF ENEMY FORCES IN THE VICINITY. IT IS BELIEVED THAT KONGO IS THE ONLY CAPITAL SHIP LIKELY TO BE MET. THREE ATAGO TYPE, ONE KAKO TYPE, AND TWO ZINTU TYPE CRUISERS HAVE BEEN REPORTED. A NUMBER OF DESTROYERS POSSIBLY OF FLEET TYPE ARE LIKELY TO BE MET.

3. MY OBJECT IS TO SURPRISE AND SINK TRANS-PORTS AND ENEMY WARSHIPS BEFORE AIR ATTACK CAN DEVELOP. OBJECTIVE CHOSEN WILL DEPEND ON AIR RECONNAISSANCE, INTEND TO ARRIVE OBJECTIVE AFTER SUNRISE TOMORROW 10TH. IF AN OPPORTUNITY TO BRING KONGO TO ACTION OCCURS THIS IS TO TAKE PRECEDENCE OVER ALL OTHER ACTION.

4. SUBJECT TO C.O.'S FREEDOM OF MANOEUVRE IN AN EMERGENCY, FORCE Z WILL REMAIN IN CLOSE ORDER AND WILL BE MANOEUVRED AS A UNIT UNTIL ACTION IS JOINED. WHEN THE SIGNAL 'ACT INDEPENDENTLY' IS MADE OR AT DISCRE-TION OF C.O. REPULSE WILL ASSUME FREEDOM MANOEUVRE REMAINING IN TACTICAL SUPPORT

BUT ENGAGING FROM A WIDE ENOUGH ANGLE TO FACILITATE FALL OF SHOT.

5. INTEND TO OPERATE AT 25 KNOTS UNLESS A CHASE DEVELOPS AND SUBSEQUENTLY TO RETIRE AT MAXIMUM SPEED ENDURANCE WILL ALLOW.

6. CAPITAL SHIPS SHOULD ATTEMPT TO CLOSE BELOW 20,000 YARDS UNTIL FIRE IS EFFECTIVE BUT SHOULD AVOID OFFERING AN END-ON TARGET. SHIPS MUST BE PREPARED TO CHANGE FROM DELAY TO NON-DELAY FUZES ACCORDING TO TARGET.

7. PRINCE OF WALES AND REPULSE ARE EACH TO HAVE ONE AIRCRAFT FUELLED AND READY TO FLY OFF IF REQUIRED. IF FLOWN OFF, AIRCRAFT MUST RETURN TO LAND BASE. KOTA BHARU AERODROME IS UNDERSTOOD TO BE OUT OF ACTION.

8. TENEDOS WILL BE DETACHED BEFORE DARK TO RETURN INDEPENDENTLY TO SINGAPORE.

9. REMAINING DESTROYERS MAY BE DESPATCHED DURING THE NIGHT 9TH/10TH SHOULD ENEMY INFORMATION REQUIRE A HIGH SPEED OF ADVANCE. IN SUCH CASE THESE DESTROYERS ARE TO RETIRE TOWARDS ANAMBA ISLANDS AT 10 KNOTS UNTIL A RENDEZVOUS IS ORDERED BY W/T.

TO PRINCE OF WALES AND REPULSE   FROM C IN C E.F.

INFORM SHIPS COMPANIES AS FOLLOWS: BEGINS

THE ENEMY HAS MADE SEVERAL LANDINGS ON THE NORTH COAST OF MALAYA AND HAS MADE LOCAL PROGRESS. OUR ARMY IS NOT LARGE AND IS HARD PRESSED IN PLACES. OUR AIR FORCE HAS HAD TO DESTROY AND ABANDON ONE OR MORE AERODROMES. MEANWHILE FAT TRANSPORTS LIE OFF THE COAST. THIS IS OUR OPPORTUNITY

BEFORE THE ENEMY CAN ESTABLISH HIMSELF.
WE HAVE MADE A WIDE CIRCUIT TO AVOID AIR
RECONNAISSANCE AND HOPE TO SURPRISE THE
ENEMY SHORTLY AFTER SUNRISE TOMORROW
WEDNESDAY. WE MAY HAVE THE LUCK TO TRY
OUR METAL AGAINST THE OLD JAPANESE BATTLE
CRUISER KONGO OR AGAINST SOME JAPANESE
CRUISERS AND DESTROYERS WHICH ARE REPORTED
IN THE GULF OF SIAM. WE ARE SURE TO GET
SOME USEFUL PRACTICE WITH THE H.A. ARMA-
MENT.
WHATEVER WE MEET I WANT TO FINISH QUICKLY
AND SO GET WELL CLEAR TO THE EASTWARD
BEFORE THE JAPANESE CAN MASS TOO FORMID-
ABLE A SCALE OF ATTACK AGAINST US. SO SHOOT
TO SINK. ENDS.

TO REPULSE AND PRINCE OF WALES   FROM
C IN C E.F.

FROM DAWN ACTION STATIONS AND THROUGH
DAYLIGHT TOMORROW WEDNESDAY ALL RANKS
AND RATINGS ARE TO WEAR CLOTHING SUCH AS
OVERALLS OR SUITS WHICH KEEP ARMS AND LEGS
COVERED AGAINST RISK OF BURNS FROM FLASH.

TO REPULSE, ELECTRA, VAMPIRE,
PRINCE OF WALES, EXPRESS, TENEDOS.
FROM C IN C E.F.

COURSE WILL BE ALTERED TO 320 DEGREES AT
18.00 BY SIGNAL. COURSE IS TO BE ALTERED TO
280 DEGREES AT 19.30 AND SPEED INCREASED TO
24 KNOTS WITHOUT SIGNAL. AT 22.00 DESTROYERS
ARE TO PART COMPANY WITHOUT SIGNAL AND
PROCEED TO SOUTHEASTWARD SUBSEQUENTLY
ADJUSTING COURSE AND SPEED SO AS TO R/V AT
POINT C AT 16.00/10 UNLESS OTHERWISE ORDERED*

* Point C was near the Anamba Islands.

TO REPULSE, PRINCE OF WALES   FROM C IN C
E.F.

UNLESS FURTHER INFORMATION IS RECEIVED,
INTEND TO MAKE SINGORA AT 07.45 AND SUBSE-
QUENTLY WORK TO EASTWARDS ALONG COAST. I
HAVE KEPT TO EASTWARDS SO AS TO TRY AND
REMAIN UNLOCATED TODAY WHICH IS THE MOST
IMPORTANT THING OF ALL.

Not only Captain Tennant, but every man on the six ships of Force Z, now knew what was in the mind of their commander. The five signals require little amplification; there is not much to be read between the lines on this occasion. The fourth signal, ordering the destroyers to part company after dark, shows that Admiral Phillips had finally decided that it would be better to make the final attack without destroyers. A memorandum at the Public Record Office later written by Captain L. H. Bell, a senior member of Admiral Phillips's staff, shows the reasoning behind that decision.

The Admiral's plan had been to detach the destroyers at midnight 9/10th and make a high-speed descent on Singora with the less vulnerable *Prince of Wales* and *Repulse* only. He considered the destroyers would be very vulnerable to air attack; with the exception of *Electra* they were not fully worked up and their operational [fuel] endurance was a perpetual anxiety. The Admiral relied on the speed and surprise of the battleships to avoid damage to these ships sufficient to slow them down, believing that Japanese aircraft would not be carrying anti-ship bombs and torpedoes and that the Force, on retirement, would only have to deal with hastily organized long-range bombers from bases in Indo-China.*

The low cloud and bad visibility had persisted through the afternoon, but at about 16.45, less than two hours before sunset, the cloud and misty conditions disappeared

---

* Public Record Office ADM 199/1149.

and were replaced by a brilliantly clear tropical evening. While this new development made the British apprehensive about the possibility of their being spotted, it did not alter the factual balance of the operation. The Japanese knew that the British were in the area from I.65's signals and had by now mounted their big search operation. Force Z was being hunted, but did not yet know it.

A more important development occurred about one hour later when *Prince of Wales*'s radar screen picked up the traces of three aircraft. The British hoped that these were friendly, but when the first aircraft was sighted visually, low down on the horizon, it was seen to be a small single-engined seaplane. The three aircraft were all Japanese Aichi E13A seaplanes (codenamed 'Jakes' by the Allies), which had been catapulted off from the Japanese cruisers to follow up I.65's sighting report. The seaplanes kept well out of range of the British guns and calmly plotted the speed and course of the British ships. It was now that a standing patrol of R.A.F. or Fleet Air Arm fighters could have been useful, either by shooting down the Japanese shadowers before they could get off their reports, or at least by driving them away so that Force Z could make a change of course unobserved. But the only friendly aircraft seen that evening was one Catalina flying boat.

Now the balance of knowledge really had changed. The Japanese had gained a further confirmation of the presence of the British ships and an up-to-date position, but, more importantly, the British now knew that their presence was no longer a secret. The one remaining condition of Admiral Phillips for the continuation of his operation appeared to have gone.

The sun set a few minutes after 6 p.m. The gathering darkness, coming so soon after the sighting of the enemy planes, brought a sense of foreboding. What lay beyond the horizon? What strength could the Japanese gather around the small force of British ships in the darkness?

Two men, an officer aboard *Prince of Wales* and a rating aboard *Repulse*, describe their feelings at this time.

We stood on the upper deck and watched the Jap float-plane in the now fading light. Our 5·25-in. guns traversed silently and menacingly, but the range was too great and, alas, we had no fighter aircraft available. We could well imagine the excitement, the conjectures, and of course the preparations the Japanese airman's radio messages would arouse at his base. And we cursed the fact that sheer chance had revealed us in that short, clear period before darkness fell.

We were to be at our action stations all night then, and I wandered into the wardroom for supper, by now a bleak, comfortless wardroom, with pictures, books and trophies taken down and all movable objects firmly lashed, in the usual preparations for impending action. There was a cold, uninteresting help-yourself supper, the stewards and attendants being already employed on their various jobs in gun turrets, ammunition hoists and shell rooms.

I didn't feel hungry. But I thought what a curse a vivid imagination could be and wished we could hurry up and get on with it. Everyone seemed rather quiet. I went down to my cabin, put on some warm clothing and stuffed some chocolate, a torch, a hypodermic syringe and a packet of tie-on casualty labels into my pockets, adjusted my uninflated lifebelt round my waist, and went out, taking a last look at my cabin with all its personal belongings and wondering vaguely, 'What the hell will you look like this time tomorrow?' (Surgeon Lieutenant-Commander E. D. Caldwell)

I remember discussing the likely battle with the Master Gunner, who had joined *Repulse* the same day as myself, a quiet, cool, appraisal in which he in as many words stated that 'with surprise on our side we could give a good account of ourselves', meaning *Repulse* mainly as *Prince of Wales* even then was regarded as not fully worked up, but it was unlikely we would get back to base. This was just 'matter-of-fact' discussion but prompted me for the first time in thousands of miles of U-boat waters to prepare for a likely sinking, i.e. I wore my small inflatable lifebelt *constantly* and waterproofed my pound notes in the prescribed sick-bay manner [in a condom] and decided which would be the abandon route or alternative. (Sick Berth Attendant W. Bridgewater)

Half an hour after sunset, the destroyer *Tenedos* swung out from her position in the screen and turned back south.

The old ship had performed a useful function in helping to escort the two capital ships for twenty-four hours and across 420 miles of sea, but her fuel capacity was so limited that she would become a liability in the event of high-speed work, and so Admiral Phillips ordered her to make her own way back to Singapore. Phillips had passed a signal to *Tenedos* which the destroyer was to transmit to Singapore at 08.00 on the following day asking Rear-Admiral Palliser to arrange for as many destroyers as possible, including the American destroyers expected at Singapore, to come out and meet *Prince of Wales* and *Repulse* at a point north of the Anamba Islands at dawn of the 11th. The added destroyer protection would be required to escort the two capital ships past any Japanese submarines that might be stationed in the approaches to Singapore. The detachment of *Tenedos* at this time and with this signal reveals that, despite the recent appearance of the Japanese aircraft, Admiral Phillips had still made no decision to abandon the operation.

Lieutenant Richard Dyer, captain of *Tenedos*, watched Force Z disappear into the darkness. He little suspected that his own ship would be the first to see action.

At 18.50, a further half-hour after *Tenedos* left, the pre-arranged course change was made and the five ships turned north-west, course 320 degrees, and the speed was worked up to 26 knots. Force Z was now heading towards the invasion beaches and into the very heart of enemy-dominated waters, and there was no sign from the flagship that the operation would not still go ahead as planned, despite their sighting by Japanese aircraft. But within only minutes of the course change, an incident occurred that Admiral Phillips would have to take into consideration. The lookouts on *Electra* sighted a flare estimated to be five miles ahead; the light seemed to hover for a few moments just above the surface of the sea and then it died out. The flagship ordered all ships to make an emergency turn to port in order to pass well clear of the flare's position.

Even while Admiral Phillips was pondering the significance of this new development, another signal arrived from Rear-Admiral Palliser.

TO C IN C E.F.   FROM C.O.S.

MOST IMMEDIATE

ONE BATTLESHIP, 'M' CLASS CRUISER, 11 DESTROY-
ERS AND A NUMBER OF TRANSPORTS REPORTED
CLOSE TO COAST BETWEEN KOTA BHARU AND
PERHENTIAN ISLAND BY AIR RECONNAISSANCE
AFTERNOON.

This was the long-awaited signal, giving what Phillips hoped was the latest news about the Japanese landing areas. He had always believed that the Singora area in Siam was the scene of the most important Japanese landing; this signal did not mention Singora, but indicated that a large force was now supporting the landing at Kota Bharu; Perhentian Island was a few miles south of Kota Bahru. A further signal, fifteen minutes later, corrected the time of the air reconnaissance and stated that the Japanese ships had been seen at 10.30 that morning. Kota Bharu was actually 130 sea miles nearer to Singapore than Singora, and a diversion to this target would give the British ships a far less hazardous run when daylight came. What Admiral Phillips did not know was that, since the air reconnaissance at Kota Bharu that morning, the Japanese landing there had been all but completed and most of the ships involved were either on their way back to Indo-China or at that very moment hunting Force Z itself.

It was as well for their peace of mind that the British were unaware of the intense Japanese activity all around and above them. On the other hand, the Japanese had taken the most outrageous risks in launching their ships and aircraft into this hastily prepared and uncoordinated hunt. But, just as the main aim of the British had been to get among the transport shipping supporting the landings, so the main Japanese aim was to protect their landings whatever the risks involved.

It was the seaplane from *Kinu*, the cruiser acting as a submarine flagship, which had got off the first sighting report well before dusk.

FOUND 2 ENEMY BATTLESHIPS. POSITION WSM. COURSE 340 DEGREES. 13 KNOTS. 3 ESCORTING DESTROYERS.

This report surprised Vice-Admiral Ozawa; he did not know that *Kinu*'s captain had sent his seaplane to join in the search. It was as well for the Japanese that he did so since the search plan for the seaplanes of the five other cruisers was spread like a fan to the west of Force Z's true position and they would most probably not have found Force Z before dark. The navigation of the submarine I.65 had been in error and she had been broadcasting sightings at incorrect positions.

The report of *Kinu*'s seaplane was quickly followed by two more, from *Suzuya*'s and then *Kumano*'s aircraft, although the last report contained an error in estimating the British ships' course as 50 degrees and counting the destroyers in the escort as five. (There were still four; these sightings were before *Tenedos* left.) This successful seaplane search had been costly for the Japanese. *Kumano*'s plane was lost; *Yura*'s hit a mountain on Procondor Island and was seriously damaged; and *Sazuya*'s force-landed on the sea later and the destroyer *Hamakaze* had to be detached to rescue it.

Despite the various errors in the seaplane reports, Vice-Admiral Ozawa had been able to plot the northerly progress of the British ships before the British turned west after dark. Using their radios freely in the attempt to draw the British into battle, Ozawa's cruiser and destroyer force turned north-east to intercept them. When Admiral Phillips did make his turn to the west after dark, Ozawa's ships were only a few miles away to the east and now directly in the path of Force Z.

Meanwhile, the land-based Mitsubishis from Saigon continued their search after dark. It was a dangerous task because it was now completely dark with four hours to go to moonrise. One of the reconnaissance planes met with an accident – of which no details are available – and this dislocated the search plan. But another reconnaissance aircraft, piloted by Lieutenant Takeda, flying just above the surface of the sea, suddenly flew over two bright lanes of white foam – the wakes of large ships! Takeda banked and flew carefully up the wakes and soon found the two black shadows of what he took to be British ships. He was not spotted and climbed away to get off a sighting report.

The fifty-three torpedo- and bomb-carrying aircraft of the main attacking force had by now reached the area. Lieutenant Sadao Takai of the Genzan Corps was again one of the pilots.

The sun had dropped below the horizon. Visibility was very poor, and we were flying in three-plane formation.

Unfortunately, there was still a serious problem to be solved. We had not decided, when the operation began, on any definite measures for differentiating between the enemy vessels and our own warships during close-range sea battles, when such identification can be extremely difficult. We did not know the definite location of the enemy warships; furthermore, we had no information as to the location of our own ships this night. How were we to distinguish one from another?

Not having received any training on this matter, and not having had time to discuss warship identification before we took off, our air and sea forces were rushing into the battle blindly. It seemed as if we might be caught in our own traps!

The clouds seemed to stretch endlessly over the ocean. We could not emerge from them, and the task of observing the ocean surface was becoming increasingly difficult. We could not fly much higher than 1,000 feet. Under such conditions our chances for discovering the enemy fleet were doubtful unless we happened to fly directly over the British ships, or crossed their wakes.

However, the situation was not hopeless. We had many planes searching the ocean and any one of them might sight the enemy forces. There was also the chance that we might discover the enemy inadvertently in the event that he sighted our planes and fired upon them. When one flies in almost total darkness one feels that the enemy might appear suddenly and without warning before one's eyes.

Farther and farther we flew southward in search of the enemy fleet.

A radio report from one of our searching bombers brought jubilation to our hearts. The anxiously sought enemy vessels had been sighted!

The radio report continued: 'We have dropped a flare.'

Vice-Admiral Ozawa promptly received a great fright. It was his flagship, the cruiser *Chokai*, that was being illuminated by the flare and on to which Lieutenant Takeda was directing the other Japanese aircraft. This was also the flare seen by *Electra* which caused Admiral Phillips to sheer off to the south. Admiral Ozawa's reaction was to turn away to the north, and at the same time to send a frantic signal to Saigon:

THERE ARE THREE ATTACKING PLANES ABOVE CHOKAI. IT IS CHOKAI UNDER THE FLARE.

At Saigon, Rear-Admiral Matsunaga read this signal and realized that his hastily mounted intervention in the night hunt had to be brought to an end. He ordered the air search to be discontinued.

It was some time before all the aircraft received this order, but no more sightings took place and no harm was done. The aircraft now had to wait until moonrise, two and a half hours later, before they could land, but they all did so safely, their crews frustrated and tired. The naval commanders too had been badly shaken by the incident. Vice-Admiral Ozawa decided it would be more prudent to withdraw at least until the moon rose, but Vice-Admiral Kondo, the overall commander, who was still well to the north with the battleships *Kongo* and *Haruna*, now stepped in and imposed his will on these confused activities. Kondo sent out orders that all Japanese forces were to prepare for the encounter which he now expected would take place immediately after dawn of the following day, the

10th. The Japanese Official History contains an interesting summary of Admiral Kondo's thoughts at that time.

The British warships' guns were judged to be far superior to ours but we were far superior in supporting units. In other words, greater fire power for them and greater torpedo and air power for us. But much difficulty was expected for our destroyer torpedo attacks because of the great speed of the British ships and they were also believed to be equipped with radar.

So, in a sea battle in bad visibility and rain, our side would be at a great disadvantage. Even in our Navy at that time not everyone believed that air attack was the best method of effectively sinking a large battleship; in fact such men were in a minority. In addition, this battleship was the *Prince of Wales*, the so-called unsinkable battleship. So we prepared with much determination for the battle next morning.*

The intervening hours would enable Admiral Kondo with his two battleships to steam nearer to the expected battle area, some of his destroyers to refuel from tankers, and the air units to be refuelled for further operations – but this time by daylight with much less danger of attacking their own ships.

Lieutenant Takeda's flare and then Admiral Kondo's new plans had finally ruled out all chance of a night encounter. Neither side realized how close they had been to what could well have been one of the decisive sea battles of the war. When the flare dropped and caused both sides to sheer away, there had been only five miles between Force Z and the Japanese cruiser force; indeed, it is surprising that *Chokai* had not been picked up on *Prince of Wales*'s radar, which had a theoretical range of up to twenty-five miles. If there had been no flare and the two sides had met, the result of the battle can only be conjecture. The British had the heavy 14-in. and 15-in. guns; the best the Japanese cruisers had were 8-in. Moreover, the British gunnery could be radar-controlled in darkness, and although this type of fighting was still in its infancy, the use of radar

* Japanese Official History, p. 437.

generally would have been an immense advantage to the British in a night action.

What could have been the possible outcome of such a battle between a British battleship, battle cruiser and three destroyers and six Japanese cruisers with their destroyer escorts? If the British guns could have got to work at close range, they might have blown the Japanese ships out of the water. If the Japanese torpedoes had found their marks, the British ships might well have been crippled, or at least slowed down for the morning. And what might the Japanese aircraft have achieved in a confusing night action? If they had carried out torpedo attacks that night, one effect might have been crucial. There were only enough aerial torpedoes in this theatre of war for just one torpedo to each aircraft. Every torpedo launched would have been one less for future use, and if they had been dropped wholesale, and had failed to score hits on the British ships in the darkness, then it really could have changed the course of future events.

But there was no battle. *Chokai* and the other Japanese cruisers continued on their northerly course. Admiral Phillips was soon to make a further and much more significant course change.

When Force Z turned to port to avoid the area where the flare had been seen, everyone on the British ships was expecting that the original course would eventually be resumed. But during these few minutes Admiral Sir Tom Phillips took what was probably the most important and possibly the most difficult decision of his life. There was no lack of courage in him, or of willingness to fight, and there was certainly much of the old naval tradition that an admiral would never go far wrong if he laid his ships alongside those of his enemy. But a modern admiral needed more than these traditional qualities. With Britain's naval strength stretched so thin, with the only sizeable ships in this theatre of war under his hand, Tom Phillips needed to show discretion as well as valour.

It was really quite simple. Constant fighter cover he knew he could not have. Surprise he knew he no longer possessed. Although he did not know how close around him were the Japanese ships and aircraft, he certainly knew that they would all be there in the morning. Japanese warships he could gladly fight, and the aircraft too if necessary, but there was one other factor. Phillips knew that any prudent enemy admiral would by now have scattered the merchant ships, that the Japanese would have cleared the waters off Singora and Kota Bharu. Even if *Prince of Wales* and *Repulse* did fight their way through, Phillips knew that there would be no targets for their big guns in the morning. A risk incurred for a great prize was certainly acceptable, but the possible loss of two ships for nothing was not. The various factors must have been tossed about in Tom Phillips's mind, but the trained mind of a high-ranking professional naval officer could only lead him to one conclusion. There was no longer any chance of success. This operation must now be called off – and quickly. They had already lost nearly two valuable hours of darkness, hours in which his ships could have been speeding back to the comparative safety of Singapore to fight another day.

Admiral Phillips had actually been thinking of taking this course of action ever since the Japanese seaplanes spotted Force Z late that afternoon, and had told his staff that he would turn back for Singapore at midnight unless there was any change in the situation. It was a bitter moment for the British admiral. In a few hours he might have been making a glorious name for himself; now he would be known as an admiral who brought his fleet home after deliberately avoiding action with the enemy. The decision also marked the final failure of twenty years of British naval policy for the Far East, but as taken by Tom Phillips it showed a great deal of moral courage. The next twenty-four hours would tell whether it had been delayed too long.

The original course was never resumed. At 20.05 a reduction in speed to 20 knots was ordered, and fifteen minutes later a new course given that would take Force Z back to Singapore via the Anamba Islands. At 20.55 a blue night-signalling lamp blinked out this message to *Repulse*:

I HAVE MOST REGRETFULLY CANCELLED THE OPERATION BECAUSE, HAVING BEEN LOCATED BY AIRCRAFT, SURPRISE WAS LOST AND OUR TARGET WOULD BE ALMOST CERTAIN TO BE GONE BY THE MORNING AND THE ENEMY FULLY PREPARED FOR US.

Captain Bell, the officer on Admiral Phillips's staff who later filed a memorandum on the operation, stated that this signal brought 'a spontaneous signal from *Repulse* which cheered the Admiral as it showed that the Captain of *Repulse* appreciated the difficulty of the decision and agreed with it'.

8

Kuantan

The five ships of Force Z steamed on to the south, away from the scene of a battle that might have been. The moon crept above the horizon to improve visibility, but there was nothing to be seen by the British lookouts; there were no Japanese eyes to witness the British withdrawal. Some of the 3,000 or more men on the British ships were asleep, but most were at or near their Action Stations and had ample opportunity to digest the implication of the recent course change and the news that they were returning to Singapore. It is not possible to generalize on the sailors' reactions to this latest change in their prospects; a feeling of disappointment by many who had nerved themselves to face action was probably balanced by the more basic human reaction of relief that this particular battle was not now to be fought.

It was now almost thirty hours since Rear-Admiral Palliser at Singapore had last seen his chief. Palliser was keeping in touch as best he could with all developments of the two-day-old war, and was keeping Force Z informed by signal of those events which he thought would be of interest to Admiral Phillips. Palliser knew that Phillips would not break radio silence until it became compelling to do so, and he had to try and imagine what decisions Phillips would be making on receipt of each of his signals – a mental exercise that became progressively more difficult as the hours passed and the number of dispatched signals piled up. Palliser must have been aware of the difficult choices that had faced his superior that evening, and at 21.45 he sent a further signal.

1. ONLY SIGNIFICANCE OF ENEMY REPORT IS CONTAINED IN MY 11.26z 9TH. ENEMY APPAR-

ENTLY CONTINUING LANDING IN KOTA BHARU AREA WHICH SHOULD BE FRUITFUL AS WELL AS SINGORA.

2. ON THE OTHER HAND ENEMY BOMBERS ON SOUTH INDO CHINA AERODROMES ARE IN FORCE AND UNDISTURBED. THEY COULD ATTACK YOU FIVE HOURS AFTER SIGHTING AND MUCH DEPENDS ON WHETHER YOU HAVE BEEN SEEN TODAY. TWO CARRIERS MAY BE IN SAIGON AREA.

3. MILITARY SITUATION AT KOTA BHARU APPEARS DIFFICULT. AERODROME IS IN ENEMY HANDS.

4. ALL OUR NORTHERN AERODROMES ARE BECOMING UNTENABLE DUE TO ENEMY AIR ACTION. C IN C FAR EAST HINTS HE IS CONSIDERING CONCENTRATING ALL AIR EFFORTS ON DEFENCE OF SINGAPORE AREA.

5. EXTREMELY DIFFICULT TO GIVE YOU CLEARER PICTURE BECAUSE AIR RECONNAISSANCE COMMUNICATIONS ARE SO SLOW DUE PARTLY TO DAMAGE TO AERODROMES.

There is more here than a gentle hint of restraint by Palliser. He was pointing the finger at Kota Bharu, much nearer than Singora, as a possible target for Force Z, and then spelling out in some detail the dangers from Japanese aircraft and the deteriorating position of the R.A.F. The unwitting errors in this signal were that there were no Japanese aircraft carriers at Saigon, only comparatively harmless seaplane tenders, and that the Japanese had now completed their main landing at Kota Bharu. In fact all the information was now irrelevant since Admiral Phillips had already called off the main operation and Force Z was steaming south. The signal is of interest, however, in that it reveals that Palliser was well in step with his chief by sending this information within two hours of the time that Phillips had been faced with the important decision of whether or not to carry on with the operation. It is also of interest in that it seems to indicate that Palliser was only too well aware of the potential danger from Japanese aircraft.

The all-important factor of how much in tune with each other's thoughts were Admiral at sea and Chief of Staff ashore was soon to be put to a further test as Palliser now had a new, and startling, item of information to send.

IMMEDIATE

ENEMY REPORTED LANDING KUANTAN. LATITUDE 03.50 NORTH.

Kuantan was a town on the east coast of Malaya, exactly half-way between Kota Bharu and Singapore. There was there a small harbour, an important R.A.F. airfield, and several roads running not only north and south along the coast but also inland, right across the peninsula. A successful landing by the Japanese at Kuantan could cut off the British forces in northern Malaya and bring the Japanese to within 180 miles of Singapore.

The Kuantan signal was received in *Prince of Wales* just before midnight, and tired as he must have been, Admiral Phillips realized at once the implications of this latest development. It is easy to deduce Phillips's reaction. Kuantan was not far from Force Z's return route and the British ships could easily appear off Kuantan early the next morning. The Japanese, as far as Phillips knew, had last spotted Force Z well to the north, still steaming north and presumably about to make a sortie into the Gulf of Siam. The Japanese could have no means, on the intelligence they held at that moment, of expecting the British ships to appear off Kuantan in five hours' time. This assessment by Phillips was perfectly justified. Moreover, Kuantan was four hundred miles from the Japanese airfields in Indo-China, which Phillips might have reckoned was a safe distance from Japanese torpedo bombers at Saigon, and certainly a safe one from the two Japanese aircraft carriers that Palliser believed to be off Saigon.

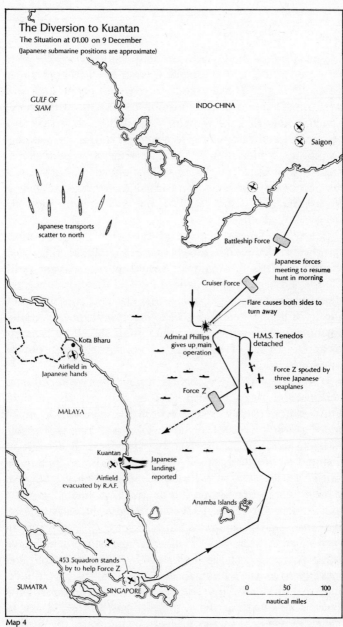

The Diversion to Kuantan

The Situation at 01.00 on 9 December

(Japanese submarine positions are approximate)

GULF OF
SIAM

INDO-CHINA

Saigon

Japanese transports
scatter to north

Battleship Force

Japanese forces
meeting to resume
hunt in morning

Cruiser Force

Flare causes both sides to
turn away

Admiral Phillips
gives up main
operation

H.M.S. Tenedos
detached

Force Z spotted by
three Japanese
seaplanes

Kota Bharu

Airfield
in Japanese hands

Force Z

MALAYA

Kuantan

Japanese
landings
reported

Airfield
evacuated by R.A.F.

Anamba Islands

453 Squadron stands
by to help Force Z

SUMATRA

SINGAPORE

0   50   100

nautical miles

Map 4

Tom Phillips made up his mind quickly. Force Z was to turn towards Kuantan, speed was to be increased to 25 knots. *Prince of Wales* and *Repulse* would attempt to surprise the Japanese in the morning and might still achieve a victory and make a valuable contribution to the defence of Malaya and Singapore. We know Phillips's reasoning, we know his decision. We can assume that he was immensely heartened by this fresh turn of events. Now it was the Japanese who had overreached themselves. *Prince of Wales*'s signal lamps blinked out the fresh orders to *Repulse* and the destroyers.

But what did not happen at this time is rather more significant than what did happen. To signal this fresh change of plans to Singapore would mean breaking radio silence. To break radio silence might, if they picked up the signal, reveal to the Japanese that the British ships were now two hours steaming to the *south* of their last known position. This could well rob the proposed dash to Kuantan of any element of surprise, so no signal went out to Singapore.

It was now that the mental rapport between Admiral Phillips and Rear-Admiral Palliser was put to the test. The Kuantan area was well within the area which, if not under absolute control of the R.A.F., was at least capable of being patrolled from the air. The British aircraft at Kuantan airfield had actually been withdrawn to Singapore on the 9th because of Japanese bombing attacks, but had it been known that Force Z was about to steam into that area at dawn on the 10th, the Buffalo fighters of 453 Squadron at Singapore, earmarked for the support of Force Z and kept out of all other fighting, could have flown patrols over the British ships next morning and possibly have used Kuantan as a forward base for refuelling. Admiral Phillips had served for two years as a senior staff officer at the Admiralty and had often had to make assessments of the future movements of fleets that were at sea and keeping radio silence. It is quite possible that Phillips assumed that Palliser would automatically arrange for the Buffaloes to be patrolling off Kuantan next morning. It is not known whether Palliser did consider this, but certainly nothing was done about it. R.A.F. Headquarters at Singapore had no idea at all of where Force Z was, and the Buffaloes remained on the ground at Singapore next morning.

There is one more factor that may have been at work. When at the Admiralty, Phillips had often had a hand in directing the operations of ships at sea; the Admiralty liked to have centralized control of such operations. Although London was half a world away, Phillips was well aware that the Operations Room at the Admiralty would be monitoring all Pallisers' signals and following this operation closely. If Phillips now signalled his future intentions to Palliser at Singapore, the Admiralty also would get to know of them. It can only be conjecture that Tom Phillips wanted to keep control of this operation himself, and by making sure that the Japanese did not know where Force Z was bound, was also ensuring that the Admiralty did not know and were less likely thereby to interfere in his decisions. But the R.A.F. were also prevented from knowing the movements of Force Z.

When the Japanese had harnessed all their forces to hunt down the British ships the previous evening, the submarines in the patrol lines farther south had been ordered to move north, to spread out and keep their eyes open for the British ships. Mindful, no doubt, of the two-hour delay in receiving I.65's sighting report the previous afternoon, the Japanese had also ordered a new and much tighter signal procedure.

One of these submarines was I.58, captained by Lieutenant-Commander Sohichi Kitamura. The Japanese Official History says that I.58 sighted the British as early as 23.52 (Singapore Time), which was while Force Z was on a southerly course after Admiral Phillips had given up the idea of raiding the Japanese invasion beaches to the north but before the course was altered to the south-west towards Kuantan. I.58 had been on the surface when her lookouts spotted the dark shadows of two large ships only 600 metres away. Kitamura dived immediately, examined the ships through his periscope and correctly identified them as the British ships he was searching for, not heading north, as he had expected, but south. He immediately prepared to carry out a submerged torpedo attack on the leading ship, *Prince of Wales*, which was coming into an ideal target position. But I.58 was an old submarine; she had been launched in 1925 and was now one of the veterans among Japanese submarines on active service. To the frustration of her crew, one of the torpedo-tube hatches jammed and the British battleship passed out of range. *Repulse* also steamed by while the Japanese were struggling with the faulty hatch, and by the time the trouble was cleared, *Repulse* was no more than a stern target drawing rapidly away. Five torpedoes were fired; all missed. Neither the radar of the British capital ships nor the Asdic sets of the destroyers had detected the submarine.

Lieutenant-Commander Kitamura had got a sighting report off before making the torpedo attack, but this first report was only picked up by a ship of the Japanese 3rd Destroyer Division and was either not forwarded to a higher command or not picked up by that command until much later. Kitamura continued to shadow on the surface and sent out three more signals.

OUR POSITION FU.MO.RO.45. HAVE LAUNCHED 5 TORPEDOES AT REPULSE BUT MISSED. ENEMY COURSE 180 DEGREES, SPEED 22 KNOTS. 03.41. [02.11 Singapore Time]

ENEMY FLEET NOW STEAMING 240 DEGREES, EMITTING MUCH BLACK SMOKE WHICH WE ARE FOLLOWING. 04.25. [02.55]

WE HAVE LOST SIGHT OF THE ENEMY. 06.15. [04.45]

The first and last of these three signals were received safely by the relevant naval and air headquarters, but not the vital second one which would have told the Japanese that the British had changed course to the south-west. Again, that signal was picked up by the 3rd Destroyer Division, but again not forwarded properly up the Japanese chain of command.

I.58 had done a fine job in hanging on despite her age for nearly five hours to a battle fleet steaming at 25 knots.* The Japanese commanders now knew that the British had given up their foray to the north and were returning, but again because of their faulty signal procedures, did not appreciate that the British ships were steaming south-west towards the Malayan coast and not due south to Singapore.

Completely unaware of I.58's activities, Force Z steamed through the early hours of 10 December in the direction of Kuantan. The crews were at second-degree readiness the whole time – a period of tension, lassitude and the low spirits often found in those last hours before dawn. For some it was a time for routine work. Cook J. H. Larthwell came on duty in *Repulse* at 02.00 and baked 800 pounds of bread in the next four hours. 'I reckoned I was the last man to bake bread in the *Repulse*.'

Yet another signal was relayed to *Prince of Wales's* signal office, this time from the Admiralty in London.

PERSONAL FROM FIRST SEA LORD

AS TORPEDO AIRCRAFT ATTACK ON SHIPS AT ANCHOR IN JOHORE STRAIT CANNOT BE RULED OUT, I AM SURE YOU HAVE IN MIND M/LD. 02033/ 41, DATED 22 APRIL 1941, PARAGRAPH 18-(14), WHICH YOU TOOK SO MUCH INTEREST IN.

---

* I.58 was renumbered I.158 in 1942 and relegated to the role of training submarine the same year. In the last months of the war she was, like I.65(I.165), adapted to carrying Kaiten midget submarines and returned to active service. She was surrendered to the U.S. Navy at the end of the war and later scuttled.

Did Tom Phillips smile when he read this signal? Could he imagine Sir Dudley Pound in London, nervous, not about the possibility of *Prince of Wales* and *Repulse* being caught at sea by Japanese aircraft, but at the chance of them being attacked while at anchor as the Italian battleships had been caught by the Fleet Air Arm at Taranto – the incident which probably inspired the document referred to in this signal? The staff officer who took this signal to Admiral Phillips remembers that both he and the admiral could not understand the relevance of this signal and that Phillips said something about 'the first Sea Lord going off at half-cock'. This was an important signal, however, because it *might* have meant that the Admiralty were in possession of intelligence information that the Japanese aircraft in Indo-China had a torpedo-carrying capability. If this was so, then it was a tragedy that the Admiralty did not spell out the danger more clearly. No one on board *Prince of Wales* paid any further attention to the signal.

The receipt of this signal was the only incident before dawn.

An early breakfast had been served on the British warships an hour before dawn, and there was a noticeable heightening of tension. 'We had visions of surprising a large number of Jap transports and warships at dawn, sinking the lot and beating a hasty retreat south.' But, again, for many men it was just a time of normal routine. A group of communication ratings on watch in *Prince of Wales* had tested all their lines and then settled down to share out some private delicacies that one man had brought on watch. Lieutenant-Commander Hancock, the Fleet Wireless Officer, suggested that a fund be started for such refreshments to be purchased on a regular basis, and every man gave a shilling to start the kitty.

Full Action Stations were manned just before dawn, which broke at about 05.00. It was cool, and the light gradually spread from the horizon behind the ships to bring forth a calm day with excellent visibility. To everyone's relief the lookouts could see nothing in any direction. Force Z was still some sixty miles from Kuantan and the coast not yet in sight. The sun climbed higher and began to warm the gun crews and the lookouts in their exposed positions. There was every promise of a hot day to come.

At 05.15 four dots were spotted on the horizon to the north; they were at first judged to be a cruiser and three destroyers, and, if so, could only be Japanese. Admiral Phillips ordered his force to turn towards this sighting, but within minutes the dots were identified as a large tug or small steamer towing three barges – Japanese invasion barges perhaps? Phillips spent only the shortest time coming to his next decision. If these were Japanese they were not at that stage worth the attention of the British ships; more important targets were probably just over the horizon in the direction of Kuantan. The original course was resumed.

Soon after 06.30 there was a further ripple of excitement and some apprehension when *Repulse*'s lookouts spotted an aircraft low on the horizon, apparently shadowing the British ships. The aircraft could not be identified, but remained at the same distance for perhaps half an hour – reports vary – before disappearing. The implications were enormous. If the aircraft was Japanese and had reported to its base, as it was reasonable to assume, then the enemy once more knew the exact location and course of the British ships. But no action of any kind was taken by Admiral Phillips. Radio silence was still maintained and no R.A.F. air cover was requested.

After the strange aeroplane had departed, the Walrus amphibian aircraft aboard *Prince of Wales* was hauled on to its catapult and prepared for flight. Its Fleet Air Arm pilot, Lieutenant C. R. Bateman, received his orders – fly to Kuantan and inspect the beaches and harbour, report back to *Prince of Wales*, then fly to Singapore or a friendly airfield to land. At 07.18 the Walrus was catapulted off. Bateman and his crew did not take long to fly to Kuantan, but they could see no Japanese ships and soon reported

back to *Prince of Wales*. The Walrus then flew away and
is believed to have landed in a minefield near Singapore;
the crew were picked up by a launch, but the Walrus was
abandoned.

Forty minutes later Force Z was itself within sight of
land, but again nothing out of the ordinary could be seen;
there was certainly no obvious warlike activity. *Prince of
Wales* and *Repulse* could not approach too close to the shore,
and turned to steam parallel to the coast at 15 knots.
Despite the report of the Walrus, Admiral Phillips decided
that he wanted a closer examination of the shore and, in
particular, of Kuantan's small harbour. This could be seen
from *Prince of Wales* only as a small break in the dense
trees of the mainland. The destroyer *Express* was ordered
to steam well in to reconnoitre.

As *Express* creamed her way across the blue water towards the land there were hundreds of pairs of eyes peering
intently at the shore. One man with binoculars could see
'a nebulous stretch of tropical coastline, nothing but sand,
surf and tropical vegetation', and another, 'a solitary
motor cyclist scampering along the road between beach
and jungle'.

Express was away just an hour.

We sailed into the shore and took a good look around. Could we see
Japanese landing craft on the beaches? All I could see was dead
vegetation and not a movement of life – not even Dorothy Lamour.
(Able Seaman J. M. Farrington)

Another *Express* man says that he saw 'just one solitary
white man waving'. Lieutenant-Commander Cartwright
finished his search, set course back to the open sea and
signalled *Prince of Wales* that all he had found was 'complete peace'. One version of the signal quotes it as being:

ALL IS AS QUIET AS A WET SUNDAY AFTERNOON.

Many men aboard the ships waiting for *Express* were
unhappy at this prolonged examination; the destroyer had

done no more than confirm what the Walrus had already found.

The longer we were hanging about there the less I liked it. There was absolutely nothing, ashore or at sea, to arouse a scrap of suspicion – except this very fact itself! Despite frequent changes of course, our reduced speed made us feel like sitting ducks and I felt that, having been sighted once, we should have been making straight back to Singapore. (Ordinary Seaman D. F. Wilson, H.M.S. *Prince of Wales*)

So here we were, those two great ships with mighty little surface screen and no air cover, nonchalantly meandering about off that empty coast, executing such ponderous peacetime manoeuvres as 'Turn 135 degrees to starboard in succession' – sitting targets for submarine or air attack for which we were not prepared. Even to the likes of me it seemed extraordinary that we were wandering about the sea so lackadaisically in such circumstances. (Lieutenant J. O. C. Hayes, H.M.S. *Repulse*)

But, despite the fact that they might have been reported by the aircraft seen three hours earlier or the possibility that Japanese submarines were in the area, Force Z did not immediately resume its voyage to the south. It was Captain Tennant of *Repulse*, with two suggestions signalled to the flagship, who prompted a further diversion. The first signal, an eminently practical one, was that *Repulse* should now catapult off one of her two Walrus aircraft to fly an anti-submarine patrol around Force Z. Admiral Phillips agreed and the Walrus was soon off. Tennant's second suggestion was that the small ship and three barges seen earlier should be investigated more closely before Force Z finally left the area. Again Admiral Phillips agreed, and the five British ships, instead of turning south-east for the Anamba Islands and the comparative safety of Singapore, took a course of 080 degrees, slightly north of due east. A battleship, a battle cruiser and three destroyers were setting out to examine one small ship and three barges – on the face of it a ludicrous risk to take on an errand that one destroyer could have performed, but clear evidence of two assumptions that must have been in

Admiral Phillips's mind at that time: that the barges, if Japanese, might be the forerunners of a larger Japanese force which his big guns could then smash; and that, at this range from Indo-China, there was little danger to Force Z from Japanese aircraft.

After Force Z had been steaming away from the coast for thirty minutes, the complacency of the second assumption was badly shaken by a signal received at 10.05. The destroyer *Tenedos*, which had detached from Force Z when short of fuel the previous evening, had rounded the Anamba Islands early that morning and signalled to Singapore the now partly out-of-date information that Force Z had broken off the main operation into the Gulf of Siam. Now *Tenedos* was signalling that she was being bombed by Japanese aircraft at a position 140 miles southeast of Force Z's present position. The implications of this report were that Japanese aircraft were about, and, furthermore, at a range considerably farther from Indo-China than Force Z. If the Japanese could reach *Tenedos*, they could easily reach Force Z.

Within minutes of this news being received, a lookout sighted an approaching aircraft.

Before leaving the subject of Kuantan for good, some explanation of the reported landings should be given. The Kuantan area was defended by the understrength 22nd Indian Brigade with two infantry battalions, the 5/11th Sikhs and the 2/18th Royal Garhwal Rifles, supported by a few guns. The brigade commander was Brigadier G. W. A. Painter. The Indian units had never seen action before. Their main purpose was to guard Kuantan airfield, which had been the base of three squadrons of aircraft until these had been badly bombed and machine-gunned the previous day, the 9th, and the remnants of the squadrons withdrawn to Singapore before nightfall.

At 19.00 that evening an observation post manned by the Garhwal Rifles had reported seeing several small ships and lighters towing barges approaching the

coast, and three hours later firing had broken out, directed
on to what the Indians believed to be a Japanese landing
craft. This was the foundation for the report sent by Vice-
Admiral Palliser to Force Z regarding the 'Japanese landing at Kuantan'. Firing continued spasmodically during the
night, but there was no firm evidence that any fire had
come from the sea. When dawn broke the 'landing craft'
had disappeared and no Japanese troops were to be found.
The somewhat shamefaced Indians claimed that they had
beaten off a small Japanese reconnaissance party. Four
days later several small boats were found some miles to
the south; some of these were bullet-riddled, and one contained Japanese rifles, a Japanese postcard and some items
of Japanese uniforms.

It is possible that these small boats had been put ashore
by the trawler – which was Japanese – seen that morning
by Force Z, and that it was an attempt to create diversions
at various points on the east coast of Malaya. If this is so,
then the ruse brought the Japanese rewards out of all
proportion to the effort involved, since it was this that
caused Force Z to come to Kuantan that morning.

The Japanese trawler and the boats she was towing will
be met again in a later chapter. The little town of Kuantan
did not feature again in the Malayan campaign until
Japanese troops from the north advanced upon it two weeks
later.*

The vital piece of information received by the Japanese
commanders during the night was the sighting report by
submarine I.58 saying that the British ships had reversed
course and were apparently returning at speed to Singapore. This signal had been received by Vice-Admiral
Kondo at 02.11, but he had never received I.58's subsequent signal about the British diversion south-west

---

* The recreation ground at Kuantan was the setting used by the
novelist Nevil Shute for the crucifixion by Japanese soldiers of the
Australian Joe Harman in his fictional work *A Town Like Alice*.

towards Kuantan. When he had received I.58's first report, Admiral Kondo immediately ordered his cruisers and two battleships to give chase, and these set off to the south at 24 knots; Vice-Admiral Ozawa's cruiser force was much the nearer to the British, but despite an increase in speed after dawn to 28 knots, Kondo soon realized that the Japanese ships would never catch the British before they reached the safety of Singapore. Moreover, he had no intention of risking his surface vessels so close to the British airfields. Only half an hour after ordering the 28 knots, Kondo ordered that the chase be abandoned and his ships turned back north. Had Kondo known that the British were at that time dallying off Kuantan, he might well have pressed on and the naval engagement that had so nearly taken place the previous night might well have occurred after all. But, as it turned out, the hunting of the British ships was now to be left in the hands of the submarines and the aircraft based in Indo-China.

The supposedly Japanese reconnaissance aircraft seen by the British soon after dawn had not sent a sighting report, or, if it did, the report did not find its way through to Admiral Kondo. In fact it is not certain that the aircraft was Japanese, though it could well have been an army aircraft flying from the newly captured Kota Bharu airfield. If it had been Japanese, then the failure to get a sighting report through to the naval command was to be the cause of much trouble and anxiety to the Japanese later that morning.

From the Japanese viewpoint, this operation to track down and bring to battle the small, fast fleet of British ships was entering the final phase, and it was becoming very much a catch-as-catch-can type of operation. The surface warships, which had been so close to engaging the British the previous night, were now out of the reckoning; the submarines had performed some useful spotting duty but had failed to slow down the British and were now well scattered. Any future success the submarines might gain would be the product of random fortune and not of careful planning. The last Japanese hope now lay with the land-based naval air units far to the north on the airfields around Saigon. The aeroplane, regarded in a lowly light by several of the naval commanders on each side, was now to have the chance to show that it had the speed, range, flexibility and hitting power to succeed where the Japanese warships had failed.

Despite the fact that his aircrews were desperately tired and had only landed in the early hours from their last flight, Rear-Admiral Matsunaga realized that the next few hours were crucial. He gave orders for every available Mitsubishi bomber of his three air corps to be refuelled and prepared for take-off soon after dawn. Out of his total strength of ninety-nine bombers, Matsunaga found that ninety-four were fit for operations. This figure represents a very high rate of serviceability after the continuous operations of recent days and says much for the robust construction of the Mitsubishis and the skill of their ground crews.

For the coming day's operations, Matsunaga's initial plan had been to allocate his available aircraft in the following roles:

17 aircraft to reconnaissance flights
17 aircraft as high-level bombers
60 aircraft as torpedo bombers

The reconnaissance aircraft were to have full fuel loads, and the only bombs they carried were two small 50-kg. ones; they were to take off first, spread out in a huge fan and search the area in which the British ships were believed to be steaming to Singapore. The attack aircraft were to follow later, and because of their heavy bomb or torpedo loads, would be forced to fly with a reduced fuel load. Their endurance, particularly that of the torpedo-carrying aircraft, would be strictly limited, but the captured airfield at Kota Bharu would be available to them in an emergency. Much would depend on the ability of the reconnaissance aircraft to find the British quickly, and then to guide in the attack aircraft. When the attacks did start it was intended

that the high-level bombers would smash up the upperworks of the British ships and cause casualties to their gun
crews. There were no armour-piercing bombs available –
they had all been allocated to the Pearl Harbor attack;
there were not even the ordinary 800-kg. bombs that the
Mitsubishis could carry and Matsunaga's men would have
to manage with 500-kg. bombs, one per aircraft, or, in
some cases, two 250-kg. bombs. The real punch was
expected to be in the force of torpedo aircraft. Much has
been written about the surprise among the Allies in 1941
over the effectiveness of some of the Japanese naval torpedoes, but those to be carried by the Mitsubishis that day
were the relatively humble Modified Type 91, some being
the Model 1 with a 149.5-kg. (330-lb.) warhead, and
others the Model 2 with a warhead weighing 204 kg.
(450 lb.). While the aircrews snatched a few hours' sleep,
the ground personnel worked hard to refuel and arm the
Nells and Bettys.

Just before take-off, however, Matsunaga changed his
mind about the allocation of aircraft and decided that he
needed more high-level bombers. Eight aircraft were
withdrawn from the reconnaissance force, and nine from
the torpedo force. The weakening of these two in favour
of the bombers was almost to prove a mistake.

The final line-up was as follows:

RECONNAISSANCE FORCE

9 Mitsubishi Type 96 G3M2 (Nell) aircraft of the Genzan Air Corps.
Take-off from Saigon airfield at 05.00 (Singapore Time).

GENZAN AIR CORPS ATTACK GROUP

Commander: Lieutenant-Commander Nakanishi
Aircraft Type: Mitsubishi Type 96 G3M2 (Nell)

Squadron	Leader	No. of aircraft	Role
1st	Lieutenant Ishihara	9	Torpedo attack
2nd	Lieutenant Takai	8	Torpedo attack
3rd	Lieutenant Nikaido	9	Bombing

Take-offs from Saigon airfield soon after 06.25.

KANOYA AIR CORPS ATTACK GROUP

Commander: Lieutenant-Commander Miyauchi

Aircraft Type: Mitsubishi Navy Type 1 G4M1 (Betty)

Squadron	Leader	No. of aircraft	Role
1st	Lieutenant Nabeta	9	Torpedo attack
2nd	Lieutenant Higashimori	8	Torpedo attack
3rd	Lieutenant Iki	9	Torpedo attack

Take-offs from Tu Duam airfield soon after 06.44.

MIHORO AIR CORPS ATTACK GROUP

Commander: none designated

Aircraft Type: Mitsubishi Type 96 G3M2 (Nell)

Squadron	Leader	No. of aircraft	Role
1st	Lieutenant Shirai	8	Bombing
2nd	Lieutenant Takeda	8	Bombing
3rd	Lieutenant Ohira	9	Bombing
4th	Lieutenant Takahashi	8	Torpedo attack

Take-offs from Tu Duam airfield between 06.50 and 08.00.

Total: 9 reconnaissance aircraft
        34 bombing aircraft
        51 torpedo aircraft

The Japanese airmen were woken and wearily took themselves to the briefing rooms where they were addressed by as many as five officers; it is recorded that the younger airmen became quite bored with the lengthy instructions, never realizing that this day they would make history. Captain Kosei Maeda, the commanding officer of the Genzan Air Corps, asked Rear-Admiral Matsunaga for permission to fly as a passenger in one of the high-level bombers, and was allowed to do so. There was speculation over how far south the British ships might have reached, and much anxiety, especially among the crews of the torpedo aircraft, that the British might even have reached Singapore itself and that the torpedo bombers might have to carry out a hazardous low-level attack over the defended harbour.

The crews picked up their flight rations of *Ohagi* – rice cakes coated with tasty bean paste – and thick sweet coffee in flasks. At 06.25 the first attack aircraft, piloted by Lieutenant Ishihara, took off from Saigon; the reconnaissance aircraft had left an hour and a half earlier. On this occasion there was no crowd of army officers to wave the Mitsubishis on their way, only the loyal ground personnel. It was 08.00 before the last attack aircraft took off; these were the nine Nells of Lieutenant Ohira's squadron from Tu Duam. They had been delayed by the decision to change the squadron's loads from torpedoes to bombs.

The Japanese airmen were pleased to find that the weather was fine; they flew straight out to sea on a course slightly west of south that would take them right to the approaches of Singapore Naval Base. The Nells and Bettys flew in formations of eights or nines, and climbed steadily until they reached 10,000 feet. The visibility was excellent with only small patches of low cloud. The Mitsubishis flew steadily south at the most economical speed and engine settings their pilots could manage. It was up to the nine reconnaissance aircraft to find the enemy; these attack aircraft could only cruise on and hope the sighting came before too much fuel was consumed.

There was no radio silence for the Japanese airmen; the reconnaissance planes were reporting back regularly on their progress and on the weather encountered, but the hours passed with no reports of battleships sighted, only a submarine believed to be British (it was not). Saigon ordered the reconnaissance planes to try farther south. Lieutenant Takai was leading one of the Genzan torpedo squadrons:

What is the matter with our reconnaissance planes? Still no sign of the enemy. In spite of the good weather and clear visibility, is it possible the reconnaissance planes still cannot find the British warships? By now our planes should be more than five hundred nautical miles from Saigon. Lieutenant-Commander Nakanishi, flying just ahead of my bomber, must also be growing very impatient.

We have passed the danger line of four hundred nautical miles from Saigon. Still no report on the enemy ships. It is as though we were enveloped in complete darkness. The pilots are becoming more and more anxious about their remaining fuel. We measured the rate of fuel consumption as carefully as possible and reduced it to the lowest possible level. It was not the best way to treat the engines, but we had little choice. Perhaps because of our severe mixture control, one of my bombers developed engine trouble and was forced to leave the formation and return to base. I could not send even one plane as escort. Including my own, the number of aircraft in my squadron was reduced to seven.

It was at this stage that I.58's last signal, reporting that the British had turned towards Kuantan, or a report from the mystery plane which had been sighted by the British soon after dawn, would have been most useful to the Japanese, but the area off Kuantan where the British now were was not in the path of the outward flight of any of the nine Japanese reconnaissance aircraft.

The fourth plane in the search pattern had reached the southern limit of its search area, near the island of Tioman, turned east and flown a short leg before turning north for the return flight. At 09.43 it spotted a small ship below and correctly identified it as a British destroyer. The Japanese pilot made a careful approach and released his two 50-kg. bombs. They missed. He reported the sighting to Saigon and continued his flight north, still searching for the main force of British ships.

Flying down from the north and passing the reconnaissance plane on the opposite course were the three attack squadrons of the Genzan Air Corps, twenty-five aircraft strong. Lieutenant Takai again:

At 10.15 we sighted a small vessel off to our left. The sea was absolutely calm. The ship appeared to be a cargo vessel of about five or six hundred tons. Singapore was near. Since it was possible that other enemy vessels might be in the vicinity, I ordered my men to stay alert. No other object could be seen; this was unusual.

Keeping a sharp lookout above and behind us for enemy planes, we tightened all formations and maintained our flight due south.

Without warning the entire 3rd Squadron dropped out of the mass formation and flew toward the small cargo vessel. Soon they circled over the ship. I could not understand what the squadron leader could possibly be doing.

The enemy vessel suddenly changed its course, and no sooner had it begun its twisting evasive action than a salvo of bombs fell more than seven hundred feet away from the ship without inflicting any damage! What was wrong with the 3rd Squadron leader? Nine 500-kilogram bombs were lost, dissipated without results, after all the trouble of carrying them for such a long time!

Lieutenant Nikaido's 3rd Squadron was the one in which Captain Maeda, the commanding officer of the Genzan Air Corps, was flying as a passenger. It is not known whether Maeda had given the order to attack or not. The nine Mitsubishis that had bombed turned for home. They were now out of the reckoning.

The 'cargo vessel' of Lieutenant Takai's account that had just been bombed was really the destroyer *Tenedos* on her way back to Singapore. She had had an exciting morning. Her Asdic had earlier detected what was believed to be a submerged submarine, and Lieutenant Dyer had ordered two depth-charge attacks on the contact. As the object remained in the same place throughout the attacks, Dyer came to the conclusion that it had not been a submarine after all and continued his voyage. He was correct; no Japanese submarine reported being attacked at this time.

Then the Japanese aircraft attacked, and so well did Dyer handle his ship that the Japanese formation had had to make three passes over the twisting destroyer before deciding to release their bombs all in one salvo. Lieutenant Dyer writes:

The bombing of *Tenedos* was my first real experience of heavy aircraft attack at sea and, I believe, I found this particular incident exciting rather than frightening. It was my first command and she handled like a dream and the Almighty was with us.

The Japanese had been flying too high for *Tenedos*'s guns to open fire and the bombs had fallen over a hundred yards out to the port side. One of *Tenedos*'s sailors had been hit in the thigh by a bomb splinter but he was the only casualty.

Tenedos broadcast four signals giving full details of the attack and of the larger formation of Japanese aircraft – the remainder of the Genzan Air Corps – that had been seen. These signals were received by Force Z, but apparently not in Singapore, only 120 miles away, for no British fighters were sent out after the Japanese. *Tenedos* increased speed so that she could land her wounded seaman more quickly at Singapore.

One by one the remaining eight Japanese reconnaissance planes were reaching the southern legs of their search patterns and turning back towards home, each taking a slightly different return route so as to cover as much ocean as possible. Of the three attack formations, the Genzan and Kanoya aircraft had by now flown down to a position level with Singapore; their crews could quite clearly see the Malayan mountains to the west, and even the Dutch island of Sumatra farther south. They would soon be at the 'point of no return' and would shortly have to abandon the operation and turn about. The Mihoro squadrons, which had taken off later, were farther to the north.

It was the crew of Midshipman Masame Hoashi, in the third plane out from the Malayan coast in the search pattern, who finally made the vital discovery. After reaching the limit of his outward flight near the Malayan coast, Hoashi had turned north-west to fly farther up the coast before turning back for Saigon. At 10.15 his crew spotted ships below and out went three radio signals:

ENEMY FLEET SPOTTED AT LAT. 4N. LONG. 103.55E. COURSE 60 DEGREES.

ENEMY FORCE CHANGED COURSE TO 30 DEGREES.

ENEMY FORCE ESCORTED BY 3 DESTROYERS. ORDER OF FORMATION IS KING-TYPE BATTLESHIP, REPULSE.

Yet again the Japanese signals system failed to function properly. Hoashi's reports were received clearly at Saigon and Tu Duam airfields, but it soon became obvious to the operations officers there that many of the attack planes had not picked up Hoashi's signals or could not understand them. Hoashi was ordered to abandon the use of codes and to broadcast his reports in plain language. He was also ordered to emit a continuous signal on long-wave on to which the direction-finders of the attack planes could home. These measures met with some success, but because of the initial delays, the seventy-six remaining aircraft of the Japanese attack force would only arrive in the sighting area in dribs and drabs over a period of an hour and a half, and all would be short of fuel. There would be no opportunity for them to execute the carefully planned and coordinated combination of high-level bombing and low-level torpedo attacks.

Lieutenant Yoshimi Shirai's squadron of the Mihoro Air Corps, with eight high-level bombers, was first on the scene forty minutes after Hoashi had first spotted the British ships.

When the Japanese reconnaissance plane was first seen by the British ships, Force Z had been steering a course of 080 degrees towards the position of the small ships seen earlier. This course was altered at once to 095 degrees, and soon afterwards to a south-easterly course. This last change was not a move to escape the shadower, which would have been impossible, but to investigate a small ship just sighted. This turned out to be a British merchant ship, the S.S. *Haldis*. The *Haldis* was on the run from her home port of Hong Kong and was hoping to make the safety of Singapore. Her crew were about to have a grandstand view.

The crews of the British warships had been stood down from Action Stations after leaving Kuantan, and many men had been given a second, cooked, breakfast. Some of the off-duty men had then been able to rest or take a stroll along the deck, chatting in the warm sunshine, although several remember that the usual high spirits were absent on this occasion; there seemed to be 'an unusual quietness, a sense of foreboding'. This was especially true when the Japanese reconnaissance plane was spotted high in the sky to the south.

Twenty-five minutes after the plane had been sighted the echoes of a formation of aircraft were picked up by radar. A general order was issued at once by the flagship: 'ASSUME FIRST DEGREE ANTI-AIRCRAFT READINESS'. On the bridge of *Prince of Wales*, sixteen-year-old Bugler Squires of the Royal Marines was ordered by Captain Leach to blow the call for 'Action Stations. Repel Aircraft' over the ship's Tannoy, and soon the men of Force Z were rushing to the stations they would man against aircraft attack – a drill they had all performed dozens of times in the past.

The call to Action Stations came just as the issuing of the rum ration was starting. This happy event was immediately suspended, the rum barrels were locked up and the keys removed. Only a few men had managed to receive their rum issue, among them Leading Torpedo Operator 'Scouse' Holehouse in *Prince of Wales*: 'I was always a bit of a fiddler. I managed to get two tots that morning and felt like meeting Tojo all on my own.'

Also in *Prince of Wales*, Marine John Wignall was taking a shower when he heard the call to Action Stations.

I was rather surprised and hesitated at first, not really focusing on what was happening, and by the time I had gathered my things together Damage Control were in operation, closing all watertight doors including the deck hatch leading down to the bathroom I was using. I heard the cleats being fastened on the outside and by the time I had dashed up the ladder I realized that I was well and truly locked in. I hammered on the hatch with my shoe in desperation, and fortunately someone running by heard me and let me out or I would have been there to this day.

Leading Seaman Basil Elsmore in *Prince of Wales* also remembers:

10.45, 10 December 1941. Kuantan, East Malaya, the bugler sounds 'Action Stations, Aircraft'. 'Bomber overhead. Bomber overhead,' the bugle seems to say. Quickly the calls come to the Transmitting Station (Gun Control), 'So-and-so station closed up and cleared away.' In perhaps two minutes at the most this great, floating home-cum-gun-platform was ready.

Was 'Jeff' Jefferies, in the Ring Main Breaker Space, right when he said, 'Cheerio Bas. Watch your step. Take care'? The hatch closed. Did you know, Jeff? Did you survive, Jeff?

It was just after 11.00 hours when the eight Mitsubishis were spotted approaching from ahead, high up and glistening in the sun. The Japanese planes were soon close enough for the control officers of the high-angle guns in *Prince of Wales* and *Repulse* to start their 'plot'. 'Enemy aircraft in sight. Range 16,500 yards. Height 10,000 feet. Speed 200. Commence. Commence. Commence.'

But no signal of any kind had gone out from the flagship to Singapore. That radio silence, so important in the mind of Admiral Phillips, was still being observed.

9

The First Round

The late take-off by some of the Japanese aircraft from their airfields, the long flight over the featureless ocean waiting for news of the British ships, then the false alarm caused by *Tenedos* – all these factors had tended to scatter the Japanese squadrons. Even when Midshipman Hoashi had found the British ships, the hit-or-miss nature of the Japanese communications system brought their attack aircraft to the scene, not in any carefully planned and co-ordinated manner, but in the most haphazard of ways. Many of the Japanese aircraft were running low on fuel, and all their crews were physically weary after so much flying during recent days and nights. The British sailors were also tired after long hours at Action Stations, particularly those men whose duties had kept them below decks in the inadequately ventilated *Prince of Wales*. But all these men – Japanese and British – were young and fit; fatigue or morale would not decide the outcome of the coming encounter, nor even courage. Equipment, skill and training would make more impact, but the elements in this coming battle were, with one exception, all long-established ones: armoured capital ships, destroyers and aircraft, guns and machine-guns, shells, bombs and torpedoes. The only new factor was radar, and radar was to play virtually no part on this clear, sunny day.

What was at issue, and what would decide the outcome, was a theory, a philosophy: could capital ships at sea survive in the face of determined air attack? As has already been indicated, the testing in action of certain theories had been surprisingly long delayed, but the day of reckoning had now arrived. Surprisingly, perhaps, it was to turn out to be a very straightforward and uncomplicated action.

.   .   .

The first Japanese formation to approach Force Z was Lieutenant Yoshimi Shirai's squadron of eight Nell bombers of the Mihoro Air Corps. The squadron had been last but one to take off from the airfield at Tu Duam, and had still been well to the north when it picked up the sighting signals. It was probably the first squadron to pick up the signals, and this was why Shirai's planes came on to the scene before other squadrons who had been much nearer at the moment of sighting. Shirai had then led his squadron well behind the ships in order to make his bombing run from a more southerly direction and from out of the sun. These aircraft were the only ones of the Japanese bomber attack squadrons that were each carrying two 250-kg. bombs instead of one 500-kg. bomb. The formation consisted of only eight aircraft because one was unserviceable. Most of the reports of the British ships record that nine bombers took part in this first attack; only the destroyers *Express* and *Electra* reported the correct number. Lieutenant Shirai decided to attack the second of the British capital ships, possibly because he recognized it as *Repulse* whose main deck was known to be more thinly armoured than that of *Prince of Wales*. Settling into the tight formation they had used so often in practice, the Japanese started their bomb run.

The British ships had been following the Japanese formation both by radar and visually for some time. It is probable that *Repulse* saw the aircraft first when Shirai's squadron passed behind Force Z before coming into attack.

I had gone to B gundeck with the other watchkeeping fraternity for a smoke and a yarn. While we were up there an able seaman called our attention to the yardarm which was flying the signal 'A' with three digits which meant, and at this distance in time I'll swear to it, 'Aircraft presumed to be hostile, sighted on bearing (3 figures).' It struck me as odd that the person in our group who saw the signal was the one non-communicator present – and the one who could have pleaded ignorance of its significance. Almost immediately we turned and saw a large group of aircraft approaching and I did not stop to ask their business.

When I reached my Action Station – the Transmitting Room was traditionally well below the waterline for safety reasons – guns were firing, klaxons sounding, and I thought this was great. Action at last! (Boy Telegraphist W. C. Tinkler, H.M.S. *Repulse*)

On sighting the enemy, both big ships had hoisted the White Ensign – the traditional battle ensign – to fore and main masts, and more signal flags were soon flying, this time from *Prince of Wales*. The signal was 'BT3'; this was an order from Admiral Phillips to Force Z: 'SHIPS TURN TOGETHER 30 DEGREES TO STARBOARD'. The two great ships and the three destroyers started their turns towards the approaching enemy. Here was the old Navy in action, but it was not the old Navy's methods of manoeuvring battle squadrons by flag signal that was needed that morning.

The final approach by the Japanese from the south had placed *Prince of Wales* closer than *Repulse* to the enemy. Before the BT3 signal began to take effect, the Japanese bombers had been approaching *Prince of Wales* from the starboard bow; the four 5·25-in. turrets on her starboard side could all train on the approaching enemy. These were the sophisticated high-angle, dual-purpose guns of such high reputation and on which the hopes of the men in Force Z to defend them from aircraft attack mainly rested. It was a young R.N.V.R. officer, Lieutenant E. J. Kempson, the Starboard Forward High-Angle Control Officer, who started the action by reporting the first information about the approaching formation to the High-Angle Plotting Table situated below decks: 'Range 16,500 yards. Height 10,000 feet. Speed 200. Commence. Commence. Commence.'

This information was fed into the calculators of the Plotting Table and a constant stream of fuze setting calculations was soon being produced for the 5·25-in. turrets. When Lieutenant Kempson judged that his rangefinder was getting a really reliable range at about 12,000 yards,

Kempson ordered fire to be opened. The gunners in the turrets set the latest fuze settings and, as each gun was loaded, a lamp came on in Kempson's control position to indicate it was ready to fire. When all his lamps were lit, a hooter blew, Kempson pressed a button and all guns fired automatically at the precise moment that the fuze setting calculation was valid. More information was meanwhile being fed to the Plotting Station, fresh fuze-settings came back to the turrets and the eight starboard guns settled down to fire steady salvoes. Years of training were being put into practice.

Repulse's older and less numerous 4-in. guns were soon in action too, opening fire at about 11,000 yards. Initially only one gun would bear, but after it had fired four rounds a second gun also came into action. Sub-Lieutenant G. H. Peters, *Repulse*'s Forward High-Angle Control Officer, has recorded the effects of his fire. He saw immediately that his bursts were well to the right of the approaching Japanese aircraft, but though he kept correcting to the left, his shells continued to explode to the right of the Japanese. The same thing was probably happening to *Prince of Wales*'s fire. It was not that the Japanese aircraft were taking any evasive action; they continued to fly a straight course towards *Repulse*. What was happening was that both ships were swinging right in answer to the BT 3 signal and the Control Officers' corrections to the left were thus being counteracted. This turn soon caused all the guns on the starboard side of both ships to cease firing as the superstructure of their ships masked their line of fire.

When *Prince of Wales*'s 5·25-in. guns first opened up, they were the first naval guns that Admiral Phillips had heard fired in anger at sea since 1915. He soon realized that he had made a mistake in ordering the turn and countermanded it. More signals flags were hoisted: '5BT': 'SHIPS TURN TOGETHER 50 DEGREES TO PORT.' But a big ship cannot reverse course quickly, and *Prince of Wales* and *Repulse* continued to swing right, so much so their port-side guns were able to come into action and fire a few rounds. But then the turn to port started taking effect; the port-side guns had to cease fire; no guns fired for a few moments and finally the starboard-side guns came into action again. By now, of course, the Japanese had completed their approach and were about to bomb. Those officers in the British ships who had been in action against aircraft before were much disheartened by Admiral Phillips's handling of the situation. The correct action would have been to allow each ship freedom of action and so make best use of their anti-aircraft armament. These cumbersome fleet manoeuvres by flag signal had robbed the gunnery officers of the opportunity to settle down to the long 'run' of firing that would have enabled corrections to be steadily applied and more effective fire brought to bear. The unswerving approach of the compact formation of Japanese aircraft at a constant speed and height was really a gunner's dream. Admiral Phillips had made a fiasco out of his first handling of ships in action, but he was the first to acknowledge it and he gave orders that in future attacks captains were to have freedom of manoeuvre.

The Japanese bombers flew almost directly over the *Prince of Wales*. It was a terrifying few seconds for those above deck who were not engaged on some duty. They could only stand with a feeling of absolute helplessness and wait for the worst. But the bombs did not fall on *Prince of Wales*; *Repulse* was the target. The Japanese aircraft were just low enough for the bombs to be seen leaving their bomb bays. It was the bomb-aimer of Lieutenant Shirai's aircraft who chose the moment of release, and the remaining aircraft dropped their bombs with his.

Men on all the British ships watched in fascination as the salvo of bombs fell through the air. There is no evidence that Captain Tennant tried to avoid the bombs; he probably felt that a ship as big as *Repulse* could do little to avoid such a salvo in the few seconds available. The men aboard *Prince of Wales* and the destroyers watched the huge fountains of water, first one on the starboard side of *Repulse*, then several more on the port side; but there were no stabs of fire to indicate direct hits. As *Repulse* emerged from the spray, however, a small plume of smoke was seen coming from her upper deck near the aircraft hangar on the starboard side.

Each of Shirai's aircraft had only dropped one of its two bombs. Shirai intended to come round and bomb again later so that he could cause the maximum confusion among the British ships. Just one of the eight bombs had struck *Repulse*. It had cut through both the roof and the floor of the hangar and then the Marines' mess deck without exploding while leaving neat holes fifteen inches in diameter. The bomb finally burst on the armoured deck. If it had been an armour-piercing bomb, or one of the 500-kg. bombs that the other Japanese aircraft were carrying, it might well have burst through the one inch of steel plating which was all that was protecting the lightly armoured battle cruiser at this point and have exploded inside one of the boiler rooms. But this did not happen and the bomb caused no serious structural damage. The explosion had been so slight that, when the flagship asked for details, Captain Tennant's initial report was that his ship had only been damaged by a near miss. *Repulse* had been fortunate; her speed was unaffected and she steamed on with just the curl of smoke to show she had been hit.

When they released their bombs, the Japanese planes were seen to surge upwards like a flock of birds, and then to fly steadily away to the north. The high-angle guns of both ships and of the destroyers continued to fire for a few moments, but then stopped to conserve ammunition. *Prince of Wales*'s single Bofors guns, mounted on the quarterdeck and manned by Royal Marines, had opened fire and even her pom-poms had let off a few defiant rounds when the Japanese had been directly overhead though still out of the pom-poms' range. The 5·25-in. guns of *Prince of Wales* had fired 108 rounds and the 4-in. guns of *Repulse* thirty-six rounds. The British gunners were probably disappointed at failing to shoot down any of the

Japanese, but they had actually done quite well. No less than five of Lieutenant Shirai's eight aircraft had been hit by the fire, two so seriously that they left the scene of action and flew straight back to their airfield.

It is not possible to be precise about the effects of *Repulse*'s bomb hit. The official documents are not comprehensive and private accounts are sometimes contradictory. It is certain that small fires were started on the catapult deck, in the Marines' mess deck and in a near-by fan casing. Two men were trapped in the wrecked Torpedo Office and the Engineer's Office. A dynamo room was damaged and reported to be flooding, probably from the water of a fire party's hoses. Commander Dendy, in command of Damage Control, detailed five damage control parties and one shipwright's party to attend to the fires and the damage. *Repulse*'s remaining Walrus aircraft was a hazard. The blast of the bomb had knocked it half off its catapult trolley and its tanks were leaking petrol over the deck. The Walrus was hooked on to a crane and swung out over the side, and a Fleet Air Arm pilot, Sub-Lieutenant 'Ginger' Holden, a New Zealander, climbed out along the arm of the crane and released the Walrus, which was thus dumped into the sea.

Several men had been injured by blast and at least one was killed outright. The worst suffering came from the fracture of several steam pipes in the boiler room below the armoured deck; these were caused either by the shock wave from the bomb burst above the boiler room or by the resulting distortion of the framework supporting the pipes. Some stokers were terribly scalded and found great difficulty in getting out to reach medical attention. It was several minutes before the crew of a 4-in. gun detailed to help with the damage were able to get the burned stokers up on deck.

During the lull, to our amazement, some of the stokers had managed to climb up through the uptakes or ventilation system and were screaming for us to let them out. These uptakes were covered with heavy wire netting and I remember them trying to tear the wire away with their bare hands. They were like monkeys in a cage. Ginger Wilkinson soon took the initiative and we found a rope and weaved it through the wire and the twelve of us ripped the wire away and helped these poor fellows out. It was only then did we realize that they were naked and all badly burnt and screaming in agony. It was a horrible sight; they had been burnt by steam from broken steam pipes down below in the boiler room. We did our best to make them comfortable on the deck until the first-aid 'tiffys' arrived and took them down to the Sick Bay. (Able Seaman S. C. Baxter)

So ended the first attack. The Japanese had pressed it home in the most resolute fashion and had dropped their bombs with great accuracy. So much for the myth that the Japanese would be incompetent and ill-equipped adversaries, even though the small 250-kg. bomb that had hit *Repulse* had not caused any serious damage. Her guns and gun crews were all intact to face future attacks and her damage control parties would all be finished work and available for future demands before they were needed again. Despite the partial loss of steam pressure from one boiler room and the injuries to some of her stokers, *Repulse*'s steaming performance was hardly affected. The British ships had not been well handled by their admiral, but he had been taught a valuable lesson and had not had to pay too dearly for the learning of it.

This first encounter had lasted just twenty minutes from first to last sight of Lieutenant Shirai's formation. But while it had ended inconclusively, it was no more than a curtain-raiser. Besides the six remaining aircraft of Lieutenant Shirai's squadron there were seventeen more high-level bombers and no less than fifty torpedo bombers still looking for the British ships.

There was a small breathing space after the bomb attack and Force Z was able to steam a few miles nearer to its base at Singapore. Within ten minutes, however, *Prince of Wales*'s radar had picked up an even larger force of aircraft approaching, not from the north, as might have been expected, but from the south-east. There may have been momentary hopes that these were friendly fighters looking for the British ships but any such hopes were soon dashed when two separate formations of twin-engined aircraft similar to those that had just bombed *Repulse* were seen flying at about 10,000 feet. The time was 11.38.

These aircraft were more Nells, but this time from the three Genzan squadrons .that had flown together to a position so far south as to have been level with Singapore. The high-level bomber squadron of the Genzan Corps that had wasted its bombs on the destroyer *Tenedos* was now on its way home. The two remaining squadrons were both armed with torpedos – the Modified Type 91 Model 1 with the 149·5-kg. (330-lb.) warhead – so there would be no chance for the Genzan Corps to carry out the combined high-level bomb and low-level torpedo attack it had often rehearsed. The first of the Genzan squadrons was commanded by Lieutenant Kaoru Ishihara and was at the full strength of nine aircraft. On board one of Ishihara's planes, possibly in Ishihara's, was Lieutenant-Commander Niichi Nakanishi, the commander of the Genzan Corps who would coordinate the attack of the two squadrons. The second squadron was led by Lieutenant Sadao Takai, but it had started out with only eight aircraft, and one of these had been forced to turn back with mechanical trouble.

When Midshipman Hoashi had first transmitted the report placing the British ships just off the Malayan coast, one of the torpedo-bomber crews had radioed back to the airfield at Saigon asking to be told the depth of the water in the area where the British ships had been located. The reason for his request was that, if the water was less than a certain depth, the torpedo attack would have to be carried out at a lower level and at a slower speed than normal, otherwise a torpedo could strike the sea bottom and explode when it first entered the water and before it had settled to its running depth of six metres (about twenty feet). The Japanese Operations Officer at Saigon was surprised that the airmen should have paid attention to such a detail at this exciting time and was immensely heartened by the signal.

Lieutenant Sadao Takai recorded his emotions as his squadron was on its approach flight to the British ships.

In spite of repeated warnings to the crew members not to relax for a moment their vigilance to the rear and above our aircraft, everybody was straining to look ahead of our bomber to sight the enemy fleet. Everybody wanted the honour of being the first to see the British warships.

It was just past 1 p.m. [11.30 Singapore Time]. Low clouds were filling the sky ahead of us. Fully five hours had passed since we left Saigon that morning. The enemy fleet should become visible any moment. I became nervous and shaky and could not dismiss the sensation. I had the strongest urge to urinate. It was exactly like the sensation one feels before entering a contest in an athletic meeting.

At exactly 1.03 p.m. a black spot directly beneath the cloud ahead of us was sighted. It appeared to be the enemy vessels, about twenty-five miles away. Yes – it was the enemy! Soon we could distinguish the ships. The fleet was composed of two battleships, escorted by three destroyers, and one small merchant vessel. The battleships were the long-awaited *Prince of Wales* and the *Repulse*!

The 1st Squadron picked up speed and moved ahead of my squadron. Lieutenant-Commander Nakanishi ordered, 'Form assault formation!' A little later, 'Go in!'

The enemy fleet was now about eight miles away. We were still flying at 2,500 metres and were in the ideal position to attack. As we had planned, Nakanishi's bomber increased its speed and began to drop toward the enemy fleet. He was headed to the right and a little ahead of the warships. Trying to maintain the same distance and not be left behind, the bombers of my squadron also increased their speed as I started a gradual dive. I headed toward the left flank of the enemy formation. It was a standard practice among us for the 1st Squadron to attack the largest vessel, and the 2nd Squadron the next largest.

All crew members searched the sky vigilantly for the enemy fighters which we expected would be diving in to attack us at any moment. Much to our surprise not a single enemy plane was in sight. This was all the more amazing since the scene of battle was well within the fighting range of the British fighters; less than 100 nautical miles from both Singapore and Kuantan.

The small merchant ship seen by Lieutenant Takai and

thought by him to be part of the British fleet was the *Haldis*, now steaming hard to get away from this battle of which she had no wish to be a part. Takai is a little in error over his distances; Kuantan was only seventy nautical miles away, but the distance to Singapore was 150 miles.

The two Japanese squadrons separated while well out of the range of the British guns and manoeuvred themselves so as to approach the British force from different directions. The intention was to make simultaneous attacks on *Prince of Wales* and *Repulse* in a pincer-like movement to split the British gunfire, but for reasons which will be explained later, the attack of Lieutenant Takai's squadron on *Repulse* was a little late. We can thus leave his seven aircraft on one side for the moment and concentrate on those about to attack *Prince of Wales*.

The men on the British ships watched as this formation flew up from the south-east and then across the bows of their ships though still well out of range. The Japanese could be seen steadily losing height and at the same time forming themselves into a line-astern formation. Admiral Phillips was sitting in his own chair on *Prince of Wales*'s compass platform; Captain Leach and several other officers were stood near by – all were watching the Japanese aircraft. Admiral Phillips had already ordered Force Z to work up to 25 knots to present a more difficult target in this next attack, and all captains now had freedom to handle their ships independently. Phillips was observed to be 'very composed, very calm'. Lieutenant-Commander R. F. Harland, *Prince of Wales*'s torpedo specialist officer, remarked, 'I think they're going to do a torpedo attack.' Harland cannot be sure of the exact wording of Phillips's reply, but believes it to have been, 'No they're not. There are no torpedo aircraft about.'

The Japanese squadron continued to lose height, however, flew into some low cloud and then reappeared off *Prince of Wales*'s port bow. The deployment was completed when the line turned in three neat turns, three aircraft to each turn, to face *Prince of Wales*. Despite Admiral Phillips's belief, nine torpedo bombers, in a huge extended arc, were now flying steadily towards his flagship.

The Japanese planes now presented a good, no–deflection, target for the eight 5·25-in. guns on *Prince of Wales's* port side. These guns were controlled in two groups. Sub-Lieutenant G. H. Hopkinson was in charge of the after group, and post-action report shows that the Japanese aircraft were soon within range and he had commenced his 'run' of information to the plotting table; but 'permission to open fire from the Air Defence Position was so slow in being passed that I had to request it. Not till then was it given. Fire could have been opened earlier but for this.'* All eight 5·25-in. guns eventually opened fire with a crash and settled down to fire salvoes at the approaching Japanese. They were soon joined by the single Bofors gun on the quarterdeck, manned by the Royal Marines, then four sets of eight-barrelled pom-poms steadily pumping out their 2-pounder shells, and, finally, the Oerlikons and machine-guns.

The guns were all firing well, but no planes were seen to be hit during the first phase of the Japanese approach. On *Prince of Wales's* bridge, Captain Leach had the classic problem of how to manoeuvre his ship. On this occasion, this meant deciding at what point to turn to meet the Japanese attack so that the torpedo tracks could be combed. To turn before the torpedo bombers had committed themselves to dropping would be too soon and would also spoil the aim of his gunners. To turn too late might leave *Prince of Wales* as an easy broadside-on target for the Japanese torpedoes. It was a problem to which every Royal Navy captain gave much thought; now Captain Leach had to make the decision. When he decided the correct moment had arrived he ordered the helm 'hard-

---

* These reports continue to come from Public Record Office ADM 199/1149 unless otherwise stated.

a-port'. The great ship, steaming at 25 knots, started to come round. The next three minutes would show whether Captain Leach had chosen wisely.

Many of the British were amazed at the approach of the Japanese aircraft. The standard British naval torpedo bomber, the Swordfish, was a slow, lumbering aircraft whose torpedo approach had to be made at a speed of less than 100 miles per hour and at a height of only fifty feet, and, in their training, the British gunners had become used to this low and slow approach. It is obvious that the British did not believe that the Japanese had anything better than the Swordfish, and there was much surprise when these modern, two-engined aircraft commenced their approach at a far greater speed and at a greater height than anything expected. The Japanese Official History records that their planes carried out this attack at 150 knots (180 miles per hour), while the average torpedo release height was 33 metres (108 feet). Many men on the *Prince of Wales* believed that they were facing a low-level bomber attack rather than a torpedo attack.

The Japanese pilots released their torpedoes at distances varying between 1,500 metres (1,640 yards) and 600 metres (656 yards) from *Prince of Wales*. The destroyer *Express* was in the line of approach and may have been responsible for causing some of the Japanese to drop their torpedoes too early. Lieutenant-Commander Cartwright recorded that one torpedo exploded near his ship on first hitting the water, and this may be correct, though none hit *Express*. The turn ordered by Captain Leach caused the Japanese planes nearest *Prince of Wales*'s bow to lose its aim and this aircraft banked away and made for *Repulse* (its torpedo missing *Repulse*) while the other planes' torpedoes ran on towards *Prince of Wales*, set to run at a depth of 6 metres (nearly 20 feet) and a speed of 25 knots. The white lines of bubbles from the compressed air expelled by the torpedoes could clearly be seen on the surface, but the actual position of each torpedo was well ahead of its visible tracks. The torpedo dropped by the most daring of the Japanese pilots would take just over two minutes to reach its target.

The Japanese planes were too large and too fast, and their turning circle too great, for them to pull away quickly to safety, and to climb too soon would slow them down and expose their soft underbellies to British gunfire. The pilots now swept even lower, some of them straight at the *Prince of Wales*, machine-gunning as they came. The British gunfire rose to a crescendo. After firing twelve salvoes, the 5·25-in. guns had given up the controlled fire at individual planes and had gone over to 'barrage fire' in which shells were fired to explode in a wall ahead of the approaching aircraft in an attempt to make them drop their torpedoes too early. It is easy to use dramatic phrases like 'curtain of fire' and 'wall of death', but the Japanese seemed to fly straight through the 5·25s' barrage and the increasing fire of the close-range guns apparently unharmed. Certainly they were not deterred from dropping their torpedoes within range. Whether it was the unexpected height and speed of the Japanese approach or the wheel to port that *Prince of Wales* was now making, but this battleship was certainly not fighting off this aircraft attack.

A further difficulty was that many of the pom-poms were having problems with their ammunition; their small shells were becoming separated from their cartridges while being fed into the quick-firing weapons and were jamming the barrels. There were frequent stoppages; one of *Prince of Wales*'s pom-poms suffered twelve such failures, another suffered eight. This was particularly unfortunate because the low-flying Japanese aircraft were ideal targets for pom-poms. The weapon mounted on top of B Turret jammed just as one of the Japanese aircraft swept low over *Prince of Wales*'s bow, and the officer in charge, Lieutenant Ian Forbes, later claimed that 'this could have been shot down with ease'.

Several men describe their experiences during that attack. Ordinary Seaman W. E. England was acting as a lookout for the Lewis gun manned by the boxer Johnny King:

I focused my glasses at about 090 degrees to port and there, like dots on the horizon, I could see a formation of about ten planes skimming low on the water towards us. I had, of course, seen this low type of V formation before and awaited with excitement the massacre of this echelon monster that would frighten the life out of lesser mortals. But, no, not us; let them get nearer, catch them on the upsweep. A deafening crescendo of noise erupted into the heavens. Eight 5·25s fired simultaneously. I watched the shells burst – but not a plane was hit. To me they seemed *well* off target. The planes came on remorselessly as all the pom-poms, machine-guns and the Bofors gun opened up. All hell seemed to be let loose at once but nothing seemed to stop them and, as they passed over the masts, I could see the faces and goggles of the Japanese pilots looking down at us. Johnny King with his machine-gun might as well have had a pea-shooter for all the effect that he had on the oncoming horde.

Ordinary Seaman Derek Wilson recollects:

I was at the very top of the after superstructure, just between the two after 5·25 Control Positions on a circular platform about ten feet across. We had two old Lewis machine-guns mounted on tripods but mine was out of action so I had to act as an anti-aircraft lookout.

The torpedo planes approached at a lower level than those that had attacked *Repulse* and in looser formation. Our guns were deafening as they passed over. In this bewildering racket there can be few whose ears were more exposed to these detonations. Most other high positions had some protection from sound blast up to neck height. I recollect that one of my colleagues jumped on me to duck me as our own machine-gun, following its target, was swinging round towards me. At point-blank range, I just could not hear it above the racket.

I remember a feeling of relief as these planes passed over without bombing.

Yeoman of Signals E. A. Randall was on the Signal Bridge when it caught a burst of Japanese machine-gun fire.

I saw one of the bridge lookouts fall with four bullet holes in a pattern round his stomach and one of my signalmen also went down. His face, what was left of it, was just dripping blood, causing me to vomit.

But the Japanese did not get away entirely without loss.

One Nell was seen to lose height and to crash into the sea on the starboard side of *Prince of Wales*. Many accounts say that two Japanese planes were shot down in this attack, but it was not so.*

The aircraft that did crash was piloted by Petty Officer Katsujiro Kawada and there were no survivors. The Japanese Official History claims that Kawada's plane was hit soon after releasing its torpedo, and the pilot, realizing he was going to crash, attempted a suicide attack on *Prince of Wales* but never made it. Three of the remaining eight Nells were damaged by *Prince of Wales*'s gunfire, but none seriously.

Prince of Wales did not escape this attack unscathed. It had taken the Japanese aircraft about twenty-five seconds to reach the battleship after releasing their torpedoes; the torpedoes would take about one and a half minutes longer to reach or pass the ship. Captain Aylwin of the Royal Marines was with the pom-pom on the top of Y Turret, the 14-in. turret at the rear of the ship, where his men were in action.

We awaited the approach of nine torpedoes with baited breath, knowing that the Captain on the bridge would be doing his best by alterations of course to avoid all. Suddenly there was the most terrific jolt accompanied by a loud explosion immediately where I was standing on the port side. A vast column of water and smoke shot up into the air to a height of about 200 feet, drenching the quarterdeck, and a vast shudder shook the ship. At least one torpedo had hit us. The jolt received was just as though the ship had encountered a rock below the surface and, though hitting it, the ship's momentum was sufficient to clear it. When the smoke and spray had dispersed it was evident that the ship had taken on a 10-degree list to port and speed was considerably reduced.

Many other men remember this explosion. 'It was as if the ship had collided with a very solid object coupled

---

* The Compass Platform Narrative of *Prince of Wales* which was kept throughout the action is one report that erroneously records two planes shot down. The narrative is given in Appendix One.

with a leap in the air.' 'The ship appeared to be on springs; it lifted into the air and settled down again.' 'She seemed to bounce three or four times and then steadied herself.' 'There was a great thump and the ship's structure whipped violently like a springboard.'

Immediately after the explosion every man aboard *Prince of Wales* felt a most unnatural vibration running through the ship, 'like a boy running a stick along a stretch of corrugated iron, although much magnified'. This horrible sensation lasted perhaps thirty seconds and then ceased. In that half-minute, the ship had lost much speed and had taken on a violent list to port; there was also a distinct settling by the stern. Instruments soon recorded that the speed had dropped from 25 to 15 knots, that the list was an amazing 11½ degrees (some reports say 13 degrees) and that the stern had settled so much that the deck was only two feet above sea level instead of the normal twenty-four feet! Almost immediately it was clear that there were further dire after-effects of the explosion. Men in many parts of the ship found that their electrical supply had failed – there were no communications in these places, no lights, no power for many of the guns, no forced ventilation below decks.

So the first part of the first torpedo attack ended. The time between the first sighting of the two squadrons of Japanese torpedo bombers and the explosion in *Prince of Wales* had been a mere six minutes, but it has been worthwhile describing those minutes in detail since what happened during them is of much significance. On the Compass Platform of *Prince of Wales*, Admiral Phillips and Captain Leach were observed to say little over the effects of the torpedo hit, both appearing 'somewhat stunned'. This is not surprising when they must have known that their ship had taken in a massive tonnage of water and that severe damage had been done to at least one propeller shaft – for that, they knew, must be what the strange vibration had been. Reports would soon reach them moreover that most of their anti-aircraft guns were now without power.

What was reputed to be one of the most efficient fighting ships in the world had been crippled by a cylinder of steel and 330 pounds of explosive. The men on the bridge of *Prince of Wales* could now see another formation of Japanese torpedo bombers preparing to attack *Repulse*; they had no means of knowing that there were a further thirty-four torpedo bombers and twenty-three high-level bombers still in the area.

Prince of Wales will be left in her pitiful state and the fortunes of *Repulse* chronicled in the attack she was now about to face.

Repulse had witnessed the whole course of the torpedo attack on *Prince of Wales*. Captain Tennant, now that he had permission to manoeuvre freely, had drawn well away to starboard and *Repulse* was now perhaps a mile south of the flagship. (No accurate records of the relative courses and positions of the two ships exist and these details are based on estimates rather than reliable documents.) The initial deployment of the two formations of Japanese torpedo planes had been watched carefully, one *Repulse* officer remarking that 'they seemed to circle our ships like Red Indians about to attack wagons'; but it could be seen that the second Japanese squadron would not attack at exactly the same time as the first. The reason for the second squadron's delay may be found in the account of Lieutenant Sadao Takai who was piloting the formation's leading aircraft.

Coordinating my movements with those of the 1st Squadron, I led my squadron to the attack so that the enemy ships would be torpedoed from both flanks. The 1st Squadron was circling about four miles to the left and forward of the enemy ships and was about ready to begin its torpedo run. Anti-aircraft shells were exploding all around the circling bombers. The planes could be seen between the flashing patches of white smoke as the shells exploded.

Not a single anti-aircraft shell exploded near my squadron. Perhaps the clouds hid us from the enemy gunners. . . .

A long, narrow plume of white smoke drifted upward from the second battleship. Later I discovered that this was due to a direct hit scored by the high-level bombers of the Mihoro Air Corps which had made the first attack.

There was no doubt that it was a battleship. However, when I studied carefully the details of the vessel, it resembled – it even appeared to be – our battleship *Kongo*! We were completely unaware of the whereabouts of our own surface forces in this area; it was not impossible that it was actually the *Kongo* below us. The narrow escape of the *Chokai* from our bombers last night was still fresh in my memory, and my blood ran cold at the thought that we might be attacking our own vessels.

However, the 1st Squadron bombers were plunging into the attack, one after the other, and the enemy gunners (if it really was the enemy!) were filling the sky with bursting anti-aircraft shells.

I was still undecided about attacking. I called our observer and inquired as to the identity of the ship below us stating that it greatly resembled the *Kongo*. I was shocked to hear the observer reply, 'It looks like our *Kongo* to me, too.'

It was a terrible situation to be in. I could not decide whether or not the vessel was a British battleship or actually the *Kongo*. I had been on the *Kongo* three years ago, and was trying to remember details of the battleship. To confess, I had not studied to any extent the details of British warships, but had concentrated instead on American vessels. My knowledge of the British vessels was very meagre. . . .

The clouds were increasing steadily, and visibility was already reduced. It would be to our disadvantage to attack from the sterns of the enemy ships. Boldly the formation circled out from the protection of the clouds, and checked once again the position of our targets. We were able to get a very good look at the battleship.

I was greatly relieved. I was sure of it – the vessel below was not the *Kongo*.

It may be that the Takai Squadron's failure to come in at exactly the same time as the Ishihara Squadron was due to the fear that the ships below were Japanese, but it is also possible that, on this occasion, Lieutenant Takai just did not manage to achieve the simultaneous attack that he had practised so often with the other Genzan squadrons. Whatever the cause, there was a delay of about twelve minutes before his seven Nells were running in to attack *Repulse*. Captain Tennant prepared to turn his ship, this time to starboard, to meet the attack. Lieutenant Takai resumes his description.

I was nervous and upset and starting to shake from the excitement of the moment. . . . The *Repulse* had already started evasive action and was making a hard turn to the right. The target angle was becoming smaller and smaller as the bow of the vessel swung gradually in my direction, making it difficult for me to release a torpedo against the ship. It was expected that the lead torpedo-bomber would be compelled to attack from the most unfavourable position. This was anticipated; and it enabled the other planes following me to torpedo the target under the best of conditions.

The air was filled with white smoke, bursting shells, and the tracers of anti-aircraft guns and machine-guns. As if pushed down by the fierce barrage thrown up by the enemy, I descended to just above the water's surface. The airspeed indicator registered more than two hundred knots. I do not remember at all how I was flying the aircraft, how I was aiming, and what distance we were from the ship when I dropped the torpedo. In the excitement of the attack I pulled back on the torpedo release. I acted almost subconsciously, my long months of daily training taking over my actions.

Repulse's anti-aircraft armament opened up but no one had ever claimed that *Repulse* was a well-provided ship when it came to dealing with aircraft attack. It was true that she had twenty 4-in. guns compared with the sixteen 5·25-in. guns of *Prince of Wales*, but some of *Repulse*'s guns could not elevate to high level and others could not depress sufficiently to engage low-flying aircraft. All these old guns had either old-fashioned control systems or none at all, and many were not even power-operated but had to be trained by hand. It is probable that Captain Tennant put his main hope in the avoidance of the torpedoes by vigorous ship handling rather than in his anti-aircraft armament.

As the Japanese flew in those 4-in. guns that could bear opened fire and were soon joined by the close-range weapons. These, too, had their troubles, however; the best-placed pom-pom immediately had stoppages in six of its eight barrels because of separated cartridges – the same complaint suffered by *Prince of Wales*'s pom-poms. The only other pom-pom's electrical motor had been damaged by the earlier bomb hit and the changeover to manual operation had not yet been implemented. The result of all these problems was that *Repulse* was able to put up only the weakest of barrages.

The *Repulse* had been due for a refit and much better A.A. armament – six 4-in. hand-worked A.A. guns for a ship of that size! Some attacks were too low for these so we opened up with our triple 4-in. mountings – a surface-ship armament – without fused shells. They made a lot of noise and flashes; might have frightened some pilots but not the Japanese. Some took no avoiding action at all, flew over us and waved, aluminium shining in the dazzling sun and the Rising Sun painted on their rudders. Ye gods, and we couldn't shoot them down. Our Oerlikon guns were going right through their fuselages. (Petty Officer A. T. Skedgell)

A small mystery should be mentioned at this point. The Japanese Official History covers in some detail the separate attacks of each squadron of Japanese aircraft, and the attack of all of these, except one, fit in with British descriptions of events. The exception is a torpedo attack by eight Mitsubishi Nells of Lieutenant Takahashi's squadron of the Mihoro Air Corps which is supposed to have attacked *Repulse* within a few minutes of Lieutenant Takai's squadron. It is possible that in the confusion and stress of the attacks no one on the British ships noticed the arrival of Takahashi's squadron, and it may be that one of the squadrons, or perhaps some planes from each squadron, did not press home their attack but released their torpedoes from extreme ranges. As the planes of Lieutenant Takahashi's squadron were not hit by any anti-aircraft fire, it may be that their torpedoes were dropped from more distant positions at the same time as Lieutenant Takai was attacking. If this is the case, then fifteen Mitsubishis in all were aiming torpedoes at *Repulse*.

Once more the white lanes of torpedo tracks could be clearly seen marking the surface of the calm blue sea.

Once again, also, some of the Japanese pilots flew on close to the British ship and their gunners opened fire with machine-guns. Aircraft flew down both sides of *Repulse* and the exposed positions on the battle cruiser's decks and superstructure suffered far more severely than had *Prince of Wales* a few minutes earlier.

When we heard machine-gun bullets being sprayed along the upper deck by the Japanese torpedo bombers, my God, did we move! As one man we all rushed for cover in the well-hole of the 4-in. gun underneath the breech block. We heard the bullets ricocheting off the gun shield but we were lucky as no one was hurt. After the firing had stopped we had a look to see what had happened. It was a good job we had that steel plate round our gun and we were behind it, otherwise we would all have been killed. One of our big launches immediately behind our gun was riddled with bullet holes and we just couldn't believe how lucky we had been. (Able Seaman S. C. Baxter)

Another gun position was not so fortunate and a Royal Marine had 'half his head blown away' by a bullet which entered the turret through a small gap. His comrades took the body outside and laid him down in a quiet corner, and a sailor from a near-by ammunition party placed a heap of cotton waste over his face. This Royal Marine was only one of many gunners killed or wounded by the machine-gun fire. Others to suffer were a party of men keeping one of the anti-aircraft guns supplied with ammunition by carrying shells up from the deck below: there were no sophisticated mechanical hoists direct to this old weapon and several of the ammunition party were killed.

It was now, with the Japanese torpedoes approaching, that Captain Tennant's judgement in shiphandling was of the utmost importance. The man who was at the wheel in the armoured conning tower just below *Repulse*'s bridge was Leading Seaman John Robson.

The conning tower rapidly filled with officers and ratings. I was not relieved at the wheel and the P.O. Quartermaster stood by the bridge voicepipe passing wheel orders to me as we took avoiding turns. The noise was terrific when the guns fired. I always remember the

P.O. Quartermaster only a foot from me shouting the wheel orders to me – his face red with the effort to be heard above the noise all around us.

I thought about the Engineer Commander's orders given a long time ago, about going easy on wheel movements, as the steering mechanism engines were long past their best, but the Captain was giving alternate wheel orders against the torpedoes·approaching us as though we were a destroyer. The whole ship shuddered with the effect of twisting to port and starboard.

Many observers have praised the skill displayed by Captain Tennant on this occasion. He had managed to dodge the 'overs' from the attack on *Prince of Wales* and now he managed to avoid every one of the torpedoes dropped by these two Japanese squadrons. Captain Tennant later submitted his own, somewhat modest report.

The second attack was shared by *Prince of Wales* and *Repulse* and was made by torpedo-bomber aircraft. I am not prepared to say how many machines took part in this attack but, on its conclusion, I have the impression that we had succeeded in combing the tracks of a large number of torpedoes, possibly as many as twelve. We were steaming at 25 knots at the time. I maintained a steady course until the aircraft appeared to be committed to the attack, when the wheel was put over and the attacks providentially combed. I would like to record the valuable work done by all bridge personnel at this time in calmly pointing out approaching torpedo-bombing aircraft which largely contributed to our good fortune in dodging all these torpedoes.

These torpedoes were not the only hazard survived by *Repulse* at this time because a small formation of high-level bombers had flown over her at 12,000 feet and carried out a bombing attack at the very moment when the torpedo bombers were making their attacks. These six aircraft involved were from Lieutenant Shirai's squadron that had already made one attack on *Repulse*. This was the only squadron to have been carrying two bombs for each aircraft, and Shirai had brought the six aircraft that remained after two had flown home with serious damage from the first attack to achieve a perfect coordination with the low-level torpedo attacks. The six 250-kg. bombs failed to hit

Repulse, but they did fall in a tight group around the battle cruiser and it was a good example of precision bombing.

Lieutenant Takai's personal account does not mention the bombing attack, and he was probably never aware of it. After his gunners had machine-gunned *Repulse*'s deck, he sheered away from *Prince of Wales*, which loomed ahead of him and from which one or two guns opened fire on him briefly, but was able to climb away to safety. He then saw the spray of Lieutenant Shirai's bombs and presumed it was caused by torpedo hits scored by his squadron. He relaxed.

Suddenly my observer came stumbling forward through the narrow passageway, crying 'Sir! Sir! A terrible thing has happened!' When I looked at him in surprise, he shouted, 'The torpedo failed to release!'

I felt as though cold water had been dashed over my head and entire body. We were still carrying the torpedo! I forced myself to be calm and reversed our course at once. I passed on my new orders to the men. 'We will go in again at once.'

I began to lower our altitude as we flew through the clouds. The second torpedo run on the battleship would be very dangerous; the enemy gunners were fully alert and would be waiting for us. I did not like the idea of flying once again through a storm of anti-aircraft fire which would be even worse than before.

We dropped below cloud level. We were on the side of the enemy battleship, which was just swinging into a wide turn. Our luck was good – no better chance would come!

I pushed the throttles forward to reach maximum speed and flew just above the water. This time I yanked hard on the torpedo release. Over the thudding impact of bullets and shrapnel smashing into the aircraft, I felt the strong shock through the bomber as the torpedo dropped free and plummeted into the water. It was inexcusable that we did not notice the absence of this shock during the first torpedo run.

Repulse's lookouts saw Lieutenant Takai's aircraft coming in again, and at least one pom-pom and several smaller weapons opened fire on him but without causing serious damage. Takai too was unlucky. His torpedo missed. Another plane in his squadron had even more trouble with its torpedo release mechanism and the torpedo never did drop. Four planes from this squadron suffered slight damage from anti-aircraft fire.

The time that had elapsed between the first sighting of the torpedo bombers and the departure of Lieutenant Takai was approximately twenty-two minutes. The Japanese claimed no less than seven torpedo hits on *Repulse* – four of them by the squadron of Lieutenant Takahashi, whose attack cannot be pinned down in British accounts. In fact, only *Prince of Wales* had been hit. Twenty-five torpedo bombers and eight high-level bombers had now completed their attacks at a cost of one aircraft shot down, two seriously damaged and ten slightly damaged. It was now forty-seven minutes since the first attack on the ships had occurred and the British were still far from being out of danger. Twenty-six further torpedo bombers and seventeen high-level bombers remained to be reckoned with, although none of these had yet found the British ships and all would soon be running low on fuel.

But this first phase of hectic action was now to be followed by a lull.

10

The Lull

It was almost exactly noon when Lieutenant Takai turned from his second torpedo run and flew away, pursued by the few last rounds of *Repulse*'s anti-aircraft fire. Then it became uncannily quiet and the crews of the British ships were able to recover their breath. *Prince of Wales* wallowed sluggishly along at her reduced speed, and *Repulse*, possibly three miles away, emerged from the smoke of her own gunfire and from the hectic twisting and wheeling that had evaded so many torpedoes. The weather had now become very hot, and although the patchy low cloud was gradually extending, it was neither low enough nor thick enough to give any protection to the British ships. The sea continued to be as calm as the open sea ever could be.

The lull enabled both ships to survey their damage and the state of their anti-aircraft armament. Gunnery officers hurried across decks that a few minutes before had been swept by machine-gun bullets and visited their gun positions, calling for specialist ordnance or electrical ratings to repair damage and the many defects. Casualties among gun crews were replaced. Great heaps of empty cartridges were cleared from around the guns and dumped overboard.

Large numbers of spare men were detailed to form extra ammunition parties for those gun positions where the power hoists had failed, or where the normal supply route had been affected by damage and a makeshift alternative had now to be found. The pom-poms and Oerlikons in particular had consumed large quantities of ammunition and had to be resupplied. It was a laborious task, manhandling the cases of ammunition for the smaller guns or the heavy, greasy shells for the larger guns from magazines deep down in the ships up through several deck levels to the gun positions. At least one party had to improvise their supply by hauling individual boxes up a long plank by ropes, and as many as four parties of men might be required to keep one chain of supply going. Everyone knew it was a vital task and worked with a will though it was exhaustingly hot work in the lower decks.

The following report by Sub-Lieutenant G. H. Peters, who was in charge of *Repulse*'s forward group of 4-in. high-angle guns, is maybe typical of the decisions being taken; once this type of battle had opened, much depended on such young officers.

My impression is that there was an appreciable interval now, during which time the T.S. reported that circuits had failed at two of the 4-inch guns (which I don't know). I told the captains of these two guns that if an attack developed again before a Leading Torpedo Operator had fixed them up they were to do the best they could on local control at anything directly menacing the ship. I passed down to the T.S. to get hold of all available ammunition.

I reviewed the ammunition situation and, bearing in mind previous orders on the conservation of ammunition, decided that it was all or nothing as, if we did get away, fighter protection might have reached us by then. I therefore decided that I should from now on develop maximum rate of fire on all aircraft in range.

In the interior compartments of both ships there was also much activity. The main medical parties were stationed well below the armoured deck and had only sent small emergency parties out on specific calls for help while the ships had been in action. Now, with this lull, they were able to open the armoured hatches that protected them and take in more casualties or to send out larger parties under surgeons to establish new aid posts near the scenes of major damage.*

The Damage Control officers in *Prince of Wales* found

---

* Surgeon-Lieutenant S. C. Hamilton, one of *Repulse*'s doctors, wrote up a full report after the action of the first-aid arrangements in his ship and the way these worked during the action. This report is reproduced in full in Appendix Two.

their ship to be in a state that they would never have believed possible. The column of water seen to be thrown up by the explosion on the port side was at a part of the ship well covered by a new system of protection against underwater attack known as the 'liquid sandwich'. In this, a strengthened inner hull around the ship's vitals was itself surrounded by an inner air space; then with a belt of tanks always kept filled with either fuel oil or water; and finally with an outer belt of air-filled compartments.

Research had shown that a torpedo or mine explosion should dissipate its force in these three belts, that the resulting flooding should be very limited and the inner hull should remain intact. A torpedo hit near Y Turret should have been followed by only a slight list, a little flooding of the outer compartments and certainly not by any of the flooding of inner compartments now clearly taking place. The exact cause of this horrifying state of affairs on *Prince of Wales* has since been the subject of much learned investigation and speculation, and while there is no full agreement on the finer points, there is a general consensus about the broad reasons for the extensive damage. Before describing the full details of the damage and its effect upon *Prince of Wales*'s capacity as a fighting unit, it would be useful to look carefully at the probable cause.

Many observers have told of the huge column of water thrown up, presumably by a torpedo explosion, on the port side of *Prince of Wales* at a point roughly level with the mainmast. There is also the evidence of the peculiar lifting sensation of an explosion followed by the tremendous vibration. Finally, from a post-war investigation, it is known that there is a hole twelve feet in diameter with jagged edges bent inwards near *Prince of Wales*'s stern on the port side and close to where the port-outer propeller shaft leaves the hull, *even though no column of water was ever seen at this point*.

It is clear that the hole near the propeller shaft must have been caused by a direct hit from one Japanese torpedo. The absence of a column of water at this point is probably

Prince of Wales in First Torpedo Attack

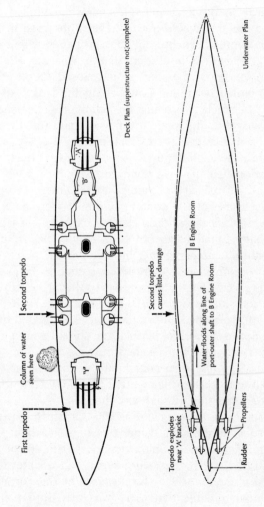

Deck Plan (superstructure not complete)

First torpedo

Second torpedo

Column of water seen here

'A'

'B'

'Y'

Underwater Plan

Second torpedo causes little damage

B Engine Room

Water floods along line of port-outer shaft to B Engine Room

Torpedo explodes near 'A' bracket

Propellers

Rudder

Diagram 1

explained by the fact that the ship's side here slopes steeply inwards to the keel and the somewhat muffled explosion under the ship would not have been observed in the white water being churned up by four propellers running almost at full speed. It is certain that it was the effect of this explosion under the stern which caused *Prince of Wales* to whip violently up and down along the length of her hull. The 'A' bracket securing the outer propeller shaft to the hull snapped, the shaft itself was bent, and the propeller was probably damaged. This distorted shaft, still being driven almost at full power, was the cause of the tremendous vibration felt by everyone in the ship. The propeller probably came off soon afterwards.

The cause of the column of water seen some 140 feet farther forward is not so easy to explain. No jagged hole has been found here, but it is known that four near-by watertight compartments became flooded. It is probable that, by coincidence, there was a second torpedo explosion at this point, the actual explosion being several feet out from the side of *Prince of Wales*. It may be that the shock-wave of the torpedo hit farther astern detonated this second torpedo just before it reached the ship. The explosion just away from the ship's side threw up a column of water higher than any seen later, and the underwater effect was probably to spring the rivetted plates over the four water-tight compartments that soon flooded.

There are even theories that a third torpedo was exploded at the same time, this one also being near the stern. There is no visible evidence, but the theory is based on estimates that the severe damage at the stern of *Prince of Wales* could not have been caused by one torpedo alone. It is just possible that there was this third torpedo, but for present purposes we must assume that there was only the direct hit at the stern and the explosion of a second torpedo near the hull farther forward.

What was of more importance to the men in *Prince of Wales* were the effects of the torpedo blasts. The first was seen in B Engine Room which was at the forward end of the 240-foot shaft that had been distorted by the explosion. Lieutenant Dick Wildish was in charge here.

All the main machinery set had an appalling, thumping-vibration and great clouds of muck, smoke, cordite fumes and dust poured out from the ventilation trunking. It was clear that the shaft had suffered serious damage and I gave orders for it to be stopped. This took some doing at 25 knots. I did this on my own authority. There was no time to consult. Once stopped, the vibration stopped. Then, and as my boiler room was still intact, and with thoughts of trying to maintain ship's speed during the attack, I decided to try running up the shaft again. As we reduced the 'astern' steam holding the shaft stopped, it started revolving again (I suppose indicating that the propeller was still there). However, as we started it going again, a rating reported that water was entering at the after end of the engine room. He was dead right. It was pouring through the flexible watertight shaft gland in the bulkhead. I rather think that we tried to tighten up on this but it was hopeless.

So we started all pumps on bilge suction – including putting the main circulator pump on bilge, instead of sea, suction. It soon became clear that the pumps could not control the flooding so we prepared to evacuate. There were certain steps to be taken to enable machinery to run on for as long as possible under flooded conditions. These concerned stopping sea-water entering the lubricating oil and boiler-feed water systems. Clearly, as my boiler room was still intact, it would help if my machinery could run on during the attack.

By the time we had done this, water was up around the control platform and rising fast. I gave the order to evacuate. As I followed the rest up, my Unit E.R.A. just ahead of me, the water swirled up in oily confusion just behind us. I have once since experienced a flooded machinery space and it is a horrifying, terrifying sight

Lieutenant Wildish's B Engine Room was not the only one in trouble. There were three other engine rooms – A, X, Y – each with its own boiler room. Each of the engine rooms was also connected to an 'action machinery room' where huge dynamos converted steam power to the electricity which was the source of power for the gun turrets, the ammunition hoists and the multitude of other pieces of equipment that enabled a warship to live and fight. In this area also were two reserve 'diesel dynamo rooms' and the harbour machinery room, which also provided electrical power. These vital compartments, deep in the heart of the ship, were well protected by steel armour and the 'liquid sandwich', and were normally considered safe from danger. Yet, not only was B Engine Room flooded, but Y Boiler Room, Y Action Machinery Room and one of the diesel dynamo rooms were also flooding fast; the harbour machinery room was flooding more slowly and Y Engine Room was losing its steam pressure: its turbines were shaking violently and a fractured oil pipe was robbing the turbines of lubrication. The engines in this room were quickly shut down. Thus, within a few minutes of first being hit, one of the world's most powerful and advanced battleships had lost half its primary power, and three of the seven machinery rooms that supplied electricity for the guns and the rest of the ship were also out of action. In addition, three out of the eight 5·25-in. magazines and a multitude of small compartments were also flooding.

This flooding was all the result of damage caused by the port-outer shaft during the few seconds when it ran amuck and before Lieutenant Wildish was able to stop it. The violent vibration of the 240-foot shaft had opened up bulkheads and smashed oil and fuel pipes right along its length. The passage in which the shaft was housed was a long corridor, the rear eighty feet of which was 'wide enough for three men to walk down side by side'. The stern torpedo explosion had torn open the rear end of this shaft passage and a tremendous rush of water along it was flooding the damaged compartments above, below and on both sides. The second torpedo explosion farther forward had flooded four watertight compartments, but the weight of water in these was almost as nothing compared to the vast quantity that had entered at the stern. Two levels of the ship, the hold and the lower platform, were flooded on the port side for a length of 270 feet, and, above these, water was forcing its way upwards through damaged ventilation trunks as high as the compartments on the middle deck.

Prince of Wales – Extent of initial horizontal flooding in hold level. (Based on survivors' reports to Bucknill Committee)

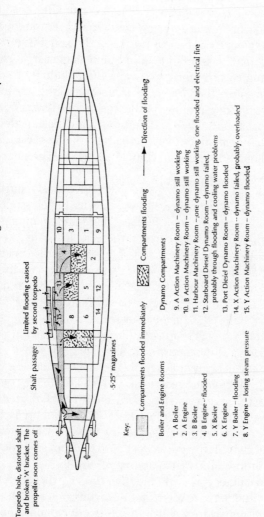

Torpedo hole, distorted shaft and broken 'A' bracket. The propeller soon comes off

Shaft passage

Limited flooding caused by second torpedo

5.25" magazines

Direction of flooding

Key:

☐ Compartments flooded immediately

▨ Compartments flooding

Boiler and Engine Rooms

1. A Boiler
2. A Engine
3. B Boiler
4. B Engine – flooded
5. X Boiler
6. X Engine
7. Y Boiler – flooding
8. Y Engine – losing steam pressure

Dynamo Compartments

9. A Action Machinery Room – dynamo still working
10. B Action Machinery Room – dynamo still working
11. Harbour Machinery Room – one dynamo still working, one flooded and electrical fire
12. Starboard Diesel Dynamo Room – dynamo failed, probably through flooding and cooling water problems
13. Port Diesel Dynamo Room – dynamo flooded
14. X Action Machinery Room – dynamo failed, probably overloaded
15. Y Action Machinery Room – dynamo flooded

Diagram 2

One of the worst upward escapes of water was found to be at places where circular discs in the trunking that were intended to be in place during action had been removed by seamen trying to obtain more fresh air, and there is also evidence that watertight doors and hatches were left open in the rush by men to escape the flooding.

It is probable that *Prince of Wales* took in 2,400 tons of water within four minutes of being hit and that, after this first big rush, a further steady flow was entering the ship as more compartments succumbed to the water pressure around them. The damage control parties had plenty to do.

Although *Prince of Wales* had been grievously hurt, the position should have been by no means hopeless. Repair work could contain any further flooding; pumping and counter-flooding could correct the list. Two of the four boilers with their engines and shafts were still capable of driving the ship along. None of the guns had actually been damaged and the ship should still have been able to defend herself. All of this might have been achieved had *Prince of Wales* not suffered a further severe, and again completely unexpected, setback, right on the heels of the first.

The electrical system of a King George V Class battle-ship had never been exposed to the stress of severe battle damage until this moment. As with the hull construction, the electrical arrangements were more sophisticated than in any previous ship.* Unfortunately, they simply failed to stand up to the strain imposed by the intense shock and vibration caused by the torpedo explosion and the sub-sequent inflow of a vast quantity of water.

The machinery rooms and the reserve diesel dynamo rooms contained between them six turbo-generators and two diesel generators which drove the dynamos supplying all the ship's electricity. Four of these eight dynamos failed immediately when the compartments in which they were situated flooded and a fifth dynamo went soon afterwards

* The electrical system was 220 volts on D.C.

for reasons which are not known because the two men tending it did not survive. * The four dynamos supplying the rear half of *Prince of Wales* were among those that had failed. In theory, it should have been possible to transfer power from the three remaining dynamos by means of ring-main breakers, but this was never satisfactorily done; such a major failure at one stroke had never been visualized and the design of the electrical system failed to cope with this emergency.

Prince of Wales's damage control organization never managed to overcome the electrical failure, and except for the battery-powered emergency lighting which functioned where the shock of the torpedo explosion had not ruined it and the occasional temporary supply brought in by emergency leads, no significant amount of electricity ever again reached the rear half of the ship. A warship lives on electricity and exactly half of *Prince of Wales* was dead.

These are some of the after-effects of the electrical failure:

Pumps

Prince of Wales had fourteen 350-tons-an-hour pumps and four bigger 1,000-tons-an-hour emergency bilge pumps – a total pumping capacity of 8,900 tons per hour – but every pump in the rear half of the ship was without power and could not operate.† Some pumping was attempted in the flooded midship sections, but no progress was made against the volume of water entering at the stern.

* The five dynamos that failed were No. 4 Turbo Dynamo in the harbour machinery room, port side; No. 5 Diesel Dynamo in the starboard diesel room; No. 6 Diesel Dynamo in the port diesel dynamo room; and Nos. 7 and 8 Turbo Dynamos in X and Y Action Machinery Rooms respectively.

† The pumps that failed were Nos. 9, 10, 11, 12, 13 and 14 Salvage Pumps, X and Y Emergency Bilge Pumps and Y Fire and Bilge Pump.

Counter-Flooding

One of *Prince of Wales*'s greatest needs was a level or almost level platform so that the guns could be trained. With the 11½ degree list at that time, not one of the eight power-operated 5·25-in. gun turrets could be trained. Captain Leach immediately ordered compartments in the starboard side of the ship to be flooded to correct the list and some counter-flooding was possible in the forward and midship compartments on the starboard side. The list was thus reduced to 10 degrees, but there was so much water in the port side of the ship that no further improvement was possible.

Communications

There was no telephone communication at all with the after part of the ship. Messages had to be passed by hand and much effort and time was wasted. Details of the damage in the rear half of the ship were thus slow to arrive at the damage control centre and repair parties were often working on less serious tasks when more urgent ones were left unattended. One example of this occurred when electrical repair parties were dragging emergency cables to individual 5·25-in. turrets while hardly any effort was being made to correct the more fundamental ring-main faults which were preventing power being supplied to the entire rear half of the ship.

Ventilation and lighting

There was no powered ventilation and only emergency lighting in all the compartments below deck in the after half of the ship. This was particularly serious for the repair parties, who rapidly became exhausted and therefore less effective, and for the men manning X Boiler Room and Engine Room and A Engine Room. These were in perfect running order, but became so hot that men collapsed with the heat or had to be relieved every few minutes – temperatures as high as 150°F (66°C) were recorded. The relief method did not last long and these compartments had to be left with machinery unattended, except for the occasional visit of an engineering officer or senior rating. Even this system failed eventually since the men who made these short visits had to have fifteen minutes' recovery time in the open air after each visit.

Another place affected by the lighting and ventilation problems was the after medical station which was forced out of its safe place below deck to the ship's chapel on the next deck up, but the many wounded and semi-suffocated men here soon overflowed on to the next deck above and had to be placed in a space known as the Cinema Flat. This was later to have tragic consequences.

Steering

Although the rudder may not itself have been damaged by the stern torpedo explosion, both the steering motors immediately went dead following the electrical failure. After several messages had been passed by hand between the main and the after steering positions, an attempt was made to change over to emergency steam-operated steering, though this was probably never achieved.

Anti-aircraft armament

The four 5·25-in. turrets in the after half of the ship – P3, P4, S3 and S4 – were all without power and were too big and heavy to be trained manually. Two of the four forward turrets suffered temporary failures, but even while these were soon rectified, the list of the ship was so steep that none of the four forward turrets could swing its gun from side to side although all the weapons could be elevated. Some of the pom-poms suffered temporary power failures, but these mostly remained in action, though continually plagued with stoppages as a result of their faulty ammunition belts.

Such was the plight that poor *Prince of Wales* found herself in during the lull in the action: not sinking, not completely out of commission, and not in a completely hopeless position, but certainly a cripple at this stage. At 12.10 the two black balls which told the other ships of Force Z that *Prince of Wales* was 'NOT UNDER CONTROL' were hoisted. The Japanese pilot who had put his torpedo into the battleship's port-outer propeller shaft while that shaft was revolving at 204 revolutions per minute had set off a chain reaction that had brought this great ship to her knees. It is unlikely that a hit at any other part of the ship could have had such serious consequences.

In some of those parts of *Prince of Wales* not directly affected by the damage and flooding, there was now an air of unreality and aimlessness. One man says that, 'There seemed to be lots of people with nothing to do and nowhere to go; many laid down and seemed to sleep on mess tables and stools.' It is probably an exaggeration to say that the organization of the ship was breaking down, but it was certainly under a great strain and it was at this time that the lack of a proper working-up period was felt. Telegraphist C. V. House is a good observer of the scene in the forward part of the ship below decks. He had been fallen out from duty and, with several other spare men, was shut in a mess deck. He had felt the torpedo explosion.

For a few moments my brain worked fast – would there be an internal explosion? Shut in a steel box below the water-line, was I going to be drowned like a rat? Seconds ticked away, and then I noticed the chap still sitting on his haunches in the gangway and as white as a ghost. I went over and spoke to him asking if there was anything I could do. I tried to chat but it didn't seem to ease the position at all.

I asked him if he thought there was any possibility of our getting out of the mess deck on to the upper deck, but he said, 'No. Not an earthly!' By then the ship had begun to list, not the usual kind of roll that I had always been used to, but a gradual tilt one way, steadily increasing, until the ship was canting at an alarming angle. I remember seeing a streak of red running across the deck and following it up found it to be beetroot juice which had spilled from one of the mess shelves. Seeing there was nothing to be done but to sit and wait events, I entered one of the messes and sat down, looking at the pictures in an American magazine, *Life*.

It was about this time that a bunch of engineer officers made their way into the mess deck in order to open up various valves and flood several starboard compartments – bathrooms and such like – in an effort to correct the list and trim the ship off. The first arrivals had no spanner with which to turn the wheels, or the knowledge (apparently) of which wheels to turn. The arrival of a warrant engineer who knew his job saved them from ridicule and the flooding commenced. It definitely stopped the listing, and after a while the ship appeared to level up a little, although she never came back to an even keel. It was about then that I noticed the Leading Tel. previously mentioned had left the mess-deck; apparently he managed to slide out as the flooding party came in. By now it was dinner time, but as the cooks had all been busy as 'repair parties' or 'first aid parties' there was no possibility of getting anything to eat.

There were men in *Prince of Wales* who were beginning to think that the ship might not survive.

I think I realized the ship was going to sink very early on because the list we had taken on showed we were badly crippled and the torpedo bombers could easily run a shuttle service until we were finished, even if it took days. Naturally there was a sensation of astonishment that our tremendous ship was knuckling under so easily and apprehension at what was going to happen to me personally. However, there was no time to sit and think it all out! (Sub-Lieutenant G. A. E. Brooke)

Many others were not so pessimistic and there was excited anticipation by some that *Prince of Wales* might be 'going to Aussie for repairs'.

If *Prince of Wales* contained men who were full of gloom, *Repulse* did not. This great-hearted ship had performed well and her crew knew it. There was immense pride in the ship-handling qualities of Captain Tennant, and there was much excited talk of how many torpedoes had so far been dodged – 'nineteen' is the figure quoted by *Repulse* men. Those men above decks on *Repulse* were shocked to see the state of *Prince of Wales* and many have recorded their disappointment in the performance of this new battleship with its high reputation. *Repulse* knew that its own anti-aircraft armament was primitive and weak, but great things had been expected of the modern high-angle anti-aircraft armament of *Prince of Wales*.

During the lull, *Repulse* completed most of the immediate repair work connected with her one bomb hit, though a small fire persisted and some men remained trapped in a compartment below the catapult deck. The medical work was well in hand, as was the repair of gun faults and the restocking of anti-aircraft ammunition. On her flag bridge, three passengers had had a grandstand view of this aircraft *versus* warship engagement. The *Daily Express* reporter, O'Dowd Gallagher, and the American, Cecil Brown of the Columbia Broadcasting System, were making notes of the action, and Lieutenant Horace Abrahams, the naval photographer, had taken many priceless photographs.

Repulse had emerged from the first phase of the battle almost unscathed. All her engines and armament were in working order and her crew's morale was high. Captain Tennant turned his ship towards *Prince of Wales*, still about three miles away, to see how he could help the flagship. But *Repulse*'s lamp signals asking about *Prince of Wales*'s damage and whether her wireless was out of action brought no reply. It was as though the flagship was too preoccupied with her grievous condition to have time to answer solicitous inquirers.

Captain Tennant had asked his signal office what signals *Prince of Wales* had sent to Singapore during the recent attacks and was astonished to be told that the flagship had still not transmitted. Tennant decided he must now send a signal, and at 11.58 what was the first message to be sent by Force Z since it had left Singapore two days earlier was tapped out from *Repulse*.

FROM REPULSE   TO ANY BRITISH MAN OF WAR
ENEMY AIRCRAFT BOMBING. MY POSITION
134 N Y T W22X09.

Prince of Wales's wireless aerials had been partially

affected by the shock of the torpedo explosion, but it is certain that her ability to send signals had not been affected. Petty Officer Telegraphist Arthur Best was the senior of the ratings in charge of the two transmitting rooms inside the armoured citadel, and he states that 'up till a few minutes before she sank, H.M.S. *Prince of Wales* was capable of sending any form of wireless message over any distance'. It is an important point because the impression is sometimes created that Admiral Phillips had not been able to send this initial emergency signal as *Prince of Wales*'s transmitter was out of action. The truth is simply that Captain Tennant had taken matters into his own hands and had got this first vital signal away without receiving permission from the flagship. The view in *Repulse* over the long delay in sending the first signal was that 'had Captain Tennant been in command of the force, as he invariably had been in command of much larger forces for the last two years, the story might have been different'.

It took six minutes for the Naval Signal Station at Kranji on Singapore Island to decode and process the signal. It was the first news received in Singapore of Force Z since the signal from *Tenedos*, earlier that morning, which had stated that the British ships were returning directly to Singapore. It was the first indication that there had been a diversion to Kuantan or that Japanese aircraft were attacking, although Force Z had first been shadowed by Midshipman Hoashi's aircraft nearly two hours earlier.

It took a further fifteen minutes for the signal to reach the operations room in Air Headquarters at Sime Road. An immediate order was sent to Sembawang airfield, where the Australians of 453 Squadron had been standing by for two days to help, and their eleven serviceable Brewster Buffaloes had all taken off within five minutes. The formation was led by Flight Lieutenant Tim Vigors, an Irishman and an ex-Battle of Britain pilot in temporary command of the squadron. But it was 150 nautical miles, one hour's flying time, to the area off Kuantan where Force Z was in trouble. The R.A.F., who had kept a scarce fighter squadron out of the fighting to help the Navy, were very annoyed at not being kept informed of Force Z's progress and at not being called upon to help earlier. Yet had it not been for Captain Tennant's breaking of Force Z's self-imposed radio silence, the Buffaloes would still not have taken off even by this late stage.

The contest so far had been almost exclusively between the Japanese attack planes and the two capital ships. The closest of several less fully engaged participants were the three destroyers. These were keeping a sharp watch by Asdic for submarines, but the Japanese submarines had not managed to reach the scene of this action. The destroyers had tried hard to help defend the bigger ships and had opened up with every gun which could engage aircraft.

Express had been in the direct line of the first wave of torpedo bombers attacking *Prince of Wales*, and her log shows she believed that three torpedoes had been deliberately aimed at her, one of them seeming to pass directly under the destroyer but evidently not running shallow enough to strike. The Mitsubishi had then flown straight over *Express*, machine-gunning as she went but causing no casualties. Stoker Robert Burnett had been helping to keep one of the 4·7-in. guns on *Express* supplied with ammunition.

I had to stand on a table maybe one yard square. There was a pole at one corner fastened to the deck; it had a belt on the pole fastened to my waist to keep me from falling off if the ship lurched. While another stoker and I were handing shells and cordite from the hoist to the gun, there was a big Australian seaman lying on the deck screaming. I wondered at times where the biggest danger was coming from – him or the bombers. Anyhow, our doctor came up and gave him a needle that quietened him down. Funny thing about that Aussie, before there were any signs of action he walked round the upper deck with a large sheath-knife in his belt saying what he was going to do with the Japs if we clued up with them.

I kept on handing shells and cordite up, wringing with sweat, till I heard a voice shout, 'Are you going to send some bloody H.E.

shells up here?' I looked up and saw Gunner Petty Officer Appleby. I told him I was giving what was handed to me. He then replied, 'They are bloody star shells.' I found out that they were the only shells we had left.

Surgeon-Lieutenant T. E. Barwell also remembers the Australian seaman as well as another incident.

The only casualty *Express* had was an acute 'shell-shock'. He was a giant of a man we had embarked on the way out and was obviously mentally unfit to be at sea. We had sent him ashore on arrival at Singapore but he had been returned to us. When the Japs came over he became quite helpless with fright and I was called to see what I could do as he was standing in the way with a 4·7-in. shell in his arms simply quaking with fright. We managed to get him down below, where I gave him an injection of a half-grain of morphine to keep him quiet.

There was one amusing episode. When we first arrived in Singapore the captain, Lieutenant-Commander Jack Cartwright, sent his servant Clingham ashore to buy him a papya, or 'pawpaw' as Clingham called it as he came from St Helena and that was the South African name I think. He took it into Cartwright next day at breakfast time, but was told to take it away and bring it back when it was ripe. In the middle of the action, amidst all the gunfire, Clingham arrived on the bridge with the pawpaw, saluted, and said, 'Captain, sir. Your pawpaw's ripe. Will you have it now, sir?'

Electra and the Australian ship *Vampire* had also been firing on the Japanese aircraft with all they had, and had been machine-gunned in return; *Vampire* claimed to have damaged at least two enemy planes. During the lull, both of these ships were ordered to search in the wake of *Prince of Wales* for men believed to have been blown overboard by the shock of the torpedo explosion, but nobody was found and it may be that the 'man overboard' scare resulted from a mistaken report in *Prince of Wales*, though several witnesses say this did happen.

A less involved observer of the battle was *Repulse*'s Walrus aircraft which had been flying an anti-submarine patrol around Force Z when the action opened. The petty officer who was piloting the Walrus – his name is not recorded – continued to circle the area throughout the entire action. The Walrus was seen by many of the Japanese pilots, but was completely ignored by all of them and the slow, lightly armed Walrus could do nothing to attack the faster Japanese aircraft. *Repulse* never got the chance to take her aircraft back again, and the Walrus eventually flew off towards Singapore, but ran out of petrol on the way and landed on sea. A friendly Catalina found her and dropped food and water, and the destroyer *Stronghold* eventually towed the Walrus into Singapore.

The crew of another aircraft witnessed the action, or most of it. This was Midshipman Hoashi's aircraft which had first spotted the British ships. Back in Saigon, Vice-Admiral Matsunaga ordered Hoashi to maintain contact until 13.30 and sent off another plane to relieve Hoashi at that time. It was now essential for the Japanese to keep in touch with the British until the conclusion of the action, whenever that might be. It was their greatest good fortune that no British fighters had yet appeared to drive away the shadower. The Japanese were operating at about 450 nautical miles from their main base; the British were 150 miles from their Singapore airfields and only sixty miles from Kuantan, where there was a military airfield built specifically for the defence of Malaya!

Just before the present lull, Hoashi had left the scene of action and flown to Kuantan airfield where he dropped his two 50-kg. bombs. This small contribution was to deter any British aircraft that might have been there from taking off, but the initiative was wasted. Kuantan airfield was empty. The Japanese pilot returned to the British ships after an hour's absence and resumed his watching and reporting.

There was a final spectator. The old steamer *Haldis* had been near enough to see all these bombing attacks and her log records the main events as seen from her bridge. It identifies the two big British ships by name, but the destroyers only by the pennant numbers painted on their fo'c'sle sides. The master of the *Haldis*, Captain A. Hall, got the two big ships mixed up after the air attacks started, however, and each is recorded as being the recipient of the other's attacks. Captain Hall, declining to become involved in this dangerous-looking action, had pushed on as fast as he could and *Haldis* soon disappeared from the scene.

11

The Final Round

Any hopes that the men in the British ships may have had that they had seen the last of the Japanese aircraft, or that help in the form of friendly aircraft might arrive before the next Japanese attack, were soon dashed. At 12.20 hours, after the lull had lasted just twenty minutes, look-outs on all the British ships saw a large formation of aircraft to the east. These aircraft soon lost height and split into two formations as though preparing to make further torpedo attacks.

Prince of Wales and *Repulse* were still about two miles apart. *Prince of Wales* could just manage 15 knots on her starboard engines, but could not steer and still had a huge list to port. *Repulse* was in fine form and had been coming across to see if the flagship could be helped in any way when the Japanese aircraft were sighted. It was exactly at this moment that the flight of Buffalo fighters was taking off from Sembawang airfield 150 miles away.

The aircraft seen approaching were the entire strength of the Kanoya Air Corps: twenty-six Mitsubishi Bettys led by Lieutenant-Commander Shichizo Miyauchi. The Kanoya aircraft were all carrying the heavier Model 2 torpedo with the 204-kg. (450-lb.) warhead. These were the aircraft which had been detached at the last moment from the Philippines operation and diverted to Indo-China at the time when the Japanese learnt of the arrival at Singapore of *Prince of Wales* and *Repulse*. The Kanoya crews had actually been flying back to Indo-China from well to the south when they somewhat belatedly picked up Midshipman Hoashi's signals. They had immediately turned west, but had at first been unable to find the British ships below the thickening cloud cover and had been on the verge of abandoning the search because of low fuel tanks.

Then a solitary aircraft, flying at a lower level, was seen through a gap in the cloud. Lieutenant-Commander Miyauchi turned towards it. It was *Repulse*'s Walrus, still on her anti-submarine patrol. Soon, three destroyers and finally the two bigger ships came into sight.

There were three Kanoya squadrons, commanded by Lieutenants Nabeta, Higashimori and Iki, with Lieutenant-Commander Miyauchi flying in one of Lieutenant Nabeta's aircraft. Miyauchi could not take too long preparing for the attack of his air corps because of the fuel position, and it is possible that the attack which developed was not the result of specific orders from Miyauchi but an 'every man for himself' affair. The Kanoya aircraft quickly split themselves into two groups. The first contained the seventeen aircraft of Lieutenant Nabeta's and Lieutenant Higashimori's squadrons and made as if to approach *Prince of Wales*, though some of them were intending to turn away at the last minute and attack *Repulse*. The third squadron, Lieutenant Iki's with nine aircraft, was farther away. Most British reports record the approach of the two formations, but there were so many aircraft approaching, and changing courses as they did so, that the British observers, used by now to seeing flights of eight or nine Japanese aircraft at a time, mostly recorded two groups of nine aircraft making this attack, not realizing that an extra squadron was present. No one recorded that these Bettys were a different type of aircraft from all those that had attacked before.

The attacks on *Prince of Wales* would develop just two minutes before those on *Repulse*, so it is the attack on the flagship that must come first in our narrative.

The hurried and somewhat ragged development of the Kanoya aircraft did not give *Prince of Wales* much time to prepare for action, though there was little she could have done in any case. The remaining engines were worked up from 204 to 220 revolutions to push along the sluggish, waterlogged cripple a little faster, and the gunners once more stood by ready to open fire, but only two of the four 5·25-in. turrets on the starboard side, from which the Japanese attack appeared to be coming, were still workable, and the close-range weapons were not in much better shape. Ordinary Seaman Derek Fox was a lookout on *Prince of Wales* and compares this attack with the earlier neat, line-abreast approach of the earlier torpedo assault on his ship.

The attacking policy of the Japanese seemed to change to individual but simultaneous approaches from many different angles. As *we* were not in a position to manoeuvre, this may have been adopted to confuse our central gunnery control. I was surprised how quickly these attacks developed and later formed the impression that there might have been a slight haze at this time, but this impression might have been caused by the confusing manner of approach.

The few guns aboard *Prince of Wales* that could do so opened fire. The four 5·25s of S1 and S2 turrets did their best, but the angle of the deck prevented any of them from depressing below 5 degrees of elevation and they could not hit the low-flying Japanese aircraft. S3 and S4 turrets were without power, and although their crews had sweated to drag the turrets round by rope or chain to bear on the approaching targets, they never opened fire. Several of the pom-poms were also without power, and others soon jammed again with the old ammunition faults. *Prince of Wales* was in such a poor state that she was virtually incapable of defending herself and it is not surprising that no Japanese aircraft was shot down in this attack.

The first six Mitsubishis came in at differing heights and from different angles, but all were aiming at the starboard side of *Prince of Wales*. Some of the Japanese pilots came right in to 500 metres (under 550 yards), almost point-blank range for torpedo dropping, before releasing and starting to break away. So close did the Japanese release their torpedoes that one Lewis gun on *Prince of Wales*, manned by Petty Officer Coles, fired at a torpedo when it was released in a vain attempt to detonate it before it entered the water. Once again some of the Japanese pilots had to fly almost over the battleship, but on this occasion there was no machine-gunning. As the attackers flew away, the tracks of several torpedoes approaching *Prince of Wales* could be clearly seen. There was nothing Captain Leach could do; the steering gear of his ship was completely useless. Hundreds of men held their breath and waited for the worst.

The torpedoes could hardly miss. British reports are again confusing, but it seems that the first hit was well forward, near the stem of the ship, and that the explosion at this narrow point blew a hole clean through the ship and out on the port side. The second hit was just forward of the bridge and produced a huge tower of water and what appeared to be oil from a ruptured fuel tank. A third torpedo attack struck farther aft, alongside the rear 14-in. gun turret, and this again threw much water up into the air to descend on the deck and soak every man near by. (One sailor is believed to have been washed overboard by this deluge.) A fourth torpedo struck just forward of the stern, bending the outer propeller shaft inwards and jamming it between the inner shaft and the hull. The turbines in A Engine Room stopped dead. The whole effect of these four successive explosions on the starboard side of the ship was 'quite stupendous, the ship appeared to jump sideways several inches, rather in the manner of an earth tremor'.

There is no need here for a long technical description of the damage and after-effects. The earlier counter-flooding of many of the watertight compartments in this side of the ship now aggravated the damage of the latest hits. The effect of an explosion against a water-filled compartment was more extensive than that against an air-filled one and the consequent damage done by these explosions had therefore extended much farther into the ship. Certainly many of the fuel tanks were pierced so that not only water but thick diesel oil was also entering the ship. It has been estimated that *Prince of Wales* had, with the earlier flooding, now taken in almost 18,000 tons of water. Apart from this huge amount of flooding, only one of her four engines was now giving power and only two of the eight dynamos were supplying electricity for guns, lights, ventilation and the all-important pumps that could alone save the ship.

There was only one small benefit from these hits: the inrush of water on the starboard side almost entirely corrected the previous list to port. In addition, the explosions had caused no great loss of life; some men had been trapped and drowned in the isolated compartments which were their Action Stations, but they had not been many and there had been no internal explosions. But *Prince of Wales* could now only make 8 knots and was settling still deeper in to the water. The pumps and repair parties were not winning the mariner's age-old battle with the sea.

From the first sighting of the Japanese aircraft to its conclusion, this attack on *Prince of Wales* had taken only five minutes. Only six of the twenty-six Kanoya aircraft had dropped their torpedoes, and it is a measure of how helpless was *Prince of Wales*, and how close-pressed the attack, that four torpedoes out of six had scored hits. The remaining Kanoya crews now turned their attention on the second big British ship.

The attack by the remainder of the Kanoya aircraft on *Repulse* was a confused affair and not easy to describe in any simplified way. Eight Bettys from the leading group of Kanoya aircraft – probably three from Lieutenant Higashimori's squadron and five from Lieutenant Nabeta's – turned away almost immediately from that group, joined up with the nine aircraft of Lieutenant Iki's squadron and formed themselves into one loose attacking force approaching *Repulse* from many different angles but most heading for the battle cruiser's starboard side. Captain Tennant had seen the first group of Japanese aircraft flying across his bows making for *Prince of Wales*, and could also see the second group approaching the starboard side of his own ship. Once again he started manoeuvring and turned

Repulse into the attack. *Repulse* was still fully effective, had so far only been hit by the one small bomb thirty minutes earlier and her guns were firing well. Able Seaman S. C. Baxter was on a 4-in. gun on the starboard side boat deck during this attack.

We continued with our rapid fire until we had a misfire. There was a shell in the breech and the firing mechanism which had operated should have fired the shell. The drill here, according to the book, was to go through the misfire drill and, if it still had not fired, to wait half an hour before opening the breech to remove the shell in case of a premature explosion, but that all went by the board under the circumstances. Ginger Wilkinson opened the breech and out popped the shell, which in no uncertain terms was immediately dumped over the side with a sigh of relief from all of us.

Repulse started her turn to starboard, but the eight Japanese planes on that side did not press their attack and released their torpedoes at about 2,280 metres (2,500 yards) out, the Bettys then turning away without any being shot down. But, just at this moment, three of the Japanese aircraft suddenly peeled off from the group that had appeared committed to attacking *Prince of Wales*, quickly switched towards *Repulse*'s port side and dropped their torpedoes. Everyone who saw it said how neatly the feint towards *Prince of Wales* and then the attack on *Repulse*'s exposed side was carried out.

Repulse was now in an impossible position. There was no chance that she could manoeuvre to avoid both salvoes of torpedoes. The Japanese move had been so precisely executed that Captain Tennant could do no more than continue in his attempt to avoid the eight torpedoes dropped earlier. In his post-action report he summarizes the incident:

About three miles away, the Japanese had split up into two formations and I estimated that those on the right would launch their torpedoes first and I started to swing the ship to starboard. The torpedoes were dropped at a distance of 2,500 yards and it seemed obvious that we should be once more successful in combing their tracks. The left-hand formation appeared to be making straight for *Prince of Wales* who was at this time abaft my port beam. When these aircraft were a little before the port beam at a distance of some 2,000 yards, they turned straight at me and fired their torpedoes. It now became obvious that, if these torpedoes were aimed straight, *Repulse* would be most certainly hit as any other alteration of course would have caused me to be hit by the tracks of those torpedoes I was in the process of combing. One torpedo fired from my port side was obviously going to hit the ship and it was possible to watch its tracks for about a minute and a half before this actually took place. The ship was hit amidships, port side. The ship stood this torpedo well and continued to manoeuvre and steamed at about 25 knots.

It is a calm description of a hectic moment. *Repulse's* guns had been crashing away in a desperate attempt to put off the Japanese aim; she had actually worked up to $27\frac{1}{2}$ knots and Captain Tennant did well to avoid all eight of the torpedoes dropped on the starboard side. His helm orders had again been bellowed down from the bridge to the steering position below, and the old battle cruiser had swerved one way and then the other but had been unable to avoid that one torpedo. The other two torpedoes from the portside attack missed. It was *Repulse's* first torpedo hit after avoiding at least sixteen aimed directly at her and several more 'overs' from attacks on *Prince of Wales*.

Ordinary Seaman Stanley Dimmack had been in a gunnery control position and had watched the attack.

Suddenly there were more tracks heading straight for us and I knew there could be no avoiding them. As they disappeared under the sheer of the bow, I held my head between my arms and gritted my teeth, expecting one almighty explosion, but much to my surprise the ship hardly shuddered and ploughed steadily on.

Repulse was well protected by her old-fashioned torpedo bulge at the point hit by the torpedo; this was why the explosion had not seriously shaken the whole of the ship. Water poured into the bulge through the torpedo hole and the ship began to list, but Commander Dendy's damage control organization immediately started counter-flooding on the opposite side to compensate and *Repulse* had still not been seriously hurt. The ship had actually come very close to being hit by a second torpedo.

I remember seeing a Japanese torpedo which had hit the ship at such an oblique angle that it had failed to explode. I remember looking over the ship's side from my Action Station and seeing this ominous weapon with its yellow head, gently nosing its way up the ship's side, in and out. Each time it came back in I expected an explosion but it never came. I was told afterwards that it was caught in the paravane chains forward. (Lieutenant R. A. W. Pool)

But *Repulse*'s luck was running out fast. There still remained the third of the Kanoya squadrons, the nine aircraft of Lieutenant Iki. Iki had been intending to attack *Prince of Wales* and had initially led his squadron towards that ship but soon found that he was not well positioned. At the same time, the fountains of water thrown up at the battleship's side told him that the attack of the other Kanoya squadrons on *Prince of Wales* had been successful. Iki decided to change targets and try instead for the *Repulse*. He ordered his formation to split up and take on the battle cruiser from different angles. Six aircraft attempted to work their way round to *Repulse*'s starboard side and Iki led the remaining three straight into the port side. It was probably the most skilfully executed attack of the day.

Less than two minutes had elapsed since the last attack and Lieutenant Iki's flight of three aircraft was on to *Repulse* even while the ship was shaking off the last attack. The three Bettys came right in to about 600 yards (500 metres) before releasing their torpedoes. What developed next was the most dramatic incident of the day. Lieutenant Iki managed to bank quickly and turn away, so close to the British ship was he that he could see sailors on her deck throwing themselves down to avoid the fire of his machine-gunners; his plane was slightly damaged by *Repulse*'s fire. But two other pilots could not turn quickly enough and flew right over *Repulse*'s bows.

It was an important principle of anti-aircraft gunnery that as soon as a torpedo bomber had released its torpedo and ceased to be a danger, fire should be switched from that target to other aircraft that had yet to release their torpedoes. Lieutenant Pool was fire distribution officer at one of *Repulse*'s pom-poms, a lethal weapon at short range.

It became obvious that the Japanese aircraft were firing their torpedoes out of our effective pom-pom range. Almost immediately, another attack developed . . . As the ship's position appeared hopeless, I did not shift target after these aircraft had dropped their torpedoes. As the two aircraft passed by the ship we hit and set on fire both of them and they crashed.

The first of the pom-pom's victims was the aircraft piloted by Petty Officer Satoshi Momoi; it exploded in a spectacular ball of fire leaving only a few fragments of aircraft to splash into the sea and then a huge red circle of burning petrol on the surface. The second aircraft hit was piloted by Petty Officer Ryochi Taue. This caught fire at the rear of its fuselage and gradually lost height with the fire eating its way rapidly up towards the cockpit and wings until the plane hit the sea in a huge cloud of spray. One report says that a Japanese airman from this aircraft was later seen standing on a floating wing and waving for help, but even if this is true, no one had time for a solitary Japanese that morning.

The cheers of *Repulse*'s crew at this double shooting-down were short lived. All three torpedoes dropped by this flight of aircraft exploded against *Repulse*'s port side – one near the engine room, one abreast of her rear 15-in. turret and one nearer the stern. This last hit, believed to be the torpedo dropped by Lieutenant Iki himself, jammed the rudder, and *Repulse*, though able to steam on, could not be steered. Because she had been turning to starboard when Iki's torpedo jammed the rudder, *Repulse* could now steam only in a wide circle.

These three hits were soon followed by a further blow. The six other aircraft of Lieutenant Iki's squadron had earlier launched their torpedoes from more distant firing positions and one of these now arrived and scored a hit, this time on the starboard alongside E Boiler Room.

The old battle cruiser had been grievously injured. Water was pouring into the ship through five holes made by torpedo explosions, and she had not been designed to withstand such severe damage. The list to port increased – 7 degrees, 9 degrees, then 12 degrees. Captain Tennant's report again:

I knew now that she could not survive and at once gave the order for everyone to come on deck and to cast loose Carley floats. It had been learnt that the broadcasting apparatus was still working throughout the ship, with the exception of the compartments down below aft, but word was quickly passed down from Y Turret and the After Control. The decision for a commanding officer to make, 'Cease all work in the ship below', is an exceedingly difficult one, but knowing the ship's construction, I felt very sure that she could not survive four torpedoes.

Captain Tennant obviously did not realize that his ship had been struck by five and not four torpedoes.

One gets the impression that the Kanoya Air Corps was a particularly skilled and audacious unit. Its twenty-six aircraft had scored nine torpedo hits – four on *Prince of Wales* and five on *Repulse*. Two of its aircraft had been shot down, three more seriously damaged (one of which would crash on landing at its airfield) and five more slightly damaged.

The action involving *Repulse* had been compressed into a time far shorter than the description of it takes to read. She had been hit by five torpedoes in four minutes. There is no need to conceal the fact that *Repulse* was about to sink, but the description of her sinking will be left over for the next chapter.

It was just 12.30 when this last devastating series of torpedo attacks died away – one and a half hours after the opening of the action. During those ninety minutes all fifty of the Japanese torpedo bombers had completed their attacks but only eight of the high-level bombers had done so, although six of these had bombed twice. *Repulse* was now sinking and *Prince of Wales* was not in much better shape. It would be forty-five minutes at least before the Australian fighters could arrive. Midshipman Hoashi, in the Japanese shadowing plane, had not yet returned from his bombing of Kuantan airfield. There remained two squadrons of Japanese high-level bombers that had not yet attacked – the Mihoro Air Corps squadrons of Lieutenants Ohira and Takeda with nine and eight Mitsubishi Nells respectively. Each plane was loaded with one 500-kg. bomb.

These two squadrons had recently arrived in the area of action, but just too late to coordinate their attacks with those of the Kanoya torpedo bombers. Lieutenant Ohira's nine aircraft were the first to start their bomb run, and there are two Japanese accounts of what happened next. Their Official History says that Ohira spotted a British ship through a gap in the cloud at 12.33 hours and his squadron dropped their nine bombs on that target but without scoring any hits. But Lieutenant Takai's personal account of the action states that, while running up to bomb, the bomb aimer in Lieutenant Ohira's aircraft accidently pressed his bomb release. His bomb then dropped far too soon and the other eight aircraft all followed suit. Takai states that the bombs of this squadron fell harmlessly in the sea well away from any target. Although Takai was miles away by then, his version is certainly the correct one since several observers on the British ships noted the explosion of these bombs harmlessly on the horizon. Their conclusion was that a damaged Japanese aircraft had jettisoned its bomb load.

The next stage of this dying action now centred around *Prince of Wales*, still unable to steer, just creeping through the water, settling more and more by the stern and with her list to port increasing again despite the four torpedo holes in the starboard side. Large sections of the ship had ceased to function, and there were many men idly waiting for the next development. Some of the more seriously wounded had now been brought on deck and the ship's Carley floats, and some of the smaller ship's boats, were being prepared for launching so as to get the wounded away if *Prince of Wales* should go down. Lookouts and gun crews were still vigilant, but very few of the guns were now capable of being fired.

Repulse could be seen some miles away to the west with two destroyers standing by. The battle cruiser was obviously sinking. One seaman in *Prince of Wales* watched *Repulse* heeling over and thought sadly about the many boy seamen he had once trained with who were now aboard her, though Captain Aylwin of the Royal Marines says 'it was difficult to describe exactly what my feelings were on seeing *Repulse* bottom up. I don't think I was particularly affected in any way. She was sinking and that was that. The enemy could now concentrate all their efforts on *Prince of Wales*.'

It is not possible to state exactly what was happening on *Prince of Wales*'s bridge at this time. No doubt a constant stream of reports was coming from various parts of the ship, but few, if any, of these could have contained cheering news for Admiral Phillips or Captain Leach. Once a flagship had become crippled, as *Prince of Wales* clearly now was, many admirals would have been transferring with their staff to another ship so as to remain mobile and effective. Yet it is obvious that Admiral Phillips was planning no such move; with *Repulse* sinking, he really had nothing much left to command. One can only guess at the emotions being experienced by Tom Phillips at this time. Seldom can a naval officer have experienced such a reversal of fortunes in such a short time, and by means of a type of enemy action that he had considered to be impossible.

The flagship had at last broken its radio silence when, at 12.20, this signal was transmitted.

EMERGENCY

HAVE BEEN STRUCK BY A TORPEDO ON PORT SIDE.

NYTWO22RO6. 4 TORPEDOES. REPULSE HIT BY 1
TORPEDO. SEND DESTROYERS.

The two amazing aspects of this signal are the delay before
it was sent at all – it was twenty-two minutes after Captain
Tennant in *Repulse* had broken radio silence – and that the
appeal was for destroyers, not aircraft cover. It was a very
revealing signal.

At 12.41 *Prince of Wales*'s lookouts reported two more
dangers. Eight high-level bombers were seen approaching
from ahead, and what was believed to be a submarine
periscope on the starboard quarter was also sighted. The
bombers were real enough – Lieutenant Takeda's squadron had seen *Prince of Wales* and were starting their
bombing run – but the periscope report was almost certainly a false one. *Prince of Wales* opened fire with what
guns were still in action; three of the 5·25-in. turrets fired
well but one of them, P2, soon had to stop firing because of
a bad oil leak in the turret hydraulic gear, and the others,
S1 and S2, were hampered in their firing as the range-taker
had been wounded in his right eye and an estimated height
had to be used. Some of the pom-poms and other close-
range weapons also joined in, though this was more an act
of defiance than anything else as Takeda's bombers were
flying at over 9,000 feet. The helpless *Prince of Wales*
would be an easy target for them. Many men saw the
attack developing and there was time for them to seek some
protection. On the bridge it was Captain Leach who
watched the bombs coming down; he turned to Admiral
Phillips and said the one word 'Now!' Everyone laid flat.

Men in other parts of the ship also remember that
moment.

While I was helping to cut the lashings on the boats, I heard shouts
about more aircraft. I could see them – high this time – approaching
in line abreast from forwàrd, their purpose obvious. 'Why? Oh why?'
We were sinking already! The forward 5·25s and pom-poms opened
fire, but clearly the fire-control calculators were not functioning as
the shell bursts were quite erratic. Each plane detached one large

bomb. In such close formation at least one bomb would hit the ship. It was inevitable that hundreds of men now alive would be dead in a few seconds and for the one time in my life I completely lost my temper, screaming impotent abuse at them. As the bombs got nearer, a group of us dived for cover in a rope store and waited. (Ordinary Seaman D. F. Wilson)

Before the final bombing attack, I remember our pom-pom director was useless so, as we saw bombs leaving the aircraft, we all lay flat on the deck in and around the director. An officer rounded on us royally for our cowardice, and we arose, shamefacedly, to our feet. I wandered through the bridge flat to see a friend of mine on a starboard director, only to find the deck there littered with officers and men also lying prone! Whilst these air attacks were being carried out, everyone on the lower deck was cursing the lack of air support. I am afraid that poor Admiral Tom Phillips was not popular at this stage, as the lower-deck rumour had it that the Admiral had told his peers that we could manage without air cover! I repeat that this was the lower-deck rumour. (Able Seaman R. H. James)

A hand klaxon or warning device sounded from the bridge. I thought 'Lord, not again.' But, looking up into a perfectly cloudless sky, high up, very high, we could just see eight or ten planes with wings tip to tip. As we watched, something that looked like snowflakes (impossible) fell from them. We watched fascinated and then I awoke – Bombs! Falling on us! I shoved the lads into the bos'n's steel cabin and banged the door, then there was a crash like thunder and a tearing of metal. It took a while for my ears and senses to come back to normal, but I suddenly thought that we might be sinking. I unwrapped somebody's legs from around my neck (the cabin was only very small and we had all tried to jam in together). I managed to get the door open and we spilled on to the deck to behold a scene of desolation, with fire and smoke pouring from air vents. The boat deck was all right and we made our way to look into the 'waist' where we found the bombs had missed us by only a few feet but had gone right through the armoured deck of the plane-launching apparatus down into the cinema flat where the wounded had been mustered. (Ordinary Seaman W. E. England)

Lieutenant Takeda's squadron had dropped seven bombs; the release mechanism of the eighth aircraft had failed. It was a well-aimed salvo and one 500-kg. bomb had penetrated the catapult deck on the port side and exploded on the 5-in. thick armoured deck below. The explosion pushed up the catapult deck 'like a small mountain'. Underneath the armoured deck and not far from the position of the explosion was X Boiler Room, the only one still being manned; the flash and fumes of the explosion forced their way through shafts into this boiler room causing more injuries, and this last source of power for the battleship was put out of action. Lieutenant Takeda later claimed two bomb hits, but this was not so, though two further bombs which were near misses on either side of the ship aft probably caused further damage to the hull of *Prince of Wales*. Takeda's squadron flew away, its crews probably not realizing that they had carried out the last action of a historic battle. No less than five of these aircraft had been damaged by *Prince of Wales*'s anti-aircraft fire – a very creditable performance by the turrets that had remained in action.

From a technical point of view the explosion of this one bomb had not caused much damage, but the human effects of it were terrible. It could hardly have burst in a worse place, for the actual explosion took place in the large compartment known as the Cinema Flat, being used at the time as an overflow casualty station and as a rest place for men suffering from heat exhaustion. There were between 200 and 300 men in the Cinema Flat, and the casualties here and in the adjoining corridors were frightful – blast, burns and shrapnel. The area had been reduced to a bloody shambles. Two men who survived describe their experiences.

The next thing was that I seemed to see a terrific flash and a tremendous explosion, with screams being forced out of everyone's throats and a great burning sensation all round and inside my lungs. I must then have become instantly unconscious, for how long I don't know, but the time came when I realized that I could see a faint glimmer of daylight which I made my way towards. (Marine R. B. Wade)

Lieutenant Dick Wildish was one of those who had

become affected by the heat in the engine rooms and had been ordered to the Cinema Flat to recover.

I lay down on the deck alongside the Senior – Lieutenant-Commander (E) R. O. Lockley. There were many people there and the padre was going round with a welcome can of grog – very acceptable. Then the bomb arrived – although I was sure at the time that there were two bombs not one – the structure above us fell in on us – the Senior and I. I turned to look at him and was sure he had been killed. I couldn't move myself for a while but managed to extricate myself from the debris and nauseating shambles and get to the quarterdeck where I met Lieutenant-Commander Terry. He was the Q.D. officer, I recall, and had presumably had to clear out of his Action Station. I told him of the appalling mess below and I thought that Lockley had been killed. I believe that Terry organized a rescue team and was delighted to find out later that the Senior had been found and brought out alive. I was in no great shape myself by then – stone deaf from bomb blast and therefore unable to exercise or hear orders, extensively burned, and with minor shrapnel wounds. Also, I suppose, shocked pretty badly. I remember little constructively after this.

Many men remember an uncanny silence in *Prince of Wales* after the bombing. The guns had ceased firing. The engines had stopped. The huge battleship was settling still deeper by the stern, with water creeping up along the port-side deck from the stern 'as though the tide was coming in'. *Prince of Wales* had sent out another signal asking for 'all available tugs', and then a further signal that was coded up wrongly in the rush so that it never was understood at Singapore what type of help was being requested – perhaps aircraft at last? No mention was made in any of *Prince of Wales*'s signals that *Repulse* had sunk twenty minutes earlier; it was left for the destroyer *Electra* to send out this bad news.

The destroyer *Express* was the only one still in her screening position off *Prince of Wales*'s starboard bow, and even before the last Japanese bombing attack, Lieutenant-Commander F. J. Cartwright had made up his mind that *Prince of Wales* was sinking.

I decided that *Prince of Wales* was in serious trouble and I could already see men jumping off the ship. I decided to go alongside to see if I could be of any assistance. I could see the Japanese bombers approaching and we held off until their attack was over; I didn't want to give them a bigger target. Then, after the bombs had dropped, I circled round and secured alongside *Prince of Wales*'s starboard quarter. As we did so, a signal was flashed down at us from *Prince of Wales*'s bridge – 'WHAT HAVE YOU COME ALONGSIDE FOR?' I told them, 'IT LOOKS AS THOUGH YOU REQUIRE ASSISTANCE.' I don't think they realized how serious the situation was.

Excepting a miracle, nothing could now save this once fine battleship. Captain Leach ordered that the wounded were to be got away, and soon these were being floated off the stern in Carley floats; other wounded were sent across to *Express* on stretchers. Captain Leach had come down from the bridge to the quarterdeck where a large crowd of his men had congregated. He told them that *Prince of Wales* had been badly hit but was still a fighting unit, and he asked for volunteers to stay aboard to try and get the ship back to Singapore. Many men tell of the dignified way in which Captain Leach spoke to them at this sad moment. There were some volunteers, but they all knew that it was hopeless and Captain Leach soon realized he was going to lose his ship. Paymaster-Lieutenant J. G. Baskcomb remembers 'the distinct picture I have in my mind of the little hopeless gesture he made as he turned away and ordered that everyone had better blow up their tubes'.

Captain Leach gave permission for those men not needed to man the guns or other vital services to get across to *Express*, and then he climbed back up to the bridge to rejoin Admiral Phillips. Phillips had not made any appeal to the men; it was not his place to do so. This was no longer an affair of admirals but of a captain and his ship's company. One report says that Admiral Phillips had sent someone below to fetch up his best cap.

At 13.15 the list to port that *Prince of Wales* had experienced since the first torpedo hit an hour and a half earlier suddenly started to increase. The ship was now beyond the help of aircraft, destroyers, tugs or anything else. She was going. Those dread words that every sailor hopes never to hear were soon passed around: 'Abandon Ship!'

12

'Abandon Ship'

When Captain Leach ordered his crew to abandon ship, the rescue work around the site of *Repulse*'s sinking had been in progress for forty minutes with the British destroyer *Electra* and the Australian *Vampire* hard at work picking up survivors. *Prince of Wales*, with *Express* standing by her, would survive for just eight more minutes. The only outside witnesses to the sinkings of these two great ships were the crews of several Japanese aircraft, who had remained as curious observers, and the first of the Brewster Buffalo fighter pilots who arrived just as *Prince of Wales* was disappearing beneath the sea.

The loss of any large ship is a sad and tragic event. When it is the result of a battle, then the actual sinking can come very quickly and the lives of large numbers of men are at risk – risk of being trapped inside a sinking ship, risk of being choked to death by the thousands of tons of diesel oil from ruptured fuel tanks, risk of further hostile action by the enemy, risk of drowning or exposure, and in these tropical waters, the risk of shark attack. Nearly 3,000 *Repulse* and *Prince of Wales* men had to face these many hazards. We will now look at the last moments of both ships, the efforts of their crews to save themselves and the help given by the three destroyers. The fact that *Prince of Wales* sank forty-eight minutes after *Repulse* went down is not important here, and incidents concerning both ships will sometimes be described simultaneously.

The battle cruiser *Repulse* had been a fully effective fighting unit until just before the end. Despite her poor anti-aircraft armament and the early bomb hit, she had played a full part in the battle for well over an hour. Captain Tennant's well-drilled, mainly pre-war crew had kept the old ship in action until the last series of Japanese attacks when five torpedoes had transformed her into a wreck. There was not for *Repulse* the lingering agony of *Prince of Wales*. At 12.23 she had been a fine, live ship. Four minutes later she was foundering.

With his ship heeled over to the port side but still moving ahead at about 6 knots, Captain Tennant announced over the loudspeaker system: 'All hands on deck. Prepare to abandon ship. God be with you.' In compartments all over the ship – in gun positions, plotting positions, damage control parties, signal offices, ammunition magazines and rooms, in what was left of engine and boiler rooms and in all those small places where men had done their duty – officer or senior ratings fell their men out and ordered them to get to the decks. Not one account by anyone who was in *Repulse* says that a single man left his place of duty until ordered to do so. Dozens of men now came pouring up through hatches from below or scrambling down ladders from the upperworks, but still no one went over the side. Captain Tennant's report reads:

When the ship had a 30-degree list to port I looked over the starboard side of the bridge and saw the Commander and two or three hundred men collecting on the starboard side. I never saw the slightest sign of panic or ill discipline. I told them from the bridge how well they had fought the ship and wished them good luck.*

Captain Tennant then ordered: 'Abandon ship.'

There was no delay once this order had been given and the first rush of men was soon away. Every man had, or should have had, an old-fashioned but efficient rubber lifebelt that he had been under orders to wear at all times for the past twenty-four hours. It took only a few seconds to blow these up. There were also a number of Carley floats which could easily be slipped overboard, but the motor boats and whalers could not be launched quickly and it is believed none of these was used.

* British Official History, p. 197.

For most men it was a case of going into the sea over the side, and to have the best chance of saving himself each man now had to do something that was against all natural inclinations. The automatic tendency was to run *down* the sloping deck to the listing port side and then jump or dive into the sea a few feet below. But this would entail the risk of being caught by *Repulse*'s massive superstructure or by the suction that would occur when the ship sank. The safer way was to climb *up* the sloping deck to the starboard side, climb over the guardrails and then face a frightening slide down the side of the ship and into the sea. The huge side of *Repulse* was soon alive with men slipping down on their bottoms. At one spot where many men were leaving there was a huge torpedo hole in the ship's side just beneath the surface of the sea. An alert petty officer still on the deck noticed that several men who jumped into the sea near this spot promptly disappeared as they were sucked into the hole, and he stood by at the danger spot and warned men to keep away from it. It was not long before *Repulse* listed farther to port and the jagged torpedo hole and the huge torpedo bulge appeared above the surface.

Lieutenant Abrahams, the Admiralty photographer, was trying to save his priceless photographs of the recent action.

When the order came to abandon ship, I knew I could not keep afloat because of the weight of camera and metal slides so I placed the camera and unexposed slides in an empty steel lifebelt locker near a pom-pom gun on the main deck – some of the gun's crew were dead – and took the slides containing pictures of the action with me when I went over the side.

There were a few wits – 'See you in Singapore, mate' and 'Now you can draw the dole.' I slipped down the ship's side until I was on the protruding bulge but, as I saw one of these gaping, jagged holes made by a torpedo, I walked further aft on the beam and then went in the sea. As I came to the surface I saw a man jumping from the deck above – he had hobnailed boots on and must have been a Royal Marine. He hit me hard, split my Mae West and closed one eye. I came to the surface minus the camera slides and lost sight of the man who had hit me amongst hundreds of bobbing heads all black with fuel oil.

Sergeant H. A. Nunn of the Royal Marines was one of several men trying to put floatable objects over the side.

In happier times B Gundeck was the Chief P.O.'s smoking space and, as such, there were large wooden garden-type seats. A seaman and myself dragged one of these to the guardrail and dropped it over the side as we thought it might be of assistance to somebody in the water, but to our consternation it sank like a stone so our effort was all in vain.

By this time it was time for me to go over the side so I kicked off my shoes and climbed over the guardrail. It was possible to walk part-way down the ship's side, but I had to finish the rest of the journey on my seat, regardless of the rips and tears to my person and clothing. I had my lifebelt with me but I had no qualms about going into the water as I was a strong swimmer. I didn't even think of the possibility that there may be sharks in the vicinity; my only concern was to try and get away from the ship and the oily patch that was beginning to spread out over the surface of the water.

Hundreds of men got safely away from *Repulse* in these few minutes. It was all quite orderly, with no panic, no pushing, with men waiting their turn to go down the side 'like queueing up for the pictures'. The ship's physical training instructor found a young marine without a lifebelt, handed over his own and the two jumped together from *Repulse*'s bow. A stoker found a young seaman standing on the torpedo bulge, afraid to enter the water and crying; he had also lost his lifebelt and had never learned to swim. The stoker handed over his lifebelt and told the youngster to jump with him, but when the stoker surfaced the other had vanished.

The speed of events and the fact that the loudspeakers had broken down in some parts of the ship resulted in many compartments below being late to realize that the order to abandon ship had been given. The men in such compartments, particularly those deep down in the ship, often had a struggle to escape being trapped. Each level of the ship was separated from the level above by hatches which had been closed during the action and now had to be forced open, often against the list of the ship. The heavy steel hatches of the main armoured deck, many of which could only be opened with chains and pulleys, were a particular hazard. Dozens of men from below only just got out in the nick of time after frantic climbs up ladders or shafts and dashes along corridors, sometimes in pitch-dark conditions. For such men it was literally a race for life.

Leading Supply Assistant Leonard Sandland had been in a party of men below loading shells on to a conveyor for one of *Repulse*'s anti-aircraft guns when the torpedoes struck.

One bloke shouted, 'The conveyor. Look!' For a second we all froze as we realized that the gun's crew up aloft must have caught a packet. No one was offloading the shells any more and they were just going up from us, straight over the top still on the conveyor, and then crashing down again. Nobby, a leading seaman member of our team, and myself had a hurried conference, wondering whether the gun's crew *had* been wiped out, or if the order had been given to abandon ship. It was obvious that we were in a bad way, though how bad we had no way of knowing. Nor did we fancy being trapped down there either.

We wondered what best to do, when suddenly our minds were made up for us. Another reverberating crash, the ship gave a terrific shudder, and the vertical wall in front of us was no longer vertical but was leaning over at an angle of about 30 degrees. That decided us. We dropped everything and made for the shaft, the top of which we could just see, leaning over us, and up we went. We had then one fear, that we might find that the hatch at the top had been clamped down, but luck was with us, probably only because the lads up top had also been so busy that they hadn't had time to secure it. Anyway, we made it to the top, lifted the hatch, and found that the lower deck into which it emerged had no lighting and we were in total darkness.

I think all our lads had been on the *Repulse* about twelve months and you get to know a ship inside out in that length of time, which was just as well. Anyway, in pitch blackness we felt our way round the bulkhead until we came to the big hatch which we knew would let us out on to the upper deck, and this one was a real stinker. It was extremely heavy and was sealed over us because of the heavy list.

We had to exert every last ounce of our combined strength to push it upwards. But we made it, and out we shot into brilliant sunshine.

Able Seaman Tom Barnes had been working at a plotting table in the main transmitting station, feeding information to the anti-aircraft guns.

We'd been hit again, sounded like the other side. Feels like she's turning on her side. Hang on to anything – not a man amongst the team has made a move. Then, over the loud hailer, 'Abandon Ship.' Through B Space, up the steel ladder on to the mess deck, a scramble for the ladder leading to the main deck starboard side, along the P.O.'s mess flat. *Repulse* is listing steeply now; am I going to make it to the upper deck? The door to the P.O.'s mess is hanging open and a glimpse inside shows a deadlight up and a porthole open – in, and scramble through the porthole almost vertically, on to the ship's side and down to the bulge – a jump and that's it. I'm in the sea.

Stoker Mechanic George Avery had been in one of the condenser rooms.

We had heard the various thumps of the torpedoes hitting the ship. Down below we had a big porthole between the two condenser rooms and my best friend, Patrick Sheam from Cork, was down the other condenser room. I looked through the porthole; he waved to me. Then there was a big load of smoke and bits flying around. A torpedo explosion had entered the other condenser room. I sat down and cried.

I noticed the steam dropping back on the evaporators; the more I opened the valves it didn't make any difference to the pressure so I said to the Chief Mech who was in charge, 'I think it's time to leave.' He said, 'Let's wait for orders.' The Tannoy system had broken down and I said it would be too late if it wasn't too late already. There were seven of us down in the compartment. We opened the big hatch from down below to the next flat up and the hatch above us was closed but the small round manhole was open and all we could see was the water rushing through. We climbed through the manhole and the water just pulled us back inboard. I grabbed something on the half-deck and the pressure of the water broke the gold ring on my finger but it saved me being pulled back into the mess deck.

Unfortunately there were many men, like Stoker Avery's friend in the next condenser room, who never made it.

There were the badly wounded, the stunned, the men trapped in the deepest compartments of the ship – the magazines, shell-handling rooms, boiler and engine rooms. There were the men who ran up and down corridors, hammering at bulkheads and armoured hatches until overtaken by the water now rushing through the ship. Some of those on duty in the 15-in. transmitting station were Royal Marine bandsmen who, just before the action started, had been having a cheerful off-duty 'jam session', but now, in contrast, were in extreme danger. Sixteen-year-old Boy Seaman Heydon was among them.

We had counted another two torpedoes before we felt a movement of the ship heeling over. With a look of utter disbelief on the faces of all around me, I waited during a shattering silence and with great concern for someone to say something – anything. The next voice to speak, however, was that of the Captain ordering, 'Prepare to abandon ship.' None of us could move because of the unreality of the whole thing until I, as the youngest member of the T.S. crew, was ordered 'out and over the side'. The fact that I was a messenger had taught me all the short cuts around the ship and I scrambled up an escape pipe wide enough to take only one person at a time. Several people were following me by the time I came to the door leading out to B Gun Deck – the door was above me at about 45 degrees. The only way I could reach up to it was to recruit the aid of the one below me, a personal chum of mine, another boy, to give me a push. Unfortunately, having done so, he lost his footing and fell back taking about another dozen with him. I still dream of the sight of those people falling, never to make it up again. When I slid into the water from the gun deck I was alone and felt sick at the thought that they had lost their lives to save mine. I still suffer remorse.

At least *Repulse* was spared the massive internal explosions that had completely destroyed three battle cruisers at Jutland and, more recently, the *Hood*, but almost four out of every ten men in *Repulse* died, an unknown but substantial proportion of this loss being crew trapped inside the ship. Perhaps the most tragic cases were those who were trapped in small compartments that retained air but who had no means of escape when water filled the ship. *Repulse* sank in 185 feet of water, and the pressure at that depth would not have been so great as to bring immediate death. There are unfortunately no dramatic tales of under-water rescues or miraculous escapes to the surface in the *Repulse* story.

The last few men were now escaping from *Repulse*'s deck as she rolled still farther over to the port side. Commander R. J. R. Dendy was one of these.

I remember seeing the starboard 4-in. triple mounting on the Flag-deck break away and go crashing over to the port side. Simul-taneously, a great wall of water came up from aft and swept me away. I remember how light in colour was this wave and I realized I was not being taken down but swept away from the ship in surface water. Eventually I came to the surface.

Lieutenant J. O. C. Hayes had made sure that the Con-fidential Signal Books would go down in the ship's safe before he set out to save himself.

My movements were then dictated by gravity, like one of those balls on a bagatelle table which bounces off pins – the funnel, red-hot from fast steaming, then against the port flag lockers by which time, nor-mally some fifty feet above the waterline, they were almost awash, and so overboard helplessly and down for what seemed a long time. When I bobbed up, the great iron structure of the main top, separating the mainmast from the main topmast, normally some hundred feet above the waterline, skidded just above my head as the ship plunged on and down with the screws still turning.

Many men speak of the courage of a young Australian, Midshipman R. I. Davies, who was last seen strapped to his Oerlikon gun still firing at a Japanese aircraft and cursing anyone who got in the way of his sights. He was never seen again.*

Repulse gave a sudden lurch and now lay on her beam ends – that is, exactly on her side with masts, funnel and superstructure at water level. Men who had yet to leave

---

* Robert Ian Davies, aged eighteen, was from Greenwich, New South Wales. He was awarded a posthumous Mention in Dispatches.

could now stand on the exposed starboard side of the ship, and many compared the scene to the classic photograph of the German armoured cruiser *Blücher* sinking at the Battle of the Dogger Bank in January 1915 which showed a great crowd of German sailors standing on the side of the sinking ship – 'that magnificent but awful photograph'.

Able Seaman D. W. Avery was on *Repulse's* side.

We made our way on to the starboard bilge, which was now out of the water with the ship lying on her port side. I didn't seem to be able to pluck up enough courage to join the struggling men in the water, so I sat on the bilge and tried to blow up my lifejacket, but it was no good; it had perished with the heat of the tropics and I hadn't a new issue.

As I sat there wondering what to do to save myself, Cecil Brown, an American reporter who had joined the ship at Singapore, came along and sat beside me, took off his boots, put them neatly beside him, stood up, turned to me and said, 'Good luck, pal,' then dived into the water and swam for the nearest destroyer. This, and the fact that the ship was getting lower into the water, made my mind up for me and I dived off. But I didn't seem to be able to come to the surface; I kept going down and down with my eyes open. I could see the light going duller and duller, then I began to panic and struggled madly to get to the surface and my lungs seemed to be bursting. I stopped panicking and kicked to the surface, but it was no good, I was beginning to pass out. I had to breathe so I let out the air in my lungs slowly; this helped but it was no good, I had to take a deep breath. I then realized I was breathing air yet I wasn't at the surface. I had been sucked under with the ship as she was sinking and while I was struggling I must have got caught in an air bubble.

Sick Berth Attendant Walter Bridgewater had been one of the last away from the Forward Medical Station.

One by one the casualties were helped to the door and with hardly a word being exchanged were then assisted, by magazine workers passing up, to get up the first set of wooden ladders. The last two I had to push up myself, and then I remember one of the seamen shouting at me that, 'Abandon Ship had been piped, didn't I know?'

Back to the Sick Bay Action Station for the last patient, but he was in a coma and could not help himself in any way. I will always remember his helpless, pathetic look. By then, the ship, which up till then had seemed quite stable, started to shudder, the deck then was at a tilt and the dressing bins and stands were rolling about and, worse still, the antiseptic liquids had spilled and the deck was wet and very slippery with the yellow acraflavine liquid, etc.

No one had gone by the door all this time and I just could do nothing with the last casualty and when the ship gave quite a shudder I just decided I'd better get out myself and I left the last one propped up in the corner.

Bridgewater then describes his escape up several decks until he reached a porthole.

Just as I was trying to pull and push myself through, the ship listed heavily and I found myself with my right arm jammed into the angle bar on my inside bicep and I was stuck there with the sea thudding down on top of my head and bending my neck nearly to my chest. Two shipmates who must have 'slept in' like myself and who were trying to get out at the same time, were just washed back and out of sight just after reaching the portholes.

I was held rigid in this awkward, arm-held, head-bent position for several minutes and I remember deciding, 'Well you've had it this time, son,' and I prepared to swallow as much water as quickly as possible and get it over with. The last thought I had was quite a selfish one, 'Well, I'll never marry Muriel now,' and I said a quick prayer as the water reached up to my nose.

Then, all of a sudden, I felt my right arm free and I grabbed at the port and was out in a split second, possibly the last to leave the old ship alive.

Walter Bridgewater also received a Mention in Dispatches, for having stayed so long with the wounded, and he did marry his Muriel.

The end came quickly. The roll of the ship continued with the great weight of the upperworks pulling *Repulse* completely over. The stern reared up with the propellers still turning, then disappeared, leaving the bows hanging in the air, glistening in the sun and showing the red-painted hull. It is possible that the stern struck the sea bottom before the bows finally disappeared because *Repulse*'s length was more than three times greater than the sea's depth here. The bows finally disappeared just eleven minutes after *Repulse* had been first hit by torpedoes. There were a few cheers from the men in the water for this much-loved old ship, but most survivors were too busy swimming away for fear of suction, though this danger turned out to be a negligible one, probably because of the shallowness of the water. 'She went down quite peacefully, as though glad it was all over.'

There remained nothing of the battle cruiser *Repulse* but a few great gulps of air and oil fuel coming to the surface.

After *Repulse* had gone down, one man describes the scene as 'bodies and debris everywhere. Most of the crew were covered in black oil and looked like a party of negro jazz-singers with just the whites of their eyes showing.' Those men who could swim or were calm enough to trust to their life-jackets found the water 'warm and relaxing' once they were clear of the oil fuel. There were those who had always believed that they were non-swimmers but now found they could swim after all. Lieutenant Jim Davis of the Royal Marines was swimming away from the *Repulse* when, as he turned to watch her sink, he was overtaken by a burly seaman who was swimming at high speed and shouting. 'Help me. Help me. I can't swim a stroke.' There were soon the usual jokes – 'Just think you're at Blackpool, lads' – and some singing, but officers tried to stop this, warning their men to save energy and avoid swallowing the oil. There was much fear of sharks and desperate moments of panic whenever a swimmer imagined that something had brushed against his legs under the water; some men deliberately swam into the patches of oil to avoid sharks. There are some reports of one or two dead monsters being seen floating at the scene, presumably killed by the recent bomb and torpedo explosions, but the live sharks had all been frightened off by the same explosions, at least for the present.

Repulse carried at least twelve large Carley floats. These were rectangular, doughnut-shaped rings made of

cork covered by canvas, with an open slatted-floor interior. They were practically unsinkable and capable of
carrying a large number of men. The swimmers set out to
reach the sanctuary of the Carley floats and these soon
became little communities of oil-soaked, sometimes
wounded men. There soon came a moment of fear when a
formation of Japanese aircraft was seen approaching at sea
level. Many men jumped off the Carley floats, fearing they
were about to be machine-gunned, but the Mitsubishis
roared overhead without firing.

The destroyers *Electra* and *Vampire* came in to start
rescuing *Repulse*'s survivors. It is a convenient time to
leave this scene and turn to that a few miles to the south-
east, where *Prince of Wales* was sinking.

Compared with the sinking of *Repulse*, which had happened
within eleven minutes of her first torpedo hit, the men in
Prince of Wales had plenty of time to prepare for the end of
their ship. *Prince of Wales* had been crippled fifty minutes
before *Repulse* sank, and she lingered for a further fifty
minutes after that.

For some time the Carley floats had been filled with
wounded and then floated gently off the flooded stern, the
screams of the burned and scalded men when they entered
the water being the most ghastly memory of many involved
in this work. Then Captain Leach had made his appeal for
volunteers to help get *Prince of Wales* back to Singapore,
but had given permission to leave the ship to those who
were not in a position to help, though there are several
reports of unwounded men jumping into the sea before
this time.

The 'non-essentials' made their way in large numbers to
the destroyer *Express*, now tied up to *Prince of Wales*'s
starboard side and with several gangplanks spanning the
gap between the two ships. There was some anger among
the ratings still needed on board *Prince of Wales* when they
saw an officer clad in immaculate 'whites' calmly walking
across to *Express*, carrying what appeared to be an attaché

case. This sight brought 'hoots of derision', and there were calls of, 'Come back you yellow bastard.' But non-essential personnel had been released by Captain Leach, and this officer may well have been ordered across to *Express* with essential documents.

Preparations to abandon ship were now in full swing. More and more men were forced up from below by the advancing water, and there was soon a large crowd on the diminishing deck. The lashings on the ship's launches and whalers were released so that these would float off when *Prince of Wales* sank; a party of men unroped a stack of timber near the boat deck and started dumping the planks over the side to provide help to men who would have to take to the water later. One man counted each plank as he helped lift it overboard – twenty-four planks one side and the same number the other. Not far away, Ordinary Seaman James Cockburn was in another party of men at work.

I had come up through the armoured hatch, made my way to the upper deck and found myself in the wardroom where some men were forming a chain to pass wardroom furniture out on to the quarterdeck. Anxious to do something, I joined this chain and passed on a number of chairs. I sensed, rather than saw, that the forward end of the wardroom was a gaping hole. I took one chair out on to the quarterdeck, there being no one to pass it to, and found what was happening to the furniture. It was being thrown overboard. This was my first view of sea and sky since we had closed up at Action Stations. Blazing tropical daylight and not a Japanese plane in sight. The ship was still under way, listing to port, and stretching a long way astern was a string of jetsam, including the wardroom furniture.

There remained much uncertainty even after Abandon Ship was finally ordered. Many parts of the ship never received the order and well-disciplined and panic-free compartments continued to function. Some officers or petty officers realized that something was wrong and ordered their men out; some stayed to the end and paid with their lives accordingly. As in *Repulse* there were several examples of men being rescued from below. Stoker Desmond Ulrick was on deck when he passed an open

hatch from which the ladder to the compartment below
had been destroyed.

Three or four men were hauling on a rope and pulled out a member
of the crew. He was pretty far gone but, before collapsing, said there
were other men below, trapped behind lockers. I and two or three
other men were then lowered back down the hatch by rope to try and
find them. The only man I remember finding, however, was a rating
sat in the power control room, in front of the telephone switchboard
and heel and trim indicators. This must have been his Action Station.
He did not appear to know what was going on and seemed very surprised when we told him the ship was sinking and the order was
'Abandon Ship'.

I remember the strangeness of this second. The lights were out,
all was black, water could be heard pouring from somewhere and,
above all, there was the quietness, like a blacked-out and deserted
town. We were pulled up again through the hatch by the rope.

Men who passed by the canteen at this time could help
themselves to unlimited cigarettes and chocolate, and the
canteen manager was even giving away bundles of English
and Singapore banknotes to anyone who had time to stop
and put them in pockets or the moneybelts that many sailors
wore, though one witness states that 'nobody seemed to
bother much'. Chief Petty Officer Hill and his Food Supply
Party H.Q. on the middle deck were still preparing an
issue of tea and sandwiches when they noticed a sudden
lurch of the ship, ran like mad and just had time to escape
through some open portholes.

As the list to port steepened, the starboard side of *Prince
of Wales* rose farther out of the water and the lower side of
the battleship started to come up underneath the *Express*
secured alongside. Her captain, Lieutenant-Commander
Cartwright, had a delicate decision to make. To remain
indefinitely would endanger his own ship, but to leave too
soon would stop the flow of wounded and other survivors
still coming across. The gangplanks fell into the sea as
the gap widened, but men continued to swing across on
ropes and the cable that still joined the two ships. Others,
more daring, were jumping the gap, but the results of the

occasional failure were horrible. As the cable tightened, men on the foc's'le of *Express* tried to release it, but it proved impossible to do so and the cable eventually snapped with a resounding crack. Engine Room Artificer Robert Woodhead was one of the last men to try his luck at leaping across.

I looked over the side and was horrified. The oil was thick on the water, some bodies were floating in it, and some of the other chaps around said there was no chance of living in that stuff. As I said earlier, I had no lifebelt, but on looking around I saw the destroyer alongside just beginning to move off. So I ran along the decks to a clear space to give myself a run at the empty space where the rails had been. Some fellows there shouted to me not to be foolish as the *Express* was already under way and I would be under the screws, but I just ran as fast as I could and jumped out and down.

I know now (have done ever since that day) that there is divine guidance for us. My heels landed on the ropes around the side of the *Express* and I pitched forward on to two chaps who were near, thus breaking my fall. When I recovered from this fright, I looked up at the *Prince of Wales*, which was receding astern very fast, and the first thing I noticed was the group of chaps who had cautioned me not to jump still standing there.

Express was indeed backing away. Lieutenant-Commander Cartwright had been watching the list on *Prince of Wales* increasing and her bilge keel coming up and under *Express*, and was judging the latest moment when he could safely leave the battleship. Able Seaman John Farrington was at the wheel of *Express*.

I watched the confused exodus – men scrambling on any line they could find and the cries of hell as some dropped between the heavy ships, squashed in a surging torrent of sea, oil and blood. *Prince of Wales* lurches badly now and we anxiously await orders. I have one eye on the wheelhouse door and one hand on the telegraph. My opposite number, 'Bungy' Williams, eyes me with a threat, 'Don't move.' Then, 'Full Steam Astern' cracks the order from the bridge, and with a crashing bump we slide off the heaving keel of *Prince of Wales*.

At this point we witness truly a brave sight – Admiral Tom Phillips is leaning over the bridge, chin resting on hands, looking like some gold-braided 'What-Ho', a signalman at his side flashing out hurried messages to our bridge.

Express had very nearly capsized when *Prince of Wales* heeled over, and several survivors on the destroyer's deck were either tipped into the sea, or else they jumped in, thinking that the destroyer was indeed capsizing. But Lieutenant-Commander Cartwright, by what was considered by many onlookers to be a superb piece of ship-handling, had judged the moment nicely. *Express* backed away with no more than a twenty-foot gash in her hull plating. As *Express* pulled away, Cartwright received a calm wave, presumably of approval, from Admiral Phillips.

There were still several hundred men aboard *Prince of Wales*. For a minute or so, they stood in large groups on the foc's'le and on the starboard-side quarterdeck, whence there came a shout from some wag to the departing *Express*, 'Does anyone want a cheap ship?' Then a large-scale evacuation over the starboard side of the ship commenced. Men jumped or swung down on ropes until the list of the ship became so steep that they could slide down on their bottoms – a perilous journey down the forty-five-foot steel side.

I walked or slid down on to the armoured plating which jutted out from the ship's side. From there my intentions were to make my way along to where two ropes secured on the upper deck led down almost to the water. But, as I neared them, I saw about a dozen men scrambling to get a hold on the rope and, one by one, sliding down to the sea. Another lurch of the ship decided me and with scarcely another thought I moved and, in a sitting position, let myself go. The ship was then at an angle of about 45 degrees, the sides thick with oil, so that the speed with which I shot down the ship's side is best left to the imagination. As I started, I remember seeing dozens of heads bobbing about below me but it was too late to call a halt and, at terrific speed, I shot down and by some miracle missed all obstructions. (Telegraphist C. V. House)

A large party of men had found its way to the foc's'le, which was now the highest part of *Prince of Wales*'s deck clear of the water. Many survivors remember an officer here, 'a big, red-headed lieutenant', who was keeping excellent order and controlling the men.* Surgeon Lieutenant-Commander Dick Caldwell was also there, tending the last of the wounded who would leave *Prince of Wales*.

The foc's'le now presented an amazing sight, with hundreds of sailors standing placidly smoking and chatting on the sloping deck – they had mostly been driven up from below by the encroaching, rising water. The guns' crews on the upper deck were still at their posts and there was nothing for the remainder to do but wait for the ship to sink. We enlisted several of them into stretcher and first-aid parties for the wounded. Someone told us there was a man with a broken leg lying in one of the compartments. We tended him, launched him and two of his pals in a float into the sea, now lapping all along the port side of the foc's'le.

Men started climbing over the rails and diving and jumping thirty or forty feet into the sea below; but 'diving' off the high side of a sinking ship is a euphemism! I took off my cap and my shoes and looked carefully round for somewhere to put them - an extraordinary action which I have read and heard of other people doing. I stood for a minute in the orderly crowd waiting their chance and heard a sailor say to his pal, 'Come on, chum. All them explosions'll have frightened the blinkin' sharks away.'

The ship was heeling over more now, and I climbed over the guard-rails and slid down to a projection on the ship's side. I stood there and looked down on dozens of heads, arms and legs in the water, still far below. Then I said to myself, 'Please God. Don't let me be drowned!' – took a deep breath, and dived into the oily water.

The final preparations were made to leave the dying ship. The gun crews were at last released from duty; one observer comments particularly on the orderly behaviour of the Royal Marine gun crew of P1 5·25-in. turret, whose gun captain, Sergeant Brooks, was seen falling in and counting off his men, including the magazine party, to

---

* This officer has been identified as Lieutenant E. J. Kempson, R.N.V.R., whose father had been Director of Studies at the Royal Naval College, Dartmouth, before the war. Lieutenant Kempson survived the sinking.

ensure that all were safely up on deck before ordering them to blow up their lifebelts and get over the side. Sergeant Thomas of S1, the other 5·25-in. turret manned by the Marines, had kept his turret in action to the end because it was the only one of the eight 5·25-in. turrets to have functioned properly throughout the action. S1's gun crew escaped, but ten of its working-chamber men were trapped and lost. Lieutenant W. M. Graham dismissed the crews of the close-range guns for which he was responsible, and these also joined the men leaving *Prince of Wales*.

The last few men who would ever get out from below decks did so at this time. One party of telegraphists who tried to reach the upper deck found their way barred by a determined commissioned gunner, who was still trying to pass ammunition by hand up to the now silent anti-aircraft guns. He turned the telegraphists back saying, 'Guns before men'. One or two managed to get past the gunner, but the remainder were never seen again. Leading Telegraphist Bernard Campion had been in the transmitting room.

Astonishing though it may be to recall, there was no mad rushing and the evacuation seemed to be absurdly leisurely considering the circumstances. As we climbed the ladders – with difficulty, as the ship was now almost lying on her port side – I found myself getting a little worried as to whether I would reach the upper deck before she turned right over and I remember playfully flicking the backside of the bloke in front of me – or rather above me – and muttering, 'Get a move on, Jan, for God's sake.' (I didn't know who it was, of course, but 'Jan' was a sort of general label in a West Country ship.)

Anyhow, when at last I emerged through the port door of the fore superstructure, I was wondering how on earth I was going to get into the water – whether to dive in over the port side or scramble up the deck as best I could and walk down the starboard side – and for a few brief seconds I stood on the side of a mushroom vent, kicking off my shoes and blowing up my lifebelt. Before I could make any further decisions the ship decided for me, as the port guardrails disappeared under the water and I was sucked down for what seemed ages in a mass of wreckage, with a derrick boom wedged firmly over my thighs and all kinds of loose spars belting me about.

I must confess that I gave up hope of ever surfacing again and hoped it would all be over swiftly. However, my inflated lifebelt served its purpose and what seemed several minutes later I did break surface in a thick mass of brown oil fuel, with a black eye, a broken thigh, and a lot of deep cuts and bruises. Incidentally, when I broke surface everything had been ripped off me except my lifebelt and my right sock!

Prince of Wales heeled right over on her port side, but not as quickly as *Repulse* had done, and several dozen men were able to walk calmly down the huge starboard side of the ship. Lieutenant W. M. Graham was one of those who took this strange walk.

I was able to muster most of my close-range guns' crews over on the starboard side and remember quite clearly walking over the bilge keel, keeping pace with the roll and thinking how clean the ship's bottom looked as I swam away. The last time I had seen the underside of the *Prince of Wales* was when I saw her being launched at Cammell Laird's yard in Birkenhead in 1939!

I should like to place it on record that there was no confusion or panic during the action and, when the time came to abandon ship, it was done quietly and almost as if hands had been piped to bathe! I suppose that many felt, like me, that this just could not be happening to them as it seemed like a bad dream – a long swim brought one back to reality!

There has been much speculation over what happened to Admiral Phillips and those around him. It is known that about ten minutes before *Prince of Wales* capsized he leant over the side of the compass platform, where he had spent the entire action with Captain Leach, and called down to the staff bridge where his immediate Fleet Staff had been working. Phillips dismissed these officers and told them to 'look after yourselves'. Commander H. N. S. Brown, Fleet Gunnery Officer, says that there was no particular expression on the admiral's face or his tone of voice, 'it was more matter of fact than anything else'. Most of these officers were saved. Various survivors saw Admiral Phillips after this. His coxswain has said that Admiral Phillips refused to put on a lifebelt, and that both he and Captain Leach were seen 'silent and impervious to entreaties to abandon ship before it was too late'.

There are several stories that Admiral Phillips, Captain Leach and Captain Simon Beardsworth, the admiral's secretary, were seen walking side-by-side down the ship's side and into the water but this cannot be confirmed. Commander Hilary Norman, Fleet Torpedo Officer, definitely saw Phillips, slumped on a stool and 'in deep despond', at a very late stage and then saw the admiral's body in the sea after *Prince of Wales* sank. Norman thought of swimming to the body and taking off it a signet ring or some other souvenir for the family but then decided that this was a little macabre and gave up the idea. He does not remember whether the body was wearing a lifebelt but presumes from its floating position that it was. Many people agree that there had been plenty of time for Admiral Phillips to save himself if he had wished to do so.

Lieutenant W. M. Graham later found Captain Leach's body, lying face downwards in the water but with a partially filled navy-pattern lifebelt around his chest. Graham and some sailors turned the body over and found the mouth clogged with vomit, the nose full of froth and the face purple; the neck may also have been broken. They tried to tow the body to H.M.S. *Express* but became exhausted, and Lieutenant Graham ordered the attempt to be abandoned. Captain Leach's son does not believe that his father would have deliberately gone down with the ship – he is certain that his father would have regarded that as an unnecessary waste of life – but he feels that, out of loyalty to Admiral Phillips, his father would not have left the compass platform until released. It is probable that this vital permission was given, but too late to save Captain Leach, who was obviously dragged down when *Prince of Wales* sank. Phillips's flag lieutenant, who had once been a university swimming 'half-blue', was later seen swimming strongly towards *Express*, but he collapsed and died on the destroyer, possibly from heart failure. Two yeomen of signals, observed at a late stage on *Prince of Wales*'s bridge, were never seen again.

There are several reports of the courage of Commander H. F. Lawson who was in command of damage control. He was attempting to repair *Prince of Wales*'s steering, deep down in the stern of the ship, but ordered the ratings with him up to safety and was last seen continuing to work alone at this impossible task. The ship's padre, the Rev. W. G. Parker, a New Zealander, was tending badly wounded men at the bottom of a shaft passage and refused to come up when the hatch at the top of the passage had to be closed. He, too, was never seen again. And a Royal Marine who survived can 'never forget the terrible screaming and shouting coming up the ventilation shafts from the men trapped down below'. But, with the slower sinking of *Prince of Wales* and the help given by *Express* in taking so many men straight over the side, four out of every five men on *Prince of Wales* were saved.

The end was near. The slow roll to port continued until *Prince of Wales* was lying upside down with her flat bottom completely exposed.

May I say it is something I will never forget now, for the ship was completely upside down. I was standing on the bottom – almost falling into a large torpedo hole – and I could see the propellers slowly turning. I had the feeling that I was the only one there but I could still hear screams from inside the torpedo hole and there appeared to be lots of people in the water. As the stern began to disappear, I realized the water would reach me standing there, so I began to swim for it. (Petty Officer L. V. Leather)*

Several of the last men on the ship's bottom were non-swimmers, or were determined to leave the ship as late as

* Mr Leather's christian names are Loos Verdun; he is one of the many First World War children named after battles on the Western Front.

possible. Leading Stoker Harry Roberts sat with several of these on the ship's bottom, calmly opened a tin of Craven A cigarettes and handed them around. Another stoker, a non-swimmer, walked up towards the bows until overtaken and sucked down by the water and, with no thoughts of surviving, began drinking in sea water to hasten his death. He was caught in an air bubble, brought to the surface and found himself next to a convenient plank of wood. A well-known character, Signalman Cole, was seen calmly standing with his white cap still on his head and, being another non-swimmer, simply stood still, trusting to his lifebelt to save him. Cole disappeared beneath the water, but also came to the surface safely.

Hundreds of men in the water and on *Express* witnessed the end. Leading Seaman Basil Elsmore remembers that 'our ship did not go easily. My last memory picture is of a huge football pitch – the ship's bottom – with all the players and spectators sliding down to one end.' The bows of *Prince of Wales* reared high in the air, the great torpedo hole in her forepeak clearly visible; then there was 'a fantastic noise' to be heard, obviously made by the inside fixtures tearing loose, and the battleship slipped quietly beneath the sea. One officer in the water was seen to salute, to the amazement of a near-by stoker who thought that 'that sort of thing only happened in books'. One survivor says that 'there were plenty of tears', and another remembers it as 'a terrible sight and, for any sailor, not possible to contemplate a worse'.

13

The Rescue

Several of the Japanese aircraft that had made the successful attacks on the British ships had remained in the area. These onlookers were either crews from the Mihoro Air Corps, which had taken off late, and therefore had more fuel remaining, or from the Kanoya Air Corps, which had delivered the last devastating torpedo attacks on *Prince of Wales* and *Repulse*. The Japanese airmen realized that there was now little danger from the anti-aircraft guns of the sinking British capital ships and still no sign of British fighter aircraft. They circled to watch the drama still unfolding below.

It was one flight of these aircraft that had swept low over the scene of *Repulse*'s sinking when the survivors believed that they were about to be machine-gunned. But the Mitsubishis had flown over their heads without opening fire, and one *Repulse* survivor is certain that he saw a Japanese pilot saluting the spot where *Repulse* had sunk. The Japanese could certainly have caused a large number of casualties among the trained and valuable seamen then in the water, but neither then nor at any time later were survivors fired upon. Commander C. W. May, captain of *Electra*, later submitted this report.

Several formations of Japanese aircraft were in the vicinity until about 13.10 but no attempt was made to bomb or machine-gun destroyers and survivors. Possibly no bombs remained but it is certainly considered that enemy aircraft purposely refrained from any hostile act during rescue work.

This restraint on the part of the Japanese is interesting because it is out of character with many other Japanese acts in the opening months of the war. The reason for it is not known. Perhaps these Japanese professional naval officers and men had some regard for their British contemporaries; perhaps they were so stunned by the complete success of their recent attacks that the idea of continuing the fight against the men in the water never occurred to them. A large number of the British survivors confidently told the authors of this book that one Japanese aircraft had even signalled to the rescuing destroyers, 'CEASE FIRING. PICK UP SURVIVORS'; and that some sort of truce had then followed. The wording of the reputed signal in many accounts was always the same. This would have made a good story, but unfortunately there is no truth in it and there was never any communication between the two sides in the battle.

Midshipman Hoashi, who had flown off to Kuantan airfield to drop his two small bombs there, returned soon after *Repulse* had gone to the bottom and resumed his duty of signalling reports of the action to Saigon. He reported that *Repulse* had sunk, that *Prince of Wales* was clearly sinking, and then details of the rescue work, adding his opinion that there would not be room on the three destroyers for all the *Repulse* survivors and that the *Prince of Wales* survivors would fail to be rescued.

This leisurely Japanese viewing of the scene was rudely interrupted at about 13.20, about three minutes before *Prince of Wales* sank, by the arrival on the scene of the Australian-piloted Brewster Buffalo fighters that had taken off from Sembawang airfield an hour earlier. One of the Buffaloes had been forced to turn back with engine trouble soon after leaving Sembawang, but the other ten, led by Flight Lieutenant Tim Vigors, all reached the scene of the recent battle. The departure from Sembawang had been so hurried that there had been no briefing; Vigors was simply told to fly to a position sixty miles south-south-east of Kuantan and find the British ships which were under Japanese air attack. There was no time to tell the other pilots anything, and they simply took off and followed Vigors. Vigors has written the following impression of his arrival on the scene.

When we reached the scene everything was a hell of a mess. The *Repulse* had been sunk long before. I just saw the last of the *Prince of Wales* as she put her nose in the air and slid in backwards. The scene was fairly sickmaking particularly as I realized the immensity of the disaster and knew that it need never have occurred. If I had been allowed to keep a standing patrol over the Fleet we could have kept the shadow aircraft away. Even had the Japanese been able to establish an exact position without shadow aircraft, their torpedo bombers had no fighter escort and were very heavily laden. Even six Buffaloes could have wrought merry hell with them and certainly prevented a lot of the torpedo strikes. The *Repulse*, which was much less heavily armoured, would probably have bought it anyway, but I have no doubt in my mind that we could have saved the *Prince of Wales* and got her back to Singapore.

One or two of the Buffalo pilots saw Hoashi's Mitsubishi, but the Japanese made off at high speed and, although the Buffaloes were slightly faster, Hoashi's aircraft soon disappeared into a cloud. The other Japanese aircraft in the area may have left by then, or they may have made their escapes like Hoashi, but they were not seen by the Buffaloes. Vigors split his formation into smaller groups to patrol at various heights in case any more Japanese planes appeared, but he took his own plane down low and flew around the desolate scene of the recent sinkings. He could see the hundreds of men in the sea quite plainly, and the men in the sea could see him. What the shipwrecked sailors and the pilot thought of each other is of some interest.

A few sailors, uninjured and more resilient than most, may well have waved and cheered when Vigors flew over their heads, but the majority saw in the belated arrival of these few fighter aircraft the cause of all their troubles and of the loss of the two great ships that had, until a few minutes earlier, been their homes, but which were now the tombs for so many of their shipmates. They jeered, booed and swore at the solitary pilot circling above. Able Seaman R. H. James, late of the *Prince of Wales*, sums up the feelings of so many men at this moment.

If, as I sincerely hope, the pilot of that aircraft is still alive, his ears must still be burning. Not that he was in any way to blame but, for a moment, he merely became the focal point of all the despair and frustration felt by the bulk of the survivors at the complete lack of support from the air.

This resentment at the fighter pilots was not felt only by the survivors of the sunken ships; a *Prince of Wales* man on *Express* noted that 'if the gun crews on the destroyer had had their way they would have opened fire on the Buffaloes'.

Flight Lieutenant Vigors completely misinterpreted his reception from the men in the water, but this will be more conveniently described later. After almost an hour over the rescue scene, the Buffaloes had to leave because of fuel shortage. No more Japanese aircraft had been seen. The fighters investigated the steamer *Haldis* while on their return flight, and then flew on to land safely back at their airfield.

The first stage of the rescue work was carried out with the destroyers *Electra* and *Vampire* working at the scene of *Repulse*'s sinking, and *Express* at that of *Prince of Wales*. This was a sensible arrangement. While there had been more *Prince of Wales* survivors to be picked up, their ship had gone down slowly and boats, Carley floats and much floatable gear had been got into the water. *Express* had, moreover, taken aboard a number of crew directly from *Prince of Wales* before she sank. Many survivors believe that the two ships went down within a mile of each other, or two miles at most, but the wreck of *Prince of Wales* now lies nearly eight miles to the south-east of that of *Repulse*. The final actions had taken place about four miles apart, with *Repulse* sinking while still turning to starboard and away from *Prince of Wales*, and the tidal current probably carried *Prince of Wales* a further two miles away during the fifty minutes between the sinking of the two ships.

The *Repulse* men in the water, or already aboard *Electra* or *Vampire*, had seen *Prince of Wales*'s bow rise into the the air and then watched as the great ship sank. The event was viewed with mixed feelings by some of the *Repulse* survivors; they had always regarded *Prince of Wales* as a 'Jonah', and on *Electra* 'there was a mass exodus to the upper deck where a hearty cheer bade her farewell'. One survivor aboard *Electra* has 'a very vivid memory of an almost naked man dancing up and down and screaming for a camera' to photograph the sinking battleship. This may have been the American reporter, Cecil Brown of C.B.S., but whoever it was never got his picture of a lifetime and the sinking of neither ship was photographed, though the Japanese took one or two indistinct photographs of the battle that have survived and Sub-Lieutenant P. F. C. Satow took one excellent one from the bridge of his ship, *Express*, while still alongside *Prince of Wales*.

When *Prince of Wales* sank, Commander C. W. May of *Electra* became Senior Officer Force Z. Although *Electra* was working at the scene of *Repulse*'s sinking, *Electra* had been broadcasting signals on behalf of the flagship since 13.00. May sent this last simple, but world-shattering, signal from *Electra* at 13.18:

H.M.S. PRINCE OF WALES SUNK.

This was received in the War Room at G.H.Q. Singapore three minutes later. Nine signals had been sent in all; not one had requested the assistance of the R.A.F.*

The many swimmers from both ships had mostly made their way to the Carley floats or to the few ship's boats that had been got away and awaited their turn to be picked up by the destroyers.

I kicked my shoes off whilst in the water and swam around in the oil fuel for about an hour making my way forward to one of the Carley floats with men already on it. The only fear that was in my mind at that moment was the sharks. When I got to the float, I hung on to the side to get my wind back. I noticed the Warrant Bosun was hanging on to a piece of wood twenty yards from the float. He was

* Appendix Three gives the full text of these signals.

delirious through consuming oil fuel. I swam towards him and brought him back on the Carley float. He said, 'If I'm too much trouble, let me go back in the water and drown.' I held him between my legs up on the float and, with the float rolling and my knees sticking into his stomach, it made him bring all the oil fuel up. Within ten minutes, he was as right as rain. (Marine J. Powell, H.M.S. *Repulse*)

After nearly being knocked senseless by a booted man who had jumped on top of me, I managed to swim to an empty Carley float but could not get in it as it floated too high out of the water, so I held on to the lifelines, then two bluejackets reached the float and their combined weight brought one end down; they got in and hauled me in also. We picked up many swimmers, including one midshipman with a stomach wound; his blood was colouring the water which was waist high for the taller men and armpit high for smaller men. A movement on the raft caused the water, blood and oil to splash our faces. We picked up a few dead sailors, but slid them back into the sea to make way for the living. As senior rank on the raft, I went to the wounded midshipman, who could only mutter, 'Thank you sir, I'll be all right.' I heard the poor lad died next day. (Lieutenant H. Abrahams, H.M.S. *Repulse*)

There was one chap up the front of the raft paddling like mad and he kept screaming for everybody else to paddle to the nearest land (which we could just see in the distance). Nobody was paying much attention to him, except to tell him to shut up. (Boy Seaman B. N. Millard, H.M.S. *Prince of Wales*)

The impression that remains uppermost in my own mind about the affair – it was strong then and it is equally strong now over thirty years later – was the incredible calmness and good humour with which the lads took to the water. Although we were all covered from head to foot in thick black oil, and many of us were in pain, I heard nothing but wry joking from the chaps who shared my crowded Carley float. One of them was grumbling lugubriously because the so-and-so's had chosen 'tot-time' [the time when the rum issue was normally made] to launch their attack and the Navigating Officer was dispassionately telling us roughly what our position was at the time of the sinking. Another chap, a signalman, was balancing himself precariously on the heaving raft and making a semaphore message to the nearest destroyer to say that we had one or two casualties among us, including myself on whom that same resourceful signalman had already tied a crude but effective splint made from a spar of wood and some strips of torn shirt. (Leading Telegraphist B. G. Campion, H.M.S. *Prince of Wales*)

The man semaphoring to the destroyer was the resilient Signalman Cole, who had earlier been seen standing calmly on the flat bottom of *Prince of Wales* still with his white hat on and trusting to his lifebelt to float him safely off.

Lieutenant Ian Forbes of *Prince of Wales* joined up with his Gunnery Officer, Lieutenant-Commander Colin Mc-Mullen, on a Carley float.

We had an agreeable time there for, perhaps, two hours as rescue operations were conducted by the escorting destroyers. We were fully aware that the Japanese planes would not return (why should they?) and so there was an air of pleasurable release, sitting in a warm and sunlit sea. A British aircraft flew over from time to time, which was greeted with waving and ribald remarks. This, I believe, was reported as being a sign of wonderful 'morale'. I don't suppose our morale was any different from the rest of the Fleet but, when released from such an event, no one solemnly considers, at that moment, the vast historic implications, such as the fall of Singapore, the total ending of all Colonial possessions, etc. All hands are happy to be alive and to wave and cheer accordingly.

Perhaps the most bizarre story to come out of the Carley floats is that of Able Seaman Alexander White, a radar operator from *Prince of Wales*.

When I joined the Navy, an aunt presented me with the caul that covered my grandfather at birth and which had been saved. Apparently there is an old seafarers' superstition that he who carries a caul will never drown. This was attached to a covering letter which I carried in my wallet which happened to be in the pocket of my trousers when I went over the side. While in the float I found the letter floating – the wallet and the caul having disintegrated. I still have the letter with the ink smeared by the water!*

---

* CAUL: The amnion or inner membrane enclosing the foetus before birth. This, or a portion of it sometimes enveloping the head of a child at birth, is regarded as lucky and supposed to be a preserva-tive against drowning' – *Shorter Oxford English Dictionary*

The three destroyers worked hard to get all the survivors out of the water. The calm sea, warm weather and
absence of Japanese aircraft made this a straightforward
operation for trained seamen rescuing their colleagues.
Scrambling-nets were let over the sides and the fit men
climbed aboard. Lines were thrown to single swimmers
who were not near to scrambling-nets, but these lines were
very difficult to grasp for oil-soaked men.

I even had my own moment of humour when *Electra* (and how
superb those destroyers were that day) found time to get around to
my vicinity where I was trying to help a very large, unconscious
Royal Marine, wounded and clogged with oil. Expertly handled,
Electra glided alongside me and threw me a rope. Wrestling to get
it underneath the man's armpits and prematurely anticipating success,
I shouted 'Haul away' a little too eagerly only to find that the noose
had slid up round his neck. Just in time. There were ribald comments
on my performance by friends in the water and already on deck, and
then we were both safe. (Lieutenant J. O. C. Hayes, H.M.S. *Repulse*)

Unfortunately there were several men who made it to
the bottom of the nets or to the lines, but, who then reaching the limit of their strength, fell back and disappeared.

The most badly wounded on the destroyers were taken
below for treatment, but most survivors were unceremoniously hauled away from the side and dumped on the
decks to be left while further men were saved from the
water. There were soon dozens of exhausted men laying
out on the hot metal decks, retching and coughing the oil
out of their lungs. Rum was found to be an excellent
remedy for swallowed oil; a stiff tot often brought forth a
violent sickness and prompt recovery. Once survivors had
recovered, they started to rub the worst of the foul-
smelling oil off their skins, to wander around looking for
missing pals, to search for a drink or a cigarette. Many
recovered survivors helped with further rescue work. On
all the rescuing destroyers it was noticed that survivors
usually gravitated towards familiar positions to offer help.
For example, *Repulse*'s Royal Marines manned the after
guns on *Electra* in case of further air attack and thus

released the destroyer's seamen gunners for rescue work.

Able Seaman James from *Prince of Wales* was one of the survivors who tried to help in rescue work.

I finished up on the fo'c'sle of the *Express* and there made what was probably my one constructive contribution to the proceedings. Three of us heaved a man aboard from the ratlines over the side and he promptly collapsed on the deck. The three of us took it in turns to apply artificial respiration, and I was amazed how much water came out of this man, forming a small continuous stream running down to the gunwale. After what must have been at least twenty minutes, he finally sat up and said, 'Thanks mate. Got a cigarette?' This we were able to provide, thanks to the generosity of the Canteen Manager on *Express*, who was distributing them freely by the packet.

Officers' Cook Wilf Greenwood of *Repulse* was rescued by *Electra*.

I remember lying on the deck and looking at the clouds and sky and thanking God for still being alive. The Steward aboard the *Electra* was a grand little chap; he assisted some survivors down into the wardroom mess and tried his best to comfort us, helping us in many ways. It was quite a sight in the messroom – bodies were everywhere. I remember seeing one big chap laid on a table, oil was coming from his mouth. Another chap who was a Chief Petty Officer looked all in and wasn't a young chap; he said, 'I've had enough of this, this is the third time for me.' Another sailor came in and said laughing, 'I've lost my bleeding teeth.' While all this was going on the radio was playing 'Ah, Sweet Mystery of Life'. It made me think.

There were many distressing, scenes in the destroyers' wardrooms, for it was here that the badly wounded men were being treated. Many scalded or flash-burned men had managed to survive this far, but were now suffering from delayed shock. There was little the doctors could do for these cases except to give them morphia to relieve the pain. On each of the rescuing ships there was soon a pitiful row of blanket-covered bodies in a quiet corner of the upper deck.

Ordinary Seaman W. E. England of *Prince of Wales* went below in *Express* to see if he could find some way of helping.

I found a messmate lying on a stretcher with his head packed in cotton wool. All the skin from his face and body had been burned off. He was, I believe, a stoker or gun-layer A.B. in the regular R.N. He told me that he had just come out of a doorway into the 'waist' of *Prince of Wales* when the flash from the last bombs caught him. He gave me his money and his watch (which was scorched and had stopped), and he asked me if I would write to his wife when I got back. I tried to comfort him and said that he was safe now and it would not be long before we were in Singapore and he was in hospital. He cheered up a bit and asked for a drink. I went off to find the bathroom on the destroyer and eventually came back with a cup of water, but I was too late. Bob had ended his story of 'life in the Navy' and passed peacefully away. I lifted his head to see what damage had been done and found his skull wide open. How had he managed to talk to me about his wife in that condition? His wife had her first child three months later.

Lieutenant J. O. C. Hayes had been 'Snotty's Nurse' in *Repulse*. One of his boys was now lying on one of the two bunks that was all that *Electra* had by way of a sick bay.

One of our young doctors was among the survivors, in no great shape himself but tackling his overwhelming task as one would expect. He came to seek me out and told me that he had a little midshipman in one of the bunks, that he was dying from bullet wounds in the groin, although sedated he was in great pain and asking to see me if I was on board. There was another dying man in the other bunk.

Among his thirty gunroom colleagues, this midshipman had hitherto appeared the least developed. Immature for his age and often in trouble – through no intention of his, but there are those who cannot avoid it – he had seemed and looked a near child and therefore had needed careful handling. He was insufficiently fledged to have an Action Station of any import and I had therefore alloted him something to do with the secondary armament, at which station he had been wounded by a machine-gun bullet.

Scarcely recognizable myself, I asked to be alone with him and took his hand. He gave me a brave smile which knifed into my heart and conscience for any previous admonishment I had had to bestow. He held on to my hand with a firm little grip as though trying to express his last tangible feeling in the young life he must have known was slipping from him. I have never before or since seen death, or the awareness of death, in that moment of truth so transform youth to man, suddenly adult, brave and silently perceptive of the tragedy in which we were both enmeshed. He died that evening.

By 14.00, nearly one and a half hours after *Repulse* had sunk, the work of rescuing her survivors was nearly over. Commander May ordered *Vampire* to carry out one last search while he took *Electra* over to the scene of *Prince of Wales*'s sinking. No other rescue ships had arrived on the scene and *Express* had been working quite alone. She was now so full of survivors as to be dangerously top-heavy. Although there were still 300 or so *Prince of Wales* men in the water awaiting rescue, Commander May ordered Lieutenant-Commander Cartwright of *Express* to make straight for Singapore while *Electra* took over the rescue work. An hour later, *Vampire* had satisfied herself that the last live *Repulse* man had been taken from the sea. She came across to *Electra*, picking up on the way two *Prince of Wales* men who had drifted out of the main rescue area. *Vampire* too was then released by Commander May to return to Singapore.

Electra stayed a further forty-five minutes, and the last few *Princes of Wales* survivors were got on board. Among the last to be picked up was a group of men who had taken refuge on one of *Prince of Wales*'s waterlogged cutters. This, although entirely below the surface, had had enough buoyancy to support the men standing in it. They were quite cheerful, and one rating was 'still mad enough to sing in defiance' until rescued. One exhausted boy seaman, however, when he had to climb *Electra*'s scrambling-net, found it 'like climbing the peak of Everest'.

At 16.00 Commander May took his ship over to the last survivors he could see, a float with a small group of men, one of whom cheerfully rolled up a trouser leg and 'thumbed a lift'. Then *Electra*'s lookout reported 'a man swimming or a drifting coconut astern'. Commander May took his ship round in one last wide sweep, and indeed found this final survivor and picked him up. *Electra* increased speed and turned towards Singapore.

The three destroyers had picked up 2,081 men who would survive the short voyage to Singapore as well as several corpses and some badly wounded who would die on the way. The smallest destroyer, the Australian *Vampire*, was the only one of the three to record the exact numbers she had picked up – from *Repulse*, nine officers including Captain Tennant, 213 ratings and one civilian war correspondent, O'Dowd Gallagher of the *Daily Express*, and two ratings from *Prince of Wales*. *Express*, which had worked alone for so long at the scene of *Prince of Wales*'s sinking, is believed to have rescued about 1,000 men, leaving *Electra* with nearly 900, of whom 571 were from *Repulse* and the remainder from *Prince of Wales*.

To mark the scene of a momentous battle there were left behind great sheets of stinking oil, drifting boats, Carley floats, flotsam of every description and many corpses, either floating face down and anonymous or bobbing about supported by their lifejackets.

14

The Aftermath

News of the disaster was becoming known in many places throughout the world even while *Electra*, *Express* and *Vampire* were still picking up survivors. Among the first to hear were the British warships in the Far East whose wirelesses had been tuned to the frequency on which the signals from Force Z had been broadcast. These messages had been decoded at once and passed to the ships' respective captains. The cruiser *Exeter* was just approaching Singapore – the first British naval reinforcement for the Eastern Fleet since the outbreak of the Japanese war. Lieutenant-Commander G. T. Cooper recounts how he received the news.

I was on the forecastle preparing the anchors and cables when the Commander came up and touched me on the shoulder.

'Had a good lunch, Number One?' he asked.

'Not particularly,' I replied.

'You better have,' he whispered. '*Repulse* sunk. *Prince of Wales* hit.'

In his own imperturbable way he moved on, leaving me standing there absolutely stunned. He obviously did not mean me to convey this information to the sailors working under me, so I continued with the cables without saying a word.

A few minutes later, I felt another nudge on the shoulder. It was the Commander again.

'*Prince of Wales* sunk too,' he said, and moved away.

A short time after, we secured alongside the dockyard wall in the Naval Base. It was not a very pleasant situation. Here we were, an 8,000-ton cruiser left as the spearhead of the British Navy against the whole naval might of Japan.

In the Operations Room at the Naval Base, Rear-Admiral Palliser was faced with the unpleasant task of having to inform the Admiralty. At 13.45, just over twenty minutes after *Prince of Wales* went down, he sent a simply worded signal informing the Admiralty that *Prince of Wales* and *Repulse* had both been sunk 'by torpedoes'; later signals gave more detail. When Lieutenant Richard Dyer of H.M.S. *Tenedos* reported to Palliser later that evening, he found Admiral Phillips's Chief of Staff 'completely stunned and virtually inarticulate; he seemed to have lost his voice and could barely nod or shake his head'. It was not known at that time whether or not Admiral Phillips had survived, and the Admiralty sent instructions that Vice-Admiral Layton, the former Commander-in-Chief China Station who had just left Singapore on the liner *Dominion Monarch*, was to be recalled to assume temporary command of the Eastern Fleet.

The authorities at Singapore had the delicate problem of how to handle the news of the sinkings, particularly in view of the existing doubts over the morale of the native populations in the Far Eastern possessions. It was assumed that the Japanese would waste no time in announcing their great victory, and it was known that three destroyers would arrive at the Naval Base later that day and discharge their hundreds of survivors – an event that could hardly be concealed from the many civilian dockyard workers. It was decided that Mr Duff Cooper, M.P., who had been the British War Cabinet's representative in Singapore since early September, should broadcast that evening on the local radio. He did so and announced the loss of the two ships without attempting to minimize the scale of the tragedy.

This is not the first time in our long history of glory that we have met with disaster and have surmounted it. Indeed there is something in our nature and of our fathers before us, that only disaster can produce.*

The local press followed this up next morning. The *Singapore Free Press* printed this editorial:

Sometimes there is news which no one will at first believe. This has happened twice during the past three days. First there was the air

* *Singapore Free Press*, 11 December 1941.

attack on Singapore early on the morning of Monday. It took everyone by surprise. Last night there was the news of the sinking of
Prince of Wales and *Repulse*. Such grievous news, it seemed, could
not possibly be true. Yet true it is, alas, and the heavy blow will long
be felt by us in the Far East, by the whole British Empire and by the
Royal Navy in particular. No words that can be printed here will
lighten the blow and no one would dare to minimize the seriousness
of the loss . . . We must face the fact that two of our best heavy warships have been sunk by the Japanese within the first three days of the
fighting in this part of the world; we must admit that the pride of the
Eastern Fleet is no more.

It was a realistic and dignified piece of journalism, but it
came all too late. British prestige in the Far East and morale
in the fighting services there had been dealt a blow from
which they would never recover.

The Japanese had actually been the first to broadcast the
news when, at 14.35 (Singapore Time), the Imperial
Navy Headquarters in Tokyo issued this statement.

From the outbreak of hostilities the movements of the two British
capital ships have been closely observed. Yesterday afternoon they
were discovered by one of our submarines carrying out a reconnaissance in co-operation with Naval surface ships and the Naval Air
Force. At 11.30 this morning our submarine again confirmed the
position of the British ships, off Kuantan on the east coast of Malaya.
Without losing a moment the Naval Air Force entered into a daunt-
less and daring attack and in a twinkling of the eye attacked at about
12.45. The *Repulse* was seriously damaged by the first bombs dropped
and shortly afterwards the *Prince of Wales* was hit and developed a
heavy list to port. The *Repulse* sank first and, shortly after, at ten
minutes to three, the *Prince of Wales* blew up and finally sank.
    The third day of hostilities has resulted in the annihilation of the
main strength of the British Far Eastern Squadron. *

It was an accurate statement in all respects save that the
Navy had credited the sighting off Kuantan that morning
to a submarine and not to Midshipman Hoashi's aircraft

* Masanobu Tsuji, *Singapore, the Japanese Version*, Constable,
London, 1962, p. 97.

and *Prince of Wales* had not blown up before sinking. This splendid news for the Japanese was immediately broadcast on Tokyo Radio, and at 15.53, while *Electra* was picking up the last of the survivors from the sea, the Japanese Domei News Agency broadcast an English-language report on its China Zone Service.

The British Foreign Office Radio Monitoring Station at Beaconsfield was one of the many places throughout the world where this report was picked up. The time was a little after 08.00 in London. The news item was immediately flashed to the Admiralty and to the Prime Minister's Office in Downing Street, but it did no more than confirm what was already known from Rear-Admiral Palliser's earlier signal. A telephone at his bedside had already woken Winston Churchill, and Sir Dudley Pound, the First Sea Lord, had given the terrible news. At first Churchill could not understand what Admiral Pound was saying, but once the message finally became clear, Churchill, as he later wrote in his memoirs, 'turned over and twisted in bed and the full horror of the news sank in on me'. Britain had lost capital ships before in this war, but never two in one day and not in such a humiliating and one-sided battle. It had been Churchill himself who had insisted that *Repulse* and *Prince of Wales* go out to the Far East.

As in Singapore, it was decided that nothing could be gained by attempting to conceal the loss from the public. Mr Churchill went down to the House of Commons, and at 11.32, immediately after prayers, he rose and made the following straightforward statement.

I have bad news for the House which I thought I should impart at the earliest moment. A report has been received from Singapore that H.M.S. *Prince of Wales* and H.M.S. *Repulse* have been sunk while carrying out operations against the Japanese attacks on Malaya. No details are yet available except those contained in the Japanese communique which claims both ships were sunk by air attack.*

* *Evening News* (London), 10 December 1941.

At the same time, an Official Admiralty communique gave much the same information to the radio and press. Such was the speed of world-wide communications that virtually everyone in England heard the news from the B.B.C.'s lunchtime news broadcasts before any of the survivors of the sinkings had reached Singapore. That afternoon it was the front-page item in all the London evening papers.

The three rescue ships were still on their way to Singapore when Winston Churchill was addressing the House of Commons. Rescuers and rescued had settled down to make the best of their eight-hour voyage to the Naval Base. Many of the survivors had to remain on deck, and only the wounded could be sure of a place below, though one old 'three-badger' rescued from *Repulse* recovered sufficiently to be observed in *Electra*'s galley calmly drying out his £1 notes. Shell-shock and reaction sometimes set in; one of *Express*'s stokers handed a cigarette to an oil-covered survivor, and was surprised to find the man was an officer who remarked bitterly, 'Don't you thank God that you weren't on *Prince of Wales*. At least you've still got your ship.'

But many of the survivors soon recovered their spirits, especially after liberal tots of rum – or whisky on the Australian *Vampire* – had been issued. *Express* was carrying the greatest load of survivors, and the issue of rum caused a queue to form along one side of the ship so that an 'alarming list' developed. Lieutenant J. R. A. Denne rushed down from the bridge, 'wondering what further disaster had hit us'. All became well after the queue had been 'wound round the funnel and the ship came upright again'. As soon as the late afternoon brought cooler conditions clothes were shared out. One *Repulse* survivor on *Vampire* was given an Australian Naval Rugby Team shirt – 'it was Number 7 and became my most treasured possession'. Food was issued, though when soup was taken to the seamen's messdeck in *Express* the younger seamen couldn't find their appetites as someone had left the body of a dead sailor laid out on the messdeck table.

Cleaned up, fed and with a tot of rum inside them, the survivors could do no more but wait for the crowded destroyers to reach Singapore. There was much fear that the Japanese aircraft would return and bomb the destroyers; casualties would have been fearful had this happened, but the Japanese were not seen again. Leading Supply Assistant Leonard Sandland, a *Repulse* survivor aboard *Electra* probably sums up well the scene at this stage.

I took a walk round the ship, seeing if I could find anyone I knew. The whole deck was covered with exhausted men, but it was difficult to recognize anybody at all because of the oil. I did eventually find one or two of my mates, but in each case I recognized them only by their voices or their outline as they walked.

I had intended to do something when and if I eventually left the Service and that was to paint a picture of some of the survivors sitting round the well of the forward gun turret for warmth – some with just a vest on, some with just underpants on, some with nothing at all on, just a row of bare bottoms sitting round that well – filthy, dead tired, but glad to be alive. It's engraved indelibly on my memory. I've never got around to painting it yet, but I will.

Vampire met again the steamer *Haldis* during the return voyage, and inquired whether any assistance was required, but the merchant ship was not in any trouble and continued with her plodding voyage to the safety of Singapore.*

Express met five destroyers heading north. These were the four American ships – *Alden*, *Edsall*, *John D. Edwards* and *Whipple* – that had arrived at Singapore that morning, and the fifth ship was H.M.S. *Stronghold*. They had all been sent out from Singapore in answer to Admiral Phillips's request for destroyer assistance. The United States Navy had thus come this close to being involved in a famous

---

* *Haldis* survived the war and sailed again in the Far East until July 1948 when she was blown ashore in a gale at Hong Kong and wrecked.

naval action. *Express* informed the destroyers that the action was over and that there was nothing they could do to help, though the five destroyers remained at sea for several hours. The four Americans searched the area where *Prince of Wales* and *Repulse* had sunk to make sure that there were no more survivors, but all they found was oil, debris and floating bodies. Early the next morning the Americans sighted what they believed to be the tracks of torpedoes fired at them, but they were not hit and no sign was found of the submarine that might have fired the torpedoes. Soon after this the U.S.S. *Edsall* found and boarded a Japanese fishing trawler, the *Shofu Fu Maru*, which had four small boats in tow. These were almost certainly the small ships seen by Force Z off Kuantan the previous morning. The *Edsall* took the Japanese ships back to Singapore where they were closely examined both by the Americans and by some British officers from H.M.S. *Mauritius* who had been out with the Americans as liaison officers. There was no sign whatsoever that the Japanese ship was other than a normal fishing trawler, with the smaller boats being used for line fishing, and the Japanese were interned. There seems to be no connection between the *Shofu Fu Maru* and the bullet-riddled boat containing Japanese army equipment found near Kuantan which had been the basis of the false report that the Japanese were landing there.*

* Three days later the four American destroyers left Singapore hurriedly, on orders from Admiral Hart at Manila, much to the disappointment of the British. *Edsall* had the most exciting time in the next few weeks. She was the first U.S. Navy destroyer to take part in the sinking of a full-sized Japanese submarine when, with three Australian corvettes, she sank I.124 off Darwin, Northern Australia, on 20 January 1942. At the end of March 1942, *Edsall* and *Whipple* were in company with the famous American ship *Langley* when it was bombed and sunk by the same Japanese naval bombers that had sunk *Prince of Wales* and *Repulse*. After transferring *Langley*'s survivors to another American ship at Christmas Island, *Edsall* had the misfortune to meet two Japanese battleships, the *Hiei* and the *Kirishima*, and was sunk in a hopeless action. *Alden* and *John D.*

Express, with her huge load of *Prince of Wales* survivors, was the first of the rescue ships to reach Singapore. Despite numerous signals sent earlier, giving the estimated time of her arrival, the destroyer found that she could get no reply from the Signal Station at Changi Point. To proceed up Johore Strait without first being 'booked in' at Changi was forbidden and would incur the risk of being shelled by coastal artillery. Lieutenant-Commander Cartwright fumed as his signaller tried in vain to get a reply to his flashing lamp signals.

We came in absolutely packed with survivors and had to stand off Changi Signal Station for nearly twenty-five minutes before we could get a reply. If I'd had any ammunition left, I'd have put a shell right through them. I was furious.

Changi eventually woke up and allowed *Express* to proceed. The destroyer reached the Naval Base at 23.10 and secured alongside. *Vampire* soon followed, and then Commander May brought *Electra* in and berthed at exactly midnight.

Survivors of shipwreck always seem to have a dazed, anonymous appearance when landing and the men of *Prince of Wales* and *Repulse* were no exception. Many were only partially dressed, few had badges of rank, most were exhausted and filthy from the fuel oil. They came ashore by the hundreds on to the quayside of the Naval Base; one wonders whether the planners and naval strategists had ever envisaged such an ignominious scene as this one.

There was, of course, the greatest sympathy and much help for the survivors. The crew of the recently arrived H.M.S. *Exeter* – another Devonport-manned ship – were prominent at the scene, as were the permanent staff of the Naval Base. The wounded came off on stretchers; the

Edwards both fought in the Battle of the Java Sea and, with *Whipple*, eventually returned to the United States. These three ships spent most of the remaining war years as escorts on Atlantic convoys.

H.M.S. *Stronghold* was sunk by Japanese warships on 4 March 1942 while attempting to escape to Australia after the Japanese invasion of Java.

dazed were helped ashore or even carried pick-a-back. One filthy survivor, walking gingerly barefoot over the gravel chippings of the quayside, was offered a lift by an officer. The survivor protested that the officer would ruin his spotless white uniform '. . . . the uniform. Get up on my back.' A lonely figure on the quayside was the young Midshipman Leach, searching for his father.

When *Express* pulled in to secure, someone had shouted up from the quayside, 'How big was the Jap Fleet you clued up with?' The reply, from someone on the destroyer, was, 'A bloody big air fleet.' And, when *Electra*'s load of survivors were going ashore, one of her crew shouted, 'Come back tomorrow, you shower of B's, and clean our ship of oil fuel'; but another man remembers that the landing was carried out 'in a grim sort of silence with no laughing or yelling'. The last survivors were soon ashore and the crews of the destroyers were allowed to rest; most fell at once into a deep sleep, and the authorities were sympathetic enough not to disturb them for twelve hours. One *Express* crew member remembers the desolate scene aboard his ship – 'The breeze blowing discarded bandages flapping from the upper superstructure, blood smeared across paintwork, and that smell of anaesthetic everywhere.'

Once ashore, the survivors were given sandwiches, cigarettes and more rum, the latter in almost unlimited quantities, perhaps in order to force men to vomit again and get rid of the last of the oil they had swallowed. The staff of the base had set up a row of tables and chairs under arc lights and had been waiting for the survivors. Each survivor made his way to this reporting centre and gave his rank, name and service number. All this activity was taking place in the middle of the night after the most traumatic day in the lives of most of them, and many were now near the end of their tether. One disillusioned member of the base staff describes them as 'a drunken, oil-sodden, undisciplined rabble but this was not surprising in view of the events'; and an officer from H.M.S. *Mauritius*, who was helping, observed among the survivors 'a feeling of shame and, in a few cases, some tears'.

After giving in their names, the survivors were led away to the Fleet Shore Accommodation and put to bed.

The contrast between the mood at Singapore and that among the Japanese involved in the recent action can easily be imagined. As long as the action had continued, there had been furious activity with the Japanese directing their submarines and surface vessels to the scene of the battle off Kuantan. Plans were actually made to rearm the returning aircraft and carry out a second strike at the British ships. The Japanese had been desperately anxious to finish off *Prince of Wales* and *Repulse* in any way possible so that their operations could be resumed in the way intended before the untimely arrival of the two British ships at Singapore.

It was a stroke of good fortune for the Japanese that the Buffaloes of 453 Squadron did not arrive on the scene a few minutes before they did; Midshipman Hoashi had just had time to see *Prince of Wales* capsize and float bottom upwards before escaping into the cloud. He knew there could be no survival for the battleship and was thus able to signal to his base that both the British capital ships had been destroyed. Had the Buffaloes arrived a little earlier, this valuable piece of information would not have reached Saigon. The Japanese would thus have had to continue with their efforts to finish off *Prince of Wales*, but Hoashi's report released them from this anxiety. The submarines and surface warships were recalled; the merchant ships supplying the Japanese invasion forces were ordered to resume work; the plan for the second aircraft strike was abandoned. The whole of the Japanese naval effort in this area could now be directed without fear of interference on the next stage of their war plan. This was the first fruit of the victory the airmen had achieved off Kuantan.

These airmen had also picked up Hoashi's signal while flying back to Saigon. They could hardly believe what they heard – these two great warships both sunk by their aeroplanes in just one series of attacks! The feelings of jubilation among the Japanese aircrews may also easily be imagined.

Saigon had ordered that any returning aircraft short of fuel could divert to the recently captured R.A.F. airfield at Kota Bharu, and several pilots took advantage of this. The remainder flew on to Indo-China and landed there to a great welcome from the ground staffs. One Mitsubishi Betty of the Kanoya Air Corps, seriously damaged by British anti-aircraft fire during the last hectic series of torpedo attacks, crashed on landing and was completely wrecked, though there is no record of casualties among its crew. Midshipman Hoashi was one of the last to land, his Nell having been in the air for thirteen hours! This young pilot and his crew had certainly served their Emperor well. There were great parties on the Japanese airfields that night. Two small statements have filtered through the intervening years: one, that 'the victory was celebrated against the current background of hatred for the British and the West'; the other that the airmen all got 'roaring drunk'.

There was one surprising sequel to the Japanese victory. Next morning, Lieutenant Iki of the Kanoya Air Corps flew again over the scene of the sinkings and dropped a wreath at the spot where so many men had died a few hours earlier. This wreath has been recorded as being a tribute by Lieutenant Iki to the bravery of the British sailors who had fought their ships to the end. It will be shown later that there were connections between the Japanese Naval Air Force and the Royal Navy, and there is no need to doubt Iki's sincerity. However, the crews of the two aircraft flying alongside Iki in his attack on the *Repulse* had both been shot down and killed before his eyes, and the Japanese pilot was almost certainly honouring these dead comrades as well as his British adversaries.

It was obvious that many high-level questions about the

recent action would soon be asked in Britain, and there was much writing of reports to be done before the survivors of the two ships were allowed to disperse. Of the *Repulse* men, it was only some of the officers who had to sit down and write out their memories of the action; it was realized that the loss of an old 1916 battle cruiser after being hit by five torpedoes was not exceptional. But the loss of *Prince of Wales*, and especially the fact of the extensive damage caused by the first torpedo hit, was not going to be passed off so lightly, and hence many of her senior ratings had also to make reports. This work was coordinated by Lieutenant-Commander A. G. Skipwith, who had been first lieutenant in *Prince of Wales* and who was her senior surviving executive branch officer. It took six days for Skipwith to take these preliminary statements, and he sent copies off to London by two different routes to ensure that at least one copy arrived safely. Skipwith's covering letter expressed the hope that these statements would 'provide valuable data for future constructions'. The documents were preserved and are now in the Public Record Office in London. They were only the first of a great mass of paperwork concerning the loss of this battleship that would eventually accumulate.

Another man busy making out a report was Flight Lieutenant Tim Vigors who had led the belated attempt by 453 Squadron to provide Force Z with fighter cover. The day after the sinkings he sat down and, on his own initiative, wrote this letter.

R.A.A.F. Station, Sembawang.
11/12/41.

To Commander-in-Chief,
Far Eastern Fleet.

Sir,

I had the privilege to be the first aircraft to reach the crews of the *Prince of Wales* and the *Repulse* after they had been sunk. I say the privilege for, during the next hour while I flew low over them, I witnessed a show of that indomitable spirit for which the Royal Navy is so famous. I have seen a show of spirit in this war over Dunkirk, during the 'Battle of Britain' and in the London night raids, but never before have I seen anything so comparable with what I saw yesterday. I passed over thousands who had been through an ordeal, the greatness of which they alone can understand, for it is impossible to pass on one's feelings in disaster to others.

Even to an eye so inexperienced as mine it was obvious that the three destroyers were going to take hours to pick up those hundreds of men clinging to wreckage and swimming around in the filthy oily water. Above all this, the threat of another bombing and machine-gun attack was imminent. Every one of those men must have realized that. Yet, as I flew around, every man waved and put his thumb up as I flew over him.

After an hour, lack of petrol forced me to leave but during that hour I had seen so many men in dire danger waving, cheering and joking as if they were holidaymakers at Brighton waving at a low flying aircraft. It shook me, for here was something above human nature. I take off my hat to them, for in them I saw the spirit which wins wars.

I apologize for taking up your valuable time, but I thought you should know of the incredible conduct of your men.
I have the honour to be,
Sir,
Your obedient servant,
Signed T. A. Vigors Flt/Lt
O.C. 453 Squadron.

This letter went first to Air Headquarters, from where it was sent to Naval Headquarters with a covering letter from Air Vice-Marshal Pulford which stated that 'the whole of the personnel under my command would like to join in' the tribute paid to the sailors by Flight Lieutenant Vigors. Vigors's letter too was preserved and was eventually published in the British Official History. When this appeared in 1957, many men who had been in the water or on Carley floats when Vigors had flown just over their heads were amused or slightly contemptuous to see that the pilot had taken their shaking fists and shouted abuse to be friendly greetings.

Flight Lieutenant Vigors had felt particularly bitter that his pilots had not been allowed to take off until long after the Japanese air attacks on the British ships had started. He had intended to carry out a more detailed investigation into this failure for his own interest rather than for official use, but he was shot down and badly burned a few days later. Until he was contacted for the research for this book, he was still firmly convinced that there had been a fifty-minute delay in passing on *Repulse*'s first signal, about being under Japanese aircraft attack, to Sembawang. The actual time-lapse was only fifteen minutes.

Half a world away there was more paperwork, but here of a far sadder nature. Petty Officer Wren Muriel Saunders was in charge of seven or eight Wrens in the Casualty Office at H.M.S. *Drake*, the naval shore establishment at Devonport which had originally provided the crews for both *Repulse* and *Prince of Wales*.

For some reason I cannot now recall, I had gone to lunch at my mother's house at the far side of Plymouth. We had the radio on and I was completely shocked to learn from an announcement by the B.B.C. that the *Prince of Wales* and *Repulse* had been sunk by the Japanese. Within half an hour, while I was still wondering what to do, a dispatch rider arrived, having been sent by the Drafting Commander to recall me to Barracks. I remember the pillion ride across town – a little unorthodox in those days. On arrival at the Barracks it was quite evident what devastating repercussions the radio announcement was to have on anxious relatives and friends of those serving in the two vessels. As for us, we could only gather together the record cards and look at the names of those involved in the action and pray. There were names of many on those cards well known to us in our section and even colleagues of previous months were on board.

The telephone lines were jammed and, indeed, I recall a family whose anxiety brought them immediately from Liverpool to stand by the barrack gates and wait.

We waited too and I remember the signals eventually arriving from Admiralty and the mounting horror, as we read the names of survivors picked up or landed at Singapore, at the magnitude of the disaster. From those survivor lists we did our grim subtraction from the total complement on board and, harassed from all sides, the pressure was then upon us. I recall the Drafting Commander putting our department out of bounds to all except the seven or eight Wrens while we plied our sorry task of typing hour after hour, over and over again, the words 'missing on war service'.

We had the Welfare Office next to our domain and at that time I trod the covered way between the two departments all too frequently. I recall meeting there a young woman some time after the next of kin had been informed who appeared to have had no news at all of a certain rating. She showed me a picture of herself with him and their children. I checked of course and my immediate suspicions were confirmed. His real wife somewhere in the North had already been told and it was evident that he had contracted a bigamous marriage. Her distress in the double disaster with which she was now faced was harrowing to say the least. I recall that he was one of those we 'presumed dead' many years later. I remember many other incidents – but perhaps my pen runs away with me and none of these recollections of mine may be of interest to you at all.

15

An Analysis

Many questions about the sinkings were being asked by British politicians and press. Why had two capital ships been sent from England to the Far East without an aircraft carrier? Why, once war had broken out, had these two ships been sent out without adequate land-based air cover? Why had the two ships and their escorts failed so miserably to defend themselves against the aircraft of a nation that had been considered so inferior in the art of waging war? How had the modern *Prince of Wales* been crippled so easily?

These were all valid questions to which the politicians and the press did receive some immediate answers and to which more detailed answers can be given here. Before doing so, however, it may be useful to summarize the factual losses of both sides in that action off Kuantan.

Within a few hours Britain had lost one First World War battle cruiser and one modern battleship. This was the first occasion since Jutland that the Royal Navy had lost two capital ships on one day. If we count aircraft carriers as capital ships, *Repulse* and *Prince of Wales* were the seventh and eighth such ships to be lost by Britain during this war. In fact it had been a disastrous few weeks for the navy because, with the aircraft carrier *Ark Royal* and the battleship *Barham* both torpedoed by German submarines in the Mediterranean in the previous month, four capital ships had now been lost in just four weeks, although the loss of *Barham* had not yet been publicly announced. In purely material terms, Britain could perhaps afford to lose the old *Repulse*; there still remained nine First World War battleships or battle cruisers. But the loss of *Prince of Wales* was a great setback as only three modern or semimodern battleships were left in service – *King George V*, *Nelson* and *Rodney* – though three more of the King George V Class would soon be available.

The two ships lost had been carrying 2,921 men when they had been sunk, and of these 840 had lost their lives (Table 1 below gives a more detailed break down). The

Table 1.

	Aboard	Lost	Percentage lost
Repulse			
Officers	69	27	39·1
Ratings	1,240	486	39·2
Total	1,309	513	39·2
Prince of Wales			
Officers	110	20	18·2
Ratings	1,502	307	20·4
Total	1,612	327	20·3

overall fatal casualty rate was 28·8 per cent, and, surprisingly perhaps, a higher proportion of officers had survived than ratings. This occurred mainly in *Prince of Wales*, and may be partly explained by the presence aboard the flagship of Admiral Phillips's staff officers – men who were without responsibility for departments and most of whom were well above deck in the armoured conning tower and were released by Phillips well before *Prince of Wales* actually sank.

Repulse's crew had suffered almost twice as heavily as had that of *Prince of Wales*. This can be accounted for by the simple fact that *Repulse* had sunk quickly after being first struck by torpedoes, crew members still being at

Action Stations a few minutes before the ship heeled over and went down. *Prince of Wales* had been virtually a hulk for some time before sinking, and a great many men had been able to come up from their posts below deck and take part in a more leisurely escape. Although Force Z had suffered several strokes of cruel luck that morning, all the factors affecting the rescue operation had been favourable. The sea was warm and calm, the Japanese aircraft had not interfered in any way with the rescue work, and there had been just enough destroyers to pick up all survivors before dark. The Japanese had estimated that the rescue work would not be so successful, and a report recorded in their Official History had concluded that the greater part of the two ships' companies would be drowned.

The warm seas into which *Repulse* and *Prince of Wales* sank are the home of several species of man-eating sharks, particularly the Great White Shark or White Pointer (*Carcharoden carcharias*). The sailors knew of this danger and there had been much apprehension over the possibility of being taken by sharks. In fact, one officer's report in the Public Record Office mentions the fins of sharks being seen and men heard screaming. The subject of sharks and the possibility that some of the survivors may have lost their lives in this way has been investigated closely by the authors, but we have not been able to find one witness who actually saw one of his friends attacked or who saw live sharks on that day. It is thought almost certain that, however many different ways in which men did perish on that day, no one died in this repulsive manner, though some dead bodies not covered in oil may later have been savaged.

A man's post above or below deck had much influence upon his chance of survival, and the most fortunate of the larger groups were probably the men of the Royal Marine detachments whose duties were mainly in gun positions on deck. No Royal Marine officer became a casualty in either ship, and only twenty-seven out of 192 marines in *Prince of Wales* died – a casualty rate well below the normal for the battleship. Age may also have been a survival factor. Only four of fourteen warrant officers aboard *Repulse* managed to survive, though, at the other extreme, thirty boy seamen from both ships and one Royal Marine boy bugler were lost. Particularly tragic were the deaths of one of the two sets of twins aboard *Prince of Wales*. Boys 1st Class Robert and James Young, only seventeen years old, had joined the Navy from a Cheltenham orphanage. The *Gloucestershire Echo*, reporting their deaths, told of the swimming and lifesaving badges the two lads had once held, but these had not saved their lives. This newspaper also reported the loss in *Prince of Wales* of Signalman R. A. Jones, the first member of the newspaper's staff to die in this war.

The youngest casualties of all were two sixteen-year-olds, Canteen Assistant George Henderson of Edinburgh, lost in *Repulse*, and Boy Bugler Gilbert Stapleton of *Prince of Wales*. The oldest casualty was fifty-four-year-old Able Seaman W. H. Jeffery, a Cornishman in *Prince of Wales*, and close behind was the Commander-in-Chief himself, Admiral Sir Tom Phillips, aged fifty-three.

The two press correspondents and the Admiralty photographer aboard *Repulse* all survived. Cecil Brown and O'Dowd Gallagher wrote their own books on the action, and, after the war, Lieutenant Horace Abrahams went, of all places, to Japan as a Keystone Press Agency photographer. In 1958, at a Tokyo hotel, Abrahams and Cecil Brown met Lieutenant Sadao Takai who had led one of the Genzan Air Corps squadrons that had attacked *Repulse* but without scoring any torpedo hits. The Japanese was at first reluctant to come, but the strange reunion went well.

The destroyers had suffered no casualties apart from the man injured when *Tenedos* had been bombed – though many miles from the main action – and the one seaman in *Express* who had become shell-shocked by the gunfire of his own ship.

Seldom can a major battle have been so one-sided in its

casualty lists. In addition to their reconnaissance planes, the Japanese had launched eighty-five Nell and Betty attack aircraft into the operation. Eighteen of these had failed to attack the main British force: nine bombers had wasted their bomb loads on *Tenedos*; nine more had released their bombs in error just short of Force Z; and one torpedo-carrying aircraft had turned back with engine trouble. Table 2 gives the performances and casualties of the attacking forces.

Table 2.

Air Corps	Took off	Attacked	Hits scored	Shot down	Damaged
A. *Torpedo Attack Aircraft*					
Genzan	17	16*	2	1	7
Kanoya	26	26	9	2	10
Mihoro	8	8	0	0	0
Totals	51	50	11	3	17
B. *Bomber Attack Aircraft*					
Genzan	9	0	0	0	0
Mihoro	25	16*	2	0	11†
Totals	34	16	2	0	11

* One Genzan aircraft's torpedo release and one Mihoro's bomb release failed to function, but they are counted here as having attacked.

† One Mihoro aircraft crashed on landing.

Eighteen airmen, all petty officers or ratings, had died in the three aircraft shot down. The Japanese Official History states that these were the result of attempted suicide attacks made by aircraft whose crews knew that their planes had been too badly hit to survive. This may be true of the first plane shot down, which crashed close alongside *Prince of Wales*, but the last two were shot down by *Repulse*'s pom-poms and crashed straight into the sea. Considering their hatred for the British at that time, their warrior code and love of Emperor, the crews of all three planes probably died happy men. Some British documents of the period mistakenly claimed seven Japanese aircraft shot down, others five. Of the Japanese aircraft that returned, one crashed on landing and twenty-seven were damaged, but all except three of these were only slightly damaged and were capable of local repair. It is not recorded that any of the crews of the returning aircraft suffered casualties.

As we have already remarked, the Japanese Official History, published in 1969, persisted in the view that no less than twenty-one of the forty-nine torpedoes launched against *Prince of Wales* and *Repulse* had scored hits, despite the fact that the British Official History, published twelve years earlier, had given a figure of ten torpedo hits – five on each ship. It is now thought that *Prince of Wales* was hit six times, counting the torpedo which exploded just a few feet away from the port side in the first attack, and eleven torpedo hits in all is probably the correct figure. The Japanese also claimed three bomb hits, though there were only two.

Despite their overclaiming – not uncommon in all forms of warfare involving hectic action – the Japanese airmen had done extraordinarily well. Russia's President Stalin, in a letter to Churchill, was convinced that aircraft flown by Japanese crews could not have achieved this great success and believed that these aircraft were either German planes that had somehow been got out to Japan in time for the opening of hostilities in the Far East, or were, at least, Japanese aircraft flown by German crews. Stalin had recently noted a lack of German air activity on the Russian Front and had been told by his advisers that Germany had sent 1,500 aircraft to Japan! It is more likely that the scarcity of German aircraft seen in Russia was the result of the Luftwaffe's troubles in coping with their first Russian winter; there were no German aircraft in the Far East.

The Japanese success had, however, been achieved by a narrow margin. Rear-Admiral Matsunaga's last-minute decision to switch one squadron of aircraft from torpedo to bomb attack had nearly caused a failure. Matsunaga had probably made the change in an attempt to neutralize the British anti-aircraft fire still further and thus give his torpedo attackers a better chance to get in close, but the high-level bombers had turned out to have very little influence on the action and every last available torpedo aircraft had been needed to achieve the two sinkings. Had there been a few more misses among the earlier torpedo attacks, then the torpedoes of that diverted squadron would really have been needed. But the lucky hit on the stern of *Prince of Wales* crippled the battleship early on in the action and thus redressed the balance. Matsunaga's switch to the old-fashioned bomb attack had had no serious ill-effects.

The Japanese Official History compares the operation against *Prince of Wales* and *Repulse* with the results of pre-war training exercises. Against target battleships steaming at 14 knots and taking vigorous evasive action, the hit rate in practice torpedo attacks had been 70 per cent. The Japanese expected that under conditions of live action this would fall by one half. The actual hit rate in this action – against ships sometimes steaming at 25 not 14 knots – was eleven out of forty-nine, only 22 per cent. Their bombing practice results – again against targets steaming at 14 knots – had been only 12 per cent and was expected to fall to 6 or even 4 per cent in action. But the actual bomb hits on *Prince of Wales* and *Repulse* was two out of twenty-three; at nearly 9 per cent this was better than had been expected.

In the end it was the Bettys of the hard-driving Kanoya Air Corps squadron, with nine torpedo hits scored in three minutes at a cost of two aircraft shot down, that really settled the issue. These were the aircraft sent to Saigon, from the Philippines attack force stationed in Formosa, when the Japanese learnt that *Prince of Wales* and *Repulse* had reached Singapore. Rarely in warfare can the diversion of such a modest force from one campaign to another have paid off so handsomely. On the other hand, if there was one Japanese activity which almost brought them failure, it was their signals procedure, which over and over again failed at crucial times.

It is absolute irony that the Japanese Naval Air Service had originally been helped into being by an American and a Briton. In 1919, a rich American, who insisted on remaining anonymous, gave the Japanese government a large sum of money to buy aircraft and train pilots as he felt that Japanese had all the right attributes to make fine aviators. Five years later, the British sent to Japan a Naval Mission headed by Commander Forbes-Sempill – Lord Sempill, known also as the Master of Sempill. He was a veteran naval pilot of the First World War, and his task was to help Japan, a country still friendly at that time, to establish its first small naval air arm. After the Second World War, a British officer was told by the famous Japanese naval airman, Commander Minoru Genda, the man who had planned the Pearl Harbor attack, that, 'Of course, it was the grandsons of the Master of Sempill who sank the *Prince of Wales* and *Repulse*.'

Although the Japanese Navy was as guilty as the other Japanese services in committing what the West would regard as war atrocities between 1941 and 1945, the crews of the Genzan, Mihoro and Kanoya Air Corps had perhaps carried forward some of the Master of Sempill's British traditions. They had fought a clean battle with no machine-gunning of survivors or any interference with the rescue work of the destroyers. Lieutenant Iki's wreath-dropping ceremony at the scene of the sinkings on the morning after the battle was a rare incident of chivalry in the Far Eastern war.

Having detailed the factual losses – two ships, so many

aircraft, so many men – there is more to be gained by a study of the larger issues such as the War Cabinet decision to send two capital ships East at that stage in the war, the decision by Admiral Phillips to sail from Singapore and his judgement concerning the danger to his ships from the Japanese aircraft known to be at Saigon. And, once the ships had sailed from Singapore, should the operation have been handled differently and could the individual ships in Force Z have been fought any better once they were attacked? What were the immediate and then the long-term effects of the loss of the only British capital ships in the Far East?

But one thing must be stated clearly: the authors of this book are fully aware of the huge advantages given to them by hindsight and by the ability to study at leisure problems which wartime commanders had to solve under pressure and always with only partial knowledge of any given situation. These wartime men had often to guess and gamble and then stake their reputations and sometimes their lives on the result. The comments that follow now acknowledge the privilege of the post-war historian's position, and any criticisms made are academic ones and have no intention of diminishing the stature of wartime leaders.

This book started by describing the changing nature of Japan in the years following the First World War when she ceased to be an active ally of Britain and the United States, and when, through jealousy, ambition and the results of Western insults, Japan moved to a position from which she threatened the Far Eastern interests of Britain, the United States and Holland. It is difficult to assess whether more skilful diplomacy between the wars could have arrested this deterioration in Japan's relations with the West; perhaps diplomacy could have slowed the process down, but it is more likely that appeasement would have been taken for weakness (as it was so taken by Hitler in the same years), and that a clash with Japan was inevitable, although the proud posture of the West and the racial insults handed out to the Japanese were unprovoked and were certainly the cause of much of the trouble.

Britain's decision to build a base at Singapore to protect her legitimate interests in the Far East as well as the peoples of Australia and New Zealand drew a bitter reaction from Japan, though it probably did no more than accelerate the inevitable decline in relations; on its own, the Singapore Naval Base was not a *causus belli*. But, once the European war had broken out, the dilemma of the War Cabinet over the use and defence of the Naval Base, the planned linch-pin of the Far Eastern defences, was a cruel one. The homeland was in real danger of defeat in 1940, and that danger had not yet fully receded in 1941. Every man, tank, gun, ship or aeroplane dispatched to the East was sent at the risk of the homeland's own safety.

But there is scope for an examination of the resources available to the three services at that time. By War Cabinet decision in August 1940, the R.A.F. had been given the main responsibility for defending Malaya and Singapore and was asked to re-equip the Far East squadrons with modern aircraft before the end of 1941 if possible. By late 1941, however, Britain was sending large quantities of modern fighters – though only a few pilots – to Russia; Fighter Command was maintaining a huge force of fighter squadrons in England in case the Luftwaffe came back and tried a second Battle of Britain; and Bomber Command was consuming ever-increasing quantities of aircraft and aircrews for the strategic bombing campaign against Germany for which Churchill and the 'bomber barons' had such high hopes. Not one modern aircraft was sent to the Far East. The R.A.F., faced with a real war in Europe and the dream of ending a modern war there by the relentless use of the heavy bomber against the industrial heartland of the enemy, chose to keep their main strength and all their modern aircraft at home. It must be emphasized that this policy had the full and active support of Churchill himself.

In supporting this policy, the Air Ministry must bear some responsibility for the failures in the Far East. When the R.A.F. was asked to take over the main responsibility for the defence of Malaya, the Army committed its main strength to the defence of airfields. A few squadrons of Spitfires or Hurricanes could have slaughtered the Mitsubishis which so casually bombed the R.A.F. out of those airfields. Modern heavy bombers could have bombed both the invasion convoys and the Japanese airfields around Saigon. That was supposed to have been the cornerstone of the new policy for the defence of Malaya. The service that was the ultimate loser by the Air Ministry's reluctance to provide modern aircraft for the Far East was the unfortunate Army – caught deployed for the defence of airfields which had no effective aircraft flying from them and which were often evacuated by the R.A.F. in the early stages.

Once the R.A.F. had virtually released themselves from their Far Eastern obligations by their failure to implement the War Cabinet decision, the War Cabinet was bound to fall back on the possibility of sending capital ships to the Far East as soon as the war clouds started gathering there in mid-1941. This was, after all, why the Singapore Naval Base had originally been built and subsequently maintained at considerable expense. And, if the ships could be got out to the East early enough and in sufficient strength, their presence might persuade the Japanese not to attack. This – the deterrent effect – was the main purpose of the dispatch of capital ships.

The next question was how many ships and of what type. The decision eventually arrived at has been detailed in an earlier chapter and may be passed over quickly. The choice of *Prince of Wales*, *Repulse* and *Indomitable* was as good as any. The choice of *Repulse* did not represent a great sacrifice to the Navy's responsibilities in the European war; she was one of many old battleships and battle cruisers – albeit faster than most – that the Navy was finding some difficulty in keeping usefully employed. It was more of a hardship to part with the modern *Prince of Wales*, but later events were to show that Churchill was correct in insisting that the absence of *Prince of Wales* would have no serious effect on the Navy's problems in Europe. The Germans never did send *Tirpitz* out in bold manner, and in purely material terms *Prince of Wales* was never missed from European waters.

In all the considerations of this affair it must never be forgotten that the Admiralty *had* allocated one of its modern aircraft carriers for the Singapore-bound force. It was the cruellest misfortune that *Indomitable* should have gone aground in the West Indies. Her repairs only took twenty-five days, but the loss of those days was never retrieved. It is fascinating to speculate how the battle off Kuantan might have turned out had *Indomitable*, with her nine Hurricane fighters, been in company with *Prince of Wales* and *Repulse*. It is significant that, as soon as war did break out in the Far East, the R.A.F. was able to find fifty Hurricanes and their pilots to put aboard *Indomitable* at Port Sudan for the belated reinforcement of Malaya.

The deterrent purpose of sending the ships East was a complete failure. The all-pervading under-estimation of Japanese ability and strength, and the fact that the Japanese were hell-bent on war, however many ships Britain sent out to Singapore, meant that there was really no naval deterrent force that Britain could have spared at that time that would have made any difference. It is true that the local Japanese commanders in the Malayan operation were concerned about the British naval reinforcements and were certainly relieved when these were disposed of, but there is no evidence that the Japanese central leadership ever seriously reconsidered their war plans on this account. Whether they would have thought twice if Britain had earlier sent Spitfires, Hurricanes and modern heavy bombers to Malaya is another matter. This is a hypothetical question to which there is no ready answer.

The sightings of the Japanese invasion convoys on 6

December 1941 provided the visible evidence that the deterrent aspect of the British ships' presence had failed. The study of events therefore now focuses on the decision to sail *Prince of Wales, Repulse* and their destroyer escorts in the attempt to catch and destroy the Japanese troop-ships. Because of the command set-up at Singapore, with the Royal Navy being excluded from the province of Commander-in-Chief Far East, and because the Admiralty in London found it difficult to control operations in an area nearly half a world away, Admiral Sir Tom Phillips was, for a naval commander, in the unique position of having almost absolute freedom in the way he handled his powerful forces. It is ironic that a man who had so often occupied the long-range control seat at the Admiralty in so many naval operations since 1939 should now be the first commander at sea able to play a lone hand in a major action. The study of events from this point until the death of Admiral Phillips must inevitably become a study of this officer's attitude to the situation in which he found himself and of the decisions he made.

The Admiralty had urged Phillips to get one or both of his ships away from Singapore before war commenced, though this was probably to lessen the risk of the ships being caught in harbour by aircraft attack or bottled up by submarines. Once the Japanese attacks in the Far East commenced, Phillips had no option but to sail from Singapore and seek out the Japanese landing forces. He had good intelligence about the Japanese mines, submarines, warships and aircraft. The mines his ships could and did avoid, submarines also. His big ships would have thrashed the Japanese surface warships if encountering them in reasonable conditions. But the air – that was the less certain element.

Again we come back to the known facts of the time: that, despite Billy Mitchell's pre-war trials, despite the warnings of R.A.F. officers, *no major warship had yet been sunk by aircraft attack while at sea and many had survived such attacks*. And the prize? If his two big ships could have got in among the Japanese shipping off the invasion beaches, there would have been a veritable slaughter, a great victory for the Navy and possibly salvation for Malaya and Singapore. Such a result would have been the complete vindication of years of naval policy. It is probable that Air Chief Marshal Brooke-Popham did try to stop Phillips, whose rank was junior to his own, but Brooke-Popham had no authority to order a naval operation to be cancelled. It might have been better if he had; the Navy could not then have been accused of failing to try their best if their local commander had been overruled.

It is clear from Japanese documents, however, that the decision taken on the morning of 8 December to sail that evening was already too late. As the Japanese quotation about the situation on the 9th, when Force Z was still eighteen hours' steaming from the invasion beaches, stated: 'Even if the British attacked from now onwards, there would be no damage done to the military units already landed and any damage would only be to empty ships and to a small quantity of supplies . . . The British naval force had lost their best chance.' The best time to sail would have been late on the 6th or on the 7th, soon after the Japanese convoys had been sighted while still at sea. But *Repulse* was away on its voyage to Australia and Phillips was at Manila conferring with the Americans. The very latest time to have sailed from Singapore and still to have had a chance of influencing the outcome of the Japanese landings would have been at dawn on the 8th, followed by a direct dash north through the Japanese minefield. But to criticize the delay until the evening departure of the 8th is to take undue advantage of hindsight; no one at Singapore guessed that the Japanese would complete the landings so swiftly.

What is more debatable is the role played in this operation by the R.A.F. and the general attitude of Admiral Phillips towards air cover. Before sailing, Phillips had asked for fighter cover and aerial reconnaissance. The latter was provided and is not the subject of any dispute, but the story of fighter cover is central to the tragedy of *Repulse* and *Prince of Wales*. The R.A.F. had earmarked the Australian 453 Squadron as 'Fleet Defence Squadron', and its commander discussed the problems and opportunities available with the Air Liaison Officer on Admiral Phillips's staff before Force Z sailed. Flight Lieutenant Vigors estimated that, if his squadron could use the airfields on the east coast of Malaya, 'I could keep a standing patrol of six aircraft over the fleet at all times during daylight providing the fleet did not go more than 100 miles north of Kota Bharu and not further than sixty miles from the coast at any time.' But this plan had not been adopted, much to Vigors's disgust. Admiral Phillips was clearly not prepared to restrict his freedom of action by staying so close to the coast – there was, after all, the Japanese minefield to consider – and not willing to risk the breaking of radio silence that might be made necessary by such cooperation. It was probably the Navy's refusal to agree on these important points that caused the R.A.F. to send, a few hours after Force Z had sailed, that well-known signal informing Phillips that fighter cover could not be guaranteed, although the heavy casualties then being suffered by the R.A.F.'s squadrons and the damage being inflicted on their up-country airfields were also factors.

So Force Z sailed into the blue, all the time keeping strict wireless silence. The coastal airfields that Flight Lieutenant Vigors had hoped to use came under even further Japanese attack; and because of this, as well as a lack of knowledge of the movements of Force Z, the R.A.F. never sent 453 Squadron to these airfields so as to shorten the flight to Force Z should the ships be attacked and call for help. The Buffaloes were kept at the disposal of the Navy, at constant daylight readiness, but at the airfield at Sembawang on Singapore Island. R.A.F. Malaya would be reduced to fifty-nine serviceable aircraft *of all types* by the morning of 10 December, and while Admiral Phillips could not have known the full details of the R.A.F.'s worsening situation in the days after he sailed, it is reasonable to assume that he knew there were some fighter aircraft available should he call for them. This point is of the utmost importance and will be referred to later.

There are few comments to be made about the first twenty-four hours of Force Z's voyage. By judicious routing, the Japanese minefield was avoided. By bad luck, the British ships were spotted by I.65, though the Japanese were slow to profit from their knowledge. But once the British ships were sighted again and shadowed by the three Japanese seaplanes on the evening of the 9th, the game was as good as up, and it seems surprising that Admiral Phillips did not turn back at that moment. Instead, he continued to sail deeper into the Gulf of Siam that night in the hope of finding Japanese shipping off the beaches next morning. But such a course was just like 'sailing the Home Fleet into the Kattegat', as had been stated at his conference aboard *Prince of Wales* just before sailing, and, moreover, with the enemy having certain knowledge that the British ships were there. The Japanese Official History contains an interesting comment upon this stage of the operation.

What was the objective of the northward moves of the British ships? Was it to hinder our landing in the Kota Bharu area? Was it to cause confusion in our rear and look for prey there? Or was it a manifestation of the British Navy's principles of war to manoeuvre the enemy cleverly into an unfavourable position? It was up to us to go and find this out. Did they know or not know that we had torpedo aircraft and a number of large cruisers and destroyers? . . . Did they think that a large number of our attack aircraft in southern Indo-China were unserviceable?

The movement of the British ships might have been reckless but its audacity was to be admired. *

It was certainly a reckless move on the part of Phillips to steam on after having been so carefully shadowed by the three Japanese seaplanes. Phillips persisted with this for a

* Japanese Official History, p. 484.

further two hours, and it is highly significant that he only gave up his course of action after seeing the flare dropped by the Japanese bomber over the Japanese cruiser *Chokai*. It was this flare, believed by Phillips to be a sign of Japanese surface warship activity, that finally caused him to turn back. It is probable that Phillips would not have persisted in his plan to raid the invasion areas next morning even if that flare had not been seen; his next signal to *Repulse* said that he had given up because of the Japanese seaplanes seen before dark. The popular view is that he had decided to give up the operation after realizing that the Japanese seaplanes had reported him before dark and that he had been intending to turn south to return to Singapore at midnight. But the two hours' further steaming towards the invasion beaches were taking Force Z ever farther from home and safety. It was a dangerous course of action, and his turn away to the south, after seeing the flare, was long overdue.

The whole affair was then complicated by the signal of a Japanese landing at Kuantan. There are no grounds for criticism in Phillips's decision to sail towards that area on his way back to Singapore; he was not to know that the report was based on false information, and he could hardly have returned without investigating.

The first of four major errors was, however, committed off Kuantan next morning. Force Z was now close enough to land to be well within the reach of any R.A.F. fighter cover, yet, when the suspected Japanese plane was seen at 06.45, no signal requesting such cover was sent. Whether or not that particular plane was really Japanese is not known, but it would certainly have been prudent at this stage to ask for air cover. Secondly, once the Walrus aircraft had reported no sign of Japanese activity in the Kuantan area, there was absolutely no need to hang about longer. Indeed, the hour lost by sending the destroyer *Express* close inshore to investigate further was to prove critical. Then, thirdly, the turn north-east by the whole of Force Z to investigate one small vessel towing a few barges was a further error. One of the three destroyers or one of the two Walrus aircraft still available could easily have done the task. The time lost in this way did not amount to much since Midshipman Hoashi's reconnaissance plane turned up a few minutes later, but the decision was none the less a bad one.

It is sometimes suggested that Rear-Admiral Palliser, Phillips's Chief-of-Staff at Singapore, was the one to blame for the disaster that followed, having failed to read his commander's mind and arrange for air patrols to be over Force Z at Kuantan that morning. We cannot agree with this view. Palliser and Phillips had been together for six weeks, and Phillips had had ample opportunity to ensure that Palliser was 'tuned in' to his likely movements and needs. No one in *Prince of Wales* has ever stated that Admiral Phillips showed any sign of disappointment that Palliser had failed to provide fighters for him that morning.

The errors committed so far were, however, nothing to what was to follow, and it was with the appearance of Hoashi's aircraft that the fourth miscalculation was made and the disaster to come sealed. There was little doubt in anyone's mind that this Mitsubishi could easily be the forerunner of the considerable force of aircraft known to be available to the Japanese and which could be expected to be out looking for Force Z that morning. Phillips did then leave the tug and barges, turn Force Z south and order his ships to man their anti-aircraft armament; but still he made no effort to summon the R.A.F. fighters that he knew were allocated to him, even though there was no need for Force Z to maintain radio silence any longer. Why did Admiral Phillips not call for the fighters? It remains the biggest question about the whole operation, and the answer to it indicates the root cause of the disaster that followed.

To answer this question it is necessary to examine two things: first, the knowledge that was available to Admiral Phillips at that time, and secondly, his general attitude to the threat of air attack.

The basic fact was that it was not really a question of the method an enemy might use to deliver explosive charges against a ship, but the form of the charges themselves. A shell and a bomb could have very similar effects upon a capital ship, and such ships were built with armoured protection around their vital compartments to withstand a considerable battering. It did not matter, therefore, whether Force Z was attacked by Japanese warships, by high-level bombers or even dive-bombers. In fact, Japanese aircraft carrying bombs were probably the least of the dangers threatening *Prince of Wales* and *Repulse*. *Prince of Wales*, particularly, had a fine outfit of high-level anti-aircraft armament, and previous experience indicated that a large proportion of any bombs dropped would miss. The actual performance later that morning of the four Japanese squadrons allocated by Rear-Admiral Matsunaga to the high-level bomber role bore this out perfectly.

What every naval officer really feared – if fear is the right word to use – was the torpedo. A bomb or shell could cause damage, and often fearful casualties, on the upper decks, but a torpedo hit will open up the side of a ship and let in water. Although their ships had anti-torpedo bulges and elaborate systems of watertight compartments to minimize the effect of one or two torpedo hits, the sailors knew that no big ship was proof against sustained torpedo attack. Such an attack could come from submarines, small fast surface vessels or torpedo-carrying aircraft. A good destroyer screen and a constant high speed was the best defence against submarines, and as we saw in earlier chapters, two Japanese submarine attacks on Force Z failed. An attack by Japanese destroyers in daylight would have been no more than suicide for the attackers, and the fine climatic conditions of that morning gave Force Z complete protection from such a threat.

That left the torpedo-carrying bomber as the one important hazard about which Admiral Phillips should have been concerned. He had excellent intelligence on the number of Japanese aircraft at the Saigon airfields. He knew that some of these aircraft had reached and bombed Singapore on the first night of the war. Did he not then wonder whether such aircraft could also carry torpedoes and might be homing in on the signals of the spotter aircraft? Should he not have known that this was possible?

To the average Royal Navy officer of Phillips's generation, torpedo aircraft were mainly slow planes of limited range that had to be borne on aircraft carriers. The standard British aircraft of this type – the Swordfish – had put paid to three Italian battleships at Taranto, *in harbour*, and within the last few days the Japanese carrier-borne torpedo aircraft had surprised the United States Pacific Fleet in Pearl Harbor. The intelligence information available to Admiral Phillips was fairly definite that no Japanese aircraft carriers were within range of Force Z, and this intelligence was quite correct. But what about land-based torpedo aircraft, which could take off from long runways with the heavily laden fuel tanks that gave a greater range than that of carrier-borne aircraft? It was known that the Italians had such aircraft – the Savoia-Marchetti Types 79 and 84 had been seen often enough in the Mediterranean convoy battles. *Prince of Wales* had actually seen them in action in the 'Halberd' operation less than three months earlier. But the Savoias had not attacked *en masse* and had suffered severely from naval anti-aircraft fire; their torpedoes had scored few successes and their performance had not impressed the Royal Navy.

The British had also developed a land-based torpedo aircraft, the Bristol Beaufort. This twin-engined plane had roughly the same performance as the Nells and Bettys at Saigon and had already been in service with Coastal Command for a year. Unfortunately, Britain was feeling her way very slowly with this warfare technique and there were many inter-service difficulties to hinder its development. The R.A.F. was more interested in the strategic bomber, the Navy in conventional warships; caught between the two, Coastal Command had not flourished. But there had been an interesting operation in June 1941 when, in cooperation with the Admiralty, Coastal Command Beauforts flying from Scotland had attacked the German pocket battleship *Lützow* off Norway. The *Lützow* was surprised by three Beauforts and severely damaged by one torpedo hit. By the time a fourth Beaufort reached the scene, German fighter protection had arrived and this Beaufort was promptly shot down. *Lützow* was in dock for seven months.

All this happened while Admiral Phillips was at the Admiralty, and he must surely have known of the operation even if he had not been directly involved. Perhaps he would have taken more notice if *Lützow* had been sunk, but this incident, together with the Italian operations in the Mediterranean, should have shown Phillips that it was perfectly feasible for land-based Japanese torpedo aircraft to operate in the area off Kuantan in which *Prince of Wales* and *Repulse* were so leisurely steaming that morning. But it is clear from Phillips's remark, when the first Japanese torpedo bombers were seen coming in to make their attack, that he considered the possibility of the Japanese having developed such aircraft to be impossible. 'No,' said Phillips. 'There are no torpedo aircraft about.'

Admiral Phillips was not the only officer in Force Z to hold this view. Many of the surviving officers, younger and possibly more aviation-minded than Phillips, speak of their astonishment when these twin-engined aircraft carried out their first torpedo attack. The reasons for their amazement were two-fold: the failure of the Navy generally to appreciate that the land-based torpedo bomber was now an operational reality, and the more widespread belief that the Japanese were so far behind the West that they could not yet have developed an aircraft like the Beaufort or the Savoia-Marchetti. In fact, while Britain, Italy and later the Germans had been moving slowly in developing the land-based torpedo bomber, the Japanese had quietly out-thought everyone and were about to put their theories into action in a thoroughly convincing demonstration.

It is just possible that Naval Intelligence had established, possibly from the American deciphering service, that the Japanese aircraft known to be in Indo-China could carry torpedoes. There had been the peculiar signal to Admiral Phillips from the First Sea Lord warning of the danger of aerial attack against Force Z while in harbour. There is also hearsay evidence that the Intelligence Officer on Admiral Phillips's staff found, on his return to Singapore after the sinkings, that the naval staff ashore had known of the presence of Japanese torpedo bombers in Indo-China while Force Z had been at sea but had not thought it necessary to send a warning signal. Unfortunately the truth of this cannot be established because the officer involved is now dead.

So far it can be shown that Admiral Phillips was no more in error about the presence of torpedo bombers than many of his officers, apart from the fact that he had access to the latest intelligence on torpedo bomber development in Europe and must have known of the Beaufort operations against the *Lützow*. If it had stopped there, and if Admiral Phillips's attitude had been no more mistaken than his contemporaries, something might yet have been saved. But, throughout the operation, Phillips continued to show a disregard, almost a contempt, for the dangers of any type of air attack. It is possible (and no more than possible, for there is no hard evidence) that Phillips had quarrelled with Brooke-Popham over the potential danger from the air. It is probable that he had made difficulties over co-operating with the R.A.F. on 453 Squadron's provision of standing patrols. It is certain that, on that morning, at a time when nothing further could be gained by keeping his presence off Kuantan a secret, he did not call for the air cover which he could so easily have had.

It is true that, just after sailing from Singapore, Force Z had received a signal stating that the R.A.F. could not supply fighter protection on 10 December. But this signal had been the answer to the requests, made by Admiral Phillips before sailing, for various types of R.A.F. assistance – reconnaissance on 9 December, reconnaissance *off Singora* (in the Gulf of Siam) at first light on 10 December and fighter protection *off Singora* during daylight on the 10th. Rear Admiral Palliser, who had sent the signal, had not felt it necessary to add the two words 'off Singora' when telling Phillips that the R.A.F. could not provide the fighter cover there. Did Phillips interpret this signal as meaning that the R.A.F. could not provide any fighter cover, anywhere, not even off Kuantan which was within 160 miles of four airfields in southern Malaya and Singapore? Did Phillips think that the Buffalo squadron allocated to him before the operation would no longer be available, that the R.A.F. could find no help at all, that it was not even worth while sending a signal asking for help? It is more likely that Admiral Phillips was confident that his ships could defend themselves and that he was determined not to ask for the help of another service.

So Force Z continued to maintain radio silence after Midshipman Hoashi had settled down to shadow and report Force Z, and even when the first high-level bombers appeared at 11.00. It was only an incredible fifty-eight minutes later that Captain Tennant of *Repulse* finally got away the first signal. *Prince of Wales* never did signal, until she was virtually sinking, and even then all Phillips's signals asked for destroyers or tugs – purely *naval* answers to all his problems! Never ever an appeal for aircraft!

While these may seem harsh findings, the facts speak for themselves: two great ships and many good men were lost because one stubborn old sea-dog refused to acknowledge that he had been wrong. Consider the following two timetables, the first being the actual timing of events that morning, the second the timetable that would have been possible had Phillips called for air support three minutes after Midshipman Hoashi settled down to shadow Force Z.

Actual timetable

10.15   Japanese shadowing plane spotted by Force Z.

11.13   First high-level bombing attack commences.
11.40   First torpedo attack.
11.58   *Repulse* signals to Singapore.
12.20   453 Squadron takes off.
12.35   *Repulse* sinks.
13.20   453 Squadron arrives.
13.23   *Prince of Wales* sinks.

Possible timetable
10.15   Japanese shadowing plane spotted by Force Z.
10.18   Force Z requests fighter support.
10.30   453 Squadron takes off.
11.13   First high-level bombing attack commences.
11.30   453 Squadron arrives.
11.40   First torpedo attack.

There is nothing spurious about this second timetable. The
only variable is the time of the first signal from Force Z;
everything else would have followed as detailed. The
Buffaloes could, in practice, have arrived after *Repulse* had
been hit by just one 250-kg. bomb and before the disastrous
first torpedo attack that crippled *Prince of Wales*. It will
never be known what effect the eleven Buffaloes could have
had on the eventual outcome, but the Japanese bombers
had no fighter support and Vigors and his Australians
could certainly have done something to break up their
attacks. The Japanese airman were determined, even
fanatical, and some torpedoes would no doubt have struck
home, but surely not the great number that finally overwhelmed the two ships.

There is not much to be said about the manner in which the
British ships were fought once the Japanese attacks com-
menced. The initial handling of the Force by Admiral
Phillips had been too rigid, but he soon realized his mistake

and allowed his ships freedom of manoeuvre, after which it
became a series of single-ship actions.

Prince of Wales was desperately unlucky in being crippled
so early in the action, and neither Captain Leach nor his
crew had much chance to show what they were worth
after that. Her 5·25-in. guns were a menace to the
Japanese aircraft to the end, and their Official History pays
this tribute.

The anti-aircraft fire of the British ships was extremely fierce and
the damage suffered by the aircraft bombing from a straight and
level approach at high altitude was very great. Consider just the
Takeda squadron of eight aircraft which bombed last, when *Prince of
Wales* had already reduced speed to about 6 knots and was sinking.
Five of Takeda's aircraft were hit. *

This damage was caused by just two turrets, S1 and S2;
how effectively might the full complement of these guns
have performed had they not been robbed of power and
denied a level platform by the early damage and the
resulting list of *Prince of Wales*.†

It is sometimes suggested that the internal organization
and morale in *Prince of Wales* broke down too quickly after
the first torpedo hits, and it is true that this is how it might
have appeared. But here was a ship that had never claimed
to have been fully worked up, that was badly under-
ventilated even when all power supplies were functioning,
and which had suffered a loss of power and, above all, of
communications that had never been envisaged and for
which no drills had prepared the crew. While there was
certainly some evidence of a lack of morale among this
mainly wartime-conscripted crew, this was before the
battle and there are no cases of outright failure of duty
during the action other than the early departure from the
ship by a few men who had probably been driven from their

---

* Japanese Official History, p. 478.

† Appendix Four contains the post-action report of Lieutenant-
Commander C. W. McMullen, Gunnery Officer in *Prince of Wales*.

place of duty below an hour before and when the ship was clearly about to sink. Any weakness in the organization of *Prince of Wales* caused by the lack of a proper working-up period, or possibly by patchy morale, made no difference in the end to the way she was fought. No gun was left unmanned, no vital position was left unattended. The end, when it came, was quite inevitable. Instead of harping too much upon the few deficiencies in *Prince of Wales*, it would be more just to remember the many acts of gallantry seen to be performed by her crew.

The only thing that might just have delayed the sinking of *Prince of Wales* was a realization by Damage Control that the efforts of the electrical repair parties would have been better spent trying to cure the root cause of the electrical failure in the ring-main-breaker system and redistributing the available supply instead of spending their time attempting to rig up emergency supplies to such out-lying services as the gun turrets. But it was a vicious circle; the communications failure caused by the loss of electricity prevented the correct appreciation and allocation of resources, and to criticize here would again be an unfair use of hindsight.

Captain Tennant and the crew of *Repulse* never put a foot wrong. Their ship, poorly armed against aircraft attack, had fought to the end and simply been overwhelmed. The lack of any further comment here is simply because this gallant ship and her crew had done their best and could have done no more. *Repulse* should never have been put in the position of having to fight off repeated air attacks without friendly air cover when that cover was so easily available. Not only was her loss tragic, it was unnecessary.

The destroyers had few chances to shine. Before the action, they had twice failed to detect Japanese submarines that had fired torpedoes and then reported Force Z's position; but these were failures resulting from a lack of advanced Asdic equipment rather than deficiencies of training or spirit. The destroyers' pop-gun armament had been quite inadequate to deal with the swarm of attacking

Japanese aircraft. Their hour came with the rescue work, which was carried out with a fine display of seamanship, and they undoubtedly helped to keep down the casualty toll.

I think that, given the design of *Prince of Wales*, with certain inbuilt vulnerabilities, and with (as with the *Bismarck* earlier) a hit in the most sensitive and vulnerable area, there was no more that we on board could have done to keep her afloat and bring her in. This does not mean that there was no room for speculation and subsequent inquiry. There was. (Lieutenant D. B. H. Wildish)

Far higher authority than Lieutenant Wildish thought that certain questions about his ship should be answered. The British press were the first to be critical. The *Daily Herald* seemed remarkably well informed in alleging a delay by Admiral Phillips in asking for fighter support, as did the *Sunday Express* in criticizing the tradition by which Admiral Phillips had gone down with his ship. There followed, on 19 December, a secret debate in the House of Commons at which there were rumblings about the original decision to send the ships East, about the failure to provide an aircraft carrier or land-based aircraft cover, about the ineptitude of the authorities generally. Churchill was by then away in the United States meeting President Roosevelt to discuss the implications of the recent outbreak of war with Japan, and it was left to Mr A. V. Alexander, the First Lord, to answer the criticisms. Alexander gave a reasoned statement of the events leading up to the disaster, but never mentioned that *Indomitable* had been earmarked for the Far East but had gone aground.

More enlightened questions were being asked in the War Cabinet and the Admiralty as to why the modern *Prince of Wales* had succumbed so easily to the first torpedo attack. The British have a neat way of dealing with such problems – they refer them to an independent judicial inquiry. Mr Justice Bucknill seemed to specialize in naval disasters, and it was he who was appointed to head the inquiry to identify the failure in *Prince of Wales* and to suggest improvements to other vessels of her class. What became known as the Second Bucknill Committee started its sittings at Grosvenor Gardens House on 16 March 1942. This was Mr Bucknill's third naval inquiry; the First Bucknill Committee had investigated the accidental loss of the submarine *Thetis* off Liverpool in 1939, and a more recent inquiry, not designated as a full committee, had investigated the failure, in February 1942, of the Navy and the R.A.F. to stop the passage of the German ships *Scharnhorst*, *Gneisenau* and *Prinz Eugen* through the English Channel from Brest to Germany.

There were two more members of Mr Bucknill's committee: Rear-Admiral W. F. Wake-Walker, who had been in the cruiser *Norfolk* during the hunting of the *Bismarck*, and Sir Maurice Denney, a celebrated marine engineer. Several of the officers and two senior ratings who had been in *Prince of Wales* were returned to England to give evidence. They attended in turn and submitted to questioning by the members of the committee in the quiet London rooms that were such a contrast to the conditions of the action being investigated. Besides questioning the *Prince of Wales* men, the committee studied the reports taken at Singapore from other survivors immediately after the sinkings, asked questions about the amount of water that had entered *Prince of Wales* when the German bomb exploded near her while she was being fitted out at Birkenhead in 1940, called for Sir Stanley Goodall, the Director of Naval Construction, and other specialists, and went to Wallsend-on-Tyne to see *Prince of Wales*'s sister ship *Anson* being completed at the Swan-Hunter yards there.

The Bucknill Committee met for some twenty days. The result of all their effort was a mass of documents that was kept secret until 1972. For the technically minded, there is now a small pot of gold in the Public Record Office.* For the more general reader, the following résumé will probably suffice.

* Public Record Office ADM 116/4554.

The two main questions that concerned the committee were:

1. How had the first torpedo hit, presumed to be by the torpedo whose explosion had been seen on *Prince of Wales*'s port side near Y Turret, caused so much damage farther to the rear of the ship and permitted such a vast quantity of water to enter the ship?

2. Why had the ship's electrical installations failed so drastically?

On the first question, there was much discussion about a certain pre-war experiment, Job 74, in which a mock-up of the side protection of the King George V Class battleships and the aircraft carrier *Ark Royal* had been subjected to an underwater explosion equivalent to a torpedo with a warhead of 1,000 lb. of explosive. The riveted construction of the torpedo protection later used in *Prince of Wales* was found to withstand the trial explosion better than the welded construction used in *Ark Royal*. The committee estimated that the Japanese torpedoes had carried a warhead of 867 lb. Why, then, had so much damage to *Prince of Wales*'s side protection occurred?

The committee could not have known two things: first, that the Japanese torpedoes contained only 330 or 450 lb. of explosive charge (which knowledge would only have increased their dilemma), and secondly, that the extensive damage and flooding had been caused not by the explosion seen on *Prince of Wales*'s port side but by the unseen torpedo hit underneath the stern. This was the torpedo that tore the 'A' bracket of the port-outer shaft away from the hull, distorted the shaft itself, and permitted the vast inrush of water. It is small wonder that the committee was baffled and that Sir Stanley Goodall could only point out lamely the urgent demands for up-to-date battleships and the restraints on contruction caused by the pre-war treaties and budgets. It was not until after the war, when *Prince of Wales*'s hull was examined, that the truth became known.

So the committee mistakenly presumed that the riveted

construction had failed despite the tests done on Job 74. It was recommended that future ships should have an extra strengthened bulkhead isolating the known vulnerability of the stern area more securely from the rest of the ship; and that, if possible, the three-shaft system of propulsion, known to be favoured by German naval constructors, be adopted in the machinery of future capital ships. (The three-shaft system was, however, never implemented.)

The Bucknill Report contains wads of material on the electrical failure in *Prince of Wales*. It transpired that the Controller of the Admiralty had laid down, in July 1938, eighteen points of principle for electrical installations in naval vessels, but because of the urgency in the building of the King George V Class ships, these had not been fully complied with. The major electrical overhauls and amendments that the remaining King George V Class ships underwent later in the war were a direct result of the failures highlighted in *Prince of Wales*.

There were many minor items. It was recommended that the officer in charge of Damage Control should have the 'prestige' to ensure that his decisions on priorities were accepted and his orders obeyed despite the claims on his organization from other departments. It was recommended that 'in future, no consideration of weight or cost should be allowed to stand in the way of making communications as safe from failure as possible'. There were comments on working-up periods and on the routing of ventilation shafts and cable passages – through which much water had passed in *Prince of Wales* – and much more. On the other hand, there was little criticism of the machinery other than a recommendation that the auxiliary services for machinery compartments should be self-contained to each compartment and the size of each engine room be reduced by placing the gearing in a separate compartment. These measures were asked for so as to restrict the effects of flooding on a ship's primary machinery.

Mr Bucknill submitted his Report and the inquiry closed. It is not known whether anyone lost his job or pension because of the failures highlighted in *Prince of Wales*, but many valuable lessons had been learnt. If the remaining King George V Class battleships had been involved in serious action later in the war, many members of their crews would have owed their lives to the experiences of *Prince of Wales*, but these other battleships were lucky in that none was ever subjected to the battering suffered by their unfortunate sister ship.

And so the action off Kuantan took its place in history. The loss of *Repulse* and *Prince of Wales*, coming so soon after the Americans had been trounced at Pearl Harbor, had far-reaching effects upon the new war. Not only had the Americans, and now the British, lost or had put out of action their entire battle fleet in the Pacific and the Far East, but these great Western nations had been publicly humiliated in an area where to lose 'face' was as serious as to lose a battle. The Allies had thus lost the respect and some of the support they might otherwise have expected from their colonial possessions. This was particularly so for the British who had the greater influence and the larger empire. For the humble natives of these countries, there could no longer be respect for a power which colonized you and traded with you, but that could not defend either herself or you when challenged by an enemy which had always been depicted as inferior. The thrashing administered in those few hours off Kuantan knocked the bottom out of British prestige in the Far East. It never recovered. This was true also in the white countries of Australia and New Zealand, though the effects were slower to appear here. These countries fought on at Britain's side loyally throughout the remainder of the war, but there was a distinct change in the post-war years and a steady move away from the close ties with Britain.

And the nature of naval warfare had changed. What Billy Mitchell and the lesser prophets had foreseen had at last come to pass. The lesson was finally learnt that the expensive battleship with a crew of one and a half thousand men had serious limitations. It could only move in two dimensions and at a speed of 30 knots at most. The cheap mass-produced aeroplane with a crew of half a dozen men could move in three dimensions, at ten times the speed of the battleship, and could deliver its load of high explosive as accurately as the battleship. There was little the battleship could do that the aeroplane could not do more efficiently, especially if that aeroplane was carrier borne. And the battleship had been proved so vulnerable; it could no longer move anywhere without constant air cover. For the Royal Navy and for navies everywhere the battleship had become obsolete. The next generation of capital ship would be the aircraft carrier, and the lifespan of even that vessel would expire while some of the survivors of *Repulse* and *Prince of Wales* were still comparatively young men.

These conclusions may be resented by some professional sailors, but surely they are the self-evident truths of the Kuantan action. It was Admiral Tom Phillips's bad luck that he had to be the one in the wrong place at the wrong time who had to learn these truths for his fellows. The fighters might have saved him, but his old dictum 'that properly-handled capital ships can defend themselves' had been proved false. For dedicated members of the Senior Service it was a bitter pill to swallow. Did Admiral Phillips think of all this as he stood on the bridge of the sinking *Prince of Wales*? Did he decide that he could not live with the shattering of all his beliefs and illusions? We shall never know, but it seems not unlikely.

It is not often that two historical milestones are reached in one day. The men of Force Z had been involved in the beginning of the break-up of an empire and in the end of the useful lifespan of the battleship. Had the Americans at Pearl Harbor not already seen the revelation of Japan as a modern military power, there would have been a third milestone to add to the list.

Those few days in December 1941 were truly historic.

16

The Years that Followed

The morning after the sinking, the officers and ratings who had survived from *Repulse* and *Prince of Wales* assembled on the parade ground at the Singapore Naval Base. They were addressed first by Captain Tennant, who told the survivors he had been ordered to fly to England to report upon the disaster and that he would do what he could to get the remains of the two ships' companies home as soon as possible for the usual survivors' leave. He was cheered by the 2,000 men on the parade ground as he left. He reached England within a few days and was never blamed for anything that had happened.*

Unbeknown to Captain Tennant, a decision had already been taken that most of the survivors were to be retained in the Far East. This policy was probably initiated by Admiral Layton, now confirmed as Commander-in-Chief Eastern Fleet, and it became his task to inform the survivors that most would not be going home. It is generally agreed by the men on the parade ground that he made a lamentably poor job of it, and there was much murmuring in the assembled ranks of survivors. After Admiral Layton had stepped down from the platform the parade was dismissed. At that moment the ship's companies of H.M.S. *Repulse* and H.M.S. *Prince of Wales* ceased to exist as formal

---

* Within two months, Captain Tennant had been promoted to Rear-Admiral and was flying his flag at sea in the cruiser *Newcastle*, escorting convoy WS. 16 out to Egypt via the Cape. In 1944 he was given the tasks of getting the components for the Mulberry Harbours across the Channel and assembled after D-Day and of supplying the invasion armies with petrol. The Naval Official History comments that he commanded 'the most oddly assorted fleet which can ever have fallen to a flag officer'. Tennant later achieved full admiral's rank and, after retirement, became Lord Lieutenant of Worcestershire. He died in July 1963.

units of the Royal Navy. It was a very unhappy and demoralized batch of sailors who drifted away to await whatever uncertain fate was in store for them in the Far East.

The survivors remained in this limbo for the next few days, mostly packed into the Fleet Shore Accommodation of the Naval Base. Commander R. J. R. Dendy was the senior officer remaining from the two lost ships. He was sent to Java to consult with the Dutch Vice-Admiral Helfrich, who had requested that some of the *Prince of Wales* and *Repulse* survivors be sent to help man the Dutch cruiser *Sumatra*, two submarines and some motor torpedo boats. But Dendy's talks with the Dutch did not proceed smoothly. The official story is that Dendy found the mechanical condition of the Dutch ships so poor that nothing could be done, but he himself states the real reason to have been that Admiral Helfrich would only allow the British seamen to sail in Dutch ships under a Dutch captain and under a Dutch flag if he received orders to that effect from Queen Wilhelmina in exile in London. The negotiations collapsed and Commander Dendy returned to Singapore to find the breaking-up of the *Repulse* and *Prince of Wales* crews already well advanced.

Two days after the sinkings, Admiral Layton received more detailed instructions from the Admiralty about the future employment of the survivors. The help to the Dutch – which had come to nothing – had been the first priority. Layton's staff were then allowed to choose officers or ratings to fill essential gaps in local naval units or in the few ships remaining in Eastern Fleet, 'or to relieve those men who had been abroad over two years'. After these outlets had been exhausted, surplus officers could be returned to England, but surplus ratings had to be found some local employment if possible.

During the next few weeks a few picked men were posted to top up the complements of the few warships at Singapore. Those who went to the cruiser *Mauritius* were the most fortunate; her engines were giving trouble and she was sent straight home to England for major repair. Others went to *Exeter*, to suffer a less happy experience, and the destroyers and smaller naval craft at Singapore all took a few men.

Others, in various categories, were selected to be sent to England. Many of the officers were so earmarked, as were most of the specialist ratings. The younger of the boy seamen were told, 'You will be sent where you belong – near your mothers'; they were delighted. Another group of men to be warned for home were the C.W. ratings.* 'C.W. candidates were not exactly popular with their mess-mates, and we could not help feeling guilty because of the preferential treatment we were now accorded. But we were not sorry to go.' All these happy groups, 900 men in all, were packed into a dirty old transport, the *Erinpura*, which sailed for Colombo on 21 December.

Morale fell badly among those left behind. They bitterly resented having to replace men who had served 'cushy' years amid the luxuries of Singapore while they had been in wartime England or involved in the sea war with Germany, to say nothing of the recent ordeal of the sinking of their ships. Many were formed into military-type units, and, with only the hastiest of training, were expected to fight as ground troops. They saw, all around them, the apathy and disorganization of a country unprepared for war and suffered the results of a service administration under severe pressure. But it was no good protesting. 'There was much muttering among the lads, who felt they were getting a rough deal, but those organizing the drafts made it known that they did not want to hear the word "survivors" again; all they were interested in was date left U.K.' The War Diary of the Eastern Fleet makes this comment:

Among naval personnel on shore and, in particular among the survivors of the *Prince of Wales* and *Repulse* who had to be ruthlessly

* C.W. ratings were named after the Navy's Commissions and Warrants Branch and these men were serving their trial periods as ratings before going on to train as officers.

re-employed on shore as soon as they were fit, morale was patchy. The survivors had, of course, had a severe shock and, by the time bombing of their accommodation at Singapore had become frequent, many were at the end of their tether.*

One small party of former *Prince of Wales* men became involved in an incident, little publicized but serious enough for those concerned. Three sub-lieutenants and some ratings were dispatched to Prai, on Malaya's west coast, to man three small ferryboats operating between Penang Island and the mainland after their civilian crews had done a bunk. The *Prince of Wales* men worked hard in the most difficult conditions of bombing, panic and disorganization, but the five or six men on one boat, the S.S. *Violet*, eventually left their posts. The sub-lieutenant in charge could not get them to return; they complained they were 'dead beat', joined a party of soldiers in a lorry and drove off to Singapore. The officer had little option but to follow them.

The Naval Officer in Charge at Penang, an elderly retired captain, had already been replaced as it was thought that he was not in sufficient control, and now the Navy decided to court martial the *Prince of Wales* officer and his men. 'Desertion' and 'desertion in the face of the enemy' were among the charges, but it is not known whether 'mutiny' was included – the papers of courts martial are not released for a hundred years. It is known that Lieutenant-Commander C. W. McMullen, the former gunnery officer of the *Prince of Wales*, defended the accused ratings, and that Surgeon-Lieutenant S. G. Hamilton, formerly of *Repulse*, had to examine the accused officer and found him medically fit. Hamilton felt annoyed at 'all this gold-braid sitting about; why weren't they doing something about the Japanese coming down the peninsula?' The accused were all found guilty, but given minimum sentences.

After the case, Admiral Layton sent this message to

* Public Record Office ADM 119/1185.

Rear-Admiral Spooner who was in charge of the Royal
Navy in Malaya.

This is not at all inspiring. Officers and men do not seem to realize
that war is not always a very pleasant game and setbacks and
dangerous experiences must be met with fortitude. Officers and men
at Hong Kong had a very unpleasant and nerve-shaking experience
which lasted for fourteen days but it did not impair their fighting
spirit. I wish to hear no more sentimental rubbish about survivors
not being fit for the next job that comes along – they should be only
too ready to get their own back. *

This minor affair still rankles, and former *Prince of
Wales* officers have asked that it not be mentioned here, or
at least placed in its correct context. They say that this was
no organized mutiny but a tiny band of men, no longer
part of an organized crew, who were at the end of their
tether. At least one of the ratings involved later petitioned
the Queen for a review of the case and for the removal of
details of it from his otherwise perfect service record sheet.

The largest bodies of men to remain together from the two
ships were their Royal Marine detachments. The marines
had been trained in the basics of soldiering and were
obviously capable of making a useful contribution to the
defence of Malaya. Few if any of the marines were
returned to England, and about two hundred, with their
original *Prince of Wales* and *Repulse* officers, were eventually merged with the remnants of an army battalion, the
2nd Argyll and Sutherland Highlanders, who had been
badly cut up in the jungle fighting in northern Malaya.
The new composite battalion was officially called 'The
Marine Argyll Battalion', but it immediately took on a far
better remembered name. The marines had all come from
Plymouth Marine Barracks, and it was inevitable that the
new unit should become known as 'The Plymouth Argylls'
after that city's football club. The marines formed two

* Public Record Office A D M 199/357.

companies of the new battalion, one of them made up entirely of *Prince of Wales* men under the command of Captain C. D. L. Aylwin, and the second mainly *Repulse* men under Captain R. G. S. Lang. The marines also provided the men for an armoured-car platoon and the battalion's machine-gun and signals section.

Singapore fell ten weeks after the sinking of *Repulse* and *Prince of Wales*. The Admiralty ordered all naval personnel to get away before the final defeat, and those left behind were mostly Royal Marines and wounded seamen. At least thirty-eight *Prince of Wales* and *Repulse* men were killed in the final stages of the fighting in Singapore, most being marines of the Plymouth Argylls who fought at least as well as the regular army units and whose exploits were to become part of Royal Marine folklore.* The survivors then passed into the hands of the Japanese when the garrison surrendered on 15 February 1942 and thus faced the horror of three and a half years in Japanese prison camps.

Among those who got away before Singapore fell was Vice-Admiral Layton and the staff of Eastern Fleet. Layton had decided that he could do no good at Singapore and sailed for Colombo. On his departure, he left this message for the naval personnel at Singapore:

I have gone to collect the Eastern Fleet. Keep your heads high and your hearts firm until I return.

It has been described as 'one of the most badly phrased signals ever to be sent during the war'. One man who was left behind writes that 'the sailors' comments were unprintable'.

Admiral Layton left Rear-Admiral Spooner, a former captain of *Repulse*, in charge at Singapore. Two nights

* Both the Royal Navy and the Army had their youngest Second World War deaths in the final fighting at Singapore. Boy 1st Class Michael Foran from Camborne, Cornwall, was only fifteen years old, and Boy W. Martin from Ipswich was a sixteen-year-old soldier in the 1st Manchester Regiment.

before the island fell Spooner arranged for every available vessel to sail from Singapore with as many service personnel and civilians as could be packed aboard them. Spooner himself, with Air Vice-Marshal Pulford (who was ordered to leave by General Percival, the senior service officer then remaining in Singapore), sailed the same night in a naval launch. Most of the ships.in that last desperate exodus ran into Vice-Admiral Ozawa's cruisers and destroyers which had so nearly clashed with Force Z the night before *Repulse* and *Prince of Wales* were sunk. Ozawa's guns slaughtered the defenceless ships and forty of them were sunk. The launch in which Spooner and Pulford were attempting to escape was bombed and wrecked and their party was left stranded upon a small island. They died of starvation.

Of the six destroyers that had escorted *Prince of Wales* from England or that had sailed with Force Z in its last action, five were sunk during the next few weeks. *Electra* and *Jupiter* were both lost in the Battle of the Java Sea on 27 February 1942. *Encounter* went the next day, the same day as the famous cruiser *Exeter*. Japanese carrier-borne aircraft sank *Tenedos* off Ceylon on 5 April, and two days later *Vampire* received the same treatment while in company with the old British aircraft carrier *Hermes*. *Express*, which had come alongside *Prince of Wales* just before she sank, was the only destroyer associated with that ill-fated operation to survive the war. In 1943 she went to the Royal Canadian Navy – under the name of *Gatineau* – and lived on to end up in a Vancouver breaker's yard in 1956.

The Australian pilots of 453 Squadron who survived the Malayan campaign were evacuated from Singapore on the old cruiser *Danae*, one of the three original China Station cruisers that had been considered too weak to go out with Force Z. *Danae* ended the war with the Free Polish Navy, but *Dragon* and *Durban* were ignominiously sunk to help form one of Admiral Tennant's breakwaters off the Normandy beaches soon after D-Day. 453 Squadron was disbanded in Adelaide in March 1942, but a new 453 Squadron, still Australian, was formed in Scotland three months later and flew Spitfires over Europe for the remainder of the war. The squadron was finally disbanded in May 1945. Flight Lieutenant Tim Vigors, who had been badly burnt ten days after *Repulse* and *Prince of Wales* were sunk, survived the war and later became a successful racehorse breeder.

The Japanese airmen who had been so successful that morning had a hard war. The Nell turned out to be a sturdy aircraft, capable of taking much punishment, but the Bettys were found to be highly inflammable; American pilots who often met them in the air battles of the Pacific campaign called them the 'one-shot lighters'. Few of the Genzan, Kanoya and Mihoro airmen survived the war, many being killed in the battles around the Solomon Islands in August 1942.

The nature of sea warfare changed dramatically after the battle off Kuantan. There were still occasional clashes between battleships, as when *Prince of Wales*'s sister ship, *Duke of York*, with a force of cruisers and destroyers caught and sunk the German *Scharnhorst* in December 1943; but such actions were the exception rather than the rule in the second half of the war. It was the R.A.F.'s 617 Squadron, with the aid of a super-bomb designed by Barnes Wallis, who put paid to the *Tirpitz* in November 1944 and finally relieved the Admiralty of the need to keep an eye on this menace. R.A.F. bombers also took care of the remainder of the German battleship force – *Gneisenau*, *Admiral Scheer* and *Lützow*.

But it was in the vast reaches of the Pacific that the new type of naval battle developed. This was the battle fought between rival fleets whose main hitting power were the air squadrons aboard their aircraft carriers. These great carrier battles, in which the rival Japanese and American fleets never saw each other and in which battleships became little more than embarrassing encumbrances, settled the outcome of the naval war in the Pacific. In revenging the

Japanese naval successes of 1941 and early 1942, American planes, mostly carrier-borne naval planes, sank six Japanese battleships, seventeen aircraft carriers and a host of minor vessels including every one of Vice-Admiral Ozawa's cruisers which had hunted *Prince of Wales* and *Repulse*.* Even the monster Japanese battleships *Yamato* and *Musashi*, each of 64,000 tons and with their upperworks covered with anti-aircraft armament, succumbed to the torpedo attacks of tiny American carrier-borne aircraft.

The battleships of Germany and Japan were swept away by air power. Those of Britain and America became little more than floating artillery batteries, as which they performed sterling work off many an invasion beach but only as long as air superiority had been won for them in advance.

The Royal Navy was not left behind in this new type of naval warfare. Within a few weeks of the loss of *Repulse* and *Prince of Wales*, the building of an entire new class of light fleet aircraft carriers was authorized. These were the ten vessels of the Colossus Class – small, fast carriers, each with forty-eight aircraft aboard. But, with the German Navy confining itself mostly to submarine warfare in the closing years of the war, the British carriers had little opportunity to shine in European waters. When Germany fell, the Royal Navy started to move its best ships East to take its place with the Americans in the war against Japan, but with the dropping of atom bombs on Hiroshima

---

* Vice-Admiral Ozawa's cruisers were disposed of as follows:

Mikuma in the Battle of Midway by aircraft of U.S.S. *Enterprise* and U.S.S. *Hornet*, 6 June 1942.

Yura in the Battle of Santa Cruz by U.S. aircraft, 24 October 1942.

Chokai (by aircraft of U.S.S. *Natoma Bay*), *Suzuya* (by aircraft of U.S.S. *Kitkun Bay*), *Mogami* (by aircraft of U.S. 7th Fleet carriers) and *Kinu* (by aircraft of U.S. 3rd Fleet carriers and U.S.A.A.F.) were all sunk in the Battle of Leyte Gulf, 25–6 October 1944.

Kumano was sunk off Luzon by aircraft of U.S. 3rd Fleet carriers, 25 November 1944.

and Nagasaki in August 1945, this war collapsed before the British really worked up to full strength in the Pacific.

The Royal Navy never lost another battleship after *Prince of Wales*. It did ask the taxpayer to provide it with one more new battleship, the 42,000-ton *Vanguard*, which was completed in 1946 at a cost of £9 million to say nothing of the cost of maintaining it until it was scrapped in 1960. It is difficult to see what role the Navy saw for *Vanguard* in wartime, but fortunately she never had to face that test.

The *Prince of Wales* and *Repulse* men who had managed to escape from Singapore spread through the ships and shore establishments of the Navy where the very fact that they had taken part in that momentous action marked them as men whose stories were worth listening to. Thus the sinking of these two ships gradually passed into the history of the Royal Navy. If it had been a victory, there would have been honours and decorations for the more worthy of the participants, but, the Admiralty obviously decided, this would not be appropriate here, despite the many acts of outstanding heroism that had been witnessed. One *Repulse* officer tried to get awards for two of his midshipmen who had lost their lives in the bravest of circumstances, but was told that 'in a disaster of such magnitude no recommendations for awards can be considered'. It was not until October 1942 that the Admiralty published a list of twenty-four men, fifteen from *Repulse* and nine from *Prince of Wales*, who had been 'Mentioned in Dispatches' – the lowest degree of recognition for courage or outstanding service that can be given to a serviceman. Thirteen of the 'Mentions' were posthumous.* There was no award for Captain Tennant, whose ship had performed so well, and many *Prince of Wales* survivors were disappointed that Lieutenant-Commander Cartwright of *Express* was not

---

* Appendix Five gives full details of the twenty-four Mentions in Dispatches.

decorated for the magnificent handling of his destroyer alongside their sinking ship, but perhaps such ability was expected as a matter of course from destroyer captains.

The war ended, the British returned to Singapore and the men who had fought off Kuantan and survived the remainder of the war mostly went home, some of the old Regulars retiring for a second time, the Hostilities Only men gladly becoming civilians again. None would ever forget that morning, and for nearly all it would be the highpoint of their lives.

At the time of writing, the wrecks of *Prince of Wales* and *Repulse* remain intact and undisturbed at the original sites of their sinkings. They have been inspected several times but, as far as is known, never entered. The Japanese were the first visitors early in 1942. The wrecks were located by their minesweepers and then buoyed. *Prince of Wales* was found to be eight miles east-south-east of *Repulse*. The Japanese salvage ship *Seishu* was involved in this work, and it is believed that the Japanese were trying to recover the radar equipment of the British ships but had little success. In June 1943 a Tokyo radio broadcast stated that Japanese engineers were attempting to refloat the *Repulse*, which lay in only thirty fathoms of water compared with thirty-six fathoms of *Prince of Wales*, but this venture did not succeed either.

In 1954 the destroyer H.M.S. *Defender* made the first of several post-war British surveys. The positions established varied very little from those recorded by the Japanese, but considerably from those reported by the destroyers of Force Z at the time of the action. The 1941 position of *Prince of Wales* was found to be two miles in error, and that of *Repulse* was eight miles out. The exact positions, fixed by H.M.S. *Dampier* using Decca radar in 1959, are:

Repulse   03° 37′ 18″ North, 104° 20′ 36″ East
Prince of Wales   03° 34′ 12″ North, 104° 27′ 48″ East

Both ships were found to be in remarkably sound and clean

condition. *Repulse* was almost completely heeled over to port, with her highest part, the starboard bilge keel, only 105 feet below the surface. *Prince of Wales* was almost upside down with her starboard bilge keel again the highest point, 155 feet below the surface. It was these post-war surveys that revealed for the first time the unsuspected torpedo hole near the *Prince of Wales*'s stern which had been the cause of the massive initial flooding.* Both ships can be seen from the air under favourable conditions. The British government regards them as Crown property and as the official war graves of the 840 men who were lost. Naval divers regularly replace the White Ensigns which are attached to rigid steel wires on a propeller shaft of each ship. Several applications for permission to salvage the ships have been refused, the most persistent applicants being the Japanese, who apparently have little idea of the offence such requests cause. But, when the question of salvage was raised in the House of Lords in October 1975, Lord Winterbottom for the government did not rule out the possibility of salvage, 'provided the bodies of the dead were reverently treated'. Many would hope that the wrecks will never be disturbed.

The men lost in *Prince of Wales* and *Repulse* are commemorated on the impressive Memorial to the Missing of the Royal Navy's Devonport Division on Plymouth Hoe, close by the depot which provided the original crews. A few men have individual graves. There are eighteen in the Kranji Military Cemetery at Singapore: sixteen of them who died aboard the rescuing destroyers or who died of injuries soon after being landed at Singapore, and two more who died later as prisoners of war. Twelve more graves have been identified in cemeteries in Siam; these were marines who were taken prisoner with the Plymouth Argylls and who died while working on the infamous Burma–Siam Railway.

---

* Appendix Six contains a report describing an examination of *Prince of Wales* made in 1966.

There is another memorial, in St Andrew's Cathedral, Singapore.

TO THE GLORY OF GOD
AND IN MEMORY OF
ADMIRAL SIR TOM SPENCER VAUGHAN PHILLIPS
K.C.B.
LIEUTENANT JOHN FORRESTER BROWNRIGG
RICHARD ALEXANDER HUNTING
AND ALL THOSE WHO GAVE THEIR LIVES IN
H.M.S. PRINCE OF WALES AND H.M.S. REPULSE
DECEMBER 10TH 1941

An altar cross and a set of candlesticks are also part of the memorial. The authors of this book spent some time looking for a possible connection between the three names on the one plaque. Lieutenant Brownrigg turned out to be an army officer in the 1/5th Sherwood Foresters, a battalion of the ill-fated British 18th Division which was sent to Singapore as a reinforcement in the final fighting. 'Jack' Brownrigg was the stepson of Admiral Sir Tom Phillips, being the son of Lady Phillips by a previous marriage. He was among the wounded in Singapore's Alexandra Military Hospital when Japanese troops broke in and massacred two hundred wounded and medical personnel. Lady Phillips gave money for a memorial to her lost son and husband.

Richard Alexander Hunting was Lieutenant Dick Hunting who had commanded the close-range anti-aircraft guns on *Repulse*. He was seen alive when *Repulse* was sinking, but never after that. Hunting was a member of the family which built up the shipowning and aviation business of that name, and his brother, while on a post-war visit to Singapore, also gave money for a memorial. There was no other connection between the Hunting and Phillips families.

What are the thoughts today of the men who survived that historic action?

Each year I spend my holidays at Plymouth and lay a wreath on the Cenotaph where the names of my comrades – sailors and marines – are inscribed. These kind of men don't live today. (Marine G. Kennedy, H.M.S. *Repulse*)

Why put the blame on anyone? We were short of ships, aircraft, soldiers because of other campaigns. Decisions were made at that time bearing this in mind. Thank God decisions were taken, wrong though some of them were with hindsight, but we might have tried to muddle through and that would have been worse. (Paymaster Sub-Lieutenant A. F. Compton, H.M.S. *Prince of Wales*)

I have, during my later years in the service, been twice over the spot where the grand old lady is resting and each time wished I could just dive and retrieve a few things from my locker, for I feel certain I would know exactly where I had to go to get to it. (Boy Seaman 1st Class C. F. T. Heydon, H.M.S. *Repulse*)

She was a great ship. (Lieutenant D. B. H. Wildish, H.M.S. *Prince of Wales*)

I found time, in hospital, to wonder – 'How?' 'Why?' and to grieve. Afterwards, I served in other ships and other theatres of war, good, efficient ships and, apart from one, they weren't sent to the bottom, but *Repulse* always did and always has seemed to be the best of ships and carried on board the best 'crowd' of men it was my privilege to serve with. (Able Seaman V. T. Barnes, H.M.S. *Repulse*)

I'm going to ask you a question I've asked myself for over thirty years. 'WHY ME?' Have I to live with the spectre of these men I lived with and learned to love, and say, 'There by the Grace of God go I.' I ask you 'Why?' I've been out today and drank myself out of my wife's favour but I can't forget. (Chief Mechanician P. Matthews, H.M.S. *Prince of Wales*)

Prince of Wales Compass Platform Narrative*

11.13.	Opened fire on eight high level bombers which attacked *Repulse*. *Repulse* was straddled by bombs and reported some damage and small fire from two near misses.
11.41½.	Opened fire on nine torpedo bombers coming to attack from port side.
11.44.	Hit by torpedo on port side aft of the bridge. (Exact position not known.)
11.44½.	One aircraft shot down, falling in sea close on the starboard side.
11.45.	Close miss past the starboard quarter by torpedo passing from forward to aft.
11.49½.	*Repulse* attacked by one aircraft which dropped one torpedo.
11.50½.	Reported – one aircraft crashed in sea Green 140. At this stage a heavy list to port had developed.
11.57½.	Opened fire on six aircraft on the starboard side thought to be attacking *Repulse*.
11.58	Ceased fire.
11.59.	Aircraft seen to have turned away.
12.05.	Man overboard port side.
12.06½.	*Vampire* ordered to pick him up.
12.10.	Hoisted 'Not Under Control.'
12.13½.	Out of touch with X Engine Room. (Out of touch with Damage Control Headquarters since shortly after hit.)
12.20.	Seven aircraft on the starboard bow.
12.21½.	Opened fire.
12.23.	Two hits by torpedoes on starboard side, a few seconds apart. One very near the stem, the other in the after part of the ship.
12.24½.	One hit starboard side under compass platform, by torpedo.
12.26½.	*Repulse* shot down two aircraft.
12.27.	*Repulse* observed to be listing to port. ? hit by two torpedoes.
12.28.	Destroyers ordered to close *Repulse*.
12.30.	Nine high level bombers on port bow.

* Public Record Office A D M 199/1149.

12.30.   X Engine Room only working.

12.32.   *Repulse* sinking.

12.33.   *Repulse* sunk.

12.41.   Opened fire on eight high level bombers on port bow.

12.44.   Hit by one bomb. (Reported as being starboard side cata-
           pult deck.)

12.50.   Asked Singapore for tugs.

13.10 (Approx.)   Order to inflate lifebelts ordered.

13.15 (Approx.)   List to port began to increase rapidly.

13.20 (Approx.)   Ship sank, capsizing to port.

W. H. Blunt
Paymaster-Lieutenant

Medical Officer's Report on the Action on 10 December 1941 when H.M.S. Repulse was sunk by Enemy Action. *

Owing to the nature of the incident, the communication is best made in the form of a personal account.

The general medical arrangements for dealing with casualties will be known from former medical journals. Briefly, there was [*sic*] two main Medical Distributing Stations, both below the armour deck which in the *Repulse* is two decks below the main mess decks. The Forward M.D.S. was situated between A and B Turrets, and the Aft M.D.S. just forward to Y Turret. The Medical parties were made up thus:

FORWARD	AFT	RESPONSIBILITY
Surg. Cdr Newberry*	Surg. Lt Hamilton	In charge
Surg. Lt Cavanagh*	Surg. Lt (D) Major	Anaesthetics
S.P.C.P.O. Trusscott	S.B.P.O. Stevens*	Instruments
L.S.B.A. Newall*	S.B.A. (D) Morgan*	Asst Instruments
L.S.B.A. Ashworth*	R.P.O. Trudgeon	Labels etc.
S.B.A. Bridgewater	P.O.Ck Hobbs	Food, water
M.A.A. Cummins*	Sy P.O. Allum	Telephones
Ch. Stwd Robertson*	Ck Blades	Emergency lighting
Ldg Wtr Marsh*	Wtr Rees	Dressings
Ldg Wtr Jackson*	Wtr Griffiths*	Dirty dressings, pans etc.
Ldg Stwd James*	Stwd Miller*	Splints
Ch. Ck Williams*		

* Became fatal casualties.

The idea was that after or during a lull in an action, the Commander would tell us which Mess deck was most suitable to convert into

* From papers kindly provided by Dr S. G. Hamilton.

a casualty ward. The necessary implements would be set up and work would commence in the shortest possible time. In theory all would stay below armour till then.

The Medical Officers, however, and the Sick Bay staff had First Aid bags ready for use should the occasion arise, to attend casualties where they might occur. From my experience, I found that these should contain simple First Aid dressings, a few larger ones made up ready for use (i.e. not rolls of gauze and wool), a bottle of flavine, triangular and ordinary bandages, and several padded splints about 18 inches long. Rubber tubing for tourniquets is more practical than the St John's type. Morphia would be carried by the Medical Officers, and it was found that rubber-capped bottles are far more convenient than ampoules. A torch or head lamp is essential.

In addition to these arrangements, First Aid boxes were available at the Gun positions and in the Engine, Condenser and Boiler Rooms and in many other parts of the ship. The Gunnery Officer, the Senior Engineer and the Padre each had morphia and a syringe and had received instruction in their use. As far as I know, only the Padre was able to make use of this facility. All men working on deck had received anti-flash gear and had been instructed to wear shirts with long sleeves, long trousers tucked into their socks, and boots or leather shoes, instead of the normal light tropical rig. Many wore boiler suits, which are very satisfactory.

At 11.00 hours on December 10th 1941, Air Raid Alarm was sounded. Action continued for one hour and twenty minutes; then the ship sank.

When the Action began I was forward in the Sick Bay with some of the Sick Bay Attendants. We had only one serious case on board viz, Sub-Lieutenant W. R. D. Page R.N.V.R. who on the previous morning had sustained a comminuted fracture-dislocation of his left wrist and bruising of his back. The forearm was in plaster of Paris. We helped him to the Forward M.D.S. and I then carried on to my station Aft.

On arrival I found all the rest of the party present. S.B.P.O. Stevens was calmly setting out medical supplies from the cupboards; the others were at their posts. The Forward M.D.S. was informed by telephone that all was correct. Very soon a loud explosion was heard. As we were over Y Magazine and smoke was beginning to enter the space from the deck above, I ordered the armoured hatch to be closed. Loudspeakers then announced that a bomb had fallen through the catapult and Marines' Mess deck and had exploded, and caused fire to break out.

Tapping was heard on the armoured hatch and we opened it to admit five casualties. The first was dead from severe head injuries so was removed again. The others, who were all frightened, consisted of a man with a lacerated wound of the forearm, a boy with a large haematoma of the buttock, caused by his being thrown to the deck by the bomb exploding near him, and two severe cases of burns. The two former were given first aid treatment, and the two cases of burns were given morphia and retained below after tannafax had been applied to the burnt areas.

One of the telephones in direct communication with Y Turret asked for help. Surg. Lieut (D) Major was despatched by way of the handling room. He found A.B. W. J. Hewitt with a compound fracture of the arm from a bullet. He applied dressings and a splint and gave morphia. Subsequently this man survived and did well in hospital.

While this was happening a warrant officer came to inform us that several casualties had collected in the Captain's lobby flat, so I proceeded there via the quarter deck and triple gun deck. I realized afterwards that it would have been better and saved time if I had taken an S.B.A. or Writer with me. On arrival we found about a dozen men; some were burnt and scalded, one had a fractured leg, another had sustained severe lacerations of the thigh and calf, and a few were more frightened than hurt and needed encouragement. Morphia and other necessary treatment were given, but the cases were not labelled because I found it took too long to do it myself, and I had hoped to return to do this. The Ward Room flat just below was full of smoke and steam but fortunately this did not come up.

Then I returned overdeck to fetch more supplies and to find out if any message had come in. En route I saw the Padre on the quarter deck and told him of the casualties and he went to see to them.

On arrival at the medical station messages came telling of the casualties in the Ward Room Cabin flat just above us, and on the half deck. Surg. Lieut Major and S.B.P.O. Stevens were despatched to investigate and deal with these.

I then telephoned to the Forward M.D.S. and heard that they were busy with about twenty casualties, mostly burns, and that Surg. Cdr Newberry with S.B.A. Ashworth were out attending casualties on the upper deck.

Then a loud explosion shook the ship, so I ordered the armoured hatch to be closed, thinking that bombs were again falling. Actually it was a torpedo somewhere amidships.

A few minutes later another bigger explosion occurred, which I considered to be a bomb through the quarter deck just aft of Y Turret. Again, in fact, it was a torpedo. The ship shook violently and lights momentarily went out.

About one and a half minutes later a still greater explosion occurred. One or two of the lights went out. Correctly we thought that this was a torpedo near us. The ship began to list, so I decided to investigate and ordered the armoured hatch to be opened by means of the winch. Water started to pour down into the station, so I ordered the hatch to be opened at full speed and everyone out. It was only just possible to climb the vertical ladder against the fall of water. Writers Griffiths and Rees, whose duty was to turn the winch, did not lose their heads and continued till there was enough space for the men to scramble out.

We proceeded to the quarter deck which was listing heavily to port to such an extent that it was difficult to reach the starboard rails. Many men had already jumped into the sea.

It has been estimated that the ship sank within seven minutes. Lifebelts were blown up though it was not very easy to do so in a hurry, and many men jumped from the starboard side of the ship and injured their heels on the bulkheads. As the ship was still moving forward, those who jumped soon were left clear, but there must have been some danger from the propellers.

Destroyers soon started to pick men up, and I was fortunate to be picked up by H.M.S. *Electra* fairly soon, and so was able to help Surg. Lieut Seymour organize resuscitation parties and afterwards to sort, treat and label the patients till we arrived in Singapore some ten hours later. S.B.A. Anderson (of *Electra*) and S.B.A. Bailey (*Repulse*) were tireless and invaluable during these hours. There were over 800 additional to the normal complement of the destroyer on board.

Most of the casualties rescued were burns, cuts and fractures. There were, in addition, men suffering from the effects of the swallowing and inhalation of oil. Two cases of severe burns died during the voyage. Fractures of the Os Calcis were frequent, caused by jumping onto the bulkhead or the ship's side. One, however, was a fractured Femur which was put in a Thomas's splint. One midshipman had a perforating bullet wound of the abdomen and required frequent doses of morphia. He was operated on by Mr Julian Taylor F.R.C.S. on arrival, but died three days later of peritonitis resulting from multiple perforation of the jejunum.

In the crowded ship we made the patients as comfortable as possible, giving morphia when required. We saw that supplies of water and hot sweet tea were continually taken round, and dressings and splints were applied and adjusted.

Although many suffered for a few days from the effects of swallowing oil fuel, there were few lasting sequels from it. Many of the men were partly naked but the warmth of the climate no doubt helped to prevent pneumonia and to lessen shock.

It was a pity that many of the men were unable to swim, as I feel that fewer lives would then have been lost.

I understand that Surg. Lieut Seymour of H.M.S. *Electra* has a full account of the casualties and the measures taken to help them in his Medical Journal.

In conclusion, I should like to express my sorrow at the loss of so many of our medical staff. From many months of loyal co-operation in all sorts of conditions I know them to have been exceptionally keen and reliable in their work.

S. G. Hamilton
Surgeon Lieutenant R.N.V.R., M.A., M.B., B.CHIR., M.R.C.S., L.R.C.P.

Log of Signals Received in Singapore from Force Z*

SECRET

MICROGRAM.

Non-Urgent.

The British Naval Commander-in-Chief, Eastern Fleet.
26th December 1941.

No. 741/4724.

The Secretary of the Admiralty.

LOSS OF PRINCE OF WALES AND REPULSE.
LOG OF MESSAGES.

In continuation of my submission No. 730/4742 of 17th December 1941, I enclose a log of the messages received in the War Room at Singapore in connection with the operations on 10th December 1941.

G. Layton VICE-ADMIRAL. COMMANDER-IN-CHIEF.

Time of receipt in War Room	From	To	Report
12.04	REPULSE	Any British Man of War.	Enemy aircraft bombing My position 134 N Y T W 22 x 09. (11.58).
12.40	PRINCE OF WALES		*Emergency* Have been struck by a torpedo on port side. N Y T W 022 R 06 4 torpedoes. Send Destroyers. (12.20.)

* Public Record Office ADM 199/1149.

Time of receipt in War Room	From	To	Report
13.04	SENIOR OFFICER, FORCE Z	Any British Man of War.	*Emergency.* Send all available tugs. My position 003° 40′ N, 104° 30′ E. (12.52.)
13.10	ELECTRA.	Any British Man of War.	*Most Immediate.* H.M.S. PRINCE OF WALES hit by 4 torpedoes in position 003° 45′ N, 104° 10′ E. REPULSE sunk. Send Destroyers. (05.30z) *
13.17	COMMANDER-IN-CHIEF, EASTERN FLEET.	CHIEF OF STAFF, Singapore.	*Most Immediate.* Am disembarking men not required for fighting ship. Send – ? – ? – fast as possible. (13.11.)
13.10	SENIOR OFFICER, FORCE Z.	Any British Man of War.	*Most Immediate.* H.M.S. PRINCE OF WALES disabled and out of control. (13.00.)
13.11	PRINCE OF WALES.	Any British Man of War.	*Emergency.* Send all available tugs. My position now is EQTW 40(?). (05.31z.)
13.17	ELECTRA.	Any British Man of War.	*Most Immediate.* My 05.30z send tugs.
13.21	ELECTRA.	Any British Man of War.	*Most Immediate.* H.M.S. PRINCE OF WALES sunk. (05.48z.)

* The 'Z' times are Greenwich Mean Time, $7\frac{1}{2}$ hours ahead of the Singapore Time used elsewhere in these signals and in the narrative of the book.

Post-Action Statement by Gunnery Officer of H.M.S. Prince of Wales.

Lt. Cdr C. W. McMullen, H.M.S. *Sultan*, Singapore, 14 Dec 1941 Draft of Gunnery Officer's letter to Senior Surviving Officer of *Prince of Wales*.*

Sir,

I have the honour to forward the following gunnery report of events leading to loss of H.M.S. *Prince of Wales*. I attach many statements taken from officers in various positions.

1. Attack No. 1. Nine bombers were observed ahead in close formation. Fire was opened by Starboard Fore Group and then Port Fore Group as own ship altered course to starboard. Finally fire was opened by Starboard Fore Group as own ship altered course back to port *Repulse* was straddled and hit by the pattern of this formation.

2. Attack No. 2. At 11.41½. About nine torpedo bombers were engaged on the starboard side and then on the port side by Starboard Fore Group and both Port Groups of 5·25-inch guns and close range weapons. One hit port side and severely shook the ship.

A good barrage was developed but this in no way deterred the enemy.

Oerlikon tracer appeared effective. Two of these machines crashed on the disengaged side after they had dropped their torpedoes. Ship assumed an 11½ degree list to port and loss of efficiency resulted in gunnery material as follows:

S3 Turret. Not possible to train in hand.

S4 Turret. Power failed and an oil leak was caused somewhere under left gun. Not possible to train uphill in hand.

P1 Turret. List of ship caused turret to jamb due to turret settling sideways onto a hydraulic pipe – this was cleared before the next attack but would not train in power against the list.

* Based on Public Record Office A D M 1/12181.

P2 Turret. Power failed to turret. Emergency leads brought power on but turret would not train until after second attack when list was reduced.

P3 Turret. Power failed and then came on again for about two minutes. It then failed for good. It was not possible to train the turret in hand.

P4 Turret. Guns continued to elevate in power but turret would not train due to list. Power then failed.

S1 and S2 not possible to depress below 5 degrees of elevation.

Ship handling. The ship could not alter course.

Between attack No. 2 and attack No. 3, fire was opened from S1 and S2 Turrets at aircraft which were attacking *Repulse*.

3. Attack No. 3. About nine torpedo bombers attacked from the starboard side. These were engaged by S1 and S2 Turrets at 12.20 and by close range weapons. Ship was at this time unmanoeuvrable and she was hit by two torpedoes three minutes later, one hitting the bow. One aft starboard side. A minute and a half later the ship was hit by a third torpedo abreast B Turret.

4. The damage caused by this attack removed power from P1 pom-poms which had become jambed in training, probably due to distortion of the roller path. Two enemy aircraft were seen to crash on the disengaged side.

5. Attack No. 4. Eight or nine high-level bombers carried out a formation attack approaching from ahead. These were engaged by P2 and S1 and S2 Turrets. The fire from S1 and S2 was not effective as an estimated height had to be used due to the rangetaker being wounded in the right eye. The 'pattern' of these bombers straddled the ship and, in addition to near misses, one bomb hit the catapult deck and exploded on the armour deck below. S1 and S2 Turrets were the last quarters to fire in *Prince of Wales*.

6. Due to the lack of an A.A. destroyer and cruiser screen, fighter escort and the determination and skill with which the enemy pressed home their attacks, it is doubtful if anything could have prevented torpedo bombers achieving their object.

The following serious deficiencies in gunnery material, however, should be put right in all ships fitted with similar equipment to that in *Prince of Wales*.

(A) Some 5·25-inch turrets failed to train in power or hand with a list of 11½ degrees on the ship (see Para 2).

(B) All pom-poms suffered from a large number of stoppages due to the shell and cartridges becoming separated, this defect showed itself in Operation Halberd but not to the same extent. Since Operation Halberd ammunition has been frequently checked for loose shells and cases.

(C) The tracer from the Bofors gun and Oerlikons was definitely seen to make some attacking aircraft jink. The pom-poms, although they were seen to hit the enemy, did not frighten him during his approach due to lack of tracer.

(D) All close range weapons should have at least 15 degrees of depression.

7. The Bofors gun on the quarterdeck fired without a stoppage. The tracer is most effective and it is considered that in KGV Class these guns should be mounted as follows:
two on top of B Turret, two on Y Turret (all on the fore and aft line) and as many as possible on the boat deck, fo'c'sle and quarterdeck in addition to the Oerlikons.

It is considered that a Bofors with tracer ammunition in local control is a more valuable weapon than an 8-barrelled pom-pom in director control without tracer, added to which a Bofors in no way relies on power and fires one-eighth of the ammunition.

8. Japanese tactics.
Torpedo bombing No. 1. Formation approached in close formation at heights between 5,000 and 7,000 feet. When at extreme gun range they formed line astern on the starboard bow and went into a shallow dive on a course at right angles to the ship and crossed from starboard to port. When on the port bow they turned to port losing height the whole time and flew on a course on the port beam reciprocal to that of the ship. Then they appeared to do a series of 'blue turns' and waves of two or three came towards the ship at a time in a rough line abreast. The deflection was at all times great up to the final moment when they turned towards the ship. They approached and dropped their torpedoes at high speed from heights of at least 100 feet from ranges of between 1,000 and 2,000 yards.
Due to the high speed of the machines, the time between their turn to a firing course and torpedo release was very small. The machines passed very close to the ship and some used their machine-guns as

they passed. A large amount of Oerlikon appeared to hit these machines.

Attack No. 2. Similar to attack No. 1 but attack from the opposite side and the number of waves is doubtful.

High level bombing attacked from a height of about 10,000 to 12,000 feet in close formation. They attacked from right ahead and released one good salvo. Similar tactics were used against *Repulse*. Before bombing they were seen to drop a salvo into the sea about 4 miles away. It is possible that this was some form of 'sighter', on the other hand it may have been a damaged aircraft jettisoning its bombs. It is not thought that the bombs were bigger than 500 pounds but this is not certain.

Type of aircraft.
The torpedo bombers were fine, robust looking craft with twin engines and rudder. They looked rather like Hudsons but larger.

9. Remarks by a Gunnery Officer on general recommendations after a year's experience as Gunnery Officer of a modern battleship in time of war.

The two statements below are not made as a result of this action but after six months' thought. I have not considered it wise to voice them before as it would be easy to be accused of 'vested interests'. Such a remark cannot now be made so here they are:—

(a) I consider that, in a. ship of the K.G.V. Class, the Gunnery Officer should be a Commander (or Acting Commander) and should have a similar status to the Commander (E). It is believed that this became the practice in big ships in the last war. It is noted also that BISMARCK had a Gunnery Commander and at least three gunnery officers under him.

(b) I consider that it is wrong for 'Damage Control' to be the sole responsibility of the Engineer Officer. It should be an executive responsibility and it would be advisable to adapt the French system of *L'Officier de L'Intérieur* who is responsible for co-ordinating all matters relating to the inside of the hull both from a domestic and fighting point of view, i.e. Messdecks, ventilation, Fire Parties, Repair Parties, Watertight doors, and to be responsible in action to the second in command for Damage Control.

As his assistants he should have an Engineer Officer, the Shipwright Officer, an Electrical or Torpedo Officer and the Commissioned Gunner.

10. I wish to state that there was one bright spark in an otherwise depressing and disastrous day and that was the excellent morale and discipline of the gunnery quarters that I saw of *Prince of Wales.* Every H.A. director, pom-pom director and pom-pom requested permission before falling out. Pom-poms and 5·25-inch crews remained in action as long as possible and the working chambers crews of S1 finally went down with the ship.

I was particularly impressed by the leadership of the following officers:

Lieutenant-Commander G. C. J. Ferguson, R.N.V.R., who was in charge of the Air Defence Position and did not manage to survive.

Sub-Lt R. C. Ripley, R.C.N.V.R., Assistant Air Defence Officer.

Lieutenants E. J. Kempson, J. B. Womersley (not a survivor), E. V. Dawson and D. C. Hopkinson, all R.N.V.R. officers in charge of H.A. Directors.

Lt W. M. Graham, R.N.V.R., who was in charge of pom-pom decks.

Lt R. C. Beckwith, 2nd Gunnery Officer, who made tremendous endeavours to get 5·25-inch Turrets back into action finally trying to train those who jambed by block and tackle.

Lt (E) A. J. Cawthra and Ord.Lt E. Lancaster who did their best to bring 5·25-inch guns back into action.

Sub-Lt A. G. C. Franklin, R.N.V.R., who organized secondary supply arrangements to P3 and P4 Turrets.

The conduct of the following Petty Officers was magnificent:

P.O. Paget and P.O. Paley, who were in charge of pom-poms. Neither survived.

C.P.O. Mantle, who was Chief Gunner's Mate on the Pom-Pom Deck.

Leading-Seaman Coles, in charge of S1 pom-pom and P.O. Stevens in charge of B pom-pom.

A.B. MacNelly (not a survivor), who manned an Air Defence Position telephone to the pom-poms until ordered to take it off as the ship started to capsize.

P.O. Spencer (not a survivor), who was in charge of lookouts and did not leave Air Defence Position until too late.

Mr F. Luxton, Commission Gunner, who organized the pom-pom supply which was kept going until the last moment when the ship started to list heavily to port. He was also a great leader in keeping people cool and cheerful below.

There were many other cases of high morale and leadership which cannot be recorded but I wish to repeat that the spirit shown by H.M.S. *Prince of Wales*'s officers and men fighting the guns during the action and at the end was in the highest tradition of the Royal Navy.

I have the honour to be sir,
Your obedient servant,

C. McMullen, Lt-Cdr R.N.

Citations for Mentions in Despatches in H.M.S. Prince of Wales and H.M.S. Repulse, 10 December 1941*

Sick Berth Attendant H. Bridgewater   H.M.S. *Repulse*

For remaining down below in the fore medical station for several minutes after the order 'everyone on deck' in order to help a wounded man on deck. Although he failed in this he only abandoned this attempt when the ship had a very heavy list and was about to sink.

Midshipman A. C. R. Bros, R.N.   H.M.S. *Repulse*   Posthumous

For showing great calmness and leadership in causing the 15″ T.S. to be evacuated in an orderly manner when the order 'everyone on deck' was given. It is considered that Midshipman Bros thereby saved many lives.

Lieutenant-Commander K. R. Buckley, R.N.   H.M.S. *Repulse*

For outstanding calmness in action under trying circumstances.

Chief Stoker Cameron   H.M.S. *Repulse*   Posthumous

Was outstanding in maintaining the efficiency of the damage control throughout the action. He is not a survivor.

Corporal W. R. Chambers, R.M.   H.M.S. *Prince of Wales*
Posthumous

The successful supply of ammunition to the 2-pdr guns was largely due to the efforts of this N.C.O. and his ability, coolness and example were outstanding. When conditions between decks became very difficult he continued to carry on, closing down magazines and shell rooms in the final effort to keep the ship afloat. His work in assisting to limit the spread of water when S3 and 4 magazines were flooded were most useful. He was lost with the ship.

Chief Petty Officer F. T. Crittenden   H.M.S. *Repulse*

Was outstanding in maintaining supply of H.A. ammunition under difficult circumstances owing to bomb damage.

* Based on Public Record Office ADM 1/12315.

Midshipman R. I. Davies, R.A.N.   H.M.S. *Repulse*   Posthumous

This very gallant young officer was last seen firing an Oerlikon gun at enemy aircraft when he and the gun mounting were slowly submerging.

Commander R. J. R. Dendy, R.N.   H.M.S. *Repulse*

For outstanding calmness in action under trying circumstances.

Writer J. I. Griffiths   H.M.S. *Repulse*   Posthumous

When the ship was listing heavily and about to sink, showed great calmness in continuing steadily to wind the winch to raise the armoured hatch over Y Space leading to the after medical station. Water was pouring down the hatch, his coolness under trying conditions enabled eleven men to escape of whom nine are survivors.

Lieutenant-Commander H. B. C. Gill, R.N.   H.M.S. *Repulse*

For outstanding calmness in action under trying circumstances.

Surgeon Lieutenant S. G. Hamilton, R.N.V.R.   H.M.S. *Repulse*

For outstanding devotion to duty on board when in action in tending the wounded and in continuing to do so for some nine hours in the destroyer *Electra* after he had been picked up.

Chief Petty Officer W. E. Houston   H.M.S. *Prince of Wales*

This Chief Petty Officer showed fine qualities of leadership in charge of an electrical repair party. He carried on his work to the end under conditions of extreme difficulty, setting a fine example to those under him. He was wounded in the last bombing attack, but is a survivor.

Lieutenant Commander (E) R. O. Lockley   H.M.S. *Prince of Wales*

This officer displayed great initiative and coolness under action conditions and it was due to him that many essential services were maintained. He showed great powers of leadership and example under arduous conditions. Although wounded, he was of great assistance in helping survivors and maintaining the high standard of morale after the ships had sunk.

Chief Mechanician Lugger   H.M.S. *Repulse*   Posthumous

Was outstanding in maintaining the efficiency of the Damage Control throughout the action. He is not a survivor.

Commissioned Electrician E. H. Marchant   H.M.S. *Prince of Wales*   Posthumous

This officer displayed great devotion to duty in conditions of extreme difficulty. He showed fine qualities of leadership and continued his electrical repair work to the end. He was last seen in an exhausted condition between decks.

Boy W. T. O'Brien   H.M.S. *Prince of Wales*

The ability, courage and coolness of this boy during the action was outstanding and his work in assisting to get up ammunition when conditions below deck were both serious and difficult, was an example to senior ratings. He remained to assist in closing down the magazines under most trying circumstances, finally taking charge of ladders and controlling the traffic leading to the upper deck. He survived and is believed to have reached Australia.

Gunner J. B. Page, R.N.   H.M.S. *Repulse*   Posthumous

As the ship was about to sink, Mr Page found Ordinary Seaman J. MacDonald on the upper deck and without life-saving belt. Mr Page took off his own belt and put it on MacDonald. Mr Page was not picked up.

Writer W. Rees   H.M.S. *Repulse*

When the ship was listing heavily and about to sink showed great calmness in continuing steadily to wind the winch over Y Space leading to the after medical station. Water was pouring down the hatch, his coolness under trying conditions enabled eleven men to escape of whom nine are survivors.

Chief Stoker S. J. Ridgeway   H.M.S. *Prince of Wales*   Posthumous

Always a man of untiring energy and devotion to duty, this Chief Petty Officer showed great qualities of leadership during the action. He was invaluable in taking charge of pumping operations and in the supply of good fuel to boilers in spite of damaged tanks and trying conditions. He continued his efforts to the end and went down with the ship.

Chief Stoker A. Russell   H.M.S. *Repulse*   Posthumous

Volunteered to enter D Boiler Room and fan flat to shut off steam in a steam-filled compartment. He is not a survivor.

Petty Officer J. S. Spencer   H.M.S. *Prince of Wales*   Posthumous

This Petty Officer was in charge of lookouts and remained at his post to the end, going down with the ship. By his example and leadership he was instrumental in maintaining the high standard of concentration displayed by the air lookouts under trying conditions.

Shipwright 1st Class A. B. Squance   H.M.S. *Prince of Wales*

This shipwright was sent to the scene of the greatest damage from his station forward. He displayed great resourcefulness and skill in stopping leaks and in organizing repair parties. By his inspiring energy, example and initiative, he proved himself a fearless leader. After the action, although wounded, he continued to further morale by his cheerfulness and morale.

Lieutenant (E) L. F. Wood, R.N.   H.M.S. *Repulse*   Posthumous

Was outstanding in maintaining the efficiency of the damage control throughout the action. Not a survivor.

Chief Shipwright L. J. Woolons   H.M.S. *Prince of Wales*
Posthumous

This Chief Petty Officer was in charge of No. 3 Shipwright Repair Party and displayed great initiative and skill in the ordering and carrying out of the shoring of hatches and the stopping of leaks. He set a fine example of leadership and carried on to the last moment despite his exhaustion. He was not saved.

Statement by Lieutenant-Commander D. P. R. Lermitte, R.N., Far East Fleet Clearance Diving Team, Following External Survey of H.M.S. Prince of Wales in 1966.*

The *Prince of Wales* was located on Sonar and marked with two mooring buoys prior to the start of the operation.

The Far East Fleet Clearance Diving Team backed up by Clearance Divers from H.M.S. *Sheraton* and the Royal Australian Navy's Clearance Diving Team No. 1, carried out the survey involving six days on a task between 25th April and 6th May this year. Diving was initially carried out from the *Sheraton*, but half way through she had to be withdrawn for operational reasons, and the team transferred to H.M.S. *Barfoil* for the remainder of the time available.

A total of sixty-four dives were carried out between 160 and 180 feet involving an overall time of thirty-three hours underwater. Most of the dives were carried out in SDDE (Surface Demand Diving Equipment – a diving suit), but the SABA (Swimmer's Air Breathing Apparatus – an aqualung) was used on a few occasions, particularly for towed diver searches from the Gemini dinghies. DUCS (Diver's Underwater Communications System) was used throughout and, when it worked effectively, found to be invaluable. The weather was fine but the ocean current, although not strong, was unpredictable and at times hindered the operation and made positioning of the diving support ship above the wreck difficult.

The *Prince of Wales* lies on a heading of 020 degrees, and bar about 15 or 20 degrees, is upside down. The shallowest part of the ship is in the vicinity of her starboard bilge keel at a depth of 155 feet. The large flat expanse of the ship's bottom is remarkably free from marine growth and, apart from the occasional sea egg, weed or small clam, is only covered with a fine layer of silt. However, the vertical surfaces and those in the dark underhanging part of the ship was well covered with small clams, weed and similar encrustation.

Owing to the vast size of this awesome ship and the problems concerned with mooring the diving support vessel above her it was only

* This is a personal statement, and we are grateful to Lieutenant-Commander Lermitte for permission to reproduce it.

possible, in the limited time available, to dive on three separate zones of the *Prince of Wales*, namely, amidships in the vicinity of the Engine Rooms, right forward on the stem and right aft in the vicinity of the propellers and rudders.

Further, owing to the sensitive nature of such an operation, our terms of reference were that we were not to enter or disturb the wreck in any way, and this fact, combined with being confined to the depth limit of 180 feet, restricted operations to the external area of the hull alone.

During the course of the survey the following evidence of war damage was seen:

(a) A large and jagged hole about twenty feet in diameter in the forepeak passing right through the ship and in one place fracturing the stem post.

(b) The starboard outer shaft crosses over the starboard inner and its propeller wedged between the inner shaft and the hull. There is a jagged hole some six feet in diameter slightly forward of where the two shafts cross over.

(c) The port outer propeller is missing entirely and the bare shaft has pulled away from the ship, snapping the 'A' bracket in the process. A few feet forward of the 'A' bracket stub is a large hole about twelve feet in diameter with the ship's side plating jaggedly bent inwards.

Diving conditions were generally good with at least a maximum horizontal visibility of forty feet on the wreck, but this would reduce to some fifteen feet when silt was stirred up by the effect of the ocean current. The wreck abounds with marine life and one was constantly accompanied by shoals of fish of all varieties. Apart from one very large and lethargic whale shark, no other kinds of shark were seen; large shoals of barracuda were frequently in attendance and on a few occasions large grouper or Jew fish were sighted. As one ascends away from the wreck and out of the milky blanket that covers her one comes into crystal clear water and visibility in excess of 120 feet.

Acknowledgements

Before all others we would like to thank the following men who were serving aboard the ships of Force Z in the action of 10 December 1941, and the men and women who were in various other positions at that time and who all helped by sending personal contributions for our research. Without this generous and always friendly help, this book could never have been written in its present form. (Contributors are listed in alphabetical order. Ranks shown are those held on 10 December 1941.)

H.M.S. *Prince of Wales*

Able Seaman H. H. Ashurst, Leading Seaman G. H. Barstow, Paymaster Lieutenant J. G. Baskomb, Stoker R. H. Bealey, Able Seaman F. W. Bennett, Petty Officer Telegraphist A. E. C. Best, Able Seaman A. J. Bidewell, Petty Officer W. G. Bigmore, Sub-Lieutenant G. A. E. Brooke, Cook P. Byrne, Surgeon Lieutenant-Commander E. D. Caldwell, Leading Telegraphist B. G. Campion, Ordinary Seaman J. Cockburn, Leading Seaman W. Dawber, Stoker Petty Officer S. Dingle, Able Seaman A. H. V. Elliott, Leading Seaman C. B. Elsmore, Ordinary Seaman W. E. England, Able Seaman R. H. Errington, Ordinary Seaman J. Everson, Lieutenant I. D. S. Forbes, Lieutenant W. M. Graham, Engine Room Artificer A. Guy (died 1974), Lieutenant-Commander R. F. Harland, Sick Berth Petty Officer W. M. Harrigan (died 1974), Able Seaman D. G. Heath, Petty Officer F. J. Hendy, Engine Room Artificer E. Holbrook, Leading Seaman G. F. Holehouse, Leading Seaman E. Housman, Ordnance Artificer D. Hunter, Ordinary Seaman J. S. Ivers, Able Seaman R. H. James, Ordinary Telegraphist W. King, Ordnance Artificer H. W. Latto, Petty Officer L. V. Leather, Ordinary Seaman H. A. Lindsay, Telegraphist J. Macmillan, Telegraphist J. A. McCall, Lieutenant-Commander C. W. McMullen, Stoker W. Malkin, Leading Sick Berth Attendant W. Mann, Boy Seaman G. D. Marks, Leading Writer J. Marsh, Chief Mechanician P. Matthews, Able Seaman J. E. Melling, Boy Seaman B. N. Millard, Able Seaman G. Mooney, Artisan Rating L. Morley, Able Seaman P. Paterson, Stoker F. Powell, Yeoman of Signals E. A. Randall, Chief Petty Officer Writer J. H. Richards, Surgeon-Lieutenant J. E. Richardson, Leading Stoker H. Rogers, Stoker Petty Officer W. A. Roseveare, Able Seaman F. Rowe, Able Seaman G. Schofield, Boy Seaman W. S. Searle, Lieutenant-Commander A. G. Skipwith, Able Seaman P. Smalley, Shipwright A. B. Squance, Shipwright Petty Officer S. R.

Stephenson, Leading Officers' Cook D. W. Thomas, Stoker D. Ulrick, Able Seaman W. Webster, Able Seaman A. F. S. White, Lieutenant D. B. H. Wildish, Officers' Steward I. E. Wilkinson, Able Seaman R. Wilkinson, Leading Signalman J. H. Willey, Ordinary Seaman D. F. Wilson, Boy Seaman R. Wilson, Engine Room Artificer R. A. Woodhead, Chief Petty Officer H. E. Wright. *Royal Marines:* Captain C. D. L. Aylwin, Marine V. T. Barnes, Marine R. Bellwood, Marine D. S. Brown, Marine E. G. Dart, Marine P. G. Dunstan, Marine G. H. Locker, Marine R. W. Seddon, Marine R. Swain, Marine R. B. Wade, Corporal R. T. Warn, Marine T. A. Webber, Marine G. F. Whitman, Marine J. Wignall, Sergeant F. Winstanley.

Fleet Air Arm: Midshipman G. A. Trevett.

Staff of Commander-in-Chief Eastern Fleet: Paymaster Sub-Lieutenant J. G. Blackburn, Commander H. N. S. Brown (Fleet Gunnery Officer), Paymaster Sub-Lieutenant A. F. Compton, Telegraphist C. V. House, Officers' Steward J. A. Murray, Commander H. Norman.

H.M.S. Repulse

Lieutenant H. J. Abrahams (attached from the Admiralty Press Division), Sub-Lieutenant G. K. Armstrong, Able Seaman D. W. Avery, Stoker Mechanic G. T. Avery, Able Seaman T. Barnes, Able Seaman S. C. Baxter, Able Seaman H. Boyd, Sick Berth Attendant W. Bridgewater, Able Seaman S. E. Brown, Able Seaman S. Burgess, Ordinary Seaman H. Cain, Petty Officer J. Davey, Commander R. J. R. Dendy, Ordinary Seaman S. C. Dimmack, Ordinary Seaman R. W. Fraser, Stoker R. G. Gage, Lieutenant-Commander H. B. C. Gill, Able Seaman F. W. Green, Officers' Cook W. Greenwood, Midshipman G. R. Griffiths, R.A.N., Ordinary Seaman H. J. Hall, Surgeon-Lieutenant S. G. Hamilton, Cook J. Harbinson, Lieutenant J. O. C. Hayes, Leading Seaman N. Heap, Boy Seaman C. F. T. Heydon, Blacksmith J. A. Howe, Ordinary Seaman T. D. Jaffray, R.N.Z.N., Cook J. H. Larthwell, Able Seaman H. G. D. Lawrence, Able Seaman G. A. McCulloch, Petty Officer A. E. Mooney, Able Seaman R. Moore, Signalman G. Morris, Able Seaman E. L. Nevin, Stoker J. Parkinson, Petty Officer B. Pester, Lieutenant R. A. W. Pool, Stoker H. Radcliffe, Chief Petty Officer R. R. Rendle, Leading Seaman J. Robson, Leading Supply Assistant L. Sandland, Petty Officer A. T. Skedgell, Leading Stoker J. Slater, Chief Petty Officer Ordnance Artificer E. L. Smith, Able Seaman

J. S. Smith, Boy Telegraphist W. C. Tinkler, Leading Seaman I. G. Tucker, Steward W. Ward, Coder R. Watson, Boy Telegraphist E. Woodworth, Able Seaman H. Wynn.
Royal Marines: Lieutenant R. J. L. Davis, Marine A. Dodgson, Marine F. W. Endacott, Marine H. W. Farrell, Sergeant J. H. Gammon, Marine J. Hayes, Lieutenant G. A. Hulton, Marine G. Kennedy, Sergeant H. A. Nunn, Marine J. Powell, Sergeant S. A. Prevett, Corporal L. T. Townsend, Marine G. Turner.

H.M.S. Electra

Leading Seaman J. Ashton, Petty Officer C. W. Braley, Leading Seaman J. P. McGrady, Leading Stoker H. S. Mantle, Leading Seaman P. H. Perkins, Radar Operator B. V. Roberts, Able Seaman J. R. Russell, Surgeon-Lieutenant W. R. D. Seymour, Petty Officer Telegraphist A. J. Smith, Stoker Petty Officer D. J. Smith.

H.M.S. Express

Surgeon-Lieutenant T. E. Barwell, Stoker K. J. R. Birtwistle, Stoker R. Burnett, Lieutenant-Commander F. J. Cartwright (died 1974), Stoker R. J. Collier, Lieutenant J. R. A. Denne, Sick Berth Attendant A. Dudman, Able Seaman J. M. Farrington (died 1974), Leading Signalman J. A. Fear, Able Seaman C. L. Fox, Stoker Petty Officer G. C. Gillett (died 1973), Lieutenant A. V. Hickley, Able Seaman W. H. Jeffery, Ordinary Seaman A. Newton, Sub-Lieutenant P. F. C. Satow, Ordinary Seaman G. Slater, Stoker A. E. Smith, Able Seaman A. Taylor.

H.M.S. Tenedos

Lieutenant R. Dyer, Chief Stoker H. Hodson.

H.M.A.S. Vampire

Leading Seaman V. Sotheren.

*

Service personnel connected with the sailing of *Prince of Wales* and *Repulse* to the Far East, or who were in Singapore or Malaya at the time of events described in the book, or who were otherwise connected with the sinking of the ships.

United Kingdom to Singapore

95 Squadron R.A.F., Freetown, Sierra Leone: Sergeant D. S. Fowler,

No. 1 Mobile Naval Base Defence Organization Royal Marines, Addu Atoll: Sergeant E. Winter.

Naval Personnel at Singapore

Shore based: Telegraphist S. C. Ball, Lieutenant-Commander D. F. Chandler, Ordinary Seaman C. L. Jones, R.N.Z.N., Ordinary Seaman J. C. Leslie, Sub-Lieutenant H. J. Lock (formerly of *Prince of Wales*), Writer G. F. Palmer, Able Seaman M. C. Robertson, R.N.Z.N. U.S.S. *Alden:* Lieutenant B. J. Anderson (temporarily transferred from H.M.S. *Mauritius*). H.M.S. *Dragon:* Chief Shipwright G. Barritt. H.M.S. *Durban:* Leading Stoker A. H. C. Rogers. H.M.S. *Exeter:* Petty Officer T. A. Andrews, Lieutenant Commander G. T. Cooper, Stoker G. Darley. H.M.S. *Mauritius:* Midshipman H. C. Leach, Lieutenant A. H. Webber. Patrol Boat 328: Engineer W. Misso.

R.A.F. Personnel at Singapore

453 Squadron R.A.A.F.: Sergeant V. A. Collyer, Sergeant S. G. Scrimgeour, Flight-Lieutenant T. A. Vigors. R.A.F. H.Q.: Leading Aircraftman A. J. Smith. R.A.F. Station Tengah: Flight-Lieutenant J. A. D. Anderson.

Army Personnel in Malaya

Signalman H. G. Rowe, 9th Indian Division Signals (in Observation Post at Kuantan, and possibly the last man on shore to see *Prince of Wales* and *Repulse*). Lieutenant G. F. Hamilton, 2/3rd Australian Reserve Motor Transport Company (at Penang Ferries).

Casualty Office, H.M.S. Drake, Devonport

Petty Officer Wren Muriel Saunders (now Mrs Holland).

PERSONAL ACKNOWLEDGEMENTS

We would like to express our thanks to people and organizations in several countries for their generous help with the preparation of this book. We think it would be invidious to attempt to place these in order of merit and hope they will forgive the following groupings by countries and in alphabetical order.

Britain

T. F. (Freddie) Abbott, of Boston, for naval advice; Group Captain H. T. Bennett, Mr T. Umehara and Mr H. Yamaguchi of London, for diligent translation of Japanese documents; Captain

N. J. M. Campbell, Ryde, Isle of Wight, for technical advice; Tommy Dean, Wickford, Essex, for initial encouragement and assistance to Patrick Mahoney, and also to his daughter Mrs Sue Bunney of Garmouth, Morayshire; Professor D. J. Gee of Leeds University; Mike Hodgson of Mareham, near Boston; Tom L. Iremonger of London; the Japan Society of London; Geoffrey F. Keay of Scarborough; Stephen Knight of the *Ilford Recorder*; Lieutenant-Commander David Lermitte of Godalming; Janet Mountain and Cherry Robinson of Boston, Lincs., for their usual efficient typing for Martin Middlebrook; Alfred Price of Uppingham; Antony Preston, editor of *Warship Profiles*; Mrs K. H. L. Painter of Camberley and Brigadier J. L. A. Painter, widow and son of the late Brigadier G. W. A. Painter, who commanded the 22nd Indian Infantry Brigade at Kuantan, for the loan of personal papers; Captain Sir Anthony Thorold, Bart, R.N. Retired, of Syston, near Grantham; Commander J. F. H. Wheeler of Alderney; Mr J. Whitton of Siebe Gorman & Co. Ltd, Chessington.

We also thank the staffs of the Ilford Central, Seven Kings and Boston Public Libraries and the Library of Australia House, the Commonwealth War Graves Commission, Imperial War Museum, the London and the Devon and Cornwall Branches of the Far Eastern Prisoner of War Association, B.B.C. Monitoring Service, Caversham (Mr S. A. G. Cook), Australian High Commission in London (Rear-Admiral C. V. Gladstone), Embassy of Japan, London (Captain H. Sato, Defence Attaché), National Maritime Museum (Mr D. J. Lyon), British Museum (Peter J. Whitehead of the Natural History Department) and Cammell Laird Ltd of Birkenhead.

We are also grateful to the following departments of the Ministry of Defence: Naval Historical Branch, Naval Home Division, Department of Naval Secretary, Department of Ships, Hydrographic Department and the Air Historical Branch.

Singapore

We would like to thank the following, mostly in connection with Patrick Mahoney's visit to Singapore in September 1974: Mr T. W. Chatterton of the Commonwealth War Graves Commission, Mr D. E. S. Chelliah, Doctor C. T. Cheng, Tim Hunt of U.K. Joint Service Public Relations, Mr B. Nair of the Ministry of Culture, Squadron-Leader D. A. Rolph, R.A.F., Peter Scanlon of the British High Commission and Miss Mary J. Yapp. The staff of the Alexandra Hospital and Singapore General Hospital, Outram Road, kindly allowed an inspection of the premises that were the scene of historic events in February 1942. Two Australian pilots, Greg McKern and Mel Dougherty of the Singapore Flying Club, together with Corporal P. R. Willett, a photographer loaned by the Royal New Zealand Air Force, made every effort to help Patrick Mahoney see and photograph the wrecks of *Repulse* and *Prince of Wales*, but sight of the wrecks was unfortunately prevented by weather conditions.

U.S.A.

Our thanks are due to William H. Garzke Jr, a naval architect of Deer Park, New York, for his valuable advice on naval construction problems; and to the Naval Historical Center, Washington Navy Yard, and the General Services Administration for the provision of official records.

Japan

We are grateful to the Senshi-Shitsu (War History Division) of the Japanese Defence Agency, Mr Shiro Ihara of Mitsubishi Heavy Industries Ltd and to Mr W. G. Jackson of Times' Publishing, Tokyo.

We wish also to acknowledge the help of the Australian War Memorial, Canberra, the Historical Section of the Australian Department of the Navy, Melbourne, and the Historical Section of the Netherlands Naval Staff, The Hague.

*

Acknowledgement for permission to include quotations from certain publications is gratefully given as follows: from the *Official History of the Second World War* to the Controller of H.M. Stationery Office; from the *Japanese Official History* to the publishers, Asagumo-Shinbunsha Co. Ltd of Tokyo; from *Zero! The Story of the Japanese Navy Air Force* to the authors, Masatohe Okumiya and Jiro Horikoshi with Martin Caidin and to E. P. Dutton and Co. Inc.; from *Singapore, the Japanese Version* to Constable Publishers; from *Japan Must Fight Britain* to Hutchinson Publishing Group Ltd; from *The Memoirs of General The Lord Hastings Ismay* to William Heinemann Ltd; and, for quotations from the London *Evening News*, the *Liverpool Daily Post*, the *Cape Times* and the *Singapore Free Press*, to the proprietors of those newspapers.

The cartoon by David Low is reproduced by arrangement with the Trustees and the London *Evening Standard*.

The authors would also like to thank those newspapers in the United Kingdom, South Africa, Australia, New Zealand, Singapore, Malaysia and Japan who published Patrick Mahoney's appeals for participants of the actions described in the book.

Bibliography

Official Histories

Japanese Defence Agency's Research Section, *The Book of Military History, The Malayan Area*, Tokyo, 1969.

Kirby, Major-General S. Woodburn, *The War Against Japan*, vol. I, H.M.S.O., London, 1957.

Morison, S. E., *History of United States Naval Operations in World War II*, vol. II, Oxford University Press, 1948–56.

Roskill, Captain S. W., *The War at Sea*, 3 vols., H.M.S.O., London, 1954–61.

Other Publications

D'Albas, Andrieu, *Death of a Navy*, Robert Hale, London, 1957.

Ash, Bernard, *Someone Had Blundered*, Michael Joseph, London, 1960.

Hough, Richard, *The Hunting of Force Z*, Collins, London, 1963.

Ishimaru, Lieutenant-Commander Tota, *Japan Must Fight Britain*, Paternoster Library, London, 1936.

Ismay, *The Memoirs of General The Lord Hastings Ismay*, Heinemann, London, 1960.

Leasor, James, *Singapore*, Hodder & Stoughton, London, 1968.

Lenton, H. T., and Colledge, J. J., *Warships of World War II*, Ian Allen, Shepperton, 1964.

Lockhart, Bruce, *The Marines Were There*, Putnam, London, 1950.

Okumiya, Masatake, and Horikoshi, Jiro, with Martin Caidin, *Zero! The Story of the Japanese Navy Air Force*, Cassell, London, 1957.

Storry, Richard, *A History of Modern Japan*, Penguin Books, Harmondsworth, 1960.

Toland, John, *The Rising Sun*, Cassell, London, 1970.

Tsuji, Masanobu, *Singapore, The Japanese Version*, Constable, London, 1962.

Watts, A. J., *Japanese Warships of World War II*, Ian Allen, Shepperton, 1966.

Index

* The references to *Electra* and *Express*, after they had been chosen
to accompany *Prince of Wales* and *Repulse* to the Far East, are so
numerous that further indexing is considered unhelpful.

* The numerous references to *Prince of Wales* and *Repulse*, after they had been chosen for dispatch to the Far East, have not been indexed.

† General references to Singapore are too numerous to be usefully indexed.

THE PLAN

www.**transworldbooks**.co.uk

THE PLAN

How Fletcher and Flower
Transformed English Cricket

STEVE JAMES

BANTAM PRESS

LONDON · TORONTO · SYDNEY · AUCKLAND · JOHANNESBURG

TRANSWORLD PUBLISHERS
61–63 Uxbridge Road, London W5 5SA
A Random House Group Company
www.transworldbooks.co.uk

First published in Great Britain
in 2012 by Bantam Press
an imprint of Transworld Publishers

A CIP catalogue record for this book
is available from the British Library.

ISBN 9780593068335 (cased)
9780593068342 (tpb)

Addresses for Random House Group Ltd companies outside the UK
can be found at: www.randomhouse.co.uk
The Random House Group Ltd Reg. No. 954009

The Random House Group Limited supports the Forest Stewardship Council
(FSC®), the leading international forest-certification organization.
Our books carrying the FSC label are printed on FSC®-certified paper.
FSC is the only forest-certification scheme endorsed by the leading environmental
organizations, including Greenpeace. Our paper procurement
policy can be found at www.randomhouse.co.uk/environment.

Typeset in 11.5/15pt Times New Roman
by Falcon Oast Graphic Art Ltd.
Printed and bound in Great Britain by
Clays Ltd, Bungay, Suffolk

2 4 6 8 10 9 7 5 3 1

To my mum. I wish you could have
read this in its finished form.
And to my dad, always an inspiration.

Contents

Acknowledgements

Firstly thank you to Scyld Berry, my colleague at the *Sunday Telegraph*, whose idea this book was, and to whom I first wrote in 1996 when wanting to work in the national press. He has been a help and inspiration ever since. But the man who gave me my first break was Peter Mitchell, of the *Sunday Telegraph*. He is now sports editor there, and I cannot thank him enough for his backing, advice and friendship. Thank you also to Ben Clissitt, Adam Sills and Jim Bruce-Ball and everyone else at the *Telegraph* for their kindness and patience in allowing me to pursue this project.

Thanks too to David Luxton, of DLA, for his determination that this book should see the light of day. But I still cannot forgive him for being part of the Christ College, Brecon side that once inflicted upon me the most humiliating defeat of my cricketing career. 'That was not a defeat; it was a surrender,' my Monmouth School cricket master said.

Thanks also to Giles Elliott at Transworld for embracing the idea. His enthusiasm from the off was extraordinary, his editing always thorough and sensible, and his knowledge outstanding. We'll go on that bike ride one day, I promise. Thanks also to Daniel Balado-Lopez for his wonderful editing.

I am indebted to many people whom I interviewed or informally spoke to for the purposes of this book: David Morgan, Hugh Morris, Ashley Giles, Geraint Jones, Marcus Trescothick, Matthew Maynard, Dean Conway, Bill and Jean Flower, Grant Flower,

Alistair Campbell, Lord MacLaurin of Knebworth, Tim Lamb, Ken Schofield, Brian Bolus, Peter Moores, Nasser Hussain, Michael Vaughan, Mark Garaway, James Boiling, Mark Wallace, Matthew Streeton, Andrew Walpole and Paul Grayson. There are also a number who wish to remain anonymous. They know who they are. Many thanks.

And thank you to a number of other journalists and commentators who have helped and advised: Richard Gibson, Simon Wilde (who passed on James Lawton's excellent advice: 'Get up at six a.m. every morning and do two hours' work before the day starts!'), Ian Ward, Paul Newman, Mike Atherton and David Lloyd. Thanks also to my parents who perused the text with their usual diligence and sharp eyes. Indeed they did, except that there is a tragic twist to this tale. My mum read the last few chapters while in hospital. She returned home, delighted that I had taken her advice and made all the suggested changes to the submitted manuscript. But a couple of weeks later, on 22 November 2011, she passed away. I hope this book would have made her proud.

A word for Duncan Fletcher and Andy Flower too, the two central characters in this story. I have known both of them for many years and regard them as close friends. Neither was interviewed directly for this book but both gladly endorsed the writing of it. Flower has told me that he does not want to write an autobiography (or authorize a full biography) after an earlier attempt was halted because of his uneasiness with the project, and his co-author, Keith Meadows, has now sadly passed away. The current England team like to be discreet (thus Flower's mild rebuke of Graeme Swann in the autumn of 2011 when, in his autobiography, he made some criticism of team-mate Kevin Pietersen) and Flower was wary of talking about his team and their methods, but we do, of course, talk. Fletcher is always willing to talk. To me at least!

Finally, thanks and apologies to my wife, Jane, and children Bethan and Rhys for their love, support and tolerance. I'll get up later from now on . . .

Introduction

I'd like 'to begin at the beginning', as Dylan Thomas did in
Under Milk Wood. And given that much of the thinking for and
indeed some of the writing of this book took place in a favourite
holiday retreat in the west Wales village of Laugharne, where
Thomas lived, it would be apt. But the truth is that we are not
beginning at the beginning. Rather we are beginning at the
bottom. At a bottom so low that it was certainly made of rock.

We begin on a day so dark that it was indeed the 'bible-black'
imagined by Thomas at the start of his celebrated play. In Test
cricket, the format that really matters, England have rarely
suffered a darker day. On Sunday, 22 August 1999 they lost a
Test match to New Zealand at the Oval, and with it the series.
Embarrassing at the best of times, yes, but that was not the half
of it. In doing so they also slipped to the bottom of what was
then called the Wisden World Championship, below even
Zimbabwe in the rankings of the nine Test-playing nations. It
was probably just as well that Bangladesh still had another year
to wait before playing their inaugural Test.

As captain Nasser Hussain went to the pavilion balcony for
the after-match presentations, he was roundly booed. It was the

appropriate sound to end a quite dreadful summer, which had begun with an unedifying row between England's players and the England and Wales Cricket Board over pay for the home World Cup. Then those very same players acquitted themselves so poorly in that tournament that, after a performance of remarkable ineptitude in defeat to India at Edgbaston, they were eliminated the day before the tournament song was released. 'Let's get things fully in proportion,' wrote John Etheridge in the *Sun*. 'This was only the most catastrophic day ever for English cricket.' He was wrong. That would actually come later in the summer, at the Oval.

And the administrators didn't exactly cover themselves in glory, producing a World Cup opening ceremony at Lord's that can only go down in the history column marked 'Cock-Ups'. It really did consist of little more than a couple of banger fireworks and a dodgy public address system that failed when Prime Minister Tony Blair tried to speak.

After the Oval defeat the ECB's chief executive Tim Lamb said that there was nothing wrong with English (and Welsh of course!) cricket 'except the shop window' (the analogy always used of the England team by ECB chairman Lord MacLaurin of Knebworth, unsurprisingly so given that he had been chairman of Tesco). It was brave defiance, but essentially misguided. Subsequent off-field improvements, like central contracts, the establishment of a National Academy and a two-divisional set-up for the county championship, which were to come soon afterwards, have proved that there was much wrong with the rest of the shop too.

The truth is that the game as a whole in England and Wales was still coming to terms with the fact that the shop window had to be of paramount importance. The state of English and Welsh cricket (from now on I will just say 'English' if that is OK, hoping my friends in the Principality will understand) is judged by the performance of its national team. And back then that window was a horrible sight. There was glass everywhere. It had been smashed to smithereens. As Lamb now admits, 'It was a disastrous summer', and MacLaurin recalls walking away from the ground to his London apartment afterwards, wanting to hide his head in embarrassment. 'It was horrific,' he says.

Alec Stewart paid for England's incompetence on the field in the World Cup with his job as skipper, and coach David Lloyd also departed with his contract time incomplete. It appears he would not have been offered a renewal anyway, judging by the haste with which the ECB accepted his resignation ('he simply had to go' says Lamb now) and agreed to pay out the remaining few months of his contract, even if that meant a coaching void for the New Zealand series, with no replacement settled upon at the time. Not since 1986 had England entered a series without a coach.

Lloyd had many good ideas as a coach, but lacked the finance and necessary support. And, if truth be told, he was a little too emotional and temperamental. He immediately moved into Sky's commentary box, and, with his natural wit, even if it sometimes borders on a lovable madness, found his true vocation.

There was some succour at hand, however. But it was not all immediate or obvious. Hussain and Duncan Fletcher were announced as captain and coach, but unfortunately only Hussain could start straight away: out of loyalty Fletcher would not leave Glamorgan until the end of the season. So England made do with selector Graham Gooch overseeing practices and chairman of selectors David Graveney acting as manager.

England won the first Test at Edgbaston, but then Hussain broke a finger in the second Test at Lord's (which New Zealand won by nine wickets), and asked Graham Thorpe to take over. The bungling selectors (Mike Gatting formed an unholy triumvirate) didn't like that, though, and instead asked Mark Butcher to captain the third Test at Old Trafford.

During that Test Gooch and Gatting were sacked as selectors. So was Butcher as captain, and indeed as a player too, as he was dropped for Hussain to return for the grim denouement at the Oval. There followed a stultifying piece of selection so that England, with three genuine number elevens in Alan Mullally, Phil Tufnell and Ed Giddins, possessed a tail longer than that of your average alligator. Debuts were handed to Giddins and Darren Maddy, as horribly miscast as a Test opener as the team's number seven Ronnie Irani was as a Test all-rounder.

Shambolic? You bet. On the Monday morning following the Oval defeat, the *Sun* devoted the whole of its front page to a mock obituary of English cricket, with a huge picture of burning bails in a parody of the famous 1882 *Sporting Times* piece that spawned the Ashes and all its subsequently rich history. 'In affectionate remembrance of English cricket which died at the Oval, 22nd August 1999,' the *Sun* said. 'Deeply lamented by a large circle of sorrowing friends and acquaintances, RIP. NB The body will be cremated and the Ashes taken to New Zealand.' Yes, English cricket was in a rare old state.

I didn't write much about it then. I was only a part-time journalist, mainly filing rushed rugby reports on chilly winter Saturday afternoons. I had begun writing for the *Sunday Telegraph* earlier that summer when providing some offerings for their World Cup pages, and I was also writing a weekly column for the *South Wales Argus* that lasted a delightful sixteen years, but that mostly concerned more parochial matters at my county, Glamorgan.

Primarily I was still a professional cricketer. Indeed I was a professional cricketer desperate to get back into that awful England team. I'd been awarded two caps the previous year, and fancied more. Heck, my county coach was about to take over.

'If you pick that Vaughan it will be an absolute disgrace,' I said to Fletcher soon after the Oval debacle and just as deliberations on the winter tour party to South Africa and Zimbabwe were being finalized. Yes, not the smartest piece of selectorial observation about a player who would go on to enjoy a highly distinguished Test career, but cricketers are mostly, by their very nature, selfish. I was thinking only of myself. And Michael Vaughan had just made the sum total of two runs in two innings for Yorkshire as we thumped them at Headingley. He hadn't looked too good in that game.

Unfortunately for me, after nearly two years at Glamorgan, Fletcher knew how good I was: an above-average county cricketer who had probably made more of his meagre talents than he should have. But, at that stage, he didn't know quite as much about many others around the county circuit, so there were a few – like Maddy, Chris Adams, Gavin Hamilton and even Graeme Swann at that stage of his career – who were extremely fortunate to board the plane that winter.

Thankfully there was, however, enough proof that England were about to enter a bright new period in terms of selection. Fletcher would never again allow England to possess a tail like that at the Oval in the summer of 1999. Lower-order runs became essential. And just watching Vaughan at net practice had been enough for him. Fletcher had seen something he liked, a talent that he could develop in readiness for Test match cricket, just as he had a week earlier when Glamorgan played Somerset at Taunton and a chunky left-hander named Marcus Trescothick had bludgeoned our bowlers, most especially Jacques Kallis in his only season for the Welsh county, to all parts. By the following summer Trescothick would be exhibiting his talents on the international stage.

Sadly Glamorgan were about to lose their coach, though. I was about to lose a travelling companion and fellow rugby addict. Fletcher might have been off to join England, but we didn't lose touch. Sometimes he might call about a bowler they were considering for selection; on other occasions we might meet in the Sophia Gardens gym as he still rented a property in

Cardiff during his England tenure, although, contrary to common perception, he never did buy one there. He wanted to, but was advised against doing so by his great friend and ally, the physiotherapist Dean Conway. Within a year or two the property which he had eyed almost doubled in value!

In 2004 Fletcher unexpectedly called asking me to ghost his autobiography. I don't think I was first choice. Mike Atherton was, but at least my old Cambridge University mate had the decency to recommend me, speaking favourably of my own autobiography, published earlier that year following my retirement from the game due to knee trouble.

There was no hesitation. Ghosting books can often be an unsatisfactory experience, but, as a journalist making his way, this was a no-brainer. When Fletcher's agent called, I simply accepted his first offer. He could easily have snared my services for much less. There began a fascinating period until the book, *Behind the Shades*, was published amid great controversy in 2007. Insight into the workings of the England cricket team does not come much sharper than straight from the coach's mouth.

I had not even heard of Fletcher when I first went to his country of birth, Zimbabwe, in 1990 to play club cricket and do some coaching in local schools. He had left the country in 1984 to work in Cape Town, but he had clearly left his mark. The admiration for him, especially among the older guard who had played under his captaincy in the national team, was evident. His name just kept cropping up in bar-room conversations. The small cricketing fraternity there yearned for his return as a coach. But, to their chagrin, his only cricket-related appearance in the country during my five winters there was as coach of Western Province on an early-season tour.

Instead I befriended the group of young Zimbabwean coaches that the Zimbabwe Cricket Union had just employed to try to spread the game's popularity to the country's more densely populated areas. Among them were two brothers, Andy and Grant Flower. They seemed decent cricketers. They seemed even better blokes.

I gleefully joined their daily rituals. Mornings were spent training maniacally at the Harare city centre gym of Zimbabwe cricketer Malcolm Jarvis. Lunchtimes were occupied with nets at Harare Sports Club, where those national cricketers with 'proper' jobs, like the trio of lawyers John Traicos, Andy Pycroft and Kevin Arnott, would fit in their extra cricket practice. Afternoons were for coaching in the various schools to which we were allocated, and then late afternoon was time for more net practice with one's club side. Evenings? Well, let us just say they were convivial. And let us say that I was quickly introduced to a favourite local drink, the soapie, a ridiculously intoxicating concoction of cane, lemon barley and soda water.

Thursday nights were different, however. They were quiet. And mostly, thanks to the wonderful kindness of Mr and Mrs Flower, Bill and Jean, they were spent at the Flower family home in the Mount Pleasant suburb of Harare, having dinner and then watching the weekly transmission of the magazine programme *Transworld Sport*. Satellite television was rare in Zimbabwe then. And on the local channels this was the only guaranteed taste of televised sport all week. In that sport-mad Flower household only the monthly arrival of the *Cricketer* magazine, as it was then called, from the UK created as much excitement.

The image of the white Zimbabwean then, before Robert Mugabe began his wicked land reclamation policies, was of a person of wealth. And many, especially those in the farming community, fitted that bill neatly. But not the Fletchers or the Flowers. There are many differences between Duncan Fletcher and Andy Flower, but here is the first of a number of similarities between the two African families that would rear two outstanding cricket coaches for England.

Both Fletcher and Flower have been prepared to challenge common political allegiances. Fletcher's family stayed loyal to the United Federal Party rather than Ian Smith's Rhodesia Front movement which oversaw white rule, and they eventually had to move into Salisbury because they became ostracized in the area.

Flower, along with Zimbabwe team-mate Henry Olonga, famously railed against Mugabe's regime and the perceived 'death of democracy' in his country when wearing black armbands in a World Cup match in Harare in 2003. But long before that both Flower and his father Bill had helped the predominantly black, high-density-area-based side Winstonians at a time when accusations of racism were rife in Zimbabwean cricket. It ended in a good deal of acrimony, as most things did in Zimbabwean cricket at the time, but the Flowers had walked avenues others would not even contemplate walking.

Both Fletcher and Flower are from big families: Fletcher was one of six children, Flower one of five. Fletcher grew up on a farm (Carswell Farm near Nyabira, north of Salisbury), but only one of 'modest return' as he puts it. The Flowers' was also an ordinary existence. Bill, an accountant and enthusiastic schoolboy coach, worked hard to provide for his family, but no silver spoons were included in that provision.

Cricket equipment is expensive at the best of times. So just imagine the cost of importing it to a third-world country like Zimbabwe, even back then when the ludicrous days of an exchange rate for Zimbabwe dollar to pound of 700,000,000,000:1 were far away and a reasonable rate of about 10:1 existed. So the Flower brothers were not the only cricketers in the country to be envious of the English professionals like me arriving with their bagfuls of kit courtesy of generous sponsorship deals.

Therefore when Zimbabwe were preparing to go to Australia and New Zealand for the 1991/92 World Cup, I did not feel it in the slightest way patronizing to offer Andy Flower a pair of my Reebok boots. He accepted readily, and wearing them duly scored 115 not out against Sri Lanka at New Plymouth. It was the closest I came to a World Cup hundred! Indeed I was watching it back in Zimbabwe with Grant, agonizingly forced to pull out at the last minute after having his arm broken by Northern Transvaal B quick bowler Chris van Noordwyk while playing for the Zimbabwe Under 24 team. He considered soapies the requisite balm to his pain. I thought I'd join him.

His brother's international playing career was ignited, even though Andy, like Grant and another batsman of huge potential, Alistair Campbell, was still paid first and foremost to coach rather than to play. And how English cricket was to benefit eventually from that rather unusual beginning to an international cricket career.

But first, what a playing career it turned out to be. Flower simply delights in surprising, and in defying perceptions and expectations. I will happily admit that the first time I saw him bat, in 1990 in a match between his Old Georgians and my team 'Bionics', he did not stand out at all. He stood out when inside-edging my Glamorgan and Bionics colleague Adrian Dale, but that was his most memorable contribution. He just looked a half-decent left-hander, with hands conspicuously low on the handle. Nostradamus himself might have been hard pushed to predict that a future number one ranked batsman in the world was in action that day. But he was. Flower ended a sixty-three-match Test career with a batting average of 51.54, higher in the lists than Sunil Gavaskar, Steve Waugh, Allan Border and Sir Vivian Richards, just to name but a few greats of the game.

The ancient French apothecary and seer might also have struggled to foresee Flower's exploits as England coach when in late 2008 and early 2009 he was Peter Moores' assistant as an almighty row erupted between the coach and captain Kevin Pietersen. Flower was being tarred with Moores' brush and, with both Moores and Pietersen sacked (although the official line was that Pietersen resigned), he could easily have lost his job altogether. Instead he uneasily took temporary charge of a tour to the West Indies where almost immediately England were bowled out for just 51 in his first Test in charge.

Ah, from the most barren soil can the most productive Flower grow. Soon he was in permanent charge, and even sooner after that he was overseeing consecutive winning Ashes series, at home in 2009 and away in 2010/11, as well as capturing a first global trophy at the International Cricket Council World Twenty20 in the West Indies in 2010. In 2011 England became the number one ranked Test team in the world. It was a remarkable *bouleversement*.

Since the debacle of 1999 England have had three coaches. It is a quirk that two of them are Zimbabwean, although Flower was actually born in Cape Town, South Africa. And just as curious that they should unexpectedly find themselves in opposition during the summer of 2011, when Fletcher arrived as coach of India to face England, after being suddenly tempted out of semi-retirement by the departure from the Indian job of one of his protégés Gary Kirsten immediately after India's World Cup triumph at home.

Even now Fletcher and Flower barely know each other. Indeed one of the few occasions when they talked at any length before becoming direct adversaries in that 2011 India series was before a T20 international against Pakistan in Cardiff in 2010 when I happened to be meeting Fletcher at the England team hotel. They chatted warmly enough, and Fletcher congratulated Flower on his achievements with England. Another occasion was in Perth in 2006 when Flower was with the National Academy squad shadowing the senior Ashes side. Fletcher was outlining his favoured batting technique of the 'forward press'; Flower wasn't entirely convinced apparently.

Flower had asked for Fletcher's telephone number before the 2009 Ashes, but did not eventually speak to him because his skipper Andrew Strauss did so first, picking Fletcher's brains on the best methods to defeat the Australians. When Strauss went with Flower to speak to Fletcher and his India captain Mahendra Singh Dhoni at Trent Bridge in the second Test in 2011, things were a little more frosty. Ian Bell had been given run out after wandering out of his crease towards the pavilion, thinking an Eoin Morgan shot had gone for four and that it was tea-time, so Strauss and Flower went asking for the decision to be overturned. I have spoken to both Fletcher and Flower privately about this incident, and neither wants his thoughts recorded, which is fair enough. But I also think it is fair enough to say that Christmas cards are unlikely to be exchanged in the future.

The other coach since that dark day at the Oval was, of course, Peter Moores, whose tenure was brief but eventful, ending in that double departure. Moores, though, appointed Flower as his assistant, and in fact undertook his first foreign coaching assignment in Zimbabwe in the mid-eighties, at Lomagundi College, while also playing for Old Hararians with Graeme Hick, then a Worcestershire colleague and close friend (Cheshire-born Moores played at Worcestershire for three seasons before enjoying a fourteen-year playing career at Sussex). He didn't meet Flower then, but when they did so later in their careers there was a huge mutual respect. To this day Flower considers Moores his coaching mentor. Moores also appointed the excellent fielding coach Richard Halsall, born in Zimbabwe but brought up in England, and made some player selections that were to be of considerable benefit then and later. There was good in his tenure.

It is by pure chance that I know Fletcher and Flower so well. As a journalist covering the England team I have been very lucky in that respect. But not as lucky as English cricket in general. Between them the two Zimbabweans oversaw three Ashes series victories in four, when the previous eight had all been lost. Their influence has been huge. They have helped transform English cricket since that day in 1999 when their own humble country of Zimbabwe was deemed, however fleetingly, better at Test cricket, with the New Zealanders sandwiched between them at the foot of the table.

There is a much-used Zimbabwean phrase called 'Making a Plan', one especially used in times of trouble. Between them Fletcher and Flower made 'The Plan' for English cricket. Between them they made England the number one ranked side in the world, a position Strauss's side reached in August 2011 when they thrashed India at Edgbaston by an innings and 242 runs to overtake the Indians at the summit. That Fletcher was present in the opposition was ironic, but there was little he could do. He had not been with that team long enough. And he did exact some sort of revenge with a thumping 5–0 defeat for England in the one-day series that followed soon afterwards in India. His presence in the heavily beaten opposition at England's moment of crowning should not in any way diminish his contribution to England cricket. He played his part all right. That he did.

1

Who's Fletcher?

England were very fortunate to acquire the services of Duncan Fletcher as coach. For it was hardly his lifetime's ambition. Indeed when his name was first mentioned as a possible candidate, he was startled. He thought it was some kind of ruse. The kid from a Zimbabwean farm as coach of the England cricket team? Pah!

The first inkling came on 17 March 1999. I remember it well because, although it was not exactly the sort of occasion to inspire Max Boyce into song, 'I was there'. It was at the Stellenbosch Farmers' Winery ground outside Cape Town where Glamorgan were playing a three-day match on a pre-season tour. Fletcher was about to begin his second season with us (having helped us win the county championship in 1997, he had taken a year off), but, because he was still coach of Western Province in the southern hemisphere summer, he was taking a short rest and only popping in for the odd day during that tour.

Back in England, the national coach David Lloyd had recently met with ECB chairman Lord MacLaurin and it had been mutually agreed that he would leave after the World Cup. So the frantic search had begun for a new coach, and, if one thinks about it, it was little surprise that Fletcher's name should have been raised as a possibility. For in place at the ECB at the time was a small Welsh enclave.

David Morgan was deputy chairman, poised to take over as chairman from MacLaurin in 2002, and already in position as technical director for two years was Hugh Morris, my old opening partner who had played under Fletcher at Glamorgan in 1997 and then made a fairy-tale ending to an excellent seventeen-year career by scoring 165 in his final match to help secure the championship. 'To Lord's with a Title' he went, as evidenced by the title of a semi-autobiographical diary he wrote of that season.

Morris and Morgan did mention Fletcher's name in ECB corridors, but so, according to MacLaurin, did Glamorgan's Robert Croft, the off-spinning all-rounder who was then a member of the England side. That is surprising given that Croft was later the only person who advised Fletcher not to take the England job, and was then hardly a close friend of Fletcher's after they had clashed on a couple of occasions during 1997, most notably in a championship match against Northamptonshire at Abergavenny when Croft, in a prevalent dressing-room prank of the time, snipped the bottoms of Fletcher's socks so that when he attempted to pull them on at the end of the day's play they flew up beyond his knees.

To say Fletcher was not impressed would be an understatement of which Jack Lemmon would have been proud. During that game I was travelling with him daily from Cardiff to Abergavenny and back, and he did not say one word for the rest of the match. He was fuming. I was sure he was about to return home. It was not just necessarily a sense of humour failure, more a feeling that his authority had been undermined, and that it had been a collective jape. It hadn't. Croft had acted independently. 'There are two things you don't mess with,' Fletcher later announced sternly. 'My woman and my kit.'

And in relating that quote, I hope I am not upsetting his delightful wife Marina, whom Fletcher positively dotes upon. In a world where machismo often dictates a supposedly cool insouciance towards relationships, I have not seen many professional sportsmen as devoted to their wives as Fletcher, or indeed so protective.

Anyway, Croft got the message. Thereafter there was always a mutual, if at times grudging, respect between them. Fletcher will even admit now that Croft altered his opinion on finger-spinners. He came to Wales considering them as relevant in the modern game as green spiked batting gloves, but Croft's skills persuaded him otherwise, even if, as regards Monty Panesar, the media would never believe as much in future years.

Morris backed Fletcher throughout the selection process, not knowing then that he would be on the interview panel. He was called only forty-eight hours beforehand to join MacLaurin, Simon Pack (ECB international teams director), Brian Bolus (chairman of EMAC, the England Management Advisory Committee), David Acfield (chairman of Essex) and Dennis Amiss (chief executive of Warwickshire) because it was felt there was a lack of coaching experience on the panel. Morris's job brief at that time was the rather large task of 'raising the standard of playing and coaching cricket from the playground to the Test arena'.

But Fletcher was not the man the ECB really wanted. MacLaurin wanted Bob Woolmer, then the coach of South Africa, although he was to resign very soon afterwards when they were bundled out of the World Cup after somehow managing to tie a semi-final with Australia that they should have won. 'I'd known Bob from my Kent days,' explains MacLaurin (who had played for Kent second eleven), 'and he was a high-flying coach at the time.' That's a rather circuitous way of admitting he wanted Woolmer. For once his chief executive Tim Lamb takes a more direct route. 'There was no doubt that Ian favoured Bob,' he says.

So MacLaurin sent Pack, the former major-general whom he'd bizarrely recruited despite a lack of cricketing experience or knowledge, to see Woolmer in South Africa about the job. The trouble was that no one else but Lamb was told, not even Bolus, who was supposed to be in charge of the new coach's recruitment.

Bolus was understandably furious when he learnt of the trip, quite by accident, from Amiss, of all people. 'I was chairman and knew nothing about this,' blasts Bolus. 'So I had a blistering row with the General [as Bolus always called Pack]. But it was not his fault. He was only acting under orders. He was a man I always admired and got on with, but he was under the influence of MacLaurin [whom Bolus often called "the Grocer"].'

Contrary to many people's opinions, most of them held to this day, Lamb says that Woolmer was not offered the job there and then. 'Simon had no mandate to offer Bob the job,' contends Lamb, 'but in hindsight it was a mistake to send him. We should have consulted the other members of EMAC. The perceived clandestine nature of the visit caused problems. I could have just had a conversation over the phone with Bob, whom I knew well from my playing days [Lamb was a seam bowler for Oxford University, Middlesex and Northamptonshire]. But I seem to recall that he [Woolmer] said, "Of course I'd be interested, but not immediately."'

What was worse was that, in going to South Africa, Pack missed an important meeting over pay for the World Cup with England's players in Sharjah, where they were competing in the Coca-Cola Cup in preparation for the World Cup.

Woolmer felt he could only begin as coach after England's tour to South Africa that winter, meaning England would have to endure another series without a coach. It should not even have been a starter. As it was, the ECB suffered enough criticism for being without a coach for one series. Just imagine if it had been for two series. But still Woolmer was slated to be interviewed. Goodness, they wanted him all right. The interviews were even arranged to fit into his schedule, 16 June being the day before that tied semi-final. But at the eleventh hour Woolmer pulled out. 'He phoned and said, "No, I can't really accept,"' says MacLaurin. 'He said, "Thanks for thinking of me."'

It is common knowledge that Bolus initially had in mind a 'dream team' as coach and team manager. As coach he wanted Jack Birkenshaw, the Leicestershire coach, and as manager James Whitaker, then still a player at the same county but having undertaken some managerial duties while suffering with the knee injury that eventually ended his career. He had done this most notably when Leicestershire won the county championship in 1998 for the second time in three years under his captaincy.

'Yes, I'd made my mind up that at that time the best management group in English cricket was Whitaker and Birkenshaw,' admits Bolus. 'They were a very good combination at a fairly impoverished county. Leicestershire were getting far more out of their players than they had any right to and it was down to those two. But if I'd have wanted Jack Birkenshaw as coach, I'd have got Jack Birkenshaw as coach.'

That last sentence is typical Bolus. A batsman who played for three counties, Yorkshire, Nottinghamshire and Derbyshire, and made seven appearances for England in the mid-sixties, he is certainly a no-nonsense, if also eccentric, character. 'He's got a screw loose,' wrote Nasser Hussain in his autobiography *Playing with Fire*, and he certainly gives that impression. 'He used to throw ideas into meetings and then sort of giggle in the corner and you never knew whether he was being serious or not,' added Hussain. 'He was a total loose cannon. We were trying to analyse people properly and getting selection back on an even keel, and this bloke was running around telling everyone what was said in meetings. The press played him brilliantly. They knew he could be quite uninhibited about what he said, and they would ring him and nearly always get something out of him.'

I know the feeling. Half the stuff Bolus told me I would not dream of repeating here, and he did say to me beforehand, 'I'll answer everything you ask, but please show some discretion in using it. I don't want any shit.' It was certainly an entertaining half hour that I spent chatting with him, as I suppose you would expect from a once-much-booked after-dinner speaker. He confused, baffled, shocked, tickled and enlightened me all at once.

What he did make clear was the situation regarding Birkenshaw. His preference for him and Whitaker held only while the World Cup was still taking place. 'I spoke to them [Birkenshaw and Whitaker] and said I was interested in them taking the job,' Bolus says. 'But then we had that debacle at Birmingham [when England tumbled out of the World Cup] and I said to Amiss and [David] Graveney, "What about this lot then?" It was obvious that the dressing room needed reform. Bob Woolmer, God bless him, had given everything to South Africa, but I felt we needed a fresh pair of legs, someone with plenty left in the tank, with ambitions to fulfil. So I went to see Jack [Birkenshaw] and said, "Sorry Jack, but I can't go along with that original suggestion. I need a different animal." Jack said, "Can I apply on my own?" I said "Yes, of course" and so we put him on the shortlist.'

Fletcher's name was mentioned to Bolus and it should be of little surprise to learn that he said 'Who's Fletcher?' and then giggled. He did know. Our 1997 championship win may have been a little surprising, but it didn't go completely unreported.

Bolus began doing some research. 'Myself and the General worked extremely hard in gathering background on him,' he says. 'It emerged that Fletcher had the reputation not just for being very successful but for being a strong man too. A lot of people gave him full marks for his attention to detail, planning and his strength of character.'

So Fletcher most definitely was in the frame, but back out in South Africa when Matthew Maynard and Dean Conway, Glamorgan's captain and physiotherapist respectively, indicated to him at Stellenbosch that this might be the case, the Zimbabwean just laughed. It was a situation laced with irony, given that Conway would become Fletcher's physiotherapist with England – indeed his presence was eventually a stipulation in Fletcher's acceptance of the job – and Maynard would one day become his assistant. But it was no joke.

Within a month Simon Pack had called Fletcher to ask if he was interested in the job. By June Fletcher was attending his interview at the ECB, with the clowning Pack famously greeting him 'Hello Dav', mistaking him for another interviewee, Dav Whatmore (Birkenshaw was also interviewed).

Fletcher was confused. Throughout this whole process he had been convinced, with some justification, that others were ahead of him in the pecking order. He had heard about the Woolmer approach and spent some forty-five minutes on the phone one day being persuaded by Morris, who, for some reason, was standing on the Western Terrace at Headingley amid the mayhem after Pakistan had beaten Australia in their World Cup pool match, that he should stay in the running and attend his interview. And when Glamorgan played Leicestershire at Grace Road, Leicester, Fletcher was somewhat perturbed to open the door of the home coach's office to find Bolus talking in serious and hushed tones with Birkenshaw and Whitaker.

But Fletcher went for his interview, and went with a very relaxed attitude. He immediately set out the principles that have always underpinned his coaching modus operandi: that the captain must be the managing director of the business that is the professional cricket team, and that he as coach must be the consultant, but must also be in charge of all off-field management, with all staff reporting to him. Fletcher told the interview panel that he would have to complete the season at Glamorgan, and then said, 'These are my current earning capacities with Glamorgan and Western Province. This is what I want.' It was thought to be an annual salary well into six figures.

Fletcher then made his way back to Canterbury where Glamorgan were playing Kent, worried that his demands had been too high. He need not have worried. Only a few hours later Pack called to offer him the job. A decision had been unanimous immediately upon the interviews being concluded.

The following day I happened to see Pack at the back of the Canterbury pavilion. I wondered why he was there. I simply could not believe that he was offering Fletcher the job so swiftly. But he was. He was offering Fletcher exactly the package he wanted in a three-year contract; not even Fletcher's added request that Conway be his physiotherapist was a problem. The ECB had clearly decided that money was no object, especially when one considers that the previous incumbent had been retained on as little as £60,000 p.a. 'We recognized that we had to pay our England coach well,' admits Lamb.

Fletcher was shocked, and asked for five days to consider. Not that anyone in the Glamorgan dressing room, skipper Maynard apart, knew. We obviously knew where he had been when he missed that day's play at Canterbury, but otherwise Fletcher was in full *omertà* mode.

It was only after Pack called again that he began to open up. He'd asked Pack for another three days: this was getting serious then. We were playing a NatWest Trophy match at Southampton against the Hampshire Board XI, and the night before Fletcher canvassed a group of senior players. He was clearly in a state of rare indecision. He never did anything without a lot of research, and it was obvious that this research had led him to a consensus that the group of England players at that time were mostly bad eggs.

I didn't really know what to say when he quizzed me. I didn't know the majority of the England players well enough to pass considered judgement, and at the back of my mind was the thought of impending trouble at Glamorgan. He had not returned to us in 1998 and we had faltered. And we were already showing such signs in 1999. We needed Fletcher to guide our youngsters.

We were to get him only for the rest of the season, and even that in hindsight was a mistake. Fletcher awoke the next morning and phoned Pack to say that he was taking the job, but he only wanted a two-year deal. 'I thought that after two years I would know whether I could do the job or not,' he later said. 'I did not want to let anyone down.'

It was probably the easiest negotiations the ECB ever had with him. 'He wouldn't take any prisoners in a business negotiation,' says Lamb now. 'He could be gruff but also very impressive. We all know that there's Duncan in a business situation and there's Duncan in a social situation. I'd be a liar if I said I didn't have some difficult moments with him.' But this was no such occasion.

Now England had to find a captain to work alongside Fletcher. He had been asked about his preference among the group and shrewdly had been noncommittal. He was never a man to make speculative judgements. And he certainly did not champion Maynard's cause as skipper. That was the word around the county circuit at the time. It was misguided rumour.

It was MacLaurin's manner to interview prospective captains. He had done so when Alec Stewart was appointed in 1998, and did so again now. There were two interviewees, Hussain and Mark Ramprakash, although in MacLaurin's rather hazy memory there were three. He thinks that Kent's Matthew Fleming was also interviewed, but he wasn't. 'Do you think I would have kept that quiet all these years?' joked Fleming when I asked him. The truth is that MacLaurin, as a Kent man, wished Fleming had been more involved in the England set-up (he won eleven one-day international caps) and at the time Fleming was chairman of the Professional Cricketers' Association, so their dealings were frequent. And it does have to be said that a man like MacLaurin – as well as being chairman of Tesco and the ECB, he has been chairman of Vodafone and the UK Sports Council and has served on the boards of Enterprise Oil, Guinness, National Westminster Bank and Whitbread – must have interviewed an awful lot of people in his time.

'Running into the interview Nasser was not favourite,' says MacLaurin. 'I think we were looking at Ramps to be quite honest with you. Nasser was not the favourite son then. But we asked them about their vision for English cricket and what they felt for the future and Nasser was fantastic, absolutely fantastic.'

This is how Hussain saw it: 'Basically I said the same stuff I told them the first time [when interviewed with Stewart the year before, clearly aware of his selfish and hot-headed reputation he had said, "You have to realize that someone, when you give them the responsibility, has it in them to behave differently"]. I think to an extent the ECB went for me as what they saw as the lesser of two evils. I gather they thought both of us would constitute a gamble but that perhaps I was calmer than Ramps by this stage of our careers and was a bit more established in the team.'

Both did indeed constitute gambles. I'd known Hussain since playing against him for Welsh Schools when he was the curly-haired leg-spinner and middle-to-late-order batsman in an English Schools Under 15 side which also included Michael Atherton. The three of us had later become team-mates in the Combined Universities side which enjoyed considerable success in the 1989 Benson & Hedges Cup. And I'm not sure our characters have changed a lot over the years: Atherton calm, studious, ever loyal and utterly confident; me quiet, always observing from a distance, utterly lacking in confidence. The

basis of Hussain's personality has remained – fiercely determined, often stroppy but with a good sense of humour when the
mood was and is right – but he has matured, and certainly found
self-deprecation a useful ally as a commentator. And along the
way as England captain he found a way to hide some of the less
appropriate parts of his character at the right times. The red
mist could be dispersed quickly if need be.

As Conway explains, Hussain's ability to alter his mood was
quite remarkable. 'Nass would be throwing things round,' he
says, 'but then he'd put his Vodafone cap on and march out of
the dressing room to a press conference and he would be
amazing. I couldn't believe the change in him sometimes. Mind
you, he'd shut the door of the press conference and he'd be
kicking off again!'

The acronym FEC on Atherton's Old Trafford locker may not
have meant what people wanted – the actual middle word was
'educated', surrounded by two unrepeatables – but there
was little doubt that he was a Future England Captain. And
back then there was little doubt in my mind that Hussain was
going to be a special cricketer. That he lost his leg-spin
completely and became a batsman instead reveals all about his
simmering desire to succeed.

If only hell hath the fury of a batsman unfairly dismissed,
then Hussain was indeed cricket's Cerberus. I was astonished
when I made my Test debut in 1998 against South Africa as to
the length and ferocity of Hussain's rage upon his first-innings
dismissal, enacted in the toilet and shower area at the back of
the Lord's dressing rooms. I remarked upon it in my autobiography, and not long after its publication I chanced upon Hussain
at Edgbaston during Twenty20 Finals Day. 'You been having a
go at me in your book Jamo?' he asked matter-of-factly. To be
truthful, I was just grateful he'd read part of my book, or at least
been informed of some of its contents. 'I was just showing that
you cared,' I blurted in response. And I was. I've not known

a cricketer who cared as much. Except maybe Ramprakash.

So it was that on Friday, 25 June 1999 Hussain and Fletcher were formally announced at Lord's as captain and coach of England. Both were very nervous. Before that morning they had never met. Hussain had been captain of Essex and Fletcher coach of Glamorgan during a tempestuous NatWest Trophy semi-final at Chelmsford in 1997, but with so much else going on – Croft and Mark Ilott pushing and shoving each other, after Darren Thomas had accidentally punched Ronnie Irani's helmet in celebration at trapping him lbw – it was little surprise that neither had taken much notice of the other. Mind you, when I spoke to Hussain for the purposes of this book, he could not even remember playing in that game! He thought he'd broken a finger around that time. He did have what he himself calls 'poppadom' fingers, mind. And he was always rather focused on playing for England.

'I was surprised when it was announced that Duncan had got the job,' wrote Hussain later. 'At that stage I wouldn't have recognized him if he'd walked in the Chelmsford dressing room, and I thought to myself, "Oh my God. Not only are you going into a job you know nothing about, but you are going to do it with a bloke you don't know at all."'

Fletcher travelled up on the train from Cardiff 'with doubts and anxieties filling my head', he later said. Before the official unveiling they were introduced by Morris and left to talk for about half an hour in his office. Fletcher outlined his philosophy and emphasized how important the captain's body language is at all times on a cricket field, because everyone, from colleagues to spectators and the media, is watching you.

'When the name Fletcher was announced, I joked that I thought they'd got Keith Fletcher!' says Hussain now, referring to the former England and Essex batsman and coach. 'But it was actually quite nice. There was a clean slate. I was worried at the time that too much of English cricket was too insular. You appointed from within, so that if you played for that county then you coached there. I wasn't a fan of all that. Now two blokes who'd never met before met at Lord's and were told: "Right, you're going to be in charge of English cricket for a while!" And straight away I knew that Fletch was different. He wasn't your average ex-cricketer talking in average ex-cricketer's clichés. He clearly had a different angle on things. He talked to me about being out of the game for a while and looking at it from the outside, and it was clear he had a business brain.'

When they then met the press, Hussain mentioned the importance of body language. Fletcher was impressed. Hussain clearly was too.

It was the start of a remarkable relationship.

2

Shiny Shoes and a Perma-tan

Nasser Hussain and Duncan Fletcher could not have transformed England cricket without central contracts. Fact. No one single decision by the ECB in recent times has been more important for the improvement of the England cricket team. Together and individually Hussain and Fletcher were pretty good anyway, but their timing was impeccable. They arrived just as this radical new initiative was about to be introduced, and they benefited accordingly. But, as always, with the gain goes the pain, and Fletcher in particular had an extraordinarily tough task in overseeing the new contracts' implementation.

Make no mistake; central contracts were a radical initiative. They were radical because since county cricket had begun in the nineteenth century, the counties had always been the players' primary employers. Some of the better players sometimes went off to play for England – for which they received some additional monetary reward – but they always returned swiftly, and went straight back into county action. They went back to their day job.

Now it was being proposed that the ECB take control of those players, maybe even deciding that they miss the odd county game so that they could be in some sort of decent physical condition for the next international. The revolutionary notion was being floated that maybe an England player could win a Test match and celebrate with his colleagues that evening rather than rush off to join his county brethren in readiness for a match the following morning. Maybe he could even report for duty for a Test match a little before noon on the day before the match. Maybe he could even report for duty feeling a little less than knackered. Goodness, maybe he could even feel part of the England team rather than some temporary intruder, as many did, including me when I played twice in 1998.

Please forgive my sarcasm. These notions seem so sensible and routine nowadays, but, believe it or not, there was a time when they were not even considered. 'We weren't really a team,' wrote Graham Thorpe of those times. 'They [Tests for England] were more like representative matches.'

Somebody had needed to see the bigger picture. And England captain Mike Atherton had. In his report after the winter tour of South Africa and then the Asian World Cup of 1995/96, he wrote: 'Although we suffered fewer injuries than on the previous tour, we do suffer more than other teams (we were the only team to send two players home from the World Cup). Clearly this is no mere accident; it is a result of overplaying. Considering especially the need to look after our premier players (in particular the fast bowlers), it seems to me the sooner we can ensure these players are under TCCB [the Test and County Cricket Board, which was incorporated into the ECB in 1997] contracts all year round the better.' But it still went down like the proverbial lead balloon.

Central contracts were considered in the Acfield Review (set up under David Acfield, then Essex's chairman of cricket, to look at the management of the England team) that was published in July 1996, but, even though there were two former England captains in David Gower and Mike Gatting on that committee, there was no recommendation for contracts, only that the chairman of selectors should have the right to withdraw players from county cricket if he felt it best for their long-term welfare. Even that idea was summarily rejected by the counties in August. And to think that Kerry Packer had lit the way for international cricketers some nineteen years previously, when using three-year contracts to entice the world's best players for his World Series Cricket. Talk about slow on the uptake.

Somehow English cricket had to be dragged kicking and screaming into the modern world, and to Lord MacLaurin, who became chairman of the ECB upon its creation in 1997, befell that fiendishly difficult task. 'Never trust a man with shiny shoes and a perma-tan' are the oft-repeated words concerning MacLaurin, as penned by Atherton in his autobiography. But, wonderful wordsmith that he has become, they were not Atherton's own, as indeed he admits if you read closely. They were prefaced by 'Someone once told me . . .', and that someone was Derek Pringle, the current cricket correspondent of the *Daily Telegraph*.

But they were still delightfully apposite. MacLaurin did have, indeed still has, both. He was, and still can be, smooth and political. But for the ECB at the time he was the perfect figure. He modernized English cricket. He made eighteen stubborn and anachronistic counties realize that the England team was much more important than them as a collective.

'I visited all the county chairmen when I took over,' MacLaurin says on a bright, sunny day when we meet near his home at Farleigh Hungerford outside Bath, 'and frankly none of them was interested in a winning England side. They were only interested in their own counties winning the championship.' Why is that not a surprise? It is still a view not exactly unknown today.

I'll tell you a little story to illustrate the point. Remember the 2005 Ashes and all its glory for England? Well, England might not have won that series had one county had its myopic way. Before the decisive fifth Test at the Oval, with England leading the series 2–1 and Australia desperate to win in order to share the series and so keep the urn that they held, Australia wanted to give their second leg-spinner, Stuart MacGill, some match practice. They were considering playing him at the Oval, but he hadn't played in any of the previous Tests.

Somerset stepped forward, eagerly offering MacGill a game (he had played one match for them against Pakistan A in 1997). Even if Auckland did give James Anderson some such match practice on England's tour of New Zealand in 2008, can you imagine an England reserve spinner being given a game or two in the Sheffield Shield while on an Ashes tour? The answer is no. A definitive no. But here were Somerset thinking only of them-selves. MacGill was actually on his way to Taunton when the deal fell through, with it becoming clear that he was available for only one week, when the ECB regulations at the time specified a minimum of three weeks for overseas signings. You do wonder what might have happened if MacGill had played in the dramatically drawn Oval Test instead of the wayward seamer Shaun Tait.

At least by 2011 Somerset had changed their outlook con-siderably, allowing the short-of-match-practice England captain Andrew Strauss to appear as a guest against India before the first Test against the same opponents.

The Somerset chairman in 2005? Giles Clarke. The same Giles Clarke who was to become ECB chairman in 2007, and the same Giles Clarke who phoned both Middlesex and Kent in outrage when they signed the Australians Phillip Hughes and Stuart Clark to play ahead of the 2009 Ashes in this country. Hughes scored a bucketful of runs for Middlesex, but was then exposed in the Tests, and dropped. Clark did not arrive because he was called up to Australia's one-day squad in South Africa.

Back to the ECB's first chairman, and MacLaurin knew that his 'shop window' needed his full attention. Otherwise the 'shambles' of an operation, as he describes the ECB then, with its budget of 'just £30 million', stood no chance.

He chaired the last meeting of the TCCB in December 1996, then thought it best to check on the well-being of the England team, who were touring Zimbabwe at the time. It did not take him long to discover it was a sick patient. He telephoned Lord's in order to organize his accommodation on the tour and was shocked to be asked where he would like to stay. 'With the team, of course,' he answered. He was then told politely that that had never happened before. The management always stayed somewhere else in much more salubrious surroundings, while the team slummed it, always sharing rooms, as well as always flying in economy class.

'The gap between the players and the administrators was quite frightening,' MacLaurin says. 'But my late wife and I booked into the team hotel. I went around all the rooms and couldn't believe it. I went to Tim Lamb immediately and said, "I'm appalled that we treat our boys like this." He said, "It's tradition." I just said, "That tradition stops now, and they will all have single rooms."' They also began to travel business class as well as enjoying a whole host of what Lamb calls 'fringe benefits'. And too right too.

In an instant MacLaurin had smashed down an unfathomable but long-lasting class barrier. At last an administrator was more concerned with the players' welfare than his perks and expenses. 'I didn't know these guys from a bar of soap,' he says, 'so I thought I'd better get to know them. I spent time with each and every one of them. I started with Mike Atherton. "What is the vision for England cricket?" I asked him. "Tell me what, if you like in business terms, is the mission statement?" He looked at me across the breakfast table and said, "Chairman, you're the first person to talk to me about that." And he'd been captain for three years!'

MacLaurin also had to alter England's image on a tour that became infamous for coach David Lloyd's 'We flippin' murdered 'em' comment after England had drawn – yes, drawn – with Zimbabwe in the Bulawayo Test. It was an outburst now termed 'disastrous' by Lamb. Relations between the two sides were probably best summed up by the home skipper, Alistair Campbell, who accused England of possessing a 'superiority complex'. And he was right. But it was a stance without foundation. England truly were a poorly performing side then.

They were also scruffy. 'If you saw the boys on the field,' says MacLaurin, 'they went out with jockey caps on. They had white helmets, pink helmets and green helmets. There was no discipline at all. I went about branding the whole thing. That was not popular with a lot of people, but a lot of things I did weren't popular.'

England may have ceased being called MCC away from home after the 1976/77 tour of Australia, but they were still wearing the club's colours of yellow and red (or egg and bacon) on their sweaters and caps with the St George and Dragon crest in Zimbabwe and later that winter in New Zealand. MacLaurin knew that had to end, with the three lions and crown always being worn, even if it inevitably upset the MCC. 'Not only did we need a winning England team but we also needed a common brand in order to attract the right sorts of sponsors,' he says.

And sponsors were leaving cricket at an alarming rate at the time. Texaco had withdrawn their sponsorship of the one-day internationals, AXA of the Sunday League and Britannic Assurance of the county championship. But, as you would expect, MacLaurin had some rather decent contacts. He was not yet chairman of Vodafone (he became so in the summer of 1998) but he knew its chief executive, Christopher Gent, a keen cricket supporter who was educated at Archbishop Tenison's

Grammar School not a stone's throw away from the Oval, well enough to broker a deal. So Vodafone's first tour as England sponsors was to the West Indies in early 1998. It was a relationship that lasted twelve years.

Even more importantly, in that same year MacLaurin persuaded Chris Smith, the Secretary of State for Culture, Media and Sport, to move cricket from the government's broadcasting A list, which restricted the live coverage of sport to terrestrial channels, to the B list. It was only on the proviso that 'the majority of Test cricket was on terrestrial TV', as MacLaurin says now.

That has obviously caused much debate and rancour since, because that is anything but the case these days with Sky ruling the roost, but this was only a gentlemen's agreement. It was hugely significant, though. Suddenly the field was open, and the sole bid was not coming from the BBC, who had first televised Test cricket in 1938 and provided sixty years of excellent coverage. Much to the chagrin of the BBC, a joint deal was done with BSkyB and Channel 4, whose unexpected bid outdid the BBC's by several million pounds. 'Our budget suddenly went up from approx £30 million to £130 million,' says MacLaurin.

The ECB had money to do things, most notably to introduce central contracts. In 2006, when terrestrial television was abandoned completely and the whole rights package sold to BSkyB in a four-year deal worth £208 million, they had even more. For the period 2009 to 2013 the deal is worth £260 million.

Like it or not, sporting excellence requires dosh. And lots of it. As an example there is none better than Clive Woodward's famous switching of hotels for his England rugby team in South Africa in 1998, paid for on his own Amex card. Only the best will do if the real mountain tops are to be reached, and this was a statement of intent that was still resonating in 2003 when England won the rugby World Cup. So in 2010 Hugh Morris, by then the managing director of England cricket, was spending

£24.8 million on all England teams. In 2005 that figure had been only £10.9 million. It makes a difference. It really does.

In October 1998 the First Class Forum had at last agreed in principle to the introduction of central contracts. Unsurprisingly the ECB did what every good English sporting organization does: they formed a committee. Yes, the Contracts Review Group was set up under the chairmanship of Don Trangmar, chairman of Sussex and a director of Marks and Spencer, and included Surrey's Paul Sheldon and Somerset's Peter Anderson. Quite naturally, the road they travelled was long and bumpy.

David Morgan was then chairman of the First Class Forum, the body that served as the guardian of county cricket until 2005 and had to provide clearance and permission to implement any significantly different changes in the game. Central contracts certainly came under that umbrella. 'Having them approved was not an easy task,' says Morgan with typical understatement. 'There were many county chairmen and chief executives – mainly those that had played at first-class level – who didn't believe it was right that Team England should be separate from the eighteen first-class counties. They believed that England had done great things in the past and would continue to do great things in the future without this.' Ah, the vision of those men.

But by May 1999 the FCF had confirmed their imminent arrival. MacLaurin was to have what he wanted, as mentioned by Morgan above: 'Team England'. In effect they were becoming the nineteenth county, and by far the most important.

'It started off whereby players would have parallel contracts with the counties and the ECB,' says Lamb, 'but that immediately led to difficulties because there were always going to be conflicts in terms of what the counties wanted from their players. It became clear very quickly that if we were going to get this thing through, we were going to have to cross the counties' palms with silver and agree to pay the players' county salaries.

That was the tipping point. When that became clear the counties had no option but to say yes.'

This was actually an episode in which Simon Pack played a role rather than the fool, cajoling and eventually persuading the counties that English cricket needed this departure from the norm. There were, after all, going to be seven home Tests a summer from 2000 (up from six) and many more home one-day internationals (in 2000 came the first triangular series of seven matches after many years of just three home ODIs per summer), and counties were hardly going to see their star players anyway. Quite rightly Pack copped a lot of flak for his work at the ECB, but speak to anyone about his work on this issue and they have nothing but the utmost praise. He ensured that the critical mass of the counties was in favour. 'The General was absolutely fantastic,' says Brian Bolus with his usual chuckle.

So finally, on Monday, 23 August 1999, the day after the debacle at the Oval with which we began this book, the counties agreed to the introduction of central contracts. The following March twelve England players were awarded ECB contracts for the first time: Nasser Hussain (captain), Michael Atherton, Andrew Caddick, Andrew Flintoff, Darren Gough, Dean Headley, Graeme Hick, Mark Ramprakash, Chris Schofield, Alec Stewart, Michael Vaughan and Craig White.

These were only six-month contracts – twelve-month contracts were not introduced until 2002 – but crucially these players were under the management and control of the England coach, Fletcher. It was a huge step forward.

There were teething problems, of course, not least that many county fans could not and would not comprehend this new arrangement. Gough even received a poison-pen letter when he missed a Yorkshire match. The central contract was a very complicated document then; goodness knows what it is like now with its clauses regarding release to the Indian Premier League. And there was the anomaly that the contracted players were on significantly less than some county players, like Chris Adams at Sussex and Alan Mullally at Hampshire, who were earning six-figure salaries at the time. For some the ECB contract was worth less than the county contract it was replacing. Counties made up the difference in those cases. For Atherton, for example, it was a straight swap. His county contract was worth £60,000; so was his new ECB contract.

An ECB contract is worth considerably more than that these days, with match fees paid on top. There was a time when the figures, including the different bands in which various players fell, were readily available. So in 2004 we know that the contracts were graded in three bands, worth between £100,000 and £150,000, with match fees paid on top. A Test match was worth £5,500 and a one-day international £2,200. For Tests abroad there was a 40% added premium, with 20% for one-day internationals, and for global trophies 50%. So, say, a player appearing in all matches in the 2002/03 season with an Ashes tour and a World Cup would have earned a basic salary in the region of £350,000.

Now the ECB are much more careful about releasing such information, and rightly so. Nonetheless it would be a surprise were the busiest players not earning, just from the ECB, some-where near £450,000 a year. Indeed in 2011 it would be just as surprising were Test captain Andrew Strauss not earning over £1 million in total for the year: a Band A Central Contract might be worth £400,000, with bonuses for appearances and wins – which are pooled and then divided up – of maybe £150,000, and sponsorship deals with Gray Nicholls, Jaguar, etc. adding up to another £500,000. These are figures no county player can ever hope to earn. And that is how it should be; the best players should earn the biggest salaries. Mind you, there are still too many mediocre county players on or near six-figure salaries. Little wonder that the counties are in so much debt.

There was also the subject of compensation, which was not

helped by the spectacularly misguided selection of Lancashire's leg-spinner, Schofield. The search for a wrist-spinner to rival Australia's Shane Warne was at its most manic at the time, and Schofield was picked on the recommendation of Gatting, tour manager of the England A trip to New Zealand the previous winter. While he was extolling the virtues of Schofield as 'the future of English cricket', as Fletcher noted in his auto-biography, Gatting was also professing he was 'not sure about this [Marcus] Trescothick'. Thank goodness, Fletcher backed his own judgement and ensured Trescothick was on the inter-national stage by the summer of 2000. Gatting has many qualities, but, sadly, in my opinion selecting and coaching are not among them.

So while Schofield was justifiably shunted from the Test scene after two Tests against Zimbabwe, it meant his county received his services for free, while other counties like Derbyshire, who lost the non-contracted Dominic Cork for four Tests, were still paying players and not receiving too much compensation (just £12,000 in Cork's case in 2000), and were then being asked to rest him at the end of the season. Thankfully that anomaly has been satisfactorily rectified over time.

Not that contention over the issue of rest has been sorted. English cricket simply does not understand the meaning of the word. Place the lads on a treadmill in April (nearly March now, with ludicrously early starts to seasons) and make damn sure they're not allowed off it until the leaves are disappearing off the trees in autumn. Don't worry if one-day matches start immedi-ately after four-day matches so that no practice or preparation is possible, so that tired players are playing on often tired pitches. Don't worry that mental tiredness is just as debilitating as its physical comrade, meaning that just the mere sight of a cricket dressing room is too much by the end.

Fletcher always made a good point in stressing that the English summer should be viewed no differently from a winter tour. England players need rest. The county season is not sacrosanct. And once burnout takes hold it is too late. The skill of the very best coaches is being able to look over the horizon and spot not just the signs long before, but also the most dangerous periods. Fletcher was extraordinarily good at this. And at first he was pleasantly surprised by the reaction from the counties at his foresight. But then came the end of the season, when promotion and relegation were being hotly contested. The mood changed. The self-interest and short-sightedness came flooding back. One county chairman told Fletcher, 'I agree with what you're doing but there is no way I could say that in front of my constituency.'

And Graham Gooch is an interesting case. When coach of Essex he was against the resting of England players. Indeed he fell out with Hussain over that very issue. Now that he is Andy Flower's batting coach he has a very different view. He understands the demands and recognizes the need for rest.

It is rather ironic, given the (Chris) Schofield scenario, that Fletcher probably had most trouble with Lancashire as regards central contracts and the resting of players. It began with their outrage at Atherton missing some National League matches in the 2000 season and continued unabated with James Anderson and others in later years.

Take this quote from Lancashire's chairman, Jack Simmons, after Fletcher had resigned from the England job in 2007. 'The introduction of Peter Moores as replacement for Fletcher has already improved relationships with the counties,' he said. 'A player improves by being out in the middle and not sat on his backside. If Mr Fletcher is hoping to return to county cricket as a coach, I don't think he needs to contact Lancashire.'

Ah, good old 'Flat Jack', the heftily built off-spinner with a penchant for fish and chips who was still playing first-class cricket at the age of forty-eight. Simmons is actually a lovely fellow, and a loyal servant to his county as both player and administrator, but in the latter role he was as old-fashioned as he was in the former.

Simmons would do well to consider the case of Glen Chapple, a fine and persevering fast bowler for Lancashire who led his county to the championship in 2011. That he has only played once for England – and that in a one-day international against Ireland – is scant reward for his talent. But he has his own county partly to blame. In 2006 he was selected for the England one-day squad, who were meeting in Southampton on Sunday, 11 June, before flying the next day to play Ireland on the Tuesday. Fletcher did not want any players to play on the Sunday. But Lancashire wanted Chapple to play in their C&G Trophy match against Derbyshire. Fletcher refused, but Simmons got involved and went to the ECB. Chapple was allowed to play, and flew down to join the team later that night. On the Monday at practice Fletcher forgot that Chapple should not bowl as many overs as the others because he had played the previous day. He broke down against Ireland, and never played again.

Geoff Miller, the current National Selector, makes a good point about the crux of Fletcher's troubled relationship with the counties: 'Whether Duncan actually said it or not, or whether it was misquoted, the feeling amongst the counties was that he had said "The standard of county cricket is poor".'

Yes, there were undoubtedly aspects of county cricket that frustrated Fletcher. But he was hardly alone in that regard. He thoroughly enjoyed his two years at Glamorgan, even if he was distracted in the latter half of his second year, with the England job looming. Indeed he will admit now that he would have been better off joining England immediately. His greatest gripe with the county game was the volume of cricket played, leading to lazy habits. He used to be enraged with the slack running between the wickets and the lack of general intensity in the fielding, always signs of tired minds as well as tired bodies. And the excuse culture, so prevalent in county cricket, used to annoy him. For example, during slip-catching practice he would often encounter fielders pusillanimously pulling out of chances that bounced in front of them, making the excuse that fingers could easily be broken. It was the sort of attitude with which Fletcher would have no truck. 'Well done, you've saved a certain wicket,' he would say sarcastically when a catch was dropped.

Fletcher used to talk about the 'cup of tea brigade' in English cricket. In other words players who would turn up to a county ground early and be more interested in having their cup of tea than actually doing some hard graft. There is a curious habit in county cricket of players arriving ridiculously early, and then doing very little. I know that the Australians who came to Glamorgan, like Matthew Elliott, Jimmy Maher and Mike Kasprowicz, simply could not understand this behaviour. It is why it makes me laugh when county championship matches start an hour later the morning after late-finishing floodlit matches the night before. It is ludicrous that this has to happen at all, but I bet all the players are there at a similar time to usual. I know I would have been. The truth is that it is very difficult to sleep after day/night matches anyway. The brain is still racing. It cannot be calmed with the flick of a switch.

Fletcher did have respect for county cricket, but the England team was more important. And central contracts have worked – it is as simple as that. 'They were the single most important thing for the good of the England side,' says MacLaurin now. Before their implementation, England won 33.5% of its Test matches. Since their introduction in 2000 and up until the end of the 2012 Pakistan series they had won 45%. Enough said.

They worked immediately, if truth be told. One only had to consider what a threat the fast-bowling duo of Darren Gough and Andrew Caddick became. They stayed fit throughout the summer of 2000, sharing sixty-four Test wickets and only having to play three county championship matches each. This naturally evoked thoughts of what might have been. Caddick was thirty-one years old and Gough thirty by 2000.

Caddick was always over-bowled at Somerset, with the line peddled disingenuously that the more overs he bowled the better he bowled. Even though I found him a bit of a prat to play against, he could have been a great England fast bowler rather than just a very good one. His omission from the Ashes tour party in 1998/99, despite 105 first-class wickets in 1998, still counts as one of the most mutton-headed pieces of selection in recent times. He bowled 59,663 balls in first-class cricket, but only 13,558 were for England. Glenn McGrath bowled 41,759 balls all told, but 29,248 of those were for Australia. That's a difference of around 47% between the two. It is a tragedy.

With central contracts has come continuity of selection. Some have, of course, accused that of being a closed shop, but it is a far and welcoming cry from the bad old days when a player was only concerned about making the side for the next Test, regardless of the result of the one in which he was actually playing. Revolving-door selections played with players' minds, none more so, in my opinion, than Hick and Ramprakash. Had central contracts been in place at the start of their careers, I'm pretty sure we would now be considering their Test-playing days in a very different light, certainly as regards Hick, who was dropped more times in his Test career than a cockney drops his aitches.

There were other significant advancements under MacLaurin's tenure. First was the splitting of the county championship into two divisions in 2000. This was not easy, of course. It had been proposed in 1997, but a vote of the First Class Forum had decided against it 12–7.

David Morgan was still against the idea. 'Both David Acfield [chairman of the cricket advisory committee] and I were opposed to two divisions because we felt you'd have a second class of first-class county,' he says. That was a very common worry at the time, easily assuaged by the promise that every county would still receive the same ECB fee payments every year. So there was no penalty for being rubbish.

At this stage there was also no penalty for squandering the money on cheap foreigners imported through the back-door. Yes, we are talking about those delightful EU passport holders and Kolpaks who have caused me so much anguish throughout my journalistic career. Some might say that I was like a broken record, such was my persistent and vociferous opposition to these chaps from abroad. But I felt it was an issue that needed urgent and plaintive addressing.

Counties were clearly making short-term decisions in search of instant success. Because the European Court of Justice's 2003 ruling in the case of Slovakian handball player Maros Kolpak allowed a sportsman from any nation with an associate trading relationship with the EU to play freely as a professional wherever he liked, they were signing cheap South Africans by the bucketload and neglecting the much longer process of producing and nurturing homegrown players. I liked Ashley Giles's phrase at the time, likening many counties' recruitment drives to 'easy internet shopping'.

I was not, and am not, xenophobic. That much should be obvious from the thrust of this book. It is, after all, about two foreigners and the tremendous good they have done for English cricket. I have always been a huge fan of overseas players in county cricket. How couldn't I be when Viv Richards turned Glamorgan's fortunes around at the start of the nineties, teaching a talented but flabby-minded team how to win, and when Waqar Younis added the cream to a long-baked cake in the winning of the county championship in 1997? But they were top-notch overseas players; the sadness is that their ilk is rarely available any more. The huge increase in year-round inter-national cricket, allied to the arrival of the IPL, has seen to that. The days of top foreigners playing full seasons and staying loyal to counties for years are gone, and in their place for a while came a host of jobbing, opportunistic mercenaries.

I have never blamed the individuals involved. They were, still are, just cricketers desperate to earn a living. Andy Flower signed initially for Essex in 2002 as an overseas player but then used his British passport to play as a local after retiring from international cricket; his brother Grant, who joined Essex in 2005, used the Kolpak ruling. They knew and know my feelings.

Top-quality individuals from abroad, in which category both Flowers undoubtedly fall, can add enormous value, of that there can never be any doubt. But as in life, it is a question of balance. When in May 2008 Leicestershire played Northamptonshire in a championship match and there were eleven players on the field not qualified to play for England, a tipping point had clearly been reached. Thankfully the system of performance-related fee payments, begun in 2005 by the ECB, has been strengthened, and, along with the tightening of entry qualifications by the Home Office, the problem has diminished.

The proliferation of Kolpaks has been my only regret regarding two divisions. I doubt that was troubling MacLaurin when he declared a two-divisional championship not to be his first-choice solution. As expressed in 1997 in his blueprint document for the England game 'Raising the Standard', he wanted a conference-style system, with three groups of six, and the six teams in one group playing the twelve other counties to make twelve championship matches a season. But this was rejected immediately by the counties; all the more funny then that it should arise again recently in discussion about the domestic structure.

But there is always discussion about the domestic structure. As I write, Morgan has just produced a review into the business of county cricket. It was not supposed to be specifically about the structure, but that is how it turned out, and it caused predictable uproar.

There always has been discussion about the county structure, and always will be, especially with eighteen counties, which is, of course, far too many. But to complain about that number is like complaining about old age. We need to get over it. I can't see the number being reduced during my lifetime.

What this does mean, though, is that there will always be compromise when considering the domestic structure. And so when the two-divisional championship was introduced, it came with the proviso of three up, three down. That was far too much fluidity, but that was what the counties wanted. Too many of them were fearful of being marooned in the second tier.

There was also a ridiculous early imbalance in the financial incentives available. The only prize money on offer was for the top two in each division, with the winner of division two receiving just £10,000 less than the runner-up in division one. The more materialistic cricketers quickly realized it was better to be in a yo-yo team, flitting between divisions, than a solid outfit in third or fourth in the first division.

Nowadays things are a little different, not least because of a significant upturn in the prize money available. Back in 2000 Surrey won £105,000 for securing the county championship. In 2010 the figure on offer was a very healthy £550,000, although it is spread between players (70%) and the county (30%), whereas before it was simply divided among the players. But it still beggars belief that in 2010 the division two winners received £135,000 for effectively finishing tenth, while the team third in division one received just £115,000. In 2011 it was slightly more complicated with the county's national insurance payment taken into account in the prize monies, but essentially the winners of the second division still earned £20,000 more than the third-placed county in division one.

Only in 2006 did the structure become two up, two down in terms of promotion and relegation. Me? I'd have one up, one down. Then we'd have an elite division, which must surely be the aim.

As it is, I suppose we should be grateful that the vote for change came at all. But it did come, in December 1998. Two counties abstained, but there were still fifteen counties in favour of two divisions, with one against. 'An historic decision heralding the most radical change in the structure of the first-class game since the championship was first rationalized in 1890,' wrote MacLaurin of it in his autobiography. 'This was, indeed, a quiet revolution.'

It was. And two divisions have been of enormous benefit. Intensity, competitiveness and professionalism have all increased. Even Morgan has been impressed. 'It hasn't quite worked out as I thought,' he says, 'and quite clearly when I talk to cricketers – and I always regard cricketers as extremely important people! [said with a smile and a knowing glance across the sitting-room of his Newport home] – they regard two divisions as a success. So I'm ready to admit that I was wrong.'

The other important initiative under MacLaurin's watch that helped improve England's fortunes was the setting up of a National Academy. Again, this was a long time in coming. The counties had approved its introduction by a vote of 16–2 as far back as 1995, and in June that year the former Australian leg-spinner Peter Philpott had been asked to be head coach at a proposed site in Shenley, Hertfordshire.

In October of that year Mark Nicholas, the recently retired former captain of Hampshire, was also asked by Dennis Silk, the chairman of the TCCB, to run the Academy. But by November the board's executive committee had performed an about-turn, reckoning Silk had overstepped the boundaries of his power, and an enraged Philpott, who had turned down other job offers, had received a fax stating that the idea was on hold.

It remained on hold until December 1999 when it was decided to try again. Hugh Morris, then the ECB's performance director, was the man tasked with its setting up. 'It was around the time that lottery funding became available,' recalls Morris enthusiastically of a project that was to prove the making of him as a cricket administrator, 'and Sport England [who were administering the Lottery Sports Fund] basically said, "Dream! We've got more money than we've ever had before. We need to hear your plans, and then we will sit down and assess them." I had to work with my staff to put a world-class performance structure together, of which the central part was the Academy. We spent over two years doing it. We looked at the Australian Academy. We looked at Liverpool FC's Academy. We did desk studies on academies around the world. We sent people to South Africa, and to America too.'

Morris was adamant that the Academy had to sit outside the first-class game, otherwise it would just become a county academy with a national badge on it. 'We wanted to rub shoulders with other sports and learn from them,' he says, 'so we began an open tender process, and had seventy-five expressions of interest from inside and outside the game. Then we sent out a very detailed invitation to tender, and that frightened a lot of people, so we got down to eight or nine serious bids.' Eventually Morris decided it was going to be at Loughborough, and after similar due deliberation the ECB's board agreed.

Next came the matter of funding. The centre was going to cost £4.52 million. Lottery funding would provide £4 million, but what about the other half a million? In stepped the Allan and Nesta Ferguson Trust with a generous grant. It wasn't going to cost the ECB or the counties anything, and for the first four years Sport England provided £2 million annually for its running.

In November 2003, fifteen years after Australia had opened its academy in Adelaide, the Queen formally opened the National Academy building at Loughborough. It was, and still is, the largest bespoke indoor cricket centre in the world, measuring approximately 70m by 25m, with six lanes in a hall long enough to accommodate fast bowlers off full runs with a wicketkeeper standing back.

For the two winters of 2001/02 and 2002/03 before the opening of the centre at Loughborough – renamed the National Cricket Performance Centre after the (Ken) Schofield Report in 2007 – the Academy was based in Adelaide. England were unashamedly copying Australia, and why wouldn't they, after just losing their seventh successive Ashes series at home that summer in 2001? So it also made sense for an Australian to run it. More to the point, the Australian who had been running the Australian Academy.

Step forward Rod Marsh, the legendary Australia wicketkeeper, who then ran the English equivalent for four years. 'There were a lot of Doubting Thomases about the Academy,' says Morris, 'so we needed somebody with real gravitas. Bringing Rod Marsh in was done specifically to raise eyebrows, and show we meant business.'

Among the first intake in 2001 were Strauss, Flintoff, Steve Harmison, Simon Jones, Ian Bell, Graeme Swann, Ryan Sidebottom, Chris Tremlett, Rob Key, Owais Shah, Alex Tudor and Chris Schofield. That's twelve players out of an intake of eighteen who went on to play for England. Seven of them went on to become Ashes winners, and eleven of them have either scored a century or taken five wickets in an innings for England.

It would be easy to conclude that the Academy was an instant success. It wasn't. It took years of tinkering and tailoring to arrive at the point in 2010/11 when England's Academy could be termed, without fear of contradiction, a world leader and an undoubted producer of world-class talent. They had long had the 'Merlyn' spin-bowling machine (which all eighteen counties now possess), which was so useful for England and their playing of Shane Warne during the 2005 Ashes, and the Hawk-Eye tracking system. Now everyone else in the world marvelled at their two latest technological advancements: the 'Pro-Batter', a virtual reality bowling machine where the batsman watches an opposition bowler running in on a screen before the ball is delivered, and 'TrackMan', a device that measures the revolutions a spinner is able to impart on the ball. In an instant Pro-Batter eliminates the age-old problem with bowling machines, that you could never time your pick-up and trigger movements as you would in a match situation. Indeed when I was a teenager, so much trouble did I have with synchronizing my movements on the bowling machine that I decided to stand with bat aloft, à la Graham Gooch.

The Pro-Batter, based on a device used by American baseball batters, is still not perfect, in that there is a small delay as the ball supposedly comes out of the bowler's hand, and some England batsmen have told me it is especially difficult to pick up bouncers from it, but, crucially, the length can be altered without any cue from the operator. England's batsmen un-doubtedly benefited from it before the Ashes of 2010/11. 'For me, the great advantage is that you can time your trigger move-ments as the bowler – be it [Mitchell] Johnson, [Ben] Hilfenhaus or whoever – is coming in,' said Strauss.

As for the TrackMan, you often hear commentators talking about a spinner getting 'good revs' on the ball. Now they can be more certain of what they are talking about. Adapted from a device used by golfers, it's a small camera placed behind the bowler's arm that can measure the revolutions per minute generated by various bowlers. It should not surprise anyone that a wrist-spinner generates more than a finger-spinner, so of the England bowlers tested in 2010 Yorkshire's leg-spinner Adil Rashid recorded the highest figure (an average of 2,312), while of the finger-spinners Swann was top (2,083), with Monty Panesar (1,750), James Tredwell (1,682) and Mike Yardy (1,350) behind him.

How today's position contrasts with the Academy's beginning. I have to admit that I was never sure about Marsh.

Yes, there was certainly merit in his bark ('You overpaid Pommie bastards!' was apparently a constant scream to his quivering academicians) and his devotion to hard work, even if its implementation was sometimes crude in the extreme, but it just seemed to be a little too much about him at the Academy. It was all about how good a job he was doing. When he became an England selector in 2003, it was obvious that he was rather keen to promote those who had come under his wing. Thus his liking of wicketkeeper Chris Read, and his infamous rant in 2004, in front of the MCC players gathered at Lord's for the season's pipe-opener against Sussex, when he discovered that Read had been dropped for Geraint Jones for the final Test of the West Indies tour in Antigua. Marsh and Fletcher never got on. They got on even less after that.

I remember calling Marsh in 2005 to ask him about a piece I was doing on players who had struggled after they had left the Academy. I was thinking about the likes of Hampshire's Derek Kenway (an academician in that original intake in 2001/02), who had a shocker of a county season in 2002, averaging just 11.82 with the bat, and was out of the professional game altogether by the end of 2005, and others like Yorkshire's Matthew Wood. Marsh thought I was specifically talking about Glamorgan's David Harrison, who'd just returned to his county after a winter with the Academy with a bowling action considerably different from that with which he'd arrived there. Suddenly he was jumping extraordinarily wide on the crease. He was half the bowler he had been previously. Glamorgan were not happy, and made their feelings clear to the Academy. Marsh thought I was stirring trouble about that, and in general questioning him as much as his methods. I wasn't. I actually had some sympathy with the situation. It was obvious to me that if Harrison were to become an England bowler, he would need to increase his pace. The Academy concurred, and that was at the heart of their work with him during that winter of 2004/05. Unfortunately it resulted in a changing of action. If you don't venture, you don't discover . . .

Marsh was in charge for two years when the Academy was based in Australia, and two at the new Loughborough centre. Early on he made a prescient comment to Morris. 'We've run an Academy in Australia for thirteen years and it's changed every single year,' he said. And that is what has happened in England. It was not always necessarily for the best, but there has certainly been considerable change, not least in the name of the side representing it abroad, whether it has been the National Academy, England A or, as now, England Lions (or Elite Player Programme side – EPP), with selection now at a point where it is very nearly a second-choice England side that takes the field on most occasions.

Cock-ups are much fewer on the ground, and the selection process much further back down the line has also been revolutionized. Gone are the days of England fielding Under 15 and Under 17 sides to play international matches. Instead, at the conclusion of the annual Bunbury Festival, so enthusiastically organized for the twenty-fifth time in 2011 by David English, an England Development Programme (EDP) squad is selected with the Under 19 side as the long-term goal. Players are added and cut as the years progress.

It is no random selection process guided by vested interests and old school ties. That used to happen, believe me. My best man, Adrian Knox, a rather rough-and-ready rugby player,went to Whitecross Comprehensive School in my hometown of Lydney in Gloucestershire. When playing for the West of England in the old regional Under 15 tournament that pre-dated the Bunbury Festival, he scored more runs than anyone else. By a distance. But he didn't make the England Under 15 team selected from that tournament. A lot of public schoolboys did.

Now it is rather different. Morris had sorted the structure of the senior team, then the Lions/Academy, so in 2010 the pathways to the national Under 19 side were his last mission. And after a disappointing ICC Under 19 World Cup performance that year, it was quite a mission. But Simon Timson, the ECB's head of science and medicine, has studied NFL scouting processes in the United States, and now the ECB are using hard evidence rather than mere selectorial whim. They use tests in the four categories of technical, physical, psychological and fielding, as well as bare cricketing statistics.

That is not to say it is foolproof just yet either. I know of a young lad who only just made his regional side for the Bunbury Festival in 2011, after much persuasion from a coach who knows his onions. He then impressed so much that he only just missed out on the fourteen players selected for the EDP. Had there been fifteen he would have been in.

Research has shown that cricketers who reach the world's top ten have usually made their first-class debuts by the age of nineteen, and by twenty-three are playing international cricket. The ECB pull no punches about the function of the EDP. It is the beginning of the line 'to produce the world's best cricketers for England by the age of twenty-seven'. Some will fall by the wayside quickly. Some may reappear as late developers in county cricket. But there is now a scientific talent identification process in place. Some might even say England have managed to put in place a system that circumvents the clunky county system. It is very clever indeed.

These days more home Lions fixtures are arranged (you can't expect strong opposition abroad if you don't provide it at home), even if they enrage the counties who are reluctant to release their players. The counties need to pipe down on that issue. Those fixtures are a vital part of the England process, and the players recognize that. They know where they stand in the pecking order, and to be selected for a home Lions match is to know that a full cap is not that far away.

At the start of the 2011 season I interviewed Craig Kieswetter, the Somerset wicketkeeper/batsman who had enjoyed a successful Lions tour of the West Indies. He had just suffered a thigh muscle strain, meaning he would miss the Lions' four-day match against Sri Lanka at Derby. He was genuinely 'gutted', as he put it. This was a chap who had already played one-day and T20 cricket for the full England team (a World Cup winner no less in T20, after England's success in the Caribbean in 2010), and he was bemoaning missing his first home Lions match. There was a time during the early years of the Academy when players simply did not want to be involved. Weeks and months of perceived incarceration at Loughborough were mind-numbing and ambition-destroying. Now Kieswetter was saying, 'To be part of the Lions set-up is unbelievable. Every player has got the same ambition to play for England. In a county set-up you get some players who are quite happy to be a county player, but with the Lions the whole atmosphere changes completely because everyone has a common goal and is training the hardest, eating the healthiest, doing everything they can to play for England. The whole environment is one of pure success and enjoyment.'

I was gobsmacked by these comments. I genuinely was. He was the first player I'd heard speak so glowingly about the Academy process. I'd heard some positive things in the past, of course – indeed my former Glamorgan team-mate Mark Wallace had written in the *Wisden Cricketers' Almanack* of 2011 that 'the winters I spent at the Academy were among the most enjoyable and rewarding periods of my career' – but this was eye-opening stuff.

I had often been critical of the Academy, especially at times of the current director David Parsons, who took over in 2007 but did not play first-class cricket. I felt there was just not the technical expertise available that players close to the England side deserve. It was probably a little harsh, because Parsons is what they call in very modern parlance an excellent 'facilitator'.

In other words he is rather like a midwife overseeing the act of childbirth. He assists in the actual delivery, but is not the producer of the end result.

The shift can be traced back to Peter Moores. After a successful spell as coach of Sussex – in 2003 they won their first county championship title in a 164-year history – he was appointed director of the Academy in 2005. He made an immediate change. 'As soon as I got there I realized that it wasn't right that it was a National Academy,' he says. 'I thought, "This has got to be a Performance Centre." It wasn't servicing the England team, and it had to do that.'

Fletcher's repeated mantra as England coach was that he should be 'putting the roofs on players' techniques, not digging their foundations'. And how right that statement is. But Fletcher was astounded at the technical naivety of many of the players picked in his England Test teams. For instance, Caddick could not bowl a slower ball. So Fletcher showed him not just how to bowl it, but also where to bowl it – ideally wide of off-stump so that the batsman, having checked his shot, then has to reach for the ball.

Moores was conscious of Fletcher's mantra. 'I thought to myself, "This is where we should be building the foundations",' he says. 'But I did not have enough coaches at my disposal. So I went to see Gordon Lord [the ECB's head of elite coach development] and said, "I've got no coaches! Who are the best candidates currently on the Level Four coaching course?"'

Lord mentioned a chap by the name of Flower, then still playing at Essex. Andy, that is. 'I watched him coach,' says Moores, 'and I liked his style. He was giving simple messages, which is what I like.'

That winter Flower began the first of two winters coaching at the Academy as a specialist batting coach. Little did anyone know then where that was going to lead.

3

The Greatest Series

I still wince at the memory. I was making my way in cricket journalism in 2005, writing a weekly column on county cricket for the *Sunday Telegraph*, as well as reporting on county matches for the *Guardian* during the week. For the week beginning Monday, 8 August 2005, I was due to cover Glamorgan against Warwickshire at Colwyn Bay. The hotel and train journey had been booked, and I was rather excited. I quite like Colwyn Bay. I scored a few runs there once upon a time. A triple century even, before my braggadocio runs riot. And I'd not been back there for a long time.

But then I received a call from Ian Prior, now the *Guardian*'s sports editor. Would I fancy changing my plans and going to the third Ashes Test at Old Trafford? Though I had done some international cricket the previous summer (my international writing 'debut' was for the *Guardian* at Trent Bridge for England's game against New Zealand in 2004 when I did a piece on fielding at short leg, of all things), I had not been in the initial plans for 2005. The big guns had quite naturally been rolled out. Goodness, Gideon Haigh was even on the roster. And he is a great cricket writer, believe me.

I dallied at Prior's suggestion. I said the hotel booking might be a problem. What about the train ticket? At that moment I wanted to go to Colwyn Bay more than I wanted to go to Old Trafford. What was I thinking? The greatest Test series ever was in progress, and I was thinking I'd prefer to watch my old team-mates in a county game. I do love Glamorgan, and years of underachievement, mainly due to poor off-field decision-making beginning in that year of 2005, have not diminished that (even if I have offered passionate criticism), but this was madness.

Thankfully Prior did not slam the phone down. He gently coaxed me, and off to Old Trafford I went to do what they termed some 'technical pieces'. I'm rather glad I did, not least because I witnessed at first hand the mayhem on the final morning when some twenty thousand people were locked out of the ground as they desperately sought to buy tickets for the denouement. Duncan Fletcher's wife Marina told him she thought there had been a bomb scare when she saw the crowds filing away in their thousands as she attempted to get to the ground. I was of much the same mind. The scenes were scarcely believable. The taxi ride from my hotel in the city centre was hardly worth it. You couldn't get near the place. 'I'll just get out here, thanks, driver,' I said about two miles away.

I suppose if I'd gone to Colwyn Bay I might have seen a fellow called Jonathan Trott make 152 for Warwickshire in their ten-wicket victory, but it was rather more pleasurable watching a Glamorgan bowler, Simon Jones, taking 6-53 in the first innings for England at Manchester.

The excitement was palpable. And that was just in the press box, where lack of emotion and disinterest are supposed to rule. One eminent cricket correspondent was all set to emigrate to New Zealand until this series suddenly and joyfully reignited his enthusiasm for the game. And sitting next to me there in Manchester was the man from the Press Association. When Justin Langer was dismissed, he turned to me and screamed, 'We're gonna win the Ashes!' And that was only in the first innings.

Of course, England did eventually win the Ashes that summer, but not until a thunderously memorable battle had been played out. The words upon the DVD sitting in my study describe it as 'The Greatest Series'. I have no argument with which to disagree. It truly was.

England were hammered at Lord's in the first Test, even though they had roughed up the Australians on the opening morning ('This isn't a war' remarked Langer to England's fielders after Ricky Ponting had been hit in the face by Steve Harmison and no one had enquired about his health). Then they won at Edgbaston in a synapses-shredder, decided when Mike Kasprowicz was caught down the leg-side with just three runs required for victory. There was a draw, with Australia nine wickets down, at Old Trafford, and then victory at Trent Bridge after Australia had followed on.

So it came down to the Oval, and only a draw required for England to regain the Ashes. Thanks to Kevin Pietersen's belligerent 158 on the final day they just about managed it. Cue the sort of celebrations never seen before or since in cricketing circles: an open-topped bus parade through many thousands of adoring spectators from the Mansion House to Trafalgar Square, a reception at Downing Street and MBEs all round (and OBEs for Fletcher, Michael Vaughan, chairman of selectors David Graveney and team manager Phil Neale). 'I stood there in Trafalgar Square and thought long and hard about what I had achieved in cricket,' said Fletcher. 'This was undoubtedly the pinnacle.'

It certainly was. And it was not something Fletcher necessarily foresaw. When he had asked me to write his autobiography in 2004, he had been planning ahead. It might be seen as an overly negative viewpoint, but he was worrying about the consequences of a poor tour to South Africa that winter and something similar in this Ashes series. It could have happened. Both opponents were formidable.

In case of failure he wanted his book deal in place. But at this stage in 2004 Fletcher did not want anyone knowing about these book plans. It would only increase speculation about his future. I dragged this secret around with me for some considerable time. Every time we met he stressed the importance of confidentiality. I'll admit that I was scared witless about its coming out.

We met for the first time at a Heathrow hotel prior to England's departure for South Africa. We talked about his early life. We talked a lot. Or rather he did. Once he starts, he can talk. I was so engrossed that I forgot about something. My Dictaphone. In those days I had one of those old-style cassette recorders. I'd turned it on at the start. But we seemed to have been talking for an awfully long time. I checked the cassette. The tape had snapped!

We had been talking for probably about an hour with no recording to show for it. It is any journalist's biggest nightmare. As a batsman will often wake up in a cold sweat having failed to get his pads on in time to be next to bat, so a journalist will dread this sort of situation.

I felt physically sick. What a first day as a ghost! Not only was there the unrecorded stuff, but also the recorded stuff that needed to be salvaged. Somehow the snapped tape had to be mended. Fletcher has a reputation for being intolerant of fools. Well, he was very tolerant of this fool on that day. He should have just sent me on my way with the words 'Sort it out yourself, you idiot!' Instead he spent the best part of an hour painstakingly fixing the cassette. Much of it was saved.

The next time I saw Fletcher was in Cape Town on the last

day of the third Test that winter. This was now serious undercover work. The need to keep the book project a secret had been intensified by speculation about Fletcher being in line to replace Ray Jennings as South Africa coach. He had even been approached about it, albeit remarkably clumsily via a security guard at one of the Tests.

Fletcher was on edge throughout my visit. He desperately wanted to beat South Africa, but his side had just been hammered in Cape Town; his mood was not lightened either by Marina falling ill with the first of many black-outs that were to affect her health over the following years. Fletcher, always so caring and protective of his wife, had rushed from the ground to attend to her. Interestingly, Harmison, with whom Fletcher never really got on, had arranged flowers for her from the players. It proved that, essentially, Harmison has a good heart. It is just that he can seem lazy, and easily led.

I was picked up at the airport by the team liaison officer and whisked into the ground to witness the last rites of England's only defeat in that series. I made a mistake, though, by wandering around the ground and bumping into Mike Dickson, then the *Daily Mail*'s cricket correspondent. I'm not sure he twigged the reason for my presence, but he most certainly would have done so had he seen me the following day.

Thanks to some hastily found prowess as a John Le Carré character, I just about ensured he didn't. Fletcher had agreed that Nasser Hussain, by now retired and working for Sky as a commentator and for the *Daily Mail* as a columnist, could come to conduct an interview at his house in the Claremont suburb of Cape Town, where I was also staying. But as he doesn't write his own stuff (although he did do so on occasions when employed previously by the *Sunday Telegraph* and considered doing so upon Mike Atherton's departure when he was also interviewed for the job I currently hold as columnist), he had to bring Dickson with him. As they were arriving through the front door,

I was leaving with Marina through the back door and into the garage. We were going to go for a coffee nearby and return when Fletcher called at the end of his interview.

However, when we opened the garage doors, we immediately realized there was a problem. Standing outside in the road was a photographer. And not any old photographer. There, lurking as only a waiting snapper can, was the always-chuckling Winston Bynorth, known to all as 'Muttley' and a fellow old boy of Monmouth School. It genuinely was a comedy moment.

There was no other choice. Into the back seat I went and ducked down as Marina drove out of the driveway and down the road, leaving Bynorth still waiting for the call to go inside and take some shots to go alongside Hussain's interview. Thankfully Bynorth did not see me. And I didn't tell him about that incident until 2008.

I met Fletcher regularly throughout 2005 to go through periods of his life and career, but without any fixed end-point. There seemed to be some confusion. I have a feeling that the publishers thought the autobiography was going to be finished after that 2005 Ashes series, come what may. And, of course given subsequent events, there are those who will argue that Fletcher might have been better off finishing then anyway.

But whatever the negotiations between Fletcher, his agent and those publishers, I was not ready for the phone call from Fletcher as I was driving to the annual Cricket Writers' Club dinner in Park Lane on 2 September 2005. 'We're going to do a diary of the Ashes as well as the autobiography,' he said. 'We've got three weeks to do it.'

Christ almighty.

Those were three of the busiest weeks of my life, even if the first week or so was rather frustrating with little work being done. That's because the final Test did not start until 8 September. The diary would still have gone ahead, I think, had

England lost that final Test and the series been drawn, but the title *Ashes Regained* obviously would not have stood.

As it was, of course, England drew that match to take the series and we managed to meet our deadline, and, while Fletcher was understandably keeping his most incendiary stuff for later, there were some intriguing insights into his and the England team's thinking that summer. It is not just the devil that is in the detail but, usually, the fascination.

So Fletcher revealed that it had been England's goal to win five Tests that summer, two against Bangladesh and three from five against Australia. Had they not been denied so agonizingly at Old Trafford they would have achieved that.

It was also the team's goal to make over 400 in the first innings of each Test in fewer than 130 overs. England did that on three occasions; Australia did not achieve it once.

England wanted one batsman to make over 150, and that was achieved twice through Vaughan at Old Trafford (166) and Pietersen's 158 at the Oval.

They also wanted three wickets from their fielding unit in every Test. By that they meant two catches – of the sort where the bowler knows he owes everything to the brilliance of the fielder (like Andrew Strauss's stunning telescopic slip catch to dismiss Adam Gilchrist at Trent Bridge) – and a run out. And we all know there was one very famous run out in this series, when substitute Gary Pratt hit the stumps at Trent Bridge prompting an outburst of expletives from the departing Ponting at Fletcher, who'd appeared on the England balcony having abandoned some toast-making inside.

Ponting had been furious at England's policy of frequently using substitute fielders throughout the series, reckoning they were merely allowing bowlers to change clothing, refresh and maybe even have a massage after spells. But that was palpably not the case here as Pratt was on for Simon Jones, who'd limped off with an ankle injury after bowling just four overs in

Australia's second innings, having taken five wickets in the first to ensure they followed on. And, if Ponting thought England were always making sure they had top-notch fielders on the field, he was wrong there too, because England had their best substitute fielder – the Zimbabwean Trevor Penney, who was also doing some fielding coaching – still in the dressing room.

There was also another run out attempt from another uncapped substitute fielder that is often forgotten in the analysis of this series. This was by Stephen Peters, then of Worcestershire, at Old Trafford, where in the mayhem of the final session, with barely six overs remaining and Australia eight wickets down, Peters' shy at the stumps just missed with Brett Lee not even in the picture. Ponting was out soon afterwards, but Lee was still there at the end. England could so easily have gone 2–1 up there, and the final series result might have been 3–1.

After that match I interviewed Peters. He told me that at the end of the match, after Lee had somehow blocked out Harmison's last offerings, Vaughan had called his shattered team into a huddle on the field and begged them to take a look at the Australian balcony. 'Look at those lot celebrating a draw,' the skipper had said. It was indeed a significant moment, a huge change in mindset.

Fletcher also divulged that every member of the squad had a copy of the poem 'The Man in the Glass' by Dale Wimbrow. After the diary's publication, he even found himself reciting the poem on Radio Five Live. Throughout the series England players could be heard shouting 'Look in the mirror!' At other times of stress the refrain 'Remember the Iceman!' could be heard. That referred to the visit the squad received before the series from Alan Chambers, who in 2000 along with Charlie Paton had reached the geographical North Pole without support, dragging their 250lb sledges across the ice from

Canada in horrendous conditions, the worst polar weather for twenty years. No Briton had ever achieved the feat before.

Then there were the secret, but crucial, one-on-one net sessions Fletcher had with Vaughan at the New Rover Cricket Club, home to the Yorkshire Academy near the Leeds outer ring road. They had done something similar before the 2004 Lord's Test against the West Indies when Vaughan scored twin centuries. Now, after Vaughan had failed twice in the first Test at Lord's, bowled for 3 and 4, they did so again.

Success was instant in county cricket where Vaughan scored a hundred for Yorkshire in a Totesport League match against Kent, even if for England he had to wait until Old Trafford for his reward. Speak to him now and he still looks back on those sessions with real affection. 'They were always Fletch enjoying his coaching most,' Vaughan says. 'They were really good fun. We'd try different things and different drills, but he always made sure I finished in a way he knew I'd get confidence from. I always had to end up playing on a high. Whenever I spent two days with Fletch there might not have been much of a technical change by the end of it, but I always felt better in myself. That was what he was good at. I always felt I would get runs afterwards. People will say, "Why didn't you do it every week?" But it was quite hard to get two days every week to hit balls with Duncan Fletcher.'

I know what Vaughan means. It was exactly the same at Glamorgan. Fletcher is the best batting-practice thrower I ever encountered. That may sound a little silly. But many professional cricketers cannot throw properly to a team-mate – many don't want to, if truth be told, because they don't like doing it. They'd rather just bat. But Fletcher has a strong arm and is unerringly accurate. Little wonder he has had the odd shoulder operation (as did Andy Flower, incidentally, at the end of the 2011 summer). He was always in demand.

*

Everyone has their own little story about that 2005 Ashes series, of how the series touched their lives, of missed appointments and the like. Mine is rather different. Mine comes from the last morning of that thriller at Edgbaston, which I watched from home. Alone in my lounge, I was not a journalist. I was just like any other supporter. And my advice to the England bowlers was becoming louder by the minute, as they appeared to be allowing the last pair of Lee and Kasprowicz to secure a victory, after having come together still with 62 required. Just as my sledging of the Australian batsmen became louder too.

At this point my six-year-old daughter Bethan entered the room. Looking at the television, she said, 'Isn't that Michael? He's your friend, isn't he? Why are you saying nasty things to him?'

As captain of Glamorgan I had signed Kasprowicz as an overseas player in 2002, and our families had become close. I can say without fear of contradiction that he is one of the nicest blokes I have come across in cricket. But here I was screaming at him. Or rather at pictures of him on the TV. Bethan was, quite naturally, rather perplexed.

When it was all over, she said, 'You'd better say sorry to him. Phone him now.'

It was, of course, no time to phone, not least because the Anti-Corruption Unit of the ICC does not permit phones to be used in the dressing room. But I did text. 'Bad luck, mate' I typed.

As it happens, it was bad luck, because the glove that deflected Harmison's delivery into wicketkeeper Geraint Jones's gloves was not actually on the bat handle at the time. Kasprowicz should not have been given out. Under today's Decision Review System, he probably would not have been given out.

But, once the initial despondency subsided, it has not done him that much harm. He now has a rather good theme for his after-dinner speeches. I emailed him some time afterwards to organize an interview on the subject. 'I would love to have a chat to you re. Edgbaston and my role in assisting the promoting of cricket for the benefit of all,' he wrote in reply, referring to the effect that the England victory had there.

So this is how that after-dinner speech now goes. 'I was approached by an Indian gentleman some time afterwards and asked whether I was Michael Kasprowicz,' he says. 'He was delighted when I replied that I was, and he immediately thanked me and said that I had single-handedly saved Test cricket. He pointed out that if we had successfully chased down the runs and won that second Test, Australia would have gone to a 2–0 series lead and, as he said, "on to win the series, leading to the slow death of Test cricket". I politely thanked him, but did feel the need to point out that the single hand he spoke of was actually off the bat at the time!' Ah, good stuff.

For many, the enduring image of the whole series occurred just after Kasprowicz was out, when Andrew Flintoff was seen with a consoling arm around the distraught non-striker Lee. 'No one came to comfort me, did they?' joked Kasprowicz. 'I was left on my own.' Crouched down, trying to bury his head in his bat handle.

Dismissing Kasprowicz was not England's only piece of fortune. There was Glenn McGrath standing on a stray ball before that game had even started, putting him out of that Test and the next one at Trent Bridge. And then soon after that there was skipper Ponting astonishingly opting to bowl, even after McGrath's injury. 'I could not believe my ears,' said Vaughan. And as Fletcher later said, 'What was he thinking? There was no doubt in our minds that we were going to bat first.'

But more than anything this was triumph for Fletcher and Vaughan, and their meticulous planning. Beforehand they had resolved to 'get into the space' of the Australians, in other words never to stand back in any confrontation. This was first manifested in a one-day international at Edgbaston in the series that preceded the Tests, when Simon Jones hurled a ball at Matthew Hayden and it hit him in the chest. Hayden was enraged and, with chest pumped out, Buzz (to his England opponents, after Buzz Lightyear) flew back at Jones.

In earlier years, and indeed sadly in the later Ashes of 2006/07, Jones might have found himself fighting a lone battle. Here he was backed as the likes of Collingwood, Strauss and Vaughan ran in to support their team-mate. The throw had accidentally hit Hayden, and Jones was about to apologize before Hayden reacted so strongly.

The truth is that Australian cricketers love to trade on their macho, aggressive on-field attitude, but once an opponent reacts in similar fashion it is as if some terribly heinous crime has been committed. They like to dish it out, but . . .

So they bristled throughout this series, with Ponting often demonstrating the Tasmanian Devil that lurks within him. His greatest frustration must have been that he was comprehensively out-captained by Vaughan. The England skipper's field placings took planning and preparation to new levels, often befuddling the Australians in the process. For instance, Hayden had a poor series that was only partially rescued by his 138 in the final Test at the Oval, as he was shackled by a series of men placed strategically 'on the drive' (in other words, in a stationary catching position much closer to the bat than they would be when saving the single), often one of them standing on the very edge of the cut strip on the off-side.

Then there was England's mastery of reverse swing. Australia had simply not reckoned with that, and in Flintoff and Jones England suddenly had two magnificent proponents of the art. Given Australia's disgruntlement with England's unexpected success, it was little surprise that there were dark mutterings over the reasons behind England's propensity to achieve this. There always are where reverse swing is concerned. But it was wide of the mark when it was suggested that Murray Mint sweets had been the reason behind its regular appearance. As illegal as it is, those sweets are used in the game, certainly in the county game. But they are used to cultivate conventional swing. The essence of reverse swing is keeping the ball dry; applying sticky sweet-laden saliva does not quite fit into that theory.

Previously in the world game reverse swing had mainly been achieved into right-handed batsmen, although Pakistan's Waqar Younis and Imran Khan could take it away a little. Now Flintoff and Jones were reversing it both ways, and a considerable distance too. Flintoff was quite superb, and not just with the ball. His century at Trent Bridge was undoubtedly his finest international innings. And, of many bewitching spells, his first over of the Australian second innings at Edgbaston will always rank as one of the greatest in Ashes history. With its first ball he bowled Langer, and with its last he dismissed Ponting caught behind. In between Ponting suffered hell on earth. It was an over that exists only in a batsman's worst nightmare.

But Jones, so shrewdly picked by Fletcher, was the real surprise. To me too. I'd seen him as the wild and woolly fast bowler of his youth. But I'd always liked him and tried to back him. In my brief stint as Glamorgan captain I only capped two players: Jones in 2002 when it was announced that he was to win his first England cap, and Mark Wallace, the wicketkeeper/batsman with whom I've become close friends as I have tried to help him on his desired path to becoming a journalist. I capped Wallace just before I announced in 2003 that I was about to enter hospital for a major knee operation, effectively ending my first-class career. 'Can I have your bats?' Wallace remarked cheekily, as I finished what was quite an emotional speech.

It was assumed that Jones learnt reverse swing from Waqar, who was at Glamorgan in 1997 and briefly in 1998. But he didn't. It is just another of those urban myths. The 'Racehorse', as Jones is known, was only a colt then. He probably only had a couple of nets in total with Waqar. Jones taught himself reverse swing while out in Australia with the National Academy in the winter of 2001/02. 'I was messing around in the nets at Adelaide with an old ball, and it was going big,' Jones says. 'That's when I did it for the first time; I hadn't really tried it before. The boys were in a bit of trouble when I was bowling it. Straussy wasn't too happy at a net session, was he?'

Indeed he wasn't, and Strauss could still recall that session some time later. 'I didn't know which way he [Jones] was swinging it,' he said. 'He bowled me a couple which swung away, and the next one started yards wide and just missed my off-stump.'

Nets are one thing, though; match situations quite another. So when it worked for Jones, firstly in a middle practice when he tied Chris Schofield in knots, and then in a match between the Academy and the Western Australia Second XI at Abbett Park in Scarborough, Perth in March 2002, he knew he was on to something. Western Australia were going along nicely at 106-1 when Jones changed the game and probably his career, quickly plunging his opponents to 146-6 on his way to 6-48, reverse-swinging the ball both ways for the first time. The Academy's manager Nigel Laughton was there. 'They couldn't get a bat on him,' he said. 'Our boys came off in disbelief; they'd never seen anything like it. It was boomeranging.'

Jones was back in Australia the following winter, this time with the full England squad, but his tour was cut as tragically short as his Test career later was, carried off on the first day of the first Test at Brisbane with a snapped anterior cruciate ligament in his right knee. Injury has bedevilled his career ever since. He never played another Test after Trent Bridge in 2005. But he was still due to play county cricket in 2012, having returned permanently to Glamorgan from Hampshire, whom he'd joined from Worcestershire.

England's bowling coach in 2005 was an Australian, Troy Cooley. He received much praise for his work that summer, not least from his bowlers, with whom he formed a close bond, as much a kindred spirit as a coach. And there was little doubt that Fletcher rated him. Fletcher did not credit Rod Marsh with much, but bringing Cooley to the National Academy was undoubtedly one move he was happy to endorse. It took just one practice session with Cooley for Fletcher to realize this was 'one quality individual', as Fletcher has said. Their views on reverse swing were similar, and Fletcher was incandescent with rage when the ECB allowed Cooley to leave in 2006. Cooley merely wanted a contract extension to take him up to the World Cup in 2007, but the ECB dithered and Cooley returned to Australia sooner than he had planned. Although, interestingly, late in the writing of this book I had a chance conversation with an ECB official who told me that he thought Cooley wanted to go home all along, whatever the length of contract that would have been offered.

But it was Fletcher, not Cooley, who initiated the plan of bowling around the wicket to Australia's left-handers during this 2005 Ashes campaign, with the reverse swing of Flintoff and Jones for the first time neutering the threat of Adam Gilchrist down the order. For years there had been a question mark next to Gilchrist's name on the whiteboard in England's dressing room detailing opposing batsmen's weaknesses.

One player involved in that series who wished to remain anonymous said, 'Troy got a lot of the credit for the bowlers in 2005, but I reckon it was more down to Fletch. For Gilchrist, the plan was not just to bowl around the wicket but to use Flintoff straight away. Fletch had seen something that meant Gilchrist struggled facing someone so close from around the wicket. It wouldn't have worked with Harmy [Steve Harmison] or Hoggy [Matthew Hoggard] because of the angle they created from wider on the crease. I know that Fletch was so confident beforehand that he said to Vaughany something along the lines of: "He [Gilchrist] won't get a run if Fred gets it right."' And

Gilchrist didn't get a fifty, averaging just 22 and being dismissed four times in the prophesied manner.

So the regaining of the Ashes in 2005 came down to the simple-looking but always-tricky-in-reality task of batting long enough on the final day of the series, Monday, 12 September, to ensure Australia could not chase down the remaining runs. It was so tense a day that even Fletcher admitted to nerves beforehand, revealing in *Ashes Regained* that he retched on the way from breakfast to his room. It was certainly no ordinary day. Not least because England had to abandon their usual plan of driving to the ground in their own cars and use a team bus because of impending celebrations. That might, of course, be the norm on tours abroad, but this was a deviation from normal practice that could easily upset the superstitious. And the leaked news that Trafalgar Square had already been booked did not help.

To tell the story of the pressure involved one needs only to consider the early stages of Pietersen's innings of 158. He would undoubtedly be the hero later in the day, but he could so easily have been given out first ball to give McGrath a hat-trick (the ball brushed shirt amid the most vociferous of appeals in those times before the DRS), then he was dropped on 0 and, probably most memorably, dropped again on 15 by Shane Warne at slip. 'Warney's dropped the Ashes' they said. And they were probably right, harsh as it might sound on the great leg-spinner who, amid a mountain of personal problems, took forty wickets in the series at an average of 19.92.

England were eventually all out for 335, leaving Australia an impossible 342 to win. They faced just four balls before bad light intervened, and at 6.15 p.m. the umpires Billy Bowden and Rudi Koertzen walked to the middle and removed the bails to spark the sort of celebrations that English cricket had long since forgotten. The Ashes had been Australia's – not physically, of course, but that is another matter – for a long sixteen years and forty-two days. At last they were England's again.

Those celebrations went on all night, and all the next day from Trafalgar Square to 10 Downing Street and on to Lord's where the symbolic gesture of handing back the Ashes to the MCC took place. The tales are legion, encapsulated by Flintoff's response to David Gower on live television that Tuesday morning: 'To be honest with you, David, I'm struggling. I've not been to bed yet and the eyes behind these glasses tell a thousand stories.'

Ah, the utter saintliness of victory. Flintoff's considerable and public inebriation – he was about as steady on his feet as Long John Silver after more than one bottle of rum – was to become the stuff of legend, the people's champion in all his glory. But really it was gory crapulence. For me this was the moment the 'Freddie' story began to spiral out of control. The reaction a couple of years later, when he drunkenly boarded a pedalo after a World Cup defeat in St Lucia, was rather different, and rightly so. Then he was pilloried and suspended.

Such behaviour in Trafalgar Square and thereafter should never have been so publicly acclaimed and glorified. But then the open-top bus parade should not have been the day after the Test finished. That was a mistake. 'It was a shambles,' said Harmison some time afterwards. 'We'd worked so hard for so long, so to tell us at the end of the game that we had to be ready to get on the bus at nine the next morning . . . I'd defy any sports team to be bright-eyed and bushy-tailed after what we'd just gone through. They should have let us sit in the hotel for two days, then we would have turned up clean-shaven, suited and booted, but too many people wanted to make a photo-opportunity out of us, especially the Prime Minister [Tony Blair] and the Mayor of London [Ken Livingstone]. Actually, I didn't think we got as rough a ride as we should have done. We got off scot-free, really. I was embarrassed. We had to celebrate it, but certain people bowed to pressure and put us straight on that bus.'

It was not the only mistake. The subsequent awarding of MBEs and OBEs was misguided. In my opinion only Vaughan, Flintoff, Trescothick, Strauss and Fletcher should have been rewarded. Bell's and Collingwood's could have come later.

And why did it take this victory for Fletcher to be granted the British passport he'd first applied for way back in 1991? He'd been coach of England for six years. His parents, his two younger brothers and sister all had British passports, but not him and his two older brothers. Apparently it was all to do with dates of birth, and whether they'd been born before 1 January 1949. Anyway, he received the good news via text during the Trafalgar Square celebrations.

Not that the rationale behind the celebrations was necessarily wrong. At the time tens of thousands filled London to acclaim their cricketing heroes. Two years later such antics were being described as those of unjustified jingoism and triumphalism, the beginning of the end for that England team. Nothing, of course, to do with an injury list containing Vaughan, Giles, Jones (S.) and Trescothick that could have prompted a souvenir issue of the *Lancet*.

Speak to Hugh Morris, now the ECB's managing director, and you discover the true impact of those Trafalgar Square celebrations. 'I remember being there at 6.30 that morning,' he says. 'There was obviously nobody around, except a few men putting some scaffolding up. And I did worry, "What if no one turns up here today?" But they did turn up, and it was an awesome sight. I remember thinking, "It's incredible how victory in international sport can inspire the nation." From that moment our every move at the ECB has been to inspire the nation. That is our vision. I thought that day was a really good thing. It showed that we'd made a lot of progress.'

Indeed they had made a lot of progress. That 2005 Ashes victory had been a long time in its planning, and its coming. It was actually the sixth Test series England had won in succession.

They had won thirteen and lost only five of the twenty-two series since Fletcher took over in 1999. To compare: in the previous twenty-two series before Fletcher arrived, they had won just six. That is some turnaround. To think that in the Schofield Report of 2007, commissioned after the 5–0 humbling at the hands of a great, bent-on-revenge Australia side, it was said there had been 'steady progress' in this period. It was just a little more than that, let me tell you.

4

Forward Press

If one Test can be pinpointed as the turning point under Fletcher, then it is surely the Lord's Test of 2000 against a West Indies side that still contained the legendary pace duo of Curtly Ambrose and Courtney Walsh. Having beaten Zimbabwe 1–0 (a draw against them at Trent Bridge betrayed the uncertainty still evident in England's cricket), England had lost the first Test at Edgbaston by an innings and 93 runs.

By the start of day three of the next Test at Lord's, having dismissed the West Indies for just 54 in their second innings the previous evening, they were chasing 188 to win on an increasingly uneven pitch. No matter that Andrew Caddick, Darren Gough and Dominic Cork had done to a decent West Indian batting line-up – including Brian Lara, Shivnarine Chanderpaul and Jimmy Adams – what West Indian attacks had been doing to England's batsmen for years: that is, roughed them up with pace and steep bounce. It would mean nothing were these runs not knocked off.

Somehow, amid agonizing tension and drama, England just

scraped home by two wickets, with that wonderful competitor Cork hitting the winning runs. The sight of the last man, the debutant Hoggard, nervously sitting just inside from the dressing-room balcony, waiting with helmet on and chinstrap in mouth, was a snapshot of the nation's cricket team at the time. It was unsure of its quality and its ability.

This was the victory that sent belief coursing through the team's veins, as well as confirming that Vaughan, with a calm second-innings 41, was a batsman of rare character. Thereafter the series result was almost a formality. The Wisden Trophy was England's after being in the West Indies' possession for twenty-seven long and painful years (many England batsmen of those times still bear the scars). A squad containing the experience and class of players like Hussain, Atherton, Stewart, Thorpe, Gough and Caddick should have been able to compete healthily on the world stage. But the complexity, sometimes selfishness, of some of these characters had been holding England back.

To take a small example from this Lord's Test. Neither Gough nor Caddick had before taken a five-wicket haul at Lord's. Neither, therefore, had his name on the famed honours board. In the first innings Gough came mighty close with 4-72. Then in the second innings Caddick at last achieved his goal with stunning figures of 13-8-16-5, offering easy evidence of the discrepancy between his bowling average in the first innings of Tests (37.06) and the second (20.81). The differential is too large to ignore; there was undoubtedly something within his mental make-up that predisposed him to react to situations rather than go out and create them himself. As Atherton observed later, he was definitely 'more sheep than shepherd'.

Anyway, Caddick entered the Lord's dressing room in un-surprisingly high spirits. 'I'm on the honours board!' he exclaimed joyfully right in front of Gough, who never did make it on to that hallowed timber. It was a miracle there wasn't a bust-up there and then. But Gough just about managed to keep his cool with his gauche New Zealand-born colleague. Watching from the corner of his eye was the all-seeing Fletcher. He recognized the playing talents of this unlikely pair – Gough short, skiddy and bustling, Caddick tall, loping and bouncy – but also the need to harness some sort of professional relationship between them. They were never going to be close mates, the heart-on-the-sleeve extroverted Gough and the introverted, insecure Caddick, but they could be as close to a world-class opening pair of bowlers as England had had for some time.

Later in the day Fletcher took Caddick out on to the balcony and advised him, among other things, on the follies of insensitivity. It was one of Fletcher's sternest lectures. Caddick had mocked Gough during the Zimbabwe Test earlier in the season when again Gough had finished with four wickets.

To me that was typical Caddick: he just speaks before he thinks. In word and deed he always seemed to lack maturity as a cricketer. His sledging was simply inane most of the time. Those who went on the 1997/98 tour of the West Indies still tell the tale of Caddick professing to know more about seam movement than both Ambrose and Walsh. Caddick, though, listened to Fletcher and later apologized to Gough. From there their partnership flourished.

'I often sit back and wonder what might have been if we had lost that Test,' says Fletcher. Indeed. Ironically the captain Hussain wasn't actually playing at Lord's, having broken his thumb in Birmingham, with Stewart deputizing. But had they lost that match England would surely have lost the series and then Hussain would have lost three out of his first four series in charge. He couldn't score a run that summer anyway, finishing with a pair at the Oval, and even in victory told Gough that he was considering quitting. He would surely have gone, with Vaughan obviously not ready to take over as he was to be in 2003, central contracts might easily have been rubbished, and Fletcher might not have been signing the two-year extension to his contract that he did sign, in October 2000.

Thankfully, none of that happened. And Fletcher could take England to the sub-continent that winter for their first tour there since 1992/93, and truly show his worth.

Whatever the reasons for England's prolonged absence from Asia, unequivocal success was certainly not among them. Since 1980 England had played twenty-three Tests in India, Pakistan and Sri Lanka, and won just four of them. They played spin as if it were spoken in a different dialect.

Fletcher was to change all that. He had been a good player of spin himself, as many Zimbabweans seem to be. Andy Flower might come to be regarded as one of the best to grace the game in that respect. Another Zimbabwean, Dave Houghton, was an excellent player of the twirlies too.

If Fletcher is famous for one particular piece of coaching advice then it is surely his urging of his batsmen to use the 'forward press'. Apologies for becoming technical here, but I do feel it is an important part of the story.

Fletcher especially advocated this trigger movement against spinners, but liked it to be used at all times if possible. It is basically a small step forward – not a lunge, because it is important that the head is kept behind the front leg – to ready the batsman before the ball is bowled.

This is how Fletcher used to explain its use to his charges. 'This is the deal, guys,' he would say. 'You have a million-pound job, but the only snag is that you can only get to work each day by bus. And there is only one bus. It arrives punctually every day at eight o'clock. If you are late for work, you lose your job. So you have a decision to make: do you get to the bus stop early, on time, or late?'

The answer, of course, is that you want to get there early – the 'there' in this case being the pitch of the ball. Ideally you would want to arrive there bang on time, but then you would run the risk of getting there late.

Trigger movements are a very modern phenomenon. Or at least the attention paid to them certainly is. In the old days batsmen were taught to stand still before the ball was bowled. And there are some players who still do that. But the truth is, however unpalatable it may be for the old-timers, that was advice dispensed in an age when all play was conducted at a slower pace. It is a dangerous policy having to make a decision so early as to where the ball will pitch when you have no idea about the degree to which the ball might swing or seam. It is much better to make small initial movements (ensuring you are momentarily still at the point of delivery, of course: a moving head means that the camera that is your eyes takes fuzzy pictures) and then another smaller movement.

That is at the heart of Fletcher's advocacy of the forward press. On turning pitches against wily spinners many wickets are often taken at the close-catching positions of silly point and short leg. If you do not move before the ball is bowled, you are taking a big stride towards the ball and therefore creating considerable momentum towards it. It is often hard in such circumstances to stop the ball deflecting to those close fielders. Fletcher's 'forward press' makes it much easier to kill the ball stone-dead in defence. How I wish I could have 'pressed' against the spinners (I think I naturally did so against the seamers). Fletcher tried to get me to do it, but I was too long in the tooth.

In the wet early summer of 2011 during yet another rain delay at one of the Tests against Sri Lanka, Sky Sports showed a re-run of the 1998 Sri Lanka Test at the Oval, my second and last Test. There I was, for my very last act in international cricket, lunging forward without a 'press' to Muttiah Muralitharan, caught at silly point off the glove. QED.

The 'forward press' also makes the sweep shot much easier. And Fletcher was hugely keen on the sweep, and indeed the sweep/slog. He was adamant that, especially on sub-continental pitches, they were the safest shots to play. Again the old-timers might advise to advance down the pitch and hit the ball straight, which is clearly sound counsel if you can get to the pitch of the ball and negate any spin. But what if you don't quite get to the pitch, and the ball is spinning sharply? By still trying to hit down the ground with a straight bat, you are actually playing across the line of the ball. By sweeping you can smother that spin and you don't need to know which way the ball is turning.

Fletcher worked out that it is better to crouch in your stance against spinners (as you naturally do in the 'forward press'). Again this went against traditional theory. Young spin bowlers are told to flight the ball above the batsman's eye-line, but Fletcher reckons it is best for the batsman to be underneath that line of the ball. He thinks it is easier to pick up its length from there, with its reference points simpler to spot.

Euclid would have been proud of Fletcher. Just like the Greek mathematician who was known as the 'father of geometry', Fletcher loves his angles. He was constantly reminding his players of the sort of alignment required to 'hit the ball back where it comes from', as the old adage goes. But that adage could be nebulous in its meaning. Fletcher made sure he was always much more specific in his advice. For example, for a left-arm seamer bowling over the wicket, the right-hander was told to try to hit the leg-stump at the far end. Not the stumps, but specifically the leg-stump. Or for the South African Makhaya Ntini, who bowls from very wide on the crease, to try to drill the ball straight back at his body.

With spinners, especially those who turn the ball prodigiously, it is more difficult. The old advice was always 'play with the spin'. Say for a right-handed batsman facing a sharp-turning off-break, that would usually mean his going across his stumps to play to leg. Or for a left-hander facing the same bowler from over the wicket to close himself off and play everything through the off-side. Well, Fletcher revealed this to be tosh. 'Try and play a straight ball with a straight bat' were always his words. So for the right-hander to the off-spinner, it would be best to stay leg-side of the ball and, if the length was right, to play through the off-side with a straight bat, even if a dozy commentator might say 'He's playing against the spin there!'

It's easier said than done, however. Marcus Trescothick had all sorts of problems understanding it, so much so that Fletcher playfully went out and bought a protractor to slip under his bedroom door on tour in Sri Lanka.

I could rarely work it out either. I recall one match in particular when I incurred Fletcher's wrath. It was at Sophia Gardens, Cardiff, in 1999, the second and last of Fletcher's summers at Glamorgan, and Durham were the visitors. In their ranks they had Simon Brown, the once-capped England left-arm swing bowler and a fine county practitioner. Bowling from the River Taff End he created such a mess in his follow-through that a huge crater appeared on a length. Consequently the ball spun from that end more than I'd ever experienced in my entire career at that ground. And off-spinner Nicky Phillips had the match of his life, taking twelve wickets.

Fletcher talked to us about how to counter this, as we chased 247 to win in the last innings, how we should stay on leg-stump to the off-spinner. I didn't get it. I felt as if I was exposing my stumps; just like when I couldn't sweep/slog, which, if played properly (think of the late Hansie Cronje hitting Warne over mid-wicket), is executed with the front leg thrown out of the way so that the arms can be freed. I got bowled around my legs trying to sweep Phillips with my body way outside off-stump. It would be wrong to say that Fletcher was fuming. Outwardly anyway. Because that was not how he operated. He merely gave me a look that told me everything I needed to know, and probably knew already.

Fletcher applied his geometry to bowlers too. Ashley Giles achieved notoriety for bowling his left-arm spinners over the wicket to right-handers. 'I still get remembered for that as much as anything else,' laments Giles now, 'even though I've gone back and counted my wickets, and it's about half and half bowling over and around the wicket to right-handers!' It was Fletcher's idea. He quite rightly reasoned that there was no difference between Giles bowling over the wicket to right-handers and any right-arm off-spinner bowling over the wicket to a left-handed batsman. The angle was exactly the same, with turn created naturally by that angle. And Fletcher had realized that Giles's bowling action involved significant crossing of his right leg across his body. If he bowled around the wicket, he would need to turn the ball an awful long way just to counteract the angle caused by his action.

So the trip to Pakistan and Sri Lanka in the winter of 2000/01 was Fletcher's chance to put all these methods and theories into practice. This was new stuff to the England players, and, while Fletcher was making it quite plain that he thought this to be the best method, he wasn't forcing it on anyone. Talk of the 'forward press', though, and two names immediately spring to mind: Trescothick and Vaughan.

Vaughan was undoubtedly the quickest of the England players to adapt to it. 'He didn't speak to me about it for a year or so,' says Vaughan, which is unsurprising since his debut had come in South Africa in the winter of 1999/2000 and before their Asian adventure England had not been faced with too much spin thereafter, 'but I think he felt I was a quick learner so he was never afraid of giving me new ideas. My thought when playing the forward press was that you were basically playing a forward defensive before the ball got there. That was Fletch's theory so that you had so much more time to decide what attacking shot to play.'

Trescothick had made his international debut the previous summer, and, as already mentioned, was very much a Fletcher pick. He hung on Fletcher's word and was very soon earning himself the nickname 'Fletcher's Son'. 'The forward press changed my game really,' he says now. 'I started learning it in Pakistan, came home and did loads of work on it over Christmas, and then went back to Sri Lanka and it clicked. I got a hundred in a warm-up match [against Sri Lanka Colts], and then my first Test hundred in the first Test at Galle.'

He had a different way of thinking about it from Vaughan. Trescothick would fake as if going down the pitch to the spinner. 'I found it really hard to get used to,' he admits. 'I got stuck at first, so I just practised. Learning the timing was key for me. When am I going to "press"?' You can 'press' too early ('fall asleep at the bus stop' as Fletcher says, going back to his original analogy).

Alastair Cook would never be termed a Fletcher acolyte – he was very friendly with Flintoff and Harmison, playing darts with them regularly on tour – but he knew the importance of the 'forward press' (as well as moving his hands lower on the bat handle, which, as Fletcher suggested, gave him more control against the spinners, and, as I mentioned, was a feature of Andy Flower's batting style too) and worked hard on its implement-ation into his game. It took him eight months, but he cracked it and still uses it now. It is pretty useful these days where the DRS is concerned, because spinners receive so many more favourable lbw decisions and so you must try and play them with your bat rather than your pad, and that is so much easier having 'pressed' first. Not that England 'pressed' at all well against Pakistan in the United Arab Emirates in early 2012 when they were white-washed by Pakistan 3–0.

Andrew Strauss, who was not to make his Test debut until 2004, did not take to Fletcher's methods of playing spin immedi-ately. He preferred to play as he'd always done. Then he embarrassingly padded up to Warne at Edgbaston in 2005 and was bowled. Having turned a huge amount out of the rough outside Strauss's off-stump, it was heralded as a ball to match Warne's first in Ashes cricket, the one that bamboozled Mike Gatting at Old Trafford in 1993, but in truth Strauss, having gone way across his stumps, had played it poorly. He went to Fletcher afterwards and admitted that he needed to change his method against spin. Hours of work on the Merlyn machine followed.

Of course, there were others who couldn't pick it up at all. Flintoff was one. Asked by reporters after scoring a hundred in a warm-up match in India in 2008 whether he had been confused by the 'forward press', he answered with another question, 'What did you think?', and laughed uproariously. But then Flintoff never was a technical cricketer, even if Flower did admit surprise to me about some degrees of subtlety in his batting when he first worked with him.

Wicketkeeper Geraint Jones, who controversially replaced Chris Read at the end of the 2004 West Indies tour, is an interesting case. 'I tried it but it never really clicked for me,' Jones says. 'I could understand the theory behind it, and I tried hard because I'd seen Tres and Vaughany play so well using it, but I struggled to do it properly. I think I probably do it naturally now, but with not as big a "press" as Fletch wanted.'

There were some players who knew what Fletcher wanted and would try everything to impress him. I remember interviewing Kent's Rob Key once, and he seemed rather keen to keep mentioning that he was using the 'forward press'. Unsurprisingly he was out of the England side at the time. Afterwards another Kent player told me he thought the interview 'embarrassing' in the way Key gave a fawning message to Fletcher. It is said that Ian Bell only employed the 'press' to satisfy Fletcher. I've never been able to confirm that, but what I will say is that Bell uses it today to spinners, and it worked pretty damned well. Until he was bamboozled by Saeed Ajmal's 'doosra' in the UAE in 2012.

It is, though, easier as a coach to destroy a player than improve him. Fletcher would never dive in and advocate radical changes to a player's technique immediately. He would always watch and observe, bide his time before making judgements and considering alterations. When he arrived in 1997 at Glamorgan he barely said a word for two weeks, standing at the back of the nets, thoroughly inscrutable. It was as if the Sphinx herself was sitting there. Skipper Matthew Maynard said to me, 'I think we've signed a mute!' But we hadn't. Only the strongest and best coaches behave in that manner. Lesser coaches feel the need to justify their position immediately.

Fletcher improved England dramatically that winter in Asia. It was not merely the playing of spin and Giles's emergence as a spinner/batsman/reliable fielder just as Fletcher wanted, but also the clever plans among the seam bowlers, with the instant abandonment of English-type plans on English pitches in favour of the modern Asian way in the use of reverse swing and cutters. Gough and Craig White were vital in that respect.

England had not won a Test in Pakistan since their very first Test in the country in 1961, yet they won the third Test at Karachi, where Pakistan had never lost any Test before, to take the series 1–0. It may have been pitch black when England triumphed, but England had shown the sort of bottle too often absent in such tense run chases in years gone by.

Crucially England had then to prove it was no fluke. They did that by winning 2–1 in Sri Lanka in a spectacularly ill-tempered but highly significant series. Not least among the positives (of which Thorpe's mastery of Muralitharan was pivotal) to come from it was the return to form of Hussain with a courageous century in Kandy. Since taking the captaincy he had made just one century, 146 not out against South Africa in Durban, and since returning from that tour up until the start of the Kandy Test he had averaged just 12.53 in eighteen innings. Throughout this time he had captained the side astutely, but even the best captains have to justify their position in the side some time, so Hussain was near to despair with his batting. He could not sleep in Sri Lanka. Team-mates recall seeing him wandering the hotel corridors at all hours of the night. Then, after more personal failure and an innings loss for the team at Galle, he went to Atherton and admitted that he was close to resignation. He wanted to know what the mood was among the players about his continuing as leader. Atherton reassured him that the team was behind him, and also reminded him of the England Young Cricketers tour they had undertaken together to Sri Lanka in 1987 and of the 170 Hussain had scored at the Asgiriya Stadium, Kandy, scene of the next Test.

It worked. Hussain made a horrible-looking and indeed downright fortunate 109 (escaping with one 'catch' to silly point), but he was back. Upon reaching the milestone Hussain 'went berserk', as he later wrote. 'I ran towards the pavilion, towards my boys,' he said. 'The hundred wasn't for me, it was for them. For ten months they had carried me with their performances. They had made me look like this great captain with the results they were earning for England and they had not said a bad thing against me or questioned my place at any time.'

Not only were England transformed as a Test team, having won four series on the trot, but so was Hussain. Selfish? Selfless, more like. A remarkable transmogrification.

But that did not mean, of course, that England could conquer the world. Between 1987 and 2005 there was always a rather large and weighty albatross on their shoulder, a bird going by the name of Australia. They arrived in 2001 and promptly thrashed England 4–1. It was a summer in which the toughness of English cricket was questioned. Australia's captain Steve Waugh pulled a calf muscle badly in the third Test at Trent Bridge, yet still managed to score a century on one leg in the final Test at the Oval.

In contrast, England's players missed Tests as a truant child does classes. Hussain was absent for two, Thorpe for four, Vaughan for the whole series and Giles for four. I too missed much of the county season that year, Caddick having broken my hand at Taunton. I'd already been out for a month with that injury when I chanced upon Fletcher in the gym at Sophia Gardens. 'How long have you been out for?' he asked. I told him, and he did not respond. He did not need to. He shook his head solemnly and walked off. He may as well have just said it: 'You English are soft cocks.' And, though he will not like Marina reading such things, that is the sort of language he sometimes uses in the dressing room, just like the word for his favourite characteristic in a cricketer: 'dogfuck'.

Of course, injuries can happen, but different people deal with them in different ways. Just after Fletcher arrived at Glamorgan he was hit on the finger while giving slip-catching practice (he always wore a batting glove on his bottom [left] hand but nothing on his top hand), and blood was pouring from it. He just carried on with the practice. We pleaded with him to get it seen to. He refused.

Fletcher was always keen on fitness, but with England he felt he rarely had the time required to supervise or instigate it. As captain of Zimbabwe he had led from the front in that regard. Macky Dudhia, a seam bowler of Indian descent who played under Fletcher in the early eighties and eventually went into cricket administration when spending time as the Bangladesh Cricket Board's chief executive, tells a wonderful story of Fletcher's maniacal attitude. 'I recall an arduous fitness session at Alexandra Sports Club nets where we had been divided into groups to undertake certain fitness training drills in rotation,' says Dudhia, who was manager of the black team Bionics in Harare whom I appeared for in the early nineties, first along with Glamorgan team-mate Adrian Dale, then with Surrey and Durham off-spinner James Boiling. 'The group I was in were not pushing themselves hard enough and as a consequence, at the end of the fitness session, we were told by Duncan that we would need to do fifteen minutes extra. We all groaned, muttered and sulked. For me who had very little air left in the lungs this was going to be very difficult indeed! As we all, most grudgingly, lined up to do these shuttle runs, Duncan, to our astonishment, joined us in the "punishment" and did the shuttle runs for the full time. To me, that spoke volumes of the man and his leadership qualities.'

With England, though, Fletcher often had to leave players to their own devices, especially between tours. And this invariably led to trouble where, say, Harmison was concerned. Sometimes he would turn up to a tour barely having bowled a ball, and certainly not having acquainted himself too regularly with his local gym. It was little coincidence that Harmison's apogee in 2004, when he became the number one ranked bowler in the world (taking sixty-seven Test wickets in thirteen Tests that year, including the remarkable 7-12 in the first Test of the West Indies tour in Jamaica), came after spending considerable time doing fitness work with the footballers at Newcastle United's training ground early that year.

Harmison was also not awarded a central contract at the beginning of that winter in 2003, and had not then impressed in Bangladesh in the first tour of three (Sri Lanka followed before the Caribbean), whence he had returned home early with a back injury. That Bangladesh trip was another important staging post in Fletcher's regime, a chance at long last to implement, in conjunction with his trusted physiologist Nigel Stockill, the sort of fitness standards he had demanded when captain of Zimbabwe.

It had not been easy under Hussain, whose attitude to fitness was not exactly enthusiastic. He almost delighted at being at the back when there was any kind of team run, even if just during a warm-up. This irked Fletcher a little, who wanted his captain to set an example (as he had advised Hussain upon first meeting him when talking of his body language). But in fairness Hussain's response was that he had been doing that for so long that to change then would have looked rather too manufactured. Ironically Hussain spends more time in the gym now as a commentator than he did when he played. He looks a lot trimmer.

Hussain had been precisely the right captain at the time, but in his successor, Vaughan, Fletcher found someone who could advance the team in other areas. During the summer of 2003 Vaughan had been to the British Grand Prix at Silverstone and had marvelled at the smartness of the Ferrari team. Just like Lord MacLaurin previously, Vaughan vowed to smarten up England again. It was not that they had returned to the sort of scruffiness MacLaurin had encountered, because Fletcher was always pretty strict on dress code. He had certainly transformed us at Glamorgan in that respect. It was just that some of the older sweats had become a little lax in their application of Fletcher's principles. So between them Vaughan and Fletcher vowed to sharpen up the England team in every respect in Bangladesh.

They trained their socks off, morning and night when they were playing, and morning, noon and night when they were not. It was an exhausting regime, but it was certainly worth it. In 2004 England did not lose a Test, drawing just two and winning the other eleven, with their eight on the bounce – the summer's seven plus the first in South Africa that winter – being a record. Their 3–0 win in the West Indies was the first series victory there since 1967/68.

It was a shame England were not that fit when they went to Australia in 2002/03. They were actually in worse shape than for that home series in 2001. They travelled with concerns over Flintoff, Gough and Simon Jones, and soon lost Jones after his horrific knee injury in the first Test at Brisbane. Giles's tour was over after one Test when he broke his wrist in the nets, John Crawley missed two Tests with a hip injury, Stewart missed one as did Caddick and Harmison. Then some replacements arrived, and they got injured too. Chris Silverwood, Craig White, Alex Tudor and Jeremy Snape were all called up for some part of the tour including the one-dayers, and all were injured.

You felt for Dean Conway. He copped some stick, some of which still rankles today. But for too long he had been asked to do too much, even if he had by now split his physiotherapist's role with Kirk Russell, who was doing the Tests while Conway did the one-dayers. He needed help. And if any good was to come out of the winter of 2002/03, it was that early in it Peter Gregory was appointed as the ECB's full-time medical officer. Now, since the appointment of science and medicine manager Simon Timson in May 2006 and Nick Pierce's replacing of Gregory later that year, England can probably boast the best cricketing medical set-up in the world.

The other significant positive to come from that winter was the fact that Vaughan was clearly a world-class batsman. Three centuries and 633 runs at 63.30 said so very loudly. But even he had his own injury worries with his knee. And he could not have known that his ascension to the captaincy would come so soon. Hussain resigned the one-day captaincy after the 2003 World Cup, and then lasted only three Tests that summer before resigning after the first Test against South Africa at Edgbaston.

In truth it was little surprise when you look back now. Hussain admitted that once Vaughan became one-day captain the situation became 'strange'. Crucially his relationship with Fletcher changed. Fletcher realized that too. Whenever he spoke to Hussain, Fletcher found himself mentioning Vaughan and what had happened with the one-day side. He felt conscious of being seen to be talking to Vaughan in Hussain's presence, so actually made a conscious decision not to do so. That's how bad things became. It was no longer just the Fletcher and Hussain show. Hussain didn't like that. I remember him saying, jokingly of course, to Fletcher, who was a consultant to the home team during the England tour of South Africa in 2009/10, 'What you doing going for dinner with Jamo? I thought I was your best mate!' He clearly felt like that about Vaughan.

So, all in a rush at Edgbaston, Hussain resigned. After four years in the job they said he was the best England captain since Mike Brearley. Simon Barnes of *The Times* went further.

'Nasser Hussain is the most significant cricketer to have played for England since the war and perhaps the finest captain to have held the office,' he wrote. 'Hussain took on an England side that was hopeless. He fought not cricketing opponents but the enemy within – the sneaking, insidious culture of defeatism, the weasel in the heart of the English pro.'

When he finished as captain, Hussain wrote to Fletcher, saying, 'Thanks for making me look a better captain than I was.' That is a little too self-deprecating. Yes, Fletcher's remarkable technical know-how dovetailed perfectly with his passion ('Hussain generated heat, Fletcher light' wrote Scyld Berry), but as Barnes writes so eloquently, Hussain fought so many important battles that were not just on the cricket field. He fought the authorities and helped alter the way of thinking in English cricket. He toughened it up.

His acme as captain was definitely the 2000/01 tours in Asia, with the series wins over Pakistan and Sri Lanka. If one session lingers longest in the memory it was when Sri Lanka were dismissed in the third Test in Colombo in only 28.1 overs. Hussain had pulled his hip flexor muscle early in the match and could barely walk by the end of it, but his unrelenting passion and desire drove his side home in blistering heat.

After a productive start with the bat in his first away series in South Africa, Hussain had lost his way with his own game. He eventually realized that more attention was required personally, and so came to string together an impressive list of tone-setting innings in series. In his last five series as skipper before the three Tests against Zimbabwe and South Africa in 2003, he scored at least a half-century in his first innings of every series. The gutsy 106 at Christchurch in March 2002 was undoubtedly a highlight, but all were incontrovertible evidence of a captain leading from the front.

Hussain acted with hugely impressive dignity and sensitivity when confronted with the tragic death of Ben Hollioake during that tour of New Zealand – Fletcher was almost in tears when recounting the details of that episode to me for his auto-biography – and, at the other end of his character traits, won plaudits for the moral victories he secured during the tour of India in late 2001. There he demonstrated the more inventive side of his captaincy. England, with a weakened team, lost the series 1–0, but they frustrated the Indian batsmen, especially the great Sachin Tendulkar, who became so flummoxed by Giles's over-the-wicket leg-stump line in the third Test in Bangalore that he was stumped for the first time in his Test career. It attracted many critics, but as Hussain says, 'I can't believe people expected me to just stand back and admire him [Tendulkar]. No, mate, you're the best player in the world and you're going to have to work for your runs.'

Hussain said it was 'the peak of my captaincy'. And if the nadir had been that day at the Oval in 1999 with which we began, he is also easily recalled as the captain who inserted Australia at Brisbane in 2002. As Australia racked up 492 he is easily pilloried, but he was hardly alone in thinking it best to bowl first. Fletcher agreed, as did many senior players. And England had sought Marsh's advice on all the Australian pitches beforehand. Of Brisbane he'd written 'if there is to be any lateral movement off the seam it will be on day one'. Waugh later admitted he would have inserted England. What is also forgotten is that Simon Jones suffered that nasty injury of his on the first day, leaving Hussain a bowler short.

Of course, Hussain was not quite finished as a player in 2003. He would play on, and play some significant innings as the senior batsman, until the summer of 2004 when he called time after making a match-winning century against New Zealand at Lord's. It might have only been the first Test of the summer, but Hussain's timing was impeccable.

Farewells in professional sport are rarely fairy tales – mine came at a dank Derby after being lbw to probably my least favourite opponent, Cork, for not very many – but Hussain's was a joyous exception. Vaughan had twisted a knee before the match and in his stead had arrived a chap named Strauss, who'd made 112 and 83 (run out by Hussain in the second innings!). Selection might have been mighty difficult for the next Test, so Hussain scored his runs and left in the grandest of manners.

5

Black Armbands

The country of Zimbabwe might have provided the England cricket team with two perspicacious coaches, but it has also provided it with untold anguish and heartache. The Cullinan Hotel on Cape Town's Waterfront describes itself as 'stylishly grand and perfectly majestic', and, having visited it myself, that is no idle boast from one of South Africa's better hotels. But for a weekend in February 2003, it became nothing less than a hell-hole for England's cricketers.

It was here that meeting after meeting was held to discuss whether England should travel from Cape Town, where the opening ceremony of the World Cup was being held, to Harare to play Zimbabwe in their opening match of the tournament. Politics engulfed sport to the extent that sport was forgotten, a mood summed up neatly, if rather crudely, by Michael Vaughan at the time. 'I'm sick of fucking meetings,' he said in a rare break from them. 'I've been in there so long I've forgotten what a cricket bat looks like.'

Zimbabwe had altered horrifically from the country I had

rushed eagerly back to during my cricketing winters in the early nineties. Robert Mugabe had begun his awful land redistribution policies in 2000, and as a result the country had begun to fall into the sharpest of declines. The economy collapsed and riots ensued. It was a social and political disaster – a word never to be used lightly, but one wholly applicable here. In a sickeningly short space of time, Africa's 'bread basket' had become a basket case.

The 2003 World Cup had been awarded to South Africa as long before as 1993, and they in turn had decided to allocate some of the ties to Zimbabwe and Kenya. That decision had been taken before Mugabe began those land policies. But given this sudden turn of events, there was considerable apprehension about the staging of matches – in Kenya as well, where there had been terrorist attacks. However, a delegation from the ICC had visited both countries and, while recognizing some deep concerns over security, deemed them safe enough to host their scheduled World Cup matches.

New Zealand declared their hand early and asked for their match to be moved from Kenya. That request was refused, so they declined to play, and forfeited the four points on offer. England too asked the ICC to move their match from Zimbabwe, citing worries over the security of all involved, spectators included. And they too forfeited four points when they eventually refused to play in Harare. But what a horrible, snaking road it was to reach that decision.

A clearly vexed Nasser Hussain devoted the first chapter of his autobiography to the issue, and in talking now to some of the other chief movers in the episode, like Tim Lamb and David Morgan, it is easy to detect their angst with a situation which could, and should, so easily have been resolved by politicians rather than by cricket administrators and, even more ridiculously, by cricketers themselves. Had it occurred five years later the government would simply have forbidden the England cricket team from going to Zimbabwe, as it did when banning Zimbabwe's tour of England in 2009, thus preventing their participation in the ICC World Twenty20 here in the same year. But in 2003 the government merely advised England not to play in Zimbabwe, even though Zimbabwe had been suspended from the Commonwealth in March 2002. They contended that they couldn't insist on England's withdrawal.

The previous December the Cabinet minister Clare Short had been outspoken in her opposition to England visiting Zimbabwe. 'I think it is deplorable and shocking,' she said. 'I think they should not go. It is like pretending everything is OK in Zimbabwe and it is not.' Pressure was added when it was made clear that the Prime Minister, Tony Blair, and the Foreign Secretary, Jack Straw, were against the fixture. Downing Street called on England's cricketers to 'reflect' on the 'humanitarian and political crisis' inside Zimbabwe. 'Seven million people are already in need of food assistance,' a Number 10 spokesman said. 'We ask them to reflect on this but ultimately it is a decision that can only be taken by the ICC and ECB. It is not for Government to tell the cricketing authorities what to do.'

What poppycock! This was Secretary of State for Culture, Media and Sport Andy Burnham in 2008 when announcing that Zimbabwe's tour should be cancelled: 'It was quite unfair to leave individual players in the position of having to make a moral judgement in the context of an awkward and un-comfortable position. The right thing to do was to provide clarity. We made the decision after giving it the longest possible time for the situation to change in Zimbabwe. The Zimbabwean Government has ceased to observe the principle of the rule of law: it has terrorized its own citizens, including the ruthless and violent suppression of legitimate political opposition. Accordingly, the UK Government has responded with a measured approach which seeks to isolate Zimbabwe inter-nationally and bring pressure to bear on supranational institutions such as the United Nations and European Union to take yet firmer action against the despotic regime, whilst ensuring that its humanitarian life-saving mission to Zimbabwean citizens continues. The UK Government considers it would be contrary to this general approach for the English cricket team to participate in bilateral fixtures with Zimbabwe. The close ties of the Zimbabwe cricket team to the Mugabe regime have also had a bearing on our decision.'

Sadly there was no such *force majeure* in 2003. And so the saga began. 'It was one of those intractable issues,' sighs the then ECB chief executive Lamb now, as we sit in a restaurant close to the London office of the Sport and Recreation Alliance, where he has been chief executive since 2005. 'We didn't get any help from the government, and there were so many dynamics and conflicting influences that contributed to make this an absolute rock-and-hard-place issue.'

England had been in Australia before the World Cup, and there in their penultimate one-day international of the tour, in Sydney, the whole squad received letters and pamphlets from a protest group called the 'Organized Resistance', outlining the situation in Zimbabwe. There were no death threats, but there was some strong propaganda, warning especially of serious unrest should the team travel to and play in Zimbabwe.

The squad travelled straight from Australia to South Africa – a source of some irritation to the players who had hoped to pop home first, particularly as the best-of-three finals of the VB one-day series against Australia had not lasted three matches. Some, like Andrew Flintoff and Ashley Giles, had been at home recovering from injuries before the World Cup. They had seen and heard that the public mood was very much against going to Zimbabwe, and they had also seen a Channel 4 documentary about some of the terrible happenings in the country. They had made up their minds that they were not going to Zimbabwe, come what may.

This was not a topic that could be dismissed easily, especially as it was likely that, if England didn't go to Harare, they would lose vital qualifying points. By not going many players would be waving goodbye to their last tilt at a World Cup. Upon arriving in South Africa, the first of the many interminable meetings took place, and at it Hussain said to his players, 'Some of you are going to have to take some serious growing-up pills and take this issue very seriously indeed. It's looking as though everyone is going to leave us to make some pretty big decisions here.'

Duncan Fletcher was in an awkward situation. On the surface it seemed ideal for England to have a Zimbabwean coach at this time. But in truth it was not. It was more complicated than it appeared for him, thus the reason why he did not make one public pronouncement on the issue, frustrating many observers in the process. The crucial thing was that, although Fletcher left Zimbabwe in 1984, he was still travelling on a Zimbabwean passport. Once inside Zimbabwe the authorities could have done what they liked with him. They were doing this on a regular basis. Imagine if he had said something the government did not like. Also, many of his wife's family still lived in Zimbabwe. In no way did he want to endanger them.

Privately Fletcher thought the game should go ahead. Although he abhorred the decline in the country he loved (in a way he had seen it coming, though, deciding to leave in 1984 when, after dislocating his shoulder, the local hospital did not have a safety pin for his sling), he thought Zimbabwe to be safe, and he was wary of cricketers making moral judgements. He thought there were many countries that England visited to play cricket you could make a case for not visiting on moral grounds. But there again he felt his view was biased. He had helped announce Zimbabwe itself as some sort of international cricketing force with his own performances at the 1983 World Cup, and he feared boycotting the match could now help destroy Zimbabwean cricket. He hardly wanted that to happen.

Fletcher offered advice to Hussain and the players – 'At no stage did he let me down,' said Hussain later – but suggested that the Professional Cricketers' Association would be of more help. So stepped forward their group chief executive Richard Bevan for a starring role. He enjoyed that. Bevan, who as I write is football's League Managers' Association chief executive, has never been one to shirk the limelight. But he is good at what he does. He took over the PCA in 1996, at a time when it had little influence or power. By the time he left eleven years later he had transformed it commercially, and begun to ask questions of the game's administrators that needed asking. He gave the players a sense of professionalism, and he gave them a proper voice.

Bevan certainly ensured the England players possessed the latter on this issue. And so on Monday, 27 January they issued this statement: 'The England players urgently request the Zimbabwe match on February 13 to be moved to South Africa. As concern has grown over the current political situation in Zimbabwe, the players request an urgent review of the World Cup schedule. Without doubt the (moral and political) issues have been weighing heavily on players' minds. Concerns are increasing daily and it is clear the situation in Zimbabwe is highly volatile. The players are greatly concerned for the welfare of the people of Zimbabwe . . . it is very important that no one comes to any harm because of a cricket match in Harare.'

It fell on deaf ears. This was, though, a period when players and administrators clashed as rarely before. It was not Lamb's finest hour, or long hours as they were, especially when he was waking Fletcher up at 3.30 a.m. (as he did one morning) to talk about the issue. He is a charming man, but his approach was a little too patrician. The 'them and us' attitude that Lord MacLaurin had been shocked to encounter when he went on the Zimbabwe tour of 1996/97 was still very much Lamb's default position. He annoyed the players on this issue with his constant references to the damage that their not playing in Harare could do to the English game as a whole.

Lamb just did not empathize enough with the players, even if his reasons for England playing the match were sound. 'I was very conscious of the consequences of not fulfilling the commitment to play the match in Harare,' Lamb says now, 'unless we had a bloody good reason which was robust and defensible. My consistent view was the same as the ICC's. At a time when British Airways was still flying into Harare, when three hundred-plus companies were still trading with Zimbabwe, when we hadn't broken off diplomatic relations with Zimbabwe, why should cricket suddenly have to be upholding the moral stance of the nation? Of course we abhorred what was happening in Zimbabwe, but is it right for cricket to make value judgements about the morality of political regimes around the world? I would contend not. Just because you carry a cricket bat, does that make you any different from a banker, insurance provider or airline pilot?'

But it was Malcolm Speed, the ICC's chief executive, who irked the England players most. Speed began a chapter of his recently published autobiography *Sticky Wicket* with the words 'Nasser Hussain does not like me'. And he is right. Hussain was enraged by Speed's perfunctory manner when he appeared at a meeting with the England players. 'No respect. No appreciation that England were in a difficult position regarding Zimbabwe,' as Hussain later wrote of him.

It was in this meeting that the England players were made aware of a letter received by Lamb back in England. It was from an organization calling themselves 'The Sons and Daughters of Zimbabwe'. In it they warned 'COME TO ZIMBABWE AND YOU WILL GO BACK TO BRITAIN IN WOODEN COFFINS!' It continued, 'Anyway, we know your Team. Come to Harare and you will die. And how safe are your families back there in the UK?' It finished with the message: 'DON'T COME

TO ZIMBABWE OR YOUR PLAYERS WILL BE LIVING IN FEAR FOR THE REST OF YOUR LIVES.'

It was dated 6 January 2003. The letter was post-marked London, sent to the ECB and received by Lamb on 20 January. He had been concealing it for nearly three weeks. 'What was the point of worrying the players? We didn't want to let it out too early,' explains Lamb, none too convincingly. 'There were one or two sensitive souls with young families, and it didn't seem sensible to share it.'

Now it did, though. Security was the only reason England could give for not going to Zimbabwe. Not that Lamb believed the threat for one minute. 'I never took that threat seriously,' he says. 'Maybe I should have burned it and put it in the bin. Why didn't I just shred that bloody letter, because I knew it was a hoax?'

Into this mess had stepped Morgan, newly appointed as ECB chairman. As a Welshman, Morgan will probably appreciate the analogy that it was like a hospital pass as first touch on debut for an international rugby fly-half. But Morgan managed to avoid the oncoming forwards pretty well. That is because naturally he seeks to avoid confrontation. Diplomacy and conciliation are his constant allies. They were good friends to him here. Without Morgan the consequences of this situation don't bear thinking about.

Call me biased, if you like, as Morgan was, of course, chairman of Glamorgan before he went on to become ECB chairman and then ICC president, but I will refer you to my father on this matter. He is an exceptional judge of character and he reckons that the two best people he has ever met in cricket are Morgan and Geraint Jones, whose first season playing cricket in England was at my own Lydney CC. The club had a habit for a number of years of employing professionals from Australia (or rather putting them up wherever they could and finding them some part-time work) and for a while Jones stayed with my parents. Jones was the only player about whom my father, as president of the club, felt moved to write a letter (to Jones's father) to pay a compliment on his behaviour and attitude.

Morgan took control. 'In the early stages all the meetings were chaired by officials of the PCA – by Richard Bevan with his lawyer – but I decided that I would chair all further meetings,' he says. 'I felt sure that if it was safe and secure for the team they should go. I interviewed players one-to-one on the importance of the match taking place. But I was persuaded by Nasser that I should not insist on one or two of the younger players coming in one-on-one, so I spoke to them as a group of three. I remember Ronnie Irani standing out as somebody who really wanted to go and play. He set a great example. He was a substantial figure in all of this.'

England also had some visitors to their Cullinan Hotel. Secret visitors, smuggled in. The first was a member of Zimbabwe's opposition party, the MDC (Movement for Democratic Change). For a long time afterwards his name was not revealed ('he must remain anonymous for his own safety,' said Hussain). But it has since emerged that it was David Coltart, now Zimbabwe's Minister of Education, Sport, Arts and Culture. He spoke to Fletcher and Hussain about the fact that he was working with two of Zimbabwe's players, Andy Flower and Henry Olonga, on making some sort of protest at the death of democracy in their country and wondered whether England might do the same if they were to play in Zimbabwe. He then led Fletcher and Hussain into another room of the hotel, and standing there were Flower and Olonga. Two England coaches, present and future! What irony. Not that the situation was laced with it then. Rather it was fear that pervaded the room, as Flower and Olonga outlined their plans. 'There go two incredibly brave people,' said Fletcher solemnly to Hussain as the pair left the room.

The idea to make such a stand had been first suggested to Flower by a chap called Nigel Hough, although Coltart's influence should never be underestimated. 'He [Flower] rates Coltart as a human being,' says Alistair Campbell, the former Zimbabwe captain. 'He rates him as one of the bravest okes he knows in fact.' 'Oke' is South African slang for bloke, if you're wondering.

Like Coltart's, Hough's was a name that had remained anonymous for a long time, indeed until Olonga revealed it in his autobiography *Blood, Sweat and Treason*, although he spelt his surname 'Huff', which may or may not have been some kind of cover-up. Flower has been careful never to mention Hough's name in public.

I knew Hough from my time playing cricket in Zimbabwe. He was a decent batsman, who occasionally bowled some leg-spin. I recall him scoring a double-hundred against the touring Durham county side for a Manicaland Select XI in 1992. I also recall him having an eccentric sense of humour. He was always saying something on the field. And for some reason I remember him once saying, 'Come on, boys, let's be alert.' There was a silence as his team-mates looked at him, as if to say 'Come on, you can do better than that'. And then Hough said, 'Yes, Manicaland needs lots of Lerts today.' Bizarre.

Hough is better known for him and his white family being the subjects of Christina Lamb's excellent book *House of Stone*, the true story of their terrible troubles during Mugabe's land redistribution policies and especially of their complicated relationship with their black maid, Aqui.

I'll allow Flower to take up the protest story, as related in a subsequent interview with the *Guardian*:

About a month before the World Cup started in South Africa I met a friend with whom I'd played Zimbabwean cricket. He'd just been thrown off his farm at the dead of night. He had lost this magnificent farm where he'd employed hundreds of people and had set up a school and clinic. He said, 'We'll take a drive and I'll show you what's happened to this once thriving community.' And he took me around and it was very sad to see. He was quite religious and he said, 'I believe you guys have an obligation to bring this to the world's attention.'

On the same day I opened a newspaper – it was the only independent paper at the time and was constantly harried by the Government. On the inside page was an article about an MP who had been arrested and tortured in police custody. It was a tiny article, hardly any space at all. And suddenly I was struck, as if for the first time, by the sheer horror of living in a nation where torture is so widespread it does not even make front page news.

He [Hough] wanted us to boycott the World Cup but I wasn't comfortable with that. We came up with a different plan. It changed my life because it was, I guess, a little scary. But once the principle had been planted in my mind, and I planted it in Henry's mind, there was no other way to go. Without sounding pious we knew it was the right thing to do. We had to do it, regardless of the consequences. I've never been able to go back to Zimbabwe – and neither has Henry. The sacrifice he made was huge.

I'll be honest and say that I was surprised when I heard Flower and Olonga were doing something together. They were not close. Flower, so I reckoned, was not alone among the Zimbabwean team in considering Olonga a little soft. Olonga seemed to succumb rather too easily to niggling injuries. If there was one thing I had learnt during my time in Zimbabwe it was that Flower, like Fletcher, abhorred any sign of softness in a sportsperson.

When Flower first asked to speak to Olonga, the black fast bowler was surprised too. 'I couldn't figure out why this guy who hadn't been prepared to give me the time of day for so long would want to talk to me now,' Olonga wrote.

'I wouldn't say Andy was my best friend, but he was my captain for years and I respected him as a player,' said Olonga later. 'How he knew I had the aptitude to make this protest, I don't know. He needed a black person, and a black person with some influence. I certainly had that: I'd sung a song and people loved it, I was the first black player to play for Zimbabwe, and if I said something it had some weight. Andy is world class, I'm not, but we'd got a combination of sport and music – Posh and Becks, if you like.'

Flower's brother Grant wanted to be part of it too. 'I asked if I could be involved,' Grant admits now, 'but they said they'd rather not. They wanted one white and one black guy and did not want it to be seen as a racist thing. None of the other black guys would have done it. One other white player, Brian Murphy, showed some interest, but no one else really knew about it.'

Indeed they didn't. It was all very secretive. It had to be. And it was not a case of Olonga being persuaded to do something he didn't want to do. He too felt strongly about the mess into which his country had descended. He made up his own mind. 'My motivation was that, two years ago, I had been handed a dossier of human rights abuses that occurred in Zimbabwe, notably the early 1980s Matabeleland massacres,' he said. 'Up to that point, I'd thought Robert Mugabe was a very fair, true, honest president.'

He and Flower thought long and hard about how they could best make a stand before coming up with the idea of a black armband protest at their first World Cup match, against Namibia in Harare on 10 February, accompanied by a statement detailing their feelings. Coltart, a lawyer by trade, helped them draw it up.

An English journalist, Geoff Dean of *The Times*, was involved too. 'Andy took me aside at nets the day before the game,' recalls Dean, 'and asked if I could do him a favour. I said, "Sure. What is it?" He said he couldn't tell me. I just laughed. But he said that if I was willing to do it, I should wait outside the entrance to the Harare Sports Club half an hour before the game was due to start the next day, and there someone whom I would know would meet me. It was all very cloak and dagger!'

The following morning Flower put about fifty pieces of paper into his cricket case. On each was printed the following statement:

Issued 9.30 a.m. February 10, 2003, at the start of Zimbabwe's opening World Cup match against Namibia.

It is a great honour for us to take the field today to play for Zimbabwe in the World Cup. We feel privileged and proud to have been able to represent our country. We are however deeply distressed about what is taking place in Zimbabwe in the midst of the World Cup and do not feel that we can take the field without indicating our feelings in a dignified manner and in keeping with the spirit of cricket.

We cannot in good conscience take to the field and ignore the fact that millions of our compatriots are starving, unemployed and oppressed. We are aware that hundreds of thousands of Zimbabweans may even die in the coming months through a combination of starvation, poverty and Aids. We are aware that many people have been unjustly imprisoned and tortured simply for expressing their opinions about what is happening in the country. We have heard a torrent of racist hate speech directed at minority groups. We are aware that thousands of Zimbabweans are routinely denied their right to freedom of expression. We are aware that people have been murdered, raped, beaten and had their homes destroyed because of their beliefs and that many of those responsible have not been prosecuted. We are also aware that many patriotic Zimbabweans oppose us even playing in the WC because of what is happening.

It is impossible to ignore what is happening in Zimbabwe. Although we are just professional cricketers, we do have a conscience and feelings. We believe that if we remain silent that will be taken as a sign that either we do not care or we condone what is happening in Zimbabwe. We believe that it is important to stand up for what is right.

We have struggled to think of an action that would be appropriate and that would not demean the game we love so much. We have decided that we should act alone without other members of the team being involved because our decision is deeply personal and we did not want to use our senior status to unfairly influence more junior members of the squad. We would like to stress that we greatly respect the ICC and are grateful for all the hard work it has done in bringing the World Cup to Zimbabwe.

In all the circumstances we have decided that we will each wear a black armband for the duration of the World Cup. In doing so we are mourning the death of democracy in our beloved Zimbabwe. In doing so we are making a silent plea to those responsible to stop the abuse of human rights in Zimbabwe. In doing so we pray that our small action may help to restore sanity and dignity to our Nation.

Andrew Flower – Henry Olonga

Once inside the ground, Flower met his father Bill. He was the man Dean would know. Dean had known the Flowers and most of the other Zimbabwean cricketers for some time, having covered their inaugural Test series against India in 1992 and having played some cricket in Zimbabwe on various tours. 'The instruction I was given was to distribute these statements to everyone in the media present that day,' says Dean, who still has a couple of the statements at home as mementos. 'I read it and straight away knew it was going to be dynamite.'

So it was. And that was just within the Zimbabwe Cricket Union. Coach Geoff Marsh, team manager Babu Meman and

CEO Vince Hogg were all shocked, pleading with Flower and Olonga not to go through with their protest. But, as the pair emphasized, it was too late. The world already knew.

Flower has obviously gone on to achieve greater fame, but for Olonga it was his defining moment. 'Did I change the world?' he asked later. 'Probably not. Did I change Zimbabwe? Probably not – but I played my part. And if I hadn't embraced the moment, I could have been a nobody, had a mediocre World Cup, and no one would have remembered. Now I'm remembered as the guy who wore a black armband.'

Not that Olonga was particularly prepared. Flower had always planned to retire from international cricket after this event, and leave Zimbabwe to play in England for Essex (and in Australia, although his stint with South Australia lasted only one of its three intended years). Olonga thought maybe he could still live in Zimbabwe. As the days passed after his protest that looked more and more unlikely. There was a vicious campaign against him in the local press and he was followed by state security agents. A few days before Zimbabwe's last qualifying match against Pakistan in Bulawayo, he knew for certain he couldn't stay. His father had received a message from someone high up in the secret police: 'Tell your son to get out of Zimbabwe now!'

Had Zimbabwe lost to Pakistan in Bulawayo they would have been out of the World Cup and Olonga would not have had a ready-made escape route. As it was, it rained, allowing Zimbabwe to progress to the Super Sixes in South Africa. 'I believe in God, and in a way I believe God sent the rain that day,' said Olonga.

That Pakistan match was on 4 March, so there had been nearly a month since the protest, time enough for Flower's father Bill to confirm that it was time to leave. 'We had been planning a withdrawal for a few years,' he says. 'The signs had been there. Then Andrew visited us one day and explained what he was going to do. One thing I was adamant about was that he should not boycott the World Cup, as Nigel Hough would have liked to have seen. But after the protest, we definitely had our phone tapped. Several times we picked up the phone to dial and we could hear them chattering at their listening posts. We always felt someone was listening in. Then when we went down to Bulawayo to watch the matches down there, we stayed with my sister-in-law and she got a phone message from an anonymous African to say something along the lines of "You are part of the Flower family and you'd better watch your back!" Then when we were watching one of the games, some Africans dressed in sharp suits came and sat either side of me and Jean [his wife]. They knew nothing about cricket and were trying to pick up what we were saying. They were from the CIA [Zimbabwe's version of the Central Intelligence Agency]. We drove back to Harare after that last match against Pakistan and packed up Andy's household with Becky [his wife], and then we all left together.'

Andy Flower still owns that house in Harare. Indeed he went back there after the World Cup had finished, much to the consternation of family and friends. 'What could they do?' he asked me later. 'Kill me?' Well, yes, they could have done.

The last I heard his house was being rented by Chris Harris, the former New Zealand all-rounder, who was out in Zimbabwe coaching the national Under 19 side and playing in the domestic Twenty20 competition. Surprise, surprise, Zimbabwe Cricket (as the ZCU became in 2004) was a little slow in paying the rent for Harris.

Of course, Zimbabwe should have played another match in Harare in their qualifying rounds. That was against England on 13 February. 'We took the decision that the England team should not get on the plane to Zimbabwe,' says Morgan. 'We took it on the basis of duty and care to our employees, the England cricketers and their support staff. The letter had been submitted to the World Cup organizing committee. And they sent it to the security unit. And on the morning of the day of the opening ceremony, Mark Roper-Drimie, our in-house lawyer, came to Tim Lamb and myself with a response from Interpol in Pretoria. The response is something I shall never forget. It said "The Sons and Daughters of Zimbabwe is an organization known to us and any threat that they pose should be taken seriously". Once we had that, we decided that all efforts to persuade the players to go should cease and we instructed them that they wouldn't be going. It was a surprise because we didn't even know it had gone to Interpol and I thought it would be declared as of no significance. It should have been plain sailing from there. But I then ran into Dr Ali Bacher [the tournament director], Malcolm Speed [ICC chief executive], Malcolm Gray [ICC president] and Percy Sonn [president of the United Cricket Board of South Africa]. They took a lot of convincing that we were right to exercise that duty of care.'

The ICC may not have been happy, but England did not go to Zimbabwe. Morgan did, though. 'As the World Cup was approaching its end,' he says, 'I was asked by Justice Ebrahim [ZCU's vice-chairman] if I would go to Zimbabwe to address their board. So I went and explained that the only reasons that we didn't turn up were safety and security. And they were the only reasons. I remember Ozias Bvute [now ZC's managing director], whom I met there for the first time, in the course of that meeting attacking Tim Lamb verbally [even though he wasn't there!]. I was unprepared to let the attack go, and I responded in a way I remain proud about. Tim Lamb is a thoroughly decent man and administrator.'

The problem was that Zimbabwe were due to tour England that summer, and South Africa, who were visiting afterwards, were threatening not to tour because of the no-show in Harare. 'That would have been a financial disaster for the ECB,' says Morgan. 'In world cricket you make your money when you host.

You don't make any money when you go away. So I had the task of making sure Zimbabwe came, because if they wouldn't come, then it was likely that South Africa would stay at home as well. In explaining that safety and security were the only reasons, they [Zimbabwe] agreed to tour. It was often said that there was another side to this, that I agreed that we would make the scheduled tour to Zimbabwe in 2004. But there was no talk about that. That was in the Future Tours Programme [FTP] and everyone knew that, short of a safety or security issue, or government intervention, England would have to fulfil those commitments.'

Yes, even though Zimbabwe did tour England without serious incident in 2003, the issue just would not go away. It had been said that there would be no repeat of the World Cup fiasco, but as the proposed tour in November 2004 approached it began to look, as many masters of malapropism have observed over the years, like déjà vu all over again. The only difference was that it was a tour rather than a one-off match, with its FTP implications as outlined by Morgan above, but all the same questions and issues remained.

The beginnings of this second Zimbabwe crisis for the ECB can be traced to the moment in June 2003 when Des Wilson was elected to the ECB's management board as chairman of the corporate affairs and marketing advisory committee. Wilson had formerly been a director of Shelter and Sport England and, among other things, had campaigned for lead-free petrol, so his appointment was always likely to be both interesting and a little dangerous. Having seen the World Cup farrago from the outside, Wilson offered his assistance to Morgan this time. He was not explicitly asked by Morgan to compile a detailed report on Zimbabwe and whether England should tour there, but was asked to maintain 'an overview of the issue'.

The result was a detailed seventeen-page report entitled 'Reviewing overseas cricket tours – a framework for rational decision-making'. It argued that 'to seek to isolate sport as an activity that stands alone in human affairs, untouched by "politics" or "moral considerations" and unconcerned for the fate of those deprived of human rights, is as unrealistic as it is (self-destructively) self-serving . . .'

There was no specific mention of Zimbabwe in it; that was to come in a second report, in the form of a letter to Morgan, in which it was argued, in Wilson's words, that 'the tour could only strengthen Robert Mugabe's regime by allowing him to claim international respectability; that it would undermine UK foreign policy in the region; that it would be contrary to the wishes of the cricket world and deeply damaging to the game's image in the UK; and that it was morally wrong to play cricket at an oasis within a country suffering such repression and hunger'.

Wilson's framework report, however, was leaked to the press before the ECB management board saw it. He was not particularly popular on the board before that; he was even less so afterwards. And the board did face a problem in that to adopt Wilson's proposals would be to perform a U-turn, after distancing itself from moral considerations during the World Cup deliberations. So they never really discussed it.

There was additional pressure exerted by the ZCU, who emailed every first-class county warning them of the financial implications should England cancel the tour. 'A claim for damages and compensation would run to millions of pounds,' said its chairman Peter Chingoka. And there was concern over the Champions Trophy, which was to be held in England in September 2004, and for which the contract had yet to be signed. The three counties responsible for holding that tournament – Hampshire, Surrey and Warwickshire – were all well represented on the management board. Guess what they wanted? They wanted England to go, of course. Self-interest and loot. They are a potent mix in the shires.

Then there was the position of Foreign Secretary Straw. Some thought he might give an instruction to the ECB not to go. Indeed when he wrote a letter to them in January 2004 Lamb announced that it was 'tantamount to an instruction' to cancel the trip. But it was not really. It said nothing new about Mugabe's regime, and concluded with the claim that the UK was 'taking a leading role' internationally against Zimbabwe, and that 'you may wish to consider whether a high-profile England cricket tour at this time is consistent with that approach'.

Morgan knew that there would be no *force majeure* from the government. 'We had various meetings with the government – known as positioning meetings,' he says. 'And finally Tim Lamb and I went to the Foreign and Commonwealth Office to meet with Jack Straw and Tessa Jowell [then Secretary of State for Culture, Media and Sport]. Both ministers knew we would have to go unless they could instruct us not to go, and Mr Straw said to us: "We do not have the legal powers to instruct you not to go. If we stop and think about it, I don't think any sport in this country would wish the government of the UK to have such powers." And so we ended that meeting with a joint media conference, where the government understood the ECB's position and the ECB understood the government's position.'

Pressure was brought upon the ECB by the ICC, who had been emphasizing the financial penalties that might be incurred if the tour were to be cancelled, that they should defer a decision on the tour until after the ICC's board meeting in Auckland in March 2004. And there a bombshell was dropped that blew any escape route for the ECB to pieces. 'Out of the blue,' says Morgan, 'it was proposed and accepted by the board by a substantial majority that the FTP should become a regulation of the ICC. And then once it became a regulation, any failure to fulfil that regulation would result in suspension.'

The suspension, in addition to already agreed financial penalties, would be for a short period. It would be long enough, though. Morgan did his maths. There would have been no 2005 Ashes. England's decision to tour Zimbabwe became as inevitable as Wilson's resignation.

But, of course, that was not the end of the matter. In May 2004 Australia toured Zimbabwe, but they went without leg-spinner Stuart MacGill, who made himself unavailable for selection. 'Whilst I fully support the ICC future tours policy that requires all member nations to play each other on a regular basis,' he said, 'and understand Cricket Australia's obligation to tour, I told them that I was uncomfortable about touring Zimbabwe at this point in time and maintaining a clear conscience.'

MacGill's stance clearly set some of the England players thinking. By then they had a new captain in Vaughan. All along he had emphasized that it was for the ECB to make a decision, and that whatever was determined, he and his players would abide by that decision. During the final Test of that summer the team met at their Grange City Hotel in London and decided that they would stick together as a team whatever decision was made.

However, during the subsequent Champions Trophy it became clear that some players were wavering. So Fletcher and Vaughan decided that it might be better to rest some of the more senior players ahead of a hard tour of South Africa and then the Ashes the following summer, as the visit to Zimbabwe was hardly likely to be taxing in terms of the opposition en-countered. That was because the whole situation had been complicated by a row: captain Heath Streak had been sacked and in all fifteen rebel white cricketers had had their contracts terminated when they expressed their displeasure at selection methods clearly designed to rid the side of whites and fill it with blacks.

England had beaten Zimbabwe easily, by 152 runs, in their first match in the Champions Trophy, so resting seemed a sensible idea to Fletcher, who was still not making any public pronouncements on Zimbabwe, but was feeling much more relaxed privately as he had just received a South African passport (his mother was born in Kimberley).

Fletcher was scuppered in his plans, however, when Steve Harmison used his newspaper column to announce that he was not going to Zimbabwe. 'In all honesty my decision was made in Cape Town over eighteen months ago when England's World Cup squad spent a horrendous four days before finally deciding not to go to Harare,' Harmison told the *News of the World*. 'Nothing has changed for me. The situation there is worse now – that's what the official reports say – and Zimbabwe's top players have been sacked. Being a personal decision, I realize I could be the only player who does not go. I'll respect what everyone else decides but I hope my refusal is not held against me.'

Both Fletcher and Vaughan were furious. So much for the team agreement earlier. This was becoming messy. Fletcher now let the ECB know of his intention to rest players. 'Duncan let me know through John Carr [ECB director of cricket],' says Morgan, 'that he wanted to rest some players for the tour, including Vaughan and Trescothick. But I decided that the tour had to be led by one of those two players. It was up to Duncan and the selectors to decide which one. I said, "You can't leave both behind. It is an extremely important tour." And it was. There were protocols in place from the government in the event of Robert Mugabe coming to the match.'

So Vaughan did lead the team. Trescothick and Flintoff were rested, while Giles went in support of his captain even though he had the option of being rested. Flintoff later admitted that he would not have gone anyway on moral grounds. Sadly it was little surprise that he should make such a public announcement when he did not need to; even less surprising that he and Harmison should be the two reluctant tourists. It was to become a familiar theme.

Originally the team were to acclimatize for the five-match Zimbabwe one-day international series in South Africa, but negotiations with the United Cricket Board of South Africa broke down, so England instead went to Namibia to play two one-day matches.

Morgan was on his way to Heathrow airport to fly to Zimbabwe when he received a call on his mobile phone (he had a driver). 'I'm on the Severn Bridge,' says Morgan, 'and the mobile goes, and it's Peter Chingoka [ZC chairman]. He said, "I'm pleased to tell you that we have clearance for visas to be issued to all your journalists with the exception of . . ." And I think the number was about fifteen. I said, "What do you mean with the exception of fifteen?" They all have to be allowed in, unless you can demonstrate good reason for them not to be allowed in.'

Morgan's phone did not stop all the way to Heathrow. The BBC were among those banned. That seemed deliberate, but the others, including my own *Sunday Telegraph* (Scyld Berry was travelling), appeared random choices.

The team heard this news just as they were leaving Namibia on a flight to Johannesburg, from where their connection to Harare had always been planned. Their initial reaction was 'We're not going', which I've always found rather amusing as most of the time they would much rather have journalists nowhere near them. But they went to Johannesburg, where they were met by Bevan. Meanwhile Morgan was flying to Zimbabwe with his deputy Mike Soper, and Carr.

The England team were in both limbo and transit. Where to have a team meeting? The smoking lounge in Johannesburg airport, of course. If that seemed bizarre – and there might have been an element of rudeness in ejecting some passengers desperately craving their nicotine fix – then some humour was soon to enter that glass-panelled lounge. This was Matthew Maynard's first tour as an assistant coach (he was still a player with Glamorgan), and Fletcher decided this was the time for him to make his first speech to the troops. He gestured to Maynard, who collected his thoughts and tried to speak. He tried again, and again. But there was not so much a frog as a cane toad stuck in the back of his throat. Nothing would come out. The room dissolved into fits of laughter. Thankfully Maynard has a remarkable ability to laugh at himself, and was soon laughing with them. Most grown men would have been mortified. I'd have simply booked a flight back to London. Not Maynard. He'd forgotten about it instantly, too. Luckily one of his management colleagues reminded me about it for the purposes of this book.

Then Morgan sent the instruction that the team should stay in Johannesburg and not fly to Harare. That was simple enough for everyone apart from team manager Phil Neale, the former Worcestershire captain who has been a willing and wonderfully diligent ever-present throughout the regimes of Fletcher and Flower up to the present day, who had to haul the mountain of bags already on the plane off again. He did so uncomplainingly, and off the team went to the nearby Caesar's Palace Hotel. It might just as well have been the Cullinan Hotel in Cape Town again. And the players were just as militant, so much so that Morgan sent Carr from Harare to speak to them.

Up in Harare, Morgan was negotiating with ZC and via the British Embassy through to Whitehall. Some thought the tour should be called off immediately, and the ICC president Ehsan Mani had indicated there might be some sympathy towards England should they take such a course of action. But Morgan was ever-mindful of the implications, and especially the 2005 Ashes.

He had, however, told the players that they would be going home unless the journalists were allowed in. ZC knew that too. So it wasn't long before the call came from Chingoka: 'David, I'm pleased to tell you that we've opened the can and all the journalists are allowed in.' 'The BBC were astonished,' admits Morgan. 'They never thought they would be let in.'

It was too late for all five ODIs to be played, even if Zimbabwe tried their hardest to do just that, as well as attempting to make sure England's accommodation in Bulawayo was as spartan as possible. But go to Zimbabwe England did, even if, since the last of those four ODIs there, England have played Zimbabwe on only one other occasion, during the ICC World Twenty20 in South Africa in 2007. In going to Zimbabwe and winning 4–0, however, England did derive one significant benefit: they gave a debut to a promising young batsman called Kevin Pietersen.

He was to prove a decent pick.

6

The Brains of Cricket

I've been called a Duncan Fletcher apologist. But I make no apology. Fletcher is quite simply the sharpest mind I have ever encountered in cricket. I learn something new from him every time we talk cricket. And I reckon I know a little bit about the game, having played it professionally for nearly twenty years. As Ashley Giles says of Fletcher, 'He is the brains of cricket.'

Fletcher is indeed that good. It is why former England charges like Nasser Hussain, Michael Vaughan, Marcus Trescothick, Andrew Strauss, Paul Collingwood and Kevin Pietersen swear by him. So too the South Africans like Jacques Kallis, Herschelle Gibbs and Gary Kirsten whom Fletcher coached at Western Province. Gibbs called him a 'legend' in his recent autobiography and Pietersen could easily have been charged with harassment, so frequent were his text messages begging Fletcher to work with him prior to England's tour of South Africa in 2009/10. There was, though, the small matter of Fletcher actually being employed by South Africa as a consultant at the time!

Hussain tells a good story of how technically sharp Fletcher is. It came on his first tour with England to South Africa in 1999/2000, where he was lumbered with a squad many of whom he hadn't seen before. 'He saw Chris Adams once in a net,' says Hussain, 'and said, "With his hands as they are, this lad might struggle outside off-stump against Allan Donald."' And twice in the first Test that's what happened – Adams was caught behind off Donald.

Interestingly, all the players mentioned in that second paragraph are batsmen. Indeed as an analyst of opposition batsmen Fletcher has few peers. 'I haven't met a coach who is as good at that or as quick at doing it,' says Geraint Jones. 'The plans he came up with were always spot on. I've never known a coach get it right as regularly as he did. Take Jacques Rudolph in South Africa in 2004/05. Fletch thought he was a massive candidate for being bowled, whereas everyone else had been saying to push the ball across him. So Fletch got us to bowl a straighter line and Rudolph hardly scored in that series [just two fifties in ten innings].'

There is a commonly held perception that Fletcher did not get on with his bowlers. It is an easy generalization, though. As England coach Fletcher always had a specific bowling coach, through whom most ideas were filtered so that the bowlers trusted that man, whether it was Bob Cottam, the late Graham Dilley, Troy Cooley or Kevin Shine. Fletcher mostly had a batting coach too, but always ensured that he himself was in charge of coaching the batsmen. That was undoubtedly his forte, but as a cricketer he was a genuine all-rounder. His finest playing hour demonstrates that amply: 69 not out and 4-42 as captain to defeat Australia in the 1983 World Cup at Trent Bridge.

Maybe it is more a matter of the characters involved. Bowlers like Andrew Flintoff, Steve Harmison and Matthew Hoggard disliked discipline. So they eventually disliked Fletcher.

Although I suspect there is more respect on both sides than is often revealed. Flintoff was as upset as the other players when Fletcher announced his resignation in the West Indies in 2007 and he resisted criticizing him heavily in his autobiography, despite Fletcher's obvious dismay with him and the revelation about his drinking exploits in his own autobiography. Mind you, maybe Flintoff was mindful of other drinking and disciplinary tales Fletcher could easily have divulged. I could have added Eric Simons to the list of devotees above. As I write he is now India's bowling coach under Fletcher. He is undoubtedly a confirmed Fletcher protégé from his time at Western Province. By way of further example, Simon Jones admits that Fletcher's advice on lengthening his run-up and grip on the ball (spreading his fingers wider) was significant in his remarkable transformation from raw fast bowler to world-class performer in the 2005 Ashes. 'He was brilliant with me,' says Jones. 'I always found him really approachable, and I remember when he changed my grip on the tour to Zimbabwe in 2004 that my control went up massively from there.'

'He had a great relationship with the bowlers,' says Matthew Maynard. 'I didn't ever see a clash – and I'm not just saying that to protect Fletch. But he had two very different characters there in Harmy and Fred. Harmy is one of the nicest blokes you could wish to meet, and he is very close with Fred, and Fred could be a pain in the arse to handle at times, but that was Fred. That was what probably made him such a good player. He wasn't quite wired the same way as everyone else. Fletch loved his bowlers because he knew they would win him matches. Batters set the game up; bowlers win it.'

Indeed when Fletcher was handed the list of potential names for the first intake of the National Academy in 2001/02, he noticed two glaring omissions: Simon Jones and Harmison. He said one thing to Rod Marsh: 'I don't care who you take, but those two must go.'

When consultant to South Africa in Australia in 2008/09 Fletcher reiterated his advice to England's bowlers in 2005 about bowling around the wicket to Australia's left-handers. The raw Morne Morkel in particular benefited, and South Africa won the Test series 2–1.

There is also little doubt in my mind that the two players who made the most noticeable technical advancements upon Fletcher's arrival at Glamorgan in 1997 were fast bowling all-rounder Darren Thomas and left-arm spinner Dean Cosker.

So Fletcher is much more than just a batting expert. Indeed his initial impact at Glamorgan was on our fielding. On a pre-season trip to Christ College, Brecon he organized the most enjoyable yet lung-bursting fielding session I or any of the other players had encountered. It was as if a new coach had arrived from a different planet such was the intensity, precision and variety of his drills. His ten-catches routine became legendary. It sounds simple but it tested even the fittest, because every catch, ten in a row without a drop, was taken at full stretch, the victim probably having run a considerable distance to try and take it. On his first England tour Vaughan was sick behind a tree having only just managed to complete the exercise, and Phil Tufnell began throwing returns over Fletcher's head in the vain hope that he would run out of balls.

The selection of wicketkeepers became a highly controversial part of his regime, especially when Geraint Jones was preferred to Chris Read, but Fletcher helped his keepers too. He talked to Alec Stewart about taking the ball standing back with his fingers pointing skywards, and to Jones about taking the ball in front of the stumps for run outs, now a trendy and highly effective tactic to save frames in television replays.

None of this, however, is to say that Fletcher does not have his faults. Of course he does. We all do. Even as a coach Fletcher had his faults. But then coaching is not an exact science. Fletcher could help players in all facets of the game, but one man's mentor can easily be another man's tormentor. Even at Glamorgan there were those who were not overly enamoured of some of Fletcher's ways, those who felt neglected. Mind you, they were usually not very good. Often those who complain about the coach are those who are not in the side.

There is a perception that Fletcher wanted yes-men around him, whether players or assistant coaches. Maynard is seen as a classic example. It is simply not true, and I will vouch for that. They were always arguing at Glamorgan. As Maynard says, 'My wife Sue always used to say when he was coming round for dinner, "You're not going to row with Fletch again tonight are you?"'

Maynard also has some interesting thoughts on Fletcher's attitude to difficult characters within the team environment. 'He used to talk about the terrorists within a team,' he says. 'You need them in your side but you know they will cause some problems too, and that you have to bring them into the circle. You can't isolate them because then they might be more destructive. It was about getting the balance right – the critical mass, as he always said. He wanted eight good characters who could drag the weaker ones through, one who might be a quieter lad and two who were tougher to handle.'

Fletcher can appear dour and grumpy and many of the other adjectives that are often bandied before his name. But, like Mike Atherton as England captain, Fletcher often played up to this part. The image had been cast early, and he was not going to alter it just to please the media. Often when I phone him he will answer mockingly with a voice as gruff as possible: 'What do you want?' And then later he'll suddenly say 'Right, you're boring me now. Time to go, Sidney from Lydney [his nickname for me, combining the actor Sid James and my hometown]' and will chuckle and hang up.

Fletcher has a lighter, more humorous side. Inside he is a happy, contented man. But because of his public image I'd need to provide examples of his successfully auditioning as a stand-up comedian to convince some of as much. I was never part of his dressing room with England, but I was at Glamorgan, and it was not the sour-faced morgue many would think. It was a wonderfully happy place, full of fun as well as hard work. I'm told it was very similar with England.

Fletcher would socialize with the team, but not for long. He knew to keep his distance, and it helped that he was forty-nine when he took the England job. His was a different generation. Only once did I see him inebriated at Glamorgan, and he still mentions it today. It was in 1999 when a lunch was held at Sophia Gardens for the Australia team who were based in Cardiff for the World Cup. He began the lunch by talking in hushed tones about the Australians who had just told us they were on an alcohol ban for the two weeks up to their opening match in the tournament. We were under no such ban, though. Every time I turned my head away Fletcher would fill my glass to the brim with red wine. Naturally I began returning the favour. It proved to be an interesting afternoon. By the time we adjourned to the nearby Beverley Hotel it was, as Dean Conway would put it, 'carnage'. I am pleased to report that Fletcher was seen eating some petunias outside the hotel later on. Pleased because it shows a side of his character few have seen. And I'm sure Fletcher will not be displeased, even if when I mentioned the incident in my autobiography he did say 'I hope Marina doesn't read that!' She knows he has got a slightly wild side. He's Zimbabwean after all.

'People only saw him on the media side and there he was stern-faced and a closed shop,' says Marcus Trescothick, 'but behind closed doors he was a completely different character. If you get to know the guy he is very jovial with a sort of sly sense of humour. He enjoys his golf, but he always got distracted if you started talking about cricket because it would mess him up. He hated it if he'd had a phone call from Grav [David Graveney] and had a bit of a disagreement about selection because he couldn't switch off then. He was completely different from what was seen in the media.'

Fletcher was strict on dress code and punctuality, and collated any misdemeanours so that they could form part of subsequent fines meetings. Fletcher loved such gatherings. At Glamorgan he would giggle when, for example, announcing that so-and-so had been fined for a PDA – a 'public display of affection' for his partner.

Such events could become rather raucous. On his first tour with England, to South Africa in 1999/2000, Fletcher asked Conway, his entertainments manager as well as physiotherapist, to organize a team meal at a restaurant in Sandton's Nelson Mandela Square in Johannesburg. It became such a riotous affair that no less a rabble-rouser than Phil Tufnell was calling for calm. Maybe he'd noticed that the press corps were dining nearby, to a man astonished to be witnessing such revelry. No one reported it, though.

This did not prevent another evening of high-jinks later in the tour, namely after the now infamous Test victory at Centurion. Nobody knew then what Hansie Cronje had been up to. There was celebrating to do, even if Atherton did observe later in his autobiography *Opening Up*, 'For the first time in my life I felt completely flat at the moment of a Test victory. It wasn't that I suspected match-fixing, but a Test match victory is a thing that has to be earned; you need to put in the hard work.' England hadn't done that really, with Cronje's generous and deviously minded declaration setting up a game.

A fines meeting ensued after the Test. As Conway relates, 'The manager of the Sandton Sun Hotel had sorted a lot of things for us: we had two sheep's heads and a pig's head on silver salvers, live birds flying around and chickens running around. I'm not really sure why we had such things, but it had been a funny tour for that sort of thing. I'd been having a running battle with Jacques Kallis [whom Conway knew from Kallis's season at Glamorgan the previous summer] and his room-mate Mark Boucher. One afternoon I'd found a snake in my bed, so as revenge I'd got into their room [both teams were staying in the same hotel] and put a [dead] chicken on their washing line in the bath and then put a meat cleaver through it so that there was blood all over their bath. I drew the shower curtain and left. Kallis told me that Boucher went for a shower later in the day and the screams could be heard on more than one floor of the hotel.'

Conway and Giles were chairmen of the meeting, in which Fletcher, all the players and management staff took a full part. For some reason everyone was asked to kiss one of the sheep's heads. 'Kiss the sheep, kiss the sheep!' was the chant that rang out as the miscreant went up to the chairmen's table. But Tufnell could not do it. 'I can't do it, Phys,' he said to Conway, which was clearly not true given his later exploits on *I'm a Celebrity Get Me Out of Here!* 'You're going to have to talk to him then,' said Conway. So, with fag dutifully at the side of his mouth, Tufnell said, 'Awright, sheep?'

In stitches with the rest of them was Fletcher. The trouble is that judgements about Fletcher's character are made about his demeanour in public, and in particular at press conferences. Those are not situations in which he is comfortable. Essentially he is a shy man. He takes some getting to know. And he will take his time getting to know you.

Speaking in public is not an easy exercise for him. Indeed I never felt he was truly at ease when speaking to the Glamorgan team as a whole. He certainly betrayed some nervousness when ending his opening address to us in 1997 with a humorous 'Let's get this road on the show then'.

He was often lambasted for his infamous 'Duncan Days', as the media labelled his press conferences, but the truth was that Fletcher would mostly be wheeled out after a poor performance.

He did not enjoy them, clearly, but he thought he should protect his players in such circumstances.

Not that he really worked out the media game. 'He was highly protective and supportive of his team,' says Giles, 'and they are great attributes as coach. Yes, to a degree you have to try and manage the media and keep them on-side, but the important stuff is to win games. Managing the media isn't going to win you games. If you can only do one or the other, he got the right one.'

At the crux of Fletcher's philosophy in life is loyalty. That was drummed into him from his schooldays at Prince Edward, Salisbury (now Harare). And he always perceived most of the media criticism as being disloyal, especially when he considered his words had been twisted. And sometimes they were, partly because that's what happens in journalism occasionally, but also because Fletcher's cricketing ruminations could be so deep that either he struggled to get his point across in such a formal forum or some journalists simply could not comprehend it.

Fletcher knew that playing the media game might help him, and that not doing so might precipitate his exit should results turn ugly, as indeed was the eventual case after the calamitous winter of 2006/07 when the Ashes were lost 5–0. And there were times when he considered a change of attitude. Jonathan Agnew, the BBC's cricket correspondent and a former team-mate of Fletcher's at the Alexandra club in Harare, often spoke to him about this. So in Bangladesh in 2003 he resolved to do something about it.

The trouble was that by the end of that short two-Test tour he had already changed his mind, upset by what he considered a 'stitch-up'. England had been hit by injuries to their bowlers on that trip, with Harmison returning home after the first Test and both Flintoff and James Anderson missing out. In their stead Hoggard won man of the series, and when Fletcher was asked afterwards by Angus Fraser, then correspondent of the *Independent*, whether England should now base their bowling attack around Hoggard, he made the mistake of not wholly endorsing that viewpoint. The headlines the next day were predictable. 'Hoggard the hero slated by Fletcher' was the general gist when all Fletcher had really said was 'I wouldn't say Hoggy is the guy we're going to build the bowling around. He bowled well yesterday and got some nice rhythm. But he's got to make the batsmen play a bit more early in the innings. That goes for all the quick bowlers. They've got to know what their roles are.'

Hoggard was no leader, as he himself explained in his auto-biography *Hoggy: Welcome to My World*, describing how his captain Vaughan saw his role: 'It was my job to keep sweeping the shop floor, grafting away at the menial work while the other bowlers were grabbing the glory upstairs in the office. I wasn't to get ahead of myself and try to show the office workers how to do their job.'

Even though Fletcher did not necessarily rate Hoggard that highly, what miffed him was that it appeared that he was criticizing one of his players in public. As Giles said, in Fletcher's scheme of things that was as forbidden as the consumption of pork in Islam. Fletcher had to phone Hoggard, who had already flown home because he was not involved in the one-day series that followed the Tests, to explain.

But there was another problem. Fletcher is never wrong. He may not like my saying that, but it is meant in the nicest possible way. He has his strong views, and, by and large, he sticks by them. And the thing is that, on cricketing matters, they are mostly right. In reality he rarely is wrong.

Early in the writing of his autobiography I often questioned him on points he was making. Always he would respond immediately with a cogent argument. I soon learnt to shut up and listen. It was his book, not mine. And he did know what he was talking about. It was always worth listening.

The book whipped up considerable controversy, not least

because its serialization was quite naturally centred upon a revelation that Flintoff, then the England captain, was still drunk at practice the day before a one-day international in Australia in 2007. I still wonder to this day whether I might have written things differently, whether I could have protected and advised Fletcher more wisely on this.

Often during the book's composition Fletcher would say things like 'I am worried that I am having too much of a go'. Because of this, many incidents (especially involving Flintoff) and observations were removed from draft versions. 'I need some advice. You're the expert,' he would often say, and I'd sometimes think to myself, 'I'm not sure if I am the expert!' The truth is that this was not a straightforward assignment. Fletcher wanted to demonstrate how difficult a job it was to coach England, and he wanted to get a considerable number of gripes off his chest. He felt his seven years in charge had been a constant battle, not just against opposition teams but against the ECB, the media, the dinosaurs still roaming county cricket and even members of his own team. He wanted to express some strong words about some supposed sacred cows of English cricket, like Flintoff, Ian Botham and Geoffrey Boycott. That was always bound to generate a strong public reaction.

And not all of it was complimentary for sure. By far the most withering book review came from Patrick Collins, an award-winning columnist for the *Mail on Sunday* and both a writer and a person whom I like and respect. But he penned an extraordinarily acerbic piece for *Wisden*. He cleverly picked out a number of instances where Fletcher mentioned that various people had apologized to him, but then let fly with this: 'But it is the tone of this ill-judged book which will linger longest in the memory: vindictive, self-justifying and relentlessly mean-spirited. In time, Duncan Fletcher may come to realize this dreadful book was his greatest mistake. And the one by which posterity will judge him.'

The book was not a mistake. Even if I say so myself, it was a damned good read. It was an honest reflection of Fletcher's life and his struggles, as well as his successes. So many sporting autobiographies are anodyne pap; here was a book full of strong opinions, one shorn of the usual flouncing platitudes towards colleagues and opponents, and one with some outstanding technical analysis. Yet it attracted some contemptuous condemnation.

It always amuses me when reviewers describe a book as self-justifying. Isn't that part of the point of an autobiography? If you don't get your point across there, when are you ever going to do so? It's your side of the story. And it hardly scuppered all future job prospects for Fletcher. Being appointed coach of the World Cup champions India in 2011, for all its initial difficulties, rather demonstrates that. And between that appointment and the publication of his book, Fletcher had worked for South Africa, New Zealand and Hampshire on a consultancy basis, while also being approached by the West Indies, Glamorgan (again) and various South African provinces. He was not exactly in coaching purdah.

To me, Fletcher has expressed only one regret about the book: the treatment of Chris Read, which might have been more sympathetic. He did not rate Read as an international keeper; a very good county cricketer, yes, but not an international. He felt his catching channel was too narrow, that he was too quiet and that his batting lacked the necessary defensive technique. But that is not to say that Fletcher disliked him as a person. 'He's a good kid,' Fletcher said to me afterwards. Between us we should have worded his faults more sensitively. After some deliberation Read, whom I know reasonably well and like, decided that he would not respond to Fletcher's comments for this book.

There was the accusation that Fletcher had betrayed Trescothick's trust by revealing details of his breakdowns in India and Australia. 'I chatted to Tres about it,' says Fletcher.

'There was a phone call that took place long before the book was completed and I said I'd mentioned some of the incidents in the book. At no stage did he say "No, I don't want it in". Whatever has been written has been out there, has been basically covered before. I said "Is that all right?" and he said "OK" and left it at that.' These are points reiterated by Trescothick himself. 'We'd had a conversation,' he says. 'I wasn't bothered. He didn't tell anything that hadn't been told before.'

Should we have included the Flintoff stuff? I still think it was right to do so. It was hardly something that happened in private; it happened at a public training session. It was the perfect example of the problems Fletcher was facing. Flintoff was out of control that winter in his off-field behaviour. In making him captain Fletcher had placed a huge amount of trust in him. He had let Fletcher down, and basically cost him the job he loved and cherished.

As Fletcher said afterwards, 'People have turned round and said, should I have brought it up? From my point of view the two [the revelation in the book and the "Fredalo" affair during the 2007 World Cup in the West Indies] were directly linked. You had a situation where an incident took place and rightly or wrongly I kept it in-house, then in three or four weeks' time we had a similar affair. I just thought it was important it was brought out in the open. If the pedalo affair hadn't happened I wouldn't have revealed it [the story of England's abandoned practice in Australia]. Having had a chat with him, if nothing had happened, I definitely wouldn't have revealed it. But they were so directly linked I was taken aback by it – enough is enough, sort of thing.'

Predictably, Flintoff's great mate Harmison was outraged when the book serialization appeared. 'The code states that what goes on in the dressing room stays in the dressing room,' Harmison said. 'It was a code very dear to Duncan Fletcher's heart and, sadly, Duncan Fletcher has broken it. For someone to be able to justify doing what Fletcher has done they would have to have a very good reason. If not, it's just telling tales out of school. Fletcher took me from a young player to someone who has won fifty-odd Test caps. And I admit I've given him a lot of problems to deal with. So it's disappointing that my relationship with him should end on such a sour note. The sadness is that Fletcher was a very good coach who did a lot for our game. But the picture he paints of Freddie is unfair and one-sided. He's said nothing about what a positive force Fred is within the dressing room, which to me, says it all.'

Well, Fletcher did actually, but not in the serialization of course. I do not think Fletcher will mind my saying that he did not contribute much to the actual writing of his two books. That's what ghosts are for. He spoke, I listened, and then I wrote. But when I wrote 'Flintoff bowled with the heart of a lion' with regard to his superhuman performance in the final Test of the 2005 Ashes at the Oval, Fletcher read it and said, 'No, that should be "the heart of three lions".' Fletcher knew all about Flintoff's talent, that is for sure.

But they were very different characters. As Simon Jones says, 'Fletch and Fred just didn't see eye to eye. Fred always respected him because he was such a good coach. I just don't think they liked each other as people. Fred is a bit of a piss taker and joker, and he'd have a laugh with most people, but I never saw him and Fletch having a giggle once.'

Flintoff himself admits as much in his book *Ashes to Ashes*: 'As far as Duncan and I are concerned, it was a case of two people who didn't get on being thrown together for eight months of the year as part of the England cricket team. We had completely different views on life, the relationship didn't work, and it came to an abrupt end after the World Cup, so it was clear he was not going to be very complimentary about me, although I've lost count of the number of times I was injured, or had jabs, while he was England coach and played to help the team. I had an inkling he was going to have a go at me, even though he once said, when the press were on his back, that the weakest way to have a go at someone was in print.'

There are and were some journalists Fletcher quite liked during his time with England. It is probably best not to name any names, but there were many he simply had no time for. He had a particular problem with many of the newspapers' number twos, who, more often than not, are promoted to pole position during the one-day series that follow Tests. Fletcher felt they understood cricket much less than their seniors. And, with the tiredness and general problems that always followed England's one-day cricket, this made for some tricky times during press conferences at the end of many tours.

Before returning to the international game with India, there were also some other awkward moments because Fletcher had to spend time in various press boxes while waiting to do summarizing stints on radio with *Test Match Special*. He did not enjoy his first experience during a one-day game at Cape Town in late November 2009. And I was not surprised. On radio you often just have to talk. Fletcher doesn't just talk. As I said earlier about the early writing of his autobiography, he can talk at length, but it has to be about a subject that is really engaging him. It is a consequence of his upbringing as much as anything. At Carswell Farm the spaces were wide and open. It was a place where very few words were required. It was a place for action and thought, not for lots of words.

But by the time of the Test there later in that tour, and the arrival of his former captain Vaughan alongside him, he was much more relaxed and comfortable on air, with his ever-so-sharp technical expertise being gently coaxed out of him. Indeed there was one lunchtime filler that the pair did about the 2005 Ashes that received much acclaim. I saw Fletcher in the Cape Town press box just afterwards. He was in unusually high spirits. 'That was so enjoyable,' he beamed.

The obvious downside for Fletcher in the *TMS* box was the

presence of Boycott. It goes without saying that never once did they exchange words; never once did Fletcher even look at the former England opener. Fletcher simply cannot stand the man. Boycott was a critic from the very moment Fletcher was appointed, questioning how he could take the job without any Test match experience. Early on in his tenure Fletcher even wrote a ghosted piece (not by me but by Mark Hodgson, then the ECB's media liaison officer) in the *Daily Telegraph* in response to some of Boycott's criticisms, especially of his resting of players from county cricket.

After the 2005 Ashes win, Boycott phoned Fletcher at his Cape Town home. Boycott has a place in a golf estate in the Western Cape and wanted to play a round on the course with Fletcher and the late Bob Woolmer, then Pakistan's coach, whose side England were about to face that winter. Fletcher was having none of it, letting rip, swearing loudly, and asking Boycott how he could try to be so friendly when he had been so vitriolic in his broadcasting and ghosted observations. Boycott realized that the golf was not going to happen, so downgraded his offer to a cup of tea somewhere. Fletcher refused and slammed the phone down.

He felt better for having stuck to his principles, but he also knew there might be further criticisms in store. Marina even mentioned this to him the minute he had put the phone down. Fletcher was sufficiently worried to phone Hussain to seek his advice. 'I'd have that cup of tea if I were you,' said Hussain. Of course Fletcher did not do that, and there was an inevitable consequence, because even before England had set off on what would be a calamitous Ashes tour in 2006/07 Boycott was calling for Fletcher's head as coach. And this while England still held the Ashes! But a bandwagon had begun its journey, and its passengers became many, varied and more and more vociferous as the winter progressed.

With some journalists, Fletcher's stance will simply never

soften. In September 2010 I was with him and a couple of other friends outside the Mochyn Du pub next to the Swalec Stadium, Cardiff when a journalist extended his hand to Fletcher, who promptly looked the other way. Now, I've had the odd difference of opinion with this journalist, but I still shake his hand.

Later that evening I spoke to Fletcher about the incident. I related a story of my own, in which my father had given me one of my biggest bollockings after a rugby match when I was playing for Lydney against Cheltenham. It had been a niggly, sometimes violent match in which I felt I'd been targeted. So when it came to a conclusion and the opposition formed their traditional tunnel to clap us off and shake hands, I skirted around it and rushed to the changing rooms in a huff. My father caught up with me in the bar afterwards. He was not happy. 'Whatever happens you still shake their hands afterwards,' he growled. 'You need to grow up.'

With my father's advice returning after all those years I told Fletcher he should have shaken the journalist's hand. 'No, no, it's different,' he replied. 'On a sports field there is a natural respect for each other. I don't respect that man. I don't see why I should shake his hand.'

The relationship between journalists and players and coaches is an interesting one. Gone are the days when they were close friends on tour. I still can't get over reading that John Woodcock, the cricket correspondent of *The Times* from 1954 to 1988, once shared a room with Brian Statham the night before a Test on tour, because Statham's room-mate Peter Loader had flu. Imagine that today.

Now there is mainly distrust. Even when Fletcher is telling me something important he will presage it with something like 'Now, Sidney, how confidential are you?' He's never been upset that I leaked something (I haven't) but he was upset with a piece I did about Matt Prior in the West Indies in 2009.

'Where has that journalist with vision I once knew gone?' he asked.

He was unhappy that, in praising Peter Moores for his promotion of Prior to the Test team in 2007, I had forgotten something: that Fletcher had wanted Prior to replace the out-of-form Geraint Jones midway through the Pakistan home series in 2006. But the selectors wanted Read, and got their wish. All the fuss about Read or Jones for the Ashes that winter might have been avoided. Prior actually played twelve one-day inter-nationals under Fletcher, opening in ten of them, and was – still is of course – Fletcher's type of combative cricketer. Fletcher wanted him for the one-day series in Australia and the sub-sequent World Cup in 2007, but was persuaded to go with the veteran Paul Nixon by skipper Vaughan.

As Fletcher said of Prior in 2009, 'It seems to have taken them [the selectors] three years to realize just how good this guy is. To have found a bloke who can bat at number seven is a huge plus. People who criticize his keeping should remember that most keepers struggle when they first come on the international scene: Alec Stewart, Brendon McCullum, Mark Boucher, even Kumar Sangakkara. All keepers miss chances, it's just that a guy like Adam Gilchrist could get away with it because Australia had an attack that covered up any mistakes he made. Prior should be cut some slack.'

Even after the calamitous 3–0 series defeat by Pakistan early in 2012, Prior still averaged 44.24 in his fifty Tests, higher than any other England keeper (Les Ames averaged 43.40) and with only his coach Andy Flower (53.70) and Gilchrist (48.60) above him among those keepers who have played ten innings. Fletcher would have liked working with Prior the Test batsman/keeper.

Being an ex-player in the media brings with it its own challenges. Players quite naturally look to you for more sympathy, and seem especially enraged when that is not necessarily forthcoming. And, of course, they may know you a little better than some other journalists. In that regard I learnt an important early lesson as a journalist. It was at Headingley in 2006, and Ian Bell had just scored his third Test century in four innings. I did a piece for the *Sunday Telegraph*, which was generally full of praise but did contain some light-hearted negativity, suggesting Bell had had a bit of fortune in reaching that century on the Saturday morning.

Twelfth man for England on the Sunday was Mike Powell, a Glamorgan player and good friend. After England had finished their pre-match practice I wandered down to the entrance from which the players used to emerge on to the ground at Headingley, where there was a curious arrangement whereby players and press could easily mingle as the press had to pass the dressing rooms to go to the toilet. I spoke to Powell to arrange dinner for that evening. He was keen and mentioned that Bell wanted to have dinner with him too.

Just a few minutes later Bell came past having finished his practice. I said hello chirpily but received only a grunt in response as Bell quickly walked past me. I was a little shocked, if the truth be told. I thought my piece had been pretty complimentary!

By lunchtime I'd spoken to Powell again. The dinner was off. Bell was unhappy with my piece and certainly did not want to have dinner with me.

The lesson I learnt was not that players are sensitive – of course they are – but that a journalist should never expect a player to speak to him. From that moment I have always made sure that if I encounter a player in a hotel or wherever I allow him to do the greeting first. If he does not want to, then I have no problem. If he feels he has been criticized unfairly, that is his prerogative. That's probably why, were I not so close to him, I wouldn't try to shake the hand of someone like Fletcher without the nod first.

7

The Terrorists Take Charge

Duncan Fletcher's reign as England coach ended after the World Cup match against the West Indies in Barbados on 21 April 2007. Two days earlier at the Police ground on the island where England were practising, Fletcher had announced to the team that he was to end his seven-year tenure. The night before that he had called captain Michael Vaughan and met him at the bar of the Hilton Hotel. He told Vaughan that he had already met with ECB chairman David Morgan to agree his terms of departure, and that the West Indies match was to be his last in charge. They reminisced for a good few hours. 'We probably had about twelve rum and Cokes,' says Vaughan with a smile now.

But the following day Vaughan was in tears as he thanked Fletcher for his work. 'I can't believe I just cried in front of grown men,' he later told Dean Conway by text. It was certainly emotional. Even Fletcher, the inscrutable 'Silver Fox', wiped a tear from his eye.

If there was sadness that Fletcher's departure from the top

job was rather inevitable, there should also have been sadness that such vast cricketing knowledge was being tossed so insouciantly out of the English game. Conway is clearly a close ally of Fletcher's but he does have a point when he says, 'Say a business institution had had a CEO like Fletch for so many years. Would they just say "Thanks for coming"? No. The ECB should have dovetailed Peter Moores in. Fletch would have been a perfect number two. He wanted a six-month handover [and India, one of the visitors in the following summer of 2007, were the only country he did not beat in a Test series]. How could the ECB presume that Moores' philosophies could take them forward from day one? Why invest so much time in one man and then do this? There is an energy you need at the top, and maybe it had dipped a bit, but you couldn't lose somebody like that with their bank of knowledge.'

One influential player told me, 'He should be at the Academy now. Imagine if he were a selector too. He'd be brilliant. There were signs at the end of the India tour the previous winter that he was tiring. The ECB should have started making moves then.'

Fletcher, of course, resigned in the West Indies, and woe betide anyone who writes that he was sacked. But the ECB hardly supported him. He had challenged too many people there. Morgan was a strong supporter, but so many others weren't. They were glad to see Fletcher go, despite the monumental task he had managed. Fletcher cared little for what others thought of him, and he paid for it in the end. He tried hard to change anachronistic English ideals, with some people more worried about keeping their jobs than actually doing them properly.

Chairman of selectors David Graveney was a classic example. He's a decent bloke. And not just because he picked me for England, even if he did phone after one Test to announce 'They [supposedly meaning the other selectors Graham Gooch and Mike Gatting] want to go with a right-hand/left-hand opening partnership' in justifying Nick Knight's inclusion ahead of me for the next Test after I'd been called up as a late replacement for the injured Mark Butcher for the Lord's Test against South Africa in 1998. Graveney was always looking to tomorrow and next week. Fletcher was looking years ahead. He viewed selection as an investment, and anyone who knows him knows how careful he is with his money! So when he said things like 'I want to know what my returns are going to be in five years' time and not next week' you knew he was thinking long and hard about that investment.

Not that Fletcher ever forced a selection upon his captain. Both Hussain and Vaughan have confirmed to me that Fletcher never did this to them once. For example, at Lord's in 2000 against Zimbabwe, Fletcher wanted Harmison to play instead of Ed Giddins. He saw Harmison as the investment, while Hussain was very much in Graveney's world then, thinking only of the horse for the course. Fletcher knew Giddins' swing might be too much for the callow Zimbabweans, but he worried that he would then have to be picked in the following series against the West Indies and get exposed. Giddins did take wickets against Zimbabwe at Lord's (7-42 in the match) and did reasonably well in the next Test at Trent Bridge, but when he was thoroughly ineffective against the West Indies at Edgbaston (0-73 from eighteen overs), Hussain had to admit that Fletcher might have been right. Giddins never played for England again.

Hussain and Fletcher rarely disagreed after that. The captain/coach bond that Fletcher preached saw to that. 'He said very early on "I want your trust. We've got to trust each other completely,"' says Hussain. And Hussain can only remember one occasion when Fletcher was upset with him. It was at a dinner in Port Elizabeth during the World Cup of 2003 after all the problems about Zimbabwe when Hussain had had too much to drink. There were others present and Hussain began bringing up private conversations that he and Fletcher had had over the issue. Fletcher gave him an icy stare and said, 'Right, that's enough of that.' And Hussain shut up immediately. 'When Fletcher said boo, I jumped,' Hussain admits now. 'If you cross him, you cross him for life. He is a very, very stubborn man.'

The commissioning of the Schofield Report was the final straw for Fletcher. He felt it thoroughly undermined him. He was right to point out that England were actually still number two in the Test rankings at the time. They'd been hammered by the number one team. The report was really all about the jerking of a number of knees.

Not that it can be denied that the winter of 2006/07 was anything other than a 'Winter from Hell', as I entitled the thirteenth chapter of his autobiography. It certainly was unlucky. England had lost the Ashes 5–0, and even though they surprisingly won the subsequent Commonwealth Bank series one-day trophy, Fletcher came in for unprecedented criticism. It wore him down. 'He defended the team a lot,' says Geraint Jones, 'but I think he got to the point in Australia where in a way he got sick of defending us and that was the first time I'd seen him in that frame of mind. I think he changed a bit on that tour. He got worn down by all the media pressure and that changed his outlook on people. I felt that approachability between the two of us had gone a bit.'

Fletcher was not the same man, or the same coach, on that trip. But it was little surprise. He'd been let down, and he was tired, as he later admitted to me when I wrote after the Ashes triumph of 2010/11 that the ECB should be careful about how they handle Andy Flower and his workload. 'You might be on to something there,' said Fletcher. 'I never realized how tired I was when I was doing the job.'

The fun, such a vital part of every dressing room in which Fletcher had been involved, disappeared a little on that Ashes trip of 2006/07. The social committee waned in its activities, and by the one-day series the tour had descended into bacchanalia, with Vaughan, returned from injury, deciding against exerting the sort of discipline he might usually have brought to bear. 'We were like a throwback to the 1970s,' wrote Vaughan. 'And we just about managed to keep it from Duncan.'

I was not on that tour. But plenty of journalists were, of course. And back home Peter Preston of the *Observer* reckoned they should have said something. 'The cosy inner circle of travelling journalists and retired England stars didn't exactly fulfil the most basic requirement their audience demands: that is, breaking a totally valid news story,' Preston wrote. Was it that bad? Some say it was, some say it wasn't. The very fact that one player was heard to joke 'This drinking team has got a cricket problem' is probably sufficient evidence.

Should Fletcher have done something? He had never imposed a curfew on any side he had coached, from the University of Cape Town upwards. He wasn't going to start in Australia. His view was that international cricketers get paid a lot of money in this day and age. With that comes responsibility. It should be obvious to any sensible person what those responsibilities are. Banning alcohol from cricket would be like taking Yorkshire pudding from a plate of roast beef.

Under Flower and Andrew Strauss England make sure the whole team celebrates personal milestones of a century or five wickets in an innings with a beer in the dressing room at the end of the day's play. 'Fitness trainers and physiologists will say that beer might make you feel more stiff the next day, but I think that's a small price to pay for genuinely celebrating one of your team-mates' successes. I brought it in pretty much straight after I became captain,' writes Strauss in his diary *Winning the Ashes Down Under*. It certainly seems better than Peter Moores' handing out of big cigars after a victory. 'It always seemed a bit forced to me,' wrote Vaughan of that.

When I met Fletcher at the team's Gatwick hotel before they left for the World Cup, he was more uptight than he had been in

South Africa in 2005. I knew it was over then. In fact I thought it best that it was over soon. This was not about the much-quoted 'coach's shelf life'. This was about a man for whom the very worst of British sport, with its passion for scapegoats and blood-letting, had become too much. He was fighting too many battles; against selectors, administrators and the media. I knew then that news of the Schofield Report had finished him off.

It was a sad day for me. I went home to my wife later that day and said, 'The book will be out this year.' And so it was. I'd finished it by the summer's end, and it was in the bookshops in time for Christmas, preceded by days of serialization that rocked the sport with their ferocity.

So where did it all go wrong? Well, the simple answer is that England were never going to win that Ashes series away to a great Australian side – and they were still great in 2006/07 – who were hell-bent on revenge after the loss in 2005, and with England missing three key players in Vaughan, Marcus Trescothick (who left the tour before the Tests) and Simon Jones. As Trescothick said to me, 'The reason we lost 5–0? We didn't have our best side out.' To emphasize: not one of England's top seven for the first Test had played a Test in Australia before.

Crucially, England did not have their captain. They had had two captains in that year, neither of whom had made a cast-iron case for the job. There was Andrew Flintoff, who'd led the side to a remarkable Test victory in Mumbai the previous winter, but then had suffered injury during the English summer. Then there was Strauss, who'd taken over in Flintoff's absence. He'd lost his first one-day series 5–0 to Sri Lanka, but had shown signs of growing into the role during the Test series against Pakistan that is always rather better remembered for an alleged ball-tampering incident that forced the abandonment of the Test at the Oval.

Flintoff was, of course, appointed for the Ashes. With the

benefit of hindsight it is a decision that has been lambasted. But I do not recall such opprobrium at the time. That Mumbai victory was enough for most observers; enough evidence of an inspirational leader.

It clearly was a tricky decision. It was certainly one which exercised Fletcher's mind throughout the summer. I remember being in his car, having done some book stuff, when he asked my opinion. In reply I asked him whether he thought Strauss could cope with the big characters in the team, in other words Flintoff and Harmison. 'He can cope with anything,' said Fletcher then.

He'd obviously changed his mind by the time the decision was made, but I could actually see why. The only way England could beat Australia was if Flintoff was firing, and if Harmison was too. There might have been the thought that Flintoff could run rampant off the field (as happened anyway) if he were not captain, but it was mainly on-field considerations that held sway.

Fletcher still stands by the decision today, even though his assistant Matthew Maynard says, 'I know that he spoke to a lot of people about that, but I haven't spoken to one person who said it should be Flintoff. I said Strauss.'

Well, the chairman of selectors, Graveney, did say Flintoff, while fellow selector Geoff Miller said Strauss.

It is here that I will ask one very important question: did Strauss really want the job then? It is my understanding that in private he was showing quite a lot of negativity towards it. He was worried about the public's support for Flintoff, their champion after all, who was making it all-clear that he wanted to be captain. And he was worried that he would not be able to control a disgruntled Flintoff and his mate Harmison. 'There was a story in the *Sun* saying Fred wanted to be captain,' says one player. 'Straussy knew then that he could not get the public on his side.'

After every tour the ECB writes a detailed report, and I have seen a copy of the report for that 2006/07 Ashes tour. This was its summation of the captaincy debate (with due apology for some over-excited use of capitals):

> It was clearly a close call between Andrew Flintoff and Andrew Strauss for the Ashes Captaincy. On balance the Selectors favoured the former as with Andrew Flintoff having his heart set on the Captaincy they felt it was the most likely way to get the best performances out of him and his close friend Steve Harmison, and they hoped that he would prove to be a talismanic leader.

Much was made of the revelation in Fletcher's book that he was swayed finally by a DVD shown at Loughborough at the end of the 2006 summer by Colin Gibson, then the ECB's head of corporate communications, with the words 'The team has to be together to beat Australia'. I'm not sure I wrote that too well. 'That was it. It had to be Flintoff,' I continued in Fletcher's voice. It left Fletcher open to easy criticism, the tale of a decision made on a whim. It was not like that. Fletcher does not do whimsy. He'd agonized over that call.

He said to Strauss 'You might thank me for this one day', although Strauss has admitted privately that he is unsure whether they were the exact words. But they were the gist. And Strauss does indeed have cause to thank Fletcher. Had he been captain in 2006/07, he would not have been captain in 2009 and in 2010/11. He would not have been an Ashes-winning captain, of that I am pretty sure.

It soon became clear that Flintoff as captain was a huge mistake, not least for Fletcher because the 'critical mass' he so often talked about was skewed against him. Flintoff was always a very persuasive voice in the dressing room, especially with the younger players coming into the side (they were easily won over by his huge presence and friendliness). His group of followers meant that Fletcher's desired number of eight good characters was seriously diminished. The terrorists were in charge.

These words from the aforementioned ECB tour report tell the story succinctly:

An off-field 'leadership vacuum' was allowed to develop on the Tour. Duncan Fletcher has always favoured empowering the captain as 'leader' whilst he plays a 'consultancy' role. Andrew Flintoff has proved not to be as natural a leader as Nasser Hussain or Michael Vaughan and not to have had as close a working relationship with Duncan Fletcher. It does not appear that sufficient time and effort was spent building team unity off the field. Andrew Flintoff has been a player who has needed 'managing' – it does not appear that the award of the Captaincy has led to him moderating his behaviour or to this situation changing. In the preparatory work prior to and at the start of the tour, the Team had agreed to take on a challenging, aggressive persona rather than a non-confrontational, friendly one that had the danger of setting a submissive tone and of isolating any England player targeted for sledging by the opposition. The Captain clearly did/does not believe in this approach and this issue was not properly ironed out in advance of the tour. The end result appears to have been a degree of disillusion and frustration for those players who believed in and aimed to carry out the original policy.

That is all so true. Only Kevin Pietersen and Paul Collingwood initially challenged the Australians verbally, but even Pietersen relented a little once he made up with Shane Warne after a spat, leaving Collingwood fighting a lone battle. There was an awful moment in Sydney when Collingwood and Warne (who was batting) were going hard at each other, with Chris Read standing between them in silence.

In Fletcher's book we used the words 'I was soon to discover he [Flintoff] was unsure of what true leadership is'. Fletcher should have been stronger, and at one stage did want to be so.

England simply had to do well in the first Test in Brisbane. Otherwise Flintoff would run away from the problem, as I believe is his wont. That is in his character. He dislikes confrontation, as well as making decisions that might prove unpopular. I'll give you a little example of something that has happened since he finished playing. Myles Hodgson is a respected cricket writer who ghosted all of Flintoff's books and has always been loyal and helpful to him. He considered himself a friend of Flintoff's. In 2009 he began working part-time for Flintoff's management company, ISM (International Sports Management). About a year later Hodgson was sacked suddenly by the company, but, as I write, he has not heard a word from Flintoff since.

England did badly in that first Test, and so Flintoff ran to the bar. He subsequently revealed that he may have been suffering from depression at the time, worsening his tendency to heavy drinking. The 'Fredalo' incident later in the winter was almost inevitable. It was also another problem that the embattled Fletcher could have done without.

The incident occurred on 16 March 2007, the night after England had lost to New Zealand in St Lucia in their opening match of the World Cup. Two days later they were to face Canada, also in St Lucia. The performance against New Zealand had been disappointing, a loss by six wickets, so when Flintoff saw a group of journalists at the Rex Resorts Hotel bar later, he told them he was not drinking that night. With laptop under arm, he was talking excitedly about 'Skyping' his family.

Flintoff, however, is easily persuaded, and did have a drink. He was soon joined by Jeremy Snape, the former England one-day spin bowler who'd been employed by Fletcher as a psychologist. Together they went to the local Lime bar, and from there to the Rumours nightclub. With them were five other players – James Anderson, Jon Lewis, Ian Bell, Paul Nixon and Liam Plunkett (although I gather one other senior player may have been there and therefore been a little fortunate to escape the flak that followed) – as well as the bowling coach Kevin Shine, who was mightily unfortunate to be caught up in all of this as it was his first night out on tour, having met up with his holidaying brother.

Flintoff can take up the story. 'Not long after I arrived at the club, I realized I'd had enough to drink and slipped out – intending to walk back to the hotel,' he wrote in his book *Ashes to Ashes*. 'Instead of walking down the road, I decided it would be nicer down the beach and come into the hotel from the back. A row of kayaks caught my eye, but none of them had any oars. Next to them were some pedalos, and I remember dragging one to the edge of the water – presumably because I fancied a ride. But for the life of me, I couldn't work out how to get on it – or my legs into it – so I let go of it, and it quickly drifted away from the shore. I think I slipped and fell over in a few inches of water, but nothing more.'

By the next morning it was obvious that the incident had not gone unnoticed. The *News of the World* had the story. How they came about it remains something of a mystery, and it was rather strange that the story appeared under the byline of David Norrie, a close friend of Flintoff's who had been on his stag 'do' to Budapest in early 2005.

The source is not important. The story was valid, and embarrassing, even if the physiotherapist Conway could extract some humour from Flintoff the next morning.

'Where were you going, Fred?' he asked.

'Preston, I think,' replied Flintoff.

In fact all Flintoff did that weekend was go back to his room. He was banned for the Canada match.

Up until 'Fredalo' there had been no greater fuss that winter than that made over England's selection for the first Test in Brisbane. England chose Geraint Jones as wicketkeeper ahead of Read, and Ashley Giles as spinner over Monty Panesar. They were seen as contentious picks because Read and Panesar had finished the English season in possession of those places. Giles had been injured for some considerable time.

Jones was also put on the team management group that Fletcher always used to help with decision-making. This was seen as ridiculous Fletcher favouritism. But I will quote that ECB report again:

> The Cricket Management Group for the Ashes comprised Andrew Flintoff, Andrew Strauss, Paul Collingwood and Geraint Jones and played just the same consultative/advisory role to Coach and captain that it has played since Duncan Fletcher established the concept when he was first appointed. The media seized on the inclusion of Geraint Jones on this group seeing it as a sign of DF's strong support for Geraint Jones. DF explains in his report the reasons Geraint Jones was on the Group – Andrew Flintoff was very keen to have him there, he is a good contributor to the group and it was felt that it would be a good move to boost his confidence.

Jones himself wishes it had not happened. 'In hindsight I wish I'd said no,' he says. 'It put a lot of pressure on me early on. I'd gone into that tour with the mindset that Readie would have the gloves and maybe I'd get a chance come Boxing Day. I just wanted to play my cricket and not worry about all the extra stuff.'

Giles was also unsure of his elevation. 'It was a bit of a surprise to me that I got the call,' he says. 'Even up to the last first-class game before the Test I didn't play. The first Test was my first first-class game in twelve months. It was quite a big ask. And just by getting picked for the first Test everyone was against me.'

In truth there were bigger issues than these two selections, which Flintoff not only agreed with, by the way, but positively pushed for. Little wonder that Fletcher eventually cracked and said 'I am not the sole selector' after the second Test in Adelaide in which he had wanted to play two spinners in Giles and Panesar, but had been thoroughly outvoted, with everyone on the management team disagreeing.

I do not think the supposed under-preparation of the team was an issue either. 'Undercooked' quickly became a cliché, but it was an easy line. There was the Champions Trophy in India just beforehand, so preparation time was limited, especially as, against Fletcher's wishes, there had to be a one-day match against a Prime Minister's XI at the start of the tour. Quite how a fifty-over match was supposed to aid Test-match preparation has never been made clear.

England did play two three-day matches, against New South Wales and South Australia. They faced some rather decent players in the shapes of bowlers Glenn McGrath, Brett Lee, Stuart Clark, Jason Gillespie and Shaun Tait, and batsmen like Phil Jaques, Simon Katich, Michael Clarke, Matthew Elliott and Darren Lehmann. Mischievously a Cricket Australia (CA) official told journalists that England had turned down the opportunity to play four first-class matches before the first Test. It was not true. In fact CA made the ECB pay for their first two days on tour, because they were two more days than England had hosted Australia for before the first Test in 2005. So this rather silences those who criticized England for going home for four days after the Champions Trophy rather than travelling straight to Australia. It would have cost more money, and Fletcher said he would have given the players four days off even if they had gone to Australia.

Another major gripe among observers was that the NSW match was a fourteen-a-side affair. But that had always been Fletcher's way. He viewed such matches as no more than practice. He preferred his players to be a little underdone going into a Test series. But it was never a popular policy, and now in Australia the brickbats flew.

When in 2010/11 England played three first-class matches

(two of them lasting three days and one four) and won two and drew the other, much was made of the preparation, but I reckon England were a little lucky. They played the same top six batsmen in all three games, therefore depriving the reserve batsman Eoin Morgan of a match before the first Test. Imagine if one of the chosen six had broken a finger the day before that first Test. Yes, Morgan showed at the start of the 2011 season that he could play first-class cricket with little preparation, returning from the Indian Premier League to score 193 for the Lions against Sri Lanka to secure a place for the first Test, but this was different. It was a gamble.

It worked, though. But there was no such luck in 2006/07. With the 5–0 drubbing completed in Sydney, at the city's Sheraton on the Park Hotel the ECB called an emergency board meeting of the seven of its twelve members present at the Test. 'The board were united on the need for a review,' says Morgan, 'and came to the conclusion that it should have a ring of independence about it. A shortlist of potential independent review leaders was drawn up and after running it past Ian Jones, a trusted Mayfair-based head-hunter, I decided to opt for Ken Schofield. And the rest is history.'

That Test in Sydney had finished on 5 January. By 11 January Schofield was receiving a call from ECB chief executive David Collier asking him to head the review. 'It came as much of a surprise to me as to all those who were equally surprised that an ageing Scotsman of doubtful cricketing pedigree could play any meaningful [part in a] review of the disappointing winter that had unfolded in Australia in terms of the Ashes defence,' Schofield wrote in his introduction to the eventual report, the full version of which I have seen, and just about waded through without falling asleep.

No matter. The Scot Schofield, the former director of the PGA European tour, was actually a decent choice. He was going to be in Australia during the one-day series anyway, having previously arranged to go there with his wife to visit their son who was on a two-year work secondment. He was given a six-man committee of Nasser Hussain, Angus Fraser, Nick Knight, Mickey Stewart, Hugh Morris and Brian Rose, all former England cricketers.

Mike Atherton declined to be on the committee, citing a conflict of interest with his media duties. And good on him for doing so. He still spoke to Schofield, as did 'between 80 and 100' other cricketing people according to the author of the report, to air some of his views. But Atherton's desire to remain on one side of the fence is depressingly rare in English cricket, indeed in cricket in general. Too many want to wear too many hats. Fraser was still cricket correspondent of the *Independent* when sitting on this report committee. Not without justification did he at the time have the nickname 'Martini', as in 'any time, any place, anywhere'. He could certainly keep a number of plates spinning at the same time. He would say that he was helping the game, and it might be partly true, but a conflict of interest is never a good thing. I have been asked to stand for the Glamorgan committee, asked to sit on Review Groups there, but have always declined. To undertake any official position brings instant compromise. I gladly offer opinion and help, but never on an official basis.

At one stage Alec Stewart managed to be a coach (at Surrey), broadcaster and an agent/mentor all at the same time, while running, alongside Alan Smith, the former manager of Crystal Palace, his sports management firm Arundel Promotions (now taken over by Essentially Group Limited). I'm not sure Stewart was actually involving himself in deals concerning players under his wing, but that can't have been right when he was looking after cricketers such as Bell, Prior and Collingwood. As I write now the likes of Warwickshire's Chris Woakes and Surrey's Jade Dernbach, two promising young bowlers for England, are in Essentially's stable where Stewart acts mostly as an ambassador, as well as offering guidance to players. Once in 2008 Stewart was particularly scathing about the performances of Bell and Collingwood. 'I call it as I see it,' he said, 'and I don't ever let any agency connections get in the way when my role is to comment on performances. The players understand that you have to be hard sometimes.'

In 2011 Surrey's director of cricket, Chris Adams, spent four days at Hove commentating for Sky Sports when his team, complete with Pietersen returning from injury amid an inevitable welter of publicity, were playing at Cambridge University. How does that work? Surrey lost too. While at Hove Adams was asked whether he thought the Surrey fast bowler Chris Tremlett should be in the side for the first Test of the summer. What was he going to say?

Away from media conflicts of interest, the case of Ashley Giles is interesting. He is Warwickshire's director of cricket, as well as an England selector. To add to the mix, after the Moores/Pietersen double sacking in early 2009, he applied to take over as England team director. Amid suggestions that he was too close to too many of the players, he was not interviewed for the role. 'With hindsight it is the best thing that could have happened to me,' he says. 'I needed more time. I felt I could do it. And I never felt the relationships with the players would have affected that. I had similar relationships with the Warwickshire players when I took over there. We all know where the line stands.'

It is a fair point, but, with Warwickshire always on the lookout to sign new players, there have been complaints from other counties that his position as a selector might attract players to his county. Some have even suggested privately that Giles might be using that position to lure players. That is ridiculous, maybe even slanderous. Giles is an unimpeachable character. But he does not take kindly to criticism. He has been one of the more sensitive England cricketers of recent times.

'You read one bad line in a newspaper and it kills you,' he says. 'You think "Shit, why do I bother?"' Mind you, when Dave Houghton said that England were better off playing with ten men after the first Ashes Test in 2005 than including him, that was pretty harsh criticism.

Less harsh was a flippant ironic throwaway line from David Hopps in the *Guardian* in 2007, which is barely worth mentioning because it was so inoffensive. But, prompted by the man from Radio Five Live with whom he was working during the Test against India, the then-retired Giles came to the press box and began what we journos love to term a PBI (press box incident). Hopps, who had ghosted Giles's *Guardian* column in 2005, reckons he's never been more angry and had to leave the box to calm down. Somehow, probably because at the time I was working for the *Guardian* too and because I think Hopps said something like 'You tell him, Jamo' as he left, I got involved. I'm not sure I told him, as Hopps asked. Indeed I'm not sure I said anything. It was all rather silly.

Giles appears a shrewd selector. We can be thankful to him for the discovery of Jonathan Trott as a Test batsman. Trott made his sensational Test debut (scoring 41 and 119) in the deciding Ashes match at the Oval in 2009, after the whole of England had seemingly given their opinion as to who should replace the out-of-form Ravi Bopara. I'm sure W. G. Grace was mentioned at one point. Or was it Mark Ramprakash?

But the truth is that decision had already been made for the previous Test at Headingley, in which England were thrashed. The batsman they had called into the squad and discarded on the morning of the match was Trott. I happened to see him leaving the ground with his pregnant wife. He was genuinely distraught. I know a few English cricketers who wouldn't have been. The pressure would have been postponed.

But as Giles said to me on a later occasion, he knew that if Trott was playing well, which he was at the time, 'he could block out all the external pressures and just bat'. And that he did rather well at the Oval. So well done to Giles.

Picking selectors is a curious business. It's not exactly a sage career choice. You can't really say 'I want to be a selector, sir' to your careers master. For Giles and James Whitaker, it is not paid well enough to be a full-time job. Poor old Graveney spent ten years as chairman of selectors on modest pay, and then the moment the role was made important after the Schofield Report and given the grander title of 'National Selector' as well as considerably more dosh, he was sacked. As I mentioned earlier, I'm not sure that Graveney was that good, but he was not that bad either. Selection definitely improved in some areas during his time, in terms of consistency and logic for sure, although I suspect Fletcher had much to do with that.

But Fletcher had nothing to do with the setting up of the Schofield Report, and that angered him. He felt it was designed solely to get rid of him. As the then team analyst Mark Garaway says, 'I've only been involved in two official reviews, and in both those the outcome was already decided and it seemed they were trying to find a way to get to that end point. One was with Somerset [where Garaway was promoted to be head coach instead of Shine, who was demoted to the Academy], and this one with England. Fletch didn't deserve this.'

Was it all about sacking Fletcher? 'I remember speaking to Mickey Stewart and us saying "If this is purely about sacking the England coach, then we don't want to be part of it",' says Hugh Morris. 'The driver was to identify key areas that had gone wrong and make sure they didn't happen again. If it was meant to sack Duncan I wasn't going to do that, nor was Mickey or Nasser for that matter.'

As Schofield himself says, 'It was the first question Nasser asked me in Melbourne. He immediately nailed his colours to Duncan Fletcher's mast, and I said to him, "We're not a hiring and firing agency." That heartened Nasser. There wasn't an overall running down of the coach during the report.'

You sense Hussain had mixed feelings about being part of the report. 'Duncan was cross,' he says, 'but he only told me that afterwards. I just got a phone call asking if I would sit on the group. I have always thought that I should help if I can, so I said yes. Hugh was on it and he was not anti-Duncan. We just went through everything that people had been critical of.'

On 24 May 2007, ECB chief executive David Collier announced the following nineteen recommendations from the Schofield Report:

Focusing on the Individual

1. Central Contracts To ensure the system of Central Contracts is maintained and developed by establishing challenging individually tailored training and preparation programmes which are closely monitored through the Performance Centre at Loughborough University, and reflect the 'needs' rather than the 'wants' of the players.

2. England Performance Squad Players outside the system of Central Contracts but selected for the England Performance Squad should have an individually tailored 12-month training and preparation programme closely monitored through the Performance Centre.

3. Skills Sets Skills Sets of players up to the age of Under 19 should be established, and have individually tailored 12-month training and preparation programmes closely monitored through the Performance Centre.

4. International Exchanges Maintain and develop links with Academies and teams throughout the World in order to provide players in England squads with the opportunity to spend time overseas developing their technical and tactical skills at appropriate times during their development.

5. Fitness and Conditioning The introduction of individually tailored strength and conditioning programmes for players within England programmes at all levels.

6. Medical Support and Screening To implement the recommendations within the ECB Science and Medicine Review, enhance the medical screening of all senior players, particularly fast bowlers, and provide 'World Class' medical support for Centrally Contracted players.

7. Player Personal Development To provide individual personal development programmes for each player in the England Performance Squad programme including media training in order to ensure the development of 'well-rounded' individuals.

8. Captaincy and Leadership Development The establishment of mentoring and development programmes for players who are in, or have the potential to be in, Captaincy and leadership roles within England cricket.

9. Coaching and Support Staff Professional Development The establishment of professional development programmes for England coaches and support staff in order for them to remain leading-edge practitioners.

10. Skill Development Supplement the coaching resources at the Performance Centre by appointing a Fielding Coach responsible for raising the standards of this discipline throughout the game.

11. Succession Planning Maintain a succession plan for all key positions within the England programme.

Focusing on the Team

12. International Programme To provide more opportunities for players to prepare, perform, repair and regenerate by reducing the amount of International cricket.

13. Establishing the National Cricket Centre as the 'Performance Centre' Refurbishment and rebranding the National Cricket Centre at Loughborough as the ECB Performance Centre, and establish the Centre as the focal point for all England player monitoring and development.

14. Domestic Competition Structure To reduce the amount of cricket played at First Class level to enable players to maintain and develop their cricket skills and fitness levels during the season, and provide competition formats and regulations which as far as possible mirror the international game.

15. Improving the Quality of Coaching A review and continual updating of the Level 4 Coaching and CPD programme to ensure the top coaches are equipped with the necessary skills and knowledge to develop 'World Class' players.

16. Improve Links/Communications with Counties Establish within a management structure, executive responsibility for promoting engagement and communication between England programmes and Counties, and raising the standards of First Class cricket.

Focusing on ECB

17. England Management Structure The establishment of a new management structure within the ECB with full accountability and responsibility for the selection and performance of the England cricket team.

18. Player Tracking Database The establishment of a player tracking database with the ability to monitor the development of every player in an England Squad.

19. Ongoing Planning Process Establish a robust biannual review process including all stakeholders and designed to take the game to the next level.

Sixteen of these were adopted immediately, and another, the 'establishment of a new management structure', was resolved in due course, but two other recommendations – 'reducing the amount of International cricket' and 'to reduce the amount of cricket played at First Class level . . . and provide competition formats and regulations which as far as possible mirror the international game' – remain on the mantelpiece, like unwanted wedding presents; gaudy-looking vases gathering dust. The volume of cricket internationally and domestically just isn't decreasing, and doesn't look as if it will by any great measure, even if Morgan's Report of 2012 suggests a reduction to 14 county championship matches. That review also proposes fifty-over county cricket, but as of 2012, county cricketers still don't play fifty-over one-day matches, as they do at World Cups. 'If I have one real regret,' says Schofield, 'it is that the counties still don't play fifty overs.'

For me the best thing to come out of the Schofield Report was the appointment of Hugh Morris as the managing director of England cricket, to fill the 'vacuum of accountability at the heart of the England set-up', as Morris has said since, and to rectify 'a distinct lack of communication between the England set-up and the ECB', and to be 'accountable for everything that comes under the broad remit of England cricket'.

I'm not just saying this because of my obvious links to Morris. It was not necessarily an appointment that was received with widespread favour. There were some who questioned how a man on the report committee could then claim the lucrative job that it recommended. 'Jobs for the boys!' screamed Hussain at the time, but his ire was probably more directed at Gatting, who was appointed managing director of cricket partnerships. They've never got on, ever since a match at the Parks in 1989 actually, a match I played in for the Combined Universities against Middlesex, when Gatting took exception to the young Hussain not walking.

Morris was deputy chief executive at the time of the report. He had first been technical director upon retiring from first-class cricket in 1997, then performance director and even acting chief executive in between the reigns of Tim Lamb and David Collier. As soon as the report was adopted, the role of deputy chief executive became redundant. He was one of fifty people to apply for the new role, with only six being interviewed. He was a worried man. Clearly had he known that a managing director would be recommended in the report, he would have had reservations about sitting on it in the first place. But he was very well qualified for the job. He'd played international cricket, he'd been heavily involved in elite coaching, he has a sports science degree and he has an MBA. And as he says, 'It's not unusual for top companies to promote from within.'

The recommendation of a managing director only came late in the Schofield Report's discussions, but it should have been one of the first. Fletcher might still be England coach today had he had such a buffer between himself and the administrators at the ECB. I asked him during the course of writing this book whether he would have liked such a person to help, and he agreed instantly. Ask those in the ECB and they will say that the increasingly autocratic Fletcher would not have entertained such a thought; indeed that it was mentioned but Fletcher refused. But it is surely more a matter of personnel. At the time of the Schofield Report Fletcher was angry with Morris, and indeed with Schofield, because they were staying in the same hotel as the team in Melbourne, and neither went to see him. Morris says there was no time, and that Stewart was due to speak to him before his departure to the Caribbean for the World Cup.

Morris as managing director and Fletcher as team director, as Flower is now titled, would have made an excellent combination. Many of the stresses that eventually dragged Fletcher down could have been taken from his shoulders. Fletcher has never openly criticized Morris to me. Deep down I think he knows he is a good man. It's just that, as already mentioned, if you cross Fletcher once, the road back is a long one.

But Morris is a good man, and a mate, even if the administrator/journalist relationship cannot be as open as most friendships are. It can be tricky at times because the easy assumption is, especially among fellow journalists, that he feeds

me information, stories even. I can assure you that never once
has he been the source of any 'story' I have obtained.

We shared some good times opening together for Glamorgan.
Over the courses of our careers we made a hundred first-class
centuries between us (forty-seven for me, fifty-three for him) and
underwent twelve knee operations (seven for me, five for him).
We had some ups and downs (the bastard dropped me!), but he
was undoubtedly the better player. I also thought him the
bravest of all the batsmen I batted with, although Atherton
clearly ran him close. Quite how brave I didn't fully realize. For
in August 2002 Morris suddenly discovered an opponent that
was to prove tougher than anything he had ever faced on a
cricket field.

One morning Morris cut himself shaving, and as he tended to
the blood, he felt a lump on his neck. Three weeks later the lump
was removed, and he was advised to return to see the surgeon in
ten days' time. But the next evening Morris was told to return
the following morning, and to bring his wife Debbie with him.

I remember in 2007 talking to Morris about Fletcher's book
and excitedly telling him that I thought some of Fletcher's early
life had been interesting, especially during the war years. 'He's
faced death, and not many of us have done that,' I said.
Immediately I realized what I had said. Morris smiled. 'I have,'
he said.

He began retelling the story of that day with the surgeon, a
man called Rogan Corbridge, when he was told he had
a secondary cancer. Biopsies were taken from his tonsils, throat,
tongue and nose, and the primary cancer was found in the
tonsils. In early 2003 he underwent a seven-hour operation,
called a bilateral neck dissection, and then had six weeks of
radiotherapy treatment.

Morris has always enjoyed a healthy appetite, and I don't
think he will mind my saying that he was never the most svelte
of cricketers. Lunch was never ready unless Morris was at the

front of its queue. There was one famous occasion at Sophia Gardens when such were his stomach's desires after a hard morning session in the field that he hurtled across the outfield, hurdled the advertising hoardings and was in that queue seemingly with the umpires still lifting the bails from their grooves.

But in early 2003 Morris lost nearly four stone in weight. That summer he came to Sophia Gardens to watch a game. I chanced upon him in the car park. I fully admit that I nearly burst into tears. The sight before my eyes was quite shocking. He looked like a man of seventy years rather than thirty-nine.

Words are not easy in such circumstances. But you know what? As soon as I spoke to him, I was convinced that he'd win his battle. For a man so clearly in such a bad way, he was remarkably upbeat. Cancer had chosen the wrong person. He was going to beat it.

And he did. On 14 May 2008, five years after he'd completed his radiotherapy treatment, Morris was given the all-clear. 'It is a date indelibly marked in my mind,' he says, with plenty of justification. English cricket has a special man overseeing its work. He gives it a perspective sport too often lacks.

8

Respect No Moores

Peter Moores' first Test as the new England coach was at Lord's against the West Indies in May 2007. The visitors won the toss and elected to field. As England's openers Andrew Strauss and Alastair Cook began their innings, I decided to take a stroll down from the Media Centre to one of the many food outlets at the Nursery End, searching ostensibly for a stronger cup of coffee than was available upstairs (yes, my name is Steve and I am a coffee addict), but also mindful that a player or coach or both might still be lurking around the net areas.

What I didn't expect to see was the head coach there. Moores was in the nets throwing to Liam Plunkett, the Durham bowler playing in his seventh Test. My heart sank. It is the kind of scenario you see every day at a county ground, and good on the coaches at that level for being so industrious. But at international level, you just cannot do that sort of thing. You have days in advance in which to do such work, and plenty of assistants to do it during the match if need be. When the Test starts you must be watching every ball. The media might be quizzing you about any aspect of the day's play later.

England had hastily installed a county coach, an extremely good county coach admittedly, in charge of the national team. At that moment I knew they'd made a mistake. I wish I'd had the courage to write as much. But I'd have looked pretty silly. Even now it seems such a petty crime on which to hang a man. But I do think it was a loud and early indication of the perils of hasty over-promotion. Moores was trying to be a county coach in the international game. It was confirmed a few years later by Michael Vaughan. 'The difference is that in county cricket you have to energize people,' he said. 'In international cricket you almost have to slow them down. With Test cricket you have to let it breathe a little. It is not all about energy.'

Goodness, Moores had been appointed less than a day after Duncan Fletcher resigned. The ECB had done this without advertisement or interview. They will point to the fact that Moores' appointment to the head of the National Academy job had come after a lengthy process of recruitment, during which for example the Australian Tom Moody, many people's favourite to succeed Fletcher, had been interviewed. Yes, it was a different role, but Moores had come out on top. 'He was very well regarded at the Academy,' says the then ECB chairman David Morgan. 'The chairman of Sussex, David Green, who was then a director of ECB, was very strong in recommending him. He was simply regarded as an outstanding candidate.'

Privately it may be a different story. One ECB official told me that had he interviewed Moores there was no way on earth he would have appointed him. While, when it came to appointing Andy Flower in 2009, a firm of head-hunters, Odgers Ray & Berndtson, were employed to recommend a shortlist of candidates. Mind you, the ECB got criticized for that too!

Things did not begin too badly for Moores. That first series against the West Indies was won 3–0. England lost the subsequent three-match series to India (home) and Sri Lanka (away) 1–0, but were never disgraced, and in one-day cricket, although they lost 2–1 to the West Indies, there were hugely encouraging series victories over India (4–3) and Sri Lanka (3–2).

It was in New Zealand in 2008 that cracks began to appear. That was actually my first overseas tour as a journalist, having just been appointed to replace Mike Atherton as the *Sunday Telegraph*'s cricket columnist. He was still in that position on that trip, however, and I went as correspondent in place of Scyld Berry who was otherwise engaged with editing *Wisden*.

England had lost the one-day series 3–1, but it was the tied match in Napier, where New Zealand managed to equal England's score of 340, that had begun to cause problems for Moores' regime. Remarkably after such a gruelling match, England's players were asked to go out and train. It didn't go down well, especially with the senior players.

It is, of course, the sort of story that is easily embellished, and it does seem that it was not a wholly compulsory session. One player told me that Moores had said 'Let's get out there and show them we're harder than them!' But team analyst Mark Garaway is not so sure those words were uttered. 'It was the sort of language Pete might have used,' he says, 'but it wasn't the full squad that went out by any stretch of the imagination. I remember it as being the group that didn't play in that match and a couple of lads who played but didn't do much.'

Graeme Swann, in his autobiography *The Breaks Are Off*, claims that everyone was ordered to do the running. 'He [Moores] announced that the whole squad was to return to the field of play,' he wrote. '"Those New Zealand boys will see us running on the square, and they will shit their pants, because they'll know that we mean business," he claimed. Shit their pants? More like piss their pants.

'The Kiwi lads thought it was absolutely hilarious as we trooped out into the middle with our fitness trainer. Our opponents sat there watching us from their dressing-room balcony, beers in hand, laughing their heads off.

'They couldn't believe what they were seeing, and I have to say it's the most humiliating and degrading session I have ever been involved in. For half an hour as we shuttled back and forth we had to ignore their mocking laughter.'

It is the gist of the story, but see what I was saying about embellishment?

Moores agreed to be interviewed for this book, which I wasn't expecting. Whether owing to the legal niceties of his departure from the ECB or not, he has rarely talked about his time as England coach since. And I was hardly his greatest supporter in the media.

He seemed to know the Napier issue would be asked about, and there does seem to be some regret on his part now. 'There are certain things I'd do differently,' he admits. 'There was an incident when we trained after one of the one-dayers [Napier]. It was sort of optional. What we were trying to do was to try and get ourselves fitter and stronger. If I'm being honest, when we first started we weren't in the right shape to be really competitive as an international unit, so the idea was that if we tagged in a quick twenty minutes then we wouldn't have to train for two days. I think the players saw it differently, especially the senior ones. That for me was a frustration.'

There was clearly a lot of frustration on that tour. It did not really become public at the time. There were murmurings, of course, but nothing explicit. Little did we know at the time that captain Vaughan was on the brink of resignation. He had texted ECB chairman Giles Clarke during the tour asking to talk. Had they done so Vaughan might have resigned there and then. Instead, before the flight home Vaughan spoke to Hugh Morris, who was also out in New Zealand, and voiced some concerns about Moores. Vaughan has since admitted that he flew home determined to resign, even though

England won the third Test in Napier to take the series 2–1.

That Test has become well known for the saving of Andrew Strauss's Test career. He made a duck in the first innings, and then 177 in the second innings. He was then batting at number three as a reluctant Vaughan opened with Cook at Moores' insistence on a right-hand/left-hand partnership. 'It was schoolboy logic,' said one player. Strauss had been dropped for the previous tour of Sri Lanka and it has since been said many times that it was good for him. I have never believed that. Listening to such an argument you'd think he came good immediately in New Zealand. He didn't. Had he got a second-innings duck, he might never have played Test cricket again. Yes, our double-Ashes-winning skipper might have been on the international scrapheap, a victim of a clash between two regimes.

As it was, Strauss managed to resurrect himself in an environment where Moores was unwisely attempting to break up the band of senior players that had been so loyal to, and generally so productive for, Fletcher.

Given what we know now I think it might have been better had Vaughan resigned after that tour. It was just not working with Moores. The next summer was simply a water-treading exercise. Just take what Vaughan wrote in a personal report, as revealed in his autobiography *Time to Declare*, before departing New Zealand: 'I feel that Peter [Moores] has been a little bit disrespectful to the old regime. He believes the Schofield report and has listened to it too much. He wants to change everything including personnel.'

Of course, following Fletcher was never going to be easy. But I have heard it said among the current England management that it was Fletcher's greatest fault that he did not create an environment where his successor could easily take over. I'm not sure about that. As mentioned earlier, Fletcher would have quite liked a hand-over period.

Moores handled the situation poorly. One comment he made

in our interview has stayed with me: 'How Duncan did the job I don't really know,' he said. He went on to say: 'It's a difficult thing to comment on coaching sometimes unless you're a player in there.' But surely it was Moores' job to find out what Fletcher did. There were clearly things that worked very well for Fletcher. It might have been an idea to incorporate some of them into his own methods.

Instead Moores, as Vaughan said, believed everything in the Schofield Report and blasted in with his methods. 'I knew how I could coach,' he says, 'and if I was not authentic to myself: one, the players would know; two, it wouldn't be me. I knew how I was going to coach and was prepared to see where it took us. I was just looking to be my own man.'

I was not in Moores' dressing room, but I was in the Glamorgan dressing room when Fletcher left in 1999 and a good-hearted but clumsy Australian called Jeff Hammond took over. It seems to me that both Hammond and Moores made the same mistakes. They railed against the Fletcher regime. I am certain Hammond felt inadequate in his shadow and I guess deep down Moores felt the same way.

Hilariously, Hammond made his first speech to us and promised a period of considered observation. Within a few minutes of the subsequent net practice he was vehemently advising our left-arm spinner that he couldn't possibly take first-class wickets with such an action and being rather rude about the stance of one of our young batsmen. Carrot and arse were mentioned in the same sentence.

Moores wasn't as tactless, of course. But he immediately tried to do things significantly differently. He was definitely not going to play Fletcher's consultant role. 'They certainly had different styles of coaching,' says Ashley Giles, who played under Fletcher and was a selector under Moores. 'Fletch's style was more sit back and watch and far more technical; Moores' style was more direct, and more directive. "This is what is going to happen now and this is what is going to happen then".'

It obviously did not sit well with his England captains. Vaughan resigned, Paul Collingwood resigned as one-day captain, and then there was the Kevin Pietersen farrago. It is actually forgotten that Strauss was Moores' first captain. For that Test mentioned at the very top of this chapter, Strauss was captain because Vaughan was injured.

The charge against Moores is that he wanted to be in charge too much. I put this to him. 'You play the role that the side needs at the time,' he said. 'It depends on the maturity of the team and where you're at. As a coach you are actively part of that team. You are in that team. I don't think coaches want the credit of the successes of their teams. Coaches don't want that. But managing anything is leading. You can't help that. Fletch was a leader. He can tell you what he wants. He was a leader. You arrive in the morning and have an influence.'

Fletcher was indeed a leader, and he does not think any coach can be worth his salt unless he is a strong leader, but it is the way you lead that is the key. In cricket the captain must still be the man in charge. It is difficult for a leadership model to work any other way. It is not like football or rugby where the manager or coach is always the leading voice and direction. It is why England's three-captains decision in 2011 was, as Andy Flower admitted at the time, 'a gamble'. It was lucky that none of the three appointed skippers – Strauss for Tests, Cook for one-day internationals and Stuart Broad for Twenty20s, which became five (Eoin Morgan and Graeme Swann also captained an ODI and two T20s respectively in the summer of 2011) – was like Nasser Hussain in character and outlook. It would have stood no chance then.

Vaughan made another point about Moores in that personal report quoted above: 'I get the feeling he would like a young captain that he can control and brainwash.' I suspect that may have been right. I think he quite fancied Ian Bell as captain.

Vaughan bears no animosity towards Moores. 'I had a decent relationship with Pete,' he says, and Vaughan phoned him before the release of his autobiography to warn him that he had been critical. 'I just think he got that job at the wrong time. It can be quite difficult for an Englishman to take it, because you almost know too much and can be too cosy with the counties, wanting to be best mates with all the coaches etc.'

None of this is to say that Moores is a poor coach. He is an exceptional coach. Talk to people at Sussex and Lancashire and they swear by him. He brought Sussex their first county championship pennant in 2003, and, in 2011, Lancashire their first title outright since 1934. He changed the culture at Sussex. They worked their socks off, especially at the disciplines like fielding and running between the wickets that are so easily improved by sheer graft. Sussex truly became a team, even if their critics will say that their success was mainly down to Mushtaq Ahmed. There is some truth in that, but truer still is that Moores took an almighty punt on Mushtaq, initially placing him on a small retainer contract with larger incentives for wickets and wins. Most observers considered him 'gone' as a cricketer when Moores signed him for the 2003 season after a few games for Surrey in late 2002.

Under Moores, Sussex did things differently. They were the trendsetters, using video analysis, a baseball coach for throwing, a vision coach, and tennis balls for fielding practice (improving reflexes and 'give' in the catch) before other counties. Once in pre-season the Sussex players arrived at the ground to find pots of paint waiting for them. The ground as a whole needed a lick and the players duly provided it without complaint. A team motto was introduced: 'United we believe, together we achieve'.

At Lancashire Moores did something similar. Nobody gave them a prayer in 2011. One esteemed former player said at the start of the season that it was the worst Lancashire side he had ever seen. They were certainly a young side, and indeed a small squad, without any stars, and it helped that they played all their home games that season away from Old Trafford (mostly at Liverpool) while it was being redeveloped, but Moores worked them hard and created a good spirit. To win the championship was a remarkable achievement given some of the great Lancashire names who had failed to win the title outright (they shared it in 1950): from the locals Brian Statham, Roy Tattersall, Jack Bond, David Hughes, David Lloyd, Mike Atherton, Neil Fairbrother, John Crawley and Andrew Flintoff to the overseas players such as Ken Grieves, Farokh Engineer, Clive Lloyd, Wasim Akram, Michael Holding, Colin Croft, Patrick Patterson and Muttiah Muralitharan. No matter that it was a poor championship year in terms of quality (if not in excitement, as it went to the final afternoon), it was still a mighty success and a romantic story.

Speak to Flower and the admiration for Moores is both huge and sincere. Indeed Flower cites no greater influence as a coach. 'I could never do what he does,' Flower once told me. 'His energy is unbelievable. He really knows how to run a cricket team.' And I don't think it's just because Moores appointed him as his assistant with England. Indeed I'm told Flower has run his England team in very much the same way Moores did his. One player told me 'Mooresy was all about getting fitness levels to a standard where we could train harder and for longer', which in essence has worked fantastically well, but the important difference is that with Flower the 'message is not so overpowering'.

Moores also made some other good appointments: Richard Halsall as fielding coach (as he had done at Sussex in 2003 too) and Mushtaq as spin-bowling coach, even if that was a controversial move because Mushtaq had been implicated in Pakistan's Qayyum Report into match-fixing in 2000. But Mushtaq has remained under Flower as an important part of the coaching team, doing a hundred days a year with the team. When the spot-fixing allegations against Pakistan arose in 2010 he quite naturally came under the spotlight again, but Flower countered with this: 'He's a cricket coach – that's what he is – and we're very comfortable working with Mushy. He's a lovely man, and a good man for our system. I'm quite happy with that.'

While his technical spin coaching may not have always worked – Adil Rashid has been a conspicuous failure, though that may not necessarily be Mushtaq's fault – he is used as much for his Test-match strategic thinking. He has a fertile cricketing brain. And he is definitely popular, ever-smiling. He calls Flower 'Mr Andy' and Swann 'Mr Swanny'; in return Swann calls him 'Mr Mushy'. On his much-talked-about Ashes 2010/11 video diaries one of Swann's best lines was to suggest that Mushtaq's long beard, with streaks of white in it, was sponsored by Adidas (after their famous three white stripes).

Moores introduced or reintroduced a number of players to international cricket. 'Swann, Prior, [Ryan] Sidebottom, Trott [picked for two T20s against the West Indies in 2007] and [James] Tredwell – a lot have carried on and had international careers,' Moores emphasizes. 'So I look at that and see it as a real positive. I don't look at that to steal anyone's thunder. I just look at it as a positive. We didn't have a lot of senior players, if I'm honest. As a coach you are trying to look for today but also looking for tomorrow. The players are only playing for today. I look back at other things and, knowing that you're going through transition and change, then there are not many supporters of it at the time. Nobody likes change. But sometimes it's a necessity. You just want things to evolve. I think they have evolved. I loved my time with England. I've got no regrets about it.' Indeed Moores has acted all along with great dignity. He has never criticized anyone or appeared bitter.

It's just a shame then that Moores could not build a relationship with any of his England captains, especially as he had had such a strong rapport with Chris Adams at Sussex. That took time, though, according to Moores. 'It became a very strong relationship,' he says, 'but at the start it wasn't like that. We had masses of disagreements. You are finding your space together and trying to make it work, like a marriage really. Relationships take time. A frustration for me was that I never got that time to build a relationship with Vaughany.'

Well, he did actually. Despite all his injury problems, Vaughan captained eighteen Tests under Moores, but by the third home Test against South Africa in 2008 he'd had enough. The Test had started on a Wednesday, so by Saturday South Africa had been set 281 to win. Nobody really expected the match to finish that day. I certainly didn't as the *Sunday Telegraph* columnist, and so set about doing a second piece for my column on Vaughan; on how, despite twin failures with the bat again, he should continue as captain.

But Graeme Smith played better than anyone could have expected, making a magisterial 154 not out, and the game was won late that Saturday evening. So late that neither I nor my colleague Berry could make the press conference on the other side of the ground at Edgbaston. While we were writing up our pieces, however, the man from the Press Association, Richard Gibson, returned from that press conference to announce, 'Something's up.' He thought some of Vaughan's responses were indicative of a man about to resign. It certainly caused some consternation in the press box. I made a couple of calls but could raise no one. As Berry later said, we should really have gone to the England team hotel that night. Instead we drove back to Bristol together where Berry dropped me off at the Parkway railway station. As I waited for my train all I could think was 'I hope he hasn't resigned'.

The following morning the dreaded text message arrived. Something along the lines of 'The ECB will hold a press conference at Loughborough at blah, blah, blah . . .' I didn't need to read the rest. It meant only one thing: Vaughan had resigned.

And the readers of the *Sunday Telegraph* were probably shaking their heads in disbelief at their cricket columnist's lack of acuity. 'Calls for his head are ridiculously premature,' I'd written. Oh no. He'd already topped himself.

Consolation came in the fact that I knew within an hour that Pietersen would be Vaughan's replacement, and indeed Collingwood's as one-day skipper, as he too had phoned Hugh Morris on that Saturday night to tender his resignation. That Collingwood went straight to Morris and did not even tell Moores speaks volumes about their relationship, or lack of it. It had stooped to its lowest level that summer when Moores forced Collingwood to apologize after a run-out incident involving New Zealand's Grant Elliott at the Oval. Elliott had collided with Ryan Sidebottom as the bowler went for the ball and the spirit of the game suggested that Collingwood should have withdrawn his appeal. But he didn't, and there was an almighty rumpus. Despite winning by one wicket, the New Zealand team slammed their dressing-room door in Collingwood's face as he left the field. Moores then told Collingwood he should apologize. He did, but he did not want to.

In the coming weeks I discovered that this had happened, and wrote as much in my column in a piece the week after Vaughan's resignation. It ran with the headline 'Discord seeps into Peter Moores' England dressing-room', because it was becoming ever clearer that that was the case. Collingwood and Moores were incensed that it had slipped out and apparently accused Flower of leaking it to me. I can say here and now to both of them that I had not got that information from Flower. But it was clearly correct.

As some consolation for my Vaughan shocker in 2008, the following year when Vaughan retired from all cricket I did at least manage to help break the story. I was sitting at home on Saturday, 27 June 2009 with no work planned for that day when a text arrived. 'Is Vaughan announcing his retirement in the Sun

Tel tomorrow?' it asked. Word was obviously being bandied around that that might be so. Vaughan was, and still is, a columnist for the Telegraph Media Group but I knew there was no planned column from him the following day. I made some calls, and, not knowing Vaughan that well, asked Berry to phone him. Vaughan confirmed that he was about to retire, but would not be quoted. Story!

My editor Peter Mitchell, the man to whom I owe everything in my journalistic career, at first thought it best for Berry to write Vaughan's 'obituary' so on such a pleasant summer's evening I decided to go for a cycle (my new fitness fix these days since those knee operations precluded running). I'd gone some distance, probably fifteen miles or so, when I came to the bottom of a steep hill near Bassaleg School outside Newport. I thought I could hear my phone ringing. Eventually retrieving it from the back of my cycling top, I discovered I'd missed sixteen calls! I was doing the Vaughan obit and I had just over an hour to complete it. I was still some way from home.

Don't panic.

I think it is fair to say that it was an interesting hour. It must have been well spent, though, because Berry later claimed it was one of my better pieces. Retirement as a sort of death for a professional sportsperson has always appealed to me as a writer, so off I went on that angle, relating along the way my favourite cricketing retirement story, that of Glamorgan's Emrys Davies, who told his skipper Wilf Wooller one July morning in 1954 after being bowled by Frank Tyson, 'I am finished. I can no longer see the ball.' The best part, though, is that Davies then went on to become a first-class umpire.

I ended the piece with this: 'Vaughan served England with distinction. He was a tough cookie, a great tactician, a very good batsman and, just as importantly, a very good bloke.' That's a pretty fair summation, I reckon.

So Kevin Pietersen was appointed. Atherton immediately

wrote with great prescience: 'I have a horrible feeling that this is going to end in tears.' It was such a contentious appointment that I understand the chairman of the ECB, Giles Clarke, seriously considered using his power of veto, as Ossie Wheatley did in 1989, in his capacity as chairman of the TCCB's cricket committee, as regards Mike Gatting, and as Morgan now wishes he might have done in relation to Andrew Flintoff in 2006/07 Down Under.

But the problem was the selectors wanted one man as captain, and with Vaughan and Collingwood gone, and Strauss not then in the one-day side, there were not too many candidates. I was told by one insider that Moores was 'adamant' he wanted Pietersen as captain. It is, I suppose, understandable, given what happened later, that Moores is rather reluctant to admit that, entering his very best cross-country mode before answering that question. 'At the time there was a strong move to unify the captaincy,' he says. 'KP got his chance, and nobody quite knew how he was going to take it. I wasn't adamant I wanted him, but we had lost a lot of seniority. One of the strengths of the Aussies over the years has been getting players to the last third of their career. Over recent times with England that has been difficult to do. It's a shame because Fletch had done so much good work and players like Tres [Marcus Trescothick] and Gilo [Ashley Giles] didn't get that last part of their international careers.'

Moores and Pietersen had to meet before Pietersen agreed to take over, and it was generally assumed that Pietersen had demanded the meeting. As he said afterwards of Moores, 'He likes to challenge us on a daily basis. We have lots of strong characters who can be very opinionated. The crux of the meeting was to decide where we can take the team together.' But I understand that it was Moores who phoned Pietersen and asked for the meeting, which eventually took place at the Hilton Hotel in Northampton.

The ECB had little time to work with – there was another Test starting at the Oval the following Thursday – but this was a rushed job. It was interesting that when England were seeking new captains for their one-day and Twenty20 teams in 2011, they conducted formal interviews with prospective candidates. That, as one ECB official has admitted to me, is what should have happened here. Despite their meeting, there were still too many grey areas between Pietersen and Moores. Pietersen thought he was in charge, and so did Moores.

Pietersen began with a bang, with a hundred and a Test win at the Oval, followed by a 4–0 series victory in the one-dayers afterwards. But trouble lay ahead, first in the form of an American chap named Stanford. I seem to recall that his first name was, and still is, Allen, although everyone at the ECB would rather forget everything about him, even if in 2011 they had to play two Twenty20 internationals against the West Indies at the end of the summer in order to fulfil contractual obligations with Sky that were a relic of the deal with the man. In the ECB's annual report for 2008 his name was not mentioned once in fifty-two pages.

But this was the man who on 11 June that year had landed his helicopter (or rather one we later discovered he had rented from nearby and to which he had had his company logo added) on the Nursery Ground at Lord's. The sight of ECB officials fawning over Stanford sickens me to this day. I know one or two of them who are mighty glad never to have been photographed with him. But there he was, arriving at the home of cricket as if on some state visit, using that old trick so favoured by American politicians of waving and pointing to make out he had some friends in the crowd. He had none.

Stanford had roped in some legends of the game to stand alongside him on stage: Sir Ian Botham, Sir Gary Sobers, Sir Everton Weekes, Sir Vivian Richards, Curtly Ambrose and Desmond Haynes. Sadly they were as gullible as the ECB's administrators, in particular chief executive David Collier, who, as others are very quick to point out now, was the driving force behind the whole Stanford deal. Money does indeed make a man blind.

Inside the Nursery Pavilion it was announced that England and a Stanford All-Stars XI would play five Twenty20 matches for $20 million each over five years. A perspex casket was brought out, supposedly with $20 million in it, and Nasser Hussain, who was presenting the ceremony, said, 'Gentlemen! If you've ever wondered what twenty million dollars looks like, here it is!' It was subsequently revealed that there may actually have been as little as $100,000 in there, and that the notes were probably fake.

Should the ECB have known that Stanford himself was a fake, as first alleged the following February when, ironically as England played a Test on the island of Antigua that had knighted him (since revoked), it emerged that he had been charged by the Securities and Exchange Commission with fraud 'of shocking magnitude'? There were certainly warning signs. South Africa, India and Australia had all spurned Stanford's offers. So had the ICC.

There had been a remarkable meeting between Stanford and ICC officials in Johannesburg on the morning of the World Twenty20 final in September 2007. He had previously met with president Percy Sonn and chief executive Malcolm Speed in the West Indies during the World Cup there earlier that year, outlining his proposals for a Twenty20 tournament involving his Stanford Super Stars. But negotiations had stumbled on the fact that Stanford wanted his team rather than the West Indies to play in this proposed competition. The ICC understandably said it could not sanction such a tournament as 'official' cricket. Stanford was not happy, but the ICC agreed to consider it further.

So another meeting was scheduled for the Sandton Sun Hotel in Johannesburg. Ray Mali (acting ICC president after Sonn had passed away in May of that year), Speed, Morgan (who was then ICC president-elect), Dave Richardson (ICC's general manager of cricket), Brian Murgatroyd and Campbell Jamieson (both senior ICC managers) were present as the ICC delegation. They were waiting for the Stanford group to arrive in the room they had hired when they were informed by a member of the hotel staff that Stanford and his cohorts were in another room. There were simply too many of them! In the other room were many great names of West Indian cricket like Richards, Weekes, Haynes, Wes Hall, Michael Holding, Lance Gibbs and Joel Garner. The president of the West Indies Cricket Board, Julian Hunte, was also present.

Mali made a polite introductory speech and then Speed got down to the business of the meeting to say that the ICC had considered carefully the offer Stanford had made. Before he could get any further, Stanford stood up, put his hand in the air and said, 'Forget all that. I now want to play the winners of today's match [the final was between India and Pakistan].'

The meeting degenerated from there. Speed tried to articulate the ICC's proposal (that the higher ranked of the two teams to tour the Caribbean each year would play the last match of their tour against the Stanford Super Stars, but it would be 'unofficial'), but Stanford lost his rag and stood up, knocking his chair over loudly in the process, and left the room. Haynes launched a rant at Speed, and Richards began banging both hands loudly on the table. 'It was the most amazing incident in which I was involved in eleven years of cricket administration,' wrote Speed. 'The walkout was childish.'

Thanks to the diplomacy of Morgan the meeting was rejoined, and Morgan calmly rebuked Haynes for his behaviour. It ended with Stanford saying that he would go to the ICC box at the final. He never did.

The ECB knew about this meeting. But as Morgan indicates, 'Had I still been chairman of the ECB I would certainly have explored Stanford. I would have been more wary after that meeting, but the ECB were still right to explore.'

As an unrepentant Collier has said since, 'Stanford had been recently knighted, Forbes referenced him as one of America's leading entrepreneurs and he had worked successfully in helping to promote West Indies cricket as well as many other sports.' And the ECB will point to the fact that they were helping the impoverished WICB as part of the deal, that it was intended to extend its own Chance To Shine scheme (promoting cricket in schools) in the Caribbean and that grassroots cricket in England and Wales, especially the funding of coaches, was to receive substantial benefits too.

There was pressure not just from the Indian Premier League but the unauthorized Indian Cricket League too. England's players were certainly miffed that they were missing out on untold riches at the IPL (none of the centrally contracted players appeared in the first instalment in 2008), typified by Chris Gayle's text messages to Pietersen at the time. First he asked why Pietersen was not playing in the IPL. Pietersen replied that he could not, so Gayle responded with a text consisting just of dollar signs. But, with England and India at each other's throats, this was about something more: about securing the West Indies' support in the fight against India's increasing dominance in cricket's politics.

My greatest gripe was with the nature of the match that was played in Antigua on 1 November 2008. Money should never be at the heart of one's desire to represent one's country. I went to the announcement of the England squad in September and felt genuinely sorry for Morris and Geoff Miller as they sat there, shuffling uncomfortably, trying to justify a match for which they should never have been asked to provide a team. That team that they did select should never have been termed 'England'. It was disrespectful to anyone who has represented England in 'official' cricket.

Miller described it as 'part of the process'. What process? 'The match has no cricketing value whatsoever,' I wrote afterwards.

'Indeed to call it cricket at all will be difficult. For Nov 1 will be the night cricket is turned into reality TV, where some grisly voyeuristic fare is served up for those of a short attention span. The ECB may come to regret this match.'

So they did. Even though one senior journalist told me it was the most attentively organized cricket trip he'd ever been on, the Stanford week was a shambles in so many other ways. England lost the match, which is probably just as well. But they were never in the right frame of mind to win it. The recession had arrived with the iciest of blasts and here were England's cricketers out in the heat of the Caribbean set to earn $1 million a man for winning a Twenty20 match. It was obscene. 'I respect what is happening in the world,' said the captain Pietersen ahead of departure for Antigua. 'I've got friends who are struggling and some who have lost their jobs and there's no way I will accept any of our players carrying on like clowns should we win this money.'

The only chap acting like a clown was Stanford, as his behaviour annoyed the England team intensely. He marched around with his own cameraman in tow, saying 'Howdy!' to everyone, trying to enter the England dressing room and then sitting Matt Prior's pregnant wife on his knee while Prior and his England colleagues were out on the field.

The ECB immediately announced it would undertake a review of its deal with Stanford, but by December the Texan had closed down his cricket office at his Coolidge ground and disbanded his Stanford board of legends, who were paid around $10,000 a month. But nobody foresaw the events of 17 February 2009. I certainly never thought I'd be standing, as I was on the morning of 18 February, in a queue outside Stanford's bank in Antigua seeking quotes from disgruntled customers as they waited to withdraw their life savings. When word came that day that he might actually be on the island, I did have wild visions of chasing him and unearthing his location on some remote part of the island. But then reality dawned. As a supporter at Newport's Rodney Parade rugby ground once advised me, 'Stick to the cricket, James!'

I called for Clarke's resignation as ECB chairman that weekend. 'Clarke should do the decent thing. But he won't,' I wrote. 'Decency departed English cricket's administration long ago: the day it prostituted itself to Stanford.' And he didn't resign. He was never going to. As I write, Clarke is still chairman of the ECB. He has recovered rather well. The ECB is in rude health, with Clarke poised for a third term in office. As for Stanford, in March 2012, he was found guilty of 13 out of 14 counts of fraud.

After that Stanford debacle in November 2008 England did at least have some 'proper' cricket: a tour to India no less. It was my first trip there. And it was going pretty much as expected by the time England were 5–0 down in the one-day series after defeat at Cuttack. The hotels in the up-country venues had been awful. 'You are staying in the second-best hotel in town,' the local agent would inform us religiously upon arrival at the airport. Translated roughly, it meant the players were in a decent establishment; we were in a shit-hole. I'd suffered Delhi-belly and England's bowlers had been smashed everywhere. Yes, the clichés were all in order.

Not even a Pietersen century had been enough to avoid defeat at Cuttack. So off we trudged from the ground to contemplate the rigours of a trip to Guwahati the next day. Then on the car journey from Cuttack to our hotel in Bhubaneswar news began filtering through of shocking events in Mumbai. Text messages from home along the lines of 'Where are you? Are you OK?' were worrying signs of something truly terrible happening.

The reasons for and the extent of that worry became apparent when we adjourned soberly to our hotel rooms and turned on the TVs. Indian TV clearly does not do picture censorship. The pictures being shown were horrifically graphic, with dead bodies being dragged across the road and blood everywhere in scenes of unfathomable butchery. Just as shocking was that the backdrop to these scenes was the Taj Mahal Palace Hotel in Mumbai, where we had stayed just two weeks earlier, indeed where the England team had left in storage their Test whites and other items of clothing for use later in the tour.

I was scared. We might have been nearly a thousand miles from Mumbai, but there was no knowing the extent of these atrocities. It was said Westerners were targets; the England cricket team and its entourage would seem easy targets in that case. I wanted to go home, and so did England's cricketers. It was the natural reaction. Of course, there were some brave comments from those sitting in the safety of their armchairs back in England. And there was the rigidity of those asserting that cricketers would never be targets. I never believed that for one minute, and appalling confirmation of as much duly came later that winter when the Sri Lankan team bus was attacked on the way to a Test match in Lahore.

But it took until 9.40 p.m. the following day in Bhubaneswar before it was finally announced that we were going home, with the two remaining one-day fixtures cancelled. It was fortunate that Morris was there in India. He played a blinder on that Thursday. Until then the question of what exactly Morris did was being asked frequently, just as it was with his counterpart at the Rugby Football Union, Rob Andrew. In rugby's case that was never fully answered, as Andrew was eventually demoted, shifted sideways and given all manner of other manoeuvrings seemingly in a bid to keep him in a job.

But Morris gave one of many compelling answers that day at the Mayfair Lagoon Hotel in Bhubaneswar in negotiations with the Board of Control for Cricket in India secretary N. Srinivasan, while keeping Clarke (on business in Colombia) and Collier (on holiday in Los Angeles) abreast of events. We the media were, of course, not staying at that hotel, but spent the whole day there lurking and listening. At one point Morris walked past and smiled. 'To think we only used to worry about scoring runs,' he said. It was indeed rather strange that the former Glamorgan opening partnership should end up in this position. But here was Morris proving that the best cricket administrators are usually those who play the game to the highest level first, then acquire the necessary management and business qualifications afterwards, as Morris did in gaining his executive MBA from Henley Management College.

Of course, everyone going home was not the end of it. There were still two Tests scheduled. Upon leaving I thought there was no way the players should return. Flintoff certainly agreed, as he told me in a rare conversation we had at the hotel bar later that night. I think the only reason he spoke to me was to tell me that the Lancashire dressing room were very unhappy with me, having been miffed at something I'd written the previous summer. 'You had a good career out of county cricket,' he said. 'Don't be so negative about it.'

We actually talked about the England A tour of Kenya and Sri Lanka in 1997/98, which we were both on and during which there was a similar situation after a huge bomb went off in Kandy where we were due to visit soon afterwards. Both Flintoff and I were keen to go home (my wife was pregnant), but it was somehow reported in the press that we had persuaded the others to stay ('an unlikely combination' we were called).

There was little doubt here who wanted to return to India, and Flintoff and his mate Steve Harmison were not among them. Pietersen did want to return, but then there were those who considered IPL riches in the next year his strongest motivation. I actually thought Pietersen led the team well in this episode. He said the right things and appeared to be in control. Apparently that wasn't the case. One player I later spoke to about him and his captaincy just giggled in response.

Confirmation of this came in Swann's autobiography. 'There

is no doubt that Kev is a good player, a really fine batsman,' he wrote, 'but he was never the right man to captain England in my opinion. Some people are better leaders of men and Kev, for all his abundant talent, is not one of those natural leaders.'

There was actually much confusion about what was happening because the atrocities were still continuing. Morris had told the players that they had to go home immediately, but they interpreted that as meaning the whole tour was off. That was never Morris's nor the ECB's intention. They always felt that, if safety and security could be guaranteed, the tour would continue at a later stage.

But it was not easy to do that. So first, after five days on every one of which each of the players had been telephoned to keep them informed of happenings, the players were flown to Abu Dhabi for a holding camp, and from there Morris and his name-sake, Sean, then the chief executive of the Professional Cricketers' Association, flew to Chennai where the first Test was scheduled to take place (the two original venues of Ahmedabad and Mumbai were replaced by Chennai and Mohali). There they met with Reg Dickason, the ECB's security adviser. Dickason, the moustachioed Australian whose ever-present smile conceals a steely character, was once easily derided as another of England's so-called unnecessary support staff, but here he proved his worth and much, much more.

Dickason demanded a 'ring of steel' of crack commando troops for the players should they return to India. And he was right to demand more security. On the day after the Mumbai atrocities a group of us journalists had accessed the England team hotel through the side entrance of an adjoining coffee shop. It hardly required the skills of Darcy Dugan to get in.

The ECB had to be sure that Dickason's security plan was going to be implemented to the letter, and Morris (Hugh that is) recalls standing before the Commissioner of Police in Chennai as Dickason went through his plans in great detail. The commissioner agreed on every point. 'Thank you very much,' said Morris. 'Now all I want is all that in writing with your signature on the bottom.' The commissioner's face dropped. It was getting late in the evening, and the two Morrises were leaving for Abu Dhabi early the following morning. They needed confirmation to present to some very nervous cricketers. Sure enough there was a knock at the door early the next morning. The signed document was there.

So the Morrises went to Abu Dhabi and addressed the players. There were two obvious dissenters in Flintoff and Harmison, with a number of other initial waverers that apparently included James Anderson, Bell, Prior, Cook and even Swann, who soon decided he rather wanted to play Test cricket. (He hadn't played at all then, remember.) But eventually all decided to go. It was a decision that was received with admiration and respect throughout the cricketing world, and beyond too. The Prime Minister, Gordon Brown, called the team 'brave and courageous'.

England lost the first Test in Chennai. It is tempting to recall the words of former England rugby skipper John Pullin, whose team went to Dublin in 1973 at the height of the political troubles there after Wales and Scotland had refused to do so the previous year. England lost 18–9, their eighth consecutive loss in the Five Nations championship, and at the post-match dinner Pullin declared, 'We may not be very good, but at least we turn up.' This England cricket team were better than that, with Strauss scoring twin centuries in the match, but India chased down 387 on the final day on a wearing pitch for victory.

However, it was not just the brilliance of Sachin Tendulkar (103 not out) that did for England there. There was trouble in the camp. Pietersen had already decided that he could no longer work with Moores. Tactically the captain had been exposed on that final day, but the die had been cast before the match when Pietersen had been to see ECB chairman Clarke and told him that Moores must go. Pietersen wanted the South African Graham Ford to take over, and told Clarke as much. England could easily have won that first Test, but Pietersen insisted even that would have changed nothing.

The ECB had naturally gone to India with much of its hierarchy. Clarke, Collier, Morris, Dennis Amiss (vice-chairman) and selector Giles were all there. But by raising the issue with Clarke (in Chennai, where the first Test was held) and bypassing Morris, Pietersen made a huge mistake. There was never going to be a simple and easy solution after that. Clarke is not a man to wear his authority lightly. This was clearly a big deal. He wanted it sorted.

Many a meeting took place in India, so that by the end of the second Test, which was drawn, Pietersen, seeing no resolution, threatened to resign. Morris had left for home by this stage, so Collier mollified Pietersen by asking him to email Morris with his plan to take England forward in 2009.

Off everyone went for Christmas, with all of us in the media still unaware of these alarming developments. Not even the announcement of the party to tour the West Indies in January, with Vaughan omitted against Pietersen's wishes, changed that. Pietersen was by now on a safari holiday in South Africa.

On Tuesday, 30 December I received a phone call from my *Telegraph* colleague Derek Pringle asking what I knew about a rift between Pietersen and Moores. At that stage all I had heard were murmurings that Pietersen was not enjoying the captaincy. I made some calls. Something was definitely bubbling. I told Pringle, who was working on the story with Nick Hoult, that they should do a speculation piece that day. You never know how long these things will last.

As they were still gathering information, they rightly waited until the next day. Unfortunately their excellent story for the New Year's Day edition was posted on the internet a little too early, at around tea-time on New Year's Eve. Both the *Daily*

Mail and the *Sun* seized on it and ran the story as 'exclusives' the following day. The cat was out of the bag.

Who let it out has been a matter of much debate ever since. 'Something was leaked, I don't know who by, I would love to find that person,' said Pietersen later. I think Pietersen thought it was Clarke. That's why he didn't speak to him for almost a year afterwards.

I'm not sure it matters who did leak the story. It certainly wasn't Pietersen, who on the day he was sacked (or resigned) issued a statement saying 'At no time have I released any unauthorized information to the media.'

The assumption has always been that the same conclusion would not have been reached had it not been leaked. From what I know now, I disagree. It is as wide of the mark as the commonly held belief that Vaughan's non-selection tipped Pietersen over the edge. As I said, once Clarke had been informed ahead of other management before the Chennai Test, there was no way that the conciliation Morris would by nature have been inclined to would suffice.

But what the leak did do was emphasize the powers of twenty-four-hour news. Quickly the story took on a life of its own. It ran more quickly than Usain Bolt ever has. Suddenly the politics of the England dressing room were being speculated upon, and Morris was canvassing some of the players to ascertain the exact details of any supposed rifts.

The truth is that many players did not even know there were such big problems. As Moores himself said to me, 'It wasn't like it was a raging feud.' But there were problems. I wrote at the time: 'For some time this England side have been unravelling like a ball of wool pawed by a frisky kitten. Forget the Oval Test win over South Africa and the subsequent 4–0 one-day success. They were mere diversionary morsels. Come the Stanford series and India the kitten was playing again. And the suspicion remains that the little beggar's name was Fred.'

Flintoff was indeed a problem. He and Pietersen never got on in the team environment, a clashing of egos as they jostled for the position of Top Cat. And Flintoff was more than happy to position himself in Moores' camp. He liked the coach from the start, especially when Moores offered to go with him to a specialist's appointment when injured. It was a level of care he never felt he'd received from Fletcher. But was Moores just being cute? Flintoff was a powerful dressing-room presence. I've heard that Moores used that relationship in his defence.

By a twist of fate Pietersen sent his email outlining his proposals on the very day the story broke in the *Daily Telegraph*. 'I really wanted to get this right for English cricket . . . In my email I said that I can't lead this team forward and take it to the West Indies if Peter Moores is coach,' he later said.

I asked Moores what the problem was. 'The whole issue revolved around respect,' he replied. 'It was about whether he felt he respected my view and whether together we could have moved it forward.' Well, there clearly was no respect. But as Moores emphasized, 'A lot of things have been said but nobody would have known that not everything was normal.'

Unsurprisingly they have not spoken since, or they hadn't when I spoke to Moores in the summer of 2011. 'Not deliberately, though, on my part,' says Moores. 'You have a county circuit and an international circuit. Occasionally they cross but generally they are different worlds.'

Pietersen was expecting to meet with ECB officials on 8 January 2009, the day he was due to return from holiday. But he never did have that meeting. Instead he was informed over the phone that his resignation had been accepted, followed by an email to that effect. Of course, he hadn't officially offered to resign, not since the end of the Mohali Test anyway, but these were mere semantics. Maybe his email had been taken as an offer of resignation, but in truth he had been sacked. And he had been warned this might happen before an ECB meeting on the evening of Tuesday, 6 January. So too had Moores, and so they were both sacked at that board meeting. A press conference at the Oval the following day confirmed as much. It would have been at Lord's but the banqueting manager was on holiday. It rather summed up the mess. Poor Morris did not take any questions. Given the dangers of employment law he would have been eaten alive.

He had been faced with the trickiest of situations. As I said earlier, he would have preferred to try to make the pair work together. There were two other options that didn't look particularly workable: firstly that Moores went and Pietersen stayed as captain, but that would have set highly dangerous precedents in terms of player power; secondly that Moores stayed as coach and Pietersen was stripped of the captaincy – but just imagine the dressing-room tension then. No, quite simply, the only option was that both men were sacked.

Of course, Pietersen came off worst. 'DeTested' screamed the *Sun*'s headline, before describing him as 'cricket's most hated man'. Much was made of those soundings Morris had taken with some players and the conclusion was reached that Pietersen had been shafted by his colleagues. I do not know what was said, but, yes, some probably did denigrate his captaincy. As I mentioned earlier it was not exactly rated inside the dressing room, but this was not the reason he was sacked. He probably should have returned from his holiday earlier, but again it is doubtful that would have made too much difference. As it was, he flew into Heathrow airport amid a welter of media scrutiny. He even had to ask for police protection via the ECB.

This imbroglio was, and still is, considered the result of his unstoppable ego. But the truth is that it was not just Pietersen. Others were just as unconvinced with Moores, as the coach himself admits. 'I've had lads turn round to me and say they loved it,' he says, 'and others who haven't.' There is little doubt that the whole affair was for the better. As I wrote at the time:

'England play cricket again in a fortnight. It might just be that they have a better captain and coach than the last time they did so.'

As Pietersen himself said, albeit with typical gaucheness, after England had retained the Ashes in Melbourne in January 2011, 'We would not be here today if I had not done what I did. I got rid of the captaincy for the good of English cricket. There is no way in this world that we would have succeeded under that regime and won the Ashes again in Australia after twenty-four years.'

Not that he had been a happy man in the intervening period. 'His conduct ever since has been terribly disappointing,' an ECB insider told me. 'He has allowed his showbiz friends to consistently convince him that he has been so badly wronged.'

Pietersen is easily disliked. I was still playing county cricket when he first came to England, and he soon acquired a poor reputation on the circuit. I actually broke his leg once in a match against Nottinghamshire at Colwyn Bay. Well, OK, he fell awkwardly when stopping one of my chinks to mid-wicket, and it was later discovered that he had broken a small bone in his leg. But the crucial point is that there didn't seem to be too much sympathy for him.

I admit that I took this attitude into my journalistic career. Early on I rarely passed up an opportunity to be critical. 'The man of the match might easily have lost England the match' I wrote at Edgbaston in 2006 when Pietersen's dismissal (for 142!) two balls after his stunning switch hit for six off Muttiah Muralitharan precipitated an England collapse.

I've come to like him, however. When on tour around the hotels and at grounds anywhere he is as polite and courteous as any England player. I think I quite like him because he is every-thing I wasn't as a cricketer. Deep down we'd all probably like to carry off that sort of cockiness and naked ambition. But it is just not an English sort of thing to do. Little wonder he was so disliked in the shires.

Pietersen is different. He craves and needs the spotlight as a child does milk. So in terms of management, he is high-maintenance. There is always something to deal with. He often engages mouth before brain. He sometimes makes poor decisions. Take what happened after his early return from the World Cup in 2011 with a hernia injury. With the Ashes and its tagged-on one-day internationals afterwards, it had been a long, long winter. Like the other England players, Pietersen was missing his family. So where does he find himself just a couple of days after returning home? In a Soho nightclub with his agent!

Add to all of this the fact that he is not English and it is easy to see why Pietersen attracts so much opprobrium. And he is not English, despite the tattoos and the early over-the-top attempts to prove as much. He's South African. I bet he still supports South Africa at rugby. Nay, I know. But we need to get over that. He came to England to play cricket. He fulfilled the qualification criteria and now scores lots of runs for England. If we feel so strongly about it, the qualification rules must be changed. Go back to seven years of residency if necessary. But the world is a smaller place now. People emigrate. People move easily. And, unfortunately for him, people are removed easily too.

The Saturday evening following the double sacking was the only occasion I have fallen out with Hugh Morris since I became a journalist. Pietersen was writing a column for the *News of the World* then and was about to pronounce his feelings about the farrago that Sunday, so all of the other Sunday journalists were under pressure to produce some sort of slant of their own on the story. 'Kevin Pietersen: I was betrayed by ECB as England captain' screamed the headline to my piece. Then on the front of the main paper: 'Betrayed!'

I had been told by a reliable source that Pietersen felt betrayed by three high-ranking ECB officials, whom I did not specifically name, but whom Pietersen felt had assured him before he went on his safari holiday that Moores would be removed as coach.

They were clearly Clarke, Collier and Morris, although I was unsure how the selector Giles fitted into the picture. Morris and I had a heated debate late on the Saturday night, when my piece appeared on the internet. He'd been copping flak all week, and I suppose a late little dagger from an old friend was not exactly what he wanted. I think we've made up now anyway. And I don't think there ever were any guarantees to Pietersen.

At his Oval press conference Morris had also said something else: 'Andrew Strauss has agreed to lead the team to the Caribbean.' Now there really was only one option, even if Strauss did mention to Morris that it might have been better to consider someone younger like Cook. The ECB cannot beat themselves up about a lack of an interview process here.

It was not headline news, of course. It was low-in-the-piece stuff compared to Pietersen and Moores. And at that moment it only referred to the Test matches in the West Indies. By the Friday it had been extended to the one Twenty20 international and the subsequent one-day internationals at the end of the tour. It had also been extended to being in charge of the tour, because Strauss left for the Caribbean very much as an old-style captain. Flower would remain as assistant coach, with no head coach appointed.

'I will be taking over a lot – the lead coach's responsibilities – but my job title is staying as assistant coach,' Flower explained at the time. 'I think it's better that way. I'm not sure if I want to apply for the job yet. I want to play it by ear and see how things go. Pete [Moores] brought me into the Academy set-up. We were good mates, and still are. I had a good think about it before I decided that I wanted to do this role. I would say it's unlikely that I would be offered the job full-time.'

Ah, the modesty of that last sentence. Just like Duncan Fletcher, albeit in very different circumstances, Flower wasn't sure whether he wanted to be coach of England. But it was the truth too. I spoke to Flower quite a lot during that period and those quotes reflect his feelings faithfully. He felt horribly awkward about immediately taking the dead man's clothes, about jumping so quickly into his mate Moores' shoes. He deliberated long and hard before accepting the role, talking at length with Morris about its parameters before doing so.

Was it awkward? I ask Moores. 'Not at all,' he responds. 'I've spoken to Andy all the way through. He is a mate. The opportunity came for him and he took it. He is a loyal bloke. We went into it as a team, and he knew it was a tough job. We went through some good times and some tough times. We had to make some really tough decisions. I mean leaving out Hoggy [Matthew Hoggard was dropped for the second Test in Wellington in New Zealand in 2008 and never played again] was a really tough decision. We thought it was right to play Jimmy [James Anderson] at the time and Stuart Broad also came in for Harmy [Steve Harmison]. They were big decisions.'

There was another complication: Pietersen had called for Flower's removal too. Flower had noticed a change in his attitude as the India tour wore on. He had become colder and more distant. And he wasn't the only one. During Moores' reign I had heard other players question Flower's ability to perform his assistant coach's role. Indeed one evening over a couple of beers one player told me in great detail how he much preferred Matthew Maynard as a batting coach. Flower himself will admit that he made mistakes early on as a coach. He was too critical, especially of some of the batsmen's techniques. But as he said then, 'When you are assistant coach you are always supportive of the coach and your most heated debates are behind closed doors, which is a healthy thing. Then you come out and speak with one voice.'

The Flower had been in its bud all that time. It was nothing new. It had been the same when he played for Essex for five seasons. There, domineering characters like skipper Ronnie Irani and Darren Gough rarely allowed him his say. 'I don't think his knowledge of the game was utilized enough in our dressing room,' admits coach Paul Grayson now. 'We had Ronnie as captain and Goughy, who both had very strong opinions in the dressing room. Maybe those two overpowered him a bit too much but whenever he did speak up it was always sensible and you always knew that when Andy was speaking everyone was listening.'

What a waste. I'd like to think that would not have been the case had Flower joined Glamorgan, which could easily have happened in 2001 when I became captain. Flower was keen (not to keep wicket, though, so as not to scupper the opportunities of our homegrown keepers, as he didn't do with James Foster at Essex), but his Zimbabwe Cricket Union contract would not permit.

But if you think Glamorgan fans might be miffed at missing out on Flower . . .

9

The Growing of a Flower

Cricketing folk of New Zealand, read this and weep. Andy Flower could so easily have been one of yours. And his brother Grant. That's because in 1978 the whole Flower family – father Bill, mother Jean and their five children Stephen, Gary, Andrew, Grant and Megan – were about to leave their home in Johannesburg in South Africa and emigrate to The Land of the Long White Cloud. The passage had been booked by liner from Durban, and all their possessions had been packed and crated. They were off to settle in Wellington where Bill had secured a job as an accountant. Melbourne in Australia had also been seriously considered, but windy Wellington it was going to be.

But there suddenly arose a problem. When Bill had made his application for a work visa, he and Jean had only four children. But in 1976 Megan had been born. At the very last minute the New Zealand authorities declined Flower senior's application, because he now had one dependant too many. Little Megan saved the day for Zimbabwe cricket. And, maybe, further down the line, England cricket too.

Mind you, the family could have stayed in South Africa, a decision that would have pleased the ten-year-old Andy. He was rather enjoying himself at Boskop primary school in Randburg (in the northern suburbs of Johannesburg). 'I didn't want to leave because we lived this idyllic outdoor life,' he said recently. 'Most white Rhodesians were making the opposite journey – leaving for South Africa [ahead of independence in 1980]. But my dad decided it was time for us to go back to Rhodesia.'

Bill accepted a transfer offer to be company secretary in Salisbury with the same international organization that had employed him for the previous ten years. Looking back, it does seem a curious decision. Whites were leaving Rhodesia in their droves, but the family had faith that things would ultimately work out for the better.

Bill, born in Johannesburg in 1937, and Jean, born in Umtali in eastern Rhodesia in 1939, had met at school in Bulawayo in 1952. Both had been brought up in Rhodesia, and eventually married in 1962. Bill swept Jean off to northern Rhodesia (now Zambia) where he was employed in the copper mines. They established a home there and produced their first two sons, Stephen and Gary. Andy was subsequently born in Cape Town, Grant in Salisbury and then Megan back in Johannesburg.

Bill was not an outstanding cricketer ('purely a league cricketer who bowled leg-spin and batted at number three or four', he says). He possessed and still does possess the most remarkable passion and energy for the game. But in 1982 he had a heart attack, and in 1984 underwent a triple bypass operation. He decided it was time to give up accountancy. 'I decided that if I stayed behind a desk I'd find an early grave,' he says, 'so I retired and applied for a job as bursar at Peterhouse [a school in Marondera, east of Harare]. I got involved in coaching sport there.' He was to become one of Zimbabwe's finest schoolboy cricket coaches.

'Wild Bill' is what Andy and Grant call him even now. But it is said in jest, in gratitude even. They know the early games they played with their father and brothers made them the cricketers they became. 'At every opportunity we'd be out in the garden kicking, hitting or chasing a ball of some description,' says Bill. 'Those family sessions set the boys off with their ball skills. I can't accentuate their importance too much. Stephen loved his cricket but never took his sport seriously and Gary, well, he never professed to be a sportsman of any description. But when it came to those family games he was up there with the rest of the family.'

No one can recall why Andy batted left-handed and bowled right-arm (some filthy medium-pace to which, to my lifelong embarrassment, I once succumbed in a club match in Zimbabwe), while Grant batted right-handed and bowled left-arm. 'Andy can play squash right- and left-handed,' says Bill, 'and he plays golf right-handed – although he can play it left-handed – and writes right-handed. Grant writes left-handed and plays tennis right-handed.'

Andy was certainly not instructed to bat left-handed, as the Flowers' great friend Alistair Campbell was by his late father 'Pol', the sagacious headmaster of the well-regarded Lilfordia School. Campbell was right-handed at everything, but his father recognized the benefits of a strong top hand in batting and so encouraged the southpaw stance. The result was one of the most graceful batting talents I've ever come across. Sadly there was not quite the temperament to match, even if there was a shrewd cricketing brain lurking within.

In their Johannesburg days the Flower family did not even have a lawn at first. Bill created one. In Salisbury they did have a lawn, but this was no typically affluent property of the white Zimbabwean. 'It was not the usual "easy street" with two house-maids,' says Bill. 'We struggled financially, so the family knew the value of money. They had to take their turns in cleaning the pool and mowing the lawn. It was good for them.'

Indeed Bill acknowledges that he was a strict father, and admits to having dished out a few deserved hidings along the way. He told me he was particularly severe if the children had misbehaved for their mother while he was away at work.

Andy went to Vainona High School in northern Harare, as did his brothers Stephen and Gary. Grant, meanwhile, went to St George's College. 'Education was beginning to turn,' says Bill. 'We foresaw problems and Grant needed to be pushed.' It was not a popular decision. 'My parents only wanted the best for me but I hated it,' says Grant. 'I wanted to go where Andrew was.' But the Jesuits did at least get Grant through his A levels.

Andy and Grant played international cricket together, at times forming an important opening partnership in one-day cricket with their rapid running and judgement between the wickets. They are so very different in character, but remain close friends, and enjoy some playful banter, which can sometimes be a little unsettling to those who don't know them.

Andy calls Grant by his nickname 'Gobs', which is short for 'Gobshite', and which in Africa is not as derogatory a word as it is in Ireland. It was given to him when he was the youngest member of the Zimbabwe side. By contrast when Andy made his first-class debut, appearing for a Zimbabwe Cricket Union President's XI against a West Indies B side as an eighteen-year-old in 1986, his older team-mates called him 'Petals'. Many of his team-mates at the Old Georgians (OGs) club where he made his debut at fifteen called him 'Maggots'. Nobody seems to know why. The Glamorgan players used to call him 'Self-raising', which always made me chuckle. Andy calls me 'Big Nose', so I call him 'Flat Nose'. Neither of us could sue. Such is the banter between sportspeople.

I met Grant for the purposes of this book in early April 2011. He'd been at the World Cup as Zimbabwe's batting coach and had just arrived back at his Chelmsford home to find a huge tax bill waiting for him. He was in a flap. He was late for our meeting. The first person he'd phoned? His brother Andrew. 'He's generally had a bit more confidence than me,' admits Grant. 'I've always hovered in the background a bit. I've got him to do things for me and I still ask him for advice, whether about cricket or life skills.'

Mind you, I did once ask Andy who he would turn to first when he was a player and was struggling with his game. The reply was instant: 'Grant.' Having witnessed the hours they spent together in the nets, it was little surprise really. 'We used to talk about cricket all the time,' says Grant. 'We knew each other's games really well.' Bill confirms this: 'They were always both very deep thinkers on the game. Grant knew Andrew's game backwards. He didn't need camcorders or any of that stuff. He could just pick up a fault by looking in the nets.'

Andy wasn't too shabby at spotting technical minutiae either. I remember sitting with him watching Worcestershire's first match of a pre-season tour against Mashonaland Country Districts at the once lovely Harare South ground, now tragically defunct as a cricket ground after being overrun by the war veterans at the height of Zimbabwe's problems. Graeme Hick, fresh from a winter with Queensland in Australia, came out to bat, and immediately Flower became quite animated. 'Look at his pick-up,' he said. 'He's flattened it out [meaning the face of the bat was not open]. They do that in Australia to counter the bounce.'

As a player, Flower was always analysing opposition batsmen's techniques, especially from his unique vantage point behind the stumps as a wicketkeeper. He noticed, for instance, that Sachin Tendulkar would gently rock back on his heels in his stance in order to maintain his balance. And early on in his Test career he marvelled at the New Zealander Martin Crowe's balance at the crease, unusual for such a big man and especially as he was hampered by knee problems late in his international career, allowing him to play peerlessly through the leg-side.

Crowe made 140 in Zimbabwe's and the Flowers' third Test in Harare in 1992 and it made a lasting impression on Andy, even if his admiration for Crowe went against the grain. Crowe was not popular among the Zimbabwean cricketing public or indeed with many of the Zimbabwean players whom he belittled in that first series between the teams. At the start of that Test, after Zimbabwe had drawn their first two Tests, a sign had been put up above one of the tents at the Harare Sports Club proclaiming Zimbabwe as 'The only unbeaten Test nation in the world!' At the match's conclusion – a New Zealand win by 177 runs – Crowe went over and pulled it down. His arrogance was not well received. But there was something Flower liked in him, a great batsman playing in a poor side. It was exactly what Flower was to become. Crowe was an inspiration.

There was also a time when Grant and Campbell called Andy 'Arrogance'. It was tongue-in-cheek from two cheeky mates, but they considered that there was some justification to it. 'He could be aloof,' says Campbell, who is not exactly short of confidence himself. 'He was one of those blokes who knew what he wanted to do and he wasn't tolerant of fools who mucked around while he was trying to achieve that.' And as Grant says, 'He did have that sort of aura about him. But most good sportspeople have a certain amount of arrogance about them.'

If only Grant had had that. It is a common assumption that Andy was the more talented cricketer of the brothers. I am not so sure about that. Talent-wise they were fairly similar, but that is not to say that the good Lord lavished too many of his cricketing gifts upon them. As I mentioned in the introduction to this book, Andy's batsmanship was not immediately eye-catching.

It is just that Andy had more confidence. And even that is, I reckon, a self-taught confidence. He is not an extrovert. He is naturally modest. Praise him and he just guffaws. Just this once, by way of illustration, I do not think he will mind my revealing a text he once sent me. When he and Andrew Strauss received OBEs in the 2011 Queen's Birthday Honours List (in which Alastair Cook also received an MBE), he replied to my congratulations with this: 'Just strange to go from OGs to OBEs!' He truly was humbled.

I have certainly never found him arrogant. In fact I've never heard anyone really say a bad word about him. But then I've never really had an in-depth conversation with Kevin Pietersen about him. There are always players who will slate a coach, at any level.

He is a loyal friend. All his friends confirm that even at the busiest times of being England coach he will always return calls and messages from his mates, however long it might take. Tickets are always sorted for those who want them – within reason, of course. And while there has obviously had to be a slight change in our relationship with me as a journalist and him as England coach, it hasn't altered dramatically. He has a gentle side. Once he came to my house in Cardiff and played golf on the Wii with my young daughter Bethan, who every time I go to cricket now says, 'Say hello to Andy for me please!'

Very early on as a cricketer Flower decided that he had to be tougher than others if he were to succeed in the game. 'I never actually had a high regard for whatever talent I had,' he once said. 'Seeing the ball, hitting it, there were plenty of other cricketers who did that far better than I did. But I thought one area where I could be better than them was to be more determined, more hungry and not give anything away.' The result was a cricketer who could not be messed with. As Campbell says, 'When he's got his "game-face" on, he's a very serious bloke.' There may have been an expletive in that quote too. A well-placed expletive, as it happens, because it does emphasize how serious Flower can be when the time comes for sporting action. Campbell is spot on. Flower's 'game-face', as a cricketer and as a coach, truly is the stuff of legend.

While Grant trained maniacally in the gym, Andy trained hard but also set about developing his mental toughness. He enlisted the help of a chap called Eugene Moody, a black belt in karate, to train differently; to train smarter.

Now I'm a bit of a fitness fanatic myself, but I can honestly say that I've never seen anyone train as hard as Grant. If I tell you that I have seen him do weights for four hours in the morning, go to net practice at lunchtime, go for a long run in late afternoon and then go for more nets in the evening, then I would not be lying. He might even fit in a game of squash somewhere too. At one stage during his time at Essex the fitness staff told him his body fat levels were 'dangerously low'. I'm not surprised. 'I overtrained,' he confesses. 'Andy trained smarter and I burnt myself out because I thought the harder you trained the better it would be, and that I just had to give myself the best possible chance. I didn't spend enough time on the mental side of things.'

Andy was always reading books on sports psychology and listening to tapes on the subject. 'He was a pioneer of self-help,' says Campbell. 'I would read the books and listen to the tapes also,' says Grant, 'but I didn't take it in as much. Andrew wanted to understand it better. I found the physical side a lot easier – to deal with and learn from.'

None of this is to say that Andy was an obviously natural leader back then. 'He goes against that perception that great leaders are born,' says Campbell. 'If you'd seen some of the things he got up to as a youngster, you'd have said "no chance". If you speak to guys who went to school with him, he was a bit of a rebel.'

Flower will admit that his youth was a little wild. I have heard of him giving talks to young aspiring England cricketers and saying as much, although he does then emphasize how he came to realize how important fitness is. I'll never forget him turning up to training at Harare Sports Club once (we visiting English pros were often allowed to train with the Zimbabwe squad) and taking his shirt off to begin a physical warm-up. He glanced down at his midriff and pinched the smallest amount of flab. 'I'm supposed to be a professional sportsman,' he said angrily to himself, and there may have been an expletive in there then too. He trained like Grant that day.

Alcohol and sport mix as easily in Zimbabwe as any other country. For me, spending winters playing there was just an extension of the five years I spent at university. There was ample time to train, play and party. The Flowers and Campbell seemed to like playing student drinking games, especially that old favourite 'Bunnies'. So with two former Combined Universities colleagues Adrian Dale and James Boiling (who now teaches at my alma mater Monmouth School) joining me in Zimbabwe for two consecutive years there were some raucous times. 'We could never get Andy drunk in those games though,' recalls Boiling. 'He was too smart. He always had his wits about him.' Flower does, though, suffer from hangovers that are as bad as the ones I have to endure. 'Alcohol poisons him,' I remember his wife Becky saying with a shake of the head one morning in Zimbabwe.

In general, however, Flower is little different from most other Zimbabweans. They have a certain streak of madness in them. As I've mentioned, Duncan Fletcher had that too. I put this to Grant, and he knew what was coming. He knew I was going to talk about a trip we took to Lake Kariba over the festive season of 1991/92. 'They weren't big crocodiles!' he said unprompted, with a laugh. He was talking about the rather inebriated habit some Zimbabweans have of catching small crocodiles at night by shining a light across the water and pouncing on the red dots the crocodiles' eyes produce. The closer together, the smaller the crocodile. 'You never know though!' Grant admits with a nervous chuckle.

On that same trip one day Andy thought it was a good idea

to cool off after a warm day's fishing and drinking by lying in the shallow waters. I'd like to think that my impassioned screams of 'Get out of the water, you mad bastard!' may have helped England become the number one ranked cricket side in the world. But the truth is that he wasn't listening.

Flower still seeks adventure as England coach. On the South Africa tour of 2009/10 he was seen climbing the floodlights at Buffalo Park in East London with wicketkeeping coach Bruce French, who is a keen climber, Huw Bevan, Richard Halsall and a player who'd probably better remain nameless (the last three only went to the top of the pole so could not be seen like Flower and French, who popped out and had their photographs taken). On tour he will often spend a day off riding huge Harley Davidson bikes with Bevan. And when in Australia for the 2010/11 Ashes he, Bevan and French went tombstone diving in Fremantle, Western Australia, as well as climbing in the Adelaide Hills.

What is it with these Zimbos? 'I just think it's the culture we were brought up in,' says Grant. 'We had an outdoor lifestyle and went on holidays to places like Kariba and Victoria Falls. People take chances. You've had a civil war to deal with and a lot of people have had trouble on their farms. If you're weak, then generally you get singled out and you don't survive and don't come through the system. It is a bit mad, yes, but people who are brought up in London are more savvy to the world. We come to England and have to do things like go on the Tube and it is a big shock to the system.'

It was actually a trip to England in 1986 that began Andy's cricketing odyssey. In his last year at Vainona he was selected for the Stragglers club tour on which they played sixteen games in three weeks. 'They blooded him on that tour,' says Bill.

It was also in England on that tour that Andy's view of the world, especially in terms of race, was challenged. 'I was billeted with a lovely family in Esher,' he said in an interview with

The Times in 2011. 'They had a son of my age and I remember having a discussion with him about interracial relationships. I was truly astonished when he said that he would contemplate having a non-white girlfriend. We argued for hours one night about it. I began to realize something was deeply wrong with my beliefs.

'It is amazing how easily racist ideology is absorbed by young people. It is a form of indoctrination because you just don't realize how your own ideas and assumptions have been coloured by what you are told and the norms of the culture you are living in. It was only when I got to my late teens and early twenties that I first started to ask the question: "What the hell am I thinking here?" My views were very backward, which is deeply embarrassing to admit today.'

Flower clearly learnt much, on and off the field, on that Stragglers tour, but returned home to work for the Anglo American Corporation as a trainee accountant. He was there for eighteen months, but the problem for him was that leave specifically for cricket would not be granted; he always had to take personal leave in order to play. Soon he decided he had had enough and went back to England to play in the Birmingham League for Barnt Green. It was a felicitous move. He was given accommodation at the club chairman's home, and Andy soon discovered that the Hampson family had a delightful daughter called Rebecca. She is now his wife and mother to three children, Jamie, Sam and Dani.

The following year (1989) Flower played in the Lancashire League for Heywood as an amateur, returning in 1992 and 1993 as a professional. In between times he spent two years in Holland, playing for Voorburg in The Hague. There followed stints with West Bromwich Dartmouth and Eastbourne (where he played alongside England fielding coach Halsall), as well as coaching posts at Epsom College and Oxford University.

This was no easy road into professional cricket. Grant was just as nomadic, taking in spells in Somerset at Winscombe, Cheltenham, Wallasey in Merseyside, Widnes and Harrogate. He also followed Andy to Voorburg and Epsom College.

But the crucial thing was that Andy was coaching, employed by the ZCU and gaining qualifications on courses run by Les Lenham, the former Sussex batsman. He coached the Zimbabwe age-group sides, visited the better schools in Harare on a rota basis, as well as youngsters in the underprivileged areas. All the while he was taking it a little more seriously than the two rapscallions Flower G. and Campbell, who were also working under the coaching director Dave Houghton. 'To be honest I didn't think about coaching then because I was playing,' admits Grant. 'It was a means to an end. I think Andrew might have thought about it a bit deeper than that. I was pretty naive and immature in those days, and Alistair [Campbell] and I were messing around. Andrew has always been a bit different.'

I'd agree with that. There was always a little bit more mystery to Andy than the others. He was certainly harder to get to know than his brother and Campbell. No harder than Fletcher, mind. 'Andrew doesn't let people in easily,' says Campbell. 'To gain his trust takes a process.'

But even Andy admits coaching was not necessarily always on his mind back then. 'I found it quite hard coaching five days a week,' he says, 'because all I really wanted to do was play. But it's interesting that when I applied for the England job I spoke about being involved in the study of coaching and maximizing my own and other people's potential for twenty years.'

In 1991 Andy was appointed to take over from Houghton as director of coaching at the ZCU. Campbell reckons this was a turning point for Flower, a time to recognize his responsibilities. 'There were no pros then so that was the highest position for a player,' says Campbell. 'My abiding memory of him is always walking around with a black Filofax under his arm. He was very structured even then. He wanted reports on where everyone was and what they were doing. He was never afraid of calling someone in and hauling them over the coals.'

I think that may mean that Campbell received the odd bollocking. And doubtless it was justified. He is an extremely humorous and gregarious fellow, but he was a lazy bugger then. His nickname is 'Kamba', which means tortoise in Shona, and it is very apt.

And none of this is to say that Flower and Campbell don't get on. They do. Famously. In 2006 they were on holiday in Mauritius with their respective families when Campbell told him he'd soon be coach of England. It was a big call given he was still playing at Essex, while doing some coaching with the National Academy. 'I told him, "You'll be England coach!"' says Campbell. 'I just thought it was a natural progression, knowing the personality and how he'd be able to distance himself from all the egos and the high life that is abundant there in the England cricket team. I knew he could bring a sense of normality.'

It was some remarkable prescience from Campbell. But as he says, he knows the character. He knows what Flower went through to become the number one ranked batsman in the world. He was his captain between 1996 and 1999, between Flower's two tenures as Zimbabwe captain.

Thinking about it, Flower must have been an awful captain. He was the only one of many I encountered in a 245-match first-class career who allowed me to bowl. Just the two balls, mind. Don Shepherd, the Glamorgan great so cruelly deprived of an England cap, took 2,218 first-class wickets at an average of just 21, so he is rather well qualified to comment on the quality of my bowling. 'The worst I have ever seen,' he once said. And he meant anywhere, not just in first-class cricket. Yes, I was rubbish – a huge disappointment given that my father had been a wicket-taker par excellence, in the Shepherd off-cutting mode as it happened, for Lydney and Gloucestershire second eleven. But

Flower allowed me to bowl, against his brother Grant of all people, at the end of a Mashonaland versus Mashonaland Under 24s match in Harare in 1994. They needed three to win. It was a surprise it took Grant two balls.

More seriously, there is something else I recall from that Logan Cup match, in which the Flowers were opposing captains. Andy won the toss and inserted the opposition on a dampish pitch at Harare Sports Club. They crawled to 284 in 152 overs. At the end of their innings as we walked from the field on the second day, I said to Andy, 'I reckon we should just get up to their score as quickly as we can, then declare.' The comment was based on two things. Firstly, a chronic lack of faith in my ability at the time. I could not score a run and was looking to take pressure from myself as the fear of failure took grip. And secondly, much less importantly in my mind, it seemed the only way for us to breathe life into a game that was dying. There just didn't seem time for much else.

So as I prepared to open with Paul Bourdillon, a Zimbabwean with whom I'd played some university cricket in England and indeed on a Combined Universities tour to Barbados captained by Mike Atherton, with Flower at number three and Trevor Penney at four in a strong side, Flower relayed this message to the team.

It went well. We were all out for 75. There was plenty of time left in the game all right. We lost by ten wickets. It has been said many times since that Flower is a good listener, but listening to a doubting, pusillanimous English pro that day was not one of his better moves.

Flower had been captain of Old Georgians at just twenty-one. He was already learning how to shape a cricket team. 'There are no mysteries,' he says. 'You need to have mutual respect for your team-mates, enjoy working together and enjoy sharing hard work.' Captaining older players is never easy, but it certainly shaped his attitude towards younger players. 'He ruled by fear a bit,' says Grant. 'Some players even left OGs because of it [I bet they weren't very good]. He didn't tolerate fools. He obviously had good knowledge, but his man management let him down sometimes.'

Flower himself will admit this. 'One of my weaknesses as captain was dealing with people,' he said recently. 'I look back and cringe at some of the things I did. I judged people too harshly, too quickly. I did not have empathy with people.'

One of the occasions he might be recalling is a Zimbabwe Under 24s match against Natal Under 24s in Durban during which he sent one of his players, Hitesh Hira, off the field. I'll let Campbell take up the story: 'Andrew felt Hitesh didn't go for a catch, so he threw his keeping gloves down, walked over to him and said: "This has been happening for too long. I'm sick and tired of you not trying. So get the fuck off the field!" Hitesh just walked off. Dave Houghton [who was coach] was in the changing room and hadn't seen what had happened. So Hitesh walks in and Houghton says, "What's wrong? Have you got a hammie [a hamstring injury]?" And Hitesh said, "Andrew has just sent me off for not trying!"'

Interestingly Fletcher also sent one of his players back to the dressing room, when he was captain of the Alexandra club side in Harare. He was a chap called Cecil Grimmer, who had been in an argument with one of his team-mates. Fletcher told him to leave the field, but Grimmer would not go. 'Get this man off the field,' said Fletcher to the umpires. Tough men, Flower and Fletcher.

Flower actually led Zimbabwe to their first Test win, in 1995, when they hammered Pakistan by an innings and 64 runs in Harare. Had I not been there I wouldn't have believed it, but I was there, with leg in plaster after partially severing my patella tendon on a glass door. It was not alcohol-related. Honest.

It was Henry Olonga's Test debut – a wake-up call, too. Not just because he was called for throwing, as he had been in the tourists' previous match against the ZCU President's XI at Harare South. He did throw at that stage of his career too, before undergoing remedial work with Dennis Lillee. I know that for certain because I had been coach of the Zimbabwe B side for the couple of years previous to that, and Olonga had played for us against Northern Transvaal B (coached by Surrey's Keith Medlycott) earlier in the month before his Test debut. It was obvious he was throwing, but I had no idea what to do. It was best I stuck to journalism, I think.

'Andy was a hard task master,' Olonga recalls of that first Test. 'He was a no-nonsense guy. He always demanded the best from his players and didn't tolerate weak excuses. I was eighteen years old and it was a case of "welcome to the world of men". Test cricket was harder than I imagined. I was a little kid and Andy didn't suffer fools gladly. You drop a catch or miss a run out and you will know about it.'

There were some weird happenings in that Test, which I thought nothing of at the time. It began at the toss. Flower tossed the coin and the Pakistan captain Salim Malik mumbled something inaudible. The match referee Jackie Hendriks immediately stepped in and put his hand over the coin, with Malik claiming he had called 'Bird' in relation to the Zimbabwe Bird, the national emblem that was on one side of the dollar coin then. A re-toss was made, which Flower won, and he and Grant put on 269 together for the fourth wicket, Grant making 201 not out and Andy 156. Both played quite superbly, but there were some curious bowling changes and tactics. Given subsequent events, it does make you think.

I was also there when Zimbabwe played their inaugural Test, against India in Harare in October 1992. For some reason, and with no idea what I was doing, I was Zimbabwe's press liaison officer. My main job was to ensure that the press box phone bills were not too expensive. I failed horribly apparently.

I was shocked that Test status had suddenly come to a group

of blokes who basically played club cricket on Sundays. It was good club cricket, I grant you, played over sixty overs, but I was genuinely worried that it was going to be too big a step up for most of them. But a flat pitch helped allay fears and Grant made 82, Andy 59, and Houghton, making his Test debut at the age of thirty-five, hit 121.

The decision to grant Zimbabwe Test cricket was, of course, politically motivated. India used it as a means of garnering another vote at the ICC's table, and duly arrived as Zimbabwe's first opponents. It shouldn't have happened, but you do wonder what might have happened had it not. What would have become of the career of Andy Flower? Would he have played for South Africa? Mark Boucher might be glad that this decision was made.

It was made, and suddenly Test and one-day international cricket was on Bill and Jean Flower's doorstep, with two of their sons as the prime actors on the stage. 'Flower Power' became a rather overused cliché. But it was always apposite. You could find no prouder and happier parents in world cricket than Bill and Jean, sitting transfixed at Harare Sports Club.

Then in 1996 tragedy struck the Flower family. At the age of just thirty-three, the eldest son Stephen was killed in an accident on his farm in Zambia. 'He was the farmer in the family,' says Bill. 'He was running a large rose operation from York Farm just outside Lusaka. And he was building a refrigeration unit on the back of his farm truck to use when he came to Harare regularly to visit family. It was a freak accident, by electrocution.'

I spoke to Bill in late March 2011. He and Jean had just moved from Lincolnshire to Surrey, to be nearer daughter Megan and her family. And Bill had just had another heart attack, on New Year's Day, in fact, while Andy was out in Australia preparing for the final Ashes Test. Andy very nearly came home. 'He asked his mother whether he should come home,' says Bill, 'and she said no, which was the correct decision.'

When I spoke to Bill he was still recovering. He was easily emotional. And recalling the tragic story of Stephen quite naturally affected him. He remembered it as if it were yesterday: 'It was a Saturday afternoon, I was being interviewed at the ZBC [Zimbabwe Broadcasting Corporation] studios about the cricket development work I was doing at the time. I was summoned to the phone. Jean had received the news. I just went to pieces . . .'

Andy and Grant are not naturally emotional people, especially Grant. Andy can be more emotional, and I have heard that occasionally he becomes so when speaking to the England team, as he did at the end of the South Africa tour in 2009/10 when talking to the team about the tour as a whole, and again in Perth on the Ashes tour. It was the fourth morning of play, with England facing defeat at 81-5. There had been an incident the previous evening when Paul Collingwood was out when he shouldn't really have been facing had nightwatchman James Anderson done his job properly and taken the single so obviously on offer. Flower apparently said, 'Jimmy messed up yesterday evening, that's OK. We all do that, but let's appreciate everything he does for us.' As Strauss related in his Ashes diary, 'He actually got quite emotional, which Andy doesn't often do. He was talking about the way Jimmy bowls, and the fact that he actually embraces the nightwatchman's role. His voice was breaking a little. It highlighted to us just how much he cares and how passionate he is about us, not only as a side but also a group of individuals.'

There was another occasion, at the Oval at the end of the 4–0 Test series win over India in 2011. As Graeme Swann was later to reveal, 'An hour or two after the Fourth Test finished on Monday, we wandered on to the outfield, supped a couple of beers and had a final reflective chat about the Test summer.

Andy Flower was quite emotional as he spoke of the pride he felt in the team. It's great that a coach can be so happy that he chokes up like that.'

When Stephen died, Andy was in England coaching at Epsom College, and Grant was playing at Wallasey. Naturally they both returned home immediately. 'They both gave the outward impression that they had everything under control,' says Bill, 'which I don't think is a good thing. You carry that grief for too long. I tried to get them to agree to counselling before they went back to the UK. But I think that by the time they came back to Zimbabwe they had had their own private grief release.'

Bill does, though, think that it played a part in shaping Andy's future management skills. 'It helps make you what you are,' he says. 'You have to learn to suffer losses like that. That's life. That's why he is so good with his man management. Players can talk to him.'

Grant, too, thinks it had an effect. 'It might have made us a bit tougher,' he says. 'It puts things into perspective. When you think things are the end of the world, well . . . We've never been the most overly emotional people, Andrew and I, and the rest of the family expected us to show our grief more. But we didn't because we tried to be strong around them. That was our method.'

Andy gave up the Zimbabwe captaincy at the beginning of that 1996/97 Zimbabwean season. It was nothing to do with Stephen's death, rather that the job had been getting too much for him as a whole. I have often been asked why Flower was not always captain of Zimbabwe, if he is such a good leader. The answer is obvious. Captaining Zimbabwe is not like captaining any other Test country. It's like captaining, say, Cambridge University in first-class cricket. You just keep losing. And that must get you down.

Flower returned to the captaincy in 1999. He intended to be in it for the long haul, but was sacked in 2000 after a pay dispute with the Zimbabwe board during the tour to England. ZCU chairman Peter Chingoka held Flower personally responsible, and, unbeknown to Flower, just before that triangular final asked Heath Streak to take over the captaincy in the upcoming season. Flower did not discover this until he returned to Zimbabwe some time afterwards following a holiday in France. To say he wasn't happy would be the grossest of understatements.

But rejection can focus the mind. Flower decided that it was all going to be about him from then on. He'd spent all that time trying to carry an under-strength side on his shoulders. So he set himself a personal goal. He wanted to become the number one ranked batsman in the world. At the time he was ninth, with Alec Stewart, Justin Langer, Inzamam-ul-Haq, Ricky Ponting, Saeed Anwar, Brian Lara, Steve Waugh and Sachin Tendulkar above him.

He began by taking a piece of paper and in the centre of it marking a huge number one. Around the number he made notes of various things he felt he needed to do in order to reach that goal, whether they were mental improvements, technical adjustments or even changes to his social habits. That piece of paper was always with him, whether he was at home or in his hotel room on tour, with only his closest friends having any knowledge of it. He kept adding notes as time moved on.

By December of that year he was up to second in the rankings, with only Tendulkar ahead of him. That was due in no small part to a couple of remarkable Tests in India, where Flower scored 183 not out and 70 in Delhi, and then 55 and 232 not out in Nagpur. It confirmed him as a quite exceptional player of spin. Anil Kumble and Harbhajan Singh may not have been playing in those Tests (at Delhi the spinners were Sunil Doshi and Murali Kartik, and at Nagpur they were Doshi and Sarandeep Singh), but Kumble, Maninder Singh and Rajesh Chauhan had been playing in 1993 in Delhi when Flower made

115 and 62 not out. And both Kumble and Harbhajan were playing when Flower made 92 at Delhi in 2002. In five Tests in India overall Flower averaged 117. It is a stunning statistic. But then few could sweep or reverse-sweep like him. In Nagpur especially he reverse-swept the Indians to distraction.

In June 2001 Zimbabwe beat India in Harare, with Flower hitting the winning runs. But unusually he was batting at number eight, having broken his thumb while keeping. Until then he had played in every one of Zimbabwe's 52 Tests and 172 one-day internationals. He missed four ODIs and two Tests before returning against South Africa in September. In the first Test in Harare he made 142 and 199 not out. Still Zimbabwe lost, but the rankings could no longer deny Flower. Since being sacked as captain in 2000, he had made 1,407 Test runs at an average of 108. He was the number one batsman in the world, and remained so until December.

That piece of paper had worked. Sound familiar? Throughout his tenure as England coach he has been seen studiously taking notes on the sidelines. Whereas before he had been plotting his own path to the top of the world, now it was England's.

10

Changing of the Guard

The West Indies is the hardest tour for a cricket newspaper journalist. Of course, it's not the hardest in terms of the lifestyle and hospitality, but it is the hardest in terms of filing to ever-shifting deadlines. In Australia you know that by the time your stuff appears in the newspaper it is dated, so you write accordingly. You write carefully! But in the Caribbean, with the time difference being about five hours behind, you are constantly filing live copy. And things can change very swiftly.

So there I was in 2009, acting as the *Sunday Telegraph*'s correspondent again, with Scyld Berry doing his *Wisden* editorship. The first Test was in Jamaica, and Saturday was the fourth day. My first edition copy had to be in by just before lunchtime. The pitch had been slow, and therefore so had the match, with most interest centring upon events far away in India where the Indian Premier League auction had taken place on the third day, with Kevin Pietersen and Andrew Flintoff both fetching a record $1.55 million each. After Pietersen had been dismissed for 97, aiming to reach his century with a six, he was memorably dubbed 'Dumbslog Millionaire', after the Oscar-winning film *Slumdog Millionaire*. Two other England players, Paul Collingwood and Owais Shah, were also bought at the auction, as was Ravi Bopara, not then on the England tour but later called up.

On that fourth morning the West Indies had only just completed their first innings, crawling to a lead of 74. The match had 'draw' written all over it so I wrote a piece suggesting as much. Just as I was finishing it, Alastair Cook was out for a duck. I was not particularly worried. Openers get ducks. Neither Cook nor Strauss had reached double figures in the first innings. The home side's opener Devon Smith had failed similarly, even if his partner Chris Gayle had made a century on his home turf.

Then for a few overs before lunch the left-arm spin of the tall Sulieman Benn was introduced. At the fourth ball of the last over before the break, Ian Bell attempted a limp cut to a wide one and was caught behind for 4. England were suddenly 11-2 at lunch, trailing by 63, and already my sports editor Peter Mitchell was on the phone advising that I tickle my 'intro' so as to reflect the possibility of some impending doom.

But nobody could have foreseen the depth and the rapidity of that doom. By 2.34 p.m. that afternoon the match was over. England had been bowled out for just 51. Only Flintoff, with 24, reached double figures. England had lost by an innings and 23 runs. Jerome Taylor recorded figures of 9-4-11-5. With the third ball after lunch he bowled Pietersen for 1 with a wicked, late away-swinging yorker. 'London Bridge is falling down' blared the music from Chester's Bar. At 26-7 soon afterwards it had collapsed.

My second edition 'intro' was rather different. 'This was an utter disgrace,' I wrote. 'Another shameful chapter of English cricketing history was written here, as England's batting collapsed inexplicably and spinelessly to 51 all out, their third-lowest score ever. Only the 45 against Australia in Sydney in

1887 and the infamous 46 in Trinidad in 1994 stand below this effort in the record books . . .'

Get stuck in, son.

After the quotes had been gathered from a despondent England press conference, Mitchell then decided, quite rightly of course, that this required a further comment piece. Another eight hundred words.

'How long have I got?' I asked.

'Twenty minutes,' came the response.

Jesus.

'Whither England now?' I wrote. 'How do you recover from such a shambles? Skipper Andrew Strauss described his dressing room as being a "pretty disconsolate place". You can bet it was a lot worse than that. It will have been a place of devastation and embarrassment . . .' I recounted a tale of my own, of how Middlesex had bowled out Glamorgan for just 31, in 1997 of all the years, the year we won the county championship, with Duncan Fletcher as our coach. I went home after that debacle and lay on my sofa for the rest of the day with my face turned inwards. I couldn't even face my wife.

Imagine how Andy Flower felt. What a first Test for the care-taker coach. Well, we discovered how he felt the very next morning in a press conference at the team's Hilton Hotel in Kingston. Let us just say that he had obviously dealt with it a lot better than I did in 1997.

The conference had been scheduled for right beside the pool, but was moved to beneath a nearby palm tree. Not even there was there any shade for Flower from what one writer described as 'the microphones and cameras that were jabbed, almost pugilistically' into his face.

As Flower had walked to his chair, he had glanced at me and smiled. I genuinely felt sorry for him. At that stage I did not think he wanted the job, and I did not think he would get it. As I wrote later that day, 'Baby-sitting should really have no place in international sport. He [Flower] is the best-paid nanny in the country, waiting until the real boss comes home.'

But I was underestimating his resilience. He was quite brilliant at that press conference. As one gnarled old hack observed, 'It's almost disarming to hear straight questions being returned with straight answers.' Yes, Peter Moores had never been particularly good at that.

Flower ducked nothing. 'As a team we've underperformed,' he said, 'and it's all our jobs to do something about that. And if we don't do it, we'll be out of jobs. What you've got to do in international cricket is handle the pressure and we didn't do that yesterday. I'm in charge – the buck stops with me.'

The last comment was impressive. It would have been so easy for him to blame others. He was, after all, only the 'assistant coach' in title. He had had no say in selection, because the squad had been chosen before the double departure of Moores and Pietersen.

It should really have occurred to me then that Flower wanted to make a fist of this. He wanted to be coach of England. Or 'team director', as the grand title now is. What's more he was clearly up to that task. Hugh Morris and Geoff Miller were standing at the back of the press conference, and they clearly thought the same. 'He was very close to getting the job that day,' admits Morris. 'He was hugely impressive in a really difficult situation. He was incredibly honest and straightforward.'

He was relaxed. There was no sense of panic. There were certainly no 'naughty-boy nets' for the players, as quite a few of them went off to play golf. 'I think after a day like yesterday it's best to stay calm,' he said, 'and reflect on what's happened and not to have knee-jerk reactions on selection. There is a time when we need to reflect on what has happened and also for the learning of the players and the coaching staff. We will have our team meeting tomorrow.'

The following day, having flown to Antigua, they did have

their team meeting. It was a meeting that was still being talked about years later. In his newspaper column in 2011, just before the third Test against India at Edgbaston, with England on the verge of becoming number one in the world, James Anderson wrote – or his ghost did anyway – of the ten steps that had brought England to that position. First on the list was the 51 all out scenario. 'After we were rolled over, assistant coach Andy Flower and Strauss led a team meeting which went something like: "You're grown men, it's time to take a bit of responsibility for yourselves, your practice, your preparation." They did not just want the captain to be the leader. Their formula was based on having a team of leaders. A key moment.'

The meeting took place at the Grand Royal Antiguan Hotel in Deep Bay, St John's. Mark Garaway was then the England team analyst, and had been since 2006. It was actually his last tour, because when Flower took over the reins permanently one of his first moves was to remove Garaway from his position. The reasons were twofold. Firstly, Garaway was very close to Pietersen, indeed they were habitual running partners in the West Indies, and it was perceived that he was heavily involved in the Moores saga. Secondly, under Fletcher, Garaway had been encouraged to coach, as well as work as the analyst. That was Fletcher's way. He liked his support staff to help out in a coaching capacity. And Garaway had been coach of Somerset, remember. But Flower didn't want that. He wanted an analyst pure and simple, even if Garaway's successor, in a job-share arrangement with Gemma Broad (Stuart's sister), was Nathan Leamon, a Cambridge maths graduate and former maths teacher at Tonbridge and director of coaching at Eton who is a qualified cricket coach. 'Numbers' the players call him, and that's what he deals in. He doesn't try to coach.

You might think Garaway is bitter. He is not. He quickly moved on to become the high performance director for Ireland Cricket (he left in 2011 to set up his own business). 'It wasn't a shock to me,' he says of his removal from the England camp. 'I'd been tipped off that was the way he [Flower] was going to go. I made no secret: I wanted to coach and I wanted to lead more importantly.'

Garaway remembers that Antigua meeting as the moment Flower stood up as a leader. 'We didn't really find out a lot about Andy in the first twenty-two months,' he says. 'During that time it was always Mooresy's message, and Andy is a loyal Zimbabwean. He never said or did anything to undermine Mooresy. But this was where we really saw what the bloke was about. I walked out of the meeting thinking, "This bloke is definitely going to get the job, and if he does get it, he is only going to get better and better."'

Strauss wrote in his Ashes diary that Flower was 'brilliant' in that meeting. 'It was the moment that we all realized that he had something special. He was very honest about his own view and some of the things that he hadn't said before, and then he encouraged other people to talk, but did it in a way that was very constructive and sympathetic to their point of view. So it wasn't "You're saying something I don't agree with, so you're talking rubbish". It was "OK, that's interesting. I don't necessarily agree with it, but I can see why you're saying that." A lot came up about the players not having bought into the team side of things. There were some pretty hard conversations going on.'

Garaway agrees it was a 'punchy' meeting. 'We all know that in cricket dressing rooms people come out with clichés,' he says, 'but here Andy and Straussy really set their stall out. A lot of the bullshit chat that had gone on before was not going to be allowed. People just wouldn't be allowed to get away with talking in vague language.'

Garaway says that everyone in the room, including the support staff, was challenged about his role. And he recalls, in particular, that Pietersen was confronted strongly. 'I remember one conversation where they were challenging KP,' he says, 'and somebody challenged him about his lifestyle, about being in the papers all the time and living in Chelsea. KP quite rightly went at them, saying, "I train as hard, if not harder, than anybody else, and I believe my results speak for themselves. I can back it up."'

Garaway then revealed that 'two or three of the senior players who didn't always see eye-to-eye with KP actually backed him up'. He was undoubtedly talking about Andrew Flintoff and Steve Harmison. 'Yes, Fred particularly,' he admitted. 'It was a very unusual thing to happen, but it was just the environment that the two Andys had decided to put in place at the time. Before that there wouldn't have been the strength of environment for them to back him up.'

As Strauss says, 'In the space of one meeting we'd gone from a team that never said anything honest to one in which people could say almost anything to each other.'

The most obvious upshot of the meeting was that Bell was dropped. Patience had run out. He was told in no uncertain terms that he needed to shape up, and toughen up. He'd played forty-six Tests by this stage of his career, with eight centuries, but with that killer statistic still hanging over his head: all of those centuries had come after a colleague had also made a century in the same innings. The accusation, which became a cliché, was that he was a piggy-backer, a soft follower rather than a tough leader. The Australian Stuart Law had once called him 'that timid little creature', and during the 2006/07 Ashes Shane Warne had nicknamed him the 'Sherminator' after the ginger-haired geek in the *American Pie* films. Mike Atherton described him as 'the man-boy'. Mentally, Bell was certainly not Flower's type of batsman at that stage.

Bell was not fit enough, or tough enough. I remember being outside the Hilton Hotel in Barbados later in the tour, talking to Flower as he prepared to leave for practice. Out of the hotel came Bell, all alone and dressed in running gear. He had a quick word with Flower, and off he ran.

'Good effort,' I said to Flower.

'Yes, he's got a lot of work to do,' was the response.

Indeed he had. For the rest of the tour barely a trip to the ground or back after play went by without a sighting of Bell running. Sometimes others were with him. Goodness, I even saw Harmison running back from the ground in Barbados once! Bell would rise early and do boxing sessions with the team security man, Reg Dickason. Bell knew the score. 'It wasn't technically that I was struggling,' he later told me. 'It was about how to make myself tougher and physically better. Reg put me in a tough place.'

It got tougher. When Bell returned from the West Indies, his Warwickshire colleague Darren Maddy put him in touch with Darren Grewcock, a rugby fitness guru with experience with the Leicester Tigers. Grewcock in turn introduced him to a cage-fighter called Barrington Patterson. By the time Bell returned to the Test team for the third Ashes Test later that year, he was a different person.

Just like Bell, the England team as a whole resolved to be different. They too resolved to be tougher. Their first step was to make themselves harder to beat. They could not win any of the three remaining Tests (four if you include the ten-ball abandoned debacle at the Sir Vivian Richards Stadium in Antigua, where the sandy outfield was soon deemed unplayable), but they did not lose any either, playing all the cricket in truth. In the hastily rearranged Test at the St John's Recreation Ground in Antigua, England had ten overs at the West Indies' last pair but, agonizingly, could not force the last wicket, and then in Trinidad the hosts were hanging on grimly with eight wickets down.

There was, inevitably, criticism of England's conservatism, with declarations seen to be too tardy, but both Flower and

Strauss were laying down markers. Test cricket is no playground. It is not like the old days of three-day county cricket, when enticing declarations were made and the result was forgotten as soon as the next match started, which was usually the next day. Test-match declarations matter. Those that lead to defeat are remembered. Everybody recalls Gary Sobers' generous declaration in Trinidad in 1968 that handed England victory, so too David Gower's at Lord's in 1984 that gave the West Indies an easy win.

At least England won the subsequent one-day series 3–2. It was the first time England had ever won a one-day series in the Caribbean, and this at the seventh attempt. In the series Strauss was the leading run-scorer (204 runs at 51, with a strike rate of 86.80) – not bad for a chap who hadn't played an ODI for nearly two years, who was ignored as soon as Moores took over after the World Cup of 2007. Between now and the 2011 World Cup, after which he retired from ODIs, he would rejuvenate his one-day batting, averaging nearly 41 in forty-nine matches with four hundreds at a strike rate of 87.68. Overall in his ODI career he averaged 35.63 with six hundreds and a strike rate of 80.94. So the improvements were obvious. He knew that he had to expand his game at the top of the order, and he did, even if I still think he was better suited to the middle order, where he batted around 2004.

Fletcher always insisted that in order to flourish as an ODI opener you need to be able to hit high and hard down the ground. So around that period in 2004 Fletcher used Strauss at number four. A game that readily springs to mind is the Champions Trophy semi-final against Australia at Edgbaston, where England chased down 260 with 3.5 overs remaining. Strauss made 52 not out from forty-two balls at number four.

Fletcher always saw his number four in one-day cricket as the lynchpin. He wanted his top three to be aggressive against the new ball in the Powerplay overs, with the realization that the number four could stabilize things if early wickets were lost. The number four also had to realize that, if the start was good, he might have to drop down the order. A lot of this applied to me at Glamorgan. A natural opener, it was Fletcher who eventually persuaded me to bat in the middle order – after much debate and argument, it does have to be said.

It always irked Fletcher that he could not improve England's one-day cricket more. And, in truth, under Flower there have been many of the same old problems, as evidenced by Fletcher's India's 5–0 win over England in the autumn of 2011. Under both coaches there have been encouraging times. But there have also been dispiriting times. Fletcher is a good one-day coach. His main worry when taking the England job was whether he could coach Test cricket. But the problem in England is that one-day cricket is the poor relation. To the counties and the ECB it is simply a money-making venture; any consideration for the standard of cricket being played often falls by the wayside. There is the difficult problem of English (and Welsh) pitches being so very different from most others around the world, and the accompanying hazards of power hitting in the Powerplay overs on seaming pitches. But that does not excuse some of the ludicrous scheduling. One-day internationals should be played as curtain-raisers to Test series, just like they were so successfully before the 2005 Ashes, not as closing credits that are so easily switched off.

The one-day series victory in the Caribbean at least gave Flower a small achievement with which to enter the interview process for England team director. The ECB had had thirty applicants for the job, but, with the help of the hot-shot recruitment agency Odgers Ray & Berndtson, who were heavily involved in the early parts of the process (presumably approaching potential candidates still under contract elsewhere and so avoiding embarrassment for the ECB), had whittled that down to a shortlist of four. The names of those four are still closely guarded today because of the jobs they were in at the time, but the New Zealander John Wright was certainly among them (he was interviewed on the phone apparently), and the then South Africa coach Mickey Arthur probably was.

The interview panel consisted of Morris, Gordon Lord (the ECB's elite coach development manager), Dennis Amiss (the ECB deputy chairman), Angus Fraser (recently appointed managing director of Middlesex after leaving the *Independent* as cricket correspondent) and Floyd Woodrow (a former head of recruitment at the SAS used by the ECB to train many of its younger cricketers. It was quite rightly felt that Woodrow knew a bit about leadership.) The candidates were interviewed for two hours, and then re-interviewed later in the day. If Flower did not already have the job, he soon did. He was informed later that evening that he was now England's new team director.

The appointment was not greeted with universal acclaim. The 'robust and transparent process', as described by the ECB, was derided. At the press conference to trumpet Flower's elevation, Morris mentioned on more than one occasion Flower's 'potential to be a world-class coach'. Not too many people believed him.

I did. That is not arrogance or my proclaiming any brilliant prescience. I believed then that potential was enough, and Flower had that. I also believed that none of the other proposed candidates were that good anyway. For the *Wisden Cricketer* I wrote, 'Those promoting a raft of better coaches out there, available or not, are spouting nonsense. Tom Moody? Ask his former Worcestershire charges in private; the Guard is changed less often than captains were there. Mickey Arthur? He does what he's told; Graeme Smith is a strong man. Graham Ford? Reliant on Kolpaks and Kent got relegated. Gary Kirsten? He was less experienced than Flower when he took the India job. John Dyson? No coach had previously lost a match single-handedly before his recent Duckworth/Lewis blunder. Andy

Moles? Twice troubled by player power in other posts before becoming New Zealand coach. And so on.'

England were ranked sixth in the world in Test cricket when Flower took over properly. They'd dropped from fifth after the 1–0 loss in the Caribbean. It had long been the ECB's stated aim to be number one in the world. First they'd said by 2007, then by 2009. But this was the first time the England team had spoken about it as a motivational tool. Flower told them that the only way they could become number one was by becoming number five first. So that was their aim for 2009. They achieved it by beating the cold and uninterested West Indians 2–0, and not even winning the Ashes at home later that year altered that position. Fifth they remained, behind India, South Africa, Australia and Sri Lanka, as 2010 dawned.

It is interesting to look back at the team Flower and Strauss picked for their first two Tests in that first home series of 2009, against the West Indies. Flintoff was unavailable, having had knee surgery for an injury sustained playing for the Chennai Super Kings in the IPL, and having missed the final two Tests of the West Indies tour with a hip injury. That quite naturally raised the old chestnut of whether to play four or five specialist bowlers. In Barbados in the first of those two away Tests, England had played six batsmen, with Ravi Bopara scoring a century from number six. He was promptly dropped for Trinidad where England preferred two spinners.

This was now a very different West Indies side away from home. In truth they were poor. They had managed to defend their 1–0 lead at home on the flattest of pitches, but now skipper Gayle set the tone, as had New Zealand's Dan Vettori the previous year, by missing the early part of the tour while staying at the IPL.

Flintoff's injury at the IPL caused much anger. He missed the ICC World Twenty20 as well as the West Indies Tests, and critical comment was only increased when it emerged that Pietersen, who like Flintoff was given a three-week window to play in part of the IPL, had an Achilles tendon problem that had been troubling him on the tour of the West Indies, where he had been clearly ridding himself of frustrations over the Moores scenario by doing a lot of long-distance running. He would not last beyond the second Ashes Test at Lord's before undergoing surgery.

The IPL is a problem, but I do not think it is now a huge problem for English cricket. Of course, dripping opulence turns heads initially, as the Stanford fiasco amply demonstrated. And because of the IPL the finer details of central contracts became hugely complicated, and for a couple of years their signing by the England players was completed about as punctually as the arrival of a train on the British rail network. But one only has to consider the deleterious effects it had on India's Test side in 2011, in particular its meaning that India's best players do not get an off-season, to realize that England's strict command that players can only go for short periods is working. For instance, before that Test series here in 2011 Virender Sehwag played eleven IPL games with an injury that required surgery, and the delay meant he missed the first two Tests. In the third he bagged a 'king pair'. Cricket does have a natural justice system after all.

Anyway, in that first home Test in 2009 England opted for five bowlers, with both Graham Onions and Tim Bresnan making their debuts in the first Test at Lord's. I think the selection was a classic case of the captain getting the side he wanted. Strauss wanted five bowlers; Flower was keener on four. It was why later in the summer, when Flintoff was deemed unfit for the fourth Ashes Test at Headingley, England again went for five. They got hammered, and presumably Strauss told Flower, 'OK, we won't be doing that again!'

Guessing that first Test squad was mighty difficult. This was my attempt in my *Sunday Telegraph* column at the third seamer because I was convinced they would select six batsmen, with Vaughan at number three and Bopara at number six:

> So to the choice of third seamer. Inked in are the excellent James Anderson and Stuart Broad, with Graeme Swann (now thankfully minus 29 loose bodies found in his troublesome elbow) as the principal spinner. But then? Panic. Firstly the injury list is lengthy. Flintoff, naturally, heads it. Ryan Sidebottom has bowled some overs after surgery, but not in Nottinghamshire's championship side. Amjad Khan and Robbie Joseph are busying Kent's physiotherapist. Ditto Simon Jones and Kabir Ali at Worcestershire, Mark Davies at Durham and Steven Finn at Middlesex. Even good old Darren Pattinson is now crocked. Charlie Shreck too.
>
> So who? Steve Harmison, one suspects, is still fighting selectorial purdah. The burly Tim Bresnan has his advocates, as has Warwickshire's thoughtful young swing bowler Chris Woakes. Matthew Hoggard, Graham Onions and Chris Tremlett are less well promoted. Justin Langer suggests Liam Plunkett. But for me Sajid Mahmood's extra pace shades it.

I was wrong. Bresnan and Onions it was, alongside Anderson and Broad, while Bopara, fresh from his IPL stint at King's XI Punjab, was selected to bat at number three, ahead of Bell and Vaughan, who was still keen to return at that stage. Bopara duly made centuries in both Tests, making it three in succession after a hundred in Barbados that winter, as England won by ten wickets and then by an innings and 83 runs.

Bresnan was, and still is to me, a fascinating selection. I'll admit that he has shocked me. And I know of many others around the county circuit who share the same feeling. On first sighting he looked ordinary, and unfit. Time in the England set-up has certainly resolved the latter problem. As for the former, Flower never saw it that way. After those first two West Indies

Tests he asked me what I thought of Bresnan, who had done decently. 'A competent fourth seamer,' I replied. Flower was aghast. 'He's the best fourth seamer in the world, if that's the case,' he responded. You have to say that he has been proved right.

Flower did get something horribly wrong in 2009, though: his selection for the World Twenty20 opener against the Netherlands at Lord's. Collingwood was by now Twenty20 captain, having been persuaded back into the job by Flower. There really wasn't much choice. Strauss had captained the sole Twenty20 international in the Caribbean but had batted at number six, and had been omitted from the thirty-man provisional squad in April. The announcements said that Strauss had stepped down voluntarily, but Flower, already showing that sentiment would play no part in his decisions, knew that he was no Twenty20 batsman. Strauss was never going to be in that squad. So, with some gentle persuasion, Collingwood returned to a leadership role.

For the first match Adil Rashid was selected ahead of Swann. England were looking forward, experimenting even. It backfired. They lost. It was a humiliation. 'England got their just deserts on Friday night,' I screeched in my Sunday column. 'Cricket has a shark's nose for those daring to treat it with complacency, and so England were easy targets. For, make no mistake, England were complacent.'

Flower learnt an important lesson, as he admitted before the next tournament in the West Indies in 2010. 'We won't mess around with selection like we did against Holland when we didn't pick Graeme Swann,' he confessed to me in an interview. Had he been cocky? I asked. 'Yes, I suppose so,' he replied with a smile. His honesty was refreshing.

In 2009 England did actually beat Pakistan, the eventual winners, in their next match, but failed to make the semi-finals. In a worrying nod to the shambles of the 1999 World Cup there was a curtailed opening ceremony because of rain, but, in fairness, the tournament as a whole was a huge success for the ECB, and much credit for that went to tournament director Steve Elworthy, the former South Africa fast bowler who is now the ECB's director of marketing and communications.

Elworthy had also organized the inaugural tournament in his homeland in 2007, where England had performed predictably miserably. It became the tournament that awoke India, the surprise winners and previous sceptics, to the wonders of Twenty20, with Yuvraj Singh striking Broad for six sixes in an over and thoughts of an IPL first emerging. But England were hapless, with a poorly selected squad relying too heavily on Twenty20 journeymen. Flintoff, incapacitated by an ankle injury, hobbled through his overs when in reality he should not have been anywhere near a cricket field. 'Give him six months off,' advised Australia's captain Ricky Ponting.

England truly were in a muddle. Wicketkeeper Matt Prior broke a thumb while receiving throw-downs from coach Moores, and even Flower was in the wars, badly damaging an Achilles tendon while playing touch rugby before a match at Newlands in Cape Town. But most embarrassing of all, captain Collingwood had been found to have been in a lap dancing club after his team lost to Australia and back in England newly elected ECB chairman Giles Clarke had to face more questions about that than other matters in his first press conference in the role.

Disciplinary matters were still sadly affecting England's preparations when it came to the 2009 Ashes at home. On a trip to Flanders Field in Belgium Bopara forgot his passport and Flintoff missed the team bus after a late night spent drinking. Bopara can be dozy (when recalled to the Test side in 2011 he said he had invested in an iPad to help sort his life out, but then in the same sentence admitted, 'But I've forgotten to charge it up and at the moment it's lying dead in my car').

Flintoff's misdemeanour was more galling. From day one of their regime Strauss and Flower had preached the need for personal responsibility. They had gone to see a conflict-resolution specialist in London immediately after the Pietersen/Moores split, and he had suggested that the team themselves draw up a charter of values. One particular mantra that arose was that 'the team is not a lease car'. In other words it was not to be treated as if it did not matter what sort of condition it was in when you left it. And whether it was intended or not, Flintoff's behaviour went against that, suggesting the sort of cynicism towards the trip that the management had been hoping to avoid, even if this sort of trip was something new to English cricket.

The Australians had first done something similar in 2001, when Steve Waugh's squad went to Gallipoli to visit Australian war graves before the Ashes, and four years later they went to Normandy. Now this was not necessarily Flower's idea – Morris had previously talked with Moores about going to Flanders – but it was certainly something Flower embraced instantly and enthusiastically. As he said afterwards, 'This visit was part of ongoing efforts designed to broaden horizons and learn more about the role of leadership and team ethics.'

It has not always been all about cricket for Flower. I interviewed him once and asked him about the greatest influences on his cricket. He talked about the coaches Zimbabwe had had during his playing days. He especially liked the plain-speaking attitude of John Hampshire, the former Yorkshire and England player. He may have been a little old-school but Flower liked his simple fondness of the basics of the game. So too before him Barry Dudleston, the former Leicestershire and Gloucestershire batsman who, like Hampshire, became an umpire. Flower admired Dave Houghton's tactical and technical expertise, and learnt much from the Australians Carl Rackemann and Geoff Marsh. Unsurprisingly he didn't mention Don Topley, the former Essex seamer, bizarrely chosen as Zimbabwe's coach for the 1992 World Cup, where at Albury Zimbabwe famously beat England, captained by Topley's Essex captain, Graham Gooch. 'I'm going to remind you about this every day next season,' said a joyous Topley afterwards, to which Gooch gave one of the classic cricketing put-downs: 'I'm not sure I'm going to be at too many second-team games this year, Toppers!'

But Flower did reel off a list of other names from Zimbabwe cricket: John Traicos, Andy Pycroft, Kevin Arnott, Malcolm Jarvis and Andy Waller – three lawyers, a gym owner and a farmer. It was not just their cricket that impressed. It was their life balance. They managed to be professional at work and in sport, as well as find time for their families and have some fun too. It would take the farmer Waller two hours to get to practice, and another two to get home afterwards, but he was always there. Jarvis had fought in the war for independence. These were not cosseted cricketers. 'I thought the balance they found was amazing,' Flower said. 'They taught me about the disciplines you need to succeed in sport and life.'

So Flanders was the beginning of that sort of process for England's cricketers, of making them more rounded characters. Broad laid a specially made stone cricket ball at the graveside of former Kent and England left-arm spinner Colin Blythe, who died at the Battle of Passchendaele in 1917, and the players attended the daily service held at the Menin Gate where wreaths were laid by Strauss, Bopara and Alastair Cook before 'The Last Post' was played and singer Sean Ruane delivered a rendition of 'Jerusalem'.

'It brought us closer as a group. It was going to be harder for the Aussies to break us down,' said Strauss afterwards. Was it mere coincidence that in the first Ashes Test in 2009 a new spirit was instantly revealed? Probably not. The Cardiff Test, as the last pair of Anderson and Monty Panesar survived sixty-nine balls and forty minutes to salvage a draw, was the first one of three 'Great Escapes' from England in a year.

It was also the first ever Test at Cardiff. This was obviously surrounded in controversy. The decision in 2006 to award this match to Cardiff rather than Old Trafford or Durham had certainly been a shock. The ECB had introduced a new 'blind bidding' system and Glamorgan had played it cleverly to surprise their rivals, bidding some £3.2 million thanks to £1.2 million from the Welsh Assembly. Lancashire bid some £1.5 million and thought they were home and hosed. They'd been pipped on the inside.

So there was outrage when the result became known. The most withering criticism came from Hampshire chairman Rod Bransgrove, even though his county had pulled out of the bidding (they would host their first Test in 2011, against Sri Lanka). 'Quite clearly the "W" in the ECB is silent, but very powerful,' he said.

I'll admit that I did not agree with Glamorgan's pursuit of Test cricket. I was still captain of the club when it was first mooted. Part of my argument against it was that they would only get Tests against Zimbabwe and Bangladesh. I was proved wrong on that one obviously! But the other part was a worry about too many Test grounds. If every one of the eighteen counties wanted Test matches, then what?

There are now nine Test grounds – Lord's, the Oval, Trent Bridge, Headingley, Old Trafford, Edgbaston, Cardiff, Durham and Southampton – as well as Bristol, which hosts one-day internationals and T20 internationals. It is probably too many. If the blind bidding system did have an upside, apart from providing easy money for the ECB, it did give grounds like Old Trafford a jolt. That ground was in serious need of re-development, which it is now receiving. And at least the bidding system has now been revised so that counties bid for packages of matches with predetermined prices.

Cardiff was the first Test in 2009 because the England management had not wanted to play at Lord's first.

England had not beaten Australia there since 1934, after all. And that was the only occasion in the twenty-seven Tests going back to 1899. That is one woeful record.

So having just avoided defeat in Cardiff – and Collingwood's gutsy 74 was as important as Anderson and Panesar's last stand – and with that sort of history looming over them, England probably did not want any extra distractions. Enter Flintoff with a huge piece of news: he was retiring from Test cricket at the end of the summer. It had emerged that he was still struggling with his knee injury, so the remaining Tests were going to be part of some grand tour of the country, with standing ovations at every turn. Roll up, roll up everyone for the last tour of Freddie's travelling circus.

The decision did not go down well. And not just with me. I've always liked the line given by former Australia fast bowler Carl Rackemann: 'You don't make a statement to let everyone know you're debuting, so why should you have to declare your intention to finish?' Especially these days when cricketers don't really retire; they just go to the IPL, or some such other Twenty20 extravaganza in the sky.

The England management weren't happy either. Plagued by injury, Flintoff had become something of an outsider to the team, rather like Meursault in Albert Camus's *The Stranger*. His closest friends had long departed. He seemed to have little understanding of the strong team ethos being developed under Strauss and Flower. He simply did his own thing.

Above that was the worry that such a decision had a history of backfiring. Both Alec Stewart and Steve Waugh had announced well in advance that they were retiring from international cricket, and it affected them and their teams, even if, of course, they departed to fervid farewells on their home grounds.

In fairness, Flintoff immediately dispelled such concerns with a performance of rare brilliance at Lord's. On the final morning England required five Australian wickets for victory, and bowling ten unchanged overs from the Pavilion End, Flintoff took three of them to end with a five-wicket haul. It was a stunning victory, courtesy of a remarkable spell of bowling, unrelenting in its accuracy and hostility. The people's champion had delivered. Fredmania swept the country as quickly as swine flu did at the time.

How Flintoff revelled in the moment. He had become a highly commercial cricketer, always with an eye for a photo opportunity, always keen to endorse some product or other. For instance he had irked the England management earlier in the summer by turning up at Lord's for the West Indies Test wearing a hooded top bearing the name of his personal sponsor rather than that of the England team, and then sitting on the balcony one along from the England dressing room.

So now for his three wickets we had three wholly photogenic poses, culminating in the bended-knee, arms-spread-wide stance that followed the wicket of Peter Siddle – a picture that has become as famous as Flintoff's consoling of Brett Lee after the 2005 Edgbaston Test.

Unsurprisingly, Flintoff was named man of the match. 'Flintoff's match' some had already christened it by the next morning. Poppycock. Strauss should have been man of the match. The beginning of the match was much more important than the ending. Of course, it was wonderful bowling from Flintoff, but his wickets on that final morning were Brad Haddin, Nathan Hauritz and Siddle. Strauss made 161 on the first day when England desperately needed to make a strong statement after Cardiff.

For some strange reason Strauss is easily maligned and over-looked as England captain. At the end of the 2012 Pakistan series he had still won exactly half of his forty-two Tests. Only Michael Vaughan has won more Tests as captain (twenty-six in fifty-one Tests), and only Vaughan (50.98), Percy Chapman (nine from 17 Tests at a winning percentage of 52.94), Mike

Brearley (eighteen from thirty-one at 58.06), W.G. Grace (eight from thirteen at 61.53) and Douglas Jardine (nine from fifteen at 60.00) of those to have captained ten Tests have a higher winning percentage.

In the West Indies it had been declarations for which he was chastised. Here it was for not enforcing the follow-on. Brearley called it 'pusillanimous'. Attitudes have altered markedly on this over the years. My instinct was always to enforce it. But maybe that was because we never had that many opportunities to do so at Glamorgan. Or maybe it was because my often overriding fear of failure preferred to postpone the moment of judgement (in other words batting) and this was always a good opportunity to do so.

Then there was, of course, the famous Test in Kolkata in 2001 when India, following on 274 behind, sensationally beat Australia by 171 runs thanks to V. V. S. Laxman's 281 and 180 from Rahul Dravid. That deterred a few from doing that again, especially after it seemed that Australia had determined never to enforce again after Mark Taylor had done so against Pakistan in Rawalpindi in 1994 and suffered as Salim Malik made 237.

Sometimes, because of time lost, you have little choice, like at the Oval in 2011 against India, which worked out fine as England won. But generally the welfare of your bowlers must be of primary concern. When Vaughan asked Australia to follow on at Trent Bridge in 2005 Simon Jones had broken down instantly. When Vaughan did the same to South Africa at Lord's in 2008, and the visitors ended up batting for three successive days, Ryan Sidebottom had got injured. When Flintoff was skipper against Sri Lanka at the same venue in 2006, he too had asked his opponents to follow on and had bowled himself into the ground (fifty-one overs in the second innings).

So you could understand Strauss's reluctance here, what with Flintoff's knee and with Anderson suffering an ankle problem. When Australia resumed on the third morning on 156-8, Strauss was of a mind to enforce the follow-on. But the weather was bright and the pitch suddenly looked very flat, as Australia added fifty-nine runs in fourteen overs for those last two wickets. Strauss nipped off the field for an over to speak to Flower, and they agreed to bat. England won the Test. No more needs to be said.

Strauss has grown into an astonishingly good leader. There was a time when he was younger that he was rather too dopey. Among his nicknames were 'Mareman' and 'Muppet'. His occasional absent-mindedness concerned Fletcher a little, I know. But not his batting. Fletcher was waiting around for an ECB meeting one day at Lord's in 2003 when he spotted Strauss batting in the middle. He recognized a Test batsman immediately, with his back-foot technique revealing strong pull and cut shots.

It was something Ed Smith, a schoolboy adversary when Strauss was at Radley and Smith at Tonbridge, had noticed years before and articulated so well in *The Times* after the Ashes triumph of 2010/11. 'When I first met him, at an England Schools trial,' wrote Smith of Strauss, 'he was not the kid in the county tracksuit earmarked for professional greatness. He just clipped the ball deftly off the back foot, a rare skill for a schoolboy, and let others big-note about county contracts and bat deals. But when we played against each other at school, I was clear about one thing: he batted better against better bowlers. My school team-mates even mocked me for suggesting that he was the best player we played against. In time, he left the flat-track bullies behind.'

So Strauss has gradually left his captaincy critics behind. He just keeps making good decisions. Some view many of them as conservative, but he is not showy as a person, cricketer or captain (giving Swann the new ball in grey, swinging conditions at Lord's against the West Indies in 2009 is the only example I can recall of him trying to be a little too clever).

'The thing about Strauss is that he is so calm and always says the right thing,' said Swann of his captain after the 2011 India Test series. And he is so right. Strauss is a highly impressive statesman, as well as the England cricket captain. He showed it so obviously during the difficult summer of 2010 when the allegations of corruption among the Pakistan team emerged, most especially when the Pakistan Cricket Board chairman Ijaz Butt then claimed in a ridiculous act of retaliation that England had deliberately lost the third one-day international at the Oval.

England very nearly did not play the fourth ODI in protest. The night before the match they were locked in talks until the early hours at London's Landmark Hotel. Strauss, quite rightly, was extremely angry. Initially, like most of his team, he did not want to play the next day. But eventually he realized that the show simply had to go on. Rather than speak to the media – there was no time really – he insisted on a carefully worded statement. It was classic Strauss:

> We would like to express our surprise, dismay and outrage at the comments made by Mr Butt yesterday. We are deeply concerned and disappointed that our integrity as cricketers has been brought into question. We refute these allegations completely and will be working closely with the ECB to explore all legal options open to us. Under the circumstances, we have strong misgivings about continuing to play the last two games of the current series and urge the Pakistani team and management to distance themselves from Mr Butt's allegations. We do, however, recognize our responsibilities to the game of cricket – and in particular to the cricket-loving public in this country – and will therefore endeavour to fulfil these fixtures to the best of our ability.

Strauss was no less impressive on the eve of the third Test against India in 2011 when riots were sweeping the land. 'I think this is an opportunity for cricket to put a feel-good factor into the newspapers and show that not everything's bad at the moment,' he said. 'Clearly it's not our proudest moment as a country. When you watch those things on the TV it's horrific. All of us agree on that and it's very disappointing to see these things happen. But they haven't affected our preparations for this Test match.'

Strauss can be flustered, though. He does not enjoy being rushed. The fourth Test at Headingley in 2009 was an example of that. The third Test at Edgbaston had been ruined by rain, and was only notable for the absence of Pietersen, whose troublesome Achilles tendon required an operation after Lord's. In the early hours of the first morning of the next Test at Headingley – at 4.45 a.m. to be precise – a fire alarm had gone off at the England team hotel, the Radisson. Then during warm-ups Prior had suffered a back spasm, and it was uncertain whether he would play. Collingwood was suddenly busily brushing up on his wicketkeeping skills when team masseur Mark Saxby was hit flush on the forehead by a stray cricket ball and carried off. It was chaos.

Australia graciously agreed that the toss be put back by ten minutes, by which time England had decided to take a gamble on Prior. It was a toss Strauss did not really want to win. It was drizzling when the players had had their early morning call, but the pitch was dry with the sun beginning to show its head. But, as happens on such occasions, he did win it. He decided to bat, and then had to conduct the various media interviews (too many in my opinion) before going off to strap on his pads.

He should have been out first ball, lbw to Ben Hilfenhaus, but was reprieved. Clearly his mental state was scrambled, and he survived only sixteen further balls before edging Siddle to slip. His team were soon all out for 102 as the ball darted around, and defeat (eventually by an innings and 80 runs) was inevitable once that had happened. It was Strauss's worst morning as England captain.

The repercussions were not as calamitous, but Strauss was similarly distracted on the opening morning of the 2010/11 Ashes Down Under. There he had won the toss and elected to bat, but had been thrown by the national anthems taking place between that and the start of play. That had happened at Cardiff in 2009 (with the Welsh national anthem played as well as 'God Save the Queen' and 'Advance Australia Fair', as well as both teams being presented to Rhodri Morgan, the first minister of Wales), and England had not batted too well. But in Brisbane it had a greater effect. Strauss admitted to being too emotional, and was out third ball.

It is easy to overlook the difficulties faced by the skipper in such circumstances. The toss usually takes place half an hour before the start of play. Captains who open the batting have to be able to compartmentalize swiftly and easily. Often as a county captain, say, you have to tell a player that he has been omitted from the final eleven. He can, of course, be disgruntled. He may even want to argue with you over it. I remember on a couple of occasions as Glamorgan skipper telling the coach, John Derrick, 'John, please go and tell so-and-so he's not playing. He's going to be mightily pissed off, but just tell him that I'll speak to him later.' But still out of the corner of my eye I'd be spying on that conversation and watching for the reaction. And then I'd try to think about batting. Not easy.

Strauss had his own selection problems at Headingley even before Prior's late injury scare. The day before, he and Flower had decided to omit Flintoff on fitness grounds. He was clearly struggling at nets the day before the game. It was decided to rest him and try to get him fit for the final Test at the Oval. Flintoff did not argue.

But then Andrew 'Chubby' Chandler, his agent, caused a fuss in an interview with *The Times*' Atherton. 'I've seen a few disappointed sportsmen over the last couple of months,' said Chandler, a former European Tour golfer, who set up International Sports Management Limited in 1989 to look after golfers mainly, 'but I've never seen anybody as low as Flintoff on Thursday night [the night before the Test] when he was told he would not be selected. He told them he was fit enough to get through, that he felt no different to how he felt at Edgbaston [where the previous Test was played] and that he could get through and do his bit. They didn't want him. He was prepared to do whatever it takes, was prepared to put whatever needed to be put into his knee. What they didn't take into account during Thursday's practice was that there was no adrenalin. That was why he looked as though he was struggling so much. His presence would certainly have lifted the crowd and the team, because without him they don't have much inspiration.'

Agents, eh? Even Flintoff admitted later, 'The article didn't do me any favours.' Too right it didn't. Flower was very quickly on the phone to Flintoff, demanding to know what on earth was going on. Likewise Strauss phoned Chandler. The England captain felt that quite a lot of Chandler's comments were inaccurate. 'We had more important things to worry about, but I felt it was important I said something to him rather than just let it lie,' said Strauss.

It is true that Chandler and his employee, the former Lancashire and England batsman Neil Fairbrother, did help Flintoff in his early years by sitting him down and spelling out some home truths about the sacrifices required to become and remain an international cricketer. And in general agents have helped international cricketers earn the sort of money they deserve (I'm not sure that is the case in county cricket, where, in my opinion, wages have spiralled out of line with what a domestic cricketer actually merits, but that is another matter). But it should also be remembered that Chandler is from a golfing background. Golf is an individual sport. Cricket is an individual sport played in a team environment. They are two very different things.

Later in 2009 the announcement came on Flintoff's own website that he had turned down the ECB's offer of an incremental central contract so that he could supposedly travel the world playing in Twenty20 tournaments, and, if he felt like it, play for England in one-day internationals and T20s some-times. He was going 'freelance', so it was said. Much was made of it, but in truth it was a non-story given unnecessary legs by what I called his 'concomitant cacophony'. Not least because Flintoff's knee never allowed him to play again after the final Test at the Oval that summer.

There is always sadness when a player's career is cut short like that, and Flintoff's case should be no different. He was an outstanding cricketer who provided some great moments and put in some great performances. He was also at times a great bloke, but celebrity changed him, as it might many of us. The England team that was to become number one in the world in 2011 was not sad to see him go. It made their absolute insistence on the team ethic so much easier. It made their insistence on supreme levels of fitness easier. With Flintoff still there, I doubt they would have been able to ignore Samit Patel purely on the grounds of sloth.

No one is irreplaceable. But it might have seemed so when England were being thrashed at Headingley without Flintoff. The lesson learnt, however, apart from ensuring Strauss is not rushed before batting, was that six batsmen must always play, despite the continuing claims of some of the game's romantics. England, with Broad at number seven, were exposed. And Flower and Strauss were spooked by the experience. Flintoff played at the Oval but thereafter until they became the world's number one team they played six specialist batsmen, a wicket-keeper and four bowlers in all of their twenty-four Tests bar one, the second Test against Bangladesh in Dhaka in March 2010, where they played two spinners. And Strauss was not actually captain then: Cook was deputizing while Strauss rested. That is a different matter anyway, having to fit in two spinners on turning pitches.

The Sunday of that Headingley Test was the last day, as England were hammered after some frolicsome, if vain, batting from Swann and Broad. It was also an interesting day in my journalistic career. 'Leaked dossier shows what the Australian team really think of England team' screamed the headline in the *Sunday Telegraph*. I suppose it could be said I had a 'scoop', even if it didn't feel like it. Indeed when I first saw the dossier that had been handed to me, I didn't think much of it. 'I'm not sure there's much in there,' I told Peter Mitchell, my sports editor. I was being very naive. In general I'd like to think I have a decent nose (yes, a big nose even) for a news story, certainly more so than some of my cricketer-turned-journalist colleagues, who often consider it stooping a little too low to become involved in such matters. But what I was forgetting here was the thrill for members of the public of being on the inside, however fleetingly; of suddenly being privy to thoughts and observations that are usually out of their reach. Every fan craves to be inside the dressing room.

I'll admit that when I first received a phone call about the dossier (that's what it was called by me and my paper, but in truth it was little more than some random thoughts) written by Justin Langer, then still at Somerset and now Australia's batting coach, I wrestled hard with my conscience. Yes, journalism is regarded as a low art, and in the wake of the phone hacking scandals its reputation has only fallen further, but it is not all about exposure. Most of us have a barrelful of stories we would never dream of publishing. Sources and contacts need to be kept, as well as protected.

I'd interviewed Langer down at Taunton earlier in the season.

He'd been engaging and interesting. But, after Mitchell had come back to me in a state of great excitement upon seeing the evidence, it seemed too good an opportunity to miss. After all, how the Australians had rejoiced and mocked when England's bowling plans had been leaked in Melbourne during the 2006/07 series.

What the hell . . .

Langer had emailed his thoughts to Australia coach Tim Nielsen, and Nielsen had printed the following off and given a copy to every member of his squad before the first Test in Cardiff. This was reproduced in full in the *Sunday Telegraph*:

Boys

Here a few thoughts from Justin Langer who captains Somerset and I have been in contact with in regard to the English squad and conditions. Have a read and use as you will

- the dukes ball usually takes a few overs to swing so don't get impatient with it. Sometimes you have to wait until the lacquer wears off before it starts to swing. England players work very hard on shining the ball after the lacquer is gone. They use Murray mints religiously to get it to shine up. Be aware of this from an opposition point of view but also from your point know the ball will shine up nicely if you work hard on it.

- English cricketers are great front runners. Because of the way they are programmed they will be up when things are going well but they will taper off very quickly if you wear them down in all apartments. Because they play so much cricket, as soon as it gets a bit hard you just have to watch their body language and see how flat and lazy they get. You can show this up by running hard between the wickets and pressurizing them in the field. They are the best in world of tapering off very quickly when things go a bit flat for them. This is also a time when most of them make all sorts of excuses and start looking around to point the finger at everyone else – it is a classic English trait from my experience.

- English players rarely believe in themselves. Many of them will stare a lot and chat a lot but this is very shallow and again will last as long as the pressure is back on them. They will retreat very quickly. Aggressive batting, running and body language will soon have them staring at their bootlaces rather in the eyes of their opponent – it is just how they are built. They like being friendly and 'matey' because it makes them feel comfortable. In essence this is maybe the key to the whole English psyche – they love being comfortable. Take them out of their comfort zone and they don't like it for a second. This can be done by aggressive bowling, confident body language and putting them back under the pump but not being too friendly with them – a good lesson learned from 2005 to 2007 series.

- Andrew Strauss is a very solid character and excellent bloke. His weakness is possibly his conservative approach. He will tend to take the safer options in most cases. He is batting well. He has played quite aggressively recently but can be cramped up just outside the off stump. He plays well through the offside, particularly off the back foot.

- Alistair Cook doesn't move his right leg towards the ball. Get him cover driving and he won't score and will also look vulnerable in the slips and gully position. He has a good all round game and very good temperament but good patient bowling full outside the off stump should bring him unstuck.

- Ravi Bopara is a good player. I have seen him caught at third man a couple of times. This might be tough at Cardiff but third man and high bouncers could be an attacking position. He will have a go at the cut and pull shots so third man and two men back behind square leg could bring him undone. He is a bit of a street fighter who is sure to wind the boys up by his strutting around but he is a respectful young guy who thrives on the chat and talk. I would leave him alone and just bowl at him rather than letting our egos take away our focus. I think you know what I mean here.

- Anderson is hugely improved and has gained a yard and is bowling well. He is swing the ball well but again can be a bit of a pussy if he is worn down. He is a classic as in my second point. Things have been going well for him so he is happy and confident but I am convinced he can be worn down and his body language could be detrimental to them if we get on top of him early.

- Swann is another one who is sure to wind us up with his ego and body language. I am not sure he likes short pitched bowling. He goes hard with the bat but will give lots of chances as he hits the ball in the air a lot. His bowling is on a par with N. Hauritz and he takes a lot of his wickets with the balls that don't spin much especially to the left handers coming back in and getting bowled or lbws

- Another point to be aware of especially for the younger guys is that the Cardiff crowd is feral and they will be brutal on you guys. They are very aggressive and it is something the boys should be aware of before the event. Awareness is the key. But they are a tough crowd. Also it might be worth the batsmen getting a good feel for the place leading up to the game because the changing rooms are a long way from the ground so it feels like you are miles away from the action. A small consideration but I know you will have plenty of time to adapt to this.

- Matt Prior – We played him a few weeks ago and I would definitely bowl wide to him. He loves to score and will go hard. A deeper point can be a catching position as can two deeper gully position. He scores a lot of runs to thirds man. He gets very very low in his stance. The key is he wants to score runs quickly and look good. He can be dangerous because he is a talented stroke player. Stop him scoring boundaries, even employing a point or deep cover boundary fielder, like Michael Vaughan did so well against us in 2005, and he will definitely give you plenty of chances. I would chip away at him about his wicket keeping and the pressure he is under to perform with the gloves on. I am not sure he actually likes keeping that much and from all accounts he has a massive ego so I would be reminding him about how his keeping could see him out of the team. I would definitely work his ego.

- Flintoff – for the batsmen who haven't faced him it takes time to get used to his pace and bounce. He has to be worn down and as we both know is the key to their attack with James Anderson.

I've not seen or spoken to Langer since. He was 'shattered' apparently. In his BBC online column he wrote this:

Having spoken to Tim on Sunday night, he was upset and sadly apologetic that our written conversation had been exposed. Because of this, I am naturally disappointed that some of my personal and private thoughts to a close friend of mine in Tim Nielsen have reached the public domain. He had copied my thoughts down and given them out to a few of the less experienced members of the team before the Cardiff Test. Obviously one of the team left these lying around and, as they say, the rest is history. What interests me is why it has taken so long for them to come out? Sure there is journalistic liberty, but if my private opinion was so relevant, why wait until England had lost a Test match? Maybe that says something about the ruthless nature of the press in this country.

From Taunton,

JL

Well, the truth, JL, is that I did not receive the 'dossier' until the Wednesday before the Headingley Test. It was published at the first available opportunity in the *Sunday Telegraph*. That it came out on the morning when England were facing a heavy defeat was a complete coincidence.

For England it must have seemed like a kick to a beaten body, although Flower never complained to me about it. He just did what he does so well: he planned how to get England out of the hole into which they'd fallen. The series stood at 1–1 with just the Oval Test to come. He did not want the players to dwell too much on their defeat, so instead of allowing them to go home immediately he called a team meeting at the hotel that evening. As ever it was frank. It was pretty obvious what had happened, aside from selection and the chaos before the toss: the players had got ahead of themselves. They had been thinking about winning the Ashes rather than how they might go about winning the Ashes. It was the classic cliché beloved of the sports psychologist: they had been focusing on the outcome, not the process. Truths were told, and they moved on to the Oval.

Flintoff duly returned to the side, but Bopara was dropped. He had endured a difficult summer at number three. As well as those three consecutive centuries, he'd also scored three ducks in succession earlier in his career. The management considered him 'mentally shot', and, after a lengthy selection meeting at Trent Bridge where Warwickshire were playing Nottinghamshire in a county championship match (with the visitors' director of cricket and England selector Ashley Giles therefore in situ) on the Friday before the Test, selected Jonathan Trott instead.

These days there is usually more secrecy surrounding England selection than an SAS mission, but this was an exception. The following morning most of the newspapers confidently named the squad ahead of Sunday's announcement. There had been a leak. Or rather someone's bins had been rummaged. At Trent Bridge a small group of journalists had decided to visit the room used for selection long after the selectors had gone. What did they find in the waste paper bin? The squad on a piece of scrunched-up paper! It was careless.

With Trott's promotion, another South African was in the England cricket team. It naturally caused considerable comment, even if Trott had already played (in Twenty20s) in 2007. It prompted that superb writer Peter Roebuck, the former Somerset captain who had become very much an Australian before tragically taking his own life in South Africa in November 2011, to dub the England side 'Durham and the Dominions'. Yes, appearing from Durham in this series were Collingwood, Onions and Harmison.

But the South African point can be stretched. Strauss

was born there, but left at the age of six, spending eighteen months in Melbourne before settling in England. He went to Caldicott Preparatory School, Radley College and Durham University. That is a very English upbringing. Little wonder that another of his nicknames to add to those I mentioned earlier is 'Lord Brocket' (after the accent of the cocky aristo-crat who came into the public consciousness around 2004 in the TV programme *I'm a Celebrity . . . Get Me Out of Here!* rather than his personality). Prior's family came from Johannesburg to England when he was eleven. He went to Brighton College.

Trott and Pietersen spent a good deal of time in county cricket before appearing for England. Trott had played for Warwickshire's seconds as long before as 2002, making 245 against Somerset on debut, as it happened. Pietersen too had played one match for Warwickshire's seconds in 2000 (scoring 92), while he was playing that season for Cannock in the Birmingham League, but Warwickshire were primarily after an off-spinner to replace Neil Smith, and so did not sign him. Mistake! Nottinghamshire instead signed him and he played four seasons for them before moving to Hampshire in the winter of 2004/05 (although he was going to join Somerset and indeed drove around for some of that winter in one of their sponsored cars). Controversy stalked his every move, mind. At the end of the 2003 season Notts' captain Jason Gallian had thrown Pietersen's kit off the Trent Bridge balcony after it became apparent Pietersen wanted to leave. And in 2010 Pietersen left Hampshire, and struggled to find a county before Surrey took him, initially on loan before eventually signing him permanently.

The Australians were still at it in 2011 when they commissioned a report, based squarely on the Schofield Report of four years earlier, into the failures of their team. When making public its recommendations, Don Argus, like Schofield a non-cricketing man placed in charge of it, joked, 'I was thinking of putting in a recommendation that we put in a Zimbabwean coach and get four South Africans into the side.' He actually forgot that England had an Irishman, Eoin Morgan, too – he might have been able to make an even better rib-tickler.

One's place of birth can, of course, be misleading. If a man is born in a stable it doesn't make him a horse, and all that. Just look at some of these England captains and their birthplaces: Gubby Allen (Australia), Freddie Brown (Peru), Donald Carr (Germany), Colin Cowdrey (India), Ted Dexter (Italy), Tony Greig and Allan Lamb (South Africa), Nasser Hussain (India). Or how about the England side that played in New Zealand in 1992 containing seven players born outside the United Kingdom: Graeme Hick (Rhodesia), Robin Smith and Lamb (both South Africa), Derek Pringle (Kenya), Chris Lewis (Guyana), Dermot Reeve (Hong Kong) and Phil DeFreitas (Dominica)?

When selected Trott was, just like Pietersen, not a popular figure on the county circuit. He was perceived to be stroppy and selfish. And, of course, South African. Very much South African according to Michael Vaughan, who wrote in his auto-biography, 'It was a sad day for English cricket when on my last day against South Africa [at Edgbaston in 2008] I saw Jonathan Trott celebrating with South Africa, when the week before he had been our 12th man at Headingley. I was going into the press conference and I saw him patting them on the back. It hit home what English cricket has become like.'

It was all a misunderstanding, though, according to Trott. 'We were standing between the changing rooms when both teams were on the field at the end,' he said. 'I've known Paul Harris [South Africa's spinner in that game] since I was sixteen and we played together at Warwickshire. I just said something like "Cheers, well done on your victory".'

I can believe it was a misunderstanding. Trott is easily

misunderstood, both as a person and as a cricketer. At the beginning of his international career I fired some arrows in his direction, just as I had with Pietersen. But Trott won me over too. It seemed at first that his whole mien was based around irritation, from his time-consuming and obsessive pre-delivery rituals to his one-paced one-day batting. But the truth is much simpler. Yes, through marriage (to Abi, Warwickshire's press officer and the granddaughter of Tom Dollery, the county's first professional captain) and fatherhood he has mellowed as a character, and therefore improved as a cricketer.

Essentially, though, Trott just loves batting. And he bats extraordinarily well. He is easily maligned because he is old-fashioned, even down to his boots and his pads. As I once wrote, 'The former look heavy and outdated, the latter rather wide and as if they should be fastened by buckles rather than Velcro.' In an age fixated with Twenty20's pyrotechnics, he is a blocker. He still plays one-day innings that divide opinion sharply. Indeed in February 2010 he played a Twenty20 innings (39 from fifty-one balls) against Pakistan in Dubai that cost him his place in that format of the game, receiving a flea in the ear from Flower for his sins. But he scores runs. He keeps scoring runs.

The fuss over Pietersen and Trott was only exacerbated early in 2011 when Craig Kieswetter, who like Trott had played for South Africa Under 19s, was selected for England's shorter-form squads almost as soon as he had finished the requisite qualification period. Even National Selector Geoff Miller was moved to say on the issue of too many South Africans, 'Yes, we have to be careful.' Others, like Jade Dernbach and Stuart Meaker, have followed.

But it is no new issue. In any sport. In 1936, for instance, Great Britain won ice hockey gold in the Winter Olympics in Germany; of their squad of thirteen, nine had grown up in

Canada. Only one was born in Canada, but eleven had previously played there. Imagine that happening now.

In cricket the South African influence began as a very different issue with the late Basil D'Oliveira, who was considered a 'coloured' under the apartheid regime and therefore barred from first-class cricket, making his England debut in 1966. He was followed by Tony Greig (and it is easily forgotten that his brother Ian, also born in Queenstown in Cape Province, played two Tests for England), the Smith brothers Robin and Chris, and Allan Lamb, all of whom made their official Test debuts for England while South Africa was excluded from international cricket.

Now, with that argument redundant since South Africa's readmission to international cricket in 1991, the reasons for moving are very different. Pietersen made it very clear that he came to England because of the quotas imposed upon provincial cricket. Trott just felt he might not make it in South Africa. Indeed when he made his debut, South Africa coach Mickey Arthur made it very clear that he would not make South Africa's team, but did voice some frustration at Trott's defection, conceding he might be 'there or there-abouts' in national selection. Arthur was rather more interested in Kieswetter, phoning the Somerset wicket-keeper during the Champions League in India in 2009. As Kieswetter once told me, 'He [Arthur] wanted to know what my plans were. He said he could get me into one of the franchise teams, as they were looking at a replacement for [Mark] Boucher. I just told him I wanted to play for England. I didn't want to be rude. I just had to say no thank you.'

Kieswetter has a Scottish mother and a British passport. His family used to visit the United Kingdom for a couple of months each year. After passing his 'matric' at the Diocesan College (Bishops), Cape Town, Kieswetter decided he wanted to come to England. He spent a term and a half at Millfield

School, trialling at Kent before Somerset signed him. In 2011 I asked him about his 'Englishness' (it should have been 'Scottishness' really). 'For five years I've answered those questions and I think there comes a time when I'd rather people write about my cricket,' he retorted sharply. He had a point.

Do we, in these days of globalization, mass immigration and widespread multiculturalism, get a little too vexed about this matter? Consider the comments of John Woodcock, the cricket correspondent of *The Times* from 1954 to 1988, on Tony Greig: 'What has to be remembered is that Greig is English not by birth or upbringing, but only adoption, which is not the same as being English through and through.' And Vaughan, later in his autobiography, discussing Trott's century at the Oval, wrote, 'I suppose you could wish he was a bit more English.'

For the associated problems you need look no further than the example of when England wanted a team song in 2005. One of the management asked a friend to come up with some lyrics reflecting what it meant to play for England. This is what he initially provided:

> Our Army's been assembled,
> From Durham down to Kent.
> A joining of all counties,
> To Lord's we have been sent.
> To play for these three Lions,
> The rose on our shoulder too,
> To play for the glory
> Of the mighty 'Navy Blue'.
>
> No matter where we travel,
> From London round to Perth,
> We take great pride in playing

For the country of our birth.
Our aim is for her triumph,
To glorify her name,
To show all those who face us
That cricket's England's game!

Somewhat hastily the first half of the second verse had to be changed to:

With the Union Jack before us,
Around the world we roam,
Taking pride in playing
For the country we call home.

I think the song was changed a bit more too, and there is now a very different song whose identity is closely guarded by the current squad. But this does rather stress the modern-day difficulties of nationality.

It is a complicated business, as I know myself, having once seriously considered playing for Zimbabwe. And I might have played all my years of professional cricket in Wales for Glamorgan, and indeed still live there, but I am fiercely proud of being English. So when I was asked to captain Wales against England in 2002 (a match we won by eight wickets, as it happened) I only did so when it was confirmed that it was an unofficial fixture. The presence of Jacques Kallis in the Wales side (he had played for Glamorgan in 1999) did rather give that game away, mind.

I also remember being a little bemused in 1997 when I went on an England training camp to Lanzarote and the one-day skipper at the time, Adam Hollioake, could not join us immediately because of visa problems concerning his Australian passport. I've recorded my thoughts already on Kolpaks, but, as I said then, rules are rules regarding international eligibility.

Cricket's are among the tightest. For instance the residency qualification to play cricket for England is four consecutive years, with at least 210 consecutive days in each of those years. By contrast for the England rugby union team it is just thirty-six consecutive months, and if you've got an England-born grandparent, you're straight in, which doesn't apply in cricket, even if a parent is England-born – presumably a reason why, when team manager Martin Johnson named his forty-five-man pre-World Cup squad in 2011, there were thirteen players born overseas in it.

As I write, the frenzy surrounding London 2012 is building. So too is the subject of what the *Daily Mail* has termed the 'Plastic Brits', athletes conveniently announcing themselves as 'British' just in time for the Olympics. Like Shana Cox, a 400m runner born and raised in the United States; or Shara Proctor, a long jumper from Anguilla; or the sprinter Tiffany Ofili-Porter, born and raised in the US to a British mother and Nigerian father. 'I've always felt I was British, American and Nigerian,' she said. 'I'm all three.'

Now that I do disagree with strongly. It is why it is good that rugby union, since the infamous 'Grannygate' scandal involving the Kiwis Shane Howarth and Brett Sinkinson, who played for Wales having falsely claimed they had Welsh grandparents, tightened its rules and deemed that you cannot play for two countries.

Technically you can still do that in cricket, but only fourteen players have ever done it in Test cricket, the first of them being Billy Midwinter, who appeared for both Australia and England, and with whom, by coincidence, I share the distinction of being the only international cricketers born in the Forest of Dean (Midwinter was born in St Briavels). Kepler Wessels was the last of those fourteen, playing for Australia and his homeland of South Africa once they were readmitted. Before him John Traicos (born in Egypt) had played for South Africa in 1970 and then Zimbabwe when they were admitted to Test cricket in 1992. In one-day internationals six players have represented two countries: Wessels, Clayton Lambert (West Indies and USA), Anderson Cummins (West Indies and Canada), Dougie Brown (England and Scotland), Ed Joyce (England and Ireland) and Eoin Morgan (Ireland and England). And in T20 internationals Dirk Nannes stands alone in this two-country representation, having represented the Netherlands and Australia.

I'll be surprised if we see another cricketer play for two countries in Tests. And I'll be even more surprised if this issue ever ceases. What fascinates me is where these players go once their playing days are finished. Lamb stayed in England, Robin Smith is now in Australia, and in 2011 Graeme Hick was planning to emigrate to Australia.

Wherever Trott goes, he will recall his debut fondly. It was a stunning entrance to Test cricket, in trying circumstances too: England's biggest Test match since four years previously when they'd reached the Oval 2–1 up with the Australians requiring a win to draw the series and retain the urn they'd had (metaphorically anyway) since 1989.

When the Australian observers weren't concerned about nationality, they were complaining about the Oval pitch. England had 'cooked the books', according to Roebuck. In other words they'd prepared a pitch to suit them. And so what? There is nothing wrong with home sides preparing pitches to suit. It was exactly what England did against India in 2011, and good on them. For too long England had been far too accommodating to its cricketing visitors. It used to irk Fletcher no end.

A draw was of no use to England. They had to win. So they requested a pitch resembling on day one the sort of wear associated with day three. They got what they wanted, with groundsman Bill Gordon receiving a standing ovation at the end-of-season dinner of the Cricket Writers' Club. It certainly began dry and spun like a top, so much so that England must have considered including a second spinner, Panesar, who was in their squad.

England were, though, grateful that they won the toss, and even more so that Australia made the unfathomable decision to omit their spinner Nathan Hauritz. Admittedly, Hauritz had not played in the victory at Headingley, but that was understandable. This was not. Swann took eight wickets in the match, including the final one of Mike Hussey, caught at short leg by Cook, on the fourth afternoon for England to win by 197 runs. For a long time afterwards the Australians were muttering darkly about what they called 'Spingate', and about the real reasons why Hauritz did not feature. It was even suggested that Hauritz, with his reticent body language, did not fancy playing.

One man who did fancy it was Stuart Broad. On the second afternoon he bowled the spell that turned the game on its head, announcing the arrival of a champion cricketer. It was supposed to be Flintoff's match, his fond farewell, but, in the general manner of these things, his was a muted exit, save for running out Ponting with a direct hit on the last day. Instead Broad took 5-37 in twelve overs of snorting hostility, combining swing and seam with a wonderfully naked spirit. It was an uplifting passage of play, forever etched into Ashes folklore. Once Australia were dismissed for just 160, and England held a first-innings lead of 172, there was no way back for the visitors. England had regained the Ashes.

It had been a curious series, though. Australia's batsmen scored eight centuries to England's two, and three Australians, Hilfenhaus, Siddle and Mitchell Johnson, stood at the top of the leading wicket-takers in the series. But England had won more of the big moments, as epitomized by Broad's spell at the Oval. You don't win the Ashes by luck. Five Tests is too many for a fluke.

But there was no open-top bus parade. And so there shouldn't have been. Strauss had been correct in saying earlier in the series that Australia had lost their 'aura'. They had. They might have begun the series ranked number one, but by the end they had slipped to number four. England began at number five, and finished there.

There was still work to be done.

11

Petals and the Weed

I should really have been thinking of the threat of spin in Asia, but instead the main question in my mind when England became the world's number one team in 2011: how would they fare against South Africa? Especially away from home if such a series had been scheduled. They'd been there in the winter of 2009/10 and drawn 1–1, with two more 'Great Escapes' beginning with 'C', at Centurion and Cape Town, to add to Cardiff in the 2009 Ashes.

At the time, though, this was actually an achievement. South Africa were number one at the start of the tour. Andrew Strauss reckoned the result to be every bit as impressive as the Ashes victory that preceded it.

Not that it showed so immediately in the grand plan. The plan to reach number one, that is. Before the tour at a meeting at Loughborough Nathan 'Numbers' Leamon, the team analyst, had gone through in great detail what was required to reach that summit. It must have been quite daunting for many of the players, not least because of the potential arduousness of Leamon's route.

As Andy Flower said at the time, 'One of the ECB's stated goals is for us to become number one and I wanted to get some idea of the task. So I asked our stats people to work out what it would take for us to get there. It was an interesting answer. Even if we win every single Test match over the next eighteen months we might still not be number one – and that's not just winning every series but every match. But I don't find that dispiriting in the least. We start by closing the gap on number four – that's our first task. We have huge scope to improve but we'd better remember exactly where we are – and that's number five in the world Test ratings. And the gap between us and number four [Australia] is huge. We're eleven points behind them.'

They were still eleven points behind Australia by the end of the series, but Australia had by then moved up to third and Sri Lanka in fourth were only seven points ahead of England. So some progress had been made.

But the ICC's rankings system is, by necessity, rather complicated. As we saw at the beginning of this book, it was once left to *Wisden* to rank the Test-playing countries, as initiated by then editor Matthew Engel in 1997. As he explained upon its introduction, 'The Wisden Championship has the advantages of simplicity, practicality – and a working model. The proposal is that each country should agree to play the other eight in at least one Test – home and away – every four years, the existing cycle for the traditional confrontations such as England v Australia. A handful of extra Tests would be needed on top of current schedules. Each series of whatever length – counting a one-off game as a series – would be worth the same: two points for winning the series, one for drawing and none for losing. The competition would be continuous, like the world ranking systems in golf and tennis, but every time a series was contested it would replace the corresponding one in the table.'

It was all admirable stuff, but it eventually encountered difficulties. In early 2003 South Africa went top of the rankings after beating Pakistan in a home series. But to everyone in world cricket it was clear that Australia were the best team by a distance, having beaten South Africa both home and away in their most recent encounters. The problem was that South Africa had played, and obviously beaten, Bangladesh and Zimbabwe in recent times, but Australia hadn't.

Change was required. So the ICC decided to adopt a system created by David Kendix, an English actuary, scorer and cricket statistician. It is a model based on the concept of a batting average, using results over the previous three or four years, with more relevance given to more recent results, but just as importantly it awards points on the strength of the opposition.

Even now it has its critics. I was one when I studied how India had reached number one status before being toppled by England in 2011. They had done most of their winning at home. And this was before England went top without winning in Asia. I contacted Kendix, and in fairness, his emailed response made sense:

There is no obvious reward that should be attached to an away win; some teams have broadly similar records home and away, others are starkly different. Also the contrast between home and away varies by fixture, so SL v India and NZ v Eng may have much less of a home advantage than say SL v Eng and NZ v India.

I don't see any problem in a team being Number 1 without beating anyone of note away from home. Being Number 1 means having a better recent record than everyone else. It doesn't necessarily mean having shown dominance in all conditions against all opponents. It just happens that during the prolonged periods of West Indian and then Australian leadership, they did indeed demonstrate that dominance, which is why they tended to lead the ratings by such large margins. Indeed, almost by definition, when the battle for Number 1 is interesting, with two or three teams closely bunched, you will not have one side who has shown a clear supremacy over the others. In a closely fought football league season, you may well have the champions who lost their away fixtures to the teams who finished 2nd, 3rd and 4th, but without it being suggested that their 1st place was in some way less worthy.

Of course, there is a similar rankings table for one-day internationals. Indeed the ICC had been using Kendix's model for ODIs since 2002. When that had begun England were sixth, and they were still sixth in September 2009 after a 6–1 drubbing at home from Australia. As of early 2012, they have never been higher than third, and have been as low as eighth. Flower had seen enough, though. It was time to make some serious alterations. England's batsmen had to be aggressive, their bowlers had to be more accurate, and their fielding had to be sharper.

Simple commands, really. But Flower wanted his batsmen to be really aggressive, his bowlers to be really accurate and his fielders really sharp. And as the start of a plan it worked pretty well. England reached the semi-final of the Champions Trophy in South Africa and then beat the hosts 2–1 in the subsequent one-day series. An important marker was put down in the dropping of Owais Shah after the Champions Trophy. He probably would have been dropped for that tournament, but ICC regulations stipulated the early announcement of squads. Shah did make 98 off eighty-nine balls when South Africa were beaten by 22 runs at Centurion, but minds had already been made up. After the Trophy semi-final against Australia he never played for England again.

I quite like Shah. He was a smiling, chirpy youngster on the England A tour I went on to Kenya and Sri Lanka in 1997/98, and it was obvious that he was a hugely talented batsman. But he is also a poor fielder (although he has competent hands at slip) and an even poorer athlete. He does tend to get run out rather often. He can be a moaner, often blaming somebody else, and not producing his best until he really needs to. Put simply, it seems to me that he is not the type of character Flower wanted in his set-up.

This period of one-day matches was also when it became clear that England possessed a seriously formidable bowling attack. They obeyed Flower's words, and more. Stuart Broad and Tim Bresnan were superb, but it was James Anderson who impressed most. This was the moment when it emerged that here was a truly world-class bowler. His 5-23 in a canter of a victory at Port Elizabeth were, and still are, his best ODI figures.

Anderson had been in the international game a long time by this stage (one-day debut in Australia in 2002, Test debut against Zimbabwe at Lord's in 2003), but, as can happen with genuine swing bowlers, his returns were infuriatingly inconsistent. It is a fiendishly difficult trade, which requires the most sensitive of treatments because the bowler's main weapon is at the mercy of a phenomenon that nobody wholly understands. Many and varied are the theories about swing bowling. The balls, the shine, the sweets used (illegally) to produce that shine, the overhead conditions, the new stands at certain grounds, a ground's water-table, its proximity to the sea when the tide is in, the bowler's action, the bowler's wrist position, and, of course, the position of the moon. OK, I might be exaggerating a little on the last point, but the others are all factors one day, and complete non-sequiturs the next. The truth is that some days the cricket ball swings, some days it doesn't.

Sometimes we writers pen a piece we later rue. And probably my worst column piece since taking over from Mike Atherton at the *Sunday Telegraph* concerned Anderson and his performance at Trent Bridge against New Zealand in 2008. But the worst thing is that I keep getting reminded of that particular piece. Just as a cricketer always insists he does not read the papers, so a journalist will always deny typing his name into an internet search engine to see what comes up. Don't believe it. Whenever

I type 'Steve James cricket' into my Google page, for some reason one of the first links to appear is a piece entitled 'Pressure and James Anderson do not mix'.

God, it was a crap piece. Anderson began the Saturday morning of that Test with all six New Zealand wickets. A fairy-tale ten-wicket haul beckoned. But Anderson was all over the place early on, and my conclusion? He'd bottled it! He did take one wicket that morning to finish with 7-43 in the first innings, as New Zealand were bundled out for 123. And he finished that series with nineteen wickets at 19. I can only apologize.

Not that Anderson was always undeserving of criticism, of course. Especially abroad, with the Kookaburra ball, he could be startlingly ineffective. He seemed to lack variation, and his body language suffered accordingly. Justin Langer's 'pussy' observation was harsh, but you could see what he was getting at.

Now in South Africa Anderson was transformed. That Kookaburra ball was not just talking; you couldn't shut the thing up. There were out-swingers, in-swingers, cutters, bouncers and slower balls. The crucial difference, in my opinion? The absence of Andrew Flintoff. Anderson was now the leader of the pack. Some bowlers shrink in the face of such responsibility. Anderson positively thrived upon it. Top dog status suited him. And one of the most important branches that helped England to the top of the tree first revealed itself here.

Anderson was not, though, England's star bowler in the drawn Test series. Surprisingly, given that the pitches at three of the four venues – Centurion, Cape Town and Johannesburg – had plenty of grass on them, that accolade fell to off-spinner Graeme Swann. At the Boxing Day Test in Durban, where England won by an innings and 98 runs, he took 9-164 in the match. After England had clung on in the first Test for a draw, nine wickets down at Centurion with Paul Collingwood reproducing his Cardiff blocking heroics with 26 not out from ninety-nine balls and Graham Onions surviving twelve agonizing deliveries, this was unexpected festive cheer from England.

I certainly needed it. Now, I am fully aware, and indeed eternally grateful for the fact, that I possess a dream job. I love cricket and rugby, and get paid to watch most of the top matches in both those sports. As a columnist rather than a correspondent, I don't even have to spend as much time away from home as many others in the profession. But there is always a downside to any job, and that Christmas of 2009 in South Africa was most certainly one. Spending Christmas Day away from your wife and two young children (Rhys was four then and Bethan eleven) is hard, and that Christmas Day, despite the efforts of the son of Denis Compton, Patrick, a South African journalist, to feed and water the travelling English press corps at his home, was one of the more depressing days of my life. That it rained was thoroughly apt.

But Boxing Day soon arrived, and with it a performance that skipper Strauss described at the time as 'not far off the best performance I've seen from an England side, certainly away from home'. That was no hyperbole. Strauss is not inclined to such stuff. There were centuries for Alastair Cook and Ian Bell, another match-turning spell from Broad on the fourth evening and, of course, Swann's continuing excellence, earning him a second successive man of the match award.

All were hugely significant performances in differing ways. Firstly, here was incontrovertible evidence, if there had not already been some during the Ashes earlier that year, that Swann was a world-class off-spinner. He'd passed fifty Test wickets in the first Test (thirty-three of those victims were left-handers), and, yes, I will admit that I was still shaking my head in disbelief. It was some transformation.

I played against Swann quite a lot in county cricket. He was different in many ways. As opposed to most other off-spinners in the English game, he bowled an attacking line outside off-stump, spinning the ball hard. He cracked a few meaty shots down the order – although the suspicion always was that, if the ball was short and fast, he was not so keen to crack anything – and he cracked more than a few jokes. Sometimes he irritated; sometimes he amused.

He was certainly chosen prematurely for England's tour of South Africa in 1999/2000. He was immature both as a cricketer and as a person. Much has been made of Duncan Fletcher's spurning of him thereafter, but it was hardly a difficult decision to do so. It was the correct decision, as Swann himself admits in his autobiography. He was what Fletcher might call a 'twit'. He was nowhere near ready as an international cricketer. 'The primary reason for me remaining on the sidelines was that at 20 I wasn't good enough,' Swann wrote, 'and my tendency to wind up the wrong people at the wrong time didn't help matters.'

Swann's move from Northamptonshire to Nottinghamshire was crucial. The pitches at Wantage Road were actually spinning too much for him. A spinner learns nothing then. Trent Bridge is where swing bowlers rule. So Swann had to learn the art of defence as well as attack. Not that it came easily. It required some stern words from Nottinghamshire's wicket-keeper Chris Read during the pre-season of 2007 for the penny to be removed from its jammed position in the slot machine. 'Stop looking for the dream ball every ball' was the main substance of the advice.

Bowling in the first innings had to become more of a holding operation. Patience became a new friend. And Swann had to learn new tricks. He needed to be able to beat the bat on both sides. So he developed the away drift from the right-hander that is such an important part of his armoury.

He has become absolutely vital to England's four-man attack, even if he has surprisingly admitted that it was a policy with which he disagreed at first. Without him England might have to consider five bowlers. But with him, because he is so adaptable as attacker and defender, and so can bowl so many overs on the first day even if the toss is lost on a flat pitch, there really is no need for a fifth specialist.

Not that Flower and Strauss recognized Swann's abilities immediately. For their very first Test in charge in Jamaica they did not pick him. Nor Anderson for that matter. Swann was not selected for the second Test either, the abandoned debacle at the beach that was the Sir Vivian Richards Stadium in Antigua. But then curiously he was included instead of Monty Panesar when the rescheduled Test at the Recreation Ground in St John's began two days later. What happened during the ten balls that were bowled at Sir Viv's stadium (not that the great man wanted to be associated with it after that) and the start of the rescheduled Test at the Rec?

Well, I'll tell you. England had a middle practice at the St John's Police Recreation Ground, and while Swann was bowling Flower called Strauss over. 'Look at how much he is troubling all the left-handers' was the gist of Flower's words to his captain. Strauss knew because he had just faced him, and struggled. As the West Indies had five left-handers in their top six, and six in their team altogether, it was a rather pertinent observation. Strauss agreed. Swann was in. He hasn't missed a Test since. Indeed he has mostly bowled like Jim Laker since.

As for Cook, the fact that he scored a hundred in Durban while undergoing a radical technical overhaul was testament to his remarkable resilience. At the end of the Ashes the previous summer he had decided, along with Flower and Graham Gooch (then just his Essex coach but soon to be appointed as England's batting coach), to make some significant changes to his technique, most notably his backlift. He tried to eradicate his natural double backlift by holding the bat aloft, as Gooch used to. But, worried that he was not holding it in the correct position, he kept glancing back at it, like some fleeing thief checking on his chasing victim. Allied to a change in his 'trigger' movements – he tried to make them earlier, avoiding his usual 'floating front foot' – he looked horrible, even uglier than normal at the crease. And that is saying something. As probably the ugliest batsman in county cricket in the nineties, I think I am well qualified to comment.

Strangely, Cook's changes appeared to bring instant success. He scored two centuries in three days for Essex in the NatWest Pro40 competition at the end of that 2009 season. It could not surely have been down to the changes so soon. It hardly fitted in with Malcolm Gladwell's theory in his excellent book *Outliers*, subtitled 'The Story of Success', that it requires ten thousand hours of practice to master a specific skill.

Indeed Cook scored two more Test centuries, away in Bangladesh, with this obviously unfamiliar method. But then came a period of sustained failure against Bangladesh and Pakistan in the home summer of 2010. The word 'drop' was even being mentioned. Not by the England team management I don't think, because I reckon they believed in him enough to have taken him to the Ashes Down Under that winter even if he had failed all that summer. But it was still a time of some crisis, as he nicely summed up later that summer in an interview I did with him. 'One day I walked into Tesco,' he said, 'and a little kid came up to me and said, "Are you Alastair Cook?" Yes, I said. "You're not playing very well are you?" he replied.' Ouch.

Before the third Test at the Oval in the summer of 2010, Cook had had enough. He went to Flower and said, 'That's it. I'm going back to how I was.' He did. He cleared his mind of all technical thoughts. He didn't glance back at his bat. His backlift was a double movement, as it always had been. He went back and across the crease, with his front foot 'floating'. He just watched the ball. And he made a century. Then he kept on making centuries, double-centuries even. Mark my words, he will score more Test runs than any England batsman (Gooch's

8,900 is the current best) and more centuries too (Geoff Boycott, Colin Cowdrey and Wally Hammond head the list with twenty-two). As I write, Cook is twenty-seven years old. He has 6,027 Test runs with nineteen centuries. With him on nineteen are Strauss and Kevin Pietersen. Bell has sixteen. And people wonder why England were so good in 2011.

One wonders whether Cook needed to go through that period of change. 'I feel pretty good that I can change my technique and still score Test runs,' he admitted to me, 'but it made me appreciate what I had before and also that you can't change things too much. You have to be true to what you are.'

'He needed to go through that,' said Flower to me later. And I could see why Cook did it. The grass is often greener for batsmen. I experimented with all manner of theories during my career. I didn't glue my top-hand glove to my bat handle, as New Zealand's John Wright once did, but I did just about everything else. It is a shame, but I cannot again watch one of Glamorgan's greatest triumphs, the claiming of the Sunday League title at Canterbury in 1993, complete with an emotional farewell from the aforementioned Mr Richards. I watched it once on tape and turned it off after watching myself face one ball. My technique was shambolic, with front foot splayed down the pitch, bat aloft, head moving, body crouching.

If there is a modern batsman I wish I could have imitated, it is Bell. He is elegance personified at the crease. That 2009/10 winter in South Africa was when he finally shed all the 'soft' tags. The century at Durban was important because he could easily have been dropped after another insipid performance at Centurion, making just 5 and 2 and being inexplicably bowled leaving the left-arm spinner Paul Harris in the first innings.

'I changed a few technical things at Centurion,' Bell said to me later in the tour. 'Sitting there watching, I was asking myself whether I needed to get my leg out of the way to Harris. But the best thing I did afterwards was to decide just to trust myself, to go back to what I normally do. I knew Durban might be my last chance – I needed a big score and something that helped the side win – but I didn't want to walk away having just feathered one negatively [as in the second innings at Centurion]. I just wanted to be positive.'

At Cape Town in the second innings of the third Test, Bell made 78. I thought his 72 in the first innings at the Oval in the Ashes decider had been a fine innings. But this was even better, as England somehow managed to save the game again, with Onions – 'Bunny' by nickname but not by nature on this trip – facing eleven of the seventeen balls that he and Swann had to survive as the last pair after Collingwood had produced another trademark low-backlift 'Brigadier Block' (as David Lloyd christened him) innings of 40 from 188 balls.

'That's it then. Argument over. Ian Bell cuts it. Anyone questioning his mental fortitude at the highest level henceforth should be dismissed with the sort of contempt reserved for irritating flies,' I wrote the next day. 'He showed the type and volume of grit England's roads could do with right now.' Yes, it was snowing back home, but in South Africa England's cricketers were working hard in the heat.

That England could not complete a series victory was a disappointment. But in Johannesburg, after all the guts they had shown previously of their own accord, they were suddenly eviscerated. The guts on show were a ghastly sight. Strauss won the toss and batted on a damp, green pitch – he was worried about later indentations – and was promptly out first ball. England were all out for 180.

Graeme Smith made a century, and that was that. Except it might not have been. Smith had made only 15 when he edged Ryan Sidebottom (a shock replacement for Onions in a decision based too much on statistics at the ground) behind, but was given not out. He did edge it. Given the loud noise, with bat well away from body as Smith attempted a cut, everybody knew he'd edged it, except umpire Tony Hill and then, on review, Daryl Harper, the TV umpire. Quite why Harper heard nothing became the subject of so many conspiracy theories that it was a surprise Dan Brown did not write a book about it. But it wasn't until six months later that the truth was confirmed: Harper had heard nothing because of a poor sound feed from the host broadcaster SABC. To compound matters, other broadcasters, especially Sky Sports, received a better sound feed so their commentators quite naturally slated Harper for what they perceived to be his mistake.

England were incensed at the time. They were firmly against the Decision Review System, and had voted against its intro-duction (it was a 9–1 vote in favour). I was never sure why, although one ICC official did mention to me that it might have been purely because Fletcher proposed the system in the first place.

Their first taste of it in the West Indies in 2009 had stirred controversy, not least because Harper was the TV umpire. Both he and the two teams failed to grasp the basic concept that the system was introduced to eradicate howlers. During the first Test in South Africa Flower had said he was 'not a fan' of the system, but here now the ECB chairman Giles Clarke dived into the debate with two feet, describing the system itself as 'damned dangerous' and its implementation here a 'shambles'.

They were unnecessary comments, not least because Clarke should leave the cricket to the experts. And it was forgetting that Collingwood's match-saving innings at Cape Town would not have lasted more than one ball without the DRS. He was given out caught at slip off Harris, but the review showed clearly the ball had hit his hip, not bat.

It was interesting how attitudes had changed by the summer of 2011 when India (with Fletcher now, of course, ironically their coach) would only accept a watered-down version of the system, while England, with Swann picking up so many of his lbws from it, were rather keener to use it. The system may still not be perfect, but it has been proven to increase the percentage of correct decisions. That has to be a good thing for the game.

It was also good, in my opinion anyway, that the day after the South Africa series concluded it was announced that Strauss was taking a break and missing the tour to Bangladesh. This was something new and different, and inevitably drew howls of disapproval from a legion of former England captains, including Mike Atherton, Nasser Hussain, Ian Botham, David Gower, Alec Stewart and Bob Willis. I thought I'd take them to task in my column. 'The old boys are talking tosh,' I began. I did, of course, give them the respect they deserve – 'Fine body of men' etc., etc. – but then 'But they are wrong. Just because they have, by various methods, been ushered to an early captaincy grave does not mean another, Strauss, has to follow them.'

The crux of this matter goes back to a point I made earlier in this book: English cricket simply does not understand the word 'rest'. Strauss was knackered. Absolutely knackered. The strain of dragging England from the mess of the Pietersen/Moores episode and trying to maintain the highest standards as an opening batsman during all that time had simply become too much.

I chanced upon him and his two young children in one of Sandton's shopping malls the day before the final Test in Johannesburg. His eldest Sam was bawling his eyes out, having hurt his arm. I wasn't sure whom to feel most sympathy for. Strauss looked shattered, not from child-minding, but just generally. I thought to myself, 'I bet he doesn't score many runs tomorrow.' As I mentioned above, he was out first ball, even if it was to a stunning catch at short leg.

Strauss is usually the most equanimous of cricketers. Neither barbs nor bouncers normally unsettle him, but in that Johannesburg Test when Morne Morkel hit him and followed it with some verbals, Strauss responded angrily. He needed a break. Yes, it was a departure from the policy adopted in 2001 by Fletcher that players could only choose formats and not tours. That was in response to Stewart and Darren Gough's desire to miss a tour of India and then travel to New Zealand later that winter. Fletcher told them they could retire from international one-day cricket if they wanted, but they couldn't pick and choose tours. It was an admirable policy, and in the end one that was well respected by the players.

But Strauss's decision was different. It was not just Strauss who made it. Flower, Hugh Morris and Geoff Miller all agreed with it. It was done with the Ashes in mind. And, let's be honest, it was done with the quality of opposition in mind. If you are going to miss a tour, if not to Bangladesh, then where? Some might scream about disrespect, but matches against lesser opposition can often be hardest for the more experienced, been-there-done-it-all players, as England showed when losing to both Bangladesh and Ireland in the 2011 World Cup. When England sent a virtual second team to play Ireland after the India Test series later that year, that was the correct call. And England won. If only narrowly in a rain-affected match.

So it was the right call to rest Strauss. It also allowed Cook some valuable leadership experience in Test matches and ODIs. When it came to choosing a new captain after that World Cup, the ECB knew their man. They quite rightly interviewed other players (including Eoin Morgan, who impressed so much that he was selected to captain in that aforementioned match in Ireland), but essentially their decision had been made. 'I think he has done brilliantly,' said Flower after Bangladesh. It was enough said.

Before that tour of Bangladesh, Flower had had reason to become excited about something else. In February 2010 England played two Twenty20 internationals against Pakistan in Dubai. They won one and lost one. I mentioned the latter match in passing earlier when talking of Jonathan Trott. He was not doing the exciting, though.

As I write, that was Trott's last T20 international, as his dawdling innings cost England the chance of victory. Flower simply does not abide selfishness, and this was never going to be swept quietly under the carpet. 'We've had some honest discussion about that, one-on-one and in front of the team,' Flower told me just before the ICC World Twenty20 three months later. 'He [Trott] got that innings wrong, no doubt about it, and that was a contributing factor to him not being in the side right now.'

Trott was then opening with Kent's Joe Denly, two players about whom I have been wrong in my predictions about their England careers. Even halfway through 2010 I was saying Trott wouldn't be in the team for the first Ashes Test that winter.

I honestly thought Denly could be the answer to England's problems at the top of their one-day order. He was aggressive, and liked to take on the short ball, and, importantly, he always seemed to score runs on television. I was at Loughborough one day in 2008 doing some interviews when Michael Vaughan walked past me as I was watching the TV as Denly took a century off Durham in the Friends Provident Trophy semi-final. 'He should be playing for England,' said Vaughan. He did play for England, but, sadly, he just couldn't cut it.

The excitement came two days before the first of those two T20s in Dubai when England had played England Lions in Abu Dhabi. The juniors had humbled the seniors, beating them by five wickets. But most importantly, Flower had suddenly seen his new T20 opening partnership. In chasing 158 to win Craig Kieswetter (a day after he had officially qualified for England) and Hampshire's Michael Lumb put on 86 for the first wicket in just eleven overs for the Lions.

Kieswetter was hastily added to England's squad for the one-day matches in Bangladesh, and when it came to the first match of the World Twenty20 in the Caribbean (against the hosts as it happened) he and Lumb became England's sixteenth T20 opening partnership in just twenty-six matches.

So much for the meticulous planning for which Flower has become famed. But as Flower said beforehand, 'We might get criticized for chopping and changing, but Twenty20s are so few and far between and there are such big chunks of time in between. We're on the search for the most effective opening combination, and that continues.'

It continued for some time afterwards actually. Since that tournament there have been a few more. Nottinghamshire's Alex Hales was the latest to be tried, in late August 2011. But Flower is right about international Twenty20. Its presence in the calendar outside of the global tournament that is now played every two years is rather arbitrary.

Indeed there are many observers who think that Twenty20 should not be played at international level at all. I tend to agree. But it's too late now, and it has become a little farcical that matches are played on their own at the start of one-day series, or in the case of England's tour to India in the autumn of 2011, at the end of it. The ICC is so worried about playing too much of it that they have set a limit on the number that can be played in a year: no more than six at home in a calendar year, and no more than three in a series.

Its introduction to the county game in 2003 was for a very specific purpose. Money. It was brought in (after a vote of 11–7 among the counties) as a means of helping ailing counties keep their finances in order. For some, like Essex, Somerset and Sussex, that has worked. But it was never about the cricket. Yes, it has extended the horizons in terms of one-day batting, but essentially it is the same game most of us played as youngsters in some local midweek league.

As Flower said before the 2010 tournament, 'There are all sorts of theories that abound about Twenty20 cricket, but I think, when you get down to the meat of the matter in the changing room, it's much more simple than people are making out.'

So England won their first global tournament by keeping things simple. It was the only way really, given that they left in late April with the county season in full swing, with some players having even played championship matches the week before. But they did possess five players – Pietersen, Collingwood, Morgan, Lumb and Bopara – who'd been appearing in the Indian Premier League beforehand. And if the captain Collingwood picked up one gem from that tournament it was that he had to have a left-arm seamer in his side. So Sidebottom played instead of Anderson. It was a surprise. But it worked. 'To me Sidebottom was non-negotiable,' Collingwood told me afterwards. 'In the IPLs so far the majority of the top bowlers have been left-armers. Right-handers struggle with their angle going across them.'

'Petals and the Weed, a strange combination to be sure,' I wrote before the final against Australia, in describing Flower and Collingwood (the England players, especially Pietersen, used to nickname Collingwood 'Weed' because of his perceived lack of hitting power) and the general surprise that England had done so well. For it was a surprise, with Collingwood having given up the one-day captaincy fewer than two years earlier when Flower was an assistant in a regime that was not universally popular. The odds on those two leading England to their first global trophy would have been long. 'Of the sort offered to the deluded father who thinks his three-year-old can play football for England,' I wrote. '"Don't be silly, but 10,000-1 anyway,"' the bookmaker might have said.

But win England did, and in some style. They benefited firstly from a settled side. They made only one change throughout the tournament, and that was because Pietersen returned home for the birth of his son Dylan, missing the match against New Zealand, with England already through to the semi-finals.

Pietersen, batting at number three after the quickfire if never lengthy opening partnerships of Kieswetter and Lumb, ended up as Man of the Tournament for his 248 runs at an average of 62 and a strike rate of just under 138.

The bowling followed a familiar but successful pattern. Sidebottom and Bresnan opened, with Broad as first change. Usually once the six Powerplay overs were over, the spin twins of Michael Yardy and Swann would operate in tandem. And the quintet had to adapt to two very different types of surface during the tournament, excluding the slow pitch in Providence, Guyana, where England played their two initial group games, and very nearly exited the competition after rain and Duckworth/Lewis tried to conspire against them, but where they only bowled 9.2 overs in total: the pace of the Kensington Oval, Barbados, which evoked memories of years gone by and the Ends named after Malcolm Marshall and Joel Garner, and something slower in St Lucia, but not as slow as Guyana. Only on two occasions did England deviate slightly from their plan: against Pakistan Collingwood bowled a single over, as did Luke Wright in the final.

It was also obvious that England were by far the fittest side on show. In the tight-fitting shirts worn these days they looked like athletes. And there was a reason for that: the work of fitness and conditioning coach Huw Bevan. If you'll pardon another brief hint of braggadocio, I'd like to take some credit for that. (But even as I write that is being taken away from me. I've asked my wife a question about Bevan and she's just replied, 'Don't try and take the credit about Bevs. That was my idea!')

To explain. In 2002 I was captain of Glamorgan, and we were looking for a part-time fitness trainer. It is crazy to think that counties did not employ full-time fitness trainers then. But they didn't. And they didn't until the ECB provided them each with £25,000 p.a. specifically for that purpose. Anyway, my wife Jane was then the physiotherapist at Cardiff RFC, and she said the best fitness trainer they'd had at Cardiff was Bevan. By then he was at Bridgend RFC before joining the Ospreys in 2003, when the Welsh game went regional. He'd been a no-nonsense hooker who'd played for Bridgend, Cardiff, Swansea and, very briefly, Llanelli. He'd also always been a keen Glamorgan CCC supporter and was living (and still lives) a stone's throw from Sophia Gardens. So one evening Jane and I were having a few drinks at the Cameo Club, a well-known watering-hole in Pontcanna near Sophia Gardens, and Bevan was there too. We got chatting and Jane just asked him if he would like to help out at Glamorgan. To say he was keen to do it would be an understatement.

So Glamorgan had a new fitness trainer. And, boy, was he good. I still talk to some of the players about the famous Friday afternoon sessions we used to endure at the David Lloyd Centre in Cardiff. They could be brutal, but they were always good fun. Jane had talked about how at Cardiff the squad would split up into forwards and backs to do 3km runs. Bevan would run with one group and finish near the front, then straight away go with the second lot and run most of them ragged too. At Glamorgan very few of us could stay with him. As for his favourite gym exercises, chins and dips, he was unbeatable.

Unfortunately in 2008 Bevan left the Ospreys. The New Zealander Andrew Hore, once the Wales team's fitness trainer, had come in as elite performance director and that was always going to spell the end for Bevan. They'd never really got on. For a while Bevan was without a job. He was beginning to fret. He had been a PE teacher at Heolddu Comprehensive in Bargoed for ten years but did not really fancy returning to the teaching profession. To fill time he did work with various Welsh tennis players and amateur boxers.

Then I mentioned to him that there was a job coming up with the ECB. He already knew. He applied, and asked me to be one of his referees. I doubt if I helped much, but in November 2008 Bevan was appointed as the National Cricket Performance Centre conditioning coach. Soon he was taking six young bowlers – Maurice Chambers (Essex), Jonathan Clare (Derbyshire), Jade Dernbach (Surrey), Chris Jordan (Surrey), Mark Turner (Somerset) and Chris Woakes (Warwickshire) – to Florida for training at the famous IMG multi-sport facility in Bradenton, where Nick Bollettieri's tennis academy is situated. That winter he also went to South Africa with the England Under 19s and to Malaysia with the Under 18s. By the time the World Twenty20 was being held in England the following year in 2009 he was being asked to work with the senior side. So impressive was his work that he has never been away from the main side again, with the man in situ, Sam Bradley, shifted back to the NCPC.

There has been no fitter England side than the one under Flower, Strauss and indeed Bevan. Not that Bevan will take any credit. He is simply not that type of bloke. Ask him and he will say it is a team effort, along with fielding coach Richard Halsall, physiotherapist Ben Langley (and before him Kirk Russell) and long-serving masseur Mark Saxby (there for many of the Fletcher years too). As he said to me during the 2010/11 Ashes, 'Under Straussy and Andy there is a very proactive culture where it is part of the players' responsibility to be in the best physical condition they can.'

But Bevan has transformed the thinking. Central to this has been the realization that cricket is actually a power sport. For a long time cricket fitness was a bit of a joke; if any was done at all, it was just some light-hearted long-distance running. When I first joined Glamorgan in the mid-eighties there was only one test conducted at pre-season training, and that was a three-mile run that had to be completed in twenty-one minutes. It was hilarious. Some of the older sweats wore their cricket whites and caps. One chap even sported his cricket spikes to wear them in on the concrete part of the course. And, of course, plenty knew a short cut, and used it too.

Cricket might be played over a long period of time, but the movements made by cricketers are actually very dynamic. They require speed and power. That is not to say endurance is not needed too, but plodding along for, say, an hour on a treadmill is a rather poor use of time unless you need to lose a considerable amount of weight. A 5km run is probably enough for those who are used to such activity, as you will often see Bevan doing with, say, Strauss on tour. You are more likely to see the bowlers performing a series of 40m sprints – say twenty-four in total, in sets of six repetitions in order to replicate bowling four overs, but with shorter rest periods.

Weight training also plays a crucial role. But here Bevan has had to endure some uninformed criticism. The easy conclusion among those who have never lifted weights seriously is that it automatically puts unnecessary muscle bulk on the participant. It doesn't. It is actually very hard to put weight on. Strength can be acquired without excess weight. Bevan does not want muscle-bound fast bowlers. He wants them lithe and powerful. It is not like rugby where bulk is obviously required.

In a remarkable new initiative during the 2010 season, Broad and Steven Finn were taken out of the game completely to work on their fitness and conditioning. That went down well among the old guard! But as Bevan explains, 'Because of all the cricket we play, it is difficult to make any gains in terms of strength, and any gains you make are difficult to maintain. Other sports will have an off-season which we don't necessarily have, so to make real improvements you need a block of time to train. We are trying to build up each of the players' training age. By that I mean if you do weights for twenty years then stop training, you won't lose strength rapidly. But if you only train for a short period of time, you will make gains quickly but also regress quickly.'

But still, whenever a bowler is injured, there is a temptation for some to criticize the training methods. So for instance when in Bangladesh Sidebottom, Broad and Onions were all lame, Flower had to defend his man, and did so very well. 'I think the game is played at a different intensity – if you look at old footage I think it is pretty obvious,' he said. 'The pace at which the game is played is such that there is a lot of stress put on bodies, especially if you play in all three forms of the game.

'I have heard some criticism of the amount of work the guys put in in their physical preparation but I think to play at the intensity required these days in both limited-overs and Test cricket people will continue to seek constant improvement in their physical shape.

'You don't want people to overtrain but you are always trying to get that balance right. Fast bowlers are going to get injured. It's a stressful job that they do. If we could morph a physical trainer and an ex-fast bowler into a package then that might be quite useful but I trust our medical staff and I certainly trust our trainer, Huw Bevan, who has been excellent and has done some really good stuff with our squad.'

These days the ECB set out what they call their 'Fitness for Selection Policy'. This is not just for the England team but, as they say, 'the minimum benchmark standards which would be expected of all professional cricketers'. It includes a minimum score of 12.5 on the dreaded Bleep Test (a continuous series of 20m shuttle runs with the pace increasing at every level); sprint scores of 1 second over 5m, 1.74 seconds over 10m and 3 seconds over 20m; and being able to bench press 80% of your body weight for five repetitions, squat 120% for five repetitions, and do five chin-ups with a 10% load added to your body weight.

The problem is that not all county cricketers are as fit as they should be. There have been a number in recent seasons who have made it into the England squad and then had to be brought up to speed (if you'll excuse the pun) by Bevan. Some counties are superb in their dedication to fitness, but some are still of the old-school view that practising cricketing skills alone is sufficient fitness.

There is also the problem of how to punish a cricketer for poor fitness levels. Nottinghamshire's Samit Patel is the classic example. England did not pick him for a long period – he should have been their second spinner at the 2011 World Cup but simply wasn't fit enough – and his county were well aware of, and indeed frustrated by, his apparent laziness. But to drop him or release him entirely would have been self-defeating because another county would instantly have signed him. He is a good cricketer after all. Indeed England were so keen to include him that they dropped the Bleep Test target to 12 for him, which he just about achieved in 2011 and so was picked for the T20s and one-day series against Sri Lanka and India.

As Bevan says, a lot of the work he does is not actually measurable. 'How do you measure athleticism?' he asks. 'There is no objective measure for the footwork and agility required for fielding.' But there is little doubt that he has formed a formidable partnership, and indeed friendship, with Halsall.

Rugby is a common talking point between those two. The Zimbabwe-born Halsall was once a promising back-row forward at Arnold School near Blackpool. He coached rugby at both Brighton College and Wellington College. Just after he began work as England's fielding coach before the 2008 season he had to take a day off to go to Twickenham to see his Wellington Under 15s beat Millfield to win the Daily Mail Under 15s Schools Cup for the second time.

Halsall was something of a surprise appointment by Peter Moores. He had become county cricket's first fielding coach when employed part-time by Moores at Sussex in 2003. And now Moores decided, quite rightly and in line with Recommendation No. 10 of the Schofield Report, that he needed someone similar with England. Another Zimbabwean, Trevor Penney, from the same Old Hararians club as Fletcher and having helped England in 2005, was approached but was unavailable as he was emigrating to Australia to be assistant to Tom Moody, with whom he'd been working for the Sri Lanka team, at Western Australia. (Ironically Penney was back in England in 2011 as Fletcher's newly appointed fielding coach for India.) Jonty Rhodes was sounded out by England too, and Gloucestershire's Mark Alleyne was interviewed, but Halsall was always going to get the job.

I'd met him a few times out in Zimbabwe in 1994 when he'd returned there for a couple of seasons. He'd left the country for England aged four, and was now there playing some representative cricket for Mashonaland Country Districts. I couldn't remember him being a particularly outstanding fielder, but as he says, 'coaching is far more than just showing'.

I interviewed him at Loughborough just after he'd got the job, and he gave me a lovely line about how he was going to put a patch over Monty Panesar's eye ('sensory deprivation stuff', he called it) in order to help his catching. How the paper loved that. But he did counter the inevitable comparisons with, say, a Rhodes by stating confidently, 'If it's about diving full length and stopping the ball then Jonty might be better. But if it was lasering the ball in from sixty metres then I'd be better than him. And as for having to write a fielding programme for a Level Three coaching module, then I'd back myself.'

Halsall has transformed England's fielding sessions into highly organized and highly scientific practices. It took some time, because I remember watching a few early on that were rather chaotic with players clueless as to what they were supposed to be doing. Now they are like military operations. Halsall uses a specially adapted bowling machine that fires balls from ground level, often on to orange ramps that deflect the balls in different directions. Sometimes they use heavier balls so that when the real ones are used they appear ridiculously light. The short leg and silly point fielders take balls off springy nets. Flower edges catches for the slip fielders left-handed, and team manager Phil Neale does it right-handed – just as Fletcher and Neale used to in a previous regime. Fletcher was, and still doubtless is for India, a quite brilliant 'nicker' for slip catches, being able to edge a ball so fine that it is a catch for a wicketkeeper standing up. Deliberately. You try to do that. It is nigh on impossible. Both Fletcher and Flower are very good at hitting catches for gully and backward point, which is also a very difficult skill to perfect.

I think Fletcher would have enjoyed working with Halsall. He was a decent cricketer. He studied sports sciences at Brighton and Cambridge, winning a Blue and also appearing for Sussex second eleven, as well as an England amateur eleven. And he is fit. When he lists one of his key tenets as 'physicality', he is well placed to comment. He spends long periods in the gym, with the players or maybe even just with Bevan. 'He doesn't like running, though,' jokes Bevan. Little wonder the players call him 'Stick', on account of his skinny legs.

Halsall's other two tenets are 'precision and sacrifice'. 'Sacrifice comes in many forms,' he says, 'but in terms of fielding it means all those extra yards that only your team-mates really appreciate. It's about diving full-length on rock-hard outfields that cut and scrape your body, chasing down what appear lost causes, sprinting forty yards to congratulate a mate, or simply backing up a throw just in case something happens. Sacrifice also means practising a skill a hundred times so you can execute it the one time in a hundred you need it.'

In that early interview Halsall talked about how England cricketers in general were poor at hitting the stumps. 'We seem obsessed with getting rid of the ball too quickly,' he said. 'You need to give yourself a photo moment as I call it – set yourself, get your base and then throw.' He has even got his players to practise archery in order to utilize the correct feet positions. He talked about how on DVD he had a perfect example of Marcus Trescothick doing so at Durham in 2005, running out Australia's Andrew Symonds from mid-off. 'It's beautiful,' he purred.

He's got a better example now, that of Trott running out Simon Katich without facing a ball on the first morning of the Adelaide Test in 2010. The fourth ball of the Test had hit Shane Watson on the pad and gone out towards square leg. As the Australian pair hesitated over a single, Trott moved around from mid-wicket, picked up the ball, took a step, stopped for that 'photo moment', took aim and hit the one stump that was visible. He ran around the ground like a striker who had just scored the winning goal in the FA Cup final.

Ricky Ponting was then out first ball to Anderson, and by the third over Australia were 2-3 (that's two runs for three wickets in the English way of telling the score, or 'three for two' as they say in Australia).

England's fielding in general during that Ashes was outstanding, their supremacy over Australia evident at every turn as England's ground fielders adopted a 'pack mentality', as Halsall likes to say, hounding the Australian batsmen, with everyone committed to saving every run possible and everyone also prepared to run huge distances to congratulate a colleague when he'd done so. Such showy slaps on the back can look a little too contrived, even a bit silly, but they can also produce a togetherness and an energy that exude purpose. That was certainly the impression given here. The statistics said that over the series England's fielders saved runs on 109 occasions compared to Australia's 68. That's a convincing victory.

England's catching was also superb. Of the ninety wickets they took in the series, sixty-six came from catches. That is a high proportion. England's wicketkeeper Matt Prior took twenty-three catches compared to Australia's stumper, Brad

Haddin, who took just eight. The best of England's catches was undoubtedly Collingwood's to dismiss Ponting at Perth, diving high to his right at third slip. His low left-handed grab off Swann to get rid of the same batsman in Adelaide wasn't bad either.

England effected four run outs to Australia's none in the series. Trott was responsible for two of them, his effort in Melbourne to run out Phillip Hughes (with a good take from Prior in front of the stumps, as Fletcher had preached to Geraint Jones all those years before) earning special praise because he had just batted for 486 minutes for 168 not out, and also because when on 46 he had dived full-length to avoid being run out. Hughes here did not dive. It told a story, as did the sight of Trott in hotel gyms early on Test-match mornings during the tour – evidence of a man who, as he later told me, had taken to heart Flower's mantra that 'fitness and fielding are non-negotiable'.

Flower was impressed. 'Trott has worked incredibly hard at his fitness and his fielding over the last year,' he said afterwards. 'He is lighter and quicker and actually hits the stumps quite often in training. The fact that he had just come off 168 not out and was still quick enough and fit enough and alert enough to effect that run out, I think is a great example of all the hard work he has put in, but also of the contributions that the back-room staff have made too. Huw Bevan has worked to get him fitter so that he can concentrate for a long time, while Richard Halsall will have done the same on his fielding. That's what makes me proud as a coach when you see something like that, rather than only his batting.'

At the World Twenty20 in 2010, England's throwing at the stumps had not appeared to be that good. In the final Australia might have been buried earlier had hits from Collingwood and Lumb (twice) been on target. But their catching and ground fielding was exceptional throughout. And as Halsall has said in convincing defence since, 'It is also useful to know how many times the people hit the stumps when it really matters. A percentage of one in four turns out to be very high – you're doing well if you can manage that.'

When he took the job, Halsall reckoned England were the fourth best fielding side in the world behind Australia, South Africa and New Zealand. By 2011 they were surely the best. And Halsall must take the credit. 'We may just have another Troy Cooley on our hands here,' I'd written at the start, 'an unknown gem of rounded knowledge and clever communication.'

Cooley had indeed been a superb bowling coach, especially in 2005. At the World Twenty20 England had a new bowling coach, David Saker. He had replaced Ottis Gibson, who had taken the job in the autumn of 2007 and had now been unable to resist the call from home, returning to the West Indies as head coach.

Gibson left with his reputation enhanced, which was a surprise to me. It might even have been a surprise to Flower, because I was never sure how highly he rated Gibson. I was never sure how well Gibson had made the transition from player to coach – unsurprising given that he had hopped between the two, coaching for the ECB for three years before returning to the professional playing game with Leicestershire in 2004.

Gibson had played for Glamorgan in 1994 and 1996, and while the raw talent was there for all to see, he was obviously no thinking cricketer. But he clearly learnt. By the time he finished his first-class career at Durham he was the canniest of fast bowlers. In that final season in 2007, at the age of thirty-eight, he took all ten Hampshire wickets in an innings at the Riverside, Chester-le-Street.

And so the ever-smiling Bajan learnt as a coach too. His early days with England were difficult, as he struggled to work with Steve Harmison and Matthew Hoggard. He would hardly have been against the decision to drop them both for the second Test at Wellington in 2008. By the time of the 2009 Ashes he was starting to earn public praise from the likes of Andrew Flintoff and Stuart Broad. Flintoff made a point of signalling to the dressing room at Lord's on the fourth morning when he dismissed Australia's Katich because a plan – bowling wider on the crease and so moving the ball across the left-hander from outside leg-stump – had been hatched that morning with Gibson. Then when England triumphed in Durban that winter, it was Gibson who was credited with outsmarting his opposite number, Vincent Barnes. England had achieved reverse swing; South Africa hadn't.

With Gibson gone, England first wanted the Australian Mike Kasprowicz. Flower phoned him and asked about his availability, but Kasprowicz eventually decided he could not justify the time away from his family. This was kept quiet at the time. The only reason I am mentioning it here is because I know Saker knows about it. Indeed he was taking the mickey out of Flower about it just before the Perth Test in 2010.

But they can laugh about it now because Saker has proved an outstanding appointment. And Saker does enjoy a laugh, especially at himself. His humorous personality is infectious. He was on a shortlist of five that also included Craig McDermott, former Warwickshire all-rounder Dougie Brown, former Gloucestershire bowler Stuart Barnes and Allan Donald, who had been England's bowling coach in the summer of 2007. So keen was Saker to land the job that he paid for his own flight from Melbourne to attend the interview.

Saker made an instant impression. 'One of the things I quite liked about him,' says Flower, 'was that he has always had a leaning towards coaching and helping other people learn, even when he was playing [in seventy-two matches for Victoria and Tasmania]. We did a lot of research on him and all the information coming back was very positive.'

Saker had coached the Delhi Daredevils IPL side of which Collingwood had been a part. Collingwood had liked what he saw. And so did England very quickly. By the start of the 2010/11 Ashes tour managing director Morris was already negotiating a new contract with Saker, and by the Test series' end he had signed for a further three years. There was to be no repeat of the Cooley impasse. Ironically, Cooley was moving on from Australia's job to their centre of excellence and there was talk Saker might apply for that. No chance. He'd already made up his mind.

Saker's great strength is that he keeps things simple. He is not a biomechanist. The art of bowling interests him more; he is more of a strategist and planner really. But he is also a fine 'people person', so important with bowlers, who can be an irascible, moody group of individuals!

Flower likes simplicity. It is why he also appointed Gooch as batting coach. That move surprised, even worried, me. I'd worked with Gooch on my only England A tour in 1997/98. I loved his work ethic, as does Bevan, who says of their now regular training sessions 'He just doesn't know when to give in!', but I was unsure what he could offer technically. Maybe he thought I'd reached a ceiling technically, and it was best not to confuse me.

Or maybe not. 'I coach run-making, not batting. Anyone can bat, but can you make runs? They are two different things,' Gooch says of his philosophy. 'We do a lot of overs practice so that the lads bat for a certain number of overs while we switch the bowling from over the wicket to around. It creates a similar environment to the middle. We also get them running between the overs, carrying bricks, or doing physical exercises. That's really to test their mind and their concentration – it's nothing to do with fitness. We call it distraction.

'Sometimes we put coloured discs down on a length when we are throwing to the batsmen. If you hit that coloured disc, the ball deviates a bit and misbehaves. But the main lesson for the players is that they've got to concentrate on the ball, not on what might be sitting on the surface of the pitch.'

Not all the England batsmen work with Gooch – Strauss and Pietersen don't – but you cannot grumble with Gooch's results in 2010/11. The batsmen had learnt to go big. I'll mention the saying once but not again because it has become a rather tiresome cliché: they are making what Gooch calls 'Daddy hundreds'.

And they are. In Tests in 2010 and 2011 England's batsmen made seven scores over 200, two each for Cook, Pietersen and Trott, and one for Bell. That is only one fewer than scores over 200 made by England players between 1986 and 2009, with Gooch himself featuring twice in that list, with his 333 against India in 1990 and 210 against New Zealand in 1994. The other six are Pietersen (226 v. West Indies, 2007), Collingwood (206 v. Australia, 2006), Rob Key (221 v. West Indies, 2004), Marcus Trescothick (219 v. South Africa, 2003), Graham Thorpe (200 n.o. v. New Zealand, 2002) and Nasser Hussain (207 v. Australia, 1997).

Double-hundreds were not required in that World Twenty20 final. Only 148 runs were needed to win there. Australia were not just beaten, they were thrashed, by seven wickets with eighteen balls remaining. After thirty-five years of failure – that is nine World Cups (a tenth went without success in 2011), six Champions Trophies and two Twenty20 World Cups – England had at last won a global one-day trophy. No wonder that the Harbour Lights nightclub in Barbados, situated conveniently close to the team's Hilton Hotel, was 'definitely lively' that night according to Collingwood. England's players celebrated long into the night. They deserved it.

What they didn't deserve were the events of the summer of 2010. The look of disgust and the slow shake of the head from

Collingwood as he spied the Pakistan team at Lord's on the morning of Sunday, 29 August said it all.

Until the night before it had been, considering the usual controversy that stalks a Pakistan cricket team, a relatively quiet season. The ball had generally darted around like a stickleback coming in and out of cover, but England had won the first two Tests comfortably before succumbing surprisingly in the third at the Oval. Now in the fourth they were in absolute control after a remarkable 332-run partnership for the eighth wicket between Trott and Broad.

I was travelling home on the train from Lord's with Scyld Berry that night when a call came. Apparently the *News of the World* had the scoop to end all cricketing scoops. But we did not know exactly what it was until 10 p.m. and the first sight of the story on the paper's website. It was shocking. There appeared to be clear evidence of two Pakistan bowlers, Mohammad Amir and Mohammad Asif, deliberately bowling no-balls earlier in the Test.

Sadly it was not a surprise. As a player I'd always considered the game clean. Corruption in cricket might as well have been on a different planet. But my experiences as a journalist, especially with Berry, of all the cricketing scribes the most relentless pursuer of fixing, as a colleague, have been very different.

Indeed earlier that season I'd almost had my own spot-fixing scoop. I'd become aware of something happening at Essex. It centred upon a NatWest Pro40 match at the end of the previous season. During the off-season concern had been raised by an Essex player about the actions of two of his team-mates. The ECB and the ICC's Anti Corruption and Security Unit were informed immediately, but they then decided to hand the matter over to the Essex Police.

It was a big story, and I had it. But it needed standing up. So on the Friday morning a call was made to the Essex Police. And they gave the following statement: 'Following allegations received about two Essex county cricket players involved in match irregularities, we have initiated an investigation and are working closely with Essex County Cricket Club and the English Cricket Board.'

The trouble was that the ECB then issued that very same statement late on the Friday afternoon. The Sunday scoop had been scuppered. The police had gone straight to the ECB to tell them that the media were on to the story.

On the Saturday morning Danish Kaneria was named as one of the players. At least I was able to name the other as Mervyn Westfield on the Sunday, but for me as a journalist it was one that got away. Kaneria was cleared but later named as the alleged corruptor when Westfield pleaded guilty and was sentenced to four months in jail.

None of this was a surprise because greed had long been the staple diet of too many cricketing people. Quite naturally that was going to spread into some dark and dirty corners into which the *News of the World* was now shining a welcome light. In February 2011 an ICC tribunal found Amir, Asif and their captain Salman Butt guilty of spot-fixing, and banned them for five, seven and ten years respectively. Butt and Asif had five and two years suspended. Then in November 2011 at Southwark Crown Court in London all three players, along with their agent Mazhar Majeed, were jailed for terms of between two years eight months and six months. They became the first sportsmen to be imprisoned for on-field corruption in the UK for almost fifty years.

To think the ECB had been helping Pakistan out by hosting their matches against Australia earlier in the summer. It was some raspberry they had been blown. But, as I kept stressing throughout the various storms that followed this horrible tempest, the show had to go on. Cricket could not cave in. There were more screams of 'Call it off!' during the subsequent one-day series than you find emanating from local councils when considering football on their pitches during a hard winter. But it was not called off, and England won a rancorous series 3–2, with a feverishly passionate display in the decider at the Rose Bowl.

England had won on and off the field. They were ready to go to Australia.

12

Sprinklings of Magic

Well, England weren't quite ready for Australia. First they had to go to Germany. Whisked away from Gatwick airport in the early hours of the morning, just a day and a bit after beating Pakistan at Southampton, and with only their barest essentials for company, they flew to Munich and from there were driven into the middle of the Bavarian forest.

The five-day trip was organized by Reg Dickason, the ECB's security adviser, and run by members of the Australian police force. None of the players knew where they were going beforehand. And, boy, did it cause some controversy, especially when it emerged afterwards that James Anderson had cracked a rib while boxing with Chris Tremlett; Tremlett himself suffered bruised ribs. It could have been worse too, or better, depending on your standpoint. Joe Calzaghe, the former world champion boxer, had been due to go to Germany with the players, but pulled out at the last minute with food poisoning.

It was reported that Anderson might miss the start of the Ashes, maybe even miss two Tests according to the wildest and most pessimistic speculation. But the truth was that he had suffered a small crack and indeed had completed all the physical work in Germany, only realizing upon his return home that he was in some pain.

Personally I was surprised that England went on this trip, especially after such an arduous summer. But the feeling among the England management was that, if they were going to do it, they had to do so immediately after the season ended so that the players could go away and rest completely for a month before reconvening for the Ashes.

But then I've always been sceptical in general about the value of such 'bonding' trips. And that's not just because I narrowly avoided nasty injury or worse on the way home from one of them in Brecon with the Glamorgan team in 2000. We'd done all the usual nonsense: orienteering, assault course, carrying logs up a steep hill, skinning chickens for supper, a night-time trek while some 'real' army men endured a mock ambush nearby, sleeping on the floor in a barn with no heating or lighting, morning aerobics in the snow, and another assault course. Then we had to go home, and drive ourselves. The player who was driving me, Keith Newell, fell asleep at the wheel on the A470 just outside Pontypridd. Thanks to the screams of Mike Powell, who was in the front passenger seat, Newell somehow managed to regain control of the car after it had hit the central reservation. Somebody really should have considered how we were going to get home after such an exhausting weekend.

A lot of baloney is spouted about the value of such things, and a lot of money is wasted. Initially it was interesting to me that two of England's best performing players in the Ashes had not seemed to gain too much from the trip. Jonathan Trott certainly didn't gain anything: he didn't go at all. His wife was expecting their first child and it would not have been possible to return swiftly had she gone into labour. So Trott stayed at home, even though his wife didn't give birth during the trip. And

Alastair Cook missed the first three days because he was attending to best-man duties at his brother's wedding. He didn't box. 'All I did was go abseiling,' he said, 'and I'm not scared of heights at all!' Graeme Swann absolutely panned the exercise in his autobiography: 'For me, it was easily the worst four days of my life. I hated every minute of it.'

But over time I have spoken to some others who were there and they have convinced me more and more of the benefits of the trip. Talking around a night-time fire can be a bit of a dreamy cliché, but those who were there said that was the best and most valuable part of the trip. The players learnt a lot about each other. And the support staff learnt a lot about the players, and, crucially, vice versa.

The team psychologist Dr Mark Bawden, an Olympic Games veteran and lead psychologist for the English Institute of Sport, was on the trip, and, if nothing else, the experience helped him gain the trust of the players. I know Andy Flower was amazed at and delighted with how easily Bawden worked with the players in Germany. After this it was noticeable how Bawden's name began cropping up in player interviews. Take Cook's explanation of his return to form in 2010. 'I went back to my old technique and worked with our sports psychologist, Mark Bawden, at the same time,' he said in the summer of 2011. 'Everything clicked. There's always a bit of a stigma seeing the guy we call the "Head Doc", but the mental side of cricket is so powerful. I've improved a lot over the last six months in that area. A lot of what we discussed was quite personal but the basic idea is to improve confidence and understanding.'

But post-Germany was the first time Flower started to cop some genuine flak. Even his father noted the shift. 'I don't buy all the papers and have the internet but I could see that turn,' said Bill. Flower had been on the defensive before the trip even began. 'First of all, I wouldn't describe it as a boot camp,' he said after the final one-day international against Pakistan.

'That's got quite a lot of negative connotations. It is designed to educate all of us, to give us a good sense of perspective on things, to allow the guys to become more self-aware, and allow the guys to understand each other better. We can live in a cosseted world, in the sporting world, and this is there to broaden minds. It's not related to the Ashes at all, it's more about our development as a group of blokes.'

In private he was a little more animated. 'It wasn't a boot camp!' he insisted to me one day. It may have been prefaced by an expression that rhymes with 'clucking bell'. Flower considered it a success, and Anderson played in the first warm-up match against Western Australia, bowling thirty-three overs in all. So really the fuss was misplaced.

I had never been to Australia before. I wish I had. A year or two playing Grade cricket might have been good for me. And I will admit that I did not see England regain the Ashes this time either. I was home for Christmas, just, after some pleading with my very sympathetic employers at the *Telegraph* had resulted in my planned return after the third Test in Perth. The only trouble was that this was around the time of the awful Arctic weather in Britain, and when I arrived at Perth airport on the evening of Monday, 20 December for my flight to Hong Kong, I was informed that it had been cancelled. 'There might be some flights available on Christmas Eve,' said the ever-so-helpful lady. Shit. I was rather looking forward to seeing my family.

But thankfully the wonderful staff at Commodore, the *Telegraph*'s designated travel company, and indeed the generosity of the *Telegraph* itself which agreed to pay extra for my return flights, ensured that I could return home via Sydney, Abu Dhabi, Brussels and Birmingham. It took a while, of course, and when a couple of current Glamorgan players, Mark Wallace and Gareth Rees, kindly arrived at Birmingham to collect me (my wife was snowed in) they declared that I'd aged at least ten years. Grey stubble can do that. You'd think the cheeky bastards would have been happy with their bar of Toblerone each, mind!

When I left, the series score was 1–1. England had just been hammered in Perth. And at dinner on my last night there was some concern among the travelling press corps. I wasn't budging from my pre-series prediction, though, as I emphasized in my last blog before leaving: 'England should not be too down-hearted, I reckon. This was one pitch on which they were always going to struggle. They are simply not used to such conditions. And crucially the lynchpin of their bowling attack, Graeme Swann, was wholly negated. I still stick by my pre-series prediction that England will win the series 2–1. Perth was always marked down as an Australia win in my book. Of course some of us got a little overexcited after Adelaide but reality has now returned. The battle is on.'

Others were less confident. But I had always been confident. Cocky even. Before I left for Australia I'd penned a piece for my Final Whistle column for the *Daily Telegraph*. The nature of that column is that it can often be tongue-in-cheek, and that was certainly the tone of this piece, with some truth, of course, lurking beneath. 'So I will travel to Australia very soon in a rare state of excitement,' I wrote.

But I will also travel in a state of some bewilderment. I'll admit it: I just don't get all the fuss. Hype and history are producing a cocktail that I'm not willing to stomach.

I'm led to believe that I'm travelling to another planet where visiting bowlers regularly disappear, sucked into some Kookaburra vortex, where batsmen become quivering wrecks on pitches simply too fast and bouncy for them, surrounded by fielders with PhDs in sledging and crowds so frightening that they all had parts in the film *Psycho*. Pah. I'm with Flower (A) on this. 'I don't think there's anything to be afraid of in Australia,' he said before departure.

The truth is that somebody needs to say it: Australia are simply not very good any more. They are losing for fun at the moment. They are the new England. Even Grade cricket is said to be going soft. Just like we used to in the eighties and nineties, they now seem to pick players out of a hat. Last Sunday they played a T20 international with players from only two states. They lost. In the past two years 45 players have represented Australia in Tests, one-day internationals and T20s. And they've only got six domestic teams! No wonder they've just sacked Merv Hughes as a selector.

Of course, the Ashes rivalry is ever-enduring, and I am indebted to Huw Turbervill, of this parish, for producing his recent book *The Toughest Tour* (Aurum, £16.99), recording the 17 post-war tours. It is full of some marvellous anecdotes and tales, certainly not 'The Toughest Read' as one of his friends mischievously ventured.

But will this be England's toughest tour? No chance. It will, though, be good preparation. India, the world's No. 1 team, are coming next summer.

Ha! I'd even fitted in a nice little plug for my *Telegraph* colleague Turbervill.

The piece caused a little bit of fuss, though. 'Below the line', as the comments sections on blogs posted on papers' websites are described, there was not exactly agreement with my sentiments. 'Juvenile' was one of the more repeatable comments. 'Steve, you know this article is going to be copied and quoted all round the Australian media? And when you get there, everyone who speaks to you is going to give you a hard time about it,' said another. Flower wasn't happy either. 'Oh yes, sure, Australia are shit!' was the gist of his sarcastic reaction. At least he reads my stuff, I suppose, and I could see why he was not keen at this stage for anyone to denigrate the Australians.

But when I did get to Australia, there was very little comment.

My feeling was that the locals knew what was coming. Of course, there was some bluster, but it was unconvincing. When the day before the first Test one of the Australian coaching staff emerged from the Brisbane nets to exclaim 'We're gonna fuck 'em!' to a journalistic acquaintance of his, the scribe just smiled obediently. He simply didn't believe him. Nobody in Australia did, really.

I have mentioned England's preparation already. It was good. They beat Western Australia. South Australia might have been beaten had it not rained on the last afternoon, and then they thrashed Australia A with their second-choice bowling attack. It was on TV too. In Australia and England, for all to see.

All the matches were eleven-a-side and accorded first-class status. When the tour began England had not won a match in whites in Australia since the last Test in 2003, a consolation victory to make the series score 4–1. They hadn't won any warm-up games on that tour either, so you had to go back to Cairns in 1998 when they scraped home by one wicket against Queensland for their last warm-up victory in whites in Australia. You could see why skipper Andrew Strauss was so keen to take these games seriously and develop a winning habit. When they beat Western Australia in their opening game it was the first time they had won their opening first-class match of the tour since 1965/66 when M. J. K. Smith's side also beat Western Australia.

But I still think the value of the preparation was rather over-hyped. England did not start the first Test well. Indeed they conceded a first-innings lead of 221. And to me the whole series turned on the first ball of England's second innings. Had Strauss been deemed to be lbw, as he so nearly was to Ben Hilfenhaus, then he would have bagged a demoralizing pair. England might never have extricated themselves from such a mess. As it was, the decision of the quite brilliant Aleem Dar, who gave Strauss not out, was vindicated upon review. Strauss had left the ball on length not line, as it cut back into him. Cook, his partner, said to me later, 'I immediately thought "That's close!"' He just about agreed with Strauss's assertion that the ball was too high. And fortunately it was. The England captain survived. Australia got him eventually but not before he made a century, and that was their only success in the second innings, as Cook made 235 not out and Trott 135 not out.

England's preparation was thorough. Just as they had before the 2009 Ashes, the England management had had a series of dinners with various groups of players looking ahead to the Ashes. Nothing was overlooked, on or off the field, from how best to use the 'Pro-Batter' machine to replicate facing the Australian bowlers before leaving to coping with the opposition's sledging, from their attitude to Twitter to dealing with the media. There was a cute move on the latter issue when, during the build-up, the press were invited to attend a training session with the team in Hobart, organized by the team sponsors Brit Insurance. One journalist remarked beforehand that it was going to be a bit like Christmas Day in no-man's land during the Great War. We journalists are easily pleased. Usually some free food will do, so this was really laying it on. The lads got a free T-shirt too!

I'm actually glad I wasn't on tour at that stage. I wouldn't have wanted to be involved. Indeed I've every admiration for my *Telegraph* colleague Derek Pringle for showing up. It's no place for an ex-pro, that sort of thing. But those members of the press corps who do not play, or have not played, seemed to enjoy it. The trouble is that I suspect, nay know, that the players were laughing at rather than with the journos, as they made fools of themselves. It was said that it helped media relations throughout the tour, and all the pieces the next day were certainly over-flowing with 'love' for the England team. But that might have had something to do with the results. It's easier to be cordial on both sides when the team is winning.

One interesting snippet, though, to emerge from the day was evidence of the remarkable accuracy of Anderson's bowling. Bowling coach David Saker had explained to the assembled throng that only three types of ball were of any use in Australia: the bouncer aimed at the head, the yorker, and the ball hitting the top of off-stump. To demonstrate he called up Anderson. To order, Anderson delivered the bouncer, hitting the badge on the helmet of a model batsman, the ball to hit the top of off-stump, and then the yorker, passing under an iron bar raised six inches off the ground on the crease. Impressive stuff.

There was also a close-up look at Graham Gooch's new toy, a device designed by a cricket-mad farmer from Writtle near Chelmsford in Essex called Frank Thorogood that appears remarkably similar to the plastic slinger used by dog-walkers to throw balls for their mutts, but is in fact something called the 'Sidearm' and is used to give throwdowns to a batsman. Quick throwdowns, in fact, with less impact on the thrower's shoulder and a trajectory that is more like a bowler's.

The proceedings were also filmed by Swann on a video camera. This was actually the third of his Ashes diaries, but it was the one that attracted most attention. Not because of the wheezing journos – and butter-fingered in the case of the *Sun*'s John Etheridge, who, for a once half-decent cricketer, had an absolute shocker in the catching part of the day – but because of the Sprinkler dance that is shown towards the end of the video. England, courtesy of Paul Collingwood so it later emerged, had created a new team dance. I actually thought the funniest part of that video was at the beginning when Swann was doing press-ups – '998 . . . 999 . . . a thousand . . . agh, [as he punches the floor in pain] the deep burn!' – but then I've seen Swann in the gym.

The Sprinkler became the craze, instant confirmation of a squad that was relaxed and happy. When they retained the Ashes at Melbourne, the whole squad performed it in front of the Barmy Army in the Great Southern Stand. It's the sort of thing you can do when you're winning.

I have heard only one murmur of dissatisfaction regarding England's build-up: that there was no game in Brisbane for the bowling attack that was sent there instead of remaining in Hobart where Australia A were being hammered. It could have been done because the Performance Programme players were in Australia until Christmas. They played a Queensland XI in a four-day match in Brisbane starting the day before the Test. Indeed Chris Tremlett (and Eoin Morgan) played. It would have been nice had Anderson, Stuart Broad, Steven Finn and Swann been able to play in such a game rather than just netting in Brisbane. But it was still a shrewd move to send them on ahead. Just as shrewd was the open declaration of strength in depth. Tremlett, Tim Bresnan, Ajmal Shahzad and Monty Panesar formed an impressive quartet. As Flower presciently observed at the time, 'Without a doubt, I would say, one or two of those guys are going to be playing Test cricket in the next couple of months – you don't have situations where the same bowling attack, or certainly not very often, play five Tests in a row.'

Indeed two of them, Tremlett and Bresnan, did play Test cricket in the next couple of months. Bresnan took the wicket that retained the Ashes in Melbourne, and Tremlett took the wicket that clinched the series in Sydney. Both were quite magnificent. Both were clever picks.

Tremlett had not been in everyone's Ashes squad. He had long been another enigma in English cricket. It is easily forgotten that he was in England's squad for the 2005 Ashes. Duncan Fletcher reckoned him the best net bowler he'd ever seen. But when it came to the crunch, the Oval that year when Simon Jones was injured, he could not be trusted. Nor could Anderson for that matter.

England went with Collingwood instead, and he was forever mocked by Shane Warne for the MBE he received as a result of his seventeen runs in two innings and four wicketless overs. He might not have deserved it then, but he certainly deserved it by the time he called time on his Test career at the end of this series. He did not have the best of series with the bat, but, with his enthusiasm never dimming and his fielding always outstanding, he departed on a high, a cricketer termed no more than 'bits and pieces' when first backed by the wise Fletcher who became an integral part of a hugely successful side. 'Few things have given me as much pleasure in my coaching career than watching Collingwood repay the faith we showed in him as a Test player by producing the goods over the years,' said Fletcher after Collingwood had announced his retirement. As for the man himself, he said, 'If, at the start of my career, someone had offered me three Ashes series wins and ten Test hundreds, I would have bitten their hands off.' It was a neat way of summing up both his modesty and his substantial achievements.

Tremlett had taken longer to fulfil his talent, including a move from Hampshire to Surrey. To me it was more about confidence in his body than anything else. Constant injury can do that to you. But when Saker watched the beanpole bowl for the first time in the nets prior to the Pakistan Test at the Oval in August 2010, he knew what he was seeing. He'd watched just three balls when he turned to Flower and said, 'This guy is coming on the Ashes tour.'

Flower replied, 'You think so?'

'Well, what I've just seen is world-class,' said Saker.

He was right. When Broad's tour was ended in Adelaide with an abdominal tear, Tremlett was the obvious choice for the next Test at bouncy Perth. The management may well have been considering him anyway. They had seriously considered using Shahzad's skiddy reverse swing in Adelaide, but Finn's six wickets at Brisbane secured his place.

England's knowledge of Australia and its conditions was vast. First there was Saker, who had played in Melbourne for six seasons for Victoria and then been assistant coach for five years. As mentioned earlier, Flower had also played a season for South Australia in 2003/04, although injury ruined it and he did not return for two more scheduled years. And Strauss had, again as previously mentioned, lived in Melbourne briefly as a child, attending Caulfield Grammar School in 1985/86, and had played for Mosman in Sydney for two seasons from 1999 to 2001. Before that he had endured a rather less fruitful season on the field with Sydney University in 1998/99 when he had been mostly stuck in the third Grade side. But off the field he had met his wife-to-be, Australian actress Ruth – a chance meeting in the Bourbon and Beefsteak, one of the late-night bars in Sydney's King's Cross, during that first season.

Strauss was one of seven players (Cook, Pietersen, Collingwood, Bell, Panesar and Anderson being the others) who had suffered during the 2006/07 Ashes, but many of the squad had also experienced Australian Grade cricket. Pietersen had played for Sydney University in 2002/03 (unlike Strauss they'd decided to play him in the first team); Collingwood had not only appeared for Richmond in Victoria but won the prestigious Ryder Medal for the competition's player of the year; Bell had played for University in Perth in 2003/04, after being recommended by John Inverarity, his Warwickshire coach; Cook played for Willetton in Perth in 2003/04; and Panesar played for Glenelg Seahorses in South Australia in 2005/06. England were not exactly entering uncharted territories.

Bresnan had always been earmarked for Melbourne by Saker. The ball was always going to reverse-swing there, but Bresnan could make the new ball bounce and bowl accurately when England required.

That was why Finn was dropped for this Melbourne Test, despite having taken fourteen wickets in three Tests. He had simply become too expensive. And England's bowling plan was very simple: attack with the new ball and defend with the old until it started reverse-swinging. Sometimes this happened very quickly; indeed in the second innings at Melbourne as early as the eleventh over.

But that was because England's husbandry of the ball was an art in itself. After the new ball had finished swinging con-ventionally (say usually in the first fifteen overs), some overs were bowled of cross-seam so that once one side of the ball was sufficiently roughed, vigorous shining began on the other (usually from fifteen to thirty-five overs). Cook, who famously does not sweat, and Anderson were in charge, holding the ball between thumb and forefinger, ensuring that not a droplet of moisture touched the ball. Hopefully for about twenty overs the ball would reverse-swing. And then for another twenty-five overs until the next new ball at eighty, England might have to revert to parsimony.

This rendered all the pre-tour fuss about the Kookaburra ball redundant (England use the Duke ball at home but had practised with Kookaburras frequently before leaving), especially about Anderson's average in Australia being 82 before the tour. He lowered it to just under 36 with twenty-four wickets, the most in Australia since Frank Tyson's twenty-eight in the 1954/55 series. Such was his timing and imperturbability that he also managed to pop home midway through the series to be at the birth of his second daughter, Ruby.

Twitter is a wonderfully modern medium, so when my colleague Scyld Berry tweeted thus: 'James Anderson has taken most wickets in a five-Test series here since Frank Tyson. Tyson was The Typhoon. Anderson is a Piercing Draught', you knew people were getting excited. About Anderson. And social networking sites.

The debate over four bowlers or five was also silenced. A lot of people, especially Berry, kept maintaining beforehand that England could not win in Australia with four bowlers. 'The last time England won an Ashes series in Australia with only four bowlers – and no all-rounder or fifth bowler of any kind – was in 1911-12,' Berry wrote, 'when grounds were open to nature. Relying on four bowlers in Australian heat, when the pitches and the make of ball favour batsmen, will put an immense strain on England's three seamers.'

Yes, it was one of Australia's cooler and wetter summers, indeed the coolest and wettest in some parts, but that should not be used as an excuse by the apologists. England were simply the better side. And you still need to score more runs than the opposition. As Strauss wrote in his Ashes diary, 'We've examined a lot of information on England teams in the past, and the statistics say that when England play five bowlers, they lose more games and they don't win any more. So the theory that it's a positive move and it's more likely to win you games doesn't stack up.'

Of course, England had some luck too. They managed to wrap up the second Test on a day recorded as Adelaide's wettest ever in December. They took the last Australian wicket at 11.27 a.m., and only a few hours later the nearby River Torrens was bursting its banks, such was the ferocity of the storms that lashed the ground.

Australia also lost their dependable opener Simon Katich after that Test to an Achilles tendon injury. And England could have lost Swann before the series had his thumb been broken rather than just bruised in the spicy nets at Perth.

And, less to do with luck but just as important, Ricky Ponting had a stinker of a series, averaging just 16, and that only because he made 51 not out when England were going through the motions at the drawn death in Brisbane. I thought before the start of the tour that he was slipping down the other side of the batting mountain, and that the series could be decided on how far that slide was from the apex of greatness. It was further than anyone could have imagined. His decision to play in

Melbourne with a fractured finger was typical of the fighter he has always been, but though he was heeding the advice of my friend Mr Thomas of Laugharne about raging against the dying of the light, his rage merely cost him 40% of his match fee for his remonstrations with umpire Dar over an unsuccessful caught-behind appeal against Kevin Pietersen. That's what can happen when you lose the Ashes three times. It didn't help that his long-determined deputy Michael Clarke averaged only 21 in the series as well.

There were also some unfathomable selections from the Australians. When they announced a squad of seventeen for the first Test, there was mirth unconfined, even if the huge number was as much to do with the desire of Cricket Australia's marketeers to hold a bells-on Ashes launch in Sydney, with a round of the Sheffield Shield still to go before the first Test, as much as the selectors' uncertainty.

But none of that explained the choice of left-arm spinner Xavier Doherty for the first and second Tests, or of Steven Smith at number six in Perth and Melbourne (he moved to number seven in Sydney), or of the clearly rather-too-well-fed Doug Bollinger in Adelaide.

Doherty's inclusion can have been for no other reason than to try and exploit Pietersen's sinistrophobia. We knew that Australia had had problems with spinners since the retirement of Warne, but this was ridiculous. Doherty was as ordinary as baked beans on toast. Indeed he was the ninth spinner they'd tried since Warne. Another shock selection and another left-armer, Michael Beer, became the tenth in Sydney. He'd been called up for the third Test at Perth, the selectors desperately claiming that it was because it was his home ground that he had been picked. It was as if he'd been bowling at the WACA since he was a nipper. He hadn't. He's actually from Melbourne and had only moved to Western Australia that season.

One of my great regrets of the series was that it rained after tea on the third day of that second Test at Adelaide. Pietersen was 213 not out, having made his first century for England since March 2009. He'd had one early scare when he got a leading edge off the spinner over cover, but by now he was treating Doherty with the sort of regard a schoolyard bully reserves for a newly arrived bespectacled nerd with a basin-bowl haircut. He was destroying him. I am convinced Pietersen would have made 300 by the close. As it was, he was dismissed for 227 the next day, but England won, with what Flower described as the 'perfect game', and with Swann taking five wickets. I think I might have mentioned that the latter might happen in my pre-match blog (or at least Swann's excited and very proud father Ray said I did when I saw him later, so that's good enough for me).

It was a busy trip. Or three Tests anyway. Blogs, daily pieces, Sunday pieces, even a debut in the Oped page of the newspaper (that is, the page opposite the editorial page). The Ashes must have been big news. So as I was heading out for dinner after the second Test had been won in Adelaide, I received a call asking if I could do a piece on how Australia as a nation was coping with defeat, especially as they had just lost out to Qatar in their bid to host the 2022 Football World Cup.

'To be a Pom in Australia right now is to dip oneself in Schadenfreude every morning,' I wrote. 'It is to walk into the Adelaide Oval and hear the gateman joke about the size of the crowds – "There must be a game on here today" – and respond with: "Yeah, but there's not much of a contest."

'The strange thing, though, is not just that the 24 years of hurt since England last won an Ashes series Down Under may be about to end. It is the way that the roles have been reversed. In response to my gag, the gateman just shrugged his shoulders. Negativity, it seems, is at last entering the Australian sporting psyche.'

Of course, very soon the Perth Test was being won and I could easily have been selecting whether I wanted the egg on my face scrambled, poached or fried. Mitchell Johnson, who'd been dropped for Adelaide, returned to the Australia side and produced a truly devastating spell of fast left-arm swing bowling, taking four wickets for just seven runs and turning the match on its head.

But it was a mere blip. By tea on Boxing Day the resignation had returned. There had been talk of a record crowd, but in the end the 84,345 on the first day at Melbourne could not surpass the 90,800 that attended the first day of the West Indies MCG Test in 1961. It didn't even beat the 2006 total of 89,155 when it was freezing cold and England were already 3–0 down.

But by just after tea there were many fewer than 84,345 in the MCG. It was estimated that some thirty thousand had already left in disgust. England had won the toss and, after some deliberation, bowled. It was a decent decision. In just 42.5 overs Australia were all out for 98, and by the close of the first day England were 157-0. Sisyphus had better days with his boulder than Australia had there. You just don't recover from that sort of position. By just before noon on the fourth day it was all over, and England had retained the Ashes for the first time for twenty-four years.

The celebrations were quite rightly long and hard. But if anyone was worried that, with the urn retained, England might relax a little in Sydney, they only had to refer back to preparations before the Melbourne Test. England had trained on Christmas Day, but not with the usual frivolity, with laughing photos taken with Santa hats on. England had practised as usual. When it comes to cricket, Flower just doesn't do frivolity.

It was right and proper that England won in Sydney by an innings and 83 runs. To win three Tests by an innings was not only unprecedented but also a fair reflection of England's superiority. The humiliation was duly completed, as Australia batted first when England would have bowled, and were summarily dismissed for 280. In reply England made 644. Yes,

644. It was their third highest total against Australia, and their highest in Australia. Cook made 189, taking him to 766 runs for the series (only Wally Hammond with 905 in 1928/29 has made more for England in any series) and making it a rather simple decision that he should be the recipient of the Compton-Miller Medal. Bell made his first Ashes hundred and Prior made a century off just 109 balls.

Australia made one more run in the second innings, 281, than their first, but just before midday on the final day it was all over when Tremlett dismissed Beer – 'replacing Beer with champagne', as one or two writers observed. England had won the Ashes, and were now ranked third in the world.

13

The Triumvirate

When Enland won in Melbourne, the first person Strauss had mentioned in interview was Flower. 'He has been immense,' the England captain said. 'He is an incredible bloke, a guy that we all respect hugely for what he has achieved but also for how he holds himself in the dressing room. Often you can't describe what he brings to the side because it is just a multitude of things, little conversations he has with people and little thoughts he puts on to paper that he actually brings into fruition in practice. The way he works with the team and back-room staff is as good as anything I have seen.'

Flower's contribution was all the more remarkable given that he had missed the second and third days of the first Test of Brisbane. A stomach bug maybe? No, skin cancer.

Gulp.

As a journalist you are obviously not supposed to reveal your sources, but I think this is an exception worth making without causing offence or rancour. I was staying in Brisbane at the Royal on the Park Hotel, and on the second morning I was waiting in reception for some colleagues to go to the ground. The huge figure who appeared through the doors was unmistakeable, if a little out of context. It was Eddo Brandes, Zimbabwe's famous chicken farmer who had destroyed England's batting on more than one occasion. He is now a tomato farmer on the Sunshine Coast.

We got chatting.

'Have you seen Andy?' I asked.

'Yes, he's in hospital having a melanoma removed.'

What?!

'I probably shouldn't have told you that,' said Brandes.

Well, it was a scoop, but it was also a shock. Even the most hardened hack would surely consider the health of their friend first. And Flower is a friend. But it was rather awkward because he was also team director of the cricket squad I was being paid to comment on, find stories on, praise and sometimes lambast.

'Is he OK?' was my only thought.

I got to the ground and made some calls. Later that afternoon I spoke to Flower himself. He was back at the team hotel watching the game on TV, with the volume turned down because of the local commentators' bias (it was that rare moment when Australia were in command). He was clearly in a lot of pain, because the operation had been performed under local anaesthetic. He said he could feel them scraping at his cheek. It was the only time I have ever detected any frailty in him. He was scared. But who could blame him?

Just consider the words of Dr Shobhan Manoharan, who operated on Flower in Brisbane, commenting on security adviser Reg Dickason's advice that Flower should get the growth under his right eye checked even though it had been there for eighteen months and he had previously received an all-clear from a dermatologist in the UK. 'For that reason, I suspect that Andy probably wouldn't have gone for another check-up for quite a while,' Dr Manoharan said. 'It's no exaggeration to say that Reg Dickason probably saved his life. I know that the England team have extremely busy schedules, so it was fortunate for everyone that we were able to get him in this week.'

Nobody had noticed on that second day that Flower was absent. Nobody in the written media, that is. During the afternoon whispers were starting to emanate from the broadcast media, who, of course, have the privilege of being out on the field before play starts, and so interact with the players a lot more. The story was not going to hold long. So I put it to Flower that I write it. He was worried because of our close relationship. He didn't want it looking like he'd given his mate a scoop. So he asked James Avery, England's excellent media liaison officer, to release the story through the Press Association. It may just have been on the *Telegraph* website a few moments before it was anywhere else.

Flower spoke to the media when the team had moved to Adelaide for the second Test. His press conference, deep in the bowels of the Intercontinental Hotel alongside the River Torrens, was a truly humbling experience for anyone present. 'I always feel lucky, every morning,' said Flower when asked whether he felt lucky that the melanoma had been diagnosed so swiftly. 'Seriously, I do. We are really lucky to be involved in cricket and get paid for it and I've always felt like that as a player. We've got so much to appreciate.'

Flower looked awful, with a large V-shaped sticking plaster over a wound with some fifty-five micro-stitches in it. 'I was surprised by being worried as much as I was,' he admitted. And, of course, he did have Hugh Morris for support and advice. 'Hugh had a much more serious issue and he was a great guy to have around,' Flower said. 'But it was more worrying for my family because they're miles away. They would have liked to have been here with me.' Mind you, if his mother Jean had been there she might have had some stern words for him. 'I don't want to make my parents feel guilty but when I was a child we were always out in the sun, all day every day, and we never used sunscreen,' he said.

Jean disagrees. When I phoned to ask if I could speak to her and Bill for the purposes of this book, she said enthusiastically, 'Yes, I'd like to put the record straight!' She would like to say that she did put suncream on her children, even if it was 'only Zimbabwean' stuff and maybe not as potent in blocking the sun's UV rays as cream purchased in more developed countries. Andrew, you have been told.

What with Bill also suffering his New Year's Day heart attack, it was a seriously stressful winter for Flower. I worried for him. It was why in January 2011 I wrote a piece suggesting he needed a break. All the talk was of how the team was tired, and indeed they were, but what about the coach? 'It was a year ago on Monday that England completed their winter tour of South Africa,' I wrote.

Since then, not including today's first one-day international in Melbourne, they have played 43 international cricket matches: that is 13 Tests, 17 one-day internationals and 13 T20 internationals.

It says much about England's improvements and consistent quality that they have lost just 10 of those matches. But it also says much about the crowded international itinerary that not one player has appeared in all 43 matches.

The closest are Paul Collingwood and Graeme Swann, with 40 appearances each, but both had to be rested last year, Collingwood skipping two home Tests against Bangladesh (he also missed a one-day international against Pakistan at the Oval due to a virus) and Swann being left out of the three home ODIs against Bangladesh.

Stuart Broad is next with 35, having sat out the same home Tests as Collingwood, while missing an ODI in Bangladesh with back trouble and then, of course, leaving the Ashes tour after the second Test with a nasty torn stomach muscle injury.

Modern cricket schedules simply do not allow players to stay on the treadmill all year. Collingwood is now to hop off for Tests, Andrew Strauss has done so for T20s for some time, but for the remainder their wellbeing and longevity are at the discretion of the team management. Like it or not, rest and rotation must now be an accepted part of international cricket.

Which brings me to England team director Andy Flower. When does the man doling out the rest periods get a rest himself?

Flower left home on Oct 28 and will fly back on Feb 7. Then there will be four nights in his own bed before leaving for Bangladesh and the World Cup. All being well, and England reaching the final, he will return home on April 3. Consider also that Flower will be away for around 100 nights next summer and that amounts to more than 250 nights away in a year.

Compare that with other sports. This year, a Rugby World Cup year, will be a busy one for Martin Johnson and his England coaching staff, but even if his team reach the final in Auckland on Oct 23 [which they didn't, of course, being knocked out in the quarter-finals], they are unlikely to be away for more than 180 nights during the year. And Johnson is reportedly on a higher salary than Flower. Fabio Capello? An obscene annual wage of £6 million for, so I'm reliably informed, just 64 nights abroad last year, including the World Cup in South Africa.

Flower did miss a one-day match in Ireland at the end of the India Test series in 2011, but he might have also liked to miss the Ireland match in Belfast in 2009, three days after the Ashes had been won. As Swann said of that, 'It was ridiculous that we went to Ireland the day after the final Test.

'All credit to the fellas who actually went out there and performed in Ireland because I know I didn't; I was in no fit state to play a game of cricket two days after the Ashes and that's how it should be, I think.

'The sad thing is that you don't get that England rugby

moment when they all got to fly home with the World Cup, passing it around. That would have been quite nice. But when it comes to cricket's schedules, there's not a lot you can do.'

I wasn't sure about too much celebration in 2009, but in 2010/11 they certainly deserved a fanfare. But they didn't get it. Instead they had to play two T20 internationals and seven ODIs out in Australia. They were knackered. But it was nothing new. In 2006/07 England had actually played ten ODIs against Australia and New Zealand before heading off to the World Cup in the West Indies. And it could have been eleven had they not beaten Australia 2–0 in the best-of-three Commonwealth Bank Series finals. Remember also that they had been at the Champions Trophy in India before the Ashes.

Understandably Flower was not happy. 'There will be a communication between me and the people who decide on these itineraries,' he said. And there clearly has been communication. The itinerary has been altered. It does mean that there will be back-to-back Ashes series home and away in 2013/14, but the cycle will be broken. Henceforth England will not arrive at World Cups broken.

The next World Cup is in Australia and New Zealand in February and March 2015. That winter England will play two T20s and five ODIs in Sri Lanka before Christmas, then go to Australia in the middle of January to play five ODIs as preparation for the tournament.

They will have a damned sight more of a chance than England did in 2011 in Asia. They were tired, and without their best one-day batsman Morgan, who had broken a finger in the very last ODI in Australia. But they were also confused. They were confused as to their best side. One match into the one-day series in Australia they had been forced by the ICC to name their World Cup squad, and had decided to pick Prior as opener, thereby dropping Steven Davies, who had done decently against Pakistan at the end of the previous summer.

The trouble was that Prior didn't do very well, so then the decision was made to open with Pietersen. And then he was injured, and had to go home after South Africa had been beaten in Chennai. Morgan returned, but it was too late. The Netherlands had already pushed England close with a score of 292, and Ireland had famously beaten them in Bangalore. Now Bangladesh beat them too. The quarter-finals were reached, but Sri Lanka strolled through by ten wickets. It was time for that drawing board to be revisited. England were still, according to the rankings, fifth in the world in ODIs. It was time for a new captain.

It had been flagged up by the *Mail on Sunday* during the tournament that Strauss was intending to step down, a story dismissed by Strauss in a TV interview as 'strange journalism'. Well, it wasn't strange, even if it pains me to add another feather to the cap covering the bald pate of the lovable Peter 'Reg' Hayter, who reckons he's scooped the resignation of every England captain since W. G. Grace decided at Trent Bridge in 1899 that fifty might be a little elderly to be skippering one's country.

It was right that Strauss went. It was time for Cook to have his chance. It was simply not possible to play both of them in the same one-day team, especially with the next man in the order being Trott, who was still being criticized as England flew home even though he was then the tournament's leading run-scorer. Clichéd or not, World Cups are staging posts. England had lost captains after the previous three World Cups (Alec Stewart in 1999, Nasser Hussain in 2003 and Michael Vaughan in 2007), and they duly lost another when Strauss eventually announced his resignation about a month later. It was his decision, but I'm pretty sure it was a decision with which Flower agreed.

Cook was made one-day captain, and in a ground-breaking tripartite arrangement (Strauss was still, of course, Test captain), Broad was given the Twenty20 captaincy. Cook's promotion was in general lampooned. I just couldn't understand the negativity of the response. Yes, he'd made a shambolic beginning in international captaincy in a Twenty20 international against South Africa at Centurion in 2009, but, as mentioned earlier, in Bangladesh in 2010 he had improved. And I always thought his batting could expand even further than Strauss's, who had made such strides after taking the one-day captaincy in 2009. Strauss was thirty-two then; Cook was only twenty-six. The evidence was immediate: England beat Sri Lanka 3–2 in the first series of the 2011 summer, and Cook made 298 runs with one century at an average of 74.50 and a strike rate of 96.75. In his previous twenty-six ODIs his strike rate had been 71.38. In the following five-match series against India England won 3–0, with a tie and an abandonment. Cook made 169 runs at 42.25, with a strike rate of 94.41. Of course, his side were then thrashed 5–0 out in India and he only made 133 runs at an average of 26.60. But at least his strike rate was 84.71. And even better was to come when Cook made two successive centuries and an 80 (at a strike rate of 88.36) in the first three matches of the series against Pakistan in the United Arab Emirates in February 2012.

Most notable among Cook's critics was my old university mate Mike Atherton, who'd described him as a batting 'plodder' and a fielding 'donkey'. Cook was furious, and so were the England management. They were harsh observations before Cook had even taken the job. But in fairness Atherton's comments were made on Sky's *Cricket Writers on TV* programme, which often lends itself to light-heartedness. He would not have used such words in print. And he was actually criticizing himself because he was worried that Cook might be another one-day captain not really worth his place, just like himself, Hussain, Vaughan and Strauss before.

Cook could not then justify a place in the Twenty20 side, but Collingwood was still captain in that format, captain of the world champions no less, and was unceremoniously sacked. Collingwood was devastated. It was 'like a juggernaut had come along at full steam and completely wiped me out', he said. 'I understand the thinking that the team moves forward and people only have a certain shelf-life. But it doesn't make it any easier to take and it doesn't mean I agree with it. I'm still very disappointed and hurt by what has happened.'

Again it was the right decision. During the World Cup Collingwood's body had been telling him things he did not want to know. Niggle had followed niggle. I could understand his disappointment, because it didn't just mean that he wasn't Twenty20 captain any more. It meant his whole international career was over. But again, that was the right decision.

If you think I am constantly praising Flower's decisions for the sake of it, then please think again. It is just that he, and indeed Strauss, just seem to make good calls. They make big calls too. This was a big call from Flower. As was dropping Pietersen at the end of the 2010 summer from the one-day internationals against Pakistan. He also missed two T20s, but that was because the second of them in Cardiff coincided with the start of a championship match for Surrey against Glamorgan at the Oval that Flower wanted Pietersen to play in in order to begin his long-form preparation for the Ashes. It was the T20 stuff that upset Pietersen most, prompting a Twitter outburst, which was quickly deleted but still landed him with a fine from the ECB. 'Done for rest of summer!! Man of the World Cup T20 and dropped from the T20 side too. Its a fuck up!!' he'd written.

Pietersen was also dropped for the India one-dayers at the end of 2011. It was said he was rested, but that was rubbish. He was dropped because he had simply not scored enough runs. Just check the figures: in 2009 in seven innings he had scored 132 runs (average 18.86), in 2010 in nine innings he made just 153 (17.00), and in 2011 in fourteen innings before being left out he scored 401 (28.64). And he still had not got a century in ODIs since his 111 not out in Cuttack in 2008, and, as one of the coaching staff present that night has pointed out to me since, even that innings was too slow (taking 128 balls), as England's 270-4 was easily picked off in just 43.4 overs by the Indians. But at least in February 2012 Pietersen got that elusive century when he made 111 not out against Pakistan in Dubai, then adding another hundred in the very next game.

There had been a lot of talk in the previous year of his one-day retirement, but he couldn't do that. It would have meant he could not have a central contract (Collingwood's Test retirement was different: both parties agreed on that). The ECB had him by the balls. So when Morgan was still injured for the away ODI series in India in the autumn of 2011, they picked Pietersen again. He only did reasonably. His 170 runs at 42.50 in four innings (he missed the last game with a broken thumb) still only took his average for the calendar year to 31.72.

Flower made another good decision in omitting Broad from the final one-dayer against Sri Lanka in 2011. He had not been bowling well, and it was said it was a tactical decision to omit him for Samit Patel on a dry Old Trafford pitch. But it was a rocket fired up Broad's backside. He went back to Nottinghamshire, and realized that he had been bowling too short. I actually always thought he was a hit-the-pitch type bowler, but he turned up for the first Test at Lord's against India with his place in jeopardy and suddenly swung the ball like Fred Trueman, taking seven wickets in the match.

Flower had been intrigued by Broad as a leader ever since an internal twenty-five-over-per-side warm-up match in the West Indies in 2009. He made Broad and Anderson skippers of the two sides in a match at the Everest club ground in Georgetown, Guyana, and the results were interesting. Before the start of the match Broad took Flower aside and asked whether he could expose some team-mates' weaknesses. There were some players he wanted to bounce, and he also wanted to test Pietersen's recently discovered aversion to left-arm spinners.

So when Pietersen came to the crease, Broad immediately

summoned Strauss to bowl his filthy left-arm spinners – and they are filthy because I faced them once in a Glamorgan v. Middlesex match that was fizzling out into a draw. One ball very nearly bounced twice. Thankfully Strauss didn't get me out, and Pietersen didn't succumb in Guyana either. But the skipper – the real skipper that is, rather than Broad – did only concede five runs from his over. Flower took note. Of Broad's captaincy, not Strauss's bowling, that is.

As I mentioned, this split captaincy could not have happened under Fletcher. His successful model of the coach being the consultant required one strong leader, with whom Fletcher formed a tight-as-a-drumskin relationship. Even during the brief Hussain/Vaughan overlap in 2003 there were problems.

But Flower operates in a very different system. The ECB now consider Fletcher's model 'old-fashioned', and Flower more accountable than Fletcher was. He is conspicuously in charge. And that has suited Strauss. It did not suit Vaughan when Peter Moores wanted to act similarly, and it certainly would not have suited Hussain.

If there was surprise at England's three captains, it was nothing compared to the shock I got while travelling up to Chelmsford on 27 April to interview Ravi Bopara, whom I'd been told was going to play in the first Test of the 2011 summer, against Sri Lanka, as England were worried about a safety-valve bowling option at number six after Collingwood's Test retirement. And I'm sure that was the plan. But Morgan's 193 for the Lions against Sri Lanka at Derby, just after returning from the Indian Premier League, was a scream that could not be ignored.

Anyway, somewhere between Newport and Paddington on that April day, I received a text message: 'Fletcher has taken India job'. I was genuinely shocked. My next thought was 'Well, he doesn't listen to me anyway.' Not that he should, of course. But he had sought my advice. I'd told him he'd be mad to take it. I'd even written a piece which, without referring to Fletcher because that would have broken a confidence, tried to warn him off.

In it I'd talked about India's superiority in world cricket, on and off the field. They were, and still are, World Cup champions. Then they were ranked number one in Tests, and had just had five players – Virender Sehwag, Sachin Tendulkar, V. V. S. Laxman, Mahendra Singh Dhoni and Zaheer Khan – selected for *Wisden's* Test XI in its 2011 edition. The same publication had named its Leading Cricketer in the World as Tendulkar, and in both 2009 and 2010 it was Sehwag. I'd talked about Gary Kirsten and how well he had done as coach, especially as he had so little experience when appointed in late 2007. He was simply missing his family too much and had returned to South Africa, where he was very soon appointed national coach. 'India now enter the coaching marketplace,' I'd continued, 'along with Sri Lanka, Bangladesh and South Africa [obviously before Kirsten's appointment there].

Presumably there are some busy cricketing agents at the moment, as well as some excited out-of-work coaches. But I wouldn't be too excited about the India job if I were them. It is surely the proverbial hiding to nothing.

It is a fiendishly difficult job, as two other foreigners, John Wright and especially Greg Chappell, found before Kirsten. Chappell attempted radical change, in particular the removal of captain Sourav Ganguly, and very quickly discovered the meaning of player power. The players are everything in Indian cricket. They are idolized to an extent that we find difficult to comprehend in this country, and so no coach can ever be bigger than them. It is the trickiest of balances, with the public's fascination and obsession easily turned to vitriolic condemnation on a whim.

For this current crop wealth and immortality are now secured. For a new coach there is only one way for the team to go, and that is downwards. A trip to the West Indies in June soon should not cause too many problems, but the visit over here to England this summer could.

I will be surprised if England do not win the four-Test series. Hopefully, as we speak, groundsmen around the country will have their thoughts and energies focused upon producing pitches with pace and bounce. That should give England the edge. Home advantage should be just that.

Well, I got the last bit right anyway, about the series result (and at the time endured the most fearful and unrelenting volleys of abuse from India's notoriously one-eyed fans) and the type of pitches produced. But I didn't get through to Fletcher.

Kirsten was a far more persuasive influence. He had been charged with helping find his own replacement. He had met with Flower over breakfast during the World Cup. Did that help Flower when he sat down with Morris at the end of that tournament to discuss the financial details of his future employment? Maybe, but not because Flower would have used it as a bargaining tool. He is not like that. The plan was to talk with Morris anyway. Flower always wanted to remain loyal to England.

Kirsten had spoken with Fletcher at length. They have always done that. They had first met at the University of Cape Town where Fletcher began his coaching career. Kirsten was batting down the order, bowling occasional off-spinners and having a lot of fun at the bar. Fletcher took him aside one day and told him he was good enough to play for Western Province as a batsman. Kirsten laughed initially, but eventually began to believe in himself and his coach. Kirsten's father had just passed away, so Fletcher became his father figure.

When Kirsten became a coach, it was Fletcher to whom he turned. 'The coach is not the man to sit on the parapets in cricket – it's not like soccer,' Kirsten told me in 2008 during England's one-day tour of India. 'Duncan taught me that. He was a great mentor to me as a player, and now he is as a coach.'

The truth is that Kirsten was the only person who could have persuaded Fletcher back into full-time international coaching. 'I just don't think I could do the year-round touring these days,' Fletcher had told me as recently as early 2010. Of course, the money was a huge factor. It made him the highest paid coach ever in world cricket. Fletcher was sixty-two when he took the India job. It was always going to be his last post. He has two grandchildren whom he adores. He wanted to make sure they are provided for.

Kirsten was adamant in his talks with Fletcher that it would be a very different role from that which he had undertaken with England. He would not be heavily involved in selection; he would only have to do minimal media duties. As well as all that, Eric Simons, whom Fletcher once described as a 'legend' from their times together at Western Province, was remaining initially as bowling coach.

'You were the only one who advised me not to do it,' Fletcher told me. 'Just like Crofty with the England job!' I was worried about the stress it might cause him, as much as anything. Marina has had her health problems, and, having been out to his new home in Hermanus during England's tour to South Africa in 2009/10, it was obvious how relaxed and happy he was. He lives between the sea and the golf course, and his study, overlooking the 15th green with the Olifantsberg mountains in the distance, possesses the most stunning view.

But he wanted one last challenge. This was it. To bring India, the number one ranked Test team in the world, to England. 'Fletcher v Flower. A big summer just got bigger,' I wrote.

Or so we thought anyway. First India went to the West Indies with a depleted side. They won the one-day series 3–2 and the three-Test series 1–0 but were far from convincing. Five days after the conclusion of that third Test in Roseau, Dominica, they were playing Somerset in a three-day match at Taunton, with Strauss playing as a guest for the home side.

I could not believe there was such criticism of Strauss playing in that match. As mentioned earlier, for me it was a rare occasion when county cricket was paying heed to the importance of the England cricket team. Without that match he would have had just one county championship match in the month between the third Test against Sri Lanka at Southampton and the first against India at Lord's. He'd struggled in that rain-ruined Sri Lanka series, which England won 1–0 thanks to an astonishing collapse by the Sri Lankans on the last afternoon in Cardiff, where they were all out for 82 in just 24.4 overs, making just twenty-seven runs in four innings. He needed the practice and got it at Taunton, making 78 and 109 not out in the match.

But as he and Arul Suppiah were putting on 101 in the first innings it was already becoming clear that this was not an India side straining at the leash for the fight. They looked tired even then, with their bowling looking as flat as a can of Coca-Cola opened the day before. I spoke to Fletcher afterwards. 'They'll be up for Lord's,' he said, while also making the very sound point that those criticizing India's attitudes to fitness and preparation (they do not exactly adhere to the old 'Fail to prepare, prepare to fail' mantra) were missing the point that Indian teams have always been like that. They were like that under Kirsten, even when winning the World Cup. I recall shaking my head on numerous occasions during that tournament, and wondering about the justice and indeed validity of a team so poor in the field and between the wickets in winning the tournament. But that is cricket's paradox: unfit cricketers can sometimes prosper. I'm not sure W. G. Grace would have done too well on the Bleep Test.

I remember talking to Kirsten about this fitness issue among the Indians in 2008. He was, and still is, a complete fitness fanatic, and had taken his friend, Paddy Upton, the former South Africa fitness trainer, to India with him to work on that, but it was a difficult process of education. 'We're trying to bring in new thinking,' he said, 'but we're not going to force them [the India players] to do it. For instance after a game Paddy might say to those that haven't played: "I'm running a shuttle school. If you want to come, come." They're physically different. They must play the game their own way. They play with enormous flair, and they've got great hands on the ball. We've got to encourage that.' It was good, then, to see how athletic the young India side, missing the likes of Sehwag, Tendulkar and Yuvraj Singh, was in the 5–0 win over England at home. Trevor Penney's influence was stamped all over some of the performances.

The Lord's Test that opened England's series against India in the summer of 2011 was not just the beginning of the fight for the number one spot in Test cricket, it was also notable for a host of other reasons. It was the 2,000th Test of all time, the 100th between England and India, and, indeed, Fletcher's 100th Test as an international coach. Tendulkar also stood on ninety-nine centuries in all international cricket – a rather contrived statistic, I grant you, because Test and one-day numbers are rarely joined together, but a remarkable statistic nonetheless, and one which kept us journalists waiting excitedly all summer. The Tendulkar colour piece was done many, many times before it became obvious that, just like for his team as a whole, it wasn't going to happen. He returned home early during the one-day series, the eighth Indian to do so in a bewildering injury roll call: Gautam Gambhir (concussion while fielding during the Oval Test), Harbhajan Singh (stomach muscle), Zaheer (hamstring), Yuvraj (finger), Sehwag (shoulder that was still troubling him when he arrived late and promptly made that king pair), Ishant Sharma (ankle) and Rohit Sharma (finger).

If Tendulkar was the highest-profile departure, then the left-armer Zaheer was the most important and most untimely. It was obvious beforehand that India were going to rely heavily on him, so when he limped off at Lord's after bowling just 13.3 overs, and having bowled superbly in swinging conditions to dismiss both England openers it has to be said, the omens for the rest of the series were not exactly propitious. The suspicion then was that India would not be able to bowl England out too often in the series.

That was certainly the case. They did bowl England out twice at Trent Bridge but on the first day the pitch had more kick than a startled horse. England were fortunate that Broad and Swann dragged them from the mire with a partnership of 73 to take the total to 221. And in the second innings England had made 544, with Bell, promoted to number three through an injury to Trott, making a magnificent 159, before they were dismissed.

Otherwise India did not look like bowling England out, and some huge scores were amassed. At Lord's in the first Test Pietersen made a double-century, in the third at Edgbaston Cook ground out a mammoth 294, and at the Oval Bell made his first Test double-century. What with Trott making an invaluable 70 at Lord's when conditions were tough before succumbing to a shoulder injury at Trent Bridge, Morgan making a century at the Oval, Prior blasting a rapid century at Lord's, Strauss eventually finding form with 87 in a 186-run opening partnership at Edgbaston, and even Bresnan making 90 at Trent Bridge, it was a summer in which England's batsmen resided on Mount Olympus.

Only the remarkable Rahul Dravid among the Indians joined them, a solid brick 'Wall' among a team of sandcastles. The rest simply could not cope with England's aggression, accuracy and relentlessness. Some of them, especially Suresh Raina, Yuvraj and to a lesser extent Abhinav Mukund, played the short ball as if suddenly placed in front of a firing squad.

England's bowlers were feasting on ambrosia and nectar too. They also quite liked the 2009 and 2010 batches of Duke balls rather than the 2011 versions which didn't swing as much. This was another example of England's attention to detail. They used the 2010 balls until stocks ran out, then switched to those from 2009.

Broad took a hat-trick at Trent Bridge (in the middle of a spell of five wickets for no runs no less) just when India looked like fashioning a decent first-innings lead, ending the series with twenty-five wickets at 13.84. Anderson, now consistently world-class, took twenty-one wickets at 25.71, and Bresnan, who could easily have played instead of Broad in the first Test but missed out and only then played in the remaining Tests because of injury to Tremlett, took sixteen wickets at 16.31. At the end of 2011 Bresnan had played in ten Tests and England had won all of them. For Bresnan read England – almost disbelievingly brilliant.

When England won the final Test at the Oval, with India entirely out of pluck by then, by an innings and 8 runs, it was England's seventh victory by an innings in their last thirteen Tests. The closest India had come in their 4–0 drubbing had been losing by 196 runs in the first Test at Lord's. Ouch.

England became the number one team in the world on a weekend at Edgbaston, having achieved the aim required before-hand of winning the series by at least two Tests. It was on Saturday, 13 August 2011, in fact, that they won the third Test. The journey from Sunday, 22 August 1999 had certainly been long and eventful.

I'll not pretend I was there when they won by an innings and 242 runs, inflicting upon India the third largest defeat in their Test history. Saturday is usually my busiest day of work, but my sister had decided to get married that day. It would be stretching a point to call her an avid cricket fan, but she followed my career closely enough to know the game pretty well. Had she envisaged England being anointed as the number one team in the world on her wedding day? Had she heck. We're only eighteen months apart in age and we grew up in an era when cricket and England meant inevitable disappointment, however promising things might appear briefly. When planning a long time before she had been more worried about a clash with the Wales versus England rugby match that day.

Not that I could be idle in the build-up to her nuptials. A column was still expected for Sunday. And rightly so. England were top of the pile, and it needed explaining. Maybe I'd told too many people about the topic of this book, because there seemed to be a lot of articles based around its timeline, of that trek from 1999. But then I suppose it was where the progress to number one status began. So that Sunday I wrote:

There really is no mystery as to why this England side are so good. Possessing an outstanding group of international cricketers is a given, but it is not always enough. Leadership is key, and this team are superbly led by Andrew Strauss and Andy Flower. The players work hard, making them the fittest team in world cricket. They adhere religiously to simple plans. And they care passionately about the team ethic. 'The team is not a lease car' is their slogan, and it is mightily apt.

This team's journey began in 2009, just after they had been humiliatingly bowled out for 51 and beaten by an innings by the West Indies in Jamaica . . .

But the longer journey had begun in the late nineties when English (and Welsh!) cricket was generally an embarrassment, so lamentable that in 1999 they were briefly ranked as the worst Test team in the world.

Which is where we came in . . .

14

Dogberry's Comparisons

A h, we're not quite done yet. There is still the awkward bit to come. The comparison, and the comparisons. As Robert Croft, my former Glamorgan colleague, said to me during the writing of this book, 'I can't wait to find out who you think is better!'

Fletcher or Flower? It's like choosing between a kindly professorial uncle and an old 'what-a-great-time-we-used-to-have' university mate. Duncan Fletcher is not my uncle, and Andy Flower did not go to Swansea or Cambridge with me, but you get the gist.

If you think Flower's England's comprehensive thrashing of Fletcher's India in the summer of 2011 (India did not win an international match in the entire tour) draws a firm conclusion then you clearly have not been reading carefully enough. As I mentioned earlier, Fletcher had had no time with his squad then, while they were ravaged by injury and fatigue. His 5–0 riposte in the one-day series in India is evidence enough of the worth of his work.

There is also another important point to be considered in

comparing the two: Fletcher has been to the end of his England tenure, Flower has not. Unless he shrewdly departs at the top, it will end in tears some time. It always does. And the 3–0 Test defeat by Pakistan early in 2012 was a chastening indicator of how swiftly things can change. 'Uneasy sits the crown' and all that.

Overall comparisons are odious anyway, or odorous, as Constable Dogberry said in the Bard's *Much Ado about Nothing*. I've always liked that malapropism and used it in 2011 when explaining the difficulties of comparing the side of 2011 with that of 2005, not least because three players – Strauss, Pietersen and Bell – played in both sides. Bell was undoubtedly a better player in 2011, but it might just be that Strauss and Pietersen were better batsmen in 2005.

The team of 2011 was undeniably a better 'team' in terms of its unity of purpose. As Matthew Maynard mentioned earlier, Fletcher has always spoken of the 'critical mass' of his team. He has always reckoned that you require eight solid characters in your side, who can then coax along the other three who might slack or disrupt. 'But as soon as that critical mass reaches seven-four or six-five you have problems,' Fletcher has said. That is unfortunately what happened in Australia in 2006/07, with Andrew Flintoff as captain.

Fletcher would have enjoyed coaching the England team of 2011. They had a critical mass of eleven; a group of genuinely good blokes. Believe me, that is rare. I have always been of the opinion that rugby dressing rooms are better places than their cricketing equivalent, because the characters found in them are generally less selfish. But the England team of 2011 seem to have bucked that theory.

Pietersen's name will obviously spring to mind in contradiction, but he trains exceptionally hard and that fits easily into the Flower and Strauss regime. One insider told me that James Anderson might once have been a problem in that critical mass respect, but apparently it is not just his bowling that has been transformed.

Sometimes as a team they might have appeared fractured on the field, because they could shout and bawl at each other when mistakes were made. I personally don't like that, and feel it was by far the most unattractive aspect of the side that went to number one. But those inside the camp insist it was just the team's methods of ensuring high standards. They say there is never any lingering animosity. And we have to believe them.

The other problem with comparing 2005 and 2011 is the standard of the opposition. In 2005 England were facing one of the greatest sides to draw breath, even if Glenn McGrath missed the two Tests England won after twisting his ankle on that stray ball at Edgbaston. Indeed before the start of that series Australia's points ranking (133) was at its highest at any time since the Test rankings were introduced. In 2011 it was an inevitable shame that India's quality was constantly questioned. They came into the series with a points ranking of 125, and finished it with 117. In direct contrast England began at 117 and finished at 125. Throughout this South Africa remained second with 118. It was close at the top, unlike, say, the end of 2004, when England were second to Australia: England had 109, Australia had 130.

In 2005, as I have touched upon, the reverse swing of Flintoff and Simon Jones was as good as anything the cricketing world had seen. The obvious differences are in the spin and wicket-keeping departments. Graeme Swann and Matt Prior would win personal duels with Ashley Giles and Geraint Jones without any argument. Anderson would have to play, as would Flintoff, who held hands with greatness for all of that series. Alastair Cook or Marcus Trescothick, though? Jonathan Trott or Michael Vaughan? Strauss or Vaughan as skipper? Steve Harmison or Stuart Broad? Tim Bresnan or Simon Jones? And so on.

In my column I went with the 2005 lot, for their individual brilliance as opposed to what I considered the more workman-like performances of 2011. 'It is 2005 for me, just, but, as Dogberry might have said, the 2011 side smell pretty good too,'

I wrote. And this even though I'd pick six from 2011 in my composite eleven: Cook, Trescothick, Vaughan (capt), Bell (2011 version), Pietersen (2005 version), Prior, Flintoff, Broad, Swann, Anderson, Jones.

Throughout the research for this book I asked many people about the similarities between Fletcher and Flower. One said 'Zimbabwean!' with a laugh, and then said that was it. They are very different, yes, but they are also surprisingly similar. Neither of them smiles much for a start. Fletcher's inscrutable gaze is well known, although he blames hereditary low jowls. He is generally happy, as it happens. And so is Flower, but the England team mock him for his miserable mien. 'Grumpy Flower' Pietersen called him jokingly after the team had reached number one and Pietersen was thanking Flower for keeping the team so grounded. And when at the post-match press conference in Sydney after the Ashes win in 2010/11 Strauss was asked why Flower was not on the field with the team, he said that it was because Flower was not very good at smiling. When told of that remark, Flower replied, with a smile, 'That's Strauss just being his cynical self.'

Scyld Berry's typically thoughtful assessment of the differences between the pair was that Fletcher is rural and Flower is urban. I have touched upon that. Fletcher grew up on a farm where words were not essential; Flower grew up in the cities of Johannesburg and Salisbury/Harare. It shows. He communicates more easily. He is more tolerant with the media, although one Sky Sports employee did tell me that getting an interview from Flower was like 'getting blood from a stone'.

'There is always a danger that by putting yourself in the paper you are aggrandizing yourself at the expense of the players,' Flower has said. 'They have to go out into the middle to play the matches; they go into the lion's den. As a coach, you should never lose sight of that.'

The majority of my interviewees reckoned Flower to be the

better man manager. I know that will irk Fletcher. He prides himself on his man management, and it was immediately proved by his treatment and the subsequently positive responses of the likes of Graham Thorpe and Phil Tufnell with England. Mike Atherton said as much in his autobiography when considering that early period when he was still an England player. Talking of Ray Illingworth's time as England manager, he wrote, 'He was as poor as Duncan Fletcher, later, was excellent.' And Fletcher's problem is that people easily remember the troubled latter stages of his tenure when he was mostly putting out fires started by the likes of Flintoff rather than the earlier more successful times.

But all those interviewees also said that Fletcher was the sharper coach. As Giles says, 'If I weighed the two up, I would say Fletch has more of the technical and less of the man management, and Andy is the opposite. But the mixes are still good, on both sides. They are just different forms of coach.'

Giles, a player under Fletcher and a selector under Flower, was interesting on their similarities. 'They have both got really good, simple disciplines,' he said. 'Respect and pride seem to be in-built into some of these Africans. There is not a lot of molly-coddling, but that doesn't mean they are not good man managers. It takes time to get to know them, and you have to break them down.'

Both keep their distance from the team. One current England player said to me, 'I wish we knew Flower a bit better,' but another told me that, as he was a young tyro, Fletcher had barely spoken a word to him.

But both have a desperate desire to win. There is a good story about Flower when he was coaching at Oxford University in 1997 (when, incidentally, he beat Fletcher as a coach for the first time when his Oxford team defeated Fletcher's Glamorgan – minus a few senior players, it does have to be said, including me! – in a run-chase after a rather generous declaration). His team had just been beaten early by Nottinghamshire and it was decided to play a game of football on the outfield between the teams. Oxford were hammered in that too, and their players headed for the showers and then, so they thought, their colleges. Flower had other ideas. He wanted to talk about the football. The players just didn't get it. It was only a game of football. 'It's about winning,' Flower told them. 'You must never, never accept losing.'

I found this story interesting because when Fletcher came to Glamorgan that year, one of the things he introduced was games of football and touch rugby as extra sessions of fitness. We had never done that before. Indeed I remember an occasion at Derby when Hugh Morris was captain and I'd brought a rugby ball along to kick around with, because I was planning a comeback season with Lydney. A game of touch was suggested. 'If you lot play touch, you'll be in trouble!' said Morris. But Fletcher encouraged it, before and after play. He encouraged the competitive side of it, splitting sides into youngsters and oldies, or East against West Wales. He'd always watch intently, scowling at slackers, enjoying the competition and never seeming to mind if tempers frayed.

Sadly you won't see England's cricketers playing football these days, as it was banned after Joe Denly was injured in a clumsy tackle by Owais Shah at the Oval in 2009. But Fletcher and Flower probably prefer rugby anyway, even if injuries prevented their playing the game for too long as youngsters.

Maynard, Fletcher's former assistant, says of the two Zimbabweans, 'I'd say there are huge similarities between them. Because Andy was more of a player in the spotlight his media stuff is far better, but, just like Fletch, he is very considered, very protective of his players and looks very well organized.'

It was the American philosopher and writer Henry David Thoreau who once said, 'The greatest compliment that was ever paid me was when someone asked me what I thought, and attended to my answer.' And that is one of Flower's great strengths. 'When you sit down with him you actively see him listening to you,' says Morris. 'And he is very considered in his response to you. He listens to people, he learns from them, he then plans meticulously and then leads that plan.'

Flower does listen, and he does seek advice in looking for what he calls 'nuggets' of information. He will talk to the likes of Ian Botham and Geoff Boycott in order to keep them onside. In both 2009 and 2010 he spoke to John Buchanan, the former Australia coach, about the Ashes series in those years and ways of planning for them. He regularly speaks to some journalists, giving them off-the-record briefings so that they understand what he is trying to do. And he has been cute in his relationship with the counties.

As Giles, as Warwickshire's director of cricket, says, 'He has managed it very well, probably better than Fletch. There is still a hell of a lot of cricket but Fletch might have got to the point where, quite rightly at the time, he said, "Sod the counties; we've got to look after these blokes for international cricket." Andy has been very clever in making the counties and the county coaches feel part of the process of producing the England team. That's how I feel anyway. When you get Bell and Trott back you feel he is doing you a favour in some ways. He is open to conversation about when you can have them back and it is more of a joined-up process. When I was playing, I might have popped back for a game but it was purely popping back for a game. They [Bell and Trott] are more Warwickshire players than I was.'

That might sound like heavy criticism of Fletcher, but it is not. Giles is an unashamed Fletcher fan. It was just, as I have said before, that Fletcher had the hardest part as regards the counties. Managing the beginning of central contracts was breaking over a hundred years of tradition, when the counties had always been in control of their players. It was always going to be messy.

Fletcher did communicate with the counties, always trying to go to every one after a winter tour, but even Maynard agrees that, with a better structure in place, it would have been good for him to have done more. He recalls speaking to Flower about this very issue when Flower was working at the National Academy in the winter of 2005/06 and Maynard had just returned from England's tour of Pakistan. 'We talked about one of the things Fletch needing to do was speak to the county coaches to make sure they knew about his philosophies and what sort of cricketers he wanted,' he says. 'But it never happened because of a lack of time.'

In 2010 Maynard was still cricket manager at Glamorgan before resigning after some shockingly underhand events at the club, whereby a new skipper, the South African Alviro Petersen, was signed in Dubai by three members of Glamorgan's hierarchy without Maynard's knowledge. Maynard was impressed that Flower made time to meet with various county representatives (it helps that he has Morris to sort out so many peripheral issues). Maynard went to dinner with Flower, Craig White (Yorkshire) and Richard Scott (Middlesex). 'I thought it was brilliant,' says Maynard. 'As a coach you could then go back to your county and say, "Right, this is what he wants."'

In one-day cricket Flower likes his explosive batsmen. And by coincidence that means he likes Tom Maynard, Matthew's son, now at Surrey after walking out from Glamorgan in disgust at the treatment of his father, and selected in 2011 for the winter Performance Programme squad. In 2010 Tom was asked to take part in a Twenty20 match situation the day before one of England's T20 internationals against Pakistan in Cardiff. Batting second, Maynard played exceptionally well, before attempting one heave too many and getting out with victory in sight. His team-mate Jos Buttler (Somerset) was bowled next ball to leave his side in trouble. Flower was not slow to communicate his feelings afterwards, using the example of the former footballer Eric Cantona. 'He [Cantona] knew he could play the magic ball,' said Flower to Maynard junior, 'but he chose to play the simple ones until he knew the time was right.'

Fletcher listens too, despite the common perception to the contrary, as Dean Conway confirms: 'I would say something to him subtly the day before, like I thought that warm-ups were too long, and he would not say "Yeah, you're right", he'd just say "OK". Then the next day that thing would have changed. I found him a good listener, but you had to be in that circle. Towards the end he got overly suspicious.'

Former team analyst Mark Garaway says that he did not become aware that Fletcher and Flower were so similar until Flower took over in the West Indies in 2009. 'I wouldn't have known before,' he says, 'but very, very quickly it was evident that we were dealing with a guy who was obviously a younger version of Fletch but had all the same beliefs. The difference between the two was that Andy was probably more prepared to challenge, irrespective of the person. So nobody got off lightly. He wasn't about respecting people's feelings. It was all about the team, and if somebody shed a tear at something he said he couldn't give a stuff. That was a very strong message to send out. I'm not saying that Fletch wasn't good at challenging, but during his time Flintoff, say, had got quite big.'

Yes, it is interesting that Flower has appeared more prepared to drop his big names. Pietersen, Broad, Collingwood, Bell and Anderson have all felt the cold steel of his selectorial axe. But in truth it is easier for him these days. England have far greater strength in depth. During Fletcher's time there was rarely that depth. That is why the team of 2005 unravelled so quickly. There was simply not the personnel to step in once injuries struck.

Garaway highlights the difference in coaching methods between Fletcher and Flower. 'It is a generational thing,' he says, 'but it is also because Andy's first coaching experience came under Pete [Moores] and that became very much a specialist and more scientific approach than Fletch's, which was a more integrated method. Pete had been a huge driver in getting the analysis department to grow and as a result we had a huge amount of people doing a lot of data mining behind myself. It was always going to go that way.'

And that is the way it has gone. Flower had been given the book *Moneyball* (Michael Lewis's tale of the statistics-driven success of the baseball team the Oakland As under their manager Billy Beane) to read by Moores and was an instant convert. Flower is cricket's Beane. It is a measure of the increased standing of statistics and statisticians that that can be seen as a compliment. In days gone by, he might have been called Mr Bean.

When interviewed for the job of team director in 2009, Flower stated that he wanted American sports science and particularly the analysis of statistics to be used more in cricket. It was a point reinforced when I interviewed him later that year. 'I think we are only scratching the surface with cricket statistics,' he said. 'They will play an increasing role in how you formulate strategy or pick people.' They have done that, courtesy of the department at the National Cricket Performance Centre at Loughborough that is solely concerned with statistics.

Not that Flower eschews technical work or talk. 'Some players are scared of talking technique,' he says, 'because they believe it will slow them down in the middle. But if there's a problem with technique – if, for example, you're playing a forward defensive and the ball keeps sliding off the bat – then something's wrong and it has to be addressed. If you've got a solid technique, your confidence will grow.'

But he will often use statistics to reinforce a point. 'It can be a very pure, a very non-judgemental form of feedback,' he says. 'I'm not saying you're a good guy or a bad guy, a great player or a bad player; these are the figures, let's talk about them.'

England's main analyst is, of course, Nathan Leamon. When England got to number one in the world, his name and his nickname 'Numbers' came to the fore. He had planned England's ascent up the rankings, and a lot else besides. He had also played all the Test matches that got them to the top on his computer even before they had been played on grass. 'We feed into the simulator information about pitches and the twenty-two players who might play, and it plays the game a number of times and tells us the likely outcomes,' Leamon told the *Sunday Times*. 'It helps us in strategy and selection. I've checked the programme against more than 300 Tests and it is accurate to within 4–5%.'

The simulations are based on those first used in the 1940s by the mathematicians John von Neumann, Stanislaw Ulam and Nicholas Metropolis, who were working on nuclear bomb projects for the Manhattan Project at Los Alamos. It was called the Monte Carlo method after Ulam's uncle, who was a hardened gambler in the casinos of Monte Carlo. 'Tell me what Monte says,' Flower will often say to Leamon when faced with a decision upon which he cannot immediately decide.

One such obvious instance is the toss. Leamon reckons that from the five hundred Tests he has looked at, you are just as likely to win the game if you've lost the toss as when you have won it. It is a logic buttressed by Strauss, who thinks that, with Test pitches deteriorating less, the days of always batting first have gone. 'If you think there's going to be something there and you bowl,' he says, 'but there isn't a huge amount there after all, you haven't actually lost a lot, because not many wickets these days deteriorate massively.' 'When in doubt, bat' might have actually become 'when in doubt, bowl'.

Leamon makes extensive use of Hawk-Eye data in preparing pitch maps for opposition batsmen, breaking down the target areas for bowlers into twenty blocks, each 100cm by 15cm. 'A lot of the old ways of looking at the techniques of opponents leads to guesswork – feet position, how they hold the bat,' says Leamon. 'Hawk-Eye enables you to come up with answers.'

It is an interesting point from Leamon. There has always been analysis in cricket. But in the old days it was conducted in the bar, and then stored in bowlers' minds if they hadn't drunk too much and could remember.

But having plans is one thing, implementing them is quite another. That is where England were so brilliant in the Ashes of 2010/11 and the India series in 2011: their bowlers were unremittingly accurate. Contrast that with 2002/03 and the infamous first Test at Brisbane, where Nasser Hussain inserted Australia. The home side made 492 but Fletcher says all of their batsmen bar Ricky Ponting fell to pre-conceived plans. 'It took so long because we did not bowl enough balls in the right place,' says Fletcher. 'Plans to dismiss a batsman do not work unless you can bowl five or six balls an over in that area.'

It was a similar problem in 2006/07 when, embarrassingly, England's bowling plans were leaked during the Melbourne Test. It would be easy to mock them in comparison to today's, especially as some of the words were misspelt, but in essence they are little different. They had the essential weaknesses of each batsman, and they had the shrewd field-placings (for example, a 'straight catcher on edge of pitch' for Matthew Hayden) that were so lauded in 2005.

However, I reckon England need to be careful. They must not give too much away. Quite clearly Loughborough and the wonderful cricketing community working from there is a hive of invention and trail-blazing initiatives. They are giving the England team and English cricket an edge. But it will not remain so if other countries are able to copy and catch up. I've always felt a little guilty about the *Ashes Regained* book I did with Fletcher after 2005. Fletcher was very careful not to reveal too much about the Australia players he knew would be playing in the next Ashes, but before that 2006/07 series his opposite number Buchanan said, 'I've made the book mandatory reading for our coaches. I think it provides a very interesting insight into

Fletcher. He discusses his own philosophies and also gives his thoughts on the current players and the way they play the game in England.' Oh dear.

In 2011 I did a small piece for my Final Whistle column on the increasing influence of mathematics in sport, and especially in cricket. I obviously mentioned Leamon and Loughborough in despatches, but I had also come across the crib sheet used by a county team before one of their Twenty20 matches that season. I found it fascinating, especially the statistical detail it went into. I did not mention the county by name but I did drop in a couple of random statistics and terms used in it. 'Dot ball limit' was one of them, and, apparently, that gave the game away. That was their term. The county in question were not happy, so I was told. And in a way I was happy about that. They were protecting their own little version of the Crown Jewels. Caveat inventor. Look what happened to Australia after we copied their Academy all those years ago.

Of more importance, though, for England to beware of is the future of Flower. As you may have noticed, I am no closer to judging him against Fletcher. It is impossible. In their different ways under different circumstances, they have both done superb jobs.

Under Fletcher, England played 270 matches of all types, winning 119 at a winning average of 44%. Under Peter Moores they played 79 and won 30 (38%). Under Flower, up until the end of the 2012 Test series against Pakistan, they have played 135 matches, winning 69. That is a winning percentage of 51.11%.

Under Flower, England have won twenty of the thirty-nine Tests played (a stunning 51.28%). In eleven series England have won eight, drawn one and only lost two. With India in 2011 in the bag they had won six series on the trot, but so did Fletcher's team in 2004 and 2005, culminating with the Ashes at home that year. In twenty-seven Test series Fletcher's team won fourteen, with six drawn, so just over half compared to Flower's 72.7%. Fletcher won forty-two of his ninety-six Tests (43.8%). By comparison in the whole of the 1990s England only won twenty-six from 107 Tests (a miserable 24.3%). In the 1980s it was twenty Tests from 104 (an even worse 19.2%). In the 1970s it was thirty-three from ninety-five (34.7%). The numbers don't lie. The improvements are huge.

The England cricket team is back, and in 2011 was better than ever (at least in the modern era). And Fletcher and Flower have put them back where they belong. So I just hope Flower is better treated than Fletcher was at the end of his tenure. Zimbabweans might well want him to return home, but I cannot see that happening, even though he does still own that house in Harare.

Of course he has hankerings for his homeland. 'I miss certain things about Zimbabwe, yes,' he has said, 'but that's sort of dwindling the longer I am out of it. The most obvious one would probably be some of my closest friends and interacting with them again. But there are also things like the smell of the rain, or the smell of the bush, and being able to go fishing or into the bush, or just go to someone's farm. The freshness and innocence of that type of lifestyle, I do miss that. And I was really lucky as a kid, so lucky to grow up there.'

But I cannot see him continuing in the main England role for too long. Just read the words of this interview he gave in March 2011. 'My kids are twelve, ten and eight,' he said. 'So it's a very important stage in their development as young people and I'm not convinced I'm doing the right thing by the family by doing this job. I'm a bit greedy because I'm trying to get the best of both worlds by helping to raise a young family and also trying to make a difference with the England cricket team. I worry about the fact this time can't be regained. I worry about the fact the kids might at some stage resent me for being away during these years.'

Give Flower no more than two years, I reckon. England

might need to start looking for another Zimbabwean coach. They do seem rather useful. Two of them have taken England from the bottom to the top.

But England already have another Zimbabwean coach. When Flower left the Brisbane Test in 2010, it was the Zimbabwe-born Richard Halsall, not Graham Gooch or anyone else, who took over. It was the same when Flower missed the short trip to Ireland in 2011. As long ago as 2009 Flower told me that Halsall could easily be a county head coach.

Could Halsall, with greater prior experience of the requirements of international coaching than Moores, step up to the national job?

We may well discover one day. But Halsall, or anyone else who takes over for that matter, will know the magnitude of his task.

They will be big boots to fill. Very big boots indeed.

Appendix: England Test series results, November 1999 to August 2011

Season	Coach	Opponent	Venue	Result	Score
1999/2000	Fletcher	South Africa	Away	Lost	2–1
2000	Fletcher	Zimbabwe	Home	Won	1–0
2000	Fletcher	West Indies	Home	Won	3–1
2000/01	Fletcher	Pakistan	Away	Won	1–0
2000/01	Fletcher	Sri Lanka	Away	Won	2–1
2001	Fletcher	Pakistan	Home	Drew	1–1
2001	Fletcher	Australia	Home	Lost	4–1
2001/02	Fletcher	India	Away	Lost	1–0
2001/02	Fletcher	New Zealand	Away	Drew	1–1
2002	Fletcher	Sri Lanka	Home	Won	2–0
2002	Fletcher	India	Home	Drew	1–1
2002/03	Fletcher	Australia	Away	Lost	4–1
2003	Fletcher	Zimbabwe	Home	Won	2–0
2003	Fletcher	South Africa	Home	Drew	2–2
2003/04	Fletcher	Bangladesh	Away	Won	2–0
2003/04	Fletcher	Sri Lanka	Away	Lost	1–0
2003/04	Fletcher	West Indies	Away	Won	3–0
2004	Fletcher	New Zealand	Home	Won	3–0
2004	Fletcher	West Indies	Home	Won	4–0
2004/05	Fletcher	South Africa	Away	Won	2–1
2005	Fletcher	Bangladesh	Home	Won	2–0
2005	Fletcher	Australia	Home	Won	2–1
2005/06	Fletcher	Pakistan	Away	Lost	2–0
2005/06	Fletcher	India	Away	Drew	1–1

2006	Fletcher	Sri Lanka	Home	Drew	1–1
2006	Fletcher	Pakistan	Home	Won	3–0
2006/07	Fletcher	Australia	Away	Lost	5–0
2007	Moores	West Indies	Home	Won	3–0
2007	Moores	India	Home	Lost	1–0
2007/08	Moores	Sri Lanka	Away	Lost	1–0
2007/08	Moores	New Zealand	Away	Won	2–1
2008	Moores	New Zealand	Home	Won	2–0
2008	Moores	South Africa	Home	Lost	2–1
2008/09	Moores	India	Away	Lost	1–0
2008/09	Flower	West Indies	Away	Lost	1–0
2009	Flower	West Indies	Home	Won	2–0
2009	Flower	Australia	Home	Won	2–1
2009/10	Flower	South Africa	Away	Drew	1–1
2009/10	Flower	Bangladesh	Away	Won	2–0
2010	Flower	Bangladesh	Home	Won	2–0
2010	Flower	Pakistan	Home	Won	3–1
2010/11	Flower	Australia	Away	Won	3–1
2011	Flower	Sri Lanka	Home	Won	1–0
2011	Flower	India	Home	Won	4–0

Bibliography

Atherton, Mike, *Opening Up* (Hodder, 2002)

Fletcher, Duncan, *Ashes Regained* (Simon & Schuster, 2005)

Fletcher, Duncan, *Behind the Shades* (Simon & Schuster, 2007)

Flintoff, Andrew, *Ashes to Ashes* (Hodder, 2009)

Hoggard, Matthew, *Welcome to My World* (HarperCollins, 2009)

Hussain, Nasser, *Playing with Fire* (Penguin, 2004)

MacLaurin, Ian, *Tiger by the Tail* (Pan Macmillan, 1999)

Olonga, Henry, *Blood, Sweat and Treason* (Vision Sports Publishing, 2010)

Strauss, Andrew, *Winning the Ashes Down Under* (Hodder, 2011)

Swann, Graeme, *The Breaks are Off* (Hodder, 2011)

Thorpe, Graham, *Rising from the Ashes* (HarperCollins, 2005)

Vaughan, Michael, *Time to Declare* (Hodder, 2009)

Index

INDEX

INDEX

INDEX

Steve James is the cricket columnist for the *Sunday Telegraph* and a sports writer for the *Daily Telegraph*.

He read Classics at Swansea University before becoming a postgraduate at Cambridge, where he won a Blue in the side captained by Mike Atherton. He played his county cricket with Glamorgan for eighteen years, scoring nearly 16,000 runs at an average of over 40, and captaining them for three seasons, winning a National League trophy in 2002, before retiring due to injury.

In 1997 James helped Glamorgan to win the County Championship for the first time in nearly thirty years and was named the Professional Cricketers' Association Player of the Year. He still holds the record for highest score by a Glamorgan batsman (309 not out against Sussex at Colwyn Bay in 2000) and also won two caps for England.